Lecture Notes in Computer Science 2433

Edited by G. Goos, J. Hartmanis, and J. van Leeuwen

Springer-Verlag Berlin Heidelberg GmbH

Agnes Hui Chan Virgil Gligor (Eds.)

Information Security

5th International Conference, ISC 2002
Sao Paulo, Brazil, September 30 - October 2, 2002
Proceedings

 Springer

Series Editors

Gerhard Goos, Karlsruhe University, Germany
Juris Hartmanis, Cornell University, NY, USA
Jan van Leeuwen, Utrecht University, The Netherlands

Volume Editors

Agnes Hui Chan
College of Computer Science, Northeastern University
Boston, MA 02115, USA
E-mail: ahchan@ccs.neu.edu

Virgil Gligor
Department of Electrical and Computer Engineering
University of Maryland, College Park, MD 20742, USA
E-mail: gligor@eng.umd.edu

Cataloging-in-Publication Data applied for

Die Deutsche Bibliothek - CIP-Einheitsaufnahme

Information security : 5th international conference ; proceedings / I3C
2002, Sao Paulo, Brazil, September 30 - October 2, 2002. Agnes Hui Chan ;
Virgil Gligor (ed.).

(Lecture notes in computer science ; Vol. 2433)
ISBN 978-3-540-44270-7

CR Subject Classification (1998): E.3, D.4.6, F.2.1, C.2, J.1, C.3

ISSN 0302-9743
ISBN 978-3-540-44270-7   ISBN 978-3-540-45811-1 (eBook)
DOI 10.1007/978-3-540-45811-1

http://www.springer.de

© Springer-Verlag Berlin Heidelberg 2002
Originally published by Springer-Verlag Berlin Heidelberg New York in 2002

Typesetting: Camera-ready by author, data conversion by PTP-Berlin, Stefan Sossna e.K.
Printed on acid-free paper   SPIN: 10870122   06/3142   5 4 3 2 1 0

Preface

As distinct from other security and cryptography conferences, the Information Security Conference (ISC) 2002 brought together individuals involved in a wide variety of different disciplines of information security to foster the exchange of ideas. The conference is an outgrowth of the Information Security Workshop, first held in Ishikawa, Japan 1997. ISC 2002 was held in Sao Paulo, Brazil, on September 30– October 2, 2002.

The Program Committee considered 81 submissions of which 38 papers were accepted for presentation. These proceedings contain revised versions of the accepted papers. The papers provide a representative sample of both the variety and the truly international scope of information security research conducted currently. The topics addressed range from e-commerce protocols to access control and trust management, and to cryptography and cryptographic algorithms.

Many people deserve our gratitude for their contribution to the success of the conference. We would like to thank the General Chair, Routo Terada, for overseeing the local arrangements, including registration and maintaining the conference website, and for the smooth running of the conference. We are grateful to Robbie Ye for his expert help in processing the electronic submissions, reviews and acceptance notifications. Robbie's enthusiasm and energy greatly simplified the Program Committee's task of conducting the on-line evaluation of the submitted papers under tight time constraints.

In evaluating the papers submitted we were fortunate to receive the help of a distinguished Program Committee. We wish to thank the committee for doing an excellent job in reviewing papers and providing useful feedback to authors. In addition to the advice of the Program Committee, we also benefited from the expert help of external reviewers, including our colleagues: Jaouhar Ayadi; Dirk Balfanz, Rakesh Bobba, Dan Boneh, M. Cassassa-Mont, C.I. Dalton, Anand Desai, Glenn Durfee, Laurent Eschenauer, David Goldberg, Guang Gong, Anwar Hasan, Hector Ho-Fuentes, Adrian Kent, H. Khurana, R. Koleva, Thiago C. Martins, Muriel Medard, Brian Monahan, Narendar, Mads Rasmussen, Joe Rushanan, David Soldera, Routo Terada, Duncan Wong, Min Wu, Robbie Ye, Muxiang Zhang, and Feng Zhu.

Most of all, we thank all the authors who submitted papers to this conference. Without their submissions, this conference could not have been a success.

July 2002

Agnes Hui Chan
Virgil Gligor

Information Security Conference 2002

September 30 – October 2, 2002, Sao Paulo, Brazil

Conference Chair

Routo Terada, University of Sao Paulo (Brazil)

Program Co-chair

Agnes Hui Chan, Northeastern University (USA)
Virgil D. Gligor, University of Maryland – College Park (USA)

Program Committee

Yolanta Beres .... HP Labs (UK)
Ricardo Dahab.. University of Campinas (Brazil)
Drew Dean...SRI (USA)
Yair Frankel.. TechTegrity (USA)
Peter Gutmann .... University of Auckland (NZ)
John Ioannidis...AT&T Labs – Research (USA)
Charlie Kaufman .... Iris Assoc (USA)
Jay Lala .... DARPA (USA)
Carl Landwehr... NSF (USA)
Teresa Lunt... PARC (USA)
Doug Maughan.. DARPA (USA)
Gary McGraw...Cigital (USA)
Cathy Meadows.. NRL (USA)
Rebecca Mercuri .... Bryn Mawr College (USA)
Radia Perlman .... Sun Microsystems (USA)
Radha Poovendran....................................University of Washington (USA)
Gang Qu .... University of Maryland (USA)
Greg Rose...Qualcomm (Australia)
Jonathan Trostle .... CISCO (USA)

Table of Contents

Intrusion Detection and Tamper Resistance

Cryptographic Algorithm and Attack Implementation

Access Control and Trust Management (I)

Authentication and Privacy

E-commerce Protocols (I)

Signature Schemes

Cryptography (I)

Access Control and Trust Management (II)

Key Management

Security Analysis

E-commerce Protocols (II)

Cryptography (II)

Real-Time Intruder Tracing through Self-Replication

Heejin Jang and Sangwook Kim

Dept. of Computer Science, Kyungpook National University,
1370, Sankyuk-dong, Buk-gu, Daegu, Korea
{janghj, swkim}@cs.knu.ac.kr

Abstract. Since current internet intruders conceal their real identity by distributed or disguised attacks, it is not easy to deal with intruders properly only with an ex post facto chase. Therefore, it needs to trace the intruder in real time. Existing real-time intruder tracing systems has a spatial restriction. The security domain remains unchanged if there is no system security officer's intervention after installing the tracing system. It is impossible to respond to an attack which is done out of the security domain. This paper proposes self-replication mechanism, a new approach to real-time intruder tracing, minimizing a spatial limitation of traceable domain. The real-time tracing supports prompt response to the intrusion, detection of target host and laundering hosts. It also enhances the possibility of intruder identification. Collected data during the real-time tracing can be used to generate a hacking scenario database and can be used as legal evidence.

1 Introduction

An identification service is a service which identifies which person is responsible for a particular activity on a computer or network [1]. Currently, most internet attackers disguise their locations by attacking their targets indirectly via previously-compromised intermediary hosts [2,3]. They also erase their marks on previous hosts where they have passed. These techniques make it virtually impossible for the system security officer of the final target system to trace back an intruder in order to disclose intruder's identity post factum. Chasing after the intruder in real time can be an alternative. The real-time tracing supports prompt response to the intrusion, detection of target host and laundering hosts. It also enhances the possibility of intruder identification.

There are several approaches that have been developed to trace an intruder. They fall into two groups such as an ex post facto tracing facility and a real-time identification service [1]. The first type of the intruder tracing approach contains reactive tracing mechanisms. In this approach, before a problem happens, no global accounting is done. But once it happens, the activity is traced back to the origin. Caller Identification System (CIS)[4] is along this approach. It is based on the premise that each host on the network has its own tracing system. The second type, the real-time identification service, attempts to trace all individuals in a network by the user ID's. The Distributed Intrusion Detection System (DIDS)[5] developed at UC

A.H. Chan and V. Gligor (Eds.): ISC 2002, LNCS 2433, pp. 1–16, 2002.

Davis is an example of a system which did this for a single local area network. It tracks all TCP connections and all logins on the network. It maintains a notion of a Network Identifier at all times for all activities on the system. Its major disadvantage is that DIDS can account the activities only when those stay in the DIDS domain. As we have seen from above, it is possible for the existing intruder tracing systems to keep track of the intruder if they are installed in the hosts on the intrusive path in advance. That is, the biggest problem in the existing real-time intruder tracing approaches is a restriction on the traceable domain.

As a solution, this paper presents the Self-Replication mechanism that meets the aforementioned requirements. It also introduces the HUNTER which is a real-time intruder tracing system based on the Self-Replication mechanism. The Self-Replication mechanism keeps track of a new connection caused by the intruder and replicates the security scheme to the target host through the connection. It broadens the security domain dynamically following the intruder's shifting path. It means that the traceable domain is extended. The HUNTER traces an intruder and gathers information about him/her. Collected data about an intruder can be used to generate a hacking scenario database and can be used as legal evidence. If an intruder attempts to access the source host while attacking the trusted domain, the System Security Officer (SSO) could determine the origin of the attack. The Self-Replication mechanism is applicable to general security solutions, such as system/network level monitoring systems, intrusion detection system, intruder tracing system and intrusion response system.

The remainder of this paper is structured as follows. Section 2 defines terminology. Section 3 proposes the Self-Replication mechanism for real-time intruder tracing. Section 4 shows that the security domain for real-time tracing is extended through the Self-Replication. Section 5 presents the architecture, the working model of the HUNTER and an implementation example. Section 6 shows performance evaluation. Finally, section 7 draws some conclusions and outlines directions for future research.

2 Preliminaries

We first define terminology.

2.1 States, Events, and Logs

We assume that the set of entities O and a set of well-formed commands E can characterize the computer system completely [6]. O is what the system is composed of and E is the set of events that can cause it to change. Following [7], a system state s is a 1-tuple (O). The collection S of all possible states is the state space. The relevant part of the system state $\sigma \subseteq s$ is the subset of (O). The collection Σ of the relevant parts of all possible system states is the relevant state space.

Monitoring activity is indispensable for security management. Monitoring is classified into two types, system state monitoring and change monitoring [7]. System state monitoring periodically records the relevant components of the state of the system. Change monitoring records the specific event or action that causes altering relevant component of the state of the system as well as the new values of those components. The output of each monitoring activity is a log $L=\{m_0, m_1, \ldots, m_p\}$, m_k ∈ I for all $k \geq 0$. Monitoring of relevant state space Σ makes the state log entry $I = N_O$ × N_V and that of relevant state space Σ and event E generate the change log entry $I = N_S \times N_O \times N_V \times N_E$. N_S are the names of users who cause events, N_O the names of the objects such as files or devices, N_V the new values of the objects, and N_E the names of the events.

2.2 A Trusted Domain and a Security Domain

We here define a trusted domain. The trusted domain D_t is composed of several domains including single administrative domains or cooperative domains. In the trusted domain, each administrator of constituent domains also has the administrative privilege in other domains.

If we consider that a security scheme is a way of controlling the security of systems or networks, the security domain [8] D_S is the set of machines and networks which have the same security scheme. Each of the heterogeneous security management systems generates its own security domain. Single administrative domain includes more than one security domain and single security domain is made up of more than one host. The security domain D_S has a static characteristic, for it does not change if the SSO does not install a security management system additionally. Those attributes of a security domain cause spatial restriction for general security management. Especially, it is the point at issue to identify intruders. If T is a security scheme, a security domain D_S controlled by T is defined by the function $dom(T)$. The result of $dom(T)$ is composed of various data representing the domain, such as network topology information N_t, network component information N_c and monitoring information M which is basically obtained by T. N_c contains information about hardware, operating system, services to be provided and etc. M is a set of log which is defined above. Since N_t and N_c have a regular effect on the extension of the security domain as expected, we consider only M that decides attributes of $dom(T)$. M consists of $m_1, m_2, m_3, \ldots, m_k, \ldots$ in which m_i is single monitoring information, i.e. a log entry. Each m_i has an occurrence time, denoted by $t(m_i)$. They are totally ordered, that is, $t(m_i) \leq t(m_{i+1})$ for all $t \geq 1$. M has spatial location as well as temporal sequence.

2.3 Real-Time Intruder Tracing

When a user on a host H_0 logs into another host H_1 via a network, a TCP connection C_1 is established between them. The connection object C_j (j ≥ 0) is constructed as *<connectionType, fromHostID, toHostID, fromUserID, toUserID, toPasswd, Time>*. *connectionType* is the type of connection and *fromHostID* and *fromUserID* are the source host id and the user id on the source. *toHostID* is the target host id, *toUserID* and *toPasswd* are the user id and the password information on the target and *Time* indicates when the connection occurs.

When the user logs from H_1 into another host H_2, and then H_3, ... , H_n successively in the same way, TCP connections $C_2, C_3, \ldots, C_n$ are established respectively on each link between the computers. We refer to this sequence of connections $CC=<C_1, C_2, \dots , C_n>$ as an extended connection, or a connection chain [9].

The task of a real-time intruder tracing is to provide intruder's movement path completely from source host to target host. In order to do this, the security domain must be secured.

3 Self-Replication

The Self-Replication mechanism supports dynamic extension of the security domain. It observes behavior of the user who is presumed as an intruder and acquires activity and identity information of the user. Using these data, it replicates itself or any other security scheme automatically into the hosts where an intruder has passed. Consequently, it broadens the security domain for data collection used for security management and intruder tracing. The Self-Replication mechanism could not only work independently but also operate together with any security scheme. The Self-Replication mechanism consists of monitoring and filtering, replication [10] and self-protection. Monitoring in the Self-Replication mechanism is a data-collecting phase for replication. It is done for specific users or all users who enter the trusted domain. The output of each monitoring activity is a log L. For replication, the Self-Replication mechanism filters some useful states or events among logs, which is related to establishing of new connections. Interesting states are aspects of important objects which can affect system security. They include states of *setuid* and *setgid* files, users with superuser privilege, or integrity of important files. Event under the close observation is the generation of new connections caused by user session creation event, account change event or intrusive behavior event. The user session creation event contains commands such as *telnet, ftp, rlogin, rexec* and *rsh*. The account change event includes gain of other user's privilege using *su* command. The intrusive behavior event comprises illegal acquisition of other user's or superuser privilege by buffer overflow attack, backdoor, and creation of malicious process or new trap.

After filtering, a point of time and a target host for replication have to be chosen. The Self-Replication mechanism decides the target host and starts to replicate itself to the host when an intruder succeeds in connecting with another host. With respect to Unix or Linux, there are various methods to connect two hosts [11]. We just take the connection through the medium object into consideration in this paper. The Self-Replication mechanism provides all users with medium objects which work normally but are controllable by this mechanism. It delivers modules and events for replication to the target host via the medium object, especially the medium object with a command processing function such as a pseudo terminal with a working shell.

Fig. 1 illustrates the event transmission through the pseudo terminal object. A lower hexahedron shows the Self-Replication mechanism running on the host. An upper hexahedron denoted as US_X is a user space in each host. It includes all actions by a specific user and every resource related to those actions. The front rectangle of the US_X is a perceptible part to the user such as standard input or standard output. As it goes back, it gets closer to the operating system. A solid arrow shows transfer of specific event $e_r \in E_R$ where E_R is a subset of E and a set of events such as copying, compiling or execution command for replication. A dotted arrow indicates forwarding of normal events $e_n \in (E - E_R)$. For example, a user U_R in a host H_R which already has the Self-Replication mechanism SM attacks a host H_T and U_R becomes U_T who has superuser privilege in H_T. A connection C_n is set up between two pseudo terminal objects, $MO_{U_R}^{C_n}$ which is allocated for U_R in the H_R by SM and $MO_{U_T}^{C_n}$ for U_T in the H_T by an operating system. Therefore, it is possible to send an event to $MO_{U_T}^{C_n}$ via $MO_{U_R}^{C_n}$ in order to remotely execute any command in H_T from H_R. A normal event e_n is delivered to H_T via $MO_{U_R}^{C_n}$ and $MO_{U_T}^{C_n}$ so that the user U_R can accomplish the event e_n with the privilege of U_T in the H_T. The event e_n is carried out in the H_T normally and the result e'_n is showed to the user U_R. For example, when a command *telnet* from H_R to H_T succeeds, a pseudo terminal is allocated [11]. Then if *ls* command is transmitted through a pseudo terminal of H_R, it is executed at H_T and the result is showed at the pseudo terminal of H_R. The SM makes the replication event e_r which is delivered to $MO_{U_T}^{C_n}$ via $MO_{U_R}^{C_n}$ and executed by means of superuser authority in the H_T. The result at H_T comes back to US_R but is not showed to U_R on $MO_{U_R}^{C_n}$ to keep any intruder from watching the whole process. It protects the replication process and SM itself from detection by U_R. As a result, SM of the host H_R replicates itself to the host H_T and duplicated Self-Replication mechanism SM' operates at H_T.

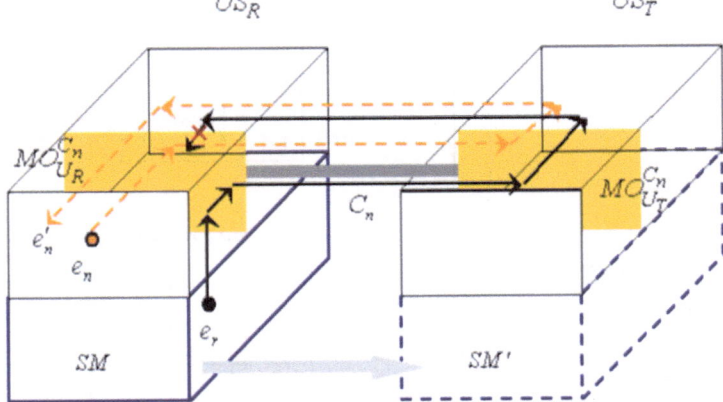

Fig. 1. Event Transmission through the Pseudo Terminal Object

Fig. 2A and 2B depict the replication protocols and their timing diagrams which are performed when the intruder succeeds in penetrating the target host H_T from the host H_R through the pseudo terminal object. RPC_X shows the replication status in each host. When a connection is established by the specific event e in the state of RPC_P, host H_R sends an *authreq* message to request the authentication for replication. If there is the same security scheme or faked scheme, H_T delivers a response message *authres* like in the Fig. 2A. H_R certifies legitimacy of the scheme and terminates the replication process. If the host H_T cannot receive *authres* during a lapse of a specific time, the host H_R enters a replication ready state of RPC_R and sends a *readyreq* message to check the intruder's environment in the H_T in the Fig. 2B. The target host enters the state RPC_R and transfers a *readyres* message which is the information about the intruder's execution environment in the target. After recognizing the intruder's environment, H_R enters a replication execution state of RPC_M and transmits modules and events for replication with *rpcout* message to H_T. H_T in the state of RPC_M executes commands from the host H_R. The Self-Replication mechanism is set up in the host H_T and starts inspecting the host and the specified intruder. And chasing an intruder continues. H_T sends *termreq* message to inform H_R of completion of the replication process. Then H_R enters a replication completion mode RPC_D and puts H_T into the state RPC_D by transmitting the *termres* message. Since the replication process is hidden from an intruder and the intruder's execution environment is maintained in the target host, the intruder cannot recognize the process. By using two self-protection methods, track erasing and camouflaging (explained in section 5.1), it protects the Self-Replication mechanism. Timing diagrams of Fig. 2A and 2B show the temporal relation among replication states of H_R, input to H_R and output from H_R.

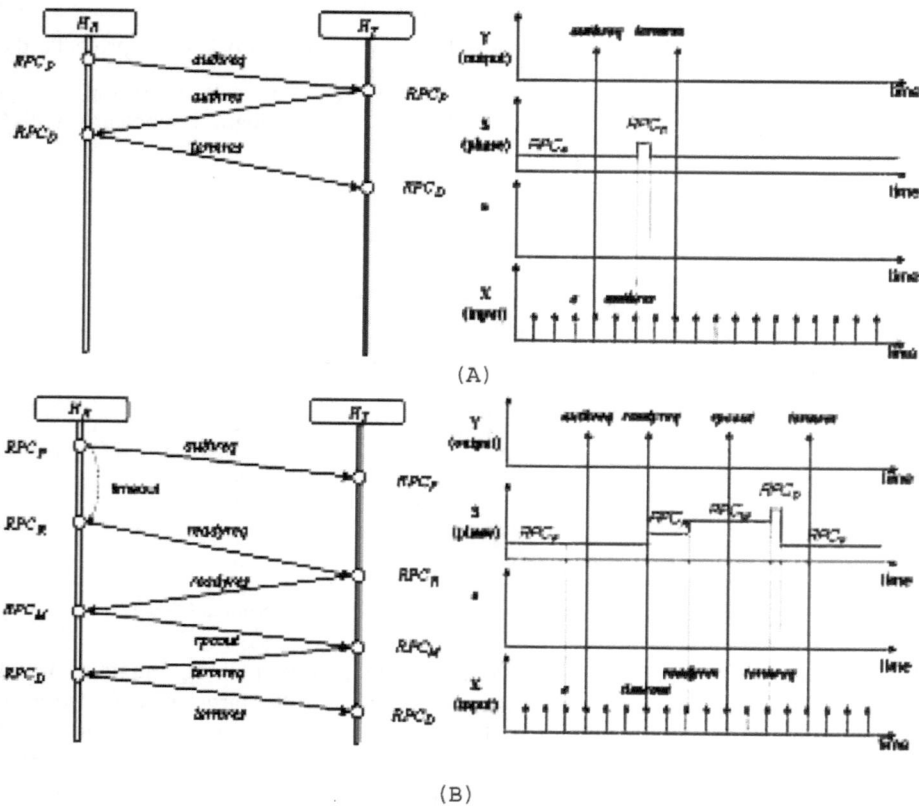

Fig. 2. (A) Replication Protocol and Timing Diagram in case there is Self-Replication mechanism in the target host (B) Replication Protocol and Timing Diagram in case there is no known Self-Replication mechanism in the target host

4 Security Domain Extension for Real-Time Intruder Tracing

In this section, we show that the security domain expands dynamically by the Self-Replication mechanism. If SS is a security scheme based on the Self-Replication mechanism, a security domain D_S controlled by SS is defined by the function $dom(SS)$. We consider only M that decides attributes of $dom(SS)$ (see Section 2.2). Given two sets of monitoring information M^{H_1} and M^{H_2} which are gathered in hosts H_1 and H_2, the merge of these two sets is partial information of M, denoted by $M^{H_1} \oplus M^{H_2}$. If we assume that login id of the user A is same in every host in the trusted domain, M_A, a set of monitoring information about the activities of a user A in only two consecutive hosts is $M_A = M_A^{H_1} \oplus M_A^{H_2}$ where $M_A^{H_1}$ is a set of monitoring information about user A in host H_1. M_A is $M_A^{H_1} \oplus M_A^{H_2} = m_{H_1 1}, m_{H_1 2}, ..., m_{H_1 k}, m_{H_2 1}, m_{H_2 2}, ..., m_{H_2 p} = m_1, m_2, ..., m_{k+p}$ if and only if there exist two sequences $H_1 1, H_1 2, ..., H_1 k$ and $H_2 1, H_2 2, ..., H_2 p$ of the sequence 1, 2, ... , $k+p$ s.t. $M_A^{H_1} = \{ m_{H_1 1}, m_{H_1 2}, ..., m_{H_1 k} \}$ and $M_A^{H_2} = \{ m_{H_2 1}, m_{H_2 2}, ..., m_{H_2 p} \}$ (see Section 2.2). The Self-Replication mechanism can recognize the changes of user's identity and monitor all behaviors of him/her while the user travels the trusted network. Therefore, if the user A passes through hosts H_1, H_2, ... , H_n ($n \geq 2$) sequentially and produces logs such as $M_A^{H_1}$, $M_A^{H_2}$, ... , $M_A^{H_n}$ in each host, the resulting set of monitoring information about user A can be extended to $M_A = M_A^{H_1} \oplus M_A^{H_2} \oplus ... \oplus M_A^{H_n}$. If an intruder begins to attack the trusted domain by penetrating the host which has a security scheme with the Self-Replication mechanism SS uniquely in the trusted domain, the result of security management by the SS is equal to that by installing and executing the scheme in every host on the intrusive path in the trusted domain. The specific user's sequence of behaviors in every host on the intrusive path is equal to the union of monitoring information sets each of which is gathered about a user in each host on the path by the Self-Replication mechanism.

Fig. 3 illustrates the security domain extension using the Self-Replication mechanism in a part of the trusted domain. Initially, there is only one host H_X with the SS in the trusted domain. We assume that an intruder passes through the host H_X first to break into the trusted domain from outside and continues to attack H_Y via H_X and then H_W via H_Y. Early security domain D_S controlled by SS is $dom(SS)$, denoted as A in the Fig. 3. When an intruder succeeds to attack via path2, the SS in host H_X replicates itself to H_Y. Let SS_{rH_Y} be the replicated security scheme in H_Y, D_S is expanded to $dom(SS) \oplus dom(SS_{rH_Y})$ (denoted as B). The D_S is enlarged to $dom(SS) \oplus dom(SS_{rH_Y}) \oplus dom(SS_{rH_W})$ (denoted as C) by the attack via path 3.

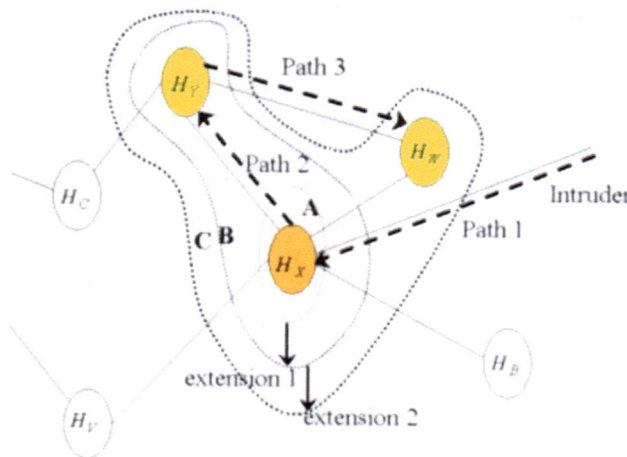

Fig. 3. Security Domain Extension for Real-Time intruder Tracing

5   Implementation

The real-time intruder tracing system, HUNTER, aims at keeping track of an intruder and, if possible, revealing the intruder's original source address and identity. Since this system is developed on the basis of the Self-Replication Mechanism, it is possible to enlarge the traceable domain following the intruder's shifting path even though a security scheme for identification is not installed in advance in all hosts within the trusted domain, unlike existing intruder tracing systems.

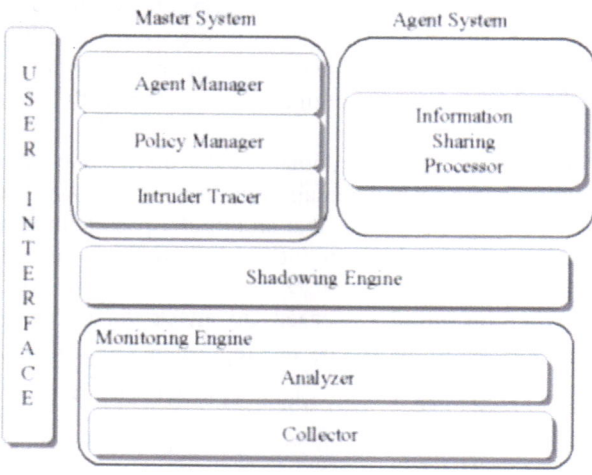

Fig. 4. System Architecture

5.1 HUNTER: Real-Time Intruder Tracing System

The HUNTER is composed of a single master system and several agent systems. This is initialized by installing a master system in the host which is the unique entrance to the trusted domain (for example, routers). Initially, there is a master system only in the trusted domain. If an intruder moves into another host via master system in the trusted domain, agent system is automatically placed into the target host through the self-replication process. As the self-replication process goes on following the intruder's movement path, the number of agent systems increase dynamically. This system is implemented in the GNU C/C++ 2.7.x.x for core modules and Java 2 SDK for the user interface on Linux 2.4.6 and Solaris 2.8. It uses MySQL 3.22.x as DBMS to store the monitoring information and JCE (Java Cryptography Enhancement) 1.2.x package for authentication and encryption between systems.

Fig. 4 describes the architecture of HUNTER. The master system and agent systems share a Monitoring Engine and a Shadowing Engine. The Monitoring Engine consists of a Collector and an Analyzer. The Collector of master system gathers activities of all users who logged in the master system. The agent system observes the user who is thought to be an intruder by any intrusion detection module. The Analyzer of master and agent systems examines each collected activity and produces the formalized object *FO*. Certain critical *FOs* are always transmitted to the master system in real-time; others are processed locally by the agent system and only summary reports are sent to the master system. A Shadowing Engine replicates the security scheme following intruder's migration. The master system manages the predefined rules to trace an intruder. The Intruder Tracer of master system extracts the useful pieces among *FOs* and constructs a connection chain which will be explained in subsequent sections. The Agent Manager controls all the distributed agent systems in the trusted domain.

The Shadowing Engine replicates the security scheme to the host on the intrusive path and supports domain extension to trace an intrusion. Fig. 5 presents the structure of the Shadowing Engine. The engine is composed of the replication module and the self-protection module.

A *FO* Filter extracts useful pieces among data sent from the Monitoring Engine and a *FO* Analyzer decides the point of time and the target host for replication. When any *FO* related to the connection is detected, *FO* Analyzer determines the target host and begins to transfer the security scheme. The Connection Manager attempts to establish the TCP connection with the target host. The Self Replication Module Manager checks the existence of the same security scheme in the target host. If there is same security scheme, the Self Replication Module Manager verifies that the installed scheme is the legal one through authentication and terminates the replication into the target host. Otherwise it lets the Remote Protocol Manager and the Remote Shell Manager send the security scheme to be copied and commands for installation, compiling and running of the duplicated modules to the target host. If above process is successful, the security scheme is set up in the target host. Since the security scheme is replicated using the pseudo terminal as a medium object, it is necessary to maintain an intruder's environment so that the intruder cannot recognize the

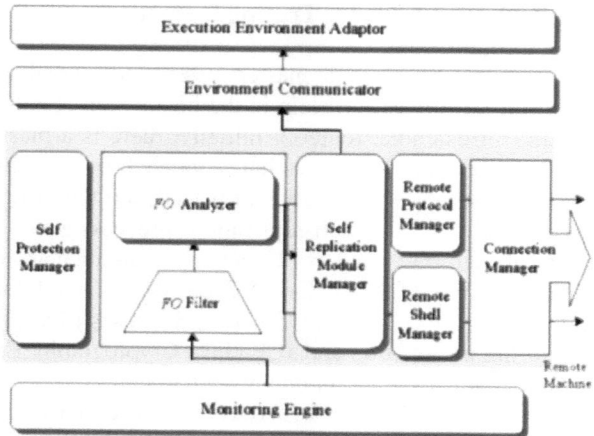

Fig. 5. Replication Engine

replication. The Environment Communicator and Execution Environment Adaptor support this maintenance. Replication protocol in the Self-Replication mechanism works as explained in section 3. Self-protection in the Self-Replication mechanism is to protect the monitoring activity itself. This plays an important role in earning some time to observe an intruder. The Self-Protection Manager in Fig. 5 attempts both to erase shadowing tracks and to blend into the normal Unix/Linux environment using camouflage. The Self-Replication mechanism carries out a number of functions to cover its trail. It erases its argument list after processing the arguments, so that the process status command would not reveal how it is invoked. It also deletes the executing binary, which would leave the data intact but unnamed, and only referenced by the execution of the Self-Replication mechanism. It uses resource limit functions to prevent a core dump. Thus, it prevents any bugs in the program from leaving telltale traces behind. In addition to erasing the tracks, camouflage is used to hide the shadowing. It is compiled under the name sh, the same name used by the Bourne Shell, a command interpreter which is often used in shell scripts and automatic commands. Even a diligent system manager would probably not notice a large number of shells running for short periods of time. Like this, it shields itself by replacing an original application program with a modified one. It sends the fake program along with the modules for replication like the trojan horse program. It can conceal processes using *ps*, *top* or *pidof* and hide files using *find*, *ls* or *du*.

5.2 Intruder Tracing by the HUNTER

This system assigns trace-id(TID) to a new user who is decided to be the intruder by any intrusion detection module and maintains a connection chain about TID. The connection chain chases the intruder's movement. The connection includes all sorts of connections which can occur through the pseudo terminal.

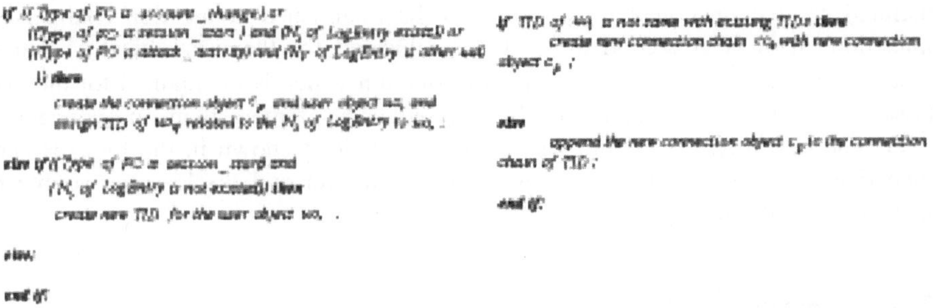

(A)   (B)

Fig. 6. (A) Rules for generating TID (B) Rules for constructing the Connection Chain

The master system monitors all users' activities on the host which the master system runs. The agent system just watches the users thought to be intruders by the master system. The targets of monitoring include attempts to connect, file access operation, process execution operation and etc. Monitoring activity records a log from which the formalized object *FO* is generated. *FO* is composed of the log collected at each agent system or the master system, the ID of the host that made the log and the *Type* field. In case of change log, *Type* may have such values as *session_start* for user session creation event, *account_change* for account change, *attack_activity* for intrusive behavior event and etc. A useful data abstracted from *FO* contains a connection object and a user object. Concerning Unix and Linux, the three ways to create a new connection are for a user to login from a terminal, console, or off-LAN source, to login locally or remotely from an existing user object legitimately, and to gain other user's privilege by illegal method such as a buffer overflow attack. These connections make new user objects and connection objects. The master system receives those objects from agent systems. It constructs a connection chain from connection objects and tries to associate the user object with an existing TID or allow the user object a new TID. We consider a user object $uo_i \in UO$ ($i \geq 0$) to be the 4-tuple *<TID, UserID, HostID, Time>* where *UO* is a set of user objects in the trusted domain. After TID generating rule is applied to the user object, value for TID is assigned.

TID and a connection chain play important parts in tracing an intruder. TID provides a unique identifier for the user who continues to attack across several hosts. Whenever a new connection object is created, new user object is formed and applicable TID is assigned to the user object. Finding an applicable TID consists of several steps. If a user changes identity on a host, the new user object is assigned the same TID as the previous one. If a user establishes a new connection with another host, the new user object gets the same TID as that of the source user object. The new user object is assigned the same TID as the previous identity in the case where the intruder obtains the superuser privilege in the remote host using vulnerabilities of the remote server. Since the user who logins from a terminal, console, or off-LAN source does not have the previous identity, new TID is assigned to the user object. Fig. 6A describes a rule with which connection objects and user objects are generated from *FO* and TID is assigned. Each TID maintains its own single connection chain to keep track of the intruder. Whenever a user with same TID sets a new connection, the generated connection object is appended to the established connection chain. New connection chain is created if new TID is allocated for the user object. A single connection chain $cc_i \in CC$ ($i \geq 0$) is the information which is maintained for the user whose TID is i. The connection chain is a sequence of more than one connection object. The rule for constructing the connection chain is shown in the Fig. 6B. The connection chain makes it possible to trace an intruder and disclose the source of attack and the intruder's identity.

5.3 Implementation Example

Fig. 7 presents the web-based user interface of HUNTER. Each of the upper frames of two big windows displays the connection chain for a specific TID. The two right bottom windows show the information of each connection object in the connection chain and intruder's activities in real time. The bottom frame of the left big window presents information about the source host and the user who begins the connection chain.

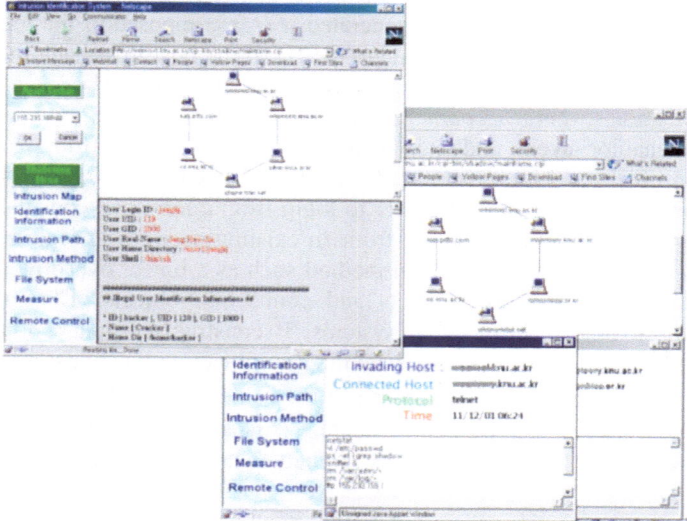

Fig. 7. User Interface (Host names are omitted for anonymity)

6 Performance Evaluations

We measured an intruder tracing rate which changes by the range of attack or intrusive path about the extent or location of the initial security domain in this experiment. An Intruder Tracing Rate Per Individual $ITRPI_i$ is a degree of tracing the intrusive path of the user i who establishes new connections within the trusted domain D_j. It is given by

$$ITRPI_i = \frac{ICC_i}{BI_i} \tag{1}$$

where BI_i is the number of connection objects generated by the user i in the D_t and ICC_i is the number of connection objects in the connection chain maintained for the user i uniquely by the HUNTER. $ITRPI_i$ has a value between 0 and 1. The value 1 of $ITRPI_i$ means that we can keep track of the specific user i completely in the trusted domain. ITR is the mean intruder tracing rate for all users who are inferred to be intruders in the trusted domain. It is given by

$$ITR = \frac{\sum\limits_{i=1}^{n} ITRPI_i}{n} \tag{2}$$

where n is the number of distinctive intruders in the domain D_t.

The target network was a class C, composed of four subnets which included 48 hosts and based on the Ethernet. It was in a single trusted domain. In this experiment, we confined network components to routers or gateways, PCs and workstations, the operating system running on each host to Solaris 2.6, Red Hat Linux 6.1 or above, and services to *telnet, ftp, www* and e-mail service. In order to lower a complexity, we assumed that an SSH secure shell 3.0.0 remote root exploit vulnerability [12] was implicit in every target and intermediary host of the attack in the trusted domain. We also presumed that the only attack used SSH secure shell vulnerability and the success rate of the attack was 100%.

6.1 Intruder Tracing Rate by the Initial Location of a Security Domain

We assessed the intruder tracing rate as the location of an initial security domain changes. We assumed an initial security domain covering only one host and a specific intrusive path within the trusted domain.

Fig. 8 shows conditions for this experiment. The path included 12 hosts which were distributed in four subnets. There was only one host X with the master system in the trusted domain. In case A, X was out of the intrusive path. In case B, X was the fifth host on the intrusive path. In case C, the intruder attacked the host X first to penetrate the trusted domain. For each case, we generated 50 different intrusive paths which satisfied the above condition. 10 different users passed through different paths.

Fig. 9 shows the result of the experiment. The x-axis presents the degree of an attack advance through the intrusive path. The ITR indicated by y-axis is 1 if every connection caused by intruders is noticed within the trusted domain. In case A, the attacks have been advanced out of the security domain. That's why the ITR is 0. In case B, not all intrusion paths could be traced. It was possible to trace the path from the point of time when the intruder has gone through the master system. In case C, when the intruder has passed through the host X first to penetrate the trusted

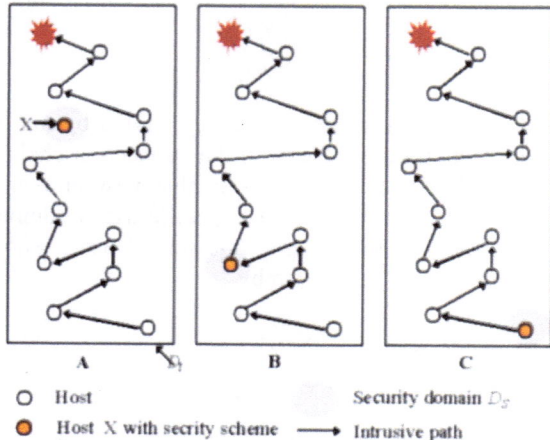

Fig. 8. Conditions for the Experiment

domain, the security domain could be extended to cover the total intrusive path within the trusted domain, making it possible to trace the intruder. This experimental result shows that the effect of the Self-Replication mechanism can be maximized if the master system is in the host which is a unique entrance to the trusted domain.

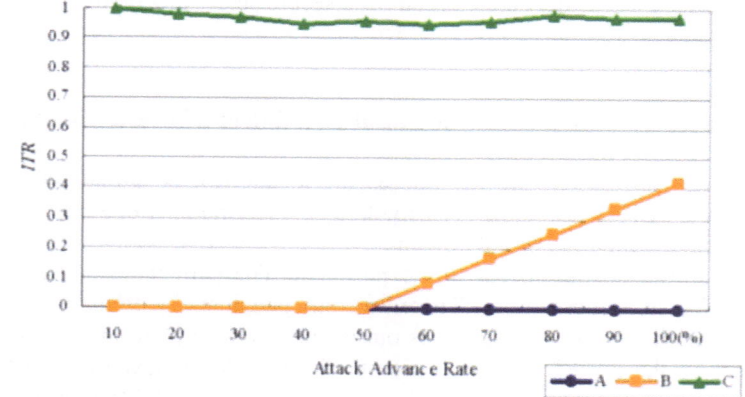

Fig. 9. Intruder Tracing Rate by the Attack Advance Rate

6.2 Intruder Tracing Rate by the Attack Range

As the attack range became wider within the trusted domain, we tested the intruder tracing rate on the condition listed in Table 1. We regarded the entire trusted domain as 100%. For the experiment, the attack range varied from 0% to 100% irrelevant to the intrusive path. However, the first penetrated host in the trusted domain was fixed and any security scheme was placed in that host in each case.

Table 1. Conditions for Evaluation

Condition Case	The number of system with security solution on the intrusive path in advance	Installed Security Solutions
A	1(2.08%)	HUNTER without Self-Replication
B	12(25%)	HUNTER without Self-Replication
C	48(100%)	HUNTER without Self-Replication
D	1(2.08%)	HUNTER

In case of D in Table 1, we installed HUNTER into the only one host in the trusted domain. In other cases, HUNTER without the Self-Replication mechanism which cannot broaden the security domain was set up in more than one host.

Fig. 10 shows the result of experiment. In case of A, there was only one host with security solution. As an intruder extended the attack range, the *ITR* dropped rapidly. About 25% of hosts including the first attacked host in the trusted domain had the security solution in the case of B. It shows that *ITR* of case B was better than that of case A but the rate still went down as the attack has advanced along the intrusive path. In case of C, we had to install the security solution into all hosts in the trusted domain in advance. It was possible to respond to the intrusion in every host in cases of C and D. However, Case D had considerable merits over case C with respect to the cost. That's because installing and executing the security solution were performed automatically through the intrusive path in case D.

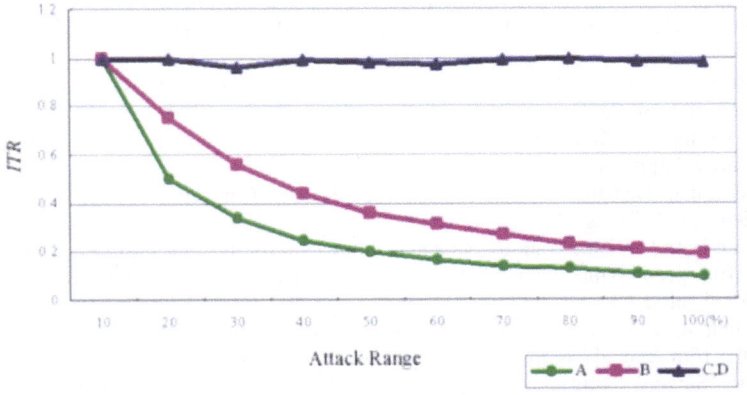

Fig. 10. The Intruder Tracing Rate by the attack range

7   Conclusions

Existing security management systems including intruder tracing systems fix their security domain after being installed in some hosts by SSOs. Therefore, it is impossible to respond to the attack properly as an intruder continues to attack across several hosts.

For this reason, this paper proposed the Self-Replication Mechanism and HUNTER which is a real-time intruder tracing system based on the mechanism. The Self-Replication Mechanism applies to the case that an intruder uses the medium object such as a pseudo terminal at least once during an attack on the trusted domain. The Self-Replication mechanism is applicable to general security solutions. The HUNTER traces an intruder and gathers information about him/her. If an intruder attempts to access the source host while attacking the trusted domain, the SSO could determine the origin of the attack. This system overcomes the restriction on the security domain under certain assumptions. Since the proposed approach in this paper traces the user who is assumed to be the intruder by any intrusion detection system, it is necessary to consult any intrusion detection system. A proper response to the attack is carried out during shadowing of the intruder.

References

1. S.S. Chen & L.T. Heberlein: Holding Intruders Accountable on the Internet. In Proceedings of the IEEE Symposium on Security and Privacy, (1995) 39–49
2. G. Eschelbeck: Active Security-A proactive approach for computer security systems. Journal of Network and Computer Applications, 23, (2000) 109–130
3. D. Schnackenberg, K. Djahandari & D. Sterne: Infrastructure for Intrusion Detection and Response, Advanced Security Research Journal, 3, (2001) 17–26
4. H.T. Jung *et al.*: Caller Identification System in the Internet Environment, In Proceedings of Usenix Security Symposium, (1993)
5. S. Snapp *et al.*: DIDS(Distributed Intrusion Detection System) – Motivation, Architecture, and an early prototype. In Proceedings of National Computer Security Conference, (1991) 167–176
6. M.R. Cornwell: A Software Engineering Approach to Designing Trustworthy Software. In Proceedings of the Symposium on Security and Privacy, (1989) 148–156
7. M. Bishop: A Model of Security Monitoring. In Proceedings of the Annual Computer Security Applications Conference, (1989) 46–52
8. S. S. Chen: Distributed tracing of intruder, Thesis of master's degree, Dept. of Computer Science, U.C.Davis. (1997)
9. K. Yoda and H. Etoh: Finding a Connection Chain for Tracing Intruders. In Proceedings of 6th European Symposium on Research in Computer Security - ESORICS 2000 LNCS - 1985, Toulouse France (2000)
10. H. Jang & S. Kim: A Self-Extension Monitoring for Security Management. In Proceeding of the 16th Annual Computer Security Applications Conference, (2000) 196–203
11. W.R. Stevens: Advanced Programming in the UNIX Environment, Addison-Wesley Publishing Company, (1992) 631–658
12. SSH Secure Shell 3.0.0 Security Advisory 2001. Found at URL: http://www.ciac.org/ciac/bulletins/l-121.shtml, CIAC, U.S. Department of Energy

On the Difficulty of Protecting Private Keys in Software

Taekyoung Kwon

Sejong University
Seoul 143-747, Korea
tkwon@sejong.ac.kr

Abstract. This paper makes simple observation on security of the
networked cryptographic device resilient to capture that was developed
to protect user's private keys by software-only techniques. That scheme
provided valuable features for secure generation of digital signatures
or decryption of messages in a way of retaining a password-protected
private key in a user-controlled device. The key idea was to exploit
network connectivity rather than tamper-resistance of the device for
securing the private key in software. However, we have found a few weak
points that are not negligible in some sense. It was difficult to protect
the private key in software even with provable security. So, we will
describe such difficulties and provide possible solutions in this paper.
Also the networked cryptographic devices will be augmented in that
fashion.

1 Introduction

Public key cryptography works well so long as a user knows intended recipient's
public key in advance. A public key infrastructure (PKI) plays an important
role for binding a public key to an entity in that sense. However, the security of
public key cryptography depends upon the security of a private key as well. If
the private key is compromised, all messages that are encrypted with its corresponding public key can be read. Also the compromised private key can be used
to forge user's digital signature. So care must be taken to manage the private
key in PKIs. However, the keying material is not favorable to human memory,
so that a kind of storage device *resilient to capture* is required for securing user's
private key [11].

It is obvious that a tamper-resistant device is a promising solution for the
purpose because the private key can never leave the portable device, for example,
a crypto smart card. However, such a device is still expensive and not ubiquitous
at this time. From a different standpoint, the tamper-resistant device could have
a surreptitious channel injected by someone at manufacturing time because it
is supposed to be a black box of which the inside can never be verified by its
users [3]. Also it can be vulnerable to the virus that infects user's computer to
modify messages exchanged with the device [7].

A.H. Chan and V. Gligor (Eds.): ISC 2002, LNCS 2433, pp. 17–31, 2002.

Currently it is usual to encrypt the private key with a symmetric key derived from a mnemonic password and retain it in a user-controlled device such as a desktop computer, notebook and handheld, in software [15]. However, the storage device is not tamper-resistant, so that the password-encrypted key is vulnerable to a dictionary attack. For example, an adversary who compiled a dictionary of likely passwords steals the encrypted private key. (S)he decrypts a candidate key, signs an arbitrary message, and verifies it with a corresponding public key. (S)he repeats this procedure until (s)he gets a correct guess. Such attacks work in a relatively small space of passwords[1]. This is the reason why we must take care when we handle the private key in a user-controlled environment.

Lately several new methods were proposed to improve security of the password-protected private key in a user-controlled environment. They include the software smart card [7] and the networked cryptographic device [11]. They postulated a remote server and exploited network connectivity in a way to cooperate with the server for performing private key operations. So, an adversary had to compromise the server as well as the password-protected private key in order to steal user's private key in the end. The main difference between them was that the server was the only entity who can verify the signature in the former scheme, while the server assisted the device only in performing its private key operation in the latter scheme. They are notable and useful when we consider a practical solution for protecting user's private key in software rather than by using a tamper-resistant device. Both of them provided security claims clearly, so that it has been known they are secure simply under postulating the remote server.

However, we have found a few weak points from them, respectively, in terms of security. For example, the software smart card was vulnerable to impersonation attacks in some practical cases [10]. This paper will scrutinize the networked cryptographic device in terms of security. The weak points may not be negligible for practical use in real world application and can be serious flaws in some sense. So, this paper will discuss the difficulty of protecting private keys in software and augment the networked cryptographic device with possible solutions. This paper is organized as follows: In Section 2 we will summarize basic notation and define a basic model that protects user's private key in software. In Section 3 we will describe the networked cryptographic device. Then we will scrutinize the weak points in Section 4 and augment the previous scheme with possible solutions in Section 5. Finally, Section 6 will conclude this paper.

2   Preliminaries

In this section we describe notation to be used in this paper and define a basic model of protecting user's private key in software.

---

[1] Password security has been studied for more than thirty years and there have been a great amount of work [12,2,6]. Recently the IEEE P1363 Standard Working Group is working on strong password protocols including SPEKE, SRP, PAK and AMP [8].

Table 1. Basic model of protecting private keys in software

Entity	Functions
User	- remembers π. - controls dvc. - types π into dvc.
dvc	- holds the password-protected private key. - communicates with svr over a public network.
svr	- holds a private key. - communicates with dvc over a public network.
adv	- holds a dictionary of likely passwords. - controls the whole network.

2.1 Notation

Let us borrow well-defined notation from [11]. Let κ be the main cryptographic security parameter such that $\kappa = 160$ while λ be a secondary security parameter for public keys, for example, $\lambda = 1024$ in that sense. Also we define a tiny parameter σ such that $\sigma = 16$. Here dvc and svr denote a user-controlled device and a remote server, respectively. Also π denote a user password while pk_{svr} server's authentic public key and sk_{svr} a corresponding private key. Here note that we will not describe in detail for public key operations of svr rather we will use $\mathcal{E}_{pk_{svr}}()$ and $\mathcal{D}_{sk_{svr}}()$ for convenience. However, we denote user's RSA public key pair as $< e, N >$ and $< d, N >$ where N is a good RSA product of two distinct odd primes, satisfying $2^{\lambda-1} \leq N < 2^{\lambda}$, and e and d are, respectively, encryption and decryption exponents, satisfying $e, d \in Z^*_{\phi(N)}$ and $ed \equiv 1 \pmod{\phi(N)}$ [16,14]. The Euler totient function is denoted by $\phi(N)$. We will use $h()$ to denote a strong one-way hash function while $\text{mac}_a()$ a specific type of keyed hash function, namely, a message authentication code (MAC). Also $E_b()$ and $D_b()$ will denote respectively encryption and decryption under a symmetric key b. A random padding is denoted by $R()$ that will pad a pre-image with random bits to a multiple of the block length of encryption system, maintaining a record of the length of the pre-image. Finally $\mathcal{C}$ denote a X.509 certificate. Additional notation that was not described here, will be declared in each part of this paper.

2.2 Basic Model

As we mentioned already, the networked cryptographic devices and the software smart cards respectively introduced valuable framework to protect user's private key in software [11,7]. They postulated a remote server and exploited network connectivity in a way of cooperating with the server to perform private key operations for a user. We define a basic model of such schemes as shown in Table 1. In this model, an adversary adv is supposed to control any inputs to dvc and svr, hear all of their outputs, and attempt a dictionary attack. Also an adversarial goal may include recovery of the private key, signature forgery, and message decryption when we consider security of a private key.

3 Protecting Private Keys in Software

3.1 Networked Cryptographic Device

Networked cryptographic devices proposed lately by Phillip MacKenzie and Michael Reiter [11] are state-of-the-art in their provable approach of protecting user's private key by software-only techniques. Their scheme was inspired by the work of [5] and so is comparable with the cryptographic camouflage [7] in their similar goals. They do not require tamper-resistance of a storage device. Instead, they exploit network connectivity by postulating a remote server that assists the device in performing its private key operation. They assumed the remote server could be untrusted. They presented three kinds of protocols in their paper [11]. Among them we will handle two kinds of protocols such as a generic key retrieval protocol and a protocol for RSA signatures. Note the basic model we described in Section 2.2.

3.2 Generic Key Retrieval Protocol

MacKenzie and Reiter presented a simple key retrieval protocol first. There are two phases such as device initialization and key retrieval for the generic key retrieval protocol of the networked cryptographic devices.

Device Initialization. The inputs to device initialization are server's public key pk_{svr}, user's password π, device's (actually user's) public key pk_{dvc}, and its corresponding private key sk_{dvc}. At device initialization time, the private key of the device is encrypted in a way that can be recovered only with the cooperation of both the device and the server. The device chooses v and a uniformly at random from $\{0,1\}^\kappa$, and computes $b = h(\pi)$, $c = f(v,\pi) \oplus sk_{dvc}$, and $\tau = \mathcal{E}_{pk_{svr}}(< a,b,c >)$ where $f()$ outputs a value of length equal to the length of sk_{dvc}. The values v, a, τ, pk_{svr} and pk_{dvc} are saved in stable storage of the device while all the others must be deleted from the device.

Key Retrieval. The device can run the following protocol with the server for retrieving the private key. Figure 1 depicts this protocol.

1. If a user types a password, the device computes $\beta = h(\pi)$ and chooses ρ at random from $\{0,1\}^\lambda$. The device computes $\gamma = \mathcal{E}_{pk_{svr}}(< \beta, \rho >)$ and $\delta = \mathsf{mac}_a(< \gamma, \tau >)$ where mac denotes a message authentication code. $< \gamma, \delta, \tau >$ is sent to the server.
2. The server decrypts τ to get $< a, b, c >$ and aborts if $\mathsf{mac}_a(< \gamma, \tau >) \neq \delta$. The server decrypts γ and aborts if $(\beta \neq b)$. The server computes $\eta = \rho \oplus c$ and sends this to the device.
3. The device computes $\rho \oplus \eta \oplus f(v, \pi)$ to get sk_{dvc}. If $M(pk_{dvc}, sk_{dvc}) \neq 1$, the device aborts where $M()$ returns 1 for correct keys. Otherwise the device returns sk_{dvc}.

The next protocol does not recover the private key even to the user and provides an interesting feature such as key disabling.

dvc   svr

$\beta \leftarrow h(\pi)$
$\rho \leftarrow_R \{0,1\}^\lambda$
$\gamma \leftarrow \mathcal{E}_{pk_{svr}}(<\beta, \rho>)$
$\delta \leftarrow \mathsf{mac}_a(<\gamma, \tau>)$

$$\xrightarrow{\quad \gamma, \delta, \tau \quad}$$

$\qquad\qquad\qquad\qquad\qquad < a, b, c > \leftarrow \mathcal{D}_{sk_{svr}}(\tau)$
$\qquad\qquad\qquad\qquad\qquad$ abort if $\mathsf{mac}_a(<\gamma, \tau>) \neq \delta$
$\qquad\qquad\qquad\qquad\qquad < \beta, \rho > \leftarrow \mathcal{D}_{sk_{svr}}(\gamma)$
$\qquad\qquad\qquad\qquad\qquad$ abort if $(\beta \neq b)$
$\qquad\qquad\qquad\qquad\qquad \eta \leftarrow \rho \oplus c$

$$\xleftarrow{\quad \eta \quad}$$

$sk_{dvc} \leftarrow \rho \oplus \eta \oplus f(v, \pi)$
abort if $M(pk_{dvc}, sk_{dvc}) \neq 1$

Fig. 1. Generic key retrieval protocol

3.3 RSA Signature Protocol

The RSA signature protocol provides an interesting ability for the user to disable a private key of the device even after an adversary has captured. For the purpose, the two-party RSA scheme is used in an additive manner, namely by splitting d into $d_1 + d_2$ [1,11]. Disabling the private key was achieved by requesting that the server should permanently ignore the device's ticket. There are two phases such as device initialization and signature generation for the RSA signature protocol.

Device Initialization. The inputs to device initialization are server's public key pk_{svr}, user's password π, and device's (actually user's) public key pair such that $pk_{dvc} =< e, N >$ and $sk_{dvc} =< d, N >$ respectively. N is presumed to be a good RSA product of two distinct odd primes, satisfying $2^{\lambda-1} \leq N < 2^\lambda$, and e and d are, respectively, encryption and decryption exponents, satisfying $e, d \in Z^*_{\phi(N)}$ and $ed \equiv 1 \pmod{\phi(N)}$ [16,14]. The Euler's totient function $\phi(N)$ must also be necessary. Then the device computes the followings:

$$t \leftarrow_R \{0,1\}^\kappa$$
$$u \leftarrow h_{dsbl}(t)$$
$$v \leftarrow_R \{0,1\}^\kappa$$
$$a \leftarrow_R \{0,1\}^\kappa$$
$$b \leftarrow h(\pi)$$
$$d_1 \leftarrow f(v, \pi)$$
$$d_2 \leftarrow d - d_1 \bmod \phi(N)$$
$$\tau \leftarrow \mathcal{E}_{pk_{svr}}(< a, b, u, d_2, N >)$$

Finally the device saves the values t, v, a, τ, pk_{dvc} and pk_{svr} on its stable storage, and erases the other values such as $u, b, d, d_1, d_2, \phi(N)$, and π. Note that the values t and τ are backed up off line for key disabling features.

vrf   dvc   svr

$$\beta \leftarrow h(\pi)$$
$$\rho \leftarrow_R \{0,1\}^\lambda$$
$$r \leftarrow_R \{0,1\}^{\kappa_{sig}}$$
$$\gamma \leftarrow \mathcal{E}_{pk_{svr}}(m, r, \beta, \rho)$$
$$\delta \leftarrow \mathsf{mac}_a(\gamma, \tau)$$

$$\xrightarrow{\gamma, \delta, \tau}$$

$$< a, b, u, d_2, N > \leftarrow \mathcal{D}_{sk_{svr}(\tau)}$$
abort if $\mathsf{mac}_a(\gamma, \tau) \neq \delta$
$$< m, r, \beta, \rho > \leftarrow \mathcal{D}_{sk_{svr}(\gamma)}$$
abort if $(\beta \neq b)$
$$\nu \leftarrow (\mathsf{enc}(m, r))^{d_2} \bmod N$$
$$\eta \leftarrow \rho \oplus \nu$$

$$\xleftarrow{\eta}$$

$$\nu \leftarrow \rho \oplus \eta$$
$$d_1 \leftarrow f(v, \pi)$$
$$s \leftarrow \nu(\mathsf{enc}(m, r))^{d_1} \bmod N$$
$$m_1 \leftarrow s^e \bmod N$$
$$m_2 \leftarrow \mathsf{enc}(m, r)$$
abort if $m_1 \neq m_2$

verify $\mathcal{C}$ $\xleftarrow{\mathcal{C}, s, m, r}$
$$m_1 \leftarrow s^e \bmod N$$
$$m_2 \leftarrow \mathsf{enc}(m, r)$$
Abort if $m_1 \neq m_2$
Otherwise, accept

Fig. 2. RSA signature protocol

Signature Generation. The device can run the protocol depicted in Figure 2, in order to generate a RSA signature and send it to an actual verifier, vrf. In this method, the signature on a message m is defined as $< s, r >$ such that $s = (\mathsf{enc}(m, r))^d \bmod N$. The parameter κ_{sig} denotes the number of random bits used in the encoding function $\mathsf{enc}()$.

Key Disabling. When the device was compromised, the user can send t and τ to the server so that the server records τ on a disabled list if $h_{\mathsf{dsbl}}(t) \neq u$.

4   On the Difficulties

In this section we scrutinize the weak points of the networked cryptographic device.

4.1   Adversaries

An adversary is presumed to have a dictionary of likely passwords for the user and control the whole network, meaning that (s)he can control any inputs to the device dvc and the server svr, hear all of their outputs, and attempt a dictionary attack. Also (s)he can *capture* certain resources in the networked cryptographic device [11]. However, (s)he cannot succeed in breaking a RSA system since such a theoretical aspect is ignored simply by assuming that RSA is safe.

Let us utilize the following definition for scrutinizing the weak points [11].

Definition 1. ADV(S) *means the class of adversaries who succeeded in capturing* S *where* $S \subseteq \{\mathsf{dvc}, \mathsf{svr}, \pi\}$. *It must satisfy* ADV($S_1$) $\subseteq$ ADV(S_2) *if* $S_1 \subseteq S_2$.

The networked cryptographic device was provably secure in meeting the security goals against the following adversary classes. Readers are referred to [11] for the details. Roman numerals denote each type of adversary classes.

I.   ADV($\{\mathsf{svr}, \pi\}$) cannot forge signatures or decrypt messages.
II.   ADV($\{\mathsf{dvc}\}$) needs on-line dictionary attacks.
III.   ADV($\{\mathsf{dvc}, \mathsf{svr}\}$) needs off-line dictionary attacks.
IV.   ADV($\{\mathsf{dvc}, \pi\}$) can be frustrated by key disabling.

However, we have found that some classes must be probed again, and the remaining classes must be observed as well.

V.   ADV($\{\mathsf{dvc}, \mathsf{svr}, \pi\}$)
VI.   ADV($\{\pi\}$)
VII.   ADV($\{\mathsf{svr}\}$)
VIII. ADV($\{\}$)

As we can see from now, there were more adversarial classes to be observed on protecting private keys in software, and some of them were real threats. We will scrutinize them by each type of adversary classes.

Class V. Firstly we define the following for observing ADV($\{\mathsf{dvc}, \mathsf{svr}, \pi\}$).

Definition 2. *An adversary in* ADV(S) *can totally break the system if* $S = \{\mathsf{dvc}, \mathsf{svr}, \pi\}$.

The total break means that either of the adversarial goals such as recovery of the private key, signature forgery, and message decryption, was achieved by an adversary in ADV(S). For example, an adversary in ADV($\{\mathsf{dvc}, \mathsf{svr}\}$) can totally break the system if (s)he succeeded in off-line dictionary attacks. All the other classes should not be derived to ADV($\{\mathsf{dvc}, \mathsf{svr}, \pi\}$) directly.

4.2   Capturing vs. Attaching

By Definition 1, we claim that each class should not be transformed to a larger class without capturing the corresponding element explicitly. For example, it must be disallowed to derive ADV($\{\mathsf{dvc}, \mathsf{svr}, \pi\}$) from ADV($\{\mathsf{dvc}, \mathsf{svr}\}$) without capturing π or attaching ADV($\{\pi\}$) to the class explicitly. In this case, "capturing π" and "attaching ADV($\{\pi\}$)" can be slightly different from each other in their respective meanings. The former must have been done by an adversary in ADV($\{\mathsf{dvc}, \mathsf{svr}\}$), while the latter must have been derived from ADV($\{\}$).

Class VI. The only possible way of deriving $\text{ADV}(\{\pi\})$ from $\text{ADV}(\{\})$, could be the aspect of social engineering, for example, by threatening a human user. This is because an adversary in $\text{ADV}(\{\})$ retains nothing for queries, assuming oracles. So, an adversary in $\text{ADV}(\{\text{dvc}, \text{svr}, \pi\})$ can do presumably all the things an adversary in $\text{ADV}(\{\text{dvc}, \text{svr}\})$ or $\text{ADV}(\{\pi\})$ could do, while the adversary in $\text{ADV}(\{\text{dvc}, \text{svr}\})$ or $\text{ADV}(\{\pi\})$ cannot do the things the adversary in $\text{ADV}(\{\text{dvc}, \text{svr}, \pi\})$ could do in some cases. Note that $\text{ADV}(\{\text{dvc}, \text{svr}, \pi\})$ can be more powerful than $\text{ADV}(\{\text{dvc}, \text{svr}\})$ in that sense. So, care must be taken when we consider adversarial classes. However, the social engineering aspect is an unavoidable threat when using a password, so that we neglect it technically in this paper as well. Here we define the followings for both capturing and attaching.

Definition 3. $\text{ADV}(\{S_1\} + S_2)$ *means that a new element S_1 was captured by* $\text{ADV}(\{S_1\})$, *and is derived to* $\text{ADV}(\{S_1, S_2\})$.

Definition 4. $\text{ADV}(\{S_1\}) + \text{ADV}(\{S_2\})$ *means that a new class $\text{ADV}(\{S_2\})$ was attached to* $\text{ADV}(\{S_1\})$, *and is derived to* $\text{ADV}(\{S_1, S_2\})$.

For example, $\text{ADV}(\{\} + \pi)$ means that an adversary in $\text{ADV}(\{\})$ has acquired π in a way of social engineering, while $\text{ADV}(\{\text{dvc}, \text{svr}\} + \pi)$ can imply ambiguously either case of social engineering or dictionary attacks for an adversary in $\text{ADV}(\{\text{dvc}, \text{svr}\})$. However, by Definition 4, $\text{ADV}(\{\text{dvc}, \text{svr}\}) + \text{ADV}(\{\pi\})$ will denote social engineering for an adversary in $\text{ADV}(\{\text{dvc}, \text{svr}\})$ while $\text{ADV}(\{\text{dvc}, \text{svr}\} + \pi)$ dictionary attacks for the same adversary. Note that both can be derived to $\text{ADV}(\{\text{dvc}, \text{svr}, \pi\})$, the total break! We summarize them where $\rightarrow$ means derivation.

- $\text{ADV}(\{\}) \rightarrow \text{ADV}(\{\} + \pi) \rightarrow \text{ADV}(\{\pi\})$
- $\text{ADV}(\{\text{dvc}, \text{svr}\}) \rightarrow \text{ADV}(\{\text{dvc}, \text{svr}\} + \pi) \rightarrow \text{ADV}(\{\text{dvc}, \text{svr}, \pi\})$
- $\text{ADV}(\{\text{dvc}, \text{svr}\}) \rightarrow \text{ADV}(\{\text{dvc}, \text{svr}\}) + \text{ADV}(\{\pi\}) \rightarrow \text{ADV}(\{\text{dvc}, \text{svr}, \pi\})$

Similar cases can be observed in the other classes, such as $\text{ADV}(\{\text{dvc}\})$ and $\text{ADV}(\{\text{svr}\})$. So, we will scrutinize them and their threats in more detail.

4.3   Finding New Threats

We will describe newly found threats on protecting private keys in software. For the purpose, two remaining classes must be observed such as $\text{ADV}(\{\text{svr}\})$ and $\text{ADV}(\{\})$.

Class VII. Any adversary in $\text{ADV}(\{\text{svr}\})$ has server's private key, sk_{svr}, so that τ or γ can be decrypted by the adversary. Then, the adversary is able to find π by dictionary attacks on β or b. See Figure 1 and Figure 2 for the details. As a result, the following derivation is possible with a few queries.

- $\text{ADV}(\{\text{svr}\}) \rightarrow \text{ADV}(\{\text{svr}\} + \pi) \rightarrow \text{ADV}(\{\text{svr}, \pi\})$
- $\text{ADV}(\{\text{svr}\}) \rightarrow \text{ADV}(\{\text{svr}\}) + \text{ADV}(\{\pi\}) \rightarrow \text{ADV}(\{\text{svr}, \pi\})$

It must be a threat when we observe the following derivation.

- $\mathrm{ADV}(\{\mathsf{svr}, \pi\}) \rightarrow \mathrm{ADV}(\{\mathsf{svr}, \pi\} + \mathsf{dvc}) \rightarrow \mathrm{ADV}(\{\mathsf{dvc}, \mathsf{svr}, \pi\})$
- $\mathrm{ADV}(\{\mathsf{svr}\}) \rightarrow \mathrm{ADV}(\{\mathsf{svr}\} + \mathsf{dvc}) \rightarrow \mathrm{ADV}(\{\mathsf{dvc}, \mathsf{svr}\})$

Simply if the device is captured, an adversary in $\mathrm{ADV}(\{\mathsf{svr}, \pi\}$ is more advantageous to total breaking than an adversary in $\mathrm{ADV}(\{\mathsf{svr}\})$. So, class VII must be considered carefully to avoid such derivation. The possible threats are as follows.

T1: The server can obtain password information by dictionary attacks, so that an adversary in $\mathrm{ADV}(\{\mathsf{svr}\})$ can do the same thing.
T2: In practice, the adversary in $\mathrm{ADV}(\{\mathsf{svr}\})$ can deny services to the device.

Class VIII. An adversary in $\mathrm{ADV}(\{\})$ can make the following derivation only.

- $\mathrm{ADV}(\{\}) \rightarrow \mathrm{ADV}(\{\} + \pi) \rightarrow \mathrm{ADV}(\{\pi\})$

It was derived in a way of social engineering, so that we can technically neglect it. However, the following threats can be observed for $\mathrm{ADV}(\{\})$ in practice.

T3: An adversary in $\mathrm{ADV}(\{\})$ replays an old legitimate message to the server. Then, the replayed message can make a server busy without detection.
T4: An adversary in $\mathrm{ADV}(\{\})$ generates a bogus message and sends it to the server. Then, the message can make a server busy without detection.

The reason for T3 is that the server could not check any time-derived information from γ. Also the reason for T4 is that the device was able to generate τ at any time, even without communicating with the server [11]. For example, an adversary in $\mathrm{ADV}(\{\})$ generates a bogus message $< \gamma', \delta', \tau' >$ such that $\tau' = \mathcal{E}_{pk_{\mathsf{svr}}}(< a', b', c' >)$, $\gamma' = \mathcal{E}_{pk_{\mathsf{svr}}}(< b', \rho >)$, and $\delta' = \mathsf{mac}_{a'}(< \gamma', \tau' >)$. Then the server cannot decline the requested service when receiving the bogus message. Though the adversary cannot obtain the previously mentioned adversarial goals, (s)he can make the server busy enough to be in serious states.

4.4   Misunderstanding Adversaries

We revisit the adversary classes of types I, II, and IV for more examination.

Class I. Security against $\mathrm{ADV}(\{\mathsf{svr}, \pi\})$ was proved in [11] in the random oracle model (See Theorem 6.1 and Theorem 6.2 in [11]). The following derivation is unavoidable to reach such a class.

- $\mathrm{ADV}(\{\mathsf{svr}\}) \rightarrow \mathrm{ADV}(\{\mathsf{svr}\}) + \mathrm{ADV}(\{\pi\}) \rightarrow \mathrm{ADV}(\{\mathsf{svr}, \pi\})$

However, the following derivation must be avoided as we mentioned with class VII (See T1 above).

- $\mathrm{ADV}(\{\mathsf{svr}\}) \rightarrow \mathrm{ADV}(\{\mathsf{svr}\} + \pi) \rightarrow \mathrm{ADV}(\{\mathsf{svr}, \pi\})$

Class II. Security against ADV({dvc}) was achieved by detecting on-line attacks in [11]. Also off-line dictionary attacks were infeasible with overwhelming probability (See Theorem 6.3 and Theorem 7.3 in [11]). However, the following threat is observed.

T5: An adversary in ADV({dvc}) sends t and τ to the server so that the user's private key is disabled.

Class IV. Security against ADV({dvc, π}) was proved in [11] as well (See Theorem 7.4 in [11]). However, as we examined above, the only possible derivation to ADV({dvc, π}) is:

– ADV({dvc}) → ADV({dvc})+ADV({π}) → ADV({dvc, π})

As a result, it is of little importance to consider this class because there is no way better than social engineering in order to derive ADV({dvc, π}) from ADV({dvc}). Also it is obvious that an adversary in ADV({dvc, π}) can achieve the adversarial goals until the private key or the corresponding public key is disabled.

5 Augmentation

In this section, we augment the networked cryptographic device against the weak points found in the previous section. The five threats are summarized as follows.

T1: The server can obtain password information by dictionary attacks, so that an adversary in ADV({svr}) can do the same thing.
T2: In practice, the adversary in ADV({svr}) can deny services to the device.
T3: An adversary in ADV({}) replays an old legitimate message to the server. Then, the replayed message can make a server busy without detection.
T4: An adversary in ADV({}) generates a bogus message and sends it to the server. Then, the message can make a server busy without detection.
T5: An adversary in ADV({dvc}) sends t and τ to the server so that the user's private key is disabled.

5.1 Augmented Password Verification

When verifying password information, the server decrypted τ and γ to compare β to b such that $\beta = b = h(\pi)$. However, the values β and b did not have sufficient entropy, so that they were vulnerable to dictionary attacks [12,2,6]. So, we slightly modify the system to derive both values as follows.

$$v \leftarrow_R \{0,1\}^\kappa$$
$$b \leftarrow h(v, \pi)$$
$$\beta \leftarrow h(v, \pi)$$

Such a modification will remove the possible threat, T1.

5.2 Augmented Initialization with a Trusted Server

When initializing the system, it was postulated that the device could initialize it alone, without communicating with the server. This property can be of interest but has critical weak points related many possible threats such as T2, T4, and T5. So, we need to modify the system to remove those threats. Let pks_{svr} and sks_{svr} denote server's signature key pair. Then the following must be abided by.

- The server must be trusted by the device, depending upon the server's authentic public key.
- The device and the server communicates with each other for initialization.
- The server signs b with sks_{svr} for the following computation.

$$\tau \leftarrow \mathcal{E}_{pk_{svr}}(< a, \mathcal{D}_{sks_{svr}}(b), c >)$$

- The device removes t from its storage while the user must back it up off line.

Then the threats, T4 and T5 can be removed. Note that T2 is unavoidable in any server-aided approaches [11]. However, postulating a trusted server is very important.

5.3 Including Time Stamps

When an adversary replayed old legitimate messages, the server was not able to detect such replays and so had to be busy with processing them. We modify the system to include time stamps so as to reduce the possible threat, T3. Let φ denote a time stamp. Then the messages should include it as follows.

$$\gamma \leftarrow \mathcal{E}_{pk_{svr}}(< \beta, \rho, \varphi >)$$
$$\delta \leftarrow \mathsf{mac}_a(\gamma, \tau, \varphi)$$

Finally, the server can verify φ when assisting the device, and request regeneration of the corresponding message if φ is out of the pre-defined range.

5.4 Augmented Key Retrieval Protocol

The augmented key retrieval protocol is as follows.

Device Initialization. The device computes the followings. Note that the server must sign b in this stage.

$$v \leftarrow_R \{0,1\}^\kappa$$
$$a \leftarrow_R \{0,1\}^\kappa$$
$$b \leftarrow h(v, \pi)$$
$$c \leftarrow f(v, \pi) \oplus sk_{dvc}$$
$$\tau \leftarrow \mathcal{E}_{pk_{svr}}(< a, \mathcal{D}_{sks_{svr}}(b), c >)$$

The values v, a, τ, pk_{svr} and pk_{dvc} are saved in stable storage of the device while all the others must be deleted from the device.

dvc   svr

$\beta \leftarrow h(v, \pi)$
$\rho \leftarrow_R \{0,1\}^\lambda$
$\gamma \leftarrow \mathcal{E}_{pk_{svr}}(< \beta, \rho, \varphi >)$
$\delta \leftarrow \mathsf{mac}_a(< \gamma, \tau, \varphi >)$

$$\xrightarrow{\gamma, \delta, \tau}$$

$< a, \mathcal{D}_{sks_{svr}}(b), c > \leftarrow \mathcal{D}_{sk_{svr}(\tau)}$
abort if $\mathsf{mac}_a(< \gamma, \tau, \varphi >) \neq \delta$
$< \beta, \rho, \varphi > \leftarrow \mathcal{D}_{sk_{svr}(\gamma)}$
abort if φ is out of range
$b \leftarrow \mathcal{E}_{pk_{svr}}(\mathcal{D}_{sks_{svr}}(b))$
abort if $(\beta \neq b)$
$\eta \leftarrow \rho \oplus c$

$$\xleftarrow{\eta}$$

$sk_{dvc} \leftarrow \rho \oplus \eta \oplus f(v, \pi)$
abort if $M(pk_{dvc}, sk_{dvc}) \neq 1$

Fig. 3. Augmented key retrieval protocol

Key Retrieval. The device can run the augmented protocol with the server for retrieving the private key. Figure 3 depicts this protocol.

5.5   Augmented RSA Signature Protocol

The augmented RSA signature protocol is as follows.

Device Initialization. The device computes the followings. Also note that the server must sign b in this stage.

$$t \leftarrow_R \{0,1\}^\kappa$$
$$u \leftarrow h_{\mathsf{dsbl}}(t)$$
$$v \leftarrow_R \{0,1\}^\kappa$$
$$a \leftarrow_R \{0,1\}^\kappa$$
$$b \leftarrow h(v, \pi)$$
$$d_1 \leftarrow f(v, \pi)$$
$$d_2 \leftarrow d - d_1 \bmod \phi(N)$$
$$\tau \leftarrow \mathcal{E}_{pk_{svr}}(< a, \mathcal{D}_{sks_{svr}}(b), u, d_2, N >)$$

Finally the device saves the values v, a, τ, pk_{dvc} and pk_{svr} on its stable storage, and erases the other values such as $t, u, b, d, d_1, d_2, \phi(N)$, and π. Note that the values t and τ are backed up off line for key disabling features.

Signature Generation. The device can run the augmented protocol depicted in Figure 4, in order to generate a RSA signature and send it to an actual verifier, vrf.

vrf   dvc   svr

$$\beta \leftarrow h(v, \pi)$$
$$\rho \leftarrow_R \{0,1\}^\lambda$$
$$r \leftarrow_R \{0,1\}^{\kappa_{sig}}$$
$$\gamma \leftarrow \mathcal{E}_{pk_{svr}}(m, r, \beta, \rho, \varphi)$$
$$\delta \leftarrow \mathsf{mac}_a(\gamma, \tau, \varphi)$$

$$\xrightarrow{\gamma, \delta, \zeta}$$

$$< a, \mathcal{D}_{sks_{svr}}(b), u, d_2, N > \leftarrow \mathcal{D}_{sks_{svr}(\tau)}$$
$$< m, r, \beta, \rho, \varphi > \leftarrow \mathcal{D}_{sks_{svr}(\gamma)}$$
abort if $\mathsf{mac}_a(\gamma, \tau, \varphi) \neq \delta$
abort if φ is out of range
$$b \leftarrow \mathcal{E}_{pks_{svr}}(\mathcal{D}_{sks_{svr}}(b))$$
abort if $(\beta \neq b)$
$$\nu \leftarrow (\mathsf{enc}(m, r))^{d_2} \bmod N$$
$$\eta \leftarrow \rho \oplus \nu$$

$$\xleftarrow{\eta}$$

$$\nu \leftarrow \rho \oplus \eta$$
$$d_1 \leftarrow f(v, \pi)$$
$$s \leftarrow \nu(\mathsf{enc}(m, r))^{d_1} \bmod N$$
$$m_1 \leftarrow s^e \bmod N$$
$$m_2 \leftarrow \mathsf{enc}(m, r)$$
abort if $m_1 \neq m_2$

verify $\mathcal{C}$ $\xrightarrow{\zeta, s, m, r}$
$$m_1 \leftarrow s^e \bmod N$$
$$m_2 \leftarrow \mathsf{enc}(m, r)$$
Abort if $m_1 \neq m_2$
Otherwise, accept

Fig. 4. Augmented RSA signature protocol

Key Disabling. When the device was compromised, the user can disable the private key by sending t and τ, while an adversary in $\mathrm{ADV}(\{dvc\})$ cannot achieve it.

6 Conclusion

In our previous study, we found that the related work named the software smart card was vulnerable to impersonation attacks when we consider an interleaved session in some practical cases [7,10]. So, in this paper, we made simple observation on the difficulty of protecting user's private key in software by scrutinizing the networked cryptographic device in details [11]. The networked cryptographic device was examined in terms of security and augmented by applying possible solutions. As we examined, it was difficult to protect the private key in software, even with provable security [11].

The private key management is important for securing user's digital identity in the cyber space. For the purpose, especially in a software-only environment, the networked cryptographic device may be useful with the proposed augmentation.

When mobility is necessary for a user, simply we may deposit the password-protected private key to a trusted server under a careful management. In order to deposit and download the private key securely, much work have been done, for example, Perlman and Kaufman used a password-based key exchange protocol [13]. Similar methods were announced in a commercial field, for instance, Entrust's SPEKE roaming, RSA's virtual smart card [17], and so on. However, they are sensitive to a server compromise because all user credentials depend upon a centered server. For the reasons, multiple server approaches are of growing interest [1,4,9]. In that sense, the networked cryptographic device can deposit the encrypted private key and the related values to another trusted server for mobility. Two different servers could improve security compared to a single server approach.

References

1. M. Bellare and R. Sandhu, "The security of practical two-party RSA signature schemes," Manuscript, 2001.
2. S. Bellovin and M. Merrit, "Encrypted key exchange: Password-based protocols secure against dictionary attacks," In Proceedings of the *IEEE Symposium on Security and Privacy*, pp.72-84, 1992.
3. S. Brands, *Rethinking public key infrastructures and digital certificates*, The MIT Press, p.11 and pp.219-224, 2000.
4. W. Ford and B. Kaliski, "Server-assisted generation of a strong secret from a password," In Proceedings of the *International Workshops on the Enabling Technologies: Infrastructure for Collaborative Enterprise*, IEEE, June 2000
5. R. Ganesan, "Yaksha: Augmenting Kerberos with public key cryptography," In Proceedings of the *ISOC Network and Distributed System Security Symposium*, February 1995.
6. L. Gong, M. Lomas, R. Needham, and J. Saltzer, "Protecting poorly chosen secrets from guessing attacks," *IEEE Journal on Selected Areas in Communications*, vol.11, no.5, pp.648-656, June 1993.
7. D. Hoover, B. Kausik, "Software smart cards via cryptographic camouflage," In Proceedings of the *IEEE Symposium on Security and Privacy*, 1999, *http://www.arcot.com* .
8. IEEE P1363.2, " Standard Specifications for Public Key Cryptography: Password-based Techniques," *http://grouper.ieee.org/groups/1363/passwdPK/index.html*, May 2002.
9. D. Jablon, "Password authentication using multiple servers," *LNCS 2020: Topics in Cryptology - CT-RSA 2001*, Springer Verlag, pp.344-360, 2001.
10. T. Kwon, "Impersonation attacks on software-only two-factor authentication schemes," *IEEE Communications Letters*, Vol.6, Iss.8, August 2002.
11. P. MacKenzie and M. Reiter, "Networked cryptographic devices resilient to capture," In Proceedings of the *IEEE Symposium on Security and Privacy*, 2001, a full and updated version is DIMACS Technical Report 2001-19, May 2001.
12. R. Morris and K. Thompson, "Password security: a case history," *Communications of the ACM*, vol.22, no.11, pp.584-597, 1979.
13. R. Perlman and C. Kaufman, "Secure password-based protocol for downloading a private key," In Proceedings of the *ISOC Network and Distributed System Security Symposium*, February 1999.
14. PKCS #1, "RSA cryptography standard," *RSA Laboratories Technical Note*, Version 2.0, 1998.

15. PKCS #5, "Password-based encryption standard," *RSA Laboratories Technical Note*, Version 2.0, 1999.
16. R. Rivest, A. Shamir, and L. Adleman, "A method for obtaining digital signatures and public-key cryptosystems," *Communications of the ACM*, vol.21, pp.120-126, 1978.
17. RSA Security Laboratories, *http://www.rsasecurity.com/* .

Intrusion Detection with Support Vector Machines and Generative Models

John S. Baras and Maben Rabi

Institute for Systems Research and
Department of Electrical and Computer Engineering
University of Maryland, College Park MD 20742, USA.
baras,rabi@isr.umd.edu

Abstract. This paper addresses the task of detecting intrusions in the form of malicious attacks on programs running on a host computer system by inspecting the trace of system calls made by these programs. We use 'attack-tree' type generative models for such intrusions to select features that are used by a Support Vector Machine Classifier. Our approach combines the ability of an HMM generative model to handle variable-length strings, i.e. the traces, and the non-asymptotic nature of Support Vector Machines that permits them to work well with small training sets.

1 Introduction

This article concerns the task of monitoring programs and processes running on computer systems to detect break-ins or misuse. For example, programs like sendmail and finger on the UNIX operating system run with administrative privileges and are susceptible to misuse because of design short-comings. Any user can pas specially crafted inputs to these programs and effect 'Buffer-overflow' (or some such exploit) and break into the system. To detect such attacks, the execution of vulnerable programs should be screened at run-time. This can be done by observing the trace (sequence of operating system calls; with or without argument values) of the program. In [3], S. Hofmeyr et.al. describe a method of learning to discriminate between sequences of system calls (without argument values) generated by normal use and misuse of processes that run with (root) privileges. In their scheme, a trace is flagged to be anomalous if its similarity to example (training) traces annotated as normal falls below a threshold; the similarity measure is based on the extent of partial matches with short sequences derived from the training traces. From annotated examples of traces, they compile a list of subsequences for comparing (at various positions) with a given trace and flag anomalous behavior when a similarity measure crosses a threshold. In [15], A. Wespi et. al. use the Teiresias pattern matching algorithm on the traces in a similar manner to flag off anomalous behavior. In both of the above, the set of subsequences used for comparison has to be learnt from the annotated set of traces (sequences of system calls) because, no other usable information or formal specification on legal or compromised execution of programs is available.

A.H. Chan and V. Gligor (Eds.): ISC 2002, LNCS 2433, pp. 32–47, 2002.

The approach advocated in this article is to obtain a compact representation of program behavior and use it (after some reduction) to select features to be used with a Support Vector Machine learning classifier.

Let $\mathcal{Y}$ be the set of all possible system calls. A trace $\mathcal{Y}$ is then an element of $\mathcal{Y}^*$ which is the set of all strings composed of elements of $\mathcal{Y}$. For a given program, let the training set be $\mathcal{T} = \{(\mathcal{Y}_i, L_i) | i = 1, \ldots, T\}$, where $L_i \in \{0, 1\}$, is the label corresponding to trace $\mathcal{Y}_i$, 0 for normal traces and 1 for attack traces. The detection problem then is to come up with a rule $\hat{L}$, based on the training set, that attempts to minimize the probability of misclassification $P_e = Pr[\hat{L}(\mathcal{Y}) \neq L(\mathcal{Y})]$. What is of more interest to system administrators is the trade-off between the probability of detection $P_D = Pr[\hat{L}(\mathcal{Y}) = 1 | L(\mathcal{Y}) = 1]$ and the probability of false alarms $P_{FA} = Pr[\hat{L}(\mathcal{Y}) = 1 | L(\mathcal{Y}) = 0]$ that the classifier provides. These probabilities are independent of the probabilities of occurrence of normal and malicious traces.

Annotation (usually manual) of live traces is a difficult and slow procedure. Attacks are also rare occurrences. Hence, traces corresponding to attacks are few in number. Likewise, we dont even have a good representative sample of traces corresponding to normal use. Hence, regardless of the features used, we need to use non-parametric classifiers that can handle finite (small) training sets. Support Vector Machine learning carves out a decision rule reflecting the complicated statistical relationships amongst features from finite training sets by maximizing true generalization (strictly speaking, a bound on generalization) instead of just the performance on the training set. To use Support Vector Machines, we need to map each variable length trace into a (real-vector-valued) feature space where Kernel functions (section 4) can be used. This conversion is performed by parsing the raw traces into shorter strings and extracting models of program execution from them.

2   Models for Attacks

The malicious nature of a program is due to the presence of a subsequence, not necessarily contiguous, in its trace of system calls. For the same type of attack on the host, there are several different combinations of system calls that can be used. Furthermore, innocuous system calls or sequences can be injected into various stages of program execution (various segments of the traces). Thus the intrinsic variety of attack sequences and the padding with harmless calls leads to a polymorphism of traces for the same plan of attack. Real attacks have a finite (and not too long) underlying *attack* sequence of system calls because they target specific vulnerabilities of the host. This and the padding are represented in a 'plan of attack' called the *Attack Tree* [12].

2.1   Attack Trees

An Attack Tree $(\mathcal{A})$[12] is a directed acyclic graph (DAG) with a set of nodes and associated sets of system calls used at these nodes. It represents a hierarchy of pairs of tasks and methods to fulfill those tasks. These nodes and sets of system calls are of the following three types:

1. $\mathcal{V} = \{v_1, v_2, \ldots, v_{k_1}\}$, the nodes representing the targeting of specific vulnerabilities in the host system, and a corresponding collection of subsets of $\mathcal{Y}$: $\mathcal{Y}^{\mathcal{V}} = \{\mathcal{Y}_1^v, \mathcal{Y}_2^v, \ldots, \mathcal{Y}_{k_1}^v\}$ representing the possible system-calls that target those vulnerabilities.

2. $\mathcal{P} = \{\wp_1, \wp_2, \ldots, \wp_{k_2}\}$, the set of instances where padding can be done along with a corresponding collection of subsets of $\mathcal{Y} \cup \{\epsilon\}$ (ϵ is the null alphabet signifying that no padding system-call has been included): $\mathcal{Y}^{\mathcal{P}} = \{\mathcal{Y}_1^\wp, \mathcal{Y}_2^\wp, \ldots, \mathcal{Y}_{k_2}^\wp\}$.

3. $\mathcal{F} = \{f_1, f_2, \ldots, f_{k_3}\}$, the final states into which the scheme jumps after completion of the attack plan along with a collection of subsets of $\mathcal{Y} \cup \{\epsilon\}$: $\mathcal{Y}^{\mathcal{F}} = \{\mathcal{Y}_1^f, \mathcal{Y}_2^f, \ldots, \mathcal{Y}_{k_3}^f\}$; a set that is not of much interest from the point of view of detecting attacks.

There may be multiple system calls issued while at a state with possible restrictions on the sequence of issue. The basic attack scheme encoded in the Attack Tree is not changed by modifications such as altering the padding scheme or the amount of padding (time spent in the padding nodes). Given an attack tree, it is straightforward to find the list ($\mathcal{L}^{\mathcal{A}} \subset \mathcal{Y}^*$) of all traces that it can generate. But given a trace, we don't have a scheme to check if it could have been generated by $\mathcal{A}$ without searching through the list $\mathcal{L}^{\mathcal{A}}$. Our intrusion detection scheme needs to execute the following steps:

1. Learn about $\mathcal{A}$ from the training set $\mathcal{T}$.
2. Form a rule to determine the likelihood of a given trace being generated by $\mathcal{A}$.

These objectives can be met by a probabilistic modeling of the Attack Tree.

2.2 Hidden Markov Models for Attack Trees

Given an Attack Tree $\mathcal{A}$, we can set up an equivalent Hidden Markov model H^1 that captures the uncertainties in padding and the polymorphism of attacks. The state-space of H^1, $\mathcal{X}^1 = \{x_1^1, x_2^1, \ldots, x_n^1\}$ (the superscript 1 corresponding to the attack model (abnormal or malicious program) and the superscript 0 corresponding to the normal program model) is actually the union: $\{x_n^1\} \cup \mathcal{V} \cup \mathcal{P} \cup \mathcal{F}$ with x_n^1 being the start state representing the start node with no attack initiated and $n = 1 + k_1 + k_2 + k_3$. We now need to describe the statistics of state transitions (with time replacing the position index along a trace) to reflect the edge structure of $\mathcal{A}$ and to also reflect the duration of stay in the vulnerability and padding nodes. The only allowed state transitions are the ones already in $\mathcal{A}$ and self-loops at each of the states. The picture is completed by defining conditional output probabilities given the state of system calls in a way that captures the information in $\mathcal{Y}^{\mathcal{V}}$ and $\mathcal{Y}^{\mathcal{P}}$. Thus we have, $\forall x_i^1, x_j^1 \in \mathcal{X}^1, \forall y_l \in \mathcal{Y} \cup \{\epsilon\}$ and $\forall t \in \mathbb{N}$

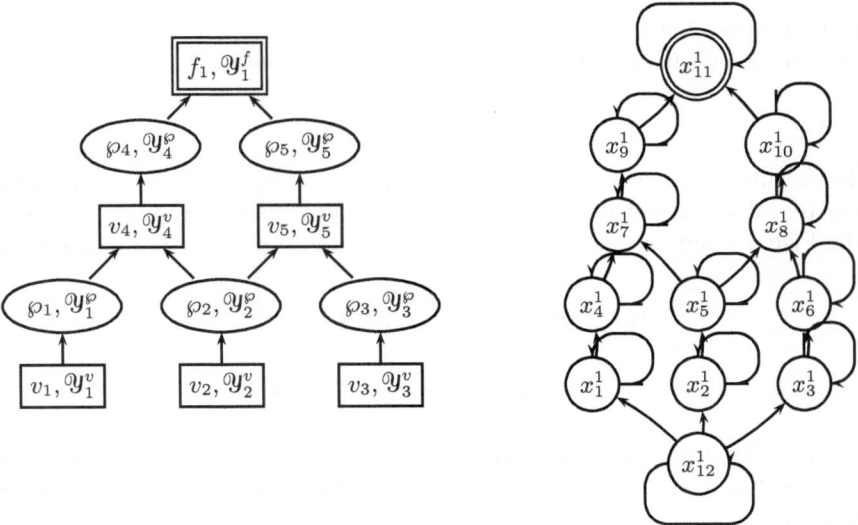

Fig. 1. An Attack Tree and its equivalent HMM with $k_1 = 5, k_2 = 5, k_3 = 1, n = 12$.

$$P[X(t+1) = x_i^1 | X(t) = x_j^1] = q_{ji}^1, \tag{1}$$

$$P[Y(t+1) = y_l | X(t) = x_j^1] = r_{jl}^1. \tag{2}$$

We can write down a similar HMM for the normal traces also. This *normal* HMM, H^0 has as its state-space a set $\mathcal{X}^0$ in general bigger than $\mathcal{X}^1$, and certainly with a different state transition structure and conditional output probabilities of system calls given the state. The associated probabilities are as follows. $\forall\, x_i^0, x_j^0 \in \mathcal{X}^0, \forall\, y_l \in \mathcal{Y}$ and $\forall\, t \in \mathbb{N}$

$$P[X(t+1) = x_i^0 | X(t) = x_j^0] = q_{ji}^0, \tag{3}$$

$$P[Y(t+1) = y_l | X(t) = x_j^0] = r_{jl}^0. \tag{4}$$

We would like to represent the probabilities for the above HMMs as functions of some vector θ of real-valued parameters so as to be able to use the framework of [4] and [5]. In the next section, we use these parametric HMMs to derive a real valued feature vector of fixed dimension for these variable length strings that will enable us to use Support Vector Machines for classification.

3   Real Valued Feature Vectors from Traces

Since we are dealing with variable length strings, we would like to extract the features living in a subset of an Euclidean space on which kernel functions are readily available enabling use of Support Vector Machines[14][1]. In [4] and [5], each observation $\mathcal{Y}$ is either the output of a parametric HMM (Correct Hypothesis H_1) or not (Null Hypothesis H_0). Then we can compute the Fisher score:

$$U_\mathcal{Y} = \nabla_\theta \log\left(P[\mathcal{Y}|H_1, \theta]\right) \tag{5}$$

as the feature vector corresponding to each $\mathcal{Y}$, θ being the real-vector valued parameter. What is not clear in this set-up is how, given only the training set $\mathcal{T}$, the Fisher score is computed. For instance, the ith entry of $U_\mathcal{Y}$ will look like

$$
\begin{aligned}
(U_\mathcal{Y})_i &= \frac{\partial}{\partial\theta_i} \log\left(P[\mathcal{Y}|H_1, \theta]\right) \\
&= \frac{1}{P[\mathcal{Y}|H_1, \theta]} \times \frac{\partial}{\partial\theta_i}\left(P[\mathcal{Y}|H_1, \theta]\right)
\end{aligned} \tag{6}
$$

This could clearly depend on θ. To use some feature like the Fisher score, we need to identify a real-valued vector parameter θ and to completely specify the computation of $U_\mathcal{Y}$.

Let the sets of malicious and normal traces in the training set be:

$$
\begin{aligned}
\mathcal{M} &= \{\,\mathcal{Y}\,|\,(\mathcal{Y}, L(\mathcal{Y})) \in \mathcal{T}, L(\mathcal{Y}) = 1\,\} \\
\mathcal{N} &= \{\,\mathcal{Y}\,|\,(\mathcal{Y}, L(\mathcal{Y})) \in \mathcal{T}, L(\mathcal{Y}) = 0\,\}
\end{aligned}
$$

Let n_1, n_0 be the sizes of the state-spaces of the attack and normal HMMs respectively. For H^1 we compute an estimate of probabilities $\hat{H}^1 = \{\hat{q}_{ij}^1, \hat{r}_{lj}^1\}$, based on the Expectation Maximization algorithm[10][2]. We obtain an updated set of estimates $\tilde{H}^1 = \{\tilde{q}_{ij}^1, \tilde{r}_{lj}^1\}$ that (locally) increases the likelihood of $\mathcal{M}$ (i.e. of the traces in $\mathcal{M}$) by maximizing the auxiliary function as below:

$$\tilde{H}^1 = \arg\max_{\underline{H}} \sum_{\mathcal{Y}\in\mathcal{M}} E_{\hat{H}^1}\left[\log P\left(\mathcal{Y}; \underline{H}\right)|\mathcal{Y}\right] \tag{7}$$

This step can be executed by the following(in the same manner as equation (44) of [10]):

$$\tilde{q}_{ji}^1 = \frac{\hat{q}_{ji}^1\left(\sum_{\mathcal{Y}\in\mathcal{M}}\frac{\partial}{\partial\hat{q}_{ji}^1}P\left(\mathcal{Y};\hat{H}^1\right)\right)}{\sum_{k=1}^{n_1}\hat{q}_{jk}^1\left(\sum_{\mathcal{Y}\in\mathcal{M}}\frac{\partial}{\partial\hat{q}_{jk}^1}P\left(\mathcal{Y};\hat{H}^1\right)\right)} \tag{8}$$

$$\tilde{r}_{ji}^1 = \frac{\hat{r}_{ji}^1\left(\sum_{\mathcal{Y}\in\mathcal{M}}\frac{\partial}{\partial\hat{r}_{ji}^1}P\left(\mathcal{Y};\hat{H}^1\right)\right)}{\sum_{k=1}^{s}\hat{r}_{jk}^1\left(\sum_{\mathcal{Y}\in\mathcal{M}}\frac{\partial}{\partial\hat{r}_{jk}^1}P\left(\mathcal{Y};\hat{H}^1\right)\right)} \tag{9}$$

where for simplicity the null output ϵ is not considered. A variant of this idea is a scheme where instead of the summation over all $\mathcal{Y} \in \mathcal{M}$, we repeat the update separately for each $\mathcal{Y} \in \mathcal{M}$ (in some desired order) as follows:

$$\tilde{q}_{ji}^1 = \frac{\hat{q}_{ji}^1 \left(\frac{\partial}{\partial \hat{q}_{ji}^1} P\left(\mathcal{Y}; \hat{H}^1\right)\right)}{\sum_{k=1}^{n_1} \hat{q}_{jk}^1 \left(\frac{\partial}{\partial \hat{q}_{jk}^1} P\left(\mathcal{Y}; \hat{H}^1\right)\right)} \tag{10}$$

$$\tilde{r}_{ji}^1 = \frac{\hat{r}_{ji}^1 \left(\frac{\partial}{\partial \hat{r}_{ji}^1} P\left(\mathcal{Y}; \hat{H}^1\right)\right)}{\sum_{k=1}^{s} \hat{r}_{jk}^1 \left(\frac{\partial}{\partial \hat{r}_{jk}^1} P\left(\mathcal{Y}; \hat{H}^1\right)\right)} \tag{11}$$

$\hat{H}^1$ is set equal to the update $\tilde{H}^1$ and the above steps are repeated till some criterion of convergence is met. We will now specify the initial value of $\hat{H}^1$ with which this recursion gets started. The acyclic nature of the Attack Tree means that, with an appropriate relabelling of nodes, the state-transition matrix is upper triangular:

$$q_{ji}^1 > 0 \Leftrightarrow i \geq j$$

or block-upper triangular if some states (padding states for instance) are allowed to communicate with each other. As initial values for the EM algorithm, we can take(the equi-probable assignment):

$$\hat{q}_{ji}^1 = \frac{1}{n_1 - j + 1}, \quad \forall i \geq j \tag{12}$$

noting that equation (8) preserves the triangularity. Similarly, we can take:

$$\hat{r}_{jl}^1 = \frac{1}{s} \quad \forall\, l, j. \tag{13}$$

Since we want to be alert to variations in the attack by padding, it is not a good idea to start with a more restrictive initial assignment for the conditional output probabilities unless we have reliable information, such as constraints imposed by the Operating System, or 'tips' of an 'expert-hacker' . Such system-dependent restrictions, in the form of constraints on some of the probabilities q_{ji}^1, r_{jl}^1 further focus our attention on the real vulnerabilities in the system. To further sharpen our attention, we can augment $\mathcal{M}$, by adding to it, its traces segmented by comparing with the traces in $\mathcal{N}$ and using any side information; essentially an attempt at stripping off padding. These segmented traces would be given smaller weights in the EM recursion (7). Going further in that direction, we can, instead of using the EM algorithm use various segmentations of the traces in $\mathcal{T}$ (into n_1 parts) and estimate the probabilities $\{q_{ji}^1, r_{jl}^1\}$. Even though we face difficulties such as a large number of unknowns, a relatively small training set, and the problem of settling on a local optimum point in the EM algorithm, we are banking on the robustness of the Support Vector Machine classifier that uses the parameters of the generative model. We can compute similar estimates($\hat{H}^0$) for the HMM representing the normal programs even though they do not, in general, admit simplifications like triangularity of the state-transition matrix.

The parameter vector we are interested in is the following:

$$\theta = \left[q_{11}, q_{12}, \cdots, q_{21}, \cdots, q_{NN}, r_{11}, \cdots, r_{sN} \right]^T \tag{14}$$

N being the larger of n_1, n_0; setting to zero those probabilities that are not defined in the smaller model. This vector can be estimated for the two HMMs $H^1, H^0 : \hat{\theta}^1, \hat{\theta}^0$ simply from $\hat{H}^1, \hat{H}^0$.

For any trace, be it from $\mathcal{T}$ or from the testing set, we can define the following feature vector:

$$U_{\mathcal{Y}} = \left[\nabla_\theta \log \left(P[\mathcal{Y}|H^1, \theta] \right) \big|_{\theta=\hat{\theta}^1} \right] \tag{15}$$

This vector measures the likelihood of a given trace being the output of the Attack Tree model and can be the basis of a *Signature-based* Intrusion Detection Scheme. On the other hand, we can use the information about normal programs gathered in H^0 to come up with

$$U_{\mathcal{Y}} = \begin{bmatrix} \nabla_\theta \log \left(P[\mathcal{Y}|H^1, \theta] \right) \big|_{\theta=\hat{\theta}^1} \\ \nabla_\theta \log \left(P[\mathcal{Y}|H^0, \theta] \right) \big|_{\theta=\hat{\theta}^0} \end{bmatrix} \tag{16}$$

which can be used for a *Combined Signature and Anomaly-based* detection. Something to be kept in mind is that the parameter vector (and hence the feature vectors) defined by (14) will contain many useless entries (with values zero) because we do not use the triangularity of the state-transition matrix for H^1 or any system dependent restrictions and because we artificially treat (in (14)) the HMMs to be of equal size. Instead, we can define different(smaller) parameter vectors $\theta_{\mathcal{M}}$ and $\theta_{\mathcal{N}}$ for the malicious and normal HMMs respectively and considerably shrink the feature vectors. Also for each feature vector in (15) and the two 'halves' of the vector in (16), there is a constant scaling factor in the form of the reciprocal of the likelihood of the trace given the HMM of interest(as displayed in equation (6)). This constant scaling tends to be large because of the smallness of the concerned likelihoods. We can store this likelihood as a separate entry in the feature vector without any loss of information. A similar issue crops up in the implementation of the EM algorithm: the forward and backward probabilities needed for the computations in (8), (9), (10) and (11), tend to become very small for long observation sequences, making it important to have a high amount of decimal precision

4   The SVM Algorithm and Numerical Experiments

Support Vector Machines (SVMs)[14] are non-parametric classifiers designed to provide good generalization performance even on small training sets. A SVM maps input (real-valued) feature vectors ($x \in X$ with labels $y \in Y$) into a (much) higher dimensional feature space ($z \in Z$) through some nonlinear mapping (something that captures the nonlinearity of the true decision boundary). In a feature space, we can classify the labelled feature vectors (z_i, y_i) using hyper-planes:

$$y_i[< z_i, w > +b] \geq 1 \tag{17}$$

and minimize the functional $\Phi(w) = \frac{1}{2} < w, w >$. The solution to this quadratic program can be obtained from the saddle point of the Lagrangian:

$$L(w, b, \alpha) = \frac{1}{2} < w, w > - \sum \alpha_i \left(y_i [< z_i, w > +b] - 1 \right) \tag{18}$$

$$w^* = \sum y_i \alpha_i^* z_i, \quad \alpha_i^* \geq 0; \tag{19}$$

Those input feature vectors in the training set that have positive α_i^* are called *Support Vectors* $\mathcal{S} = \{z_i | \alpha_i^* > 0\}$ and because of the Karush-Kuhn-Tucker optimality conditions, the optimal weight can be expressed in terms of the Support Vectors alone.

$$w^* = \sum_{\mathcal{S}} y_i \alpha_i^* z_i, \quad \alpha_i^* \geq 0; \tag{20}$$

This determination of w fixes the optimal separating hyper-plane. The above method has the daunting task of transforming all the input raw features x_i into the corresponding z_i and carrying out the computations in the higher dimensional space Z. This can be avoided by finding a symmetric and positive semi-definite function, called the Kernel function, between pairs of x_i

$$K : X \times X \to \mathbb{R}^+ \cup \{0\}, \ K(a, b) = K(b, a) \ \forall a, b \in X \tag{21}$$

Then, by a theorem of Mercer, a transformation $f : X \to Z$ is induced for which,

$$K(a, b) = < f(a), f(b) >_z \quad \forall a, b \in X \tag{22}$$

Then the above Lagrangian optimization problem gets transformed to the maximization of the following function of α_i:

$$W(\alpha) = \sum \alpha_i - \frac{1}{2} \sum \alpha_i \alpha_j y_i y_j K(x_i, x_j) \tag{23}$$

$$w^* = \sum y_i \alpha_i^* z_i, \quad \alpha_i^* \geq 0; \tag{24}$$

the support vectors being the ones corresponding to the positive αs. The set of hyper-planes considered in the higher dimensional space Z have a small estimated VC dimension[14]. That is the main reason for the good generalization performance of SVMs.

Now that we have real vectors for each trace, we are at full liberty to use the standard kernels of SVM classification. Let $u_1, u_2 \in \mathbb{R}^n$. We have the *Gaussian Kernel*

$$K(u_1, u_2) = \exp\left(-\frac{1}{2\sigma^2}(u_1 - u_2)^T(u_2 - u_2)\right), \tag{25}$$

the *Polynomial Kernel*

$$K(u_1, u_2) = (u_1^T u_2 + c_1)^d + c_2, \ c_1, c_2 \geq 0, \ d \in \mathbb{N} \tag{26}$$

or the *Fisher Kernel*

$$K(u_1, u_2) = u_1^T I^{-1} u_2; \quad I = E_Y[U_Y U_Y^T] \tag{27}$$

Having described the various components of our scheme for intrusion detection and classification, we provide below a description of the overall scheme and experiments aimed to provide results on its performance. The overall detection scheme executes the following steps:

1. For the given T_1 attack traces of system calls $\mathcal{Y}_i$, we estimate using the EM algorithm a HMM model H^1 for an attack with n_1 states.
2. For given T_0 normal traces of system calls, $\mathcal{Y}_i$, we estimate a HMM model H^0 for the normal situation with n_0 states.
3. We compute the Fisher scores for either a signature-based intrusion detection or a combined signature and anomaly-based intrusion detection using equations (15) and (16).
4. Using the Fisher scores we train a SVM employing either one of the kernels (Gaussian, Polynomial, Fisher).
5. Given a test trace of system calls $\mathcal{Y}$, we let the SVM classifier decide as to whether the decision should be 1 (attack) or 0 (normal). The Fisher scores of $\mathcal{Y}$ are computed and entered in the SVM classifier.

We performed numerical experiments on a subset of the data-set for host based intrusion detection from the University of New Mexico [13][3]. We need to distinguish between normal and compromised execution on the Linux Operating system of the `lpr` program which are vulnerable because they run as a privileged processes. In the experiments, we tried various kernels in the SVMs. The performance evaluation is based on the computation of several points of the receiver operating characteristic (ROC) curve of the overall classifier; i.e. the plot of the curve for the values of the probabilities of correct classification (detection) P_D vs the false alarm probability P_{FA}.

In our experiments with HMMs (both attack and normal), we encountered two difficulties due to the finite precision of computer arithmetic (the `long double` data type of `C/C++` for instance is not adequate):

1. The larger the assumed number of states for the HMM, the smaller the values of the probabilities $\{q_{ji}\}$. For a fixed set of traces, like in our case, increasing the number of states from say, 5 to 10 or any higher value, did not affect the EM estimation (or the computation of the Fisher score) because, despite the attacks and normal executions being carried out in more than 5 (or n) stages, the smaller values of $\{q_{ji}\}$ make the EM algorithm stagnate immedeately at a local optimum.
2. Having long traces (200 is a nominal value for the length in our case) means that values of the *forward* and *backward* probabilities [10] $\alpha_t(j), \beta_t(j)$ become negligible in the EM algorithm as well as in the computation of the Fisher score. For the EM algorithm, this means being stagnant at a local optimum and for the computation of the Fisher score, it means obtaining score vectors all of whose entries are zero.

3. While computing the Fisher scores (15,16), if any element of θ is very small at the point of evaluation, the increased length of the overall Fisher score has a distorting effect on the SVM learning algorithm. For instance, while using linear kernels, the set of candidate separating hyper-planes in the feature space is directly constrained by this. This problem is actually the result of including the statistics of non-specific characteristics (background-noise, so to speak) like the transition and conditional output probabilities related to the basic system calls like `break, exit, uname` etc.

To combat these problems of numerical precision, one can go for an enhanced representation of small floating point numbers by careful book-keeping. But this comes at the cost of a steep increase in the complexity of the overall detection system and the time taken for computations.

We propose a solution that simplifies the observations and segments each trace into small chunks with the idea of viewing the trace as a (short) string of these chunks. This solution removes the floating point precision problems.

4.1   SVM Classification Using Reduced HMMs

We describe a technique for deriving a reduced order Attack HMM (or a normal HMM) from the traces in the training set. We choose a small number of states to account for the most characteristic behavior of attacks (or of Normal program execution). We also use the observation that system-calls that constitute intrusions (attack system calls from the set $\mathcal{Y}^{\mathcal{V}}$) are not exactly used for padding (i.e. $\mathcal{Y}^{\mathcal{V}} \cap \mathcal{Y}^{\mathcal{P}} \approx \emptyset$). For every trace $\mathcal{Y}$, we can compute the ratio of the number of occurrences of a system-call s and the length of that trace. Call this number $\rho_s(\mathcal{Y})$. We can also compute the ratio of the position of first occurrence of a system-call s and the length of the trace (same as the ratio of the length of the longest prefix of $\mathcal{Y}$ not containing s and the length of $\mathcal{Y}$). Call this number $\delta_s(\mathcal{Y})$. Calculate these ratios $\rho_s(\mathcal{Y}), \delta_s(\mathcal{Y})$ for all system calls $s \in \mathcal{Y}$, and for all T_1 malicious traces in $\mathcal{T}$.

For every $s \in \mathcal{Y}$, find the median of $\rho_s(\mathcal{Y})$ over all T_1 malicious traces in $\mathcal{T}$. Call it $\hat{\rho}_s^1$. Similarly, compute the medians $\hat{\delta}_s^1 \; \forall s \in \mathcal{Y}$. We prefer the median over the mean or the mode because we want to avoid being swayed by outliers. We now propose a scheme for identifying attack states $\{v\}$. Choose $\gamma_1, \gamma_2 : 0 < \gamma_1, \gamma_2 < 1$. Find subsets $\{s_1, s_2, \ldots, s_k\}$ of $\mathcal{Y}$ such that

$$|\hat{\rho}_{s_i}^1 - \hat{\rho}_{s_j}^1| < \gamma_1 \,, \; |\hat{\delta}_{s_i}^1 - \hat{\delta}_{s_j}^1| < \gamma_2 \,, \; \forall i, j \in \{1, 2, \ldots, k\} \tag{28}$$

Increase or decrease γ_1, γ_2 so that we are left with a number of subsets equal to the desired number of states n_1. In practice, most, if not all, of these subsets are disjoint. These subsets form the attack states. However, the alphabet is no longer $\mathcal{Y}$ but $\mathcal{Y}^*$. Thus, for the state $x_j = \{s_1, s_2, \ldots, s_k\}$, all strings of the form '$w_1, s_{\pi(1)}1, w_2, s_{\pi(2)}, w_3, \ldots, w_k, s_{\pi(k)}, w_{k+1}$' are treated as the same symbol corresponding to it (with $w_1, w_2, w_3, \ldots, w_{k+1} \in \mathcal{Y}^*$ and with π a

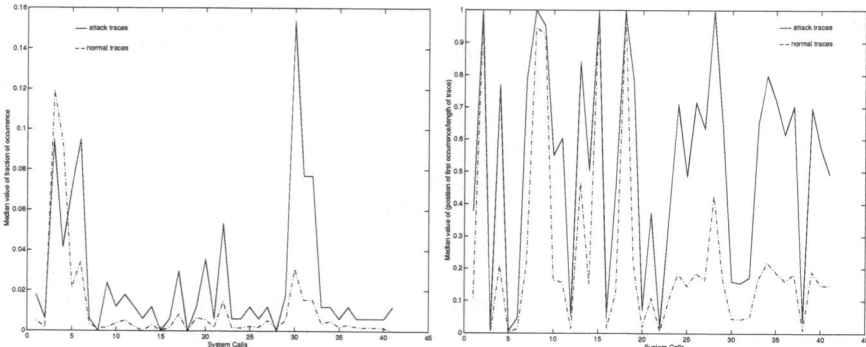

Fig. 2. Plots of the values of $\hat{\rho}_s^1$ and $\hat{\delta}_s^1$ over normal (dashed lines) and attack (solid lines) sequences used in obtaining reduced HMMs for the `lpr` (normal) and `lprcp` (attack) programs (the system call index has been renamed to ignore those system calls never used).

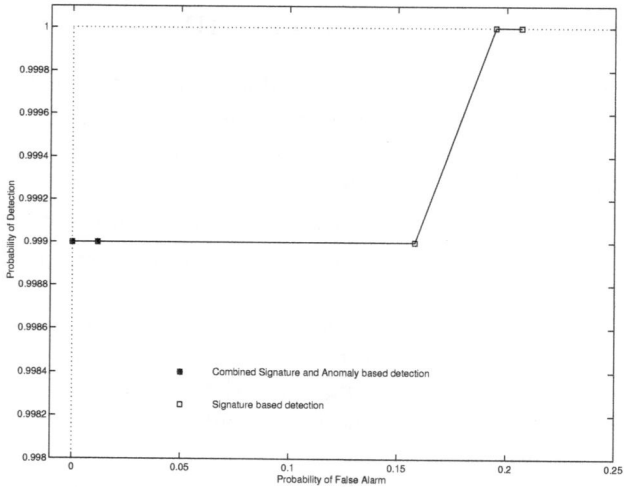

Fig. 3. Plot of ROC (for different number of hidden states) using SVMs and reduced HMMs using the computation of the medians $\hat{\rho}_s^1, \hat{\rho}_s^0, \hat{\delta}_s^1$ and $\hat{\delta}_s^0$. We used the trace dataset of `lpr` (normal) and `lprcp` (attack) programs.

permutation on $\{1, 2, \ldots, k\}$ such that $\hat{\delta}_{s_{\pi(i)}}^1$ is non-decreasing with i). We call this symbol (also a regular expression) y_j.

Now, we can assign numerical values for $\{q_{ji}\}$ and for $\{r_{jl}\}$. The transition probability matrix will be given a special structure. Its diagonal has entries of the form : τ_i and the first super-diagonal has its entries equal to $1 - \tau_i$ and all other entries of the matrix are equal to 0. This is the same as using a *flat* or *left-right* HMM [10]. We set the conditional output probability of observing the

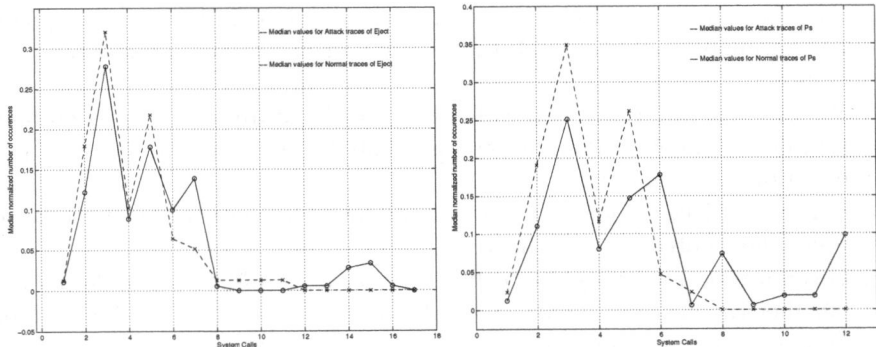

Fig. 4. Plots of the values of $\hat{\rho}_s^1$ and $\hat{\rho}_s^0$ over normal (dashed lines) and attack (solid lines) sequences used in obtaining reduced HMMs for the `lpr` (normal) and `lprcp` (attack) programs (For the `Eject` program: sys_call_12 = `pipe`, sys_call_13 = `fork` For the `Ps` program: sys_call_10 = `fork`, sys_call_11 = `fcntl`)

compound output y_j corresponding to state x_j to be $\mu_j : 0 < \mu_j < 1$. We treat all other outputs at this state as the same and this *wild-card* symbol (representing $\mathcal{Y}^* - \{y_j\}$) gets the probability $1 - \mu_j$. We can make the values μ_j all the same or different but parameterized in some way, along with the τ_is by a single variable so that we can easily experiment with detection performance as a function of the μ_j, τ_i. A point to be kept in mind all along is that we need to parse any given trace $\mathcal{Y}$ into n_1 (or more) contiguous segments. When there are different segmentations possible, all of them can be constructed and the corresponding feature vectors tested by the classifier.

The above steps can be duplicated for constructing the normal HMM also. A sharper and more compact representation is obtained if the Attack tree and the Normal tree do not share common subsets as states. In particular, consider a subset (of $\mathcal{Y}$) $x = \{s_1, s_2, \ldots, s_l\}$ that meets condition (28) for both the normal and attack traces:

$$|\hat{\rho}_{s_i}^L - \hat{\rho}_{s_j}^L| < \gamma_1^L \; , \; |\hat{\delta}_{s_i}^L - \hat{\delta}_{s_j}^L| < \gamma_2^L \; ,$$

$$\forall i, j \in \{1, 2, \ldots, k\}, \; 0 < \gamma_1^L, \gamma_2^L < 1, \; L \in \{0, 1\} \tag{29}$$

Then, x should clearly not be a state in either the Attack HMM or the Normal HMM. The signature based detection scheme would as usual use only the reduced attack HMM. The combined signature and anomaly-based approach would use both the attack and normal HMMS.

Now the overall detection scheme executes the following steps:

1. For the given T_1 attack traces of system calls $\mathcal{Y}_i$, we parse the $\mathcal{Y}_i$ into n_1 blocks and estimate using the reduced HMM model H^1 for an attack with n_1 states.

2. For given T_0 normal traces of system calls, $\mathcal{Y}_i$, we parse the $\mathcal{Y}_i$ into n_2 blocks and estimate a reduced HMM model H^0 for the normal situation with n_0 states.

3. We compute the Fisher scores for either a signature-based intrusion detection or a combined signature and anomaly-based intrusion detection using equations (15) and (16).

4. Using the Fisher scores we train a SVM employing either one of the kernels (Gaussian, Polynomial, Fisher).

5. Given a test trace of system calls $\mathcal{Y}$, we let the SVM classifier decide as to whether the decision should be 1 (attack) or 0 (normal). The Fisher scores of $\mathcal{Y}$ are computed and entered in the SVM classifier.

We performed numerical experiments on live `Lpr` and `Lprcp` (the attacked version of `Lpr`) traces in the data-set for host based intrusion detection [13][3]. We found that the quadratic programming step of the SVM learning algorithm did not converge when we used linear and polynomial kernels (because of very long feature vectors). On the other hand, SVM learning was instantaneous when we used the Gaussian kernel on the same set of traces. The value of the parameter σ in equation (25) made no significant difference. We used the Gaussian kernel (25) We selected a small training set (about one percent of the whole set of traces with the same ratio of intrusions as in the whole set). We trained the SVM with different trade-offs between the training-error and the margin (through the parameter c in [7]) and different number of hidden states for the Attack and Normal HMMs. We averaged the resulting P_D, P_{FA} (on the whole set) over different random choices of the training set $\mathcal{T}$.

We also performed experiments on the `eject` and `ps` attacks in the 1999 MIT-LL-DARPA data set [8]. We used traces from the first three weeks of training. In the case of the `eject` program attack, we had a total of 8 normal traces and 3 attack traces in the BSM audit records for the first three weeks. Needless to say, the SVM classifier made no errors at any size of the reduced HMMs. The interesting fact to observe was that the single compound symbol (28) (for the most reduced HMM) 'pipe*fork' was enough to classify correctly, thus learning the Buffer-overflow step from only the names of the system calls in the traces. The ps trace-set can be said to have more statistical significance. We had 168 normal and 3 attack instances. However, for all sizes of reduced HMMs, all of the Fisher scores for the Attack traces were the same as for the Normal ones. Here, too, at all resolutions, the buffer-overflow step was learnt cleanly: All the reduced HMMs picked the symbol 'fork*fnctl' to be part of their symbol set (28). Here too, the SVM made no errors at all. The plots of $\hat{\rho}_s^1$ and $\hat{\rho}_s^0$ in Fig.3 complete the picture. This data-set make us beleive that this approach learns efficiently buffer-overflow type of attacks. It also highlights the problem of a lack of varied training instances.

We used the SVM^{light}[7] program for Support Vector Learning authored by Thorsten Joachims.

5 SVM Classification Using Gappy-Bigram Count Feature Vectors

Here, we present an algorithm that uses a simpler feature that avoids the estimation of the gradient of the likelihoods. For any trace $\mathcal{Y} \in \mathcal{Y}^*$, we can write down a vector of the number of occurrences of the so-called *gappy-bigrams* in it. A *bigram* is a string (for our purposes, over the alphabet $\mathcal{Y}$) of length two that is specified by its two elements in order. A gappy-bigram '$r\lambda s$' is any finite-length string (over the set $\mathcal{Y}$) that begins with the alphabet s and terminates with the alphabet $\grave{s}$. Let

$$\#_{s\grave{s}}(\mathcal{Y}) = \text{the number of occurences of the gappy} - \text{bigram ' } s\lambda\grave{s} \text{ ' in } \mathcal{Y} \qquad (30)$$

where

$$s, \grave{s} \in \mathcal{Y}, \quad \lambda \in \mathcal{Y}^* \cup \{\epsilon\}, \quad \epsilon \text{ being the null string.} \qquad (31)$$

We write down the T^2-long vector of counts $\#_{s\grave{s}}(\mathcal{Y})$ for all $(s, \grave{s}) \in \mathcal{Y} \times \mathcal{Y}$.

$$C(\mathcal{Y}) = \begin{bmatrix} \#_{s_1 s_1} \\ \#_{s_1 s_2} \\ \vdots \\ \#_{s_T s_T} \end{bmatrix} \qquad (32)$$

We call the feature vector $C(\mathcal{Y})$, the count score of $\mathcal{Y}$ and use this to modify the earlier scheme using the Fisher score.

The new overall detection scheme executes the following steps:

1. We compute the count scores using equation (32).
2. Using the count scores we train a SVM employing either one of the kernels (Gaussian, Polynomial, Fisher).
3. Given a test trace of system calls $\mathcal{Y}$, we let the SVM classifier decide as to whether the decision should be 1 (attack) or 0 (normal). The count scores of $\mathcal{Y}_i$ are computed and entered in the SVM classifier.

We performed numerical experiments on live `Lpr` and `Lprcp` (the attacked version of `Lpr`) traces in the data-set for host based intrusion detection [13][3]. We found that the quadratic programming step of the SVM learning algorithm did not converge when we used linear and polynomial kernels (because of very long feature vectors). On the other hand, SVM learning was instantaneous when we used the Gaussian kernel on the same set of traces. The value of the parameter σ in equation (25) made no significant difference. Our experiments were of the following two types:

1. We selected a small training set (about one percent of the whole set of traces with the same ratio of intrusions as in the whole set). We trained the SVM with different trade-offs between the training-error and the margin (through the parameter c in [7]). We averaged the resulting P_D, P_{FA} (on the whole set) over different random choices of the training set $\mathcal{T}$. Our average (as well as the median) values of P_D, P_{FA} were 0.95 and 0.0.

2. We used the whole set of traces available for training the SVM with different tradeoffs (again, the parameter c in [7]) and used the leave-one-out cross-validation $\xi\alpha$ ([7]) estimate of P_D, P_{FA}. We obtained the following values for P_D, P_{FA} : $0.992, 0.0$.

We have only one measured point on the ROC curve. We also note that this detection system behaves like an anomaly-based intrusion detection system.

6   Conclusions

We have described a method for incorporating the structured nature of attacks, as well as any specific system-dependent or other 'expert-hacker' information, in the HMM generative model for malicious programs. Using the generative model, we have captured the variability of attacks and compressed into a vector of real values, the set of variables to be examined for flagging off attacks. We use these derived feature vectors in place of variable-length strings, as inputs to the Support Vector Machine learning classifier which is designed to work well with small training sets. We have presented a method for deriving reduced HMMs using the temporal correlations (28, 29) between system calls in traces. An alternative large-scale HMM classifier would need to use techniques from the area of large vocabulary speech recognition [6] to grapple with the numerical problems associated with full-scale generative models for attacks and normal program execution. We also presented the gappy-bigram count feature vector for SVM based classification. We need to develop versions of the above intrusion detection systems that work in real-time, and those that work on distributed programs like a network transaction.

Acknowledgments. This work was supported by the United States Army Research Office under contract number DAAD190110494 of the CIP-URI program. We express our thanks to Senni Perumal, Sudhir Varma and Shah-An Yang for suggestions and for assistance in the computer experiments. We also thank the referees for their useful comments.

References

1. N. Cristianini, J. and Shawe-Taylor. An introduction to Support Vector Machines and other kernel-based learning methods. Cambridge University Press (2000)
2. R. Elliot, L. Aggoun, J., Moore. Hidden Markov Models, Estimation and Control, Springer-Verlag.
3. S. Hofmeyr, S. Forrest, A. Somayaji. Intrusion detection using sequences of system calls. Journal of Computer Security **6** (1998) 151–180
4. T. Jaakkola, and D. Haussler. Exploiting generative models in discriminative classifiers. Advances in Neural Information Processing Systems II, San Mateo, CA. Morgan Kauffmann Publishers.

5. T. Jaakkola, and D. Haussler. Using the Fisher Kernel method to detect remote protein homologies. Proceedings of the Seventh International Conference on Intelligent Systems for Molecular Biology (1999)
6. F. Jelinek. Statistical methods for Speech Recognition. MIT Press, (1999)
7. T. Joachims. SVM^{light}. http://svmlight.joachims.org/.
8. MIT Lincoln Labs, The 1999 DARPA Intrusion Detection evaluation data corpus. http:// www.ll.mit.edu /IST /ideval
9. O. Sheyner, J. Haines, S. Jha, R. Lippmann, J. Wing, J. Automated generation and analysis of Attack Graphs. Proceedings of the IEEE Symposium on Security and Privacy, Oakland, CA, (May 2002)
10. L. Rabiner. A tutorial on Hidden Markov Models and selected application in Speech Recognition. Proceedings of the IEEE, vol: **77**, No: 2, (February 1989)
11. I. Rigoutsos and A. Floratos. Combinatorial pattern discovery in Biological sequences: the Teiresias algorithm. Bioinformatics, vol:**14**, no:1, pages:55–67 (1998)
12. B. Schneier. Attack Trees. Dr. Dobb's Journal, http:// www.ddj.com /documents /s=896/ddj9912a/9912a.htm (December 1999)
13. http://www.cs.unm.edu/ immsec/data/
14. V. Vapnik. Statistical Learning Theory. Wiley Inter-science. (1996)
15. A. Wespi, M. Dacier, H. Debar. Solutions périodiques, du An intrusion detection system based on the Teiresias pattern discovery algorithm. EICAR proceedings (1999)

Small and High-Speed Hardware Architectures for the 3GPP Standard Cipher KASUMI

Akashi Satoh and Sumio Morioka

IBM Research, Tokyo Research Laboratory, IBM Japan Ltd., 1623-14,
Shimotsuruma, Yamato-shi, Kanagawa 242-8502, Japan
{akashi, e02716}@jp.ibm.com

Abstract. The KASUMI block cipher and the confidentiality ($f8$) and integrity ($f9$) algorithms using KASUMI in feed back cipher modes have been standardized by the 3GPP. We designed compact and high-speed implementations and then compared several prototypes to existing designs in ASICs and FPGAs. Making good use of the nested structure of KASUMI, a lot of function blocks are shared and reused. The data paths of the $f8$ and $f9$ algorithms are merged using only one 64-bit selector. An extremely small size of 3.07 Kgates with a 288 Mbps throughput is obtained for a KASUMI core using a 0.13-μm CMOS standard cell library. Even simultaneously supporting both the $f8$ and $f9$ algorithms, the same throughput is achieved with 4.89 Kgates. The fastest design supporting the two algorithms achieves 1.6 Gbps with 8.27 Kgates.

1   Introduction

A 64-bit block cipher KASUMI [1-4] was developed based on MISTY [5] for the 3GPP (3rd Generation Partnership Project) standard algorithm used in the WCDMA (Wideband Code Division Multiple Access) cellular phone systems. KASUMI has an 8-round Feistel structure with nested round functions, and is suitable for small hardware implementations. A high-speed KASUMI hardware design that has eight round function blocks was reported in [6], and a throughput of 5.78 Gbps with 47.66 Kgates was obtained in pipelined operation. However, the pipelined operation cannot be applied to the confidentiality algorithm $f8$ and the integrity algorithm $f9$ where KASUMI is used in feedback modes.

In this paper, we propose three compact but still high-speed hardware architectures, and implement them using an ASIC library and FPGAs. A performance comparison between a conventional implementation [6] and ours is also done using the same FPGA platform.

2   KASUMI Algorithm

2.1 Round Functions

KASUMI has an 8-round Feistel network, and encrypts 64-bit data using a 128-bit key. Fig. 1 shows the nested structure of the KASUMI data path excluding the key

A.H. Chan and V. Gligor (Eds.): ISC 2002, LNCS 2433, pp. 48–62, 2002.
© Springer-Verlag Berlin Heidelberg 2002

scheduler. The network has a linear 32-bit function FL and a nonlinear 32-bit function FO as the main round functions. The FO function consists of a 3-round network with a 16-bit nonlinear function FI. The FI function consists of a 4-round network with two S-Boxes, S9 and S7. In the odd-numbered rounds of the 8-round main network, 64-bit data is divided into two 32-bit blocks, and the left block is transformed by FL followed by FO, and then the FO output is XORed with the right block. In the even-numbered rounds, the order of the functions is swapped with FO followed by FL. At the end of each round, the left and right 32-bit blocks are also swapped.

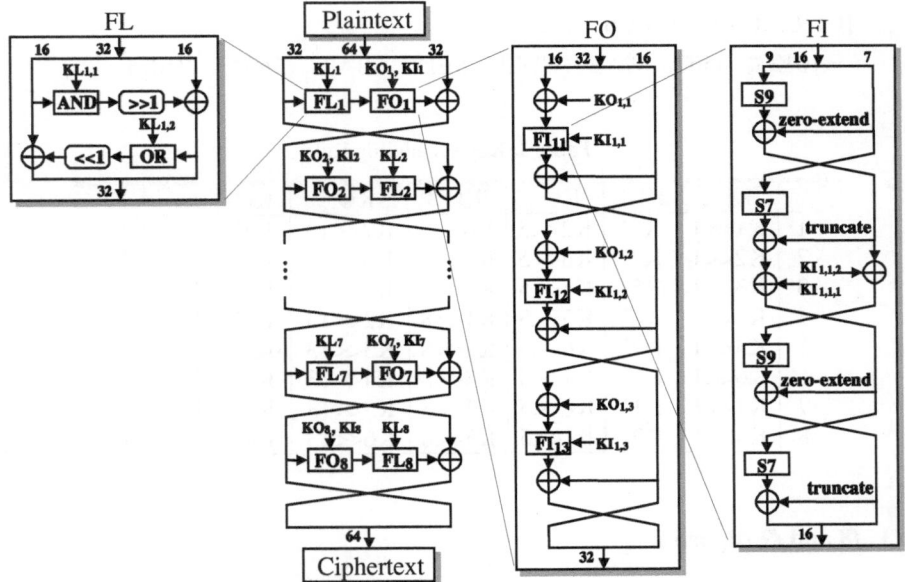

Fig. 1. KASUMI encryption data path

The FL function transforms the 32-bit data with two 16-bit sub-keys $KL_{i,1}$ and $KL_{i,2}$, using AND, OR, XOR, and 1-bit cyclic shift operations. The FO function divides the 32-bit input data into two 16-bit blocks, and then the left block is XORed with the 16-bit sub-key $KO_{i,j}$, transformed by the FI function with a 16-bit sub-key $KI_{i,j}$, and XORed with the right block. This routine is iterated three times with swaps of the left and right blocks.

A 16-bit data block entering the FI function is divided into two smaller blocks for S-Box transformations. The leftmost 9 bits become one block, and the rightmost 7 bits become another block, and then they are transformed twice using the 9-bit S-box S9 and the 7-bit S-box S7 respectively. These S-boxes are defined as AND-XOR matrix operation. The two data blocks are XORed with each other, but the bit length is different, so zero-extension is done to the 7-bit blocks by adding two '0's, and the two most significant bits of the 9-bit blocks are truncated. In the middle of the 4-round network, an XOR operation is done with the 16-bit sub-key $KI_{i,j}$ (where $KI_{i,j,1}$ is the upper 9 bits and $KI_{i,j,2}$ is the lower 7 bits).

2.2 Key Scheduling

The key-scheduling scheme of KASUMI is very simple: cyclic bit-shift and XOR with constant values are the only required operations. A 128-bit secret key is divided into eight 16-bit keys Kj ($1[j [8$), and then eight 16-bit sub-keys {$KL_{i,1}$, $KL_{i,2}$, $KO_{i,1}$, $KO_{i,2}$, $KO_{i,3}$, $KI_{i,1}$, $KI_{i,2}$, $KI_{i,3}$} for each i-th round ($1[i [8$) are generated according to Equation (1) and Table 1.

$$Kj' = Kj \oplus Cj \quad (1 \le j \le 8) \tag{1}$$

$$\{C1, C2, C3, C4, C5, C6, C7, C8\}$$

$$= \{0123_h, 4567_h, 89AB_h, CDEF_h, FEDC_h, BA98_h, 7654_h, 3210_h\}$$

Table 1. Key scheduling Rule

i	$KL_{i,1}$	$KL_{i,2}$	$KO_{i,1}$	$KO_{i,2}$	$KO_{i,3}$	$KI_{i,1}$	$KI_{i,2}$	$KI_{i,3}$
1	K1<<1	K3'	K2<<5	K6<<8	K7<<13	K5'	K4'	K8'
2	K2<<1	K4'	K3<<5	K7<<8	K8<<13	K6'	K5'	K1'
3	K3<<1	K5'	K4<<5	K8<<8	K1<<13	K7'	K6'	K2'
4	K4<<1	K6'	K5<<5	K1<<8	K2<<13	K8'	K7'	K3'
5	K5<<1	K7'	K6<<5	K2<<8	K3<<13	K1'	K8'	K4'
6	K6<<1	K8'	K7<<5	K3<<8	K4<<13	K2'	K1'	K5'
7	K7<<1	K1'	K8<<5	K4<<8	K5<<13	K3'	K2'	K6'
8	K8<<1	K2'	K1<<5	K5<<8	K6<<13	K4'	K3'	K7'

2.3 $f8$ and $f9$ Algorithms

The 3GPP standardized two algorithms, $f8$ and $f9$, using KASUMI. Fig. 2 and Equations (2)-(4) show the $f8$ algorithm used to protect the confidentiality of user data, where KASUMI is used here in a variant of the OFB (Output FeedBack) mode. "KASUMI(A)$_K$" in the equations means the data A is encrypted by using the secret key K. The input data stream (with a maximum length is 5,114 bits) is divided into n 64-bit blocks IDB_i ($1 [i [n$), and XORed with the key stream blocks KSB_i coming out of the KASUMI core, and then the encrypted output data blocks ODB_i are generated. The initial 64-bit vector IV is a concatenation of the system parameters, COUNT (32 bits), BEARER (5 bits), DIRECTION (1 bit), and a series of 26 '0's. The IV is encrypted into the 64-bit data block A by KASUMI using the key CK (Confidentiality Key) and the key modifier MK_{f8}. In every i-th cycle, the key stream block KSB_{i-1} from the previous cycle is XORed with the data A and the number i-1, and is then encrypted as the next key stream block KSB_i by using KASUMI with the key CK.

Fig. 3 and Equations (5)–(7) show the integrity algorithm $f9$ generating a 32-bit message authentication code MAC-I from the message data stream MESSAGE. KASUMI is used here in a variant of the CBC (Cipher Block Chaining) MAC mode [7] with the integrity key IK. First, the system parameters COUNT (32 bits), FRESH (32 bits), DIRECTION (1 bit), and a bit '1' followed by zero bits are added to

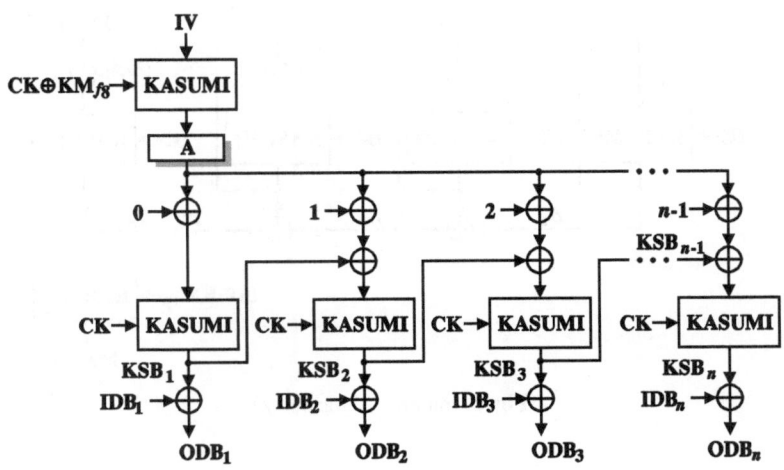

Fig. 2. Confidentiality algorithm $f8$

$$ODB_i = IDB_i \oplus KSB_i \quad (1 \leq i \leq n) \tag{2}$$

$$\begin{cases} A = KASUMI(IV)_{CK \oplus KM_{f8}} \\ IV = COUNT \| BEARER \| DIRECTION \| 0...0 \\ KM_{f8} = 55555555\ 55555555\ 55555555\ 5555555_h \end{cases} \tag{3}$$

$$\begin{cases} KSB_0 = 0 \\ KSB_i = KASUMI(A \oplus (i-1) \oplus KSB_{i-1})_{CK} \quad (1 \leq i \leq n) \end{cases} \tag{4}$$

MESSAGE to generate the padded string PS. Then PS is divided into n 64-bit blocks PS_i ($0[\ i\ [\ n$-1), and each block PS_i is XORed with a ciphertext block A_i from the previous cycle, and encrypted into A_{i+1} by KASUMI. All ciphertext blocks $A_1 \sim A_{n-1}$ are XORed together into B_{n-1} thorough $B_1 \sim B_{n-2}$. Finally, the block B_{n-1} is encrypted with the modified key IK/KM_{f9}, and then the left 32 bits of the 64-bit result become MAC-I.

3 Compact Data Path Architectures

3.1 KASUMI Encryption Data Path

The largest hardware component of the block ciphers is an S-box, and KASUMI uses two kinds of S-boxes (S9 and S7) 6 times each in the FO function as shown in Fig. 1. Therefore, the most efficient way to achieve a compact design is to share these S-boxes. The operation sequence of "XORδFIδXOR" is repeated three times in the FO function. Therefore, the hardware resource can be reduced down to 1/3 by repeatedly

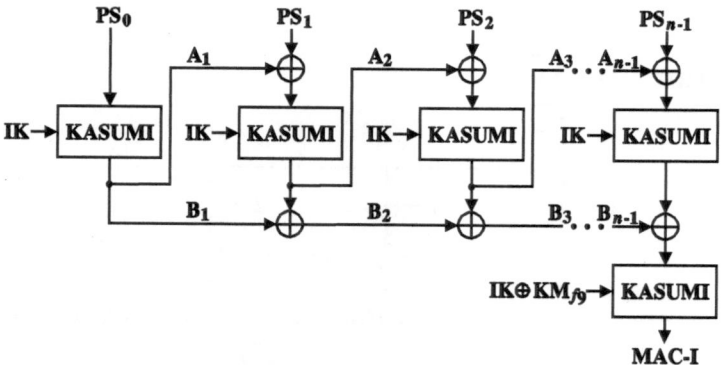

Fig. 3. Integrity algorithm $f9$

$$PS = \{PS_0, PS_1, \cdots PS_{n-1}\} \tag{5}$$
$$= COUNT \parallel FRESH \parallel MESSAGE \parallel DIRECTION \parallel 1 \parallel 0...0$$

$$\begin{cases} A_0 = 0 \\ B_0 = 0 \\ A_i = KASUMI(A_{i-1} \oplus P_i)_{IK} \\ B_i = B_{i-1} \oplus A_i \qquad (1 \le i \le n) \end{cases} \tag{6}$$

$$\begin{cases} MAC\text{-}I = LeftHalf(KASUMI(B_n)_{IK \oplus KM_{f9}}) \\ KM_{f9} = AAAAAAAA\,AAAAAAAA\,AAAAAAAA\,AAAAAAAA_h \end{cases} \tag{7}$$

using one FI core. In addition, we modify the FI function to separate it into two identical function blocks. In the FI function, the first S7 output is XORed with a truncated data block and the sub-keys $KI_{i,1}$, $KI_{i,2}$, but the second S7 output is XORed only with the truncated data. In order to make the regular repeated structure, we split off the XOR operation following the FI function from the FO function in Fig. 1, and put it into the FI function. Then the FI function can be divided into two FI' functions, and the FO function that has 6 FI' functions is obtained as shown in Fig. 4. The S7 output is XORed with the truncated data and the sub-key $KI_{i,1}$ in Fig. 1. However, the order of the XOR operations is reversed here. Because the sub-key comes faster than the truncated data that passes thorough the S-box S9 and an XOR gate.

Fig. 5 shows the entire data path of our compact KASUMI hardware design. The architecture on the left has one FI' function that contains one pair of the S-boxes S9 and S7. This architecture takes 6 cycles to execute the FO function, and one cycle for the FL, and thus in total it takes 7 cycles for one round. As a result, 56 cycles (= 7 cycles × 8 rounds) are required for the entire encryption process. The architecture on the right has one normal FI function containing two pairs of the S-Boxes, and the FO uses the FI three times. Therefore, 4 cycles (3 for the FI and 1 for the FL) are required for one round, and the entire encryption process takes 32 cycles (= 4 cycles × 8 rounds).

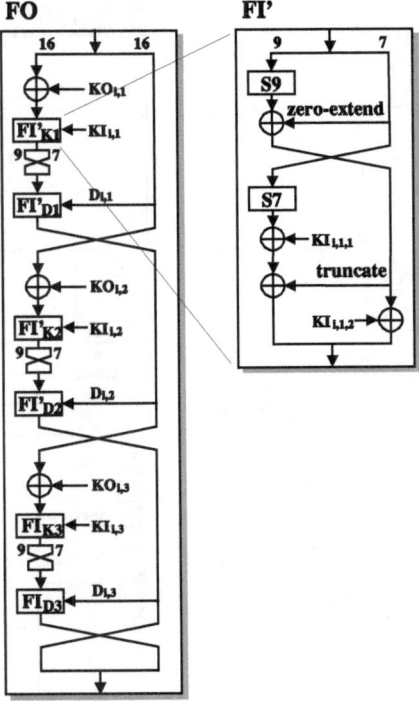

Fig. 4. Equivalent FO function

3.2 Key Scheduler

Eight 16-bit sub-keys {$KL_{i,1}$, $KL_{i,2}$, $KO_{i,1}$, $KO_{i,2}$, $KO_{i,3}$, $KI_{i,1}$, $KI_{i,2}$, $KI_{i,3}$} are generated from the 16-bit secret keys K1~K8 in each i-th round (1[i [8) by bit-rotating or XORing with the constant 16-bit values C1~C8 as shown in Equation (1) and Table 1.

One secret key generates one sub-key in each cycle, and the correspondence of the keys is shifted one by one according to Table 1. Therefore, we use a shift register architecture for the key scheduler, as shown in Fig. 6. The register data is shifted to the left in encryption, and to the right in decryption. The KASUMI specifications do not describe decryption, because the ƒ8 and ƒ9 algorithms only use KASUMI in encryption mode. However, we developed hardware supporting both encryption and decryption. This makes built-in self-test easier, and can be applied for other purposes besides the ƒ8 and ƒ9 algorithms.

In order to reduce selectors, the 128-bit secret key is loaded into the registers from the 16-bit input port Kin through the path for shift operation using 8 cycles. In the sub-key generation phase, the constant values C1~C8 are also shifted, and four of them are XORed with the key register outputs. This part is designed as a barrel shifter followed by selectors. A barrel shifter usually requires large hardware, but this circuit can be compressed into small combinatorial logic, because the inputs are all constants and the operation timing is not critical. The key registers are shifted every cycle for the normal (1 round / cycle) architecture, and are shifted every 7 or 4 cycles for the compact architectures described above.

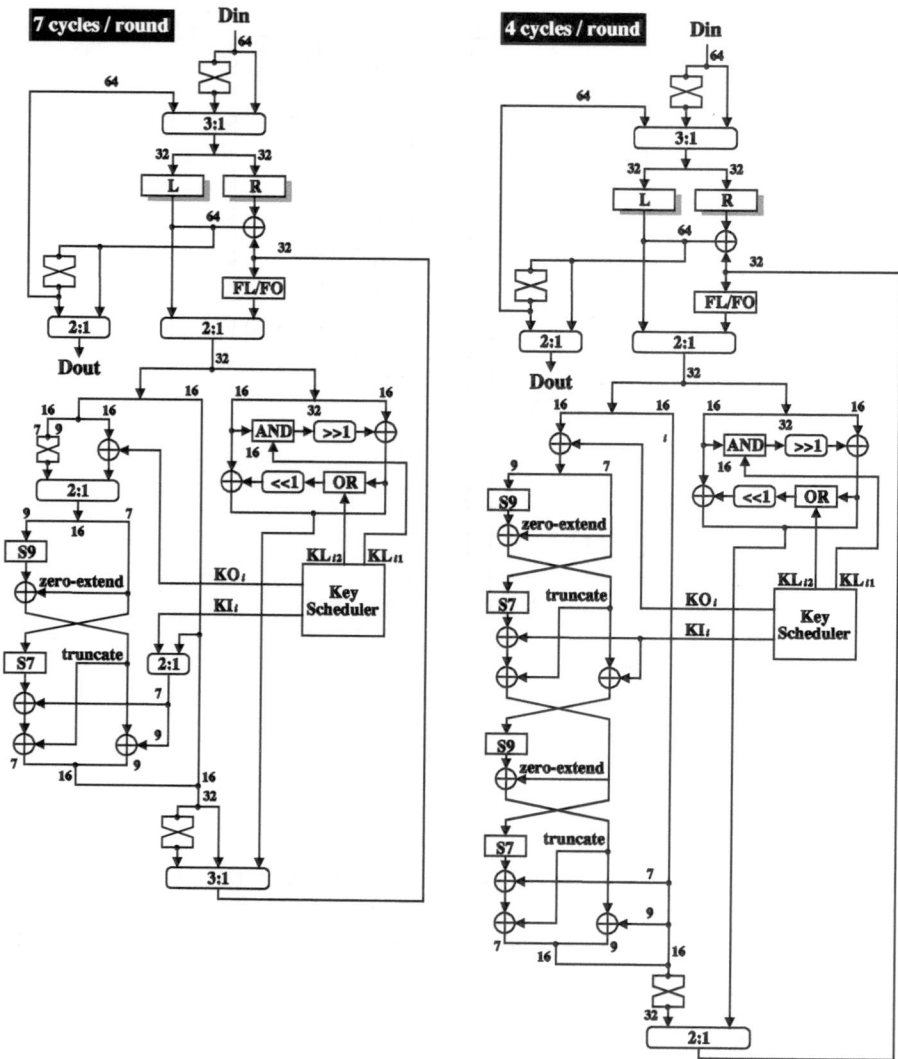

Fig. 5. Data path of proposed KASUMI architectures

3.3 Data Path Sharing between *f8* and *f9*

In order to support the *f8* and *f9* algorithms with a single small device, we share the KASUMI core, the key and data registers, XOR gates, and the controller logic between the algorithms. However, the critical path gets longer and the operating speed is reduced if selectors are inserted carelessly for the component sharing. In addition, a 2:1 selector is bigger than an XOR gate, so it should not be used simply to share an XOR gate. Therefore we use the feature of the XOR operation that one of the two inputs passes through to the output when the other input is held at '0'. Fig. 7

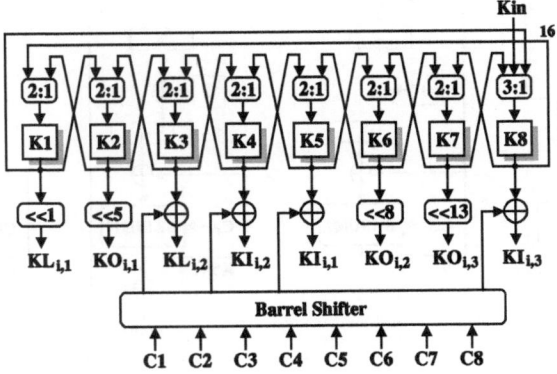

Fig. 6. Key scheduler

shows our hardware architecture where the two algorithms are successfully shared using only one 64-bit selector. The data flow is controlled by the selector and the XOR gates. The $f8$ and $f9$ operations using our merged architecture are detailed in the Figures 8 and 9.

In the $f8$ initial rounds, the secret key CK is XORed with the key modifier KM_{f8} ($=555...5_h$), and in the $f9$ final rounds, the IK is XORed with the KM_{f9} ($=AAA...A_h$) as shown in Equations (3) and (7). By these XOR operations, the values of the even bits in CK and the odd bits in IK are reversed, and then the modified keys are fed into the KASUMI key scheduler. The key scheduling is a simple linear function using bit rotations and XOR. Therefore the XOR with the constant KM_{f8} or KM_{f9} for the input key can be replaced by an XOR with the constants KM'_{f8} or KM'_{f9}, shown in Table 2, for the sub-key output. The bit patterns of KM'_{f8} and KM'_{f9} for the sub-keys $\{KL_{i,2}, KO_{i,2}, KI_{i,1}, KI_{i,2}, KI_{i,3}\}$ are the same as KM_{f8} and KM_{f9}, and the patterns are rotated by 1 bit for the sub-keys $\{KL_{i,1}, KO_{i,1}, KO_{i,3}\}$ that are rotated by an odd number of bits.

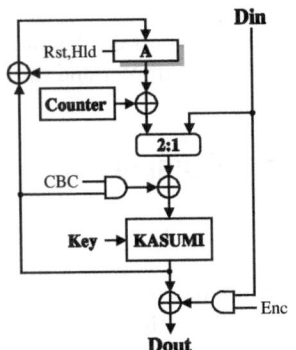

Fig. 7. $f8$ and $f9$ merged architecture

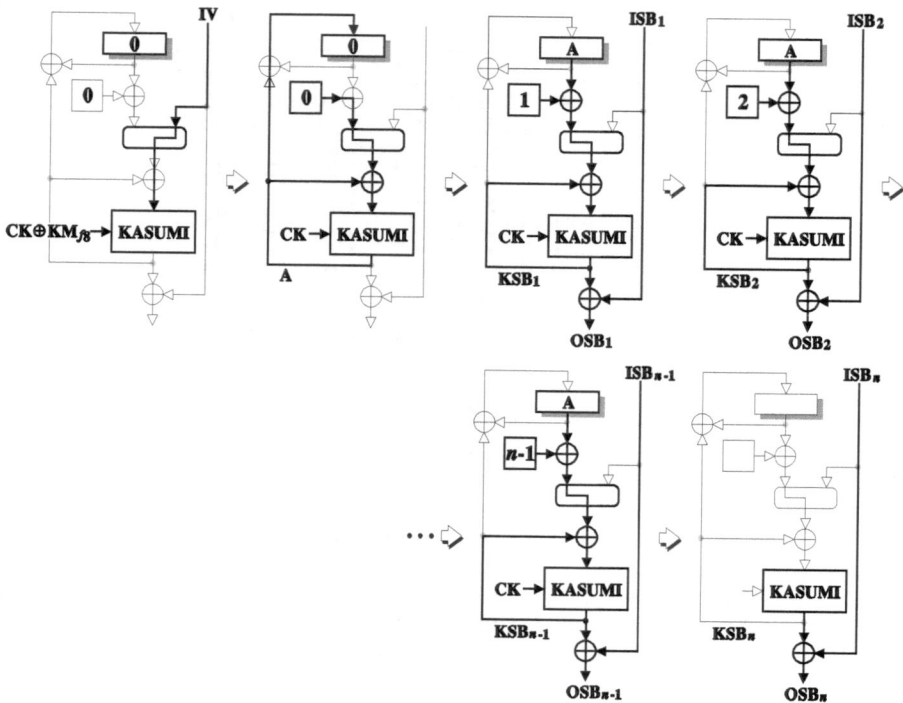

Fig. 8. f8 operation control

Fig. 10 shows the key modifier generator. When the KASUMI core is used in feedback mode, and the key modify operation is not required, the control signal FBn is assigned to '0', and then the AND outputs become '0', and all XOR operations are disabled. The signal FBn is assigned to '1' for the sub-key modification, and then KM'_8 or KM'_9 are generated when the signal f8_f9 is '0' or '1' respectively. By attaching this circuit to the output lines of the key scheduler shown in Fig. 6, the sub-key modification can be supported easily. It is possible to modify the secret key in the register directly, but our architecture is simpler and the hardware is smaller.

4 Hardware Performance Comparisons

4.1 ASIC Comparison

Our KASUMI and f8/f9 merged architectures were implemented by using a 0.13-μm CMOS standard cell library, and their performances are shown in Table 3 and Fig. 11 in comparison with the conventional approach [6]. We designed three kinds of circuits: KASUMI supporting both encryption and decryption, KASUMI supporting only encryption, and the f8/f9 combined design. Each circuit was also implemented in three data path architectures: 56-, 32-, and 8-cycle versions with one, two, and six pairs of S-Boxes respectively. Two circuits were generated from one design by

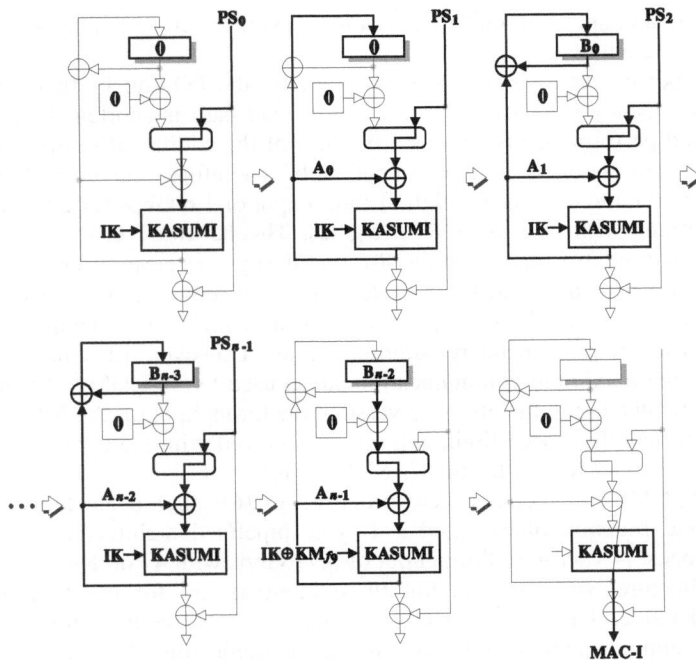

Fig. 9. ƒ9 operation control

Table 2. Key modifier KM'_ƒ8 and KM'_ƒ9 for sub-keys in ƒ8 and ƒ9

Sub-Keys	KM'_ƒ8	KM'_ƒ9
$KL_{i,1}$	$AAAA_h$	5555_h
$KL_{i,2}$	5555_h	$AAAA_h$
$KO_{i,1}$	$AAAA_h$	5555_h
$KO_{i,2}$	5555_h	$AAAA_h$
$KO_{i,3}$	$AAAA_h$	5555_h
$KI_{i,1}$	5555_h	$AAAA_h$
$KI_{i,2}$	5555_h	$AAAA_h$
$KI_{i,3}$	5555_h	$AAAA_h$

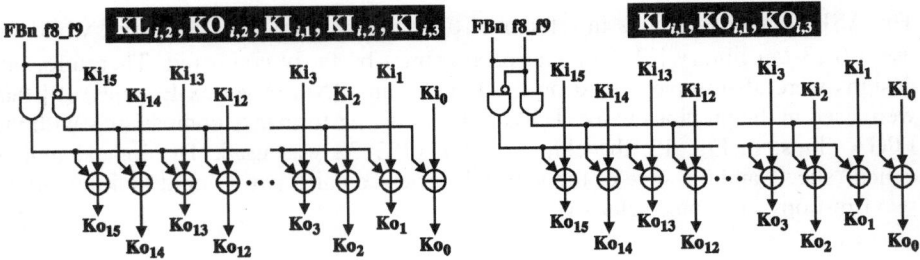

Fig. 10. Key modifier generator

specifying area or speed optimization to a logic synthesizer, so a total of 18 (= 3 × 3 × 2) circuits were obtained.

The number of cycles is increased by dividing the FO and FI functions, but the operation frequency is boosted because the critical path is shortened. However, the overall speed performance is degraded because of the additional setup and hold time for the registers inserted in the critical path. Therefore, the normal 8-cycle (1-cycle/round) version obtains the highest throughput of 1.6 Gbps for all KASUMI and $f8/f9$ algorithms with only 6.14~8.27 Kgates. The hardware efficiency defined by throughput/gate is also highest in the 8-round design, because all architectures have the same number of data and key registers, and their controllers are also almost the same. Only the size of the encryption data path is different. Therefore, the fastest design does not require so many additional gates. However, 1.6 Gbps is 800 times higher than the maximum communication speed used by W-CDMA. Even using our minimum architecture in the 56-cycle version, the throughput of 288 Mbps is still 144 times higher than this speed limit, and this is achieved with the extremely small size of 4.89 Kgates (3.07 Kgates for the KASUMI core).

Two KASUMI architectures were proposed in [6]: an 8-cycle loop architecture with 2 round function blocks, and a 1-cycle pipelined architecture with 8 round function blocks. A very high throughput of 5.79 Gbps with 47.66 Kgates using the 1-cycle architecture was reported, but these numbers are for the ECB (Electronic CodeBook) mode. The CBC and OFB feedback modes required for the $f8$ and $f9$ algorithms cannot be supported by their pipelined architecture, but the throughputs for the algorithms were misleadingly evaluated based on the pipelined operation. Therefore, we corrected the numbers by assuming the non-pipelined operation for their high-speed hardware in Table 3.

The gate counts 4.89~8.27 K for our implementations that support both the $f8$ and $f9$ algorithms is only 1/4~1/7 the size compared with the 2-cycle architecture in [6] where either $f8$ or $f9$ was supported. In addition, the number of registers in those implementations shows that only the encryption data path was included, excluding the key registers, scheduler, and control logic, while ours contains everything. In hardware efficiency defined as throughput/gate, our designs are at least 2.7~9.3 times more efficient. The superiority of our architecture is quite clear in Fig. 11.

4.2 Comparison in FPGAs

The ASIC implementations in reference [6] use a 0.25-μm CMOS library, while we use a 0.13-μm library [8], so their speed cannot be fairly compared. Therefore, our designs were also implemented on the FPGA chips (Xilinx vertex-E series) [9] that were used in the previous work. Table 4 shows the performance comparisons with the FPGA chips. In Fig. 12, the chip xcv300E-6BG432 was used. The logical unit is called "slice," and the slice of the vertex-E series contains two 4-input look-up tables, two flip-flops, and some selectors.

Table 3. Hardware performance comparison in ASICs

	Functions	Cycles	Area (gates)			Max. Freq. (MHz)	Through-put (Mbps)	Kbps / gate	Notes
			Combi-nation	Register	Total				
This work	KASUMI Enc. + Dec.	56	2,225	1,212	3,437	251.89	287.87	83.76	Area optimized
		32	2,765	1,209	3,974	250.00	500.00	125.82	
		8	4,462	1,026	5,488	142.86	1,142.88	208.25	
		56	3,344	1,350	4,694	454.55	519.49	110.67	Speed optimized
		32	4,022	1,308	5,330	370.37	740.74	138.98	
		8	5,315	1,121	6,436	200.00	1,600.00	248.60	
	KASUMI Enc.	56	1,861	1,205	3,066	251.89	287.87	93.89	Area optimized
		32	2,410	1,200	3,610	250.63	501.26	138.85	
		8	4,059	1,020	5,079	142.86	1,142.88	225.02	
		56	2,548	1,250	3,798	454.55	519.49	136.78	Speed optimized
		32	3,721	1,316	5,037	367.65	735.30	145.98	
		8	5,017	1,120	6,137	200.00	1,600.00	260.71	
	$f8 + f9$	56	3,289	1,599	4,888	251.89	287.87	58.89	Area optimized
		32	4,007	1,597	5,604	250.00	500.00	89.22	
		8	5,597	1,405	7,002	142.86	1,142.88	163.22	
		56	4,687	1,825	6,512	454.55	519.49	79.77	Speed optimized
		32	5,117	1,754	6,871	333.33	666.66	97.03	
		8	6,758	1,512	8,270	200.00	1,600.00	193.47	
[6]	KASUMI Enc.	8	14,003	1,678	15,697	90.42	723.37	46.08	Key scheduler and controller are not implemented. Area of μm^2 in [6] is incorrect.
		1	43,481	4,136	47,660	94.05	5,786.94 A	126.29	
	$f8$	8	28,918	5,376	34,328	89.15	713.20=	20.78=	
		8=	89,890	12,958	102,848	90.09	720.72=	7.01=	
	$f9$	8	28,082	4,453	32,567	88.71	709.68=	21.79=	
		8=	86,879	9,145	96,380	89.12	712.96=	7.40=	

= Authors' estimation. A ECB mode only. Is correct number 6,019.20 ?

Two independent circuits were required for the $f8$ and the $f9$ algorithms in [6], and their performances were the 164.16 Mbps throughput with a hardware area of 2,781 slices, and 165.44 Mbps with 2,671 slices respectively. The size of our implementations are only 512~742 slices which is only 18.4~26.7% of the previous work while supporting both $f8$ and $f9$ in a single circuit, and our throughput is 58.5~206.4 Mbps. As a result, our hardware efficiency (throughput/slice) is 1.8~4.7 times higher, and thus our architecture has strong advantages in both size and speed.

5 Conclusion

Small and high-speed hardware architectures for the block cipher KASUMI from the 3GPP standard were proposed, and performance comparisons in ASICs and FPGAs were made.

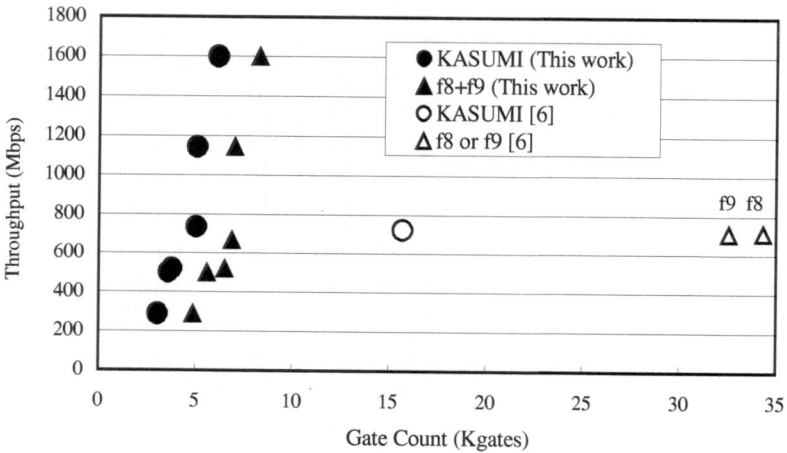

Fig. 11. Hardware performance comparison in ASICs (worst case)

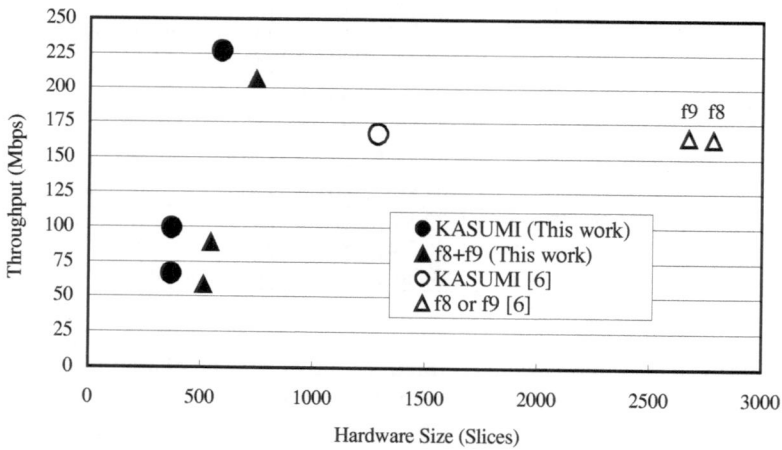

Fig. 12. Hardware performance comparison in FPGA (xcv300E-6BG432).

KASUMI has a nested structure. Its round function contains the FL and the FO functions, the FO uses the FI function three times, and the FI has two pairs of S-Boxes. Therefore we divided the FI function into two regular blocks that have one pair of S-boxes each, and designed three types of architectures containing one, three, and six pairs. The data paths for the confidentiality ($f8$) and integrity ($f9$) algorithms were successfully merged with only one additional selector. Other function blocks such as the key scheduler and controller were also optimized in size and speed.

Table 4. Hardware performance comparison in FPGAs

	Functions	Cyc-les	Area (Slice)	Max. Freq. (MHz)	Through-put (Mbps)	Kbps / Slice	Device	Notes
This work	KASUMI Enc.+ Dec.	56	435	68.13	77.86	179.00	(1)	
		32	461	57.96	115.92	251.45		
		8	665	33.14	265.12	398.68		
	KASUMI Enc.	56	368	68.13	77.86	211.58		
		32	370	58.06	116.12	313.84		
		8	588	33.14	265.12	450.88		
	$f8 + f9$	56	511	59.88	68.43	133.92		
		32	544	51.96	103.92	191.03		
		8	741	30.12	240.96	325.18		
	KASUMI Enc.+ Dec.	56	435	58.14	66.45	152.75	(2)	
		32	461	49.51	99.02	143.21		
		8	665	28.38	227.04	341.41		
	KASUMI Enc.	56	368	58.14	66.45	180.56		
		32	370	49.59	99.18	268.05		
		8	588	28.38	227.04	386.12		
	$f8 + f9$	56	512	51.15	58.46	114.17		
		32	544	44.42	88.84	163.30		
		8	742	25.80	206.40	278.17		
[6]	KASUMI Enc.	8	1,287	20.88	167.04	129.79	(2)	Key scheduler and controller are not implemented.
		1	4,032	20.86	1,335.04	331.11	(3)	
	$f8$	8	2,781	20.52	164.16=	59.03=	(2)	
		8=	8,416	20.01	160.08=	19.02=	(4)?	
	$f9$	8	2,671	20.68	165.44=	61.94=	(2)	
		8=	8,104	20.19	161.52=	19.93	(4)	

= Authors' estimation
(1)300E-8BG432 (2)300E-6BG432 (3)400E-6BG432 (4)1000E-6BG560

Using the 0.13-μm ASIC library, extremely small sizes of 3.07 Kgates for KASUMI core, and 4.89 Kgates for the $f8/f9$ algorithms were obtained. In addition, their throughput of 288 Mbps is 144 times higher than the maximum communication speed of W-CDMA. The performance of the fastest version of the $f8/f9$ achieved throughput of 1.6 Gbps with 8.27 Kgates (6.14 Kgates for the KASUMI core). Therefore KASUMI can be applied not only to WCDMA cellular phone systems but also to many other applications.

In comparison with the previous work using the same FPGA platform, the total hardware efficiency is at least 1.8~4.7 times higher, and it was shown that our architectures are superior in both size and speed.

References

1. "3GPP TS 35 201 v 3.1.1 Document 1: f8 and f9 Specification,"
   http://www.3gpp.org/TB/other/algorithms/35201-311.pdf
2. "3GPP TS 35.202 v 3.1.1 Document 2: KASUMI Specification,"
   http://www.3gpp.org/TB/other/algorithms/35202-311.pdf

3. "3GPP TS 35.203 v 3.1.1 Document 3: Implementers' Test Data,"
   http://www.3gpp.org/TB/other/algorithms/35203-311.pdf
4. "3GPP TS 35.204 v 3.1.1 Document 4: Design Conformance Test Data,"
   http://www.3gpp.org/TB/other/algorithms/35204-311.pdf
5. M. Matsui, "New Block Encryption Algorithm MISTY," *Fast Software Encryption '97 (FSE97)*, LCNS1267, pp. 54-68, 1997.
6. N. K. Moshopoulos, F. Karoubalis, and K.Z. Pekmestzi, "On the Hardware Implementation of the 3GPP Confidentiality and Integrity Algorithm," *Information Security Conference 2001 (ISC2001)*, LNCS 2200, pp.248-265, 2001.
7. ISO/IEC 9797-1:1999, "Information technology – Security techniques – Message Authentication Codes (MACs) – Part 1: Mechanisms using a block cipher."
8. "Blue Logic Cu-11 ASIC,"
   http://www-3.ibm.com/chips/products/asics/products/cu-11.html.
9. "Vertex-E Data Sheet," http://xilinx.com/partinfo/ds022.htm.

Fast Software Implementations of SC2000

Helger Lipmaa

Laboratory for Theoretical Computer Science
Department of Computer Science and Engineering
Helsinki University of Technology
P.O.Box 5400, FIN-02015 HUT, Espoo, Finland
helger@tcs.hut.fi

Abstract. The block cipher SC2000 was recently proposed by a research group of Fujitsu Laboratories as a candidate cipher for the CRYPTREC and NESSIE projects. The cipher was designed so that it would be highly flexible and fast on many platforms. In this paper we show that the cipher is really fast on the Pentium III and AMD platforms: Our C implementation of SC2000 on Pentium III is only second to the best C implementations of RC6 on the same platform, and faster than for example the world fastest implementation of Twofish in assembly. In particular, we improve the bulk encryption and decryption times by almost 1.6 times as compared to the previous best implementation by Fujitsu. Finally, we report new Rijndael and RC6 implementation results that are slightly better than these of Aoki and Lipmaa.

Keywords: Block cipher design, fast implementation, large S-boxes, SC2000.

1 Introduction

While Rijndael [DR02] has been recently approved as the new US governmental standard, Europe and Japan are in a quest for their own standards. SC2000 is one of the new block ciphers that was recently proposed by a research group from Fujitsu Laboratories [SYY$^+$01] in the context of CRYPTREC in Japan and NESSIE in Europe. The cipher features many standard constructs of modern block ciphers, mixed in a way that makes it potentially fast in many different execution environments when using suitable implementation strategies. However, such design also makes the cipher more complex than some of the rivals.

An example design decision that makes it possible to code an implementation of SC2000 that takes into account the peculiarities of the target processor is the use of two 6-bit S-boxes and four 5-bit S-boxes. All six S-boxes can be accessed in parallel. One could then use the straightforward $(6, 5, 5, 5, 5, 6)$-implementation for implementing SC2000 on low-end storage-constrained environments with only 256 different S-box entries. On high-end microprocessors with large cache size, one might instead want to use a $(16, 16)$-implementation where six small S-boxes are combined into two large S-boxes. The number of table look-ups required by such an implementation would decrease by 48 per encrypted or decrypted block, while the S-box tables would have $2^{17} = 131072$ entries. Another example of the flexibility of SC2000 is the B function that

A.H. Chan and V. Gligor (Eds.): ISC 2002, LNCS 2433, pp. 63–74, 2002.

may be implemented without or with bit-slicing techniques, depending on the concrete processor.

On the other hand, although many strategic choices are available for the implementer it is not *a priori* clear whether SC2000 will perform well on any concrete platform. As an concrete example, the designers of SC2000 [SYY+01] have reported SC2000 implementations that at least on Pentium III are severely less efficient than corresponding implementations of Rijndael [DR02], RC6 [RRSY98], MARS [BCD+98] and Twofish [SKW+99], four of the five AES finalists. Complexity of SC2000 without any referable performance advantages was probably the main reason why this cipher did not pass to the second round of NESSIE.

We have chosen to implement SC2000 in the C language. For the sake of generality, we report the results of all implementations when compiled with gcc, icc or (when available) hand-coded in assembly on both Pentium III and AMD's Athlon. (See Table 1.) However, our implementations are specifically optimized for the $(16, 16)$-strategy for the icc 5.0 compiler and for the Pentium III. Chosen processors are sufficiently powerful to enable the usage of large S-boxes and to support efficient bit-slicing, but they are not as powerful as to make the resources used by our implementations unreasonable in other common processors. In particular this means that while the $(16, 16)$-implementation strategy might seem to be luxurious when using a Pentium III or an Athlon, it will become more realistic in the near future also in the commercial setting. Additionally, we focused our work on implementing the 128-bit key version of SC2000, SC2000-128, since this version seems to be commercially the most relevant for the foreseeable future.

We show that one can significantly improve upon the implementation results of [SYY+01]. On Pentium III, we report a pure C $(16, 16)$-implementation of SC2000 that is almost 1.6 times faster than the C implementation, and approximately 1.4 times faster than the combined C-assembly implementation of Fujitsu [SYY+01]. Such a large speed-up is mainly caused by the use of large S-boxes, and demonstrates the flexible design of SC2000. We also report fast implementations of SC2000 in different implementation strategies.

Additionally, we report fast implementations of Rijndael and RC6 that are somewhat faster than the ones described by Aoki and Lipmaa [AL00]. We then compare our implementations of Rijndael, RC6 and SC2000. On the Pentium III, our C implementation of SC2000 takes 270 cycles (or runs at 543 Mbit/s) that is faster than the best *assembly* implementation of Twofish on the same platform [AL00] and is only second to the assembly implementations of RC6 and Rijndael, reported in this paper. In particular, the only well-known block cipher that can be implemented faster in C on the same platform seems to be RC6. One of the main conclusions of this paper is that given current knowledge, it seems to be relatively easy to design fast (and secure) ciphers.

Road-map. In Section 2, we will give a short overview of the programming environment and previous best results. Then, in Section 3 we will describe our new implementations. There we will also give a summary of our final results. We conclude the paper with some recommendations, further work and acknowledgments.

Table 1. Comparison of Rijndael, RC6 and SC2000 implementations on Pentium III. N/A means that corresponding entry was not implemented. Enc means that the decryption key schedule is equal to the encryption key schedule. Subscript $+$ means high optimization in terms of the spent time, with more pluses signifying better optimization

Cipher	Compiler	Encr.	Decr.	Key schedule	
				Encr.	Decr.
Rijndael	assembly	226^{+++}	239^{+}	N/A	N/A
	icc 5.0	430	453	185	319
	gcc 3.0.4	346^{++}	371^{++}	171^{++}	280^{++}
SC2000	icc 5.0	270^{++}	278^{++}	357^{++}	Enc
	gcc 3.0.4	269^{++}	376	357	Enc
RC6	assembly	219^{+}	205^{+}	N/A	N/A
	icc 5.0	257	289	1436	Enc
	gcc 3.0.4	234^{+}	265	1778	Enc

2   Environment and State-of-the-Art

2.1   Description of Target Processor

We decided to optimize our implementations for one concrete widely used processor but also test them on at least on another one. At the time of writing this paper mainstream computers shipped at least three different processor families that, while inter-compatible, were internally sufficiently different to make it necessary to use specialized implementation strategies to achieve the best performance: Namely, Intel's P6 family (of which the Pentium III was the most high-end representative), Intel's P7 family (mainly, Pentium 4), and AMD's Athlon family.

We chose the P6 family (most precisely, the Pentium III) mostly because of the wide availability of comparison materials: For example, the results of Aoki and Lipmaa [AL00] on implementing four of five AES finalists can be directly compared to ours. Our main development and target processor was a 1200 MHz Pentium III Mobile that was used in high-end laptops at this point. (The performance of our implementations on Pentium III Mobile and Pentium III (Katmai) was the same, so we will mostly omit the word 'Mobile' in the next.)

A relevant introduction of the Pentium II for cipher designers and implementers is given by Aoki and Lipmaa [AL00]. The main difference of Pentium III, as compared to Pentium II (namely, inclusion of several new multimedia instructions) has no relevance to our work: Our implementations are coded in C, and neither the Gnu C or the Intel C Compiler generated any MMX technology instructions at all. As opposed to that, a quite relevant change is the increase in size of cache to 512 KB. Larger cache size made it feasible to use the $(16, 16)$-implementation strategy (see Section 3.1). On the other hand, increased cache size has not benefitted other block ciphers as greatly: our best implementations of AES finalists on the Pentium III, while being slightly faster, take approximately as much times as the implementations of Aoki and Lipmaa on the Pentium II [AL00]. (This can be seen from Table 1.) The main reason behind that seems to be the fact that, as a rule, other block ciphers do not have specific implementation strategies that require $256\ldots512$ KB of memory.

In Section 3.2 we will also describe our results of implementing SC2000 on AMD's Athlon processor. The concrete Athlon had 256 KB cache and ran at 1400 MHz. Since we did not make any specific effort of optimization for Athlon—we stress that one could get a better performance on Athlon, after spending more time on implementation—, we will omit description of this processor family.

2.2   Description of General Environment

We have coded our implementations under the Linux operating system, by using two different compilers, gcc 3.0.4 (Gnu C Compiler) and icc 5.0 (Intel C Compiler). The choice of operating system was partially due to the envisioned scenario of using our implementations in (say) routers, firewalls and servers that often run a version of Linux. Such machines usually do not serve as workstations, they instead execute a few specialized tasks. Therefore, in such machines memory usage of $512\ldots600$ KB for one particular cipher seems to be quite reasonable if it results in 30% win in throughput. We also chose to use a high-level language with a highly optimizing compiler so as to be able to simply port our implementations to other machines and on the other hand, not to loose seriously in throughput compared to implementations coded in the assembly language.

More precisely, we tested our results on two different machines, one having a 1200 MHz Pentium III Mobile, 512 KB cache, 128 MB RAM, both gcc 3.0.4 and icc 5.0 compilers, and Linux 2.4.18 operating system. The second machine had a 1400 MHz Athlon, 256 KB cache, 1 GB RAM, gcc 3.0.3 compiler and Linux 2.4.17 operating system. The gcc compiler was used with flags

```
-O4 -fomit-frame-pointer -mcpu=XXX -march=XXX
-D__OPTIMIZE__ -fexpensive-optimizations
-funroll-loops -mpreferred-stack-boundary=2
```

where XXX corresponded to the processor type (pentiumpro or athlon). The icc compiler was used without any explicit optimization flags since their usage did not result in any gain in performance.

2.3   Overview of Related Results

As far as we know, the only optimized implementation of SC2000 on the Pentium III thus far is by the designers [SYY+01]. Their results, together with information from [Shi02], is summarized in Table 2.

Aoki and Lipmaa [AL00] implemented several AES finalists on the Pentium II, and described thoroughly their timing methods, implementation criteria (e.g., no self-modifying code), etc. We follow their sensible guidelines. This allows precise comparison of our results to theirs. We refer to [AL00] for description of the timing subroutines and other background information. Appendix A contains a short overview of the used time measurement procedures.

Table 2. The previously best implementations of SC2000-128 [Shi02], compiled with VC++ 6.0 and tested under Microsoft Windows

Processor	Strategy	Language	Encr.	Decr.	Key schedule
Pentium III (Katmai)	$(6, 10, 10, 6)$	C+assembly	383	403	427
		C	412	424	433
	$(11, 10, 11)$	C+assembly	525	535	488
		C	554	549	488
Athlon	$(6, 10, 10, 6)$	C+assembly	392	402	426
		C	383	402	426
	$(11, 10, 11)$	C+assembly	318	329	373
		C	337	358	373

3 Main Contributions

3.1 Choice of Implementation Strategy

General Strategy. We omit the full description of SC2000 and refer to [SYY+01] instead. Our implementation and its strategy, described in this subsection, follows somewhat loosely the recommendations given in that paper about implementing SC2000 on 32-bit processors.

Cipher state. Cipher state consists of four 32-bit variables that are initialized by the plaintext and then get modified by the B, $B^{(i)}$, I, M and R functions.

S-boxes. From numerous available possibilities of combining the S-boxes we chose the variant $(16, 16)$: That is, the case with two S-boxes that both contain 2^{16} elements, all elements being 32-bit integers. The total storage needed by such S-boxes, 512 KB, does not seem to be prohibitive in the target environment. However, when indeed one must save the memory, one can use also the $(11, 10, 11)$-implementation strategy when S-boxes have been partitioned into 11, 10 and 11-bit S-boxes. In this case, the S-boxes require only 20 KB of storage space, but the resulting implementation will also be 30% slower. Several intermediate strategies are possible, the most natural ones are summarized in Fig. 1. We implemented all four strategies.

Function M. We have chosen the strategy, outlined already in [SYY+01], to combine the M function and S-boxes into single table. Therefore, M function does not add any additional overhead to the implementation, compared to the S-boxes alone. Indeed, our implementation features a function called SM.

Function R. Implementing R is straightforward, since it only includes two calls to the SM function and a few Boolean operations. There was basically no choices to be done while implementing this function.

Strategy						Look−ups	#Cells
6	5	5	5	5	6	6	256
6	10		10		6	4	2176
11		10		11		3	5120
16			16			2	131072

Fig. 1. Different implementation strategies for the S-boxes, with the number of table look-ups per SM function and the total number of elements in all S-boxes

Function I. Function I consists of XOR-ing of a part of the key schedule to the internal state of the function. An implementer has almost no freedom in optimizing this subroutine either.

Function B. We chose to implement B by using bit-slicing techniques, as also suggested in [SYY+01], but improved considerably upon the example code given in [SYY+01]. Our code for B function consists of 20 instructions that belong to one of the next five available primitive operations of the target processor: a=b, a=~b, a|=b, a^=b and a&=b. Our implementation of B also uses three temporary registers.

Function $B^{(i)}$. We also use bit-slicing to implement the function $B^{(i)}$. Our code for $B^{(i)}$ function consists of 23 instructions and uses four temporary registers. As we see later, the difference in the complexities of B and $B^{(i)}$ functions seem to be relevant under the gcc compiler.

Key schedule. Our key implementation proceeds first by creating intermediate keys and then the final key. Both parts are relatively straightforward. During creation of intermediate keys, one has to apply the SM function 16 times on different inputs; this part also includes some Boolean operations. During creation of the extended key schedule, we invoke a subroutine EKEY 56 times, where every invocation of EKEY consists of four table look-ups and a few simple instructions.

Encryption. During encryption, we first invoke the "encryption meta-round" function $\phi_i = R_i \circ R_i \circ I \circ B \circ I$ six times, and then apply $I \circ B \circ I$ to the result. Here, by $\alpha \circ \beta$ we denote the serial composition of first β and then α; R_i denotes the R function with constant $0x111111 \cdot (3 + 2 \cdot (i \mod 2))$. More precisely, every invocation of I feeds a new part of the extended key schedule to I, and the four elements in the state of the cipher are permuted after each component function. The final state is stored as the ciphertext. Permuting is implemented by inputting a different permutation of the four state variables as arguments to different subroutines and therefore permuting is free. Permutations are chosen so as to minimize the amount of mov-type instructions in different functions.

Decryption. During decryption, we first invoke the "decryption meta-round" function $\psi_i = R_{i+1} \circ R_{i+1} \circ I \circ B^{(i)} \circ I$ six times, and then apply $I \circ B^{(i)} \circ I$ to the result. Therefore, our code of decryption looks very similar to our code of encryption, except of the exchange in indexes of R functions and the replacement of B with $B^{(i)}$. (Also, the permutations of $B^{(i)}$ function are different of the permutations of B function.) Thus, in all our implemented strategies, the encryption and decryption routines have exactly the same complexity except that there are 3 additional instructions in every $B^{(i)}$ function (and one additional temporary register in use) as compared to the B function.

3.2 Summary of Results

We implemented the SC2000 by using four possible strategies and compared the results obtained when using two different compilers (gcc and icc) on two different platforms (the Pentium III and Athlon). Summary results are given in Table 3 and in Table 4. We specifically optimized the $(16, 16)$-implementation for Pentium III under the icc compiler (the first row in Table 3), and no specific effort was made in optimizing results in any other row. If such effort will be made, numbers in many fields will most probably decrease significantly. We specifically expect that significantly improved performance can be achieved on Athlon.

Our results indicate that the above-mentioned difference between the B and $B^{(i)}$ functions is substantial in the case of gcc that runs short of registers in decryption routine: This can result in decryption being almost twice slower. On the other hand, when icc is used, encryption and decryption will have almost identical timings. Thus, the small number of integer registers of the target processors makes implementations extremely sensitive to proper allocation of registers.

The Intel C Compiler tends to optimize better the key schedule algorithm, while the superiority of one compiler over the another one in producing better encryption code seems to depend very much on the concrete implementation strategy. From the implementation strategies, $(16, 16)$ seems to yield the best throughput on the Pentium III, while $(11, 10, 11)$ suits better the Athlon. The difference is caused mainly by the fact that the Pentium III Mobile and Katmai feature 512 KB cache, twice as much as the target Athlon. Really, when using the $(16, 16)$-strategy, the S-boxes have size 512 KB and therefore, when using the $(16, 16)$-strategy, accessing the S-boxes produces many cache misses on Athlon.

On the other hand, this problem with the $(16, 16)$-strategy non-withstanding, Athlon seems to be a slightly better processor than the Pentium III. Our implementations (except the $(16, 16)$-implementation) run faster on the Athlon even if no special optimization was made for Athlon! More precisely, icc-compiled implementations had often better timings on Athlon than gcc-compiled implementations on Athlon (or icc-compiled implementations on Pentium III), even if icc does not optimize for Athlon! When the next

Table 3. Our SC2000 implementation results in the table form (cpb=cycles per block)

Processor	Strategy	Compiler	Encr. (cpb)	Decr. (cpb)	Key sch. (cpb)
Pentium III	$(16, 16)$	icc 5.0	270	277	356
		gcc 3.0.4	269	489	359
	$(11, 10, 11)$	icc 5.0	349	356	427
		gcc 3.0.4	452	561	501
	$(6, 10, 10, 6)$	icc 5.0	409	414	483
		gcc 3.0.4	388	609	511
	$(6, 5, 5, 5, 5, 6)$	icc 5.0	521	527	519
		gcc 3.0.4	503	824	665
Athlon	$(16, 16)$	icc 5.0	362	381	280
		gcc 3.0.3	374	543	309
	$(11, 10, 11)$	icc 5.0	319	327	361
		gcc 3.0.3	312	507	392
	$(6, 10, 10, 6)$	icc 5.0	413	376	404
		gcc 3.0.3	366	606	438
	$(6, 5, 5, 5, 5, 6)$	icc 5.0	471	478	427
		gcc 3.0.3	463	843	534

Table 4. Our SC2000 implementation results as a bar graph. It is clearly seen that the $(16, 16)$-implementation strategy is more fit for the Pentium III than for the Athlon

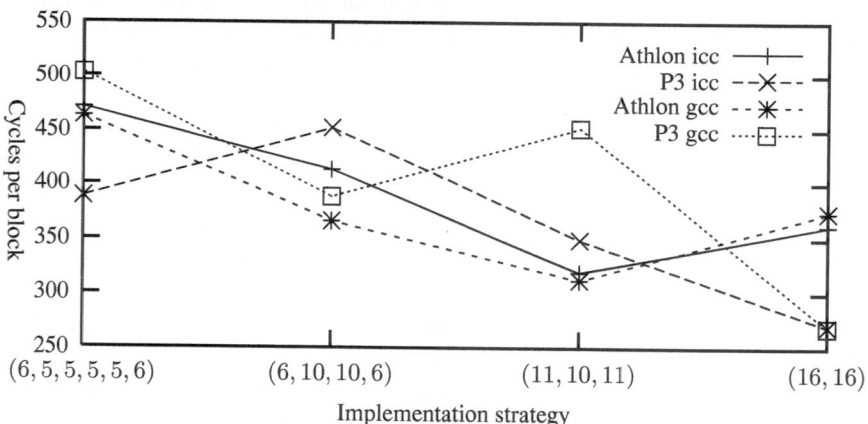

versions of gcc will be properly tuned to perform heavy Athlon-specific optimizations, we can definitely expect to see our performance numbers to improve on Athlon.

3.3 Implementations of Rijndael and RC6

We have also implemented Rijndael, the new AES, and RC6 for both Pentium III. These implementations are slightly better than the implementations of Aoki and Lipmaa [AL00] for Pentium II. For example, instead of 237 cycles, our Rijndael encryption takes 226 cycles. Also, instead of 223 cycles, our RC6 encryption takes 219 cycles. We also implemented the key schedule algorithms of Rijndael, although in C, and achieved very good results. (The Rijndael key scheduling implementation that was available for the authors of [AL00] was substantially slower.)

4   Conclusions and Further Work

4.1   Conclusions

Following Section 3.2, we can conclude that from the depicted choices, a Pentium III running the icc-compiled $(16, 16)$-implementation of SC2000 would be the best one when only raw throughput is important. If, additionally, the available memory is constrained, one might consider switching to Athlon and to the $(11, 10, 11)$-strategy. This, in particular, demonstrates the importance of the cache size in software implementations.

Our results show that after additional scrutiny from the security viewpoint, the SC2000 might be a serious contender in the block cipher arena just because of excellent throughput in different environments, as shown by this paper and by [SYY$^+$01]. (We however stress that we did not analyze the security of SC2000 at all.) Based on Table 1, on Section 3.3 and on [AL00], our C implementation of SC2000 is slower than the best assembly implementations of Rijndael and RC6, while being faster than the best C implementations of Rijndael and the best assembly implementations of Twofish and MARS [AL00] on Pentium III. This leaves us wondering how fast SC2000 could be in assembly, and also lets us conclude that nowadays it is possible to create surprisingly fast ciphers.

Our improvement, 1.6 times in encryption speed compared to the previous best is quite significant. However, we used significantly more memory than the previous implementations and therefore the implementations are not directly comparable. It is an interesting open question how efficiently can one implement (say) Rijndael, given similar amount of memory—512 KB—for internal storage.

Note that in many environments, the large S-box tables can be stored in ROM. Since ROM is potentially both cheaper and faster than RAM, this would even more decrease the price per performance ratio. Alternatively, one can create the 16-bit S-box tables from a small seed of ≈ 128 elements. (The latter strategy was used in our implementations.)

4.2   Further Work

We did not implement SC2000 in assembly, but nevertheless we made some observations. While both used compilers seemed to generate a very good code, a few things can be certainly improved in assembly:

1. Use of MMX technology would benefit in at least two ways: First, it would make more internal registers available to the cipher implementer. This would eliminate some memory accesses. Second, the MMX technology features the nand instruction that could be used to somewhat speed up the implementations of B and B$^{(i)}$.
2. Better register allocation: Even without using the MMX technology, one could reduce memory accesses by re-allocating some of the internal variables to correspond to registers.

3. Advanced optimization: Do complete optimization that would take into account trade-offs between different stages of the work of Pentium III, as described, say, in [AL00]. This would include careful instruction reordering, manipulating the length of individual instructions, etc.
4. Better bit-slicing: our implementations of B and $B^{(i)}$ might well be suboptimal. To achieve a better throughput, one might have to write a brute force program for generating (at least heuristically) close-to-optimal implementation of B and $B^{(i)}$. Here, such an implementation should both have a small number of Boolean operations but also a very small number of temporary registers. Most likely, optimal implementation depends on the processor family, chosen strategy but also on the compiler.

The fourth item in this list, finding better bit-slicing code, is also an interesting research question by itself, and does not only concern SC2000 but also some other ciphers like Serpent [ABK98].

Acknowledgments. We are thankful to Masahiko Takenaka, Takeshi Shimoyama and anonymous reviewers for useful comments. This work was partially supported by Fujitsu Laboratories. Our results were first presented at ISEC 2002 [TLT02].

References

[ABK98]   Ross Anderson, Eli Biham, and Lars Knudsen. Serpent: A Flexible Block Cipher With Maximum Assurance. In *The First Advanced Encryption Standard Candidate Conference*, Ventura, California, USA, 20–22 August 1998.

[AL00]   Kazumaro Aoki and Helger Lipmaa. Fast Implementations of AES Candidates. In *The Third Advanced Encryption Standard Candidate Conference*, pages 106–120, New York, NY, USA, 13–14 April 2000. National Institute of Standards and Technology. Entire proceedings available from the conference homepage http://csrc.nist.gov/encryption/aes/round2/conf3/aes3conf.htm.

[BCD+98] Carolynn Burwick, Don Coppersmith, Edward D'Avignon, Rosario Gennaro, Shai Halevi, Charanjit Jutla, Stephen M. Matyas Jr., Luke O'Connor, Mohammad Peyravian, David Safford, and Nevenko Zunic. MARS — A Candidate Cipher for AES. Available from http://www.research.ibm.com/security/mars.html, June 1998.

[DR02]   Joan Daemen and Vincent Rijmen. *The Design of Rijndael. AES - The Advanced Encryption Standard.* Springer-Verlag, 2002.

[RRSY98] Ronald L. Rivest, Matt J. B. Robshaw, R. Sidney, and Y. L. Yin. The RC6 Block Cipher. Available from http://theory.lcs.mit.edu/~rivest/rc6.ps, June 1998.

[Shi02]   Takeshi Shimoyama. Personal communication. April 2002.

[SKW+99] Bruce Schneier, John Kelsey, Doug Whiting, David Wagner, Chris Hall, and Niels Ferguson. *The Twofish Encryption Algorithm: A 128-Bit Block Cipher.* John Wiley & Sons, April 1999. ISBN: 0471353817.

[SYY+01] Takeshi Shimoyama, Hitoshi Yanami, Kazuhiro Yokohama, Masahiko Takenaka, Kouichi Itoh, Jun Yajima, Naoya Torii, and Hidema Tanaka. The Block Cipher SC2000. In Mitsuru Matsui, editor, *Fast Software Encryption '2001*, volume 2355 of *Lecture Notes in Computer Science*, pages 312–327, Yokohama, Japan, 2–4 April 2001. Springer-Verlag, 2002.

[TLT02]   Masahiko Takenaka, Helger Lipmaa, and Naoya Torii. The Implementation of The Block Cipher SC2000 (III). In *ISEC 2002*, Tohoku University, Sendai, Japan, 18–19 July 2002. In Japanese.

```
movd mm0, dword ptr [time];    /* warm cache and set MMX state */
xor eax, eax;
cpuid;                         /* serialize instructions */
rdtsc;                         /* read time-stamp counter */
mov dword ptr [time], eax;     /* save counter */
xor eax, eax;
cpuid;                         /* serialize instructions */
/* call to xxEnc() or xxDec() */
xor eax, eax;
cpuid;                         /* serialize instructions */
rdtsc;                         /* read time-stamp counter */
sub dword ptr [time], eax;     /* compute the difference */
emms;                          /* empty MMX state */
```

Note that time is a 4 bytes work area.

Fig. 2. Time measurement code

```
        /* push all used registers */
        cmp dword ptr [lenBlk], 0;
        jz L1;
        align 16;
L0:
        dec dword ptr [lenBlk];
        jnz L0;
L1:
        /* pop these registers once more */
```

Fig. 3. Null function

A   Timing

We use exactly the same convention of measuring the time as in [AL00] and is described in Fig. 2. The inputs and key of the cipher are generated randomly before the measurement. The input variable lenBlk was chosen to be equal to 8000. Also, time is a work area of type uint32, used in later calculations.

We would get some overhead when outputting the result of this function alone due to both high latency of the `rdtsc` instructions and also the overhead caused by looping instructions like `jnz` which are not formally part of the cipher itself. We measure this overhead by using the null function shown in Fig. 3 obtaining a value `nulltime`, and then we subtract it from the value of `time` obtained by measuring the speeds of different encryption/decryption procedures. Finally, this result is divided by the number of blocks encrypted. Intuitively, by using this method we obtain the number of cycles corresponding to unrolled implementation of the block cipher, or to the implementation where we only care about the time it takes to encrypt one block, without adding any extra overhead. The subtracted overhead number was equal to ≈ 6 on the Pentium III and ≈ 7 on the Athlon in the case $n = 8000$. One could just add this number to those presented later to get the number of cycles *with* overhead.

Finally, we did a loop of 500 times over the described measurements and then chose the smallest number for every cipher, since that corresponds most likely to the case where most of the data and code are in L1 cache and the branch prediction works successfully: i.e., to the bulk encryption speed of the cipher itself.

Comparative Analysis of the Hardware Implementations of Hash Functions SHA-1 and SHA-512

Tim Grembowski[1], Roar Lien[1], Kris Gaj[1], Nghi Nguyen[1],
Peter Bellows[2], Jaroslav Flidr[2], Tom Lehman[2], and Brian Schott[2]

[1]Electrical and Computer Engineering, George Mason University, 4400 University Drive,
Fairfax, VA 22030
{rlien, kgaj, nnguyen1}@gmu.edu
[2] University of Southern California – Information Sciences Institute
Arlington, VA 22203
{pbellows, jflidr, tlehman, bschott}@east.isi.edu

Abstract. Hash functions are among the most widespread cryptographic primitives, and are currently used in multiple cryptographic schemes and security protocols such as IPSec and SSL. In this paper, we compare and contrast hardware implementations of the newly proposed draft hash standard SHA-512, and the old standard, SHA-1. In our implementation based on Xilinx Virtex FPGAs, the throughput of SHA-512 is equal to 670 Mbit/s, compared to 530 Mbit/s for SHA-1. Our analysis shows that the newly proposed hash standard is not only orders of magnitude more secure, but also significantly faster than the old standard. The basic iterative architectures of both hash functions are faster than the basic iterative architectures of symmetric-key ciphers with equivalent security.

1 Introduction

Hash functions are very common and important cryptographic primitives. Their primary application is their use together with public-key cryptosystems in the digital signature schemes. They are also a basic building block of secret-key Message Authentication Codes (MACs), including the American federal standard HMAC [8]. This authentication scheme appears in two currently most widely deployed security protocols, SSL and IPSec [12, 16]. Other popular applications of hash functions include fast encryption, password storage and verification, computer virus detection, pseudo-random number generation, and many others [13, 16].

Cryptographically strong, collision-free, hash functions are very difficult to design. Tens of them have been proposed, and the majority of them have been broken. Only a few hash functions have gained a wider acceptance, and even fewer have been standardized.

By far the most widely accepted hash function is SHA-1 (Secure Hash Algorithm-1), a revised version of the American federal standard introduced in 1993 [4]. The original version of this function, SHA, was developed by National Security Agency

A.H. Chan and V. Gligor (Eds.): ISC 2002, LNCS 2433, pp. 75–89, 2002.

(NSA), and revised in 1995 for increased security even before any weakness was found in the open research.

SHA-1 was introduced as a federal standard about the same time as an 80-bit secret-key encryption algorithm named Skipjack [5] and the Digital Signature Standard (DSS) [6]. The security parameters of all these standards were chosen in such a way to guarantee the similar level of security, in the range of 2^{80} operations, as required by the best currently known attack.

After introducing a new secret-key encryption standard, AES (Advanced Encryption Standard) [7], with three key sizes, 128, 192, and 256 bits, the security of SHA-1 does not any longer match the security guaranteed by the encryption standard. Therefore, an effort was initiated by NSA to develop three new hash functions, with the security matching the security of AES with 128, 192, and 256 bit key respectively. This effort resulted in the publication of the draft Federal Information Processing Standard, introducing three new hash functions referred to as SHA-256, SHA-384, and SHA-512 [11].

The goal of the project described in this article was to implement the most complex of these new hash functions, SHA-512, in reconfigurable hardware, and to compare its implementation with the implementation of SHA-1, realized in the same technology.

Our comparative analysis sought, among the other, answers to the following questions:

- does the increased security of the SHA-512 hash function come at the cost of decreased speed, increased area, or decreased speed to area ratio of the hardware implementations when compared to the SHA-1 hash function;
- how does the speed of the SHA-512 hash function compare to the speed of the corresponding versions of the AES algorithm? Which transformation, encryption or authentication, is faster in hardware? Which transformation requires less area?

Our investigation is a part of the larger project [10] aimed at implementing a hardware accelerator for a new suite of cryptographic algorithms to be used in the IP security protocol, IPSec. The target throughput of this accelerator is 1 Gbit/s for both encryption and authentication. Therefore we are also interested in studying the difficulty of implementing SHA-1 and the newly proposed hash functions at the speed of 1 Gbit/s using the current FPGA devices.

Although multiple commercial and academic implementations of SHA-1 have been reported and validated by NIST [15], we are not aware of any hardware implementation of SHA-512, or its comparison with the implementation of SHA-1 implemented in the same technology, using the same optimization techniques. This article is aimed at filling this gap.

2 Functional Comparison

In Table 1, four investigated hash functions are compared from the point of view of functional characteristics. The security of these hash functions is determined by the size of their outputs, referred to as hash values, n. The best known attack against these functions, the "birthday attack", can find a pair of messages having the same hash value with a work factor of approximately $2^{n/2}$. This complexity means that in order to accomplish equivalent security, hash functions need to have an output twice as long as the size of a key of the corresponding secret-key cipher.

SHA-1 and SHA-256 have many features in common. They both can process messages with the maximum length up to $2^{64}-1$ bits, have a message block size of 512 bits, and have internal structure based on processing 32-bit words. SHA-384 and SHA-512 have even more similarities. They process messages with the maximum length up to $2^{128}-1$ bits, have a message block size of 1024 bits, and have internal structure based on processing 64-bit words. On top of that, the definition of SHA-384 is almost identical to the definition of SHA-512, with the exception of a different choice of the initialization vector, and a truncation of the final 512-bit result to 384 bits.

All functions have a very similar internal structure, and process each message block using multiple rounds. The number of rounds is the same for SHA-1, SHA-384, and SHA-512, and 20% smaller in SHA-256. The critical path in each round involves multioperand addition. SHA-1 requires two fewer operands per addition than in the remaining three functions.

A notation $k+1$ used in the table, means that the number of operands to be added is k in all but last round, and $k+1$ in the last round. Alternatively, a number of operands may be equal to k in all rounds, and an additional simplified round may be introduced for the remaining single addition.

Table 1. Functional characteristics of four investigated hash functions

	SHA-1	SHA-256	SHA-384	SHA-512
Size of hash value	160	256	384	512
Complexity of the best attack	2^{80}	2^{128}	2^{192}	2^{256}
Equivalently secure secret-key cipher	Skipjack	AES-128	AES-192	AES-256
Message size	$< 2^{64}$	$< 2^{64}$	$< 2^{128}$	$< 2^{128}$
Message block size	512	512	1024	1024
Word size	32	32	64	64
Number of words	5	8	8	8
Number of digest rounds	80	64	80	80
Number of operands added in the critical path	5+1	7+1	7+1	7+1
Number of constants K_t	4	64	80	80
Round-dependent operations	f_t	None	None	None

The number of different constants is equal to four in SHA-1, and is the same as the number of rounds in all remaining functions. As a result, implementations of SHA-256, SHA-384, and SHA-512 must include a look-up table of constants, K_t, where t=0..number of rounds. SHA-1 is also the only function that contains an operation dependent on the round number t; in all remaining hash functions all rounds perform exactly the same operations.

The following conclusions can be derived from this functional comparison. Hardware implementations of SHA-384 and SHA-512 have exactly the same performance, so only one of them needs to be implemented for the purpose of comparative analysis. Notice that the size of the message block is twice as large in SHA-512 as compared to SHA-1, the number of rounds is the same, and the critical path is only slightly longer in SHA-512. Because of this, SHA-512 (the strongest function) is likely to be significantly faster than SHA-1 (the weakest function), which would be a very positive result if true. The throughput of SHA-256 is likely to be in the same range as a throughput of SHA-1, and smaller than the throughput of SHA-512. Taking into account these estimations, we have decided to implement two of the investigated hash functions, SHA-1 and SHA-512, which lay on the opposite ends of the spectrum in terms of both security and speed, with SHA-1 being the weakest and slowest, and SHA-512 being the strongest and fastest of the four investigated hash functions.

3 Design Methodology

Our target FPGA device was the Xilinx Virtex XCV-1000-6. This device is composed of 12,288 basic logic cells referred to as CLB (Configurable Logic Block) slices, includes 32 4-kbit blocks of synchronous dual-ported RAM, and can achieve synchronous system clock rates up to 200 MHz [17]. This device was chosen because of the availability of a general purpose PCI board based on three FPGA devices of this type. This board is described in detail in Section 5.

The design flow and tools used in our group for the implementation of cryptographic modules in Xilinx FPGA devices are shown in Fig. 1. All algorithms were first described in VHDL, and their description verified through the functional simulation using Active HDL v. 5.1, from Aldec, Inc. Test vectors and intermediate results from the reference software implementations based on the Crypto++ library [1] were used for debugging and verification of VHDL codes. The revised VHDL code became an input to the Xilinx integrated environment ISE 4.1i, performing the automated logic synthesis, mapping, placing, and routing. Tools included in this environment generated reports describing the area and speed of implementation, a netlist used for timing simulation, and a bitstream used to configure an actual FPGA device. All designs were fully verified through behavioral, post-synthesis, and timing simulations, and experimentally tested using the procedure described in Section 5.

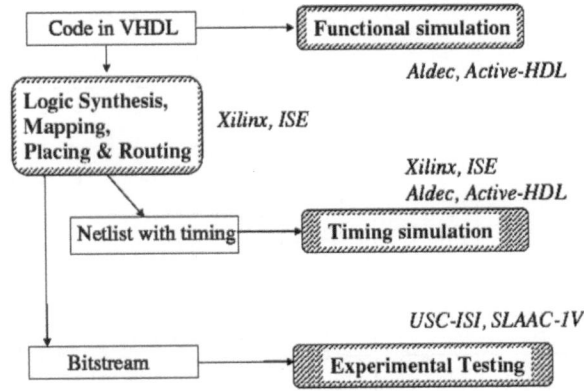

Fig. 1. Design flow and tools used in the development of cryptographic modules

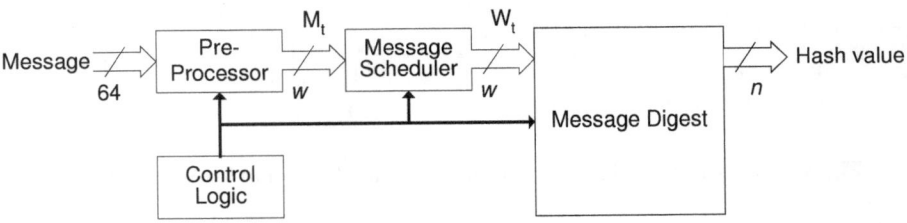

Fig. 2. General block diagram of SHA-1 and SHA-512. For SHA-1, w=32, n=160; for SHA-512, w=64, n=512

4 Hardware Architectures

A general block diagram common for all four hash functions is shown in Fig. 2. Input messages pass first through the preprocessing unit which performs padding and forms message blocks of the fixed length, 512 or 1024 bits, depending on the hash function. The preprocessing unit passes message blocks to the message scheduler unit. In our architecture, message blocks are passed to the message scheduler unit a word at a time, during the first 16 clock cycles used to process each message block. The message digest unit performs the actual hashing. It uses one clock cycle per digest round. In each round, the digest unit processes a new word W_t generated by the message scheduler unit.

The internal structure of the message digests for SHA-1 and SHA-512 are shown in Fig. 3ab. In both functions, input registers are initialized with the constant initialization vector, and are updated with the new value in each round. In SHA-1, four out of five words (A, B, C, and D) remain almost unchanged by a single round. These words are only shifted by one position down. The last word, E, undergoes a complicated transformation equivalent to multioperand addition modulo 2^{32}, with five 32-bit oper-

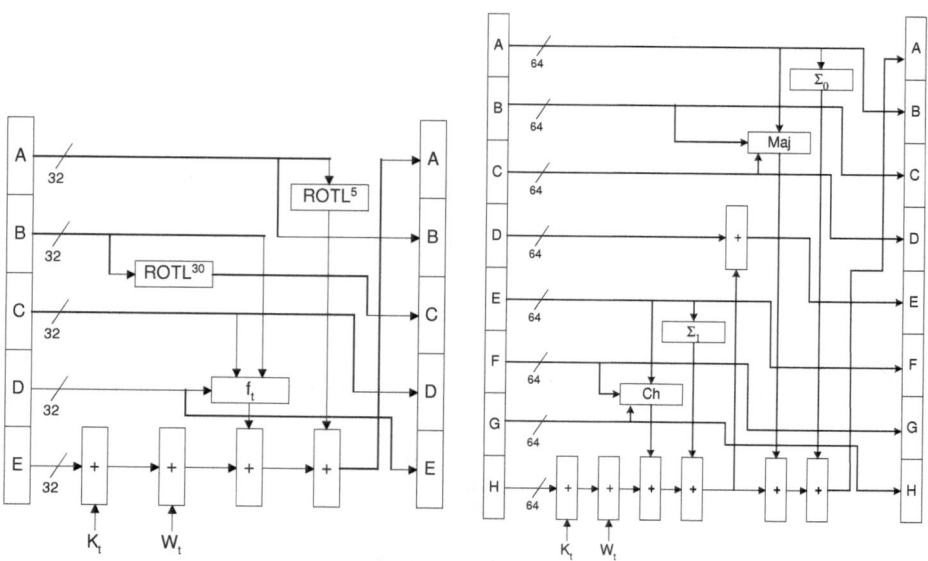

Fig. 3. Functional block diagram of the message digest unit of a) SHA-1, b) SHA-512

ands dependent on all input words, the round-dependent constant K_t, and the message dependent word W_t. The internal structure of the message digest of SHA-512 is similar. The primary differences are as follows: The number of words processed by each round is 8, each word is 64 bits long, and the longest path is equivalent to addition of seven 64-bit operands modulo 2^{64}. These operands depend on seven out of eight input words (all except D), the round-dependent constant K_t, and a message dependent word W_t. Six out of eight input words remain unchanged by a single round.

Our implementations of the message digests are shown in Figs. 4ab. The critical path in each circuit is marked with a thick line. Both circuits use the carry save representation of numbers to speed-up the multioperand addition, and minimize delays associated with carry propagation. The number of operands that need to be processed in each round has been minimized by precomputing the sum $K_t + W_t$ in the preceding clock cycle.

At the same time, the need for an additional round at the end of processing has been eliminated by introducing a conditional addition of the initial value of registers H_0-H_m (m=4 for SHA1, and m=7 for SHA-512) inside of each round. These initial values are added only in the last round of the message digest computations; in all previous rounds zero is added instead. After these two optimizations, the maximum number of operands to be added in each round is 5 for SHA-1 and 7 for SHA-512.

The straightforward use of carry save adders in case of five operand addition would lead to three levels of 3-to-2 carry save adders, followed by a carry propagate adder as shown in Fig. 5a. Instead, we have decided to use a 5-to-3 parallel counter (see Fig. 5b) [14], which reduces the number of binary digits at each position in the sum of five

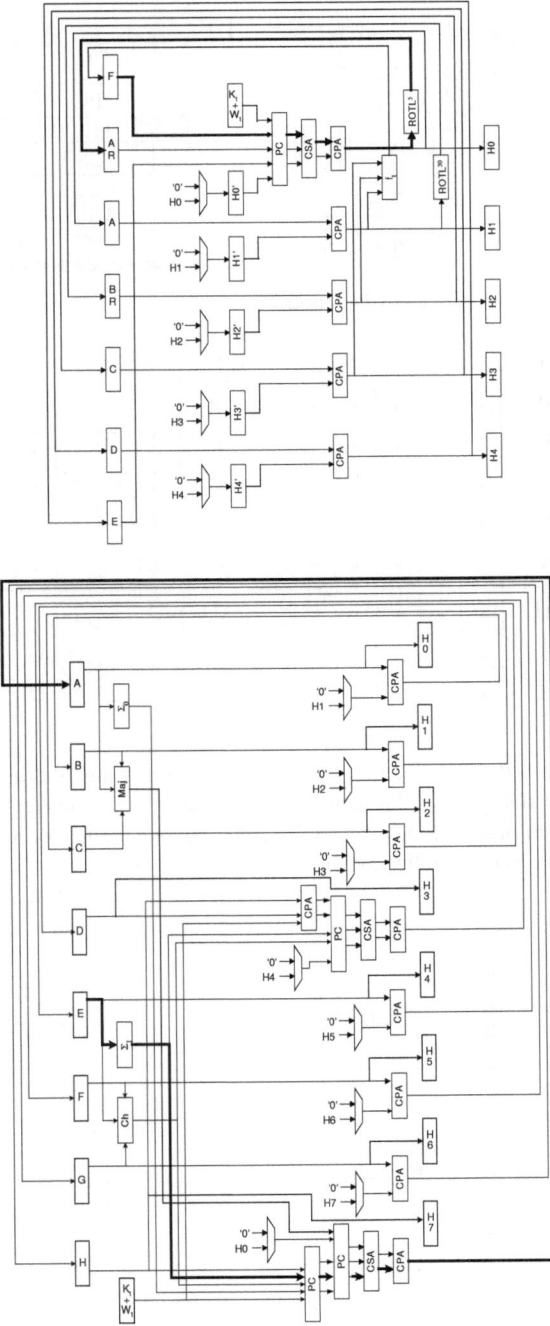

Fig. 4. Our implementations of the message digest units of a) SHA-1, b) SHA-512

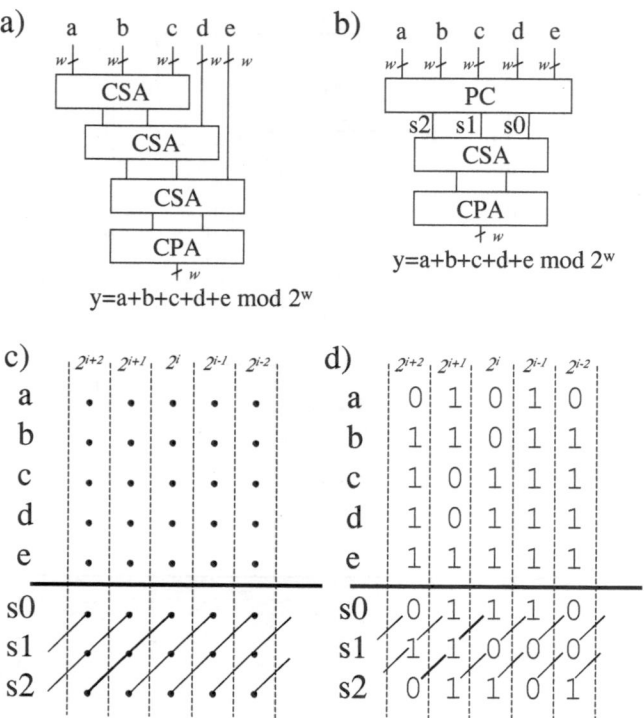

Fig. 5. Using 5-to-3 Parallel Counter. a) adding five w-bit numbers using a tree of 3-to-2 car-rysave adders, b) adding five w-bit numbers using 5-to-3 parallel counter followed by a 3-to-2 carry save adder, c) operation of the 5-to-3 parallel counter in the dot notation, d) example of the operation of the 5-to-3 parallel counter

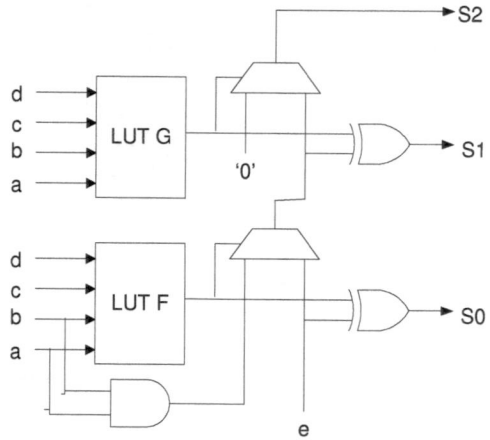

Fig. 6. Using internal structure of a single CLB slice of the Xilinx Virtex FPGA device to implement a bit-slice of a 5-to-3 Parallel Counter (PC)

operands from 5 to 3, and has approximately the same delay as a 3-to-2 carry save adder. The operation of the 5-to-3 parallel counter is shown in Fig. 5c, using the dot notation. In this notation, each dot represents a binary digit, 0 or 1 [14]. The 5-to-3 parallel counter adds five binary digits with the same weight, 2^i, and represents the result using three binary digits with three subsequent weights, 2^i, 2^{i+1}, and 2^{i+2}. An example of the operation of this counter is shown in Fig. 5d. The speed-up comes from the fact that the operation of the parallel counter can be realized in Virtex FPGAs using resources of a single CLB slice as shown in Fig. 6.

In SHA-512, a cascade of two 5-to-3 parallel counters is used to reduce the number of operands from seven to three (see Fig. 4b). As a result, the critical path is longer than in SHA-1 only by two levels of CLB slices (one level for the parallel counter, and one for the Σ_1 operation).

Further optimization of the critical path in both circuits has been accomplished by reducing the delays of interconnects. The primary optimization technique used for that purpose was the reduction of the fan-out of control signals by using buffers, duplicating portions of control logic, and placing control logic close to the controlled parts of the execution unit.

The block diagrams of the message scheduling units in SHA-1 and SHA-512 are shown in Fig. 7. Both units generate 80 message dependent words, W_t, t=0..79. The first 16 of these words, $W_0..W_{15}$, is simply the first 16 words of the input message block, $M_0..M_{15}$; the remaining words are computed using a simple feedback function, based on rotations, shifts, and XOR operations. The actual implementation of both functions is given in Fig. 8. Our implementations have been optimized for minimum area, using a shift register mode of CLB slices available in the Xilinx Virtex FPGA devices. Using this mode, a cascade of several one-bit registers, each taking normally a single CLB slice, can be reduced to a single CLB slice implementing the multi-stage shift register with up to 16 stages.

5   Testing Procedure

The experimental testing of our cryptographic modules was performed using the SLAAC-1V hardware accelerator board. The logical architecture of SLAAC-1V is shown in Fig. 9. The three Virtex 1000 FPGAs (denoted as X0, X1, and X2) are the primary processing elements.

About 20% of the resources in the X0 FPGA are devoted to the PCI interface and the board control module. The remaining logic of this device, as well as the entire X1 and X2 FPGAs, can be used by the application developer. The board control module implemented in X0 provides high-speed DMA (Direct Memory Access), data buffering, clock control (including single-stepping and frequency synthesis from 1 to 200 MHz), etc. The current 32 bit 33 MHz control module has obtained DMA transfer rates of over 1 Gbit/s (125 MB/s) between X0 and the host memory, very near the PCI theoretical maximum.

In all our experiments, the X1 FPGA was configured to contain cryptographic modules, while X0 and X2 were used only to facilitate the transfer of data between X1 and the memory of the host computer running Linux.

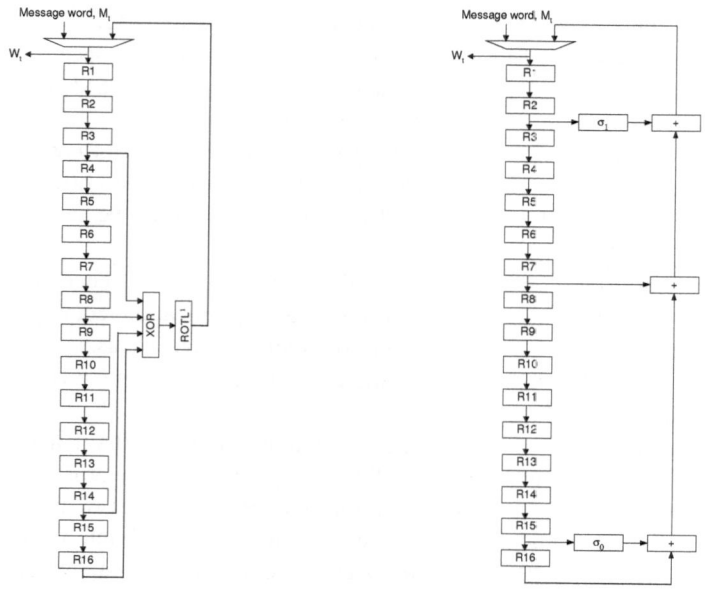

Fig. 7. Functional block diagrams of the message scheduler unit of a) SHA-1, b) SHA-512

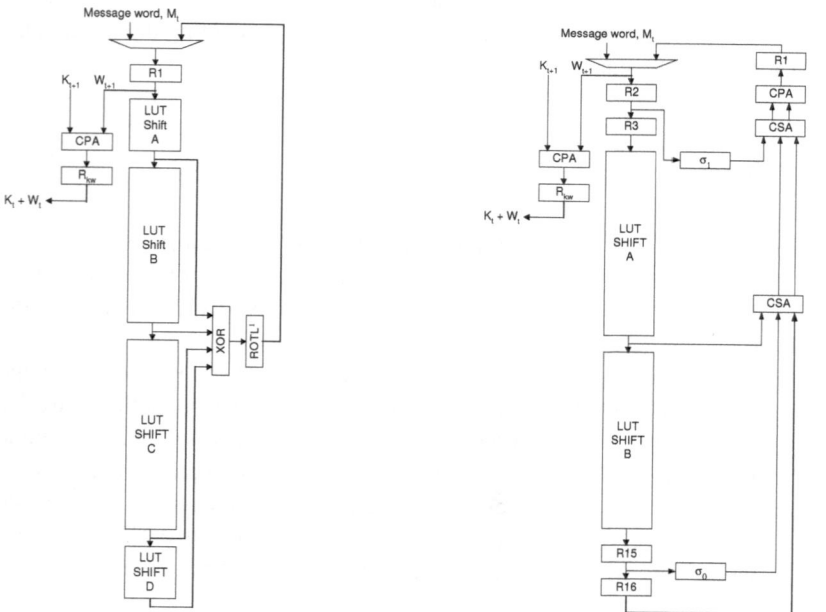

Fig. 8. Our implementations of the message scheduler unit of a) SHA-1, b) SHA-512

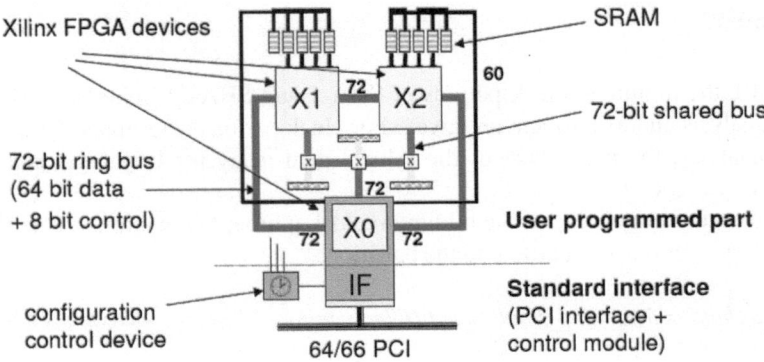

Fig. 9. SLAAC-1V Architecture

The test program written in used the SLAAC-1V APIs and the SLAAC-1V driver to communicate with the board.

Our testing procedure is composed of three groups of tests. The first group attempts to verify the circuit functionality at a single clock frequency. The goal of the second group is to determine the maximum clock frequency at which the circuit operates correctly. Finally, the purpose of the third group is to determine the limit on the maximum encryption and decryption throughput, taking into account the limitations of the PCI interface.

Our first group of tests is based on the NIST recommendations provided in [2]. These recommendations describe the comprehensive suite of three functional tests for SHA-1.

The second test is aimed at determining the maximum clock frequency of the hash function modules. Three megabytes of pseudorandomly generated data are sent to the board for hashing, the result is transferred back to the host and compared with the corresponding output obtained using software implementation of the given hash function based on the Crypto++ library [1]. This procedure is repeated 30 times using the same clock frequency to minimize the effect of input data values on the results of analysis. The next clock frequency is chosen based on the rules of the binary search, i.e., in the middle between two closest earlier identified frequencies giving different test results. The test is repeated until the difference between these two frequencies is smaller than the required accuracy of the measurement (< 0.1 MHz in our tests). The highest investigated clock frequency at which no single processing error is detected is considered the maximum clock frequency. In our experiments, this test was automatically repeated 10 times with consistent results in all iterations.

The third group of tests is an extension of the second group. After determining the maximum clock frequency, we measure multiple times and average the amount of time necessary to process 3 MB of data, taking into account the delay contribution of the 32 bit/33 MHz PCI interface.

6 Results

In Fig. 10, the minimum clock periods of SHA-1 and SHA-512 obtained using static timing analysis and experiment are given. For clock periods determined through static timing analysis, the percentage of the critical path delay used by logic and routing respectively is shown.

Based on the knowledge of the minimum clock period, the maximum data through-put has been computed according to the equation:

*Throughput = Message_block_size / (Clock period * Number_of_rounds)*

Throughput values calculated based on the minimum clock periods obtained using static timing analysis and experiment are shown in Fig. 11. In the same figure, these

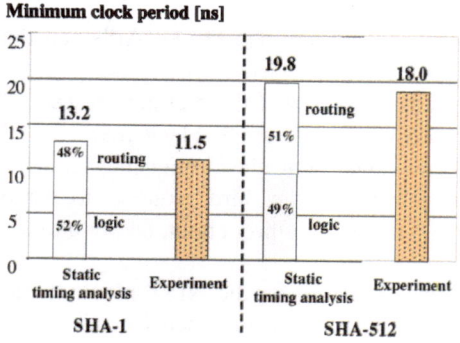

Fig. 10. Minimum clock period of SHA-1 and SHA-512: a) obtained using static timing analysis, b) determined experimentally

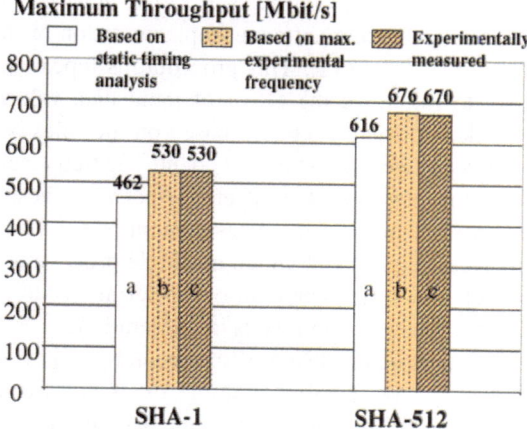

Fig. 11. Maximum throughputs of SHA-1 and SHA-512: a) obtained using static timing analysis, b) calculated based on the experimentally measured maximum clock frequency, c) experimentally measured, including the contributions of the PCI interface

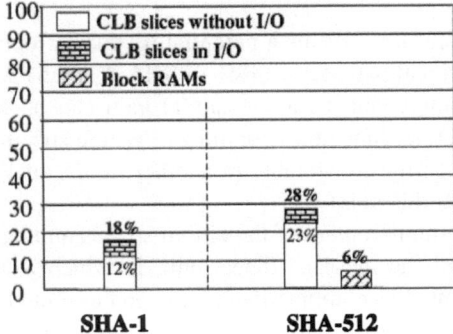

Fig. 12. Percentage of the FPGA resources used by each implementation

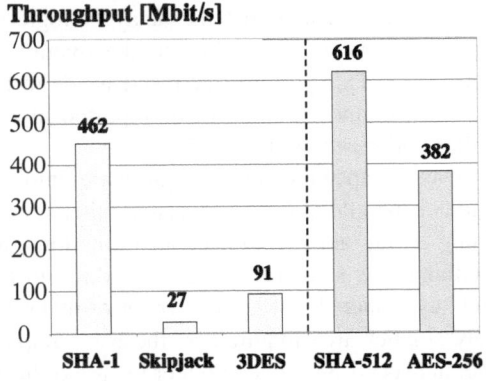

Fig. 13. Comparison of throughputs for the basic iterative architectures of old and new standards in the area of hash functions and symmetric-key ciphers

results are compared with the experimentally measured data throughputs that take into account the delay contributions of the PCI interface. This comparison demonstrates that the PCI interface provides a constant uninterrupted flow of data and has a negligible influence on the data throughput.

Our results confirm our earlier predictions that the design of strong hash functions does not involve any major trade-off between security and performance. To the contrary, the most secure function, SHA-512, is also the fastest of four investigated hash functions.

The percentage of the FPGA resources (CLB slices and Block RAMs) used by implementations of SHA-1 and SHA-512, are shown in Fig. 12. The difference in the number of CLB slices is primarily caused by the difference in the size of input and output registers in the message digest units of both functions (512 bits vs. 160 bits), and the width of the multioperand adders in the critical path of these units (64 bits vs. 32 bits). In SHA-512, two 4 kbit block RAMs are used to store 80 64-bit constants K_i.

7 Possible Extensions

The analysis of our results, reveals a potential for further optimizations. Since a large percentage of the critical path delay (48% in SHA-1 and 51% in SHA-512) is contributed by delays of interconnects, a substantial gain can be accomplished by manual floorplaning and routing. Since these optimizations are specific for a given type of the device, and are not easily transferable to another family of FPGA devices, they have not been attempted at this point.

A further radical improvement of the circuit speed can be achieved by using an unrolled architecture of the message digest unit, in which m (m=2, 4, 5, or 8) digest rounds are implemented as combinational logic and executed in the same clock cycle. As a result, the total number of clock cycles necessary to compute a digest for a single message block is reduced by a factor of m, at the cost of a significantly smaller increase in the delay of the critical path. The preliminary study of this extended architecture for SHA-1 and m=5 indicates that the delay of logic in the critical path increases by a factor smaller than 2.5, leading to the overall increase in the circuit throughput by a factor of 2. This preliminary result needs to be verified, taking into account the delays of interconnects, and will be reported in a future article together with results of a similar optimization of SHA-512.

Another popular way of speeding up the hardware implementations of cryptographic transformations is parallel processing, using either several independent execution units or pipelining. Even taking into account limitations imposed by the area of FPGA devices, pipelining was shown to permit speeding up the implementations of AES and other secret key ciphers by at least an order of magnitude [3, 9]. Taking into account the relatively smaller area required by the basic implementations of SHA-1 and SHA-512, a potential speed-up is even greater in case of hash functions.

Unfortunately, applying parallel processing to hash functions is limited by the fact that only input blocks belonging to *different* messages may be processed in parallel. In this respect, hashing is similar to encryption in the CBC (Cipher Block Chaining) mode and other *feedback* modes of secret-key block ciphers. The processing of the next message block cannot start before the processing of the previous block is fully completed. Additionally, hash functions do not possess any non-feedback modes of operation, such as ECB (Electronic CodeBook) or counter mode. Therefore, pipelining, although possible, is limited by the availability of multiple independent messages that could be processed in parallel. This availability is application specific and may strongly depend on the characteristic of the network traffic, e.g., an average size of packets exchanged in the given communication protocol.

8 Summary

An FPGA implementation of the newly proposed draft hash standard SHA-512 has been developed and compared with the implementation of the old hash standard SHA-1. An effort was made to use exactly the same technology and identical design and optimization techniques. Our implementations based on Xilinx XCV-1000-6 demonstrate that SHA-512 is 33% faster than the equivalent implementation of SHA-1 according to the static timing analysis, and 26% faster according to the experiment. At the same time, without taking into account an input/output interface, SHA-512 takes almost twice as many CLB slices as SHA-1, and requires two additional 4 kbit Block RAMs. These results have been verified experimentally using the PCI FPGA Board, SLAAC-1V, based on three Xilinx FPGA devices Virtex 1000. Our results prove that the design of a strong hash function does not necessarily involve a trade-off between the hardware speed and cryptographic security. At the same time, the more secure hash function may require substantially more hardware resources.

Further optimizations of both implementations based on loop unrolling are possible and will be reported in a future article. Our research is a part of a larger effort aimed at implementing the newly proposed cryptographic algorithms of IPSec in the form of a giga-bit rate hardware accelerator on a Xilinx FPGA-based PCI card [10].

References

1. Crypto++, free C++ class library of cryptographic schemes, available at
    http://www.eskimo.com/~weidai/cryptlib.html.
2. Digital Signature Standard Validation System (DSSVS) User's Guide available at
    http://csrc.nist.gov/cryptval/shs.html
3. Elbirt, A. J., Yip, W., Chetwynd, B., Paar, C.: An FPGA implementation and Performance Evaluation of the AES Block Cipher Candidate Algorithm Finalists. Proc. 3rd Advanced Encryption Standard (AES) Candidate Conference, New York, April 13–14, 2000.
4. http://www.itl.nist.gov/fipspubs/fip180-1.htm
5. FIPS 185, Escrowed Encryption Standard (EES), February 1994.
6. FIPS 186-2, Digital Signature Standard (DSS), February 2000, available at
    http://csrc.nist.gov/encryption/tkdigsigs.html
7. NIST, FIPS Publication 197, Specification for the Advanced Encryption Standard (AES), November 26, 2001, available at http://csrc.nist.gov/encryption/aes/.
8. FIPS 198, HMAC - Keyed-Hash Message Authentication Code, available at
    http://csrc.nist.gov/encryption/tkmac.html
9. Gaj, K., and Chodowiec, P.: Fast Implementation and Fair Comparison of the Final Candidates for Advanced Encryption Standard Using Field Programmable Gate Arrays, Proc. RSA Security Conference - Cryptographer's Track, April 2001.
10. GRIP (Gigabit Rate IP Security) project page, available at
    http://www.east.isi.edu/projects/GRIP/
11. NIST Cryptographic Toolkit, Secure Hashing, available at
    http://csrc.nist.gov/encryption/tkhash.html
12. IP Security Protocol (ipsec) Charter – Latest RFCs and Internet Drafts for IPSec,
    http://ietf.org/html.charters/ipsec-charter.html
13. Menezes, A. J., van Oorschot P. C., and Vanstone S. A.: Handbook of Applied Cryptography, CRC Press, Inc., Boca Raton, 1996.
14. Parhami, B.: Computer Arithmetic: Algorithms and Hardware Design, Oxford University Press, 2000.
15. SHS Validation List, available at http://csrc.nist.gov/cryptval/shs/shaval.htm.
16. Stallings, W.: Cryptography and Network Security, 1999 Prentice-Hall, Inc., Upper Saddle River, New Jersey. 2nd Edition.
17. Xilinx, Inc.: Virtex 2.5 V Field Programmable Gate Arrays, available at www.xilinx.com.

Implementation of Chosen-Ciphertext Attacks against PGP and GnuPG

Kahil Jallad[1,4], Jonathan Katz[2,4], and Bruce Schneier[3]

[1] The Eon Company
kajal@eoncompany.com
[2] Department of Computer Science, University of Maryland (College Park)
jkatz@cs.umd.edu
[3] Counterpane Internet Security, Inc.
schneier@counterpane.com
[4] Work done while at Columbia University

Abstract. We recently noted [6] that PGP and other e-mail encryption protocols are, in theory, highly vulnerable to chosen-ciphertext attacks in which the recipient of the e-mail acts as an unwitting "decryption oracle". We argued further that such attacks are quite feasible and therefore represent a serious concern. Here, we investigate these claims in more detail by attempting to implement the suggested attacks. On one hand, we are able to successfully implement the described attacks against PGP and GnuPG (two widely-used software packages) in a number of different settings. On the other hand, we show that the attacks largely fail when data is compressed before encryption.

Interestingly, the attacks are unsuccessful for largely fortuitous reasons; resistance to these attacks does not seem due to any conscious effort made to prevent them. Based on our work, we discuss those instances in which chosen-ciphertext attacks *do* indeed represent an important threat and hence must be taken into account in order to maintain confidentiality. We also recommend changes in the OpenPGP standard [3] to reduce the effectiveness of our attacks in these settings.

1   Introduction

Electronic mail (e-mail) has become an essential and ubiquitous communication tool. As such, users and businesses have become concerned with the privacy of their e-mail and have turned to both commercially- and freely-available e-mail encryption software to achieve confidentiality. Typical users of e-mail encryption software are not educated in good security practices; it is therefore important to design *robust* software whose security is not compromised even when the software is used in a naive manner.

It was recently noted [6] that, in principle, the secrecy provided by commonly-used e-mail encryption protocols can be completely violated by an adversary us-

A.H. Chan and V. Gligor (Eds.): ISC 2002, LNCS 2433, pp. 90–101, 2002.

ing a *chosen-ciphertext attack*[1] [7,1]. Furthermore, it was claimed that the attack could be implemented easily. We explore these claims in more detail; in particular, we attempt to implement the described attacks against GnuPG (available at `http://www.gnupg.org`) and PGP (available at `http://www.pgpi.org`) and thereby ascertain whether the attacks do in fact represent a serious concern. Our findings may be summarized as follows:

- We have successfully implemented the attack against GnuPG and PGP when files or messages are sent *without compression.*
- If compressed files are sent (e.g., a .zip file is sent using PGP), the attack still works and may be used to recover the original data.
- On the other hand, compression done by the encryption software itself (when an uncompressed file is sent) causes the attack to fail. In the case of GnuPG (when compression is used), the attack fails only due to the presence of a message integrity check which is not explicitly required[2] as part of the OpenPGP specification [3]. Without the integrity check, the attack succeeds 100% of the time.
- Implementations which strictly follow the OpenPGP specification [3] are vulnerable to the attack *even when the message is compressed during encryption.* As it turns out, the actual implementations of PGP and GnuPG deviate from this specification in significant ways, thereby (fortuitously) foiling the attack.

Our results lead us to suggest a number of changes to the OpenPGP specification.

We review the arguments of [6] as to why chosen-ciphertext attacks might be feasible in the specific context of encrypted e-mail. Imagine a user who has configured his software to automatically decrypt any encrypted e-mails he receives. An adversary intercepts an encrypted message C sent to the user and wants to determine the contents P of this message. To do so, the adversary creates some new C' and sends it to the user; this message is then automatically decrypted by the user's computer and the user is presented with the corresponding message P'. To the user, P' appears to be garbled; the user therefore replies to the adversary with, for example, "What were you trying to send me?", but also *quotes the "garbled" message P'*. Thus, the user himself unwittingly acts as a decryption oracle for the adversary. Using information obtained in this way, the adversary may be able to determine the original message.

---

[1] In such an attack, an adversary given a *challenge ciphertext* C attempts to determine the underlying plaintext $P = \mathcal{D}(C)$ by submitting different ciphertexts C' to a *decryption oracle* that returns $\mathcal{D}(C')$.

[2] At the time this is written, RFC 2440 is being revised; future drafts may require the presence of a message integrity check [2]. Note, however, that if full inter-operability with older versions of PGP is desired then a message with no integrity check (as opposed to an invalid one) will be accepted and the attack described here can proceed.

2   Overview

The term "PGP" is an all-encompassing name for several implementations of an email encryption program first written as freeware by Phil Zimmerman in 1991 [5,8]. PGP 2.6.2 was the first widely available and widely ported version, followed shortly thereafter by versions fixing previous bugs as well as "international" versions free from patent and export-law restrictions. There were several commercial PGP 4.x releases which were compatible with the 2.6.x versions. PGP 5.0 and subsequent releases were GUI based (the previous versions being command line only); note that PGP 2.x and PGP 5.x versions are considered incompatible. An IETF working group was later formed to standardize the PGP message format, resulting in RFC 2440 [3]. GnuPG is a free, open source, RFC 2440 compliant implementation. Most of the different versions of PGP, as well as GnuPG, have a fairly significant user base.

2.1   The Attack

We explicitly consider attacks on PGP 2.6.2 and GnuPG. We refer the reader to [5,8,3] for a more in-depth description of the protocols; here, we merely provide a high-level description necessary for a proper understanding of the attack. Specifically, the attack exploits the symmetric-key modes of encryption used; therefore, only this detail of the protocol is presented. Further details of the attack can be found in [6].

PGP messages are encapsulated in packets. A PGP packet has a header section and a data section. The header holds information such as the packet type and length, among other things. The data section contains the payload of the packet, which is dependent on the packet type. The specifics of the packet format are slightly different in various versions of PGP and in the OpenPGP specification, we focus here on PGP 2.6.2 packets.

Consider an e-mail message (or file) M. PGP encrypts the message as follows:

1. A random "session-key" K is generated, encrypted with the recipient's public key pk, and encapsulated in a public-key encrypted session key packet (PKESKP). The output can be represented as follows:

$$\langle \text{PKESKP HEADER}, \mathcal{E}_{pk}(K) \rangle.$$

2. Message M is encapsulated in a literal data packet (LDP), resulting in:

$$LDP = \langle \text{LP HEADER}, M \rangle.$$

3. The LDP is compressed using the DEFLATE algorithm [4], and becomes the payload of a compressed data packet (CDP):

$$CDP = \langle \text{CP HEADER}, \text{DEFLATE}(LDP) \rangle.$$

4. The CDP is encrypted with a symmetric-key encryption algorithm (i.e., block cipher) and key K, using cipher feedback (CFB) mode (described below). This gives ciphertext $C_1, C_2, C_3, \ldots$. The ciphertext is encapsulated in a symmetrically encrypted data packet (SEDP) as follows:

$$\langle \text{SEDP HEADER}, C_1, C_2, C_3, \ldots \rangle.$$

5. The following message is sent to the recipient:

$$\langle \text{PKESKP HEADER}, \mathcal{E}_{\text{pk}}(K) \rangle \langle \text{SEDP HEADER}, C_1, C_2, C_3, \ldots \rangle.$$

The recipient, reversing the above steps, uses his private key to compute K; given K, the recipient can then determine the compressed message which is decompressed to return the original message M.

A mode of encryption is necessary in step 4 (above) in order to encrypt CDPs longer than a single block. GnuPG and PGP use a variation of CFB mode which we now describe. Before encryption, the plaintext (i.e., the CDP) is prepended by a 10-octet string. The first 8 octets are random, and the 9th and 10th octets are copies of the 7th and 8th octets. This prepended data serves both as a weak "integrity check" and as the initialization vector for the cipher. We denote the resulting text by $R_1, R_2, P_1, \ldots, P_k$ where R_1 represents the first 8 octets prepended to the CDP, R_2 represents the last 2 octets (the "key check octets") prepended to the CDP, and $P_1, P_2, \ldots, P_k$ represents the CDP itself. Encryption using a CFB-like mode of encryption then proceeds as follows:[3]

Encryption: Given $R_1, R_2, P_1, P_2, \ldots, P_k$, compute:
$$C_1 = R_1 \oplus \mathcal{E}_K(0^{64})$$
$$C_2 = R_2 \oplus \mathcal{E}_K(C_1)_{[0,1]} \quad \text{(note: } C_2 \text{ and } R_2 \text{ are 2 bytes long)}$$
$$IV = C_{1[2-7]} \circ R_2$$
$$C_3 = P_1 \oplus \mathcal{E}_K(IV)$$
for $i = 2$ to k:
$$C_{i+2} = P_i \oplus \mathcal{E}_K(C_{i+1})$$
Output: $C_1, C_2, \ldots, C_{k+2}$

Decryption: Given ciphertext $C_1, C_2, \ldots, C_{k+2}$, *compute* :
$$R_1 = C_1 \oplus \mathcal{E}_K(0^{64})$$
$$R_2 = C_2 \oplus \mathcal{E}_K(C_1)_{[0,1]} \quad \text{(note: } C_2 \text{ and } R_2 \text{ are 2 bytes long)}$$
$$IV = C_{1[2-7]} \circ R_2$$
$$P_1 = C_3 \oplus \mathcal{E}_K(IV)$$
for $i = 2$ to k:
$$P_i = C_{i+2} \oplus \mathcal{E}_K(C_{i+1})$$
if $(R_2 == R_{1[6,7]})$
    Output: $P_1, P_2, P_3 \ldots, P_k$
else
    Error

---

[3] $\mathcal{E}_K(\cdot)$ represents application of the block cipher using session-key K. The notation $B_{[0,1]}$ represents the first and second bytes of a block B, and the notation $B_{[2-7]}$ represents the third through the eighth bytes of a block B.

As described previously [6], a single-message chosen-ciphertext attack can seemingly be used to decrypt any given ciphertext (for simplicity, we omit the PGP headers that are attached to the messages; these will be discussed in more detail later). Given ciphertext $<\mathcal{E}_{pk}(K), C_1, \ldots, C_k>$, to obtain the value of plaintext block P_i $(i > 1)$ one does the following:

1. Choose a (random) 64-bit number r.
2. Submit the ciphertext: $\langle \mathcal{E}_{pk}(K), C_1, C_2, C_{i+1}, r \rangle$.
3. Receive back the decryption P_1', P_2', where $P_2' = r \oplus \mathcal{E}_K(C_{i+1})$.
4. Compute $P_i = P_2' \oplus r \oplus C_{i+2}$.

(A similar attack may be used to determine P_1.)

Other chosen ciphertext attacks are also possible. For example, submitting:

$$< \mathcal{E}_{pk}(K), C_1, C_2, C_3, r_1, \ldots, C_k, r_{k-2} >,$$

where $r_1, \ldots, r_{k-1}$ are random 64-bit strings, allows the adversary, in theory, to compute the entire contents of the original message.

As described, these attacks seem devastating to the secrecy of encrypted messages. In practice, however, one might expect certain complications to arise. We discuss this in the remainder of the paper.

3   Uncompressed Data

When the message data is not compressed by PGP before encryption (e.g., the compression option is turned off by the user), the encrypted message is simply an encrypted LDP. Note that if the original plaintext is already compressed (i.e., the plaintext is a zip file), it will be treated as literal data and will not be re-compressed by PGP.[4] We demonstrate here that the chosen-ciphertext attack as described in the previous section *does* succeed in recovering the plaintext message in these cases.

The diagram below represents a PGP message without compression. In the diagram, shaded portions represent encrypted data. The numbers along the bottom of the diagram represent the lengths (in bytes) of the corresponding fields. A "?" represents a field of variable length (for example, the length of the "Name" field depends on the value contained in the "Name Length" field). CTB is shorthand for *cipher type byte*, a PGP construct used to determine the type of the packet being processed. The "Name Length" field is a single byte that determines the length of the following "Name" field; this second field contains the name of the plaintext file. See [3] for more details of PGP packet formats.

---

[4] Although compressed files *are* re-compressed in GnuPG 1.0.6, this "flaw" was subsequently corrected in GnuPG 1.0.7 (thereby allowing the attack).

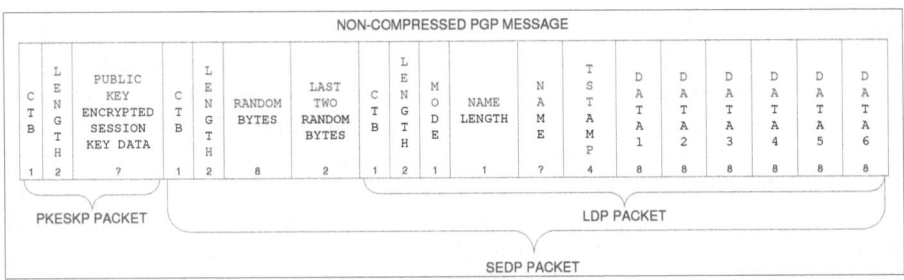

An attacker can follow the procedure given in Section 2.1 to produce a ciphertext that, when decrypted and returned, will allow the contents of the message to be determined. The diagram below represents the ciphertext that allows recovery of the entire message:

CHOSEN CIPHERTEXT MESSAGE (NON-COMPRESSED DATA)																		
CTB	LENGTH	PUBLIC KEY ENCRYPTED SESSION KEY DATA	CTB	LENGTH	RANDOM BYTES	LAST TWO RANDOM BYTES	CTB	LENGTH	MODE	NAME LENGTH	NAME	TSTAMP	R_1	DATA1	R_2	DATA2	R_3	DATA3
1	2	?	1	2	8	2	1	1	1	1	?	4		8		8		8

If this ciphertext is decrypted and somehow made available to the adversary, the first half of the original message can be obtained via the procedure described in Section 2.1. Note that PGP will not return more data than the number of bytes described in the "Length" field of the header, while inserting random blocks effectively doubles the size of the message. Therefore, a straightforward implementation of the attack will require the adversary to obtain decryptions of *two* ciphertexts in order to recover the entire message (i.e., the adversary can obtain about half the plaintext with each decrypted ciphertext he receives). Alternately, the adversary can try to modify the "Length" field. The actual length of the packet is known, so by manipulating the bits of the "Length" field in the encrypted data the adversary can potentially set the value to the length of the modified ciphertext. This is possible, however it causes the next block of data to be garbled unpredictably (thereby preventing the adversary from learning the message corresponding to that block). Furthermore, this approach will be effective only if the lengths of the modified ciphertext and the original ciphertext lie in the same range; i.e., the lengths are described by the same number of bytes. Otherwise, the attack will fail because the adversary will have to insert bytes into the encrypted header of a PGP packet, which will result in unpredictable data.

Another minor complication is that PGP checks the value of the CTB after decryption. If the value of this byte is not valid, PGP will exit with an error message. Decryption will also fail if the "Mode" byte is not recognized. Thus, when constructing the chosen ciphertext message, the adversary must take care not to garble the first block of the message which contains the header for the Literal Data Packet. This is taken into account in the above diagrams.

Finally, PGP will read the number of bytes given in the "Name Length" field from the "Name" field; these bytes will not appear in the output plaintext (rather, they are used to derive a name for the file that will contain the plaintext). If the attacker inserts data in the encrypted packet before the end of the original filename, or if the filename does not end on a block boundary, the decrypted message will not properly align with the attacker's random data. This is so because the beginning of the decrypted chosen ciphertext will actually contain part of the filename field that is not normally output by PGP. This minor problem can be avoided by repeating the packet header blocks in the chosen ciphertext and then finding the proper alignment by shifting the decrypted message (i.e., by dropping off one byte at a time from the beginning of the message), thus repeatedly trying the attack until the "Length field" (whose value is known) is found. The alignment that allows determination of the "Length" field also allows the rest of the data to be determined, and no additional chosen ciphertext messages are required.

In summary, when the plaintext message is not compressed by PGP before encryption or when the plaintext is itself a compressed file which is not further compressed by PGP, a single-ciphertext or two-ciphertext attack can be used to determine the entire contents of the original message. A program (in Java) implementing the single-ciphertext and two-ciphertext versions of the attack is available at:

http://www.cs.umd.edu/~jkatz/pgpAttack.tar.gz

Because PGP and GnuPG inter-operate, the above attack also works against a message sent via GnuPG when compression is not used. The code has been tested with PGP versions 2.6.2 and 2.6.3 as well as GnuPG version 1.0.6.

4   Compressed Data

Both GnuPG and PGP compress data by default before encrypting it (unless the data is already compressed, as described above). Compression further complicates the attack because a compression algorithm is applied before encryption and after decryption. The difficulties arise from the fact that the programs use packet headers included in the encrypted data for further processing. Modification of these headers will usually cause the attack to fail because the program cannot process the garbled headers. Additionally, GnuPG uses a message digest check to protect the integrity of the data. While a minor modification of the attack succeeds against GnuPG , the digest check fails and causes the program to output a warning message that would likely cause the user to become suspicious and fail to return the decrypted chosen ciphertext message.

4.1   PGP

A PGP message with compressed data is formed as follows:

PGP COMPRESSED MESSAGE									
C T B	L E N G T H	PUBLIC KEY ENCRYPTED SESSION KEY DATA	C T B	L E N G T H	RANDOM BYTES	LAST TWO RANDOM BYTES	C T B	A L G	COMPRESSED DATA
1	1	?	1	1	8	2	1	1	?

The compressed data is comprised of raw DEFLATE [4] blocks, the result of applying the DEFLATE algorithm to a PGP literal packet containing the plaintext. The DEFLATE algorithm compresses data via a two-step process. First, it scans the data and finds "backward matches" or sections of the data that are redundant. These are represented by ⟨length, distance⟩ pairs that describe where in the data stream the redundancy occurs. Then, both the symbols in the data and the ⟨length, distance⟩ pairs are replaced by Huffman codes. Huffman coding essentially replaces each literal token with an encoded string, where literals that are more common in the actual data are given shorter codes. The "Huffman tree" is the mapping between literals and Huffman codes. This mapping is determined based on statistical analysis of the literals in the data, or is predefined by the algorithm.

The DEFLATE RFC [4] states the following:

> Any data compression method involves the reduction of redundancy in the data. Consequently, any corruption of the data is likely to have severe effects and be difficult to correct.

The chosen-ciphertext attack requires the insertion of random blocks into the encrypted data. Insertion or modification of any data in an encrypted stream will cause the plaintext of the next block to be random. Thus, in general, it is difficult to predict the effects of random changes in a compressed file because the compressed data is very dependent on the original data. Usually, random data in a compressed file will corrupt the internal state of the inflater during decompression and cause the algorithm to fail — the more random data inserted, the higher the probability that decompression will fail. If the decompression fails, a decryption of the chosen-ciphertext message is not produced and the attack cannot continue.

Based on some heuristic tests on about 400 text files, insertion of a single 64-bit block or modification of a block at random will cause a decompression error roughly 90% of the time. The larger the original message, the more likely it decompresses improperly after modification. Files that did decompress successfully were either severely truncated or were very similar to the original message.

It is claimed in [6] that if the attacker obtains the decompressed output resulting from the attack, he can re-compress it and continue the attack. This is not actually the case. Recall that the attacker needs the decryption of the chosen ciphertext in order to perform the attack. Normally, the payload of a PGP Session Key Encrypted Data Packet is an LDP which has been compressed and then encrypted:

$$C_1, C_2, \ldots, C_k = \mathcal{E}_K(\text{DEFLATE}(\text{LDP})).$$

Decryption and decompression proceed as follows:

$$P_1, P_2, \ldots, P_k = \text{INFLATE}(\mathcal{D}_K(C_1, C_2, \ldots, C_k)).$$

When $\mathcal{D}_K(C_1, C_2, \ldots, C_k)$ is in fact a valid output of the DEFLATE algorithm, we do indeed have

$$\text{DEFLATE}(\text{INFLATE}(\mathcal{D}_K(C_1, C_2, \ldots, C_k))) = \mathcal{D}_K(C_1, C_2, \ldots, C_k).$$

On the other hand, when the ciphertext is modified (as it is when the chosen ciphertext is constructed), $\mathcal{D}_K(C'_1, \ldots, C'_k)$ is no longer a valid output of the DEFLATE algorithm. The decompression process assumes that its input consists of Huffman codes that will translate into the appropriate literals for whatever Huffman tree is in use at that point of the decompression; in other words, IN-FLATE expects to run on input that is the valid output of the deflation algorithm. Thus (with overwhelming probability),

$$\text{DEFLATE}(\text{INFLATE}(\mathcal{D}_K(C'_1, \ldots, C'_k))) \neq \mathcal{D}_K(C'_1, \ldots, C'_k)$$

and the attack cannot proceed. If the decompression does produce a result that is not badly truncated or is very similar to the original message, it may be possible to reproduce at least part of $\mathcal{D}_K(C'_1, \ldots, C'_k)$ using the decompressed output and knowledge of where the random insertion was made. This requires careful analysis of the corrupted compressed message, which is difficult and in many cases impossible.

4.2   GnuPG

A variant of the chosen-ciphertext attack is partially successful against GnuPG, although the effectiveness of the attack is mitigated by the presence of an integrity check on the data. GnuPG uses slightly longer headers on compressed data, and these headers are predictable. This allows an attacker to change the header bytes of the data to those of a literal packet (by "flipping" bits in the encrypted data that correspond to bits in the known "underlying" value), although the data section is left alone. When the data is decrypted, the algorithm will not attempt to decompress the result because the compressed packet headers have been changed to literal packet headers. The decrypted chosen ciphertext will thus be the compressed version of the original message. Since compressed data bears no resemblance to the original data, the recipient will not be suspicious of the decrypted data and is likely to send it back.

The key to this variant of the attack is that two extra bytes of the encrypted data are predictable under GnuPG's default compression algorithm, where the original message is as follows:

										GPG COMPRESSED MESSAGE		
CTB	LENGTH	PUBLIC KEY ENCRYPTED SESSION KEY DATA	CTB	LENGTH	RANDOM BYTES	LAST TWO RANDOM BYTES	CTB	ALG	METHOD	FLAGS	COMPRESSED DATA	
1	2	?	1	2	8	2	1	1	1	1	?	

The fact that the "METHOD" and "FLAGS" bytes are known in this case allows the attacker to flip bits in the underlying data to change the compressed packet header to a literal packet header, as in the diagrams detailing uncompressed data messages above.

In order to obtain the entire message, the attacker can set the filename length header to the blocksize of the algorithm and append the entire original segment of encrypted data to the (modified) first block as follows:

											GPG CHOSEN CIPHERTEXT MESSAGE		
CTB	LENGTH	PUBLIC KEY ENCRYPTED SESSION KEY DATA	CTB	LENGTH	RANDOM BYTES	LAST TWO RANDOM BYTES	NEW CTB	LENGTH	MODE	NAME LENGTH	RANDOM BYTES (MINUS BYTES 0,1)	LAST TWO RANDOM BYTES	ENTIRE ORIGINAL MESSAGE
1	2	?	1	2	8	2	1	1	1	1	6	2	?

▢ = modified encrypted data

The result of decryption will be one block of random data, followed by the compressed packet. Upon receipt of the decrypted chosen ciphertext message, the attacker can strip off the garbage data and headers, and decompress the data to obtain the original message.

There is one flaw with the above approach. By default, GnuPG includes a message digest on the encrypted data. Since this check is likely to fail for the ciphertext constructed by the attacker, a warning message will be relayed to the user. This might make the user suspicious enough not to send the message back (thereby preventing the chosen-ciphertext attack). It should be noted, however, that the message digest is not used when GnuPG inter-operates with PGP, and this might allow the attack. When inter-operating with PGP, though, ZIP compression is used (instead of ZLIB); we were unable to implement the attack when ZIP compression is used.

5   OpenPGP Vulnerabilities

The OpenPGP specification is written as a base specification for security software inter-operability. Most implementations of the specification are written with inter-operability with PGP as a basic goal, and are built along similar lines. An application written "directly from specification" would potentially be vulnerable to a chosen ciphertext attack due to a difference in the specification and the actual operation of PGP. In defining constants allowed in the "Algorithm" field of a compressed data packet, the specification states the following [3]:

```
ID    Algorithm
--    ---------
0    - Uncompressed
1    - ZIP (RFC 1951)
2    - ZLIB (RFC 1950)
100 to 110  - Private/Experimental algorithm.
```

Implementations MUST implement uncompressed data. Implementations SHOULD implement ZIP. Implementations MAY implement ZLIB.

The specification states that compliant implementations MUST implement uncompressed as one of their algorithms; that is, a compressed packet with an "Algorithm" field of 0 must be acceptable. In practice, neither GnuPG or PGP actually implement this; uncompressed data is never encapsulated in a compressed data packet. If this part of the specification were followed, however, an attack similar to the one described for GnuPG would be successful against that implementation — the attacker could change the encrypted compression algorithm header and obtain the compressed data as if it were plaintext. The attacker could then simply decompress that data and retrieve the original message. There is little chance that the user would recognize the data as "similar" to the actual message, because it would be in compressed format. The widely used programs (GnuPG and PGP) that claim to conform to the specification actually do not in this instance, and therefore fortuitously escape vulnerability to the attack.

In general, the OpenPGP standard presents compression as optional. An implementation that did not provide compression would be vulnerable to the non-compressed attack as described.

It is also important to note that the OpenPGP standard does not explicitly require an integrity check on the contents of an encrypted message.[5] An implementation of GnuPG which did not include the integrity check would be vulnerable to chosen-ciphertext attack. GnuPG includes this integrity check by defining their own packet type which is not included in the OpenPGP standard. When this packet type is encountered by the program, it actually uses a slightly different chaining mode (the re-sync step is omitted). This prevents an attacker from changing the headers on a packet with an integrity check to make it look like a non-integrity checked packet: such a packet will not decrypt properly due to the difference in chaining modes used. This is another example of an extension to the OpenPGP standard that allows the program to avoid vulnerability to chosen-ciphertext attacks in practice.

6   Recommendations

If compression is not used, or if compressed files are sent, the chosen-ciphertext attack described here succeeds against both GnuPG and PGP. GnuPG is also vulnerable if the user does not view the warning message that the encrypted

---

[5] But see footnote 2.

data fails the message integrity check. In "batch mode" operation this warning would probably go unnoticed by the user; since in this case the decrypted file is still produced, the attack would succeed. Additionally, some of the front-end programs that use GnuPG do not propagate this warning to the user. In this case, the attack is definitely feasible.

Users of GnuPG and PGP should be aware that compression should not be turned off. Compression is turned on by default, but a user sending a compressed file will still be at risk from a chosen-ciphertext attack.

The OpenPGP standard, as written, is vulnerable to chosen ciphertext attack due to the following:

1. No explicit requirement of a message integrity check.
2. Optional implementation of compression.
3. Requiring acceptance of "uncompressed" as a valid form of compression.

The first problem is basically a recognized one that has been solved in practice by those implementing the algorithm. On the other hand, precisely because the problem is universally recognized by those "in the know", it is time for the RFC to reflect this. Requiring "uncompressed" to be recognized as a valid form of compression is a minor, but clear, problem with the standard itself. Compression algorithms already allow for inclusion of non-compressed data and the standard should not try to deal with this issue because it introduces a flaw. Luckily the widely used programs that (generally) conform to the standard ignore this requirement; the standard should still be fixed so as not to cause problems in new implementations.

Developers of front-end software for GnuPG need to propagate integrity violation warnings to the users. This is important not only for protection against chosen ciphertext attacks — integrity protection is useless if the user is not warned when it has been violated!

Acknowledgments. Thanks to Jon Callas and David Shaw for their extensive comments and helpful suggestions.

References

1. M. Bellare, A. Desai, D. Pointcheval, and P. Rogaway. Relations Among Notions of Security for Public-Key Encryption Schemes. Crypto '98.
2. J. Callas and D. Shaw. Personal communication, July 2002.
3. J. Callas, L. Donnerhacke, M. Finney, and R. Thayer. "OpenPGP Message Format," RFC 2440, Nov. 1998.
4. L.P. Deutsch. "DEFLATE Compressed Data Format Specification version 1.3," RFC 1951, May 1996.
5. S. Garfinkel. *PGP: Pretty Good Privacy*, O'Reilly & Associates, 1995.
6. J. Katz and B. Schneier. A Chosen Ciphertext Attack against Several E-Mail Encryption Protocols. 9th USENIX Security Symposium, 2000.
7. M. Naor and M. Yung. Public-Key Cryptosystems Provably Secure against Chosen Ciphertext Attacks. STOC '90.
8. P. Zimmerman. *The Official PGP User's Guide*, MIT Press, 1995.

Role-Based Access Control for E-commerce Sea-of-Data Applications

G. Navarro, S. Robles, and J. Borrell

Dept. of Computer Science
Universitat Autònoma de Barcelona
Edifici-Q, 08193 Bellaterra, Spain.
gnavarro@ccd.uab.es, {Sergi.Robles,Joan.Borrell}@uab.es

Abstract. Sea-of-Data (SoD) applications (those that need to process huge quantities of distributed data) present specific restrictions, which make mobile agent systems one of the most feasible technologies to implement them. On the other hand mobile agent technologies are in a hot research state, specially concerning security. We present an access control method for mobile agent systems. It is based on Role-based Access Control and trust management to provide a reliable solution for e-commerce SoD applications. It uses SPKI certificates to implement the role system and the delegation of authorization. It is proposed as an extension of the MARISM-A project, a secure mobile agent platform for SoD application. We also show its functionality with an e-commerce SoD medical imaging data application, which is based on a scenario of the IST project INTERPRET.

1 Introduction

Sea-of-Data (SoD) applications have this common characteristics. The user is just interested in the outcomes resulting from processing a huge amount of data distributed among internetworked locations. Data never leaves these locations because a number of reasons, including legal requirements (medical images, for instance), bandwidth limitations, or even physical restrictions (data could be acquired on demand). The user is not on-line during all the time required for data processing: this process might take a considerable amount of time, or the user might be connected through a non reliable network link. SoD applications are extremely useful in many areas such as intrusion detection systems, medical image processing or satellite imagery analysis. Furthermore, SoD applications provide a new prospect for electronic commerce. Data (resource) processing can be charged to users establishing a new variant of selling of indirect services.

Restrictions in SoD applications make them hard, if not impossible, to be implemented with traditional technologies. Mobile agents systems appear to be the only feasible solution to implement SoD applications. In these systems, autonomous software entities (agents) can travel through a network of execution platforms (agencies), allowing the code in SoD applications to be borne to the data. After an agent is launched, the initial agency can be off-line. Thus, the user

A.H. Chan and V. Gligor (Eds.): ISC 2002, LNCS 2433, pp. 102–116, 2002.

may be disconnected during the execution of the application. It is also possible to parallelize the execution of processes allowing a high degree of scalability. But mobile agents systems are not a panacea. They introduce a new branch of issues concerning security [3].

One of the most important challenges that needs to be solved is the resource access control. We need a lightweight, flexible, and scalable method to control the access to data and resources in general. Traditional methods are normally based on the authentication of global identities (X.509 certificates). They allow to explicitly limit access to a given resource, through attribute certificates or Access Control Lists (ACLs). They also require a Certification Authority (CA) and a centralized control. This approach makes the system closed from the clients point of view. To be a reliable e-commerce application, it needs to provide a good solution to deal with a great variety of clients. It will be desirable for the clients to access the resource without having to be registered in a CA. Clients may be able to have a simpler key management. On the other hand, we will have a reduced and controlled number of agencies. They can afford to have keys with relatively long validity time ranges and be registered in a CA.

An alternative to implement access control are authorization infrastructures. These infrastructures are based on trust management and allow to assign authorizations (permissions or credentials) to entities and delegate trust from one entity to another. One of these infrastructures is the *Simple Public Key Infrastructure* (SPKI) [5], which seems to be one of the most accepted. SPKI provides a good base to implement the access control method. There are security frameworks providing SPKI functionalities [8], an it is probably the most standard solution to implement trust management mechanisms, such as delegation of authorizations. There are also some approaches using authorization infrastructures to implement access control methods [1], [9].

In order to make access control easier, it is also interesting to use an approach similar to Role-based Access Control (RBAC) [11]. Instead of having to provide and/or revoke specific permission to a principal, RBAC allows to determine the privileges of a principal by its role membership.

In this article, we present a solution for e-commerce SoD applications. We adapt RBAC for mobile agents using SPKI. Our model allows to authorize a mobile agent to access a given resource and control its access with quite flexibility. The mobile agent does not need to carry any kind of information with regard to the resource access. This avoids the inconveniences of storing sensitive information in the mobile agent. Our model is going to be implemented as an extension of the MARISM-A platform [14], a secure mobile agents platform. To clarify and explain our proposal, we will explain an example application based on a scenario of the project INTERPRET IST-1999-10310 (*International network for Pattern Recognition of Tumors Using Magnetic Resonance*, http://www.carbon.uab.es/interpret).

In Section 2 we give an overview of SPKI. Section 3 introduces the MARISM-A platform and the extension added to support the RBAC model through SPKI. We present our adapted RBAC model in Section 4 and the example SoD application in Section 5. Section 6 shows the functionality of the proposed model over the example application and considerations about the distribution of the model. And finally Section 7 contains our conclusions.

2   SPKI

The base to our proposal is SPKI (more formally named SPKI/SDSI) [5]. It is an infrastructure which provides an authorization system based on the delegation of authorizations and a local name model. It provides mainly two kind of certificates, authorization and name certificates. Any individual, software agent or active entity in general is called a *principal*. It is a *key-oriented* system, each principal is represented and may be globally identified by its public key. We can say that in SPKI a principal is its public key. Since it does not need a certification authority, each principal can generate and manage its keys. A key is a generic cryptographic key pair (public and private). Currently the SPKI specification supports RSA and DSA keys. The representation format used by SPKI is S-expressions [13].

An authorization certificate has the following fields:

- Issuer (I): principal granting the authorization.
- Subject (S): principal receiving the authorization.
- Authorization tag (*tag*): specific authorization granted by the certificate.
- Delegation bit (p): if it is active, the subject may forward delegate the authorization received.
- Validity specification (V): specifies the validity of the certificate through a time range and on-line tests.

It is signed by the issuer. The on-line tests from the validity specification field, provide the possibility of checking, at verification time, the validity or revocation of the certificate. We will use the 5-tuple notation: *(I,S,tag,p,V)*, to denote a SPKI authorization certificate.

In a normal situation there will be a principal controlling a resource, which delegates an authorization. The authorization may be further delegated to other principals. If a principal wants to access the resource, it needs to provide an *authorization proof*. Te proof is a certificate chain, which binds the principal controlling the resource to the one requesting the access. To find this certificate chain there is a deterministic algorithm. *Certificate Chain Discovery Algorithm*[4], which finds the authorization proof in polynomial time.

In SPKI a principal may have a local name space and define local names to refer to other principals. To define a name, a principal issues a name certificate. It has an issuer, subject, validity specification, (just as an authorization certificate) and a name. The *issuer* defines the *name* to be equivalent to the *subject*. For example a principal with public key K may define the name *Alice* to be equivalent to the the principal with public key K_A. Now K can refer to the principal K_A by the name *Alice* instead of the public key. Such a name certificate can be denoted as:

$$K \; Alice \longrightarrow K_A$$

meaning that K defines the name *Alice* in its local name space to be equivalent to K_A. If a principal wants to refer to a name defined in another name space, it just has to add the local name space owner's public key to the name as a prefix. When we say $K \; Alice$, we mean the name *Alice* defined in K's local name space.

SPKI also provides the ability of defining compound names. Names that refer to other names which may also reference other names and so on. For example, the principal K_B can define the following name in its local name space:

$$K_B \; employee \longrightarrow K \; Alice$$

It defines the name *employee* to be equivalent to the name *Alice* defined in K's local name space. Note that it is referring to K_A without knowing it.

This is a key concept in our proposal since we will consider a role as a SPKI local name.

3 MARISM-A

As said before the proposed access control model is an extension of our MARISM-A platform [14] (http://www.marism-a.org). MARISM-A is a secure mobile agent platform implemented in Java, it is implemented on top of the JADE-LEAP system (http://sharon.cselt.it/projects/jade, http://leap.crm-paris.com), which follows the standards proposed by FIPA [6].

The basic element of the MARISM-A platform is the agency, the environment for the execution of agents. An agency consists of a directory service, an agent manager, and a message transport service. An agent system has several agencies distributed on a network. Each agency in controlled by an entity (its owner).

Agents are software units executing in the agencies on behalf of their owners. Agents in MARISM-A can be mobile or static, depending on the need of the agent to visit other agencies to fulfill its task. There are several types of mobile agents according to the characteristics of its architecture: basic or recursive structure, plain or encrypted, itinerary representation method, etc. Agents can communicate each other through the agency communication service.

One of the novel aspects introduced in the MARISM-A platform is the flexibility of the agent architecture. Different security solutions have some especial agent requirements. Instead of focusing on a specific type of agent, there are different agent architectures. Some security mechanisms are applicable only for certain types of agents. Even mobility is a feature of only some agent architectures. Moreover, our design allows to have several types of agents living together in a heterogeneous environment.

Most bibliographic references on agents do not make a clear distinction between different parts of an agent. Some of them suggest the need of considering independent some internal parts, especially for mobile agents. This is the case of agent data in [15], of agent code in [2], or agent itinerary in [10]. The independence of these parts plays an important role for some agent protection mechanisms, whereas it is unnecessary for others. In MARISM-A, the architecture of the agent is an adaptable model that determines the different parts in which an agent is divided and the combination of security, integrity, or other mechanisms included in it.

All mobile agent architectures share some basic aspects, such as the differentiation of internal parts and migration mechanisms. A mobile agent consists of code, data, state, and an explicit itinerary. Code is the set of instruction describing the execution of the agent. Data is an information storage area that can be used by the agent at any moment for reading and writing and goes with it all the time. Results of executions are stored in this area, normally using some convenient protection mechanisms. State is like the data part of the agent but reserved to store the agent information related with its state. Explicit itinerary is a structure containing all agencies that are going to be visited by the agent on its life cycle. Itineraries consist of several basic structures: sequences, sets, and alternatives. These structures can be combined to build complex itineraries. In a sequence, the agent will migrate to each agency one after the other. In a set, a group of agencies will be visited by the agent in no special order. On the other hand, only one agency of those listed in an alternative will be visited by an agent, depending on some conditions.

MARISM-A considers a minimal security infrastructure to protect the communications between agencies. All the agencies are registered in a CA, and we use SSL to provide both confidentiality and authentication for agency communications.

It is important to assume that agencies untrust each other. Therefore, they might try to modify results carried by the agent, or to gain knowledge about its itinerary, to favor themselves to the detriment of the rest. It is also reasonable to assume that agencies are not malicious and they do not seek to adversely affect the owner of the agent (the client), or the agent itself.

From now on we will use the following notation:

- $E_i(m)$: encryption of m using a symmetric cipher with i's secret key.
- $P_i(m)$: encryption of m using an asymmetric cipher with i's public key.
- $S_i(m)$: signature of m using i's private key.
- $hash(m)$: hash function of m.
- $hash_{K_i}(m)$: keyed hash function of m using i's secret key.

Subsections 3.1 and 3.2 introduce the architecture of MARISM-A static agents and the mobile agents with explicit itinerary as an extension to MARISM-A mobile agents.

3.1   Static Agents

A MARISM-A static agent has the following form:

$$\text{Agent} = \text{ControlCode, State, Code, Data}$$

Because agent management code is in the agent itself, it is indifferent for the platform to deal with mobile or static agents. There are not many words to say about security in static agents. Communication and interface with other agents are provided by secure services of the agency. Data protection is assured by the agency too, and there is no itinerary to protect here.

3.2 Mobile Agents with Explicit Itinerary

Agent code is split into several pieces. There is a main code that will be executed in all agencies (Common Code), and as many code fragments as agencies are in the itinerary, each one to be executed in a particular agency (Local Code). This feature makes MARISM-A very useful in some types of application where execution is context dependent. The agent changes after a migration. This agent aspect dynamism allow several security mechanisms to be applied.

The agent has the following structure:

$$\text{Agent}_i = \text{ControlCode, StateData,}$$
$$\text{CommonCode, GlobalData, ResultsData,}$$
$$(\text{LocalCode}_0, \text{LocalData}_0, \text{Agencies}_1), \dots ,$$
$$(\text{LocalCode}_{n-1}, \text{LocalData}_1, \text{Agencies}_n),$$
$$(\text{LocalCode}_n, \text{Nil})$$

Agencies_i is the agency (or agencies, depending on the type of itinerary) the agent is going to visit (migrate) next. The agent that is sent to the next hop of the itinerary (Agent_{i+1}) has the same structure. The last host is identified because of a *Nil* next agent. CommonCode is executed by all agencies when the agent immigrates and before the specific LocalCode. Programming is simplified by using this common code to include the non agency dependent code only once. The control code in the agent deals with the functions of agent management, in this case extracting the relevant parts of the agent.

It might be interesting to protect integrity and secrecy of data that has been written in some agency. In an e-commerce application, for instance, where agencies represent shops and agents act on behalf of buyers, it might be necessary to protect offers from rival shops. The method to provide the secrecy and integrity required for this data in this agent architecture is based on a hash chain. Some of the data area is reserved to store results from executions (Results Data). Results are not stored plain, but they are firstly encrypted using agent's owner cryptographic information. Only the owner of the agent will be able to read these results. Once the result has been written a hash of the Result and previous hashed information is calculated, signed and written also. This hash has information about the identity of next agency in the itinerary, so that no agency can neither modify the result area nor remove some result. Each agency verifies during immigration that all hashes in the Results Data are correct. This is the format of the Results Data area:

$$\text{Results Data} = P_o(R_1), S_1(hash(P_o(R_1), Id2)),$$
$$P_o(R_2), S_2(hash(P_o(R_2), hash(P_o(R_1), Id2), Id3)),\dots,$$
$$P_o(R_n), S_n(hash(P_o(R_n), ..., hash(P_o(R_1), Id2), Id0)))$$

where $P_o(R_i)$ is the encryption of the result of agency i using the public key of the owner of the agent (PubKey$_o$) and $hash()$ is a hash function.

We also need a way to ensure the agent's integrity. The owner, before sending the agent, computes a keyed hash of the whole agent excluding the Results Data, $hash_{K_o}(initial\_agent)$. Then when the agent finishes its execution, the owner can verify the agent's keyed hash.

To protect the itinerary we use the following encryption schema:

$$\begin{aligned}
\text{Agent}_i = {} & \text{PubKey}_o, \text{ControlCode}, \text{StateData}, \\
& \text{CommonCode}, \text{GlobalData}, \text{ResultsData} \\
& E_1(\text{LocalCode}_0, \text{LocalData}_0, \text{Agencies}_1), \ldots, \\
& E_{n-1}(\text{LocalCode}_{n-1}, \text{LocalData}_{n-1}, \text{Agencies}_n), \\
& E_n(\text{LocalCode}_n, Nil), \\
& hash_{K_o}(initial\_agent).
\end{aligned}$$

where E_i is a symmetric encryption function using agency i symmetric key. As we will see the encryption is performed by the agency itself before the whole agent is constructed. So the symmetric key is only used by the agency and it does not need to be distributed.

A variant of this agent is the mixed one, where the list of information for agencies is scrambled. This makes it not possible to know which is the part of the agent that will be executed in a given agency.

4   Access Control for SoD Applications

One of the first problems we found when planning the authorization model, is if the mobile agents should have a SPKI key and be considered as principals. A mobile agent cannot trivially store a private key, so it cannot perform cryptographic operations such as digital signatures. There are some propositions to store sensitive information (private keys) in mobile agents [12]. But the problem arises when the mobile agent uses the private key to compute a cryptographic operation. The agency where the agent is in execution will be able to see the private key. As a result we consider that a mobile agent should not have a private key.

Our solution is to delegate authorizations directly to the agent. This way the mobile agent does not need to carry any kind of authorization information, making the agent more simple and lightweight. This issue will be discussed in section 6.2.

The main components of the access control method can be seen as independent modules. Each module is implemented as an static agent, has a SPKI key, and it is considered as a SPKI principal. The modules are:

Authorization Manager (AM): it manages the delegation of authorizations, issuing SPKI authorization certificates. It follows a *local authorization policy.*

Role Manager (RM): it manages the roles (mainly the role membership) by issuing name certificates. It follows a *local role policy.*

Certificate Repository Manager (CRM): it manages a certificate repository. Provides services such as certificate chain discovery.

Resource Manager (DM): it is an authorization manager, which controls a
resource (data), it has to verify resource access requests. Normally its authorization policy will be quite restrictive, delegating to an authorization
manager the responsibility of performing complex authorization tasks.

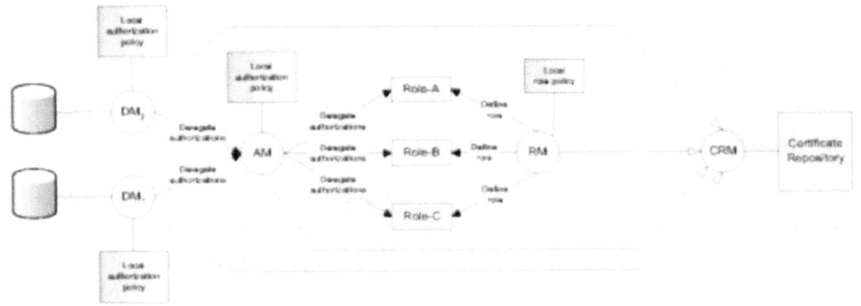

Fig. 1. Access control modules

Figure 1 shows a simple schema of the model with two DMs, an AM, a RM,
and a CRM. The RM defines the roles and determines its membership. The
DMs delegate the authorizations related to the resources to the AM, and the
AM delegates authorizations to the roles. Each static agent stores the issued
SPKI certificates in the certificate repository through the CRM (denoted by
broken lines).

4.1   Authorization Manager (AM)

The main functionality of the AM is to provide authorization certificates under
request. To obtain an authorization certificate, a principal sends a request to
the AM specifying the specific authorization, it wants to obtain. Then the AM
decides whether to issue the certificate or not, and under what conditions it has
to be issued. To do that, it follows its local authorization policy. Since the policy
is local to the AM agent, it does not need to follow any specification and its
format is implementation dependent.

We propose an authorization policy, described as a SPKI ACL, where each
rule can be expressed as an ACL entry in S-expression format. A SPKI ACL
entry is an authorization certificate without the issuer and it does not need to
be signed because it is local to the AM and stored in secure memory. It has the
following fields:

– Subject: the principal receiving the authorization. It may be a role or another
  AM.

- Authorization tag: specifies the specific authorization that the subject can obtain. SPKI allows quite flexibility to specify the authorization tag with S-expressions.
- Delegation bit: determines whether the subject may receive the right to delegate the authorization or not.
- Validity specification: allows to limit the authorization to a time range, and include some on-line tests to verify the validity or revocation of the authorization certificate.

To be more specifics, the AM will receive authorization delegation requests from a RM or another AMs. It has to delegate authorizations to roles or to other AM which will finally authorize roles.

4.2   Role Manager (RM)

The RM is responsible for assigning and managing roles, and determines the role membership. The use of roles facilitates the access control management and the specification of policies. The main idea is to exploit the advantages of Role Based Access Control (RBAC) [11] and trust management. The RM assigns a role by issuing a SPKI name certificate following its local role policy. It can also assign a role to a role defined by another RM, thus allowing the delegation of role membership management. Section 6.1 details how roles are assigned and used.

Each RM has a local role policy which determines what roles does it manage. It also includes rules to determine if a given principal requesting a role membership has to be granted or not. If we choose to describe the role policy as a SPKI ACL, it is quite similar to an authorization policy. Now the subject of the SPKI ACL entry is a principal or another role and the authorization tag determines the role that the subject can have.

4.3   Certificate Repository Manager (CRM)

A CRM implements a certificate repository. For example, one agency may have one CRM to collect all the certificates issued by agents inside the agency. The CRM provides the repository and all the services needed to query, store or retrieve the certificates in the repository. It also provides a certificate chain discovery service. A principal can make a query to the CRM to find a specific certificate chain. This way we solve the problems derived from certificate distribution and leave the task to perform chain discoveries to the CRM and not to the other principals. It decreases the communication traffic, certificates do not need to travel from one principal to another and reduces the task that generic principals need to perform.

4.4   Resource Manager (DM)

The main task of a DM is to control the access to a resource (data). It holds the master SPKI key to access the resource, delegates authorizations to AMs, and verifies that an agent requesting access to the resource has a proper authorization.

Another important feature of a DM is to issue *Certificate Result Certificates* (CRC) to agent hashes, see 6.2.

As it has to delegate authorizations issuing authorization certificates it also acts like an AM and follows a local authorization policy. But this policy is much more restricted. A DM only has to issue authorization certificates to AMs and a special certificate to mobile agents (see 6.2), which are quite straightforward operations.

5 Example Application

This example is derived from the project IST INTERPRET, which provides a clear example of a SoD application. The example application is going to be developed using the extensions of the MARISM-A platform to support the proposed access control. Consider a medical SoD application for radiology images. There are several hospitals, research centers, and companies with a radiology department which produces some kind of sensitive, and possibly expensive, radiology images such a magnetic resonances or high resolution radiologies. Each center organizes the data in a database accessed by at least one agency with DMs. The application may provide the ability for clients to process the distributed data in a variety of ways, for example testing a classification algorithm. The owner of the data may also provide itself classification services. It may have a trained classification system, which a client may use to classify a reduced set of data provided by herself.

The reason for using a mobile agent approach in this application, is due to the high quantity of distributed data, which is difficult to centralize. Also because it is quite sensitive medical data, which the hospitals are normally not allowed to give it to someone else. That is, a mobile agent processing the data, may get back to the client with the obtained results, but not with the data.

We will consider each participating entity as a principal. A principal may be a static agent or an individual (normally the owner of a mobile agent) with its own SPKI key. We consider three kinds of principals, data producers, data consumers, and process consumers:

- *data producer*: updates the database, adding new images or replacing existing ones.
- *process consumer*: provides a reduced set of data, and wants to use some processing service provided by the agency (normally a complex trained algorithm such as a classification one).
- *data consumer*: it provides a code to be executed with the data provided by the agency.

A simple definition of roles for the example application may be:

- *physician*: authorized as data and process consumer for all the resources.

- *external_physician*: authorized as process consumer for a reduced set of data.
- *radiography_technologist*: authorized as a data provider.
- *external_researcher*: authorized as data consumer for a restricted set of data.

These roles may be hierarchically extended, for example as *radiography_technologist*, there may be *radiographer*, which provides only radiographies and *mr_technologist*, which provides only magnetic resonances. Specially the *external_researcher* role, which may be seen as a client, may have several sub-roles to be able to specify several specific authorizations for different kinds of clients.

6   Access Control Management

Given the example application we will show the functionality of the access control method. The main features are the role system and the delegation of authorizations to mobile agents. A principal may be authorized to access a resource as a role member. The AM may give several authorizations to an specific role. Then a principal belonging to that role, has all the authorizations of the role. We already said that we do not consider a mobile agent as a SPKI principal. Thus we need a way to authorize mobile agents and control its access to resources.

We also consider the distribution of the access control management by distributing the modules. We can distribute several modules, or just one, for example. This makes the model easily adaptable to specific applications. Since a module is implemented in a static agent, to distribute a module means to use several static agents, which may operate independently.

6.1   Roles

An important issue of the RM is that it is the main responsible to grant access permissions to principals. When a principal requests a role membership and succeeds, it automatically has all the authorizations of the role. In some cases, specially *external_researcher* membership, the RM will need to perform some kind of economic transaction to grant the membership. That is, granting membership will require a special protocol involving a payment processes through, for example, a third party credit card issuer.

Another important issue is that the role membership can be restricted through the validity specification of the name certificate, which grants the membership. That is, it can have a *not-after* and *not-before* time range and some on-line tests [5].

6.2   Mobile Agent Authorization

A client as a principal may be member of a role or roles, say *external_client*. It may be authorized to access resource *A* with a mobile agent. Since mobile agents cannot have private keys, we can not delegate authorizations to the mobile agent or make it member of a role. Our approach is to delegate the authorization to a hash of the agent. The subject of a SPKI authorization certificate and any SPKI principal in general can be a public key or a hash of a public key. So a hash may be seen as a principal, subject of a certificate. This idea does not really follow the SPKI specifications, since it is not the hash of the public key, it is not a principal. Thus we need to extend the SPKI specifications to introduce this idea.

As we said before the mobile agent is constructed from the itinerary, separately including the code to be executed in each agency. Let m_i be the code to be executed in the agency i. The client already has an authorization to access resource A, which is controlled by DM_A. Once the client has specified all the m_is it constructs the itinerary and proceeds to get the authorization for the agent. The main idea is to request a *Certificate Result Certificate*(CRC) to DM_A having the hash of m_i as the subject. The CRC is an authorization certificate, which resumes a certificate chain, in this case the authorization proof for the client to access resource A. The process involves the following steps:

1. The client sends a CRC-request to DM_A. It includes the specific authorization it wants to obtain, the code m_i, and the client's public key. This request is signed by the client.
2. The DM_A requests the CRM to verify if the client is authorized to access the resource. That is, verifies if there is an authorization proof which allows the client to access the resource.
3. If the authorization is correctly verified, the DM_A computes the hash of the code, and issues an authorization certificate which has DM_A as the issuer and the hash of the code as the subject. The specification tag and the validity specification is the intersection between the ones from the client's CRC-request and the ones returned in the authorization proof request.
4. Finally the DM_A encrypts the code m_i with a symmetric cipher. It uses a private key only known by the DM_A. The DM_A is the only one who is able to decrypt m_i.

Once the mobile agent is constructed it will be able to access the resource. The mobile agent will travel to the agency and request access to DM_A. The DM_A just has to decrypt and compute the hash of the agent code (m_i); and check if there is an authorization certificate, which directly authorizes the hash to access. This authorization verification is straightforward, since it does not require the generation of a full authorization proof.

This approach allows to delegate authorizations to mobile agents. Note that the mobile agent does not need to include any kind of authorization information, it just has to provide the specific code so DM_A can compute the hash.

One thing we have not explicitly talked about is how to control the proper behavior of the mobile agents. In our example, how do we know that a mobile agent is not *stealing* data?. First of all, the process of authorizing a mobile agent involves the computing of the hash of the piece of code of the agent, which is going to be executed in the agency. So we can easily log this code for auditing purposes. It is also feasible for an agency to include a local monitoring system looking for anomalies in the behavior of the agents.

6.3 Distribution of Role Management

Due to the local names provided by SPKI, the role management can be easily distributed. We can have several RMs managing its local roles and use compound names to reference one local role to another. For example, consider we have two RMs, named RM_A and RM_B. Each one has its local roles definitions, RM_A may define:

RM_A radiography_technologist $\longrightarrow$ K_1
RM_A physician $\longrightarrow$ K_2
RM_A physician $\longrightarrow$ K_3
RM_A companyB_client $\longrightarrow$ RM_B ext._researcher

That is, it says that the principal K_1 is member of the radiology_technologist role; the principals K_2 and K_3 are members of the role physician. And that the name external_researcher (which is also a role) defined in the local name space of RM_B is member of the role companyB_client. Then RM_B may define:

RM_B external_researcher $\longrightarrow$ K_4
RM_B external_researcher $\longrightarrow$ K_5

So the principals K_4 and K_5 are members of the role external_researcher defined by RM_B. And they are also members of the role companyB_client defined by RM_A. Note that each RM defines independent roles, both RMs could define locally two roles with the same name, and they will be considered as different roles by the system. Is important to notice that all the roles, as SPKI names, are local to each RM. We can globally identify the role by adding the public key of the RM as a prefix of the role (just as a SPKI name). This independence of role definitions makes the system easily scalable and distributed. Note that in the example we can say that the role management is distributed over the two RMs since both of them take part in the hole role management. So independent RMs can interact in the same model without having to redefine roles.

This can be also seen as trust management, in some way RM_A trusts RM_B to manage the role RM_A companyB_client.

6.4 Distribution of Authorization Management

The distribution of the authorization management is achieved by distributing the management over several AMs. This distribution is straightforward. Each AM manages authorizations following its local policy. It can only delegate an authorizations that it has received. To be more precise an AM or any principal may delegate a certificate granting an authorization it does not have. But any principal receiving the authorization will not be able to have the proper authorization proof, since the certificate chain will be broken.

There will be no conflict between several AMs. If there is an authorization proof for one principal to access a resource, the principal will be able to access no matter which AMs or principals have interfered.

6.5   Distribution of the Certificate Repository

The distribution of the certificate repository is a complex task. All the authorization proofs are obtained from the repository. In fact it is the CRM, which performs the certificate chain discovery. To distribute the repository will considerably increase the complexity. We need to use a distributed certificate chain discovery algorithm, which adds not only complexity to the implementation but also introduces the need for more communication and process resources.

The application we are implementing does not impose the distribution of the certificate as a must. In fact it can easily be implemented with a centralized repository. So there is no need to add complexity to the system by distributing the repository.

There is some work done in relation to distributed certificate repositories and chain discovery, such as dRBAC [7], which could be used if an specific application really needs to distribute the certificate repository.

7   Conclusions and Further Work

We have proposed an access control model for e-commerce SoD applications, based on a mobile agents platform. It provides a simple, flexible, and scalable way of controlling the access to resources. It takes the advantages of RBAC and trust management ideas. The proposed model is an extension of the MARISM-A project. A secure mobile agents platform for SoD applications. We have also introduced an example application, a medical SoD imaging application based on the IST project INTERPRET.

Our solution provides a secure migration for agents with protected itineraries and we solve the secure resources access control and the authorization management. Even though, there are some problems which still being unsolved, like for example some subtle and limited replay attacks from one agency to another; or open problems like malicious hosts acting against agents. Some existing solution can solve the former problems [16] with a high cost in scalability, distribution, and complexity, but the later ones are still open problems [3].

We are working on the implementation of the proposed model. This process involves the study of additional aspects. For example considering alternatives to implement the local policies. By using SPKI ACLs, the policy is based on SPKI keys. This may be reflected in limitations of the key management. We also want to consider issues such as anonymity, specially relevant in key-oriented systems.

Acknowledgments. This work has been partially funded by the Spanish Government Commission CICYT, through its grant TIC2000-0232-P4-02, and Catalan Government Department DURSI, with grant 2001SGR 00219.

References

1. T. Aura. Distributed access-rights management with delegation certificates. In J. Vitek and C. Jensen, editors, *Secure Internet Programming: Security Issues for Distributed and Mobile Objects*, volume 1603 of *LNCS*, pages 211–235. Springer, 1999.
2. J. Baumann, F. Hohl, K. Rothermel, and M. Straßer. Mole - Concepts of a Mobile Agent System. *Special Issue on Distributed World Wide Web Processing: Applications and Techniques of Web Agents*, 1(3):123–137, 1998.
3. D. Chess. Security issues of mobile agents. In *Mobile Agents*, volume 1477 of *LNCS*, pages 1–12. Springer-Verlang, 1998.
4. D. Clarke, J. Elien, C. Ellison, M. Fredette, A. Morcos, and R. Rivest. Certificate chain discovery in SPKI/SDSI. *Journal of Computer Security*, 9(9):285–322, 2001.
5. C. Ellison, B. Frantz, B. Lampson, R. Rivest, B. Thomas, and T. Ylonen. RFC 2693: SPKI certificate theory. The Internet Society, September 1999.
6. Foundation for Intelligent Physical Agents. FIPA Specifications, 2000. http://www.FIPA.org.
7. E. Freudenthal, T. Pesin, L. Port, E. Keenan, and V. Karamcheti. dRBAC: Distributed role-based access control for dynamic coalition environments. New York University, Technical Report TR2001-819.(to appear ICDCS 2002), 2001.
8. Intel Architecture Labs. Intel Common Data Security Architecture. http://developer.intel.com/ial/security/.
9. L. Kagal, T. Finn, and A. Joshi. Trust-Based Security in Pervasive Computing Environments. *IEEE Computer*, pages 154–157, Dec. 2001.
10. G. Karjoth, N. Asokan, and C. Gülcü. Protecting the Computation of Free-Roaming Agents. In *Proceedings of the Second International Workshop on Mobile Agents*, LNCS 1477, pages 194–207. Springer-Verlag, 1998.
11. D. Rerraiolo, R. Sandhu, S. Gavrila, D. Kuhn, and R Chandramouli. Proposed NIST standard for role-based access control. In *ACM Transactions on Information and System Security*, volume 4, pages 224–274, August 2001.
12. J. Riordan and B. Schneier. Environmental key generation towards clueless agents. In *Mobile Agents and Security*, pages 15–24, 1998.
13. R. Rivest. S-expressions. Internet-draft: <draft-rivest-sexp-00.txt>. The Internet Society, 1997.
14. S. Robles, J. Mir, and J. Borrell. Marism-a: An architecture for mobile agents with recursive itinerary and secure migration. In *2nd. IW on Security of Mobile Multiagent Systems*, Bologna, 2002.
15. M. Straßer and K. Rothermel. Reliability Concepts for Mobile Agents. *International Journal of Cooperative Information Systems (IJCIS)*, 7(4):355–382, 1998.
16. M. Straßer, K. Rothermel, and C. Maifer. Providing Reliable Agents for Electronic Commerce. In *Trends in Distributed Systems for Electronic Commerce*, LNCS 1402, pages 241–253. Springer-Verlag, 1998.

An Access Control Model for Tree Data Structures

Alban Gabillon[1], Manuel Munier[1], Jean-Jacques Bascou[1],
Laurent Gallon[1], and Emmanuel Bruno[2]

[1]LIUPPA/CSySEC. Université de Pau. IUT de Mont de Marsan, 40 000 Mont de Marsan,
France.
http://csysec.univ-pau.fr
{gabillon,munier,bascou,gallon}@univ-pau.fr
[2]SIS-Equipe Informatique. Université de Toulon, 83 000 Toulon, France
bruno@univ-tln.fr

Abstract. Trees are very often used to structure data. For instance, file systems
are structured into trees and XML documents can be represented by trees. There
are literally as many access control schemes as there are tree data structures.
Consequently, an access control model which has been defined for a particular
kind of tree cannot be easily adapted to another kind of tree. In this paper, we
propose an access control model for *generic* tree data structures. This model can
then be applied to any specific typed tree data structure.

Keywords: Authorization Rule, Permission, Security Policy, Access Control,
Tree Data Structures.

1 Introduction

Trees are very often used to structure data. For instance, file systems are structured
into trees and XML documents [Bray00] can be represented by trees. There are
literally as many access control schemes as there are tree data structures:

- many access control models for XML have recently been proposed
  [GB01][Ber00a][Dam00a] [KH00]
- SNMPv3 [WPM99] proposes a View Access Control Model (VACM) for MIB trees
  (Management Information Base)
- the security model of UNIX is an access control model for hierarchical file
  structures
- LDAP [OL] includes an access control model for LDAP tree directories [Sto00]
- etc.

Historically, applications like the SNMP protocol, the LDAP protocol, WEB servers
or file systems were initially developed without integrating access control facilities.
For the developers of these applications, the most important was to organize the data
and to define primitives for manipulating them. Later on, some access control
mechanisms were added to these applications. However most of these access control
mechanisms rely on models which are not clearly defined and which are specific to a

A.H. Chan and V. Gligor (Eds.): ISC 2002, LNCS 2433, pp. 117–135, 2002.
© Springer-Verlag Berlin Heidelberg 2002

particular kind of tree data structure. Very often these models are even based on the semantics of the data.

In this paper, we propose an access control model for *generic* tree data structures. This model can then be applied to any specific typed tree data structure.

The development of an access control model requires the definition of *subjects* and *objects* for which *authorization rules* must be specified and *access controls* must be enforced. An authorization rule grants or denies a *privilege* on an object to a subject. The *security policy* consists of a set of authorization rules. Access controls enforce the security policy.

The model we define in this paper provides us with the possibility of writing security policies with a great expressive power:

- The *granularity* of the objects is very fine
- The set of privileges includes the *read* privilege but also various types of *write* privileges

Moreover, our model provides us with a *security policy control language*. We use this language to administrate the security policy. It is based on the classical GRANT/REVOKE scheme.

The remainder of this paper is organized as follows:

In section 2 we define the concept of *tree*. In this section we also suggest a language for addressing the *nodes* of a tree. In section 3, we present our model. We give the definition of a subject and an object. We present the privileges which are supported by our model. We show how we can define authorization rules by labeling the source tree with some *authorization attributes*. Finally, we present the core of our security policy control language. In section 4, we show how we can use our model to protect XML data structures. Section 5 compares our model with some related works. Section 6 concludes this paper.

2   Tree Data Structure

2.1   Definition

A tree is a type of data structure in which each datum is called a *node*. Each node is the parent of zero or more *child* nodes. Each node has one and only one parent except one fundamental node which has no parent and which is called the *root* node (or simply the root). Trees are often called *inverted trees* because they are normally drawn with the root at the top.

In figure 1, v1, v2, v3 etc. are nodes. v1 is the root. v6, v5 and v3 are nodes without a child. They are called *leaf* nodes. v2 and v3 are the child nodes of v1. v2 is the parent node of v4 and v5. v4, v5, v6 are the *descendant* nodes of v2. v1 is the *ancestor* of all the other nodes etc.

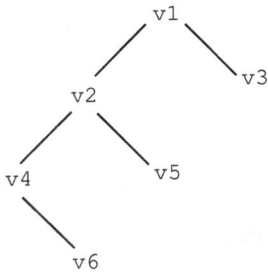

Fig. 1. Example of a Tree (1)

2.2   A Language for Addressing Nodes

The purpose of this section is to suggest a language for addressing nodes. Our language can be seen as a simplified version of XPath [CD99]. Simplification comes from the fact that in our language each node is a non typed datum whereas in XPath, each node is of a specific type (element, attribute, text etc.). Due to space limitations, we cannot formally and completely define our language here. However, the readers who know XPath can understand expressions which are written in our language without any problem. They can also predict what is going to be the expression for addressing this or that set of nodes. In this section, we only give an intuitive overview of our language by showing some examples of expressions for addressing nodes. This presentation is sufficient to understand the paper.

Nodes are individually or collectively addressed by the means of *path* expressions. Examples of path are the followings (these paths apply to the tree depicted in figure 1):

- /v1/v2. This path addresses the node v2.
- /v1/v2/*. This path addresses the child nodes of v2.
- /v1//*. This path addresses the descendant nodes of v1.
- /v1/v2//* | /v1/v2. This path addresses the node v2 and all its descendants (| is the union operator).

Let us now consider the tree of figure 2. Examples of path expressions which apply to this tree are the followings:

- /v1/v2[position()=1]. This path addresses the first node v2 starting from the left.
- /v1/v2/v4. This path addresses the two nodes v4 which are childs of a v2 node.
- /v1/*/v4. This path addresses the three nodes v4.
- /v1/v6[v4]. This path addresses the node v6 which has the node v4 as a child.

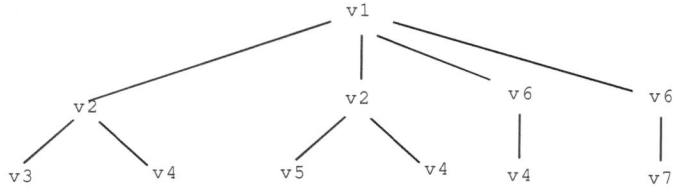

Fig. 2. Example of a Tree (2)

3   Access Control Model

In this section, we define an access control model for tree data structures. This section is organized as follows:

In section 3.1, we briefly define the concept of subject and object. In section 3.2, we first introduce the privileges which are supported by our model. We then show how we can define a security policy by labeling the source tree with some authorization attributes. In section 3.3, we define some access control algorithms which we use to enforce the security policy. Finally, in section 3.4, we suggest a security policy control language which we use to efficiently administrate the security policy.

3.1   Subjects and Objects

In our model, a subject is a user. It is not the purpose of this paper to give detailed information on how these subjects are organized. Let us mention that we could easily extend our model to take into account the concepts of user groups and/or roles.

In our model, an object is a node. As we are going to see in section 3.2, each node is associated with its own *access control list*. The node is the smallest granule of information which we can protect.

3.2   Security Policy

In our model, we define the security policy by labeling the nodes of the source tree with some authorization attributes.

An authorization attribute refers to a unique user and a unique privilege. We define an authorization attribute as follows:

An authorization attribute is a pair `<subject, privilege>`

- `subject` identifies a user.
- `privilege` takes its value from the following set: `{read, delete, insert, update}`

Authorization attributes are associated with nodes. An authorization attribute may be associated with several nodes and a node may be associated with several authorization attributes. The association of an authorization attribute with an object makes a *permission*. The set of authorization attributes associated with a node makes an access control list.

Let v be a node. Let <s,p> be an authorization attribute. If node v is associated with <s,p> then s is granted the privilege p on node v.

- if p = read then s is granted the right to see v.
- if p = delete then s is granted the right to delete the sub-tree whose root is v.
- if p = insert then s is granted the right to add a new sub-tree to v.
- if p = update then s is granted the right to update v (i.e. replace v by another datum).

Privileges should not be confused with *operations*. Operations need privileges to complete. Operations depend on the application. For example, in one application, we might need an *append* operation which always performs the insertion of a sub-tree at the last position (the rightmost position), whereas in another application we might need an insert operation which is able to perform the insertion of a sub-tree at any position. Both operations need the insert privilege to complete.

In our model what is not permitted is forbidden. If node v is *not* associated with <s,p> then s is *denied* the privilege p on v. In other words, our model always enforces the *closed* policy [Jaj97]. Note that, some other access control models (see [Dam00a] or [GB01] for instance) offer the possibility to insert explicit prohibitions in the security policy. In these models, one single authorization rule (permission or prohibition) generally addresses several subjects and/or objects. This allows the Security Administrator to *override* such an authorization rule with another more specific rule which addresses a smaller subset of subjects and/or objects. In our model, a permission is always "as specific as possible" since it addresses a unique object, a unique subject and a unique privilege.

For the sake of simplicity, we have assumed that the security policy applies to a single tree. Thanks to this assumption, we do not need to consider any kind of create-tree privilege. If we face a situation of having to define a security policy for a set of trees, then we just need to consider that these trees are actually all sub-trees of a virtual root. Under this assumption, creating a new tree means adding a new sub-tree to the virtual root.

Fig. 3. Labeled Tree

Labeling the nodes with authorization attributes allows us to define security policies which are dynamic and which are updated automatically whenever the source tree is modified. For example, let us consider the tree of figure 3. In our model, nodes are labeled with authorization attributes. The security policy is dynamic and it continues to apply even if v1 is updated and replaced by v3.

Another way of defining the previous security policy would be to write authorization rules separately as it is shown on figure 4.

```
v1
  \
   \
    \
    v2
```

```
<s, /v1, read>

<s, /v1/v2, read>

<s, /v1, update>
```

Fig. 4. Unlabeled Tree

With this approach the security policy would not be dynamic: if v1 is updated and replaced by v3 then the three rules above become invalid since their object field has become invalid.

In the remainder of this paper we shall assume that the pseudo write privilege refers indifferently to the delete, insert or update privilege.

As we mentioned at the beginning of this section, defining the security policy is done by labeling the source tree with some authorization attributes. There is no constraint which should be respected when labeling the tree. However, we add the following two rules to *every* security policy:

– **Integrity Rule 1**: A subject is forbidden to perform a write operation on a node which he is not permitted to see (even if he has been granted the corresponding write privilege on this node by the labeling process).
– **Integrity Rule 2**: The view of the source tree a subject is permitted to see has to be a *pruned* version of the original source tree.

Following comments can be made about these rules:

– These two rules may conflict with some permissions which are defined by the labeling process. However, the priority of these two rules is always higher than the priority of other rules.
– Integrity Rule 1 means that we forbid *blind writes.*
– Integrity Rule 2 means that a subject is forbidden to see a node if he is not permitted to see all the ancestors of this node. We want Integrity Rule 2 to be enforced because we want users to be provided with consistent views of the source tree.

3.3   Access Control Algorithms

In this section we propose two access control algorithms. The first algorithm, which we call View Control algorithm, computes the view of the source tree a given user is permitted to see. The second algorithm which we call Write Control algorithm is able to determine whether a given user is allowed to perform a write operation on a particular node.

View Control Algorithm

```
1.  Let S be the user for which the view has to be computed
2.  Let L be an empty list of nodes
3.  Insert the root node into L
4.  Let R be an empty list of nodes
5.  While L is not empty Do
6.     N ← the first node of L
7.     If N is associated with the attribute <S,Read> then
8.          Append N to R
9.          Replace N in L with all the child nodes of N
10.    Else
11.         Remove N from L
```

This algorithm traverses the tree in pre-order. After the algorithm finishes, R contains the pre-order list of the nodes which belong to the view.

Regarding this algorithm, we can make the following comments:

– Lines 7, 8 and 9: The `if` statement is true when N is associated with the attribute `<S,Read>`. In this case, node N has to appear in the view. Therefore, node N is appended to R. Node N is also replaced in L with all its child nodes so that the while loop can start a new iteration with the first child node of N.

– Lines 10 and 11: The `else` statement is true when N is not associated with the attribute `<S,Read>`. In this case, node N should not appear in the final view. Therefore, node N is removed from L and is not appended to R. Note that N is *not* replaced in L with its child nodes. Therefore, the child nodes of N (and consequently all the descendant nodes of N) do not appear in the view. Authorization attributes which are associated with the descendant nodes of N are not even checked. Consequently, Integrity Rule 2 is enforced. Finally, if L is not empty then the `while` loop can start a new iteration with the new first node in L.

Let us apply the `View Control` algorithm to the sample source tree in figure 5:

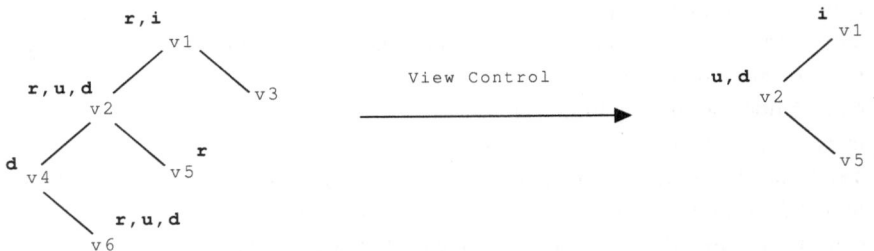

Fig. 5. View Control Algorithm

Let s be a user. Symbols **r** (respectively **i, d, u)** represent the attributes which grant `read` (respectively `insert`, `delete`, `update`) privileges to s. We can see that the sub-tree, whose root is v4, does not appear in the final view although s has been granted the privilege to read v6. Accordingly with Integrity Rule 2, the tree which is computed by the `View Control` algorithm is a pruned version of the source tree.

Let us now present the `Write Control` Algorithm.

In order to answer the question "Is user s permitted to perform an operation which requires the `delete|insert|update` privilege on node n ?", we apply the following algorithm:

Write (Insert,Delete,Update) Control Algorithm

```
1. Let S be the user performing the operation which requires
   the WRITE¹  privilege on node N.
2. Use the View Control Algorithm to compute the view of the
   source tree for user S
3. If N does not appear in the view then
4.   S is forbidden to perform the operation (node unknown)
5. Else
6.   If N is associated with the attribute <S,WRITE> then
7.       S is permitted to perform the operation
8.   Else
9.       S is forbidden to perform the operation
```

Regarding this algorithm, we can make the following comment:

− Lines 2, 3 and 4 mean that we consider only the nodes the user is permitted to see. Consequently, Integrity Rule 1 is enforced. Regarding line 4, the answer user S is provided with, should not be something like "access denied" because such an answer would reveal the existence of node N to user S. The answer should rather be "node unknown" since node N does not belong to the view user S is permitted to see.

Let us consider the previous example and use the `Write Control` algorithm to answer the following questions:

− Is user s permitted to update v2 ?
  Yes. s has been granted the privilege to update v2 and v2 belongs to the view.
− Is user s permitted to update v6 ?
  No. v6 does not belong to the view.
− Is user s permitted to add a new sub-tree to v1 ?
  Yes. s has been granted the `insert` privilege on v1 and v1 belongs to the view. Section 3.4 explains how a newly inserted sub-tree is labeled.
− Is user s permitted to delete the sub-tree of which v2 is the root ?
  Yes. s has been granted the privilege to delete the sub-tree of which v2 is the root.

However, regarding the `delete` privilege, we have to comment on the following two points:

1. If user s deletes the sub-tree whose root is v2 then nodes v4 and v6, which the user is not permitted to see, are deleted.

---

[1] Recall that WRITE stands for either INSERT, DELETE or UPDATE

2. If user s deletes the sub-tree whose root is v2, then node v5 is deleted although s does not hold the `delete` privilege on it.

Regarding point 1, it does not contradict Integrity Rule 1 which says that blind writes are forbidden. Indeed, recall that user s performs the delete operation on node v2 which belongs to the view. Now, the fact that user s indirectly deletes some data which he is not aware of, might be seen as an Integrity violation. Therefore, we could define the following Integrity Rule 3:

- **Integrity Rule 3**: A subject is forbidden to perform a delete operation on a node if this operation leads to the deletion of data he is not permitted to see.

With such a rule, s would be forbidden to delete the sub-tree whose root is v2 since this operation would lead to the deletion of v4 and v6. However, this would reveal to user s the existence of data he is not permitted to see. In other words, enforcing Integrity Rule 3 would lead to a Confidentiality violation.

Our previous `delete Control algorithm` emphasizes the Confidentiality and does not enforce Integrity Rule 3.

However, in some cases, we might need to enforce Integrity rule 3. Therefore we propose a second version of the `delete Control algorithm` which enforces Integrity Rule 3.

Delete Control Algorithm (enforces Integrity Rule 3)

```
1. Let S be the user performing the operation which requires
   the DELETE privilege on node N
2. Let T be the tree whose root is N
3. If T contains at least one node which is not associated with
   the attribute <S,READ> then
4.           S is forbidden to perform the operation
5. Else
6.           S is permitted to perform the operation
```

Regarding point 2, recall that user s performs the delete operation on node v2 where user s holds the `delete` privilege. Now, the fact that user s indirectly deletes some data on which he does not hold the `delete` privilege might be seen as an Integrity violation. Therefore, we can define the following Integrity Rule 4:

- **Integrity Rule 4**: A subject is forbidden to perform a delete operation on a node if this operation leads to the deletion of data he is permitted to see but not permitted to delete.

With such a rule, s would be forbidden to delete the sub-tree whose root is v2 since this operation would lead to the deletion of v5. In some cases, it would perfectly be acceptable to introduce Integrity Rule 4 in the security policy. Therefore, we propose a third version of the `delete Control Algorithm`:

Delete Control Algorithm (enforces Integrity Rule 4)

1. Let S be the user performing the operation which requires the DELETE privilege on node N
2. Let T be an empty tree
3. Use the View Control Algorithm to compute the view of the source tree for user S
4. If N does not appear in the view then
5. S is forbidden to perform the operation (node unknown)
6. Else
7.   T ← the View of the sub-tree whose root is N
8.   If T contains at least one node which is not associated with the attribute <S,DELETE> then
9.   S is forbidden to perform the operation
10.   Else
11.   S is permitted to perform the operation

The following fourth version of the delete control algorithm enforces both Integrity rules 3 and 4. If the security policy particularly emphasizes the Integrity then this algorithm might be needed.

Delete Control Algorithm (enforces Integrity Rules 3 and 4)

1. Let S be the user performing the operation which requires the DELETE privilege on node N
2. Let T be the tree whose root is N
3. If T contains at least one node which is not associated with the attribute <S,READ> then
4.   S is forbidden to perform the operation
5. Else
6.   Use the View Control Algorithm to compute the view of the source tree for user S
7.   T ← the View of the sub-tree whose root is N
8.   If T contains at least one node which is not associated with the attribute <S,DELETE> then
9.   S is forbidden to perform the operation
10.   Else
11.   S is permitted to perform the operation

3.4   Security Policy Control Language

In this section, we define the core of a security policy control language which we can use for administrating the authorization attributes. Before presenting this language, we need to introduce a new special privilege which we call the owner privilege.

Let v be a node. Let <s,owner> be an authorization attribute. If node v is associated with <s,owner> then s holds the owner privilege on v. This means that s is automatically granted the four other privileges (read, insert, delete and update) on v. This also means that s is allowed to grant/revoke these four privileges on v to/from other users. The owner privilege cannot be transferred.

Given a node, the user who holds the `owner` privilege is the user who created the node. If a user inserts a new sub-tree into the source tree then this user is granted the `owner` privilege (and consequently all the other privileges) on all the nodes of this new sub-tree. This defines the default labeling of a newly inserted sub-tree.

From the fact that the `owner` privilege is held by the user who has created the node and from the fact that the `owner` privilege cannot be transferred, we can easily deduce that each node has one and only one owner.

The fact that the `owner` privilege cannot be transferred may be seen as a limitation of our model. However, this has the advantage of providing us with a simple *delegation scheme* and minimizing the so-called *safety problem* [HRU76]. Nevertheless, in our future work, we might extend the delegation scheme of our model with the privilege of granting/revoking the "privilege to transfer privileges".

Our security policy control language includes the `GRANT` command and the `REVOKE` command. The syntax for these two commands is the following:

– GRANT <set of privileges> ON <set of nodes> TO <set of subjects>
– REVOKE <set of privileges> ON <set of nodes> FROM <set of subjects>

`<set of privileges>` is a subset of {`read, insert, delete, update`}.

`<set of nodes>` addresses nodes which belong to the source tree. It is an expression which is written with the language we describe in section 2.2. <set of nodes> may include nodes on which the user does not hold the owner privilege, but for such nodes, the GRANT and REVOKE commands have no effect.

`<set of subjects>` addresses users. In our future work, we plan to include the concept of *role* (see [San98] for a definition of role) in our model.

Let us consider the labeled source tree in figure 6:

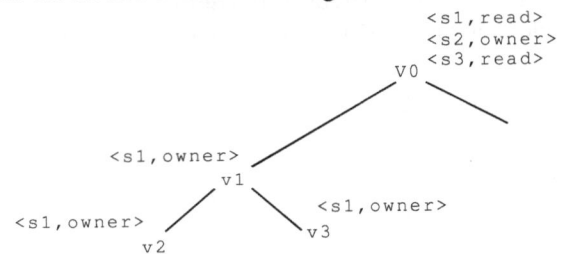

Fig. 6. Owner Privilege

User `s1` is the owner of the sub-tree of which `v1` is the root. Let us now consider some examples of commands which user `s1` may invoke:

– `GRANT read ON /v0/v1 TO s2`
– `GRANT read,update ON /v0/v1 | /v0/v1//* TO s3`
– `REVOKE update ON /v0/v1 FROM s3`

With the first command, user `s1` grants the privilege to read node `v2` to `s2`. With the second command, user `s1` grants the privilege to read and update node `v1` and all its descendant nodes to s3. With the last command, user s1 revokes the privilege to update v1 from s3. Figure 7 shows the resulting labeled tree .

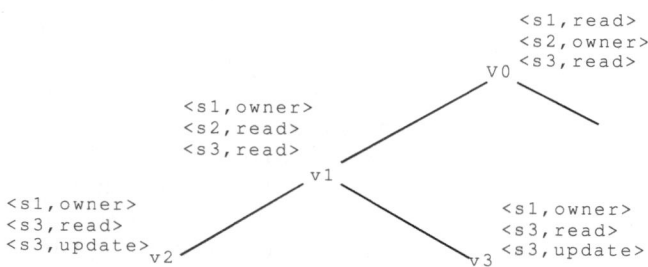

Fig. 7. Grant/Revoke Commands

4   An Access Control Model for XML Data Structures

In this section, we show through an example that we can easily apply our model to specific XML data structures.

The language we describe in section 2.2, allows us to write path expressions which can address non typed nodes of generic data structures. Now, what is important to understand is that each time we apply our model to specific data structures, we need to adapt our language so that it takes into account the fact that nodes are typed. Therefore, in this section we use the XPath language which has been specifically designed for addressing nodes of XML data structures.

Let us consider the following XML document which contains two medical files:

```
<database>
        <record id="Robert">
                <doctor>d1</doctor>
                <diagnosis>Pneumonia</diagnosis>
        </record>
        <record id="Franck">
                <doctor>d2</doctor>
                <diagnosis>Ulcer</diagnosis>
                <comment>serious case</comment>
        </record>
</database>
```

Markups like <database></database> or <record></record> are elements. Elements may have some attributes associated with them. For example the record elements which are in the document above are respectively associated with the attribute Id="Robert" and id="Franck". Strings like d1, Pneumonia are character data. More information about XML can be found in [Bray00].

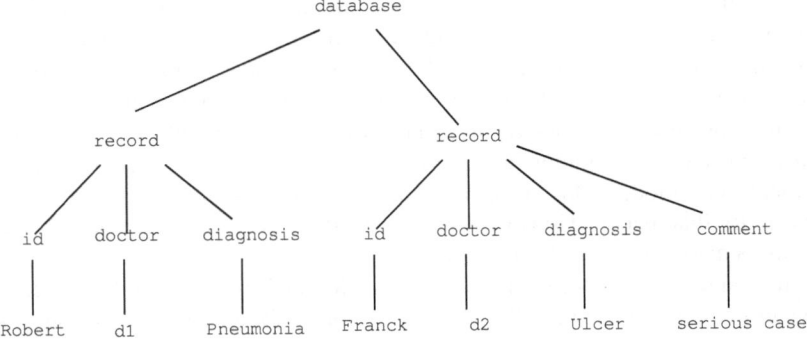

Fig. 8. Tree Representation of an XML Document (1)

There are several possible tree representations of the above XML document. Figure 8 shows one representation. Figure 9 shows another representation.

In the tree in figure 8, the granularity level is very small whereas in the tree in figure 9, the granularity level is the medical file as a whole.

Intuitively, we can choose the tree representation of our document according to the security policy which applies to the document. If the security policy addresses small portions of medical files then we definitely need to adopt the tree representation in figure 8. Now, the tree representation in figure 9 may be more convenient to define a security policy which treats each medical file as a whole.

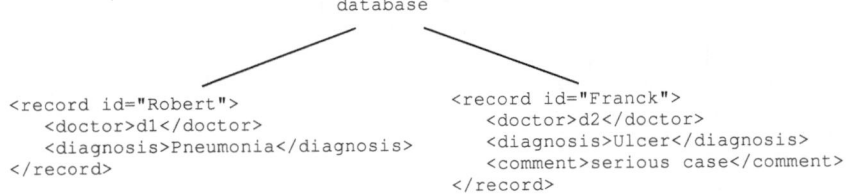

Fig. 9. Tree Representation of an XML Document (2)

The approach which consists of choosing the tree representation which best adapts to the security policy, gives flexibility to the model. However, as for XML, we do not follow this approach. We always use the XPath data model to represent an XML document, regardless of the security policy which applies to the document. Figure 10 shows the XPath tree which corresponds to our previous document. This tree is slightly different from the tree in figure 8. In the XPath tree in figure 10, each attribute and its value make a single node whereas in the tree in figure 8, each attribute and its value make two distinct nodes. Therefore, the XPath tree in figure 10 provides us with a granularity level which is almost the same as the granularity level we could obtain from the tree in figure 8.

It might look as a disadvantage to always adopt the XPath data model to represent XML documents. We reduce the flexibility of the model and we cannot define a

130   A. Gabillon et al.

security policy which separately addresses an attribute and its value. The main advantage of using the XPath data model actually resides in the fact that XPath has been designed to be used by XSLT [Clark99]. XSLT is a language for transforming XML documents into other XML documents. Therefore, we can use an XSLT processor for computing different views of the source tree and for modifying the source tree. We are currently designing a security processor for XML documents which implements our model. Due to space limitations, we cannot describe this security processor in this paper. However, let us mention that the core of this security processor is made of an XSLT processor.

Let us assume that doctor d1 is the owner of Robert's medical file and doctor d2 is the owner of Franck's medical file. Administrator a is the owner of the root node. In particular, administrator a is in charge of granting to other doctors the privilege to insert medical files.

In the tree in figure 10, symbols o, r, i, d, u respectively stand for owner, read, insert, delete, update. Figure 10 shows the initial labeling of this tree.

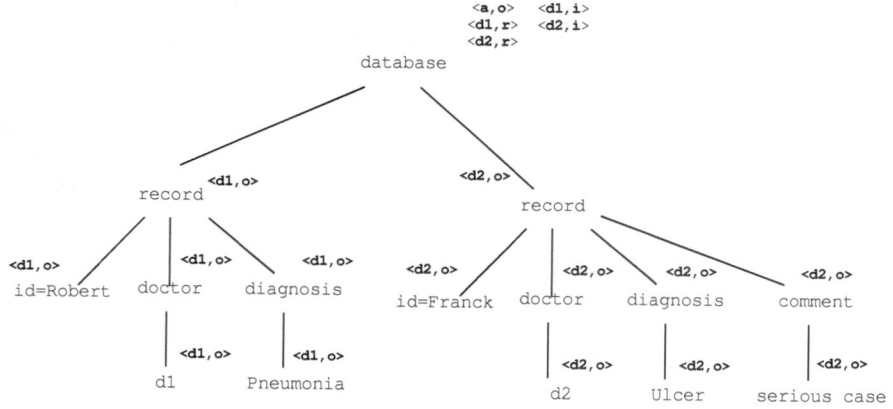

Fig. 10. Labeled XPath Tree

Let us now consider the following set of commands. Each command is prefixed with the reference of the user who types the command. We can use the XPath language to address the nodes.

d3 is another doctor and s is the secretary of doctor d2.

```
a:   GRANT read,insert ON /database TO d3

d2:  GRANT read ON /database/record[doctor='d2']/descendant-or-
     self::node() TO d3,s

d2:  REVOKE read ON
     /database/record[doctor='d2']/diagnosis/text() FROM s

d2:  GRANT read ON /database/record[id='Franck']/descendant-or-
     self::node() TO d1
```

```
d2: GRANT update ON /database/record[id='Franck']/comment/text()
    TO d1
```

The first command says that administrator a grants to doctor d3 the privilege to insert medical files. Note that, granting the sole privilege `insert` would not be enough. According to Integrity Rule 1, a also needs to grant the `read` privilege on the root node to doctor d3.

The next command says that doctor d2 grants to both doctor d3 and secretary s the privilege to see all medical files such as `doctor = 'd2'` that is, all the files doctor d2 is in charge of.

The next command says that doctor d2 revokes from secretary s the privilege to see the content of the diagnosis element from all the files doctor d2 is in charge of.

The next command says that doctor d2 grants to doctor d1 the privilege to see Franck's medical file.

The last command says that doctor d2 grants to doctor d1 the privilege to update the content of the comment element of Franck's medical file.

This simple example has shown that we can easily apply our model to XML data structures. Due to space limitations, we cannot show how we apply our model to other specific tree data structures like the hierarchical file system structure. Let us however briefly mention the two following points:

- We need to slightly adapt the language we describe in section 2.2 so that it can differentiate between the nodes which are simple files and the nodes which are folders
- For implementing our model into a UNIX system, we need to patch the kernel

5   Comparison with Related Works

There are literally as many access control schemes as there are tree data structures. Historically, applications like the SNMP protocol, the LDAP protocol, WEB servers or file systems were initially developed without integrating access control facilities. For the developers of these applications, the most important was to organize the data and to define primitives for manipulating them. Later on, some access control mechanisms were added to these applications. However most of these access control mechanisms rely on models which are not clearly defined and which are specific to a particular kind of tree data structure. Very often these models are even based on the semantics of the data.

Regarding XML, the situation is almost the same. Many access control models for XML have been defined but these models are all very recent. However, XML data are said to be *semi-structured*. This means in particular that the structure of XML trees is weakly constrained. Therefore, access control models which have been proposed for XML are certainly the most sophisticated ones and the most interesting to compare with our model.

The purpose of this section is to give an overview of all these models and to make a comparison between them and our model. However since in the previous section we have applied our model to XML data, we particularly investigate the models for XML.

View-Based Access Control Model (VACM) for the SNMP Protocol

The View-based Access Control Model (VACM) [WPM99] allows the security administrator to regulate the access to the Management Information Base (MIB). The MIB is a fixed tree data structure. The privileges are not associated with the nodes of the MIB but with all its possible views. Each view is a pruned tree of the MIB tree. VACM uses a kind of Access Matrix [HRU76] to grant privileges on the views to subjects. Only the read and write privileges are supported. The write privilege corresponds to our update privilege.

Lightweight Directory Access Protocol (LDAP)

There are as many access control schemes as there are LDAP servers. The OpenLDAP [OL] server keeps the access control lists in the configuration file and uses regular expressions for the comparison of objects and subjects while Netscape and IBM keep the access control information in the directory tree as an attribute of the entries. However, the basic ideas are similar across server implementations [Sto00]. Basically, the access control lists can control access to the entire directory tree or portions of it. There is usually a default access mode, and the access control lists are used to override that default. Privileges which are supported are more or less equivalent to the privileges of our model (including the owner privilege). However, their semantics strongly depends on the nodes' type.

Web Servers

Web servers organize the data into a hierarchical file system structure. Web servers like the Apache server [APA] allow us to regulate the access to some portions of the tree structure. This can be done by using some special .htaccess files. An .htaccess file is simply a text file containing Apache directives. Those directives apply to the documents in the directory where the .htaccess file is located and to all subdirectories under it as well. Other .htaccess files in subdirectories may change or nullify the effects of those in parent directories. Since the purpose of Web servers is to publish the information, basically, only the read privilege is supported.

Note that, the goal of the emerging WebDAV [WW98] (Web-based Distributed Authoring and Versioning) protocol is to leverage the success of HTTP in being a standard access layer for a wide range of storage repositories. HTTP gives them read access, while DAV gives them write access. See [WG99] for more information on WebDAV.

File Systems

Regarding file systems, it is also very difficult to talk about one model. Each file system has its own way of regulating the access to the data. Moreover, the semantics of privileges varies, depending on whether they apply to directories or to files. For example, the `execute` privilege of `UNIX` grants either the right to *enter* (?) a directory or to execute a file.

Regarding the write privilege, if it applies to a directory, then it generally encompasses our insert privilege on the directory itself (right to add some entries in the directory), our delete privilege on the entries (right to delete the entries) and our update privilege on the entries (right to rename the entries).

In most cases, each node (file or directory) is labeled with its own access control list.

Security Models for Object-Oriented Databases

There has been a considerable amount of work which has been done in the area of access control models for object-oriented databases (see [FGS94][Rab91] for instance). It would be too long to detailed information about each of them. Let us however mention that many of these models use inheritance of rights along tree hierarchies. We could show that some of these models have some similarities with our model when it is applied to object-oriented data.

Access Control Models for XML Documents

Recently, several access control models for XML documents have been proposed:

- In [Dam00a], Damiani et al. propose an access control model which deals with the `read` privilege. An authorization can be local (in this case it applies to an element and its attributes) or it can be recursive (in this case, it applies also to the sub-elements). The level of granularity is not as fine as it is in the model we propose in section 4. Indeed, a single granule of information includes an element, its content (text node) and its attributes. Conflicts between authorization rules are solved by a conflict security policy which applies principles like "the most specific object takes precedence" or "the most specific subject takes precedence". We believe that these policies which were first used in Object-Oriented environments are not well adapted to XML.
- In [Ber00a], Bertino et al. propose an access control model which deals with the `read` and the `write` privileges (the model includes also a `navigate` privilege. This is a kind of `read` privilege for objects which are targeted by links). Depending on the targeted object, the semantics of an authorization varies making sometimes difficult to understand the security policy. The `write` privilege is more or less equivalent to the `update` privilege we introduce in this paper.
- In [KH00], Kudo and Hada propose an access control model which deals with the `read`, `write`, `create` and `delete` privileges. These privileges are more or less equivalent to our `read`, `write`, `insert` and `delete` privileges. However,

the level of granularity is not as fine as it is in the model we propose in section 4. Indeed, attributes or text nodes cannot be considered as granules. Therefore, they cannot be independently protected. The model offers the possibility of inserting *provisional authorizations* into the security policy. A provisional authorization grants a privilege to a subject provided he or the system completes an *obligation* which is specified by the authorization rule.

– In [GB01], Gabillon and Bruno propose an access control model which deals with the read privilege. The level of granularity is exactly the same as it is in the model we describe in section 4. Each node can be independently protected (element node, attribute node, text node etc.). The conflict resolution policy is based on priorities.

None of the above models associate the nodes of the source tree with access control lists. Authorization rules match the basic pattern <subjects, objects, privilege>.

In all these models, conflicts between the rules make sometimes difficult to predict what is going to be the output of the security policy. In the model we present in this paper, authorization attributes cannot conflict with each other and neither can Integrity Rules. Only Integrity Rules may conflict with authorization attributes. However, these conflicts are always solved in favor of the Integrity Rules. This very simple conflict resolution policy makes easy to predict what is going to be the output of the security policy.

6   Conclusion

In this paper, we propose an access control model for generic tree data structures. Our model does not rely on any assumption regarding the structure of the trees. The labeling process allows us to define dynamic security policies supporting various types of write privileges. The owner privilege along with the grant/revoke commands provide us with a distributed security management scheme.

We plan to extend our work in several directions:

– Access control lists does not provide a user with a clear vision of the security policy which currently applies to the nodes he is the owner. Therefore, we shall propose a solution to translate the security policy which is expressed within the access control lists into a set of authorization rules matching the basic pattern <subjects, privileges, objects>. At any time, each user should have the possibility of being provided with the translation of the access control lists he owns. Note that a translation which is made at time t might not be valid at time t+1 since the owner may invoke new grant/revoke commands, and since the structure of the tree may change.

– We shall include the concept of provisional authorizations which Kudo and Hada define in [KH00]. A provisional authorization grants a privilege to a subject provided he or the system completes an *obligation* which is specified by the authorization rule.

– We shall include the concept of role in our model.

References

[APA]   The Apache Software Foundation. http://www.apache.org/

[Ber00a]   E. Bertino, S. Castano, E. Ferrari and M. Mesiti. "Specifying and Enforcing Access Control Policies for XML Document Sources". World Wide Web Journal, vol. 3, n. 3, Baltzer Science Publishers. 2000.

[Ber00b]   E. Bertino, M. Braun, S. Castano, E. Ferrari, M. Mesiti. "AuthorX: A Java-Based System for XML Data Protection". In Proc. of the 14th Annual IFIP WG 11.3 Working Conference on Database Security, Schoorl, The Netherlands, August 2000.

[Bray00]   T. Bray et al. "Extensible Markup Language (XML) 1.0". World Wide Web Consortium (W3C). http://www.w3c.org/TR/REC-xml (October 2000).

[CD99]   J. Clark and Steve DeRose . "XML Path Language (XPath) Version 1.0". World Wide Web Consortium (W3C). http://www.w3c.org/TR/xpath (November 1999).

[Dam00a]   E. Damiani, S. De Capitani di Vimercati, S. Paraboschi, P. Samarati, "Securing XML Documents," in Proc. of the 2000 International Conference on Extending Database Technology (EDBT2000), Konstanz, Germany, March 27–31, 2000.

[Dam00b]   E. Damiani, S. De Capitani di Vimercati, S. Paraboschi, P. Samarati "XML Access Control Systems: A Component-Based Approach" in Proc. IFIP WG11.3 Working Conference on Database Security, Schoorl, The Netherlands, August 21–23, 2000.

[FGS94]   Eduardo B. Fernández, Ehud Gudes, Haiyan Song: A Model for Evaluation and Administration of Security in Object-Oriented Databases. TKDE 6(2): 275–292(1994)

[GB01]   Alban Gabillon and Emmanuel Bruno. "Regulating Access to XML documents". Fifteenth Annual IFIP WG 11.3 Working Conference on Database Security. Niagara on the Lake, Ontario, Canada July 15–18, 2001.

[HRU76]   Harrison, M.H., Ruzzo, W.L. and Ullman, J.D. Protection in Operating Systems. Communications of ACM 19(8):461–471 (1976).

[Jaj97]   S. Jajodia, P. Samarati, V. Subrahmanian and E. Bertino. "A Unified Framework for Enforcing Multiple Access Control Policies". Proc. of the 1997 ACM International SIGMOD Conference on Management of Data, Tucson, May 1997.

[KH00]   M. Kudo and S. Hada. "XML Document Security based on Provisional Authorisation". Proceedings of the 7th ACM conference on Computer and communications security. November, 2000, Athens Greece.

[OL]   OpenLDAP. http://www.openldap.org/

[Rab91]   F.Rabitti, E.Bertino, W. Kim and D. Woelk."A model of authorization for Next Generation Database Systems.". ACM TODS vol 16, n°1. Mar 1991.

[San98]   R. Sandhu. "Role-Based Access Control". Advances in Computers. Vol 48. Academic Press. 1998.

[Sto00]   E. Stokes, D. Byrne, B. Blakley, and P. Behera. "Access Control Requirements for the Lightweight Directory Access Protocol". RFC 2820, May 2000.

[WG99]   Jim Whitehead, and Yaron Y. Goland. "WebDAV: A network protocol for remote collaborative authoring on the Web". European Computer Supported Cooperative Work (ECSCW'99) conference.

[WPM99]   B. Wijnen, R. Presuhn, and K. McCloghrie. "View-based Access Control Model for the Simple Network Management Protocol". RFC 2575, April 1999.

[WW98]   E. James Whitehead Jr, and Meredith Wiggins. "WebDAV: IETF Standard for Collaborative Authoring on the Web". IEEE Internet Computing, September/October 1998.

[xss4j]   AlphaWorks. XML Security Suite (xss4j). http://www.alphaWorks.ibm.com/tech/xmlsecuritysuite.

A New Design of Privilege Management Infrastructure for Organizations Using Outsourced PKI

Ed Dawson[1], Javier Lopez[2], Jose A. Montenegro[2], and Eiji Okamoto[3]

[1] Information Security Research Centre,
Queensland University of Technology, Australia
e.dawson@qut.edu.au
[2] Computer Science Department, E.T.S. Ingenieria Informatica
Universidad de Malaga, Spain
{jlm,monte}@lcc.uma.es
[3] Institute of Information Sciences and Electronics,
University of Tsukuba, Japan
okamoto@is.tsukuba.ac.jp

Abstract. Authentication services provided by Public Key Infrastructures (PKI) do not satisfy the needs of many e-commerce applications. These applications require additional use of authorization services in order for users to prove what they are allowed to do. Attribute certificates have changed the way in which the authorization problem has been considered until now, and Privilege Management Infrastructures (PMI) provide the necessary support for a wide use of those certificates. Although both types of infrastructures, PKIs and PMIs, keep some kind of relation, they can operate autonomously. This fact is specially interesting for companies who have taken or will take the decision to outsource PKI services. However, outsourcing PMI services is not a good option for many companies because sometimes information contained in attribute certificates is confidential. Therefore attribute certificates must be managed very carefully and, preferably, only inside the company. In this paper we present a new design of PMI that is specially suited for those companies that outsource PKI services but still need to manage the PMI internally. The scheme provides additional advantages that satisfy the needs of intra-company attribute certification, and eliminates some of the problems associated with the revocation procedures.

1 Introduction

It is well known that by using an *authentication service* you can prove who you are. Identity certificates (or public-key certificates) provide the best solution to integrate that basic service into most applications developed for the Internet that make use of digital signatures. However, new applications, particularly in the area of e-commerce, need an *authorization service* to describe what it is allowed for a user to do. In this case privileges to perform tasks should be considered.

A.H. Chan and V. Gligor (Eds.): ISC 2002, LNCS 2433, pp. 136–149, 2002.

For instance, when a company needs to establish distinctions among their employees regarding privileges over resources, the authorization service becomes important. Different sets of privileges over resources (either hardware or software) will be assigned to different categories of employees. In those distributed applications where company resources must be partially shared through the Internet with other associated companies, providers, or clients, the authorization service becomes an essential part.

Authorization is not a new problem, and different solutions have been used in the past. However, "traditional" solutions are not very helpful for many of the Internet applications. Those solutions are not easy to use in application scenarios where the use of identity certificates, to attest the connection of public keys to identified subscribers, is a must. In such scenarios, types of independent data objects that can contain user privileges would be of great help. *Attribute certificates* proposed by the ITU-T (International Telecommunications Union) X.509 recommendation [10] provide an appropriate solution, as these data objects have been designed to be used in conjunction with identity certificates.

The use of a wide-ranging authentication service based on identity certificates is not practical unless it is complemented by an efficient and trustworthy mean to manage and distribute all certificates in the system. This is provided by a *Public-Key Infrastructure* (PKI), which at the same time supports encryption, integrity and non-repudiation services. Without its use, it is impractical and unrealistic to expect that large scale digital signature applications can become a reality [13],[1].

Similarly, the attribute certificates framework defined by ITU provides a foundation upon which a *Privilege Management Infrastructure* (PMI) can be built. PKI and PMI infrastructures are linked by information contained in the identity and attribute certificates of every user. The link is justified by the fact that authorization relies on authentication to prove who you are.

Although linked, both infrastructures can be autonomous, and managed independently. Creation and maintenance of identities can be separated from PMI, as authorities that issue certificates in each of both infrastructures are not necessarily the same ones. In fact, the entire PKI may be existing and operational prior to the establishment of the PMI.

From the company point of view this is a very important fact. The reason is that, on the one hand, an "identity" tends to have a global meaning; thus, identity certificates can be issued by *Certification Authorities* (CAs) that are external to the organization. If this is the case, CAs can sometimes be under the control of private companies that offer specialized external services and facilities. In some other cases, CAs are under the control of national or regional governments, which is the most typical solution when applications run inside scenarios that are related to e-government services.

However, an "attribute" tends to have a more local meaning. Privileges are used in a more closed environment, i.e, inside an organization, or among a group of them. Therefore, there are numerous occasions where an authority entitled to attest who someone is, is not the appropriate one to make statements about what that person is allowed to do. In the case of a private company, it seems more reasonable that someone from the senior staff in the company decides on privileges and, therefore, issues a certificate containing them.

Precisely, this is the scope of the work presented here. This paper presents an attribute framework in which the PMI has been specifically designed for companies that have decided to outsource services provided by a PKI. In this case, the term "outsource" has the meaning of using an external authentication service,regardless of whether this is provided by a private organization (and hence, with some cost-per-service for the company), or by a governmental organization (a free service in many cases).

The new PMI scheme has several advantages in comparison with the scheme proposed by ITU. It makes use of a distributed architecture of authorities that satisfy the typical needs of attribute certification inside companies, avoids scalability problems associated to both extranet or company expansion, and eliminates problems associated with the revocation procedures.

The rest of the paper is structured as follows: Section 2 reviews the traditional solutions that have been used, and are actually used in many scenarios, for authorization management. Section 3 describes the initial approach of using attributes in the extensions fields of identity certificates, and why this solution is not suitable in most privilege applications. Also, this section shows how Privilege Management Infrastructures have been designed to provide a solution to those applications. In section 4 these infrastructures are studied and compared to Public Key Infrastructures, we argue about the mutual independence of the new infrastructures, and how this facilitates the outsourcing of services. Section 5 shows the new scheme we have designed that is specially suited for those companies that outsource authentication services but, because of the confidentiality of the information contained in the attribute certificates, still have to manage them internally. Finally, section 6 concludes the paper.

2   Previous Solutions for Authorization Management

Traditional authorization schemes have mainly focused on access control, that is concerned with limiting the activities of a legitimate user within a system. Access control also assumes that authentication of the user (whatever method is used) has been successfully verified prior to enforcement of access control.

Two different schemes have been commonly used. The first one, *discretionary access control* governs the access of users to information on the basis of the users' identities and authorizations. Authorizations specify, for each individual user and each object (resource) in the system, the access rights of the user, that is, what the user is allowed to perform on the object. Each activity is checked against the access rights, which are held as access control lists within each target resource. If authorization stating the user can access the object in the specified mode exists, then access is granted, otherwise is denied.

The second one, *mandatory access control* governs access on the basis of the classification of resources and users according to security levels. Thus, access to a resource is granted if the security level of a particular user stands in accordance with the security level of that object. A classification list that is typically used in military applications is unmarked, unclassified, restricted, confidential, secret and top secret [2].

As can be seen, these schemes are suitable for authorization, but only when the access control of local resources is the problem to be solved. It is reasonable to think that management of access rights under both types of authorization policies must be done by system administrators.

A *role-based access control* scheme is an alternative solution to discretionary and mandatory schemes [6]. A role policy regulates the access of users to information on the basis of the activities that the users perform in the system in pursuit of their goals. A role can be defined as a set of actions and responsibilities associated with a particular working activity. Instead of specifying all the actions that any individual user is allowed to execute, actions are specified according to roles [15].

We can see that these solutions focus on the problem of access control. For a long time, access control has been used as synonymous to authorization. However, authorization involves many issues, for instance, group membership, role identification (collection of permissions or access rights, and aliases for the user's identity), limits on the value of transactions, access time for operations, security clearances, time limits, etc. In order to provide support to applications where authorization means something else than access control, attribute certificates become an excellent solution, as we explain in next section.

3   Authorization with Attribute Certificates: From PKI to PMI

Advantages of using attribute certificates to implement authorization have become clear. Even traditional access control solutions studied in previous section have evolved in this direction. A clear example is the integration of role-based schemes with attribute certificates. After the introduction of attribute certificates in the ITU-T X.509 recommendation [9], some proposals using them for role-based access control have been presented [8],[14].

As previously stated, one of the advantages of an attribute certificate is that it can be used for various purposes. It may contain group membership, role, clearance, or any other form of authorization. Yet another essential feature is that the attribute certificate provides the means to transport authorization information to decentralized applications. This is specially relevant because through attribute certificates, authorization information becomes "mobile", which is highly convenient for new e-commerce applications.

Actually, the mobility feature of attributes has been used in applications since ITU-T 1997 recommendation. However, it has been used in a very inefficient way. That recommendation introduced an ill-defined concept of attribute certificate. For this reason, most actual applications do not use specific attribute certificates to carry authorization information. On the other hand, attributes of entities are carried inside identity certificates. The certificate field used for this purpose is the *subjectDirectoryAttributes* extension. This field conveys any desired Directory attribute values for the subject of the certificate, and is defined as follows:

```
subjectDirectoryAttributes EXTENSION ::= {
    SYNTAX     AttributesSyntax
    IDENTIFIED BY id-ce-subjectDirectoryAttributes }
AttributesSyntax ::= SEQUENCE SIZE (1..MAX) OF Attribute
```

This solution does not make entity attributes independent from identity, which can cause problems. Firstly, this is not convenient in situations where the authority issuing the identity certificate is not the authority for assigning privileges. This occurs very frequently, as we will discuss later. Secondly, even in the situations where the authority is the same one, we must consider that life of identity certificates is relatively long when compared to frequency of change of user privileges. This means that every time privileges change it would be necessary to revoke the identity certificate, and it is widely known that certificate revocation is a costly process.

Moreover, many applications deal with authorization issues like delegation (conveyance of privilege from one entity that holds a privilege to another entity) or substitution (one user is temporarily substituted by another user, and this one holds the privileges of the first one for a certain period of time).Identity certificates do not support delegation or substitution.

The ITU-T 2000 recommendation provides the solution to these problems. Attribute certificates are conveniently described, including an extensibility mechanism and a set of specific extensions are handled and a new type of authority for the assignment of privileges is defined, the *Attribute Authority* (AA).

The recommendation defines a framework that provides a foundation upon which a Privilege Management Infrastructure is built to contain a multiplicity of AAs and final users. Revocation procedures are also considered by defining the concept of *Attribute Certificate Revocation Lists* (ACRLs) which are handled in the same way as for CRLs published by CAs.

The identity and attribute certificates of one user are bound as shown in figure 1. We can see that the field *holder* in the attribute certificate contains the serial number of the identity certificate. Although linked, both certificates are independently managed. The important meaning of this is that a PKI and PMI are separate infrastructures in the sense that either structure can work on their own, or to be more precise, they can be established and managed independently. Next section describes in more detail this possibility.

4   Mutual Independence of the Infrastructures

The mutual independence of the two infrastructures is also valid when considering other ways to describe the holder of the attribute certificate. In spite of using the serial number for the identity certificate it is possible to bind the attribute certificate to any object by using the hash value of that object. For instance,

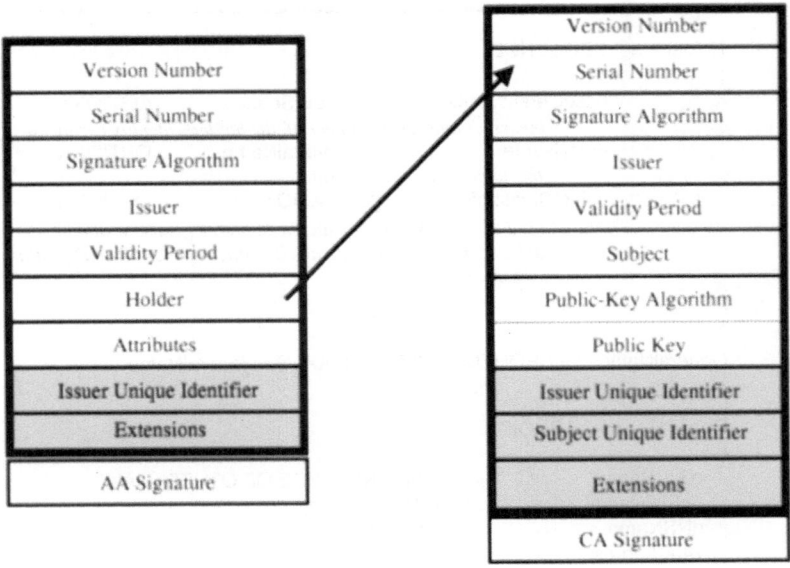

Fig. 1. Relation between identity and attribute certificates

the hash value of the public key, or the hash value of the identity certificate itself can be used. All possibilities for binding can be concluded from the ASN.1 [11] specification for the field *holder* shown in figure 2, where other related data structures are also specified. As we will see in next section, the content of this specification is essential for the scheme that we have developed.

The infrastructures are absolutely separated when considering the situation in which some other authentication method different from that one based on identity certificates is used. In these cases, a PKI is not even used, and the name of the subject is a good option to describe the holder of the attribute certificate.

The discussion about the separation of functions between PKIs and PMIs is a very relevant issue for this paper. From the point of view of the theory, the separation is possible as we have argued in previous paragraphs. From the point of view of real application scenarios separation is not only possible but, in our opinion, very convenient. We previously argued that in most cases the authority issuing the identity certificate is not the authority for assigning privileges. That is, the entity having the role of Certification Authority is not the same one as that one having the role of Attribute Certificate.

The main reason for this argument is that the identity of a user has a global meaning in most certification schemes (although a few schemes do not support this idea, for instance, SPKI [4]). Thus, the CA does not necessarily belong to the organization where the user belongs to. The identity certificate can be issued by a CA managed by a governmental organization, a public organization, or even

```
      Holder ::=  SEQUENCE
      {
                  baseCertificateID      [0] IssuerSerial      OPTIONAL,
                    -- the issuer and serial number of the holder's identity certificate
                  entityName             [1] GeneralNames      OPTIONAL,
                    -- the name of the entity or role
                  objectDigestInfo       [2] ObjectDigestInfo  OPTIONAL
                    -- used to directly authenticate the holder, e.g. an executable
                    -- at least one of baseCertificateID, entityName or objectDigestInfo
                       present --
      }


      GeneralNames ::= SEQUENCE SIZE (1..MAX) OF GeneralName


      GeneralName ::= CHOICE
      {
          otherName                  [0]   INSTANCE OF OTHER - NAME,
          rfc822Name                 [1]   IA5String,
          dNSName                    [2]   IA5String,
          x400Address                [3]   ORAddress,
          directoryName              [4]   Name,
          ediPartyName               [5]   EDIPartyName,
          uniformResourceIdentifier  [6]   IA5String,
          iPAddress                  [7]   OCTET STRING,
          registe redID              [8]   OBJECT IDENTIFIER
      }


      ObjectDigestInfo   ::= SEQUENCE
      {
          digestedObjectType ENUMERATED {
              publicKey              (0),
              publicKeyCert          (1),
              otherObjectTypes       (2) },
          otherObjectTypeID          OBJECT IDENTIFIER  OPTIONAL,
          digestAlgorithm            AlgorithmIdentifier,
          objectDigest               BIT STRING
      }
```

Fig. 2. ASN.1 specification of Holder and related data structures

by a private company specialized in providing services and facilities related to certification of identities.

On the contrary, we believe that a user attribute has non-global meaning. An attribute certificate contains some kind of user authorization, and an authorization is merely valid for an specific application, scenario or environment. Hence, it can rarely be considered to have a global meaning. In fact, it is reasonable to think that the same user will have several attribute certificates, for different applications, scenarios or environments, while using only one identity certificate for all cases. Moreover, because of the restricted scope of an attribute certificate, it is convenient that this certificate is issued by an authority that is more or less local to the scope of the user.

This argument is even more valid if user attributes are considered as confidential information. The certificate may contain some sensitive information and then attribute encryption may be needed, as proposed by PKIX [5]. That kind of confidential information should be solely managed by people belonging to the organization. These reasons, but also the fact that user privileges can change frequently, suggest that, in order to preserve some level of efficiency, authorities external to the user organization are not the most appropriate to issue attribute certificates.

Non-globality of attribute certificates is not in contradiction with the "mobility" feature argued at the beginning of this section. As we stated, this type of certificates are extremely useful for new distributed Internet applications because they facilitate that user authorization is not limited to a local computer system or to local resources. On the contrary, the mobility feature allows that authorization comprises a set of computer systems and resources geographically distributed over the network. An application running in this way, although distributed, can not be considered global.

Once we have conveniently argued that many applications need that the PKI and the PMI are established and managed independently, we consider in next subsection the idea of outsourcing the PKI while managing the PMI inside the organization.

4.1   Outsourcing the PKI

For many years big organizations have designed, deployed and managed their own security solutions. However, many of those organizations are not considering this model anymore. They have realized that they do not have the skills to evaluate the multitude of security vendor products, deploy, integrate and manage these products into their existing network infrastructure. Also, difficulties with recruiting highly skilled, costly security specialists add to the list of problems for most organizations. This is specially true for security solutions that include firewalls, virtual private networks, URL filtering and, certainly, identity certificates [12].

Therefore, many organizations try to remain focused on their own business and outsource as many security services and technologies as possible. Outsourcing is done to those security companies, typically known as *Managed Security Services Providers*, that have the resources to continuously update security-related products.

As for authentication and PKI, managed security service provide customers with third-party infrastructure to guarantee the authenticity of their clients, devices and content for a variety of applications, including remote access, IPSEC, server applications, work-flow messaging systems and e-commerce solutions. As

PKI attracts a growing number of companies and organizations, the case of outsourcing PKI becomes favourable.

The principal argument against outsourced PKI is loss of control at the customer site. Therefore, outsourced PKI products are transferring control almost entirely to the customer. However, and even with this transference of control, the argument is entirely valid for PMIs. In our opinion, a PMI and their related services should not be outsourced because in many cases attribute certificates contain information that is of special relevance for the company. That information describes the privileges of their employees, and in some cases it is sensitive enough as to be totally or partially encrypted. Some clear examples are standard attribute types, like "access identity", "group", "role", "clearance", "audit identity", "administrators group", etc., that may put in high risk information considered as confidential inside the organization. When encryption of attributes is involved, the *Cryptographic Message Syntax* is used to carry the ciphertext and associated per-recipient keying information [7].

Therefore, outsourcing the PKI but not the PMI becomes a real working environment for many organizations. Of course, this scenario does not give additional difficulties to the organization. It is quite clear that when both infrastructures exist then identity certificates must be generated in the first place.

Afterwards, the organization will create attribute certificates binding each of them to the corresponding identity certificate issued by the outsourced PKI. As previously stated, binding can be done by using serial numbers of identity certificates or, whatever alternative information, as was shown in figure 2. It is important to point out this last idea, as our solution makes use of one of those alternatives, as we will explain in next section.

5   A New Scheme of PMI

A new scheme of PMI has been designed considering some basic goals which we summarize as: (a) use of a distributed architecture of authorities that satisfy the needs of intra-company departmental certification; (b) avoid scalability problems associated to both extranet or company expansion; and (c) eliminate problems associated with the revocation procedures, specially those introduced by the use of ACRLs.

Regarding the distributed architecture of authorities, our scheme is based on the fact that the typical structure of many companies is hierarchical. In fact, companies tend to have their own structure of divisions, departments, sections, etc., as the example in figure 3 shows.

We also take into consideration that, in most of cases, it is desirable that the distributed authorization infrastructure mimics or fits the company structure. Therefore, we propose a scheme with various managers acting as Attribute Authorities and operating independently over different *domain of users* (group of employees). The location of those authorities matches with the nodes of the hierarchy in the organization, that is, each node corresponds to a division, department, etc. This facilitates that every Attribute Authority issues attribute certificates for those employees over which it has a direct control.

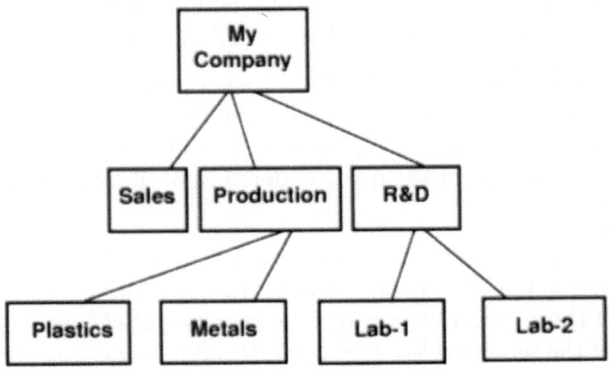

Fig. 3. A typical hierarchical company infrastructure

The main elements in our PMI design are the *Attribute Certificate Service Units* (ACSUs), which integrate attributes certification and management functions. Figure 4 shows all the components of a ACSU, which core is an Attribute Authority. More precisely, every ACSU is managed by an Attribute Authority who may be the manager in the division, department, etc.

Additionally, the ACSU contains a database to store the attribute certificates of the users local to the ACSU's domain. Each user's certificate is stored exclusively in the database of his/her ACSU, and that database is solely managed by the corresponding authority. Therefore, updating and revocation of certificates are local operations that do not affect the rest of the system. Revocation is possible, although ACRLs are not used in the system. When an attribute certificate is revoked because the user privileges change, it is deleted from a database and a new certificate is issued by the authority and stored.

The third component of the ACSU is the *Attribute Server*. Whenever a user (or a resource, an application, etc.) needs to know the privileges of certain user A in a domain X, the Attribute Server of that domain delivers the attribute certificate requested. A more detailed description of the request and deliver procedures are explained in the next Subsection.

5.1   System Operation

The operation of the system is related to the very natural way of identifying users inside the organization. For instance, according to figure 3, the employee *Alice* may belong to the department of *Metals*, which is included in the division of *Production*. In the operation of our system, this employee is identified as *Alice@metals.production.mycompany* inside the organization. This is clearly neither considered nor used as an e-mail address by our system, although we use the same format [3] because it allows to link the attribute certificate to the identity certificate. Occasionally, it may happen that in some organizations the structure of divisions, departments, etc. may coincide with the hierarchy of Internet domains, but this does not have an effect in the system.

Attribute certificates issued by authorities in our new design follow the format established by ITU and, at the same time, extend the composition of *Holder* field. Of course, this extension is not a particular one of our creation. In contrast, it strictly follows one of the alternatives under the specification of the standard as shown in figure 2.

To be more precise, in our implementation the field *Holder* of every attribute certificate generated inside the organization contains two concatenated data objects. Types of those data objects are *IssuerSerial* and *rfc822*, respectively; that is, the result of the sequence *baseCertificateID* and *entityName*. Such a sequence is totally valid according to the mentioned specification.

The first data object, an identity certificate serial number, binds the attribute certificate issued internally with the identity certificate issued by an outsourced company or organization. The second data object, which is a user identification similar to the one of the example (*Alice@metals.production.mycompany*), is used for the search of *Alice*'s privileges following the procedure that is explained next for a general scenario.

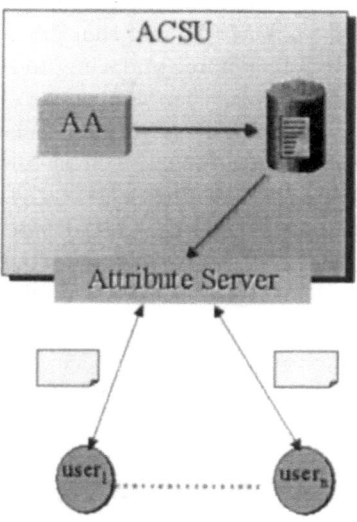

Fig. 4. Components of the ACSU

The scheme defines a special user called $AA@<\text{domain}>$ ($AA@x.y.z$ in the example shown in Figure 5), that denotes the corresponding AA in every ACSU. The certificate of any AA is stored in the database of its parent ACSU ($y.z$), except for the top-level domain ($.z$), that is the source of authorization.

The attribute certificate request process will be started by *Bob* as soon as he receives a request from *Alice*. This request has the following simplified information structure: $[Alice@x.y.z, operation]S_{Alice}$. The meaning of such structure is that *Alice* requests to *Bob* the permission to perform the operation, and digitally signs his request in order to avoid impersonation. At this moment, *Bob* needs *Alice*'s identity certificate to verify the request, and *Alice*'s attribute certificate to check if she is allowed to perform the operation.

Then, *Bob* firstly initiates the procedure to obtain *Alice*'s attribute certificate, that has been generated inside the organization. Figure 5 shows the procedure to obtain and verify it. We can see that *Bob* requests *Alice*'s certificate from his own ACSU (step 1) and this one directs the request to the ACSU located at the $x.y.z$ node (step 2). The response from the addressee's ACSU (step 3) is then forwarded to *Bob* (step 4).

Afterwards, and in the case *Bob* needs to be more confident in the certificate he has received, he can request the certificate of $AA@x.y.z$ from the ACSU located at $y.z$, obtaining a new certificate (Figure 5b). This procedure guarantees *Bob* that *Alice*'s authority has not been impersonated. This is a process of verifying the chain of attribute certificates up to the source of authority (at the top of the organization), but *Bob* can decide when he wants to stop going up.

According to the figure *Bob* must request the attribute certificate from his ACSU. This is so because access restrictions to ACSUs are set in the system, in such a way that a user can not access other ACSUs but the one in the domain where he is included.

In some circumstances it could happen that no ACSU is present at a certain node, say $y.z$. If this is the case, the certificate of $AA@x.y.z$ would be automatically requested from the parent node, that is, z. This allows for a company to use an incomplete structure without loss of functionality.

6   Conclusions

By using an authentication service you can prove who you are, but it is clear that this not enough for many of the applications in e-commerce scenarios. Additionally, it is necessary to prove what you are allowed to do or, in other words, it is necessary to use an authorization service. Although authorization is not a new problem, traditional solutions have been used for central applications, and not distributed applications. Therefore, they are not valid for the scenarios we are considering.

ITU-T has created the concept of attribute certificate in order to solve these problems. The attribute certificates framework provides a foundation upon which a Privilege Management Infrastructure (with a multitude of Attribute Authorities) can be built. In fact, the ideas followed by ITU-T when designing PMIs

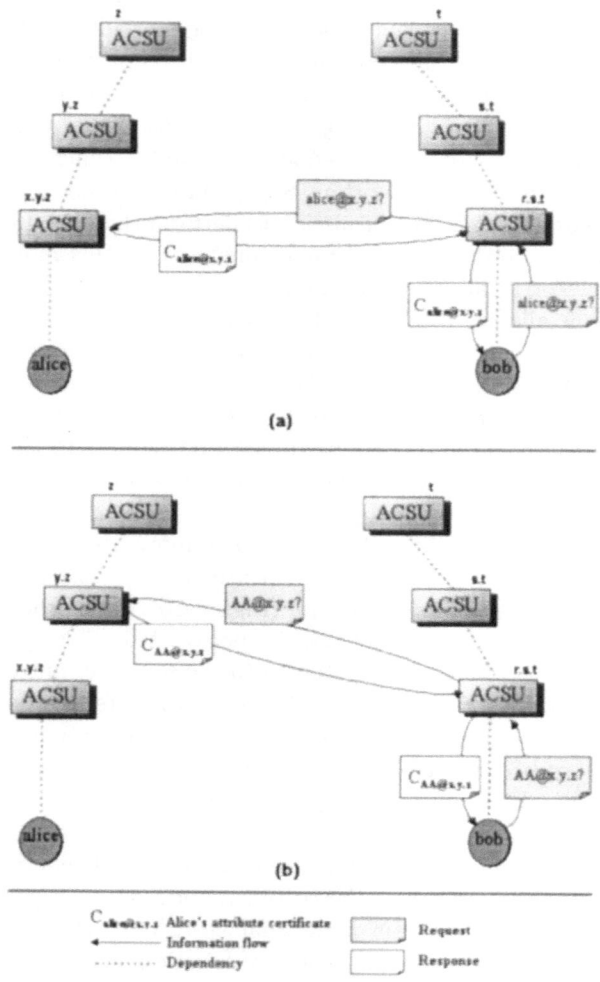

Fig. 5. a) Certificate Request b) Certificate Verification

are very likely to that one used to create PKIs. Both type of infrastructures are similar from the functional point of view, and they are linked, as the identity certificate and the attribute certificate of one user have fields with the same content.

Although linked, both types of infrastructures can operate independently. In the case of PKI services, these can be outsourced, but the case with PMI services is not the same, because much of the information contained in attribute certificates may be confidential. Therefore attribute certificates must be carefully managed and, preferably, only inside the company.

In this paper we have presented a new design of PMI that is specially suited for those companies that outsource PKI services but still need to manage the PMI internally. The new scheme has been designed considering some basic goals: (a) use of a distributed architecture of authorities that satisfy the needs of attribute certification that most companies have; (b) avoid scalability problems associated to both extranet or company expansion; and (c) eliminate problems associated with the revocation procedures, specially those introduced by the use of ACRLs. Therefore, although revocation procedures are allowed, there is no need for using ACRLs.

References

1. C. Adams, S. Lloyd, "Understanding Public-Key Infrastructure: Concepts, Standards and Deployment Considerations", New Riders, 1999
2. D. Chadwick, "An X.509 Role-based Privilege Management Infrastructure", *Business Briefing: Global Infosecurity*, 2002
3. D. Crocker, "Standard for the format of Arpa Internet Text Messages", Request for Comments 822, August 1982
4. C. Ellison et al. "SPKI Certificate Theory", Request for Comments 2693, IETF SPKI Working Group, September 1999
5. S. Farrell, R. Housley, "An Internet Attribute Certificate Profile for Authorization", Request for Comments 3281, IETF PKIX Working Group, April 2002
6. D. Ferraiolo, R. Jun, "Role-based access control", *Proc. 15th NIST-NCSC National Computer Security Conference*, 1992, pp. 554–563
7. R. Housley, "Cryptographic Message Syntax", Request for Comments 2630, IETF PKIX Working Group, June 1999
8. J. Hwang, K. Wu, D. Liu, "Access Control with Role Attribute Certificates", *Computer Standards and Interfaces*, vol. 22, March 2000, pp. 43–53
9. ITU-T Recommendation X.509, "Information Technology - Open systems interconnection – The Directory: Authentication Framework", June 1997
10. ITU-T Recommendation X.509, "Information Technology - Open systems interconnection – The Directory: Public-key and attribute certificate frameworks", March 2000
11. B. Kaliski "A Layman's Guide to a Subset of ASN.1, BER, and DER", November 1993
12. M. Lira, "Outsourcing your security to a Global Provider", *Business Briefing: Global Infosecurity*, 2002
13. A. Nash, W. Duane, C. Joseph, D. Brink, "PKI: Implementing and Managing E-Security", McGraw-Hill, 2001
14. R. Oppliger, G. Pernul, and Ch. Strauss. "Using Attribute Certificates to Implement Role-based Authorization and Access Control", *Proceedings of the 4. Fachtagung Sicherheit in Informationssystemen (SIS 2000)*, Zürich, October 2000, pp. 169–184
15. R.S. Sandhu, E.J. Coyne, H. Feinstein, C.E. Youman, "Role-based access control models", *IEEE Computer* Vol. 29, No. 2, 1996, pp. 38–47

Password Authenticated Key Exchange Based on RSA for Imbalanced Wireless Networks

Feng Zhu, Duncan S. Wong, Agnes H. Chan, and Robbie Ye

College of Computer Science
Northeastern University
Boston, MA 02115
{zhufeng, swong, ahchan, robbieye}@ccs.neu.edu

Abstract. We consider an imbalanced wireless network setup in which a low-power client communicates with a powerful server. We assume that public key cryptographic operations such as Diffie-Hellman key exchange conducted over a large multiplicative group is too computationally intensive for a low-power client to implement. In this paper, we propose an authenticated key exchange protocol such that it is efficient enough to be implemented on most of the target low-power devices such as devices in sensor networks, smart cards and low-power Personal Digital Assistants. In addition, it is secure against dictionary attacks. Our scheme requires less than 2.5 seconds of pure computation on a 16MHz Palm V and about 1 second for data transmission if the throughput of a network is 8 kbps. The computation time can be improved to 300 msec and the transmision time can also be reduced to 300 msec if caching is allowed.

1 Introduction

Classical symmetric key based authenticated key exchange protocols dictate the shared cryptographic keys to be long enough and randomly generated so that they can deter key-guessing attacks, or so-called brute force key searching attacks. They are widely used to provide mutual entity authentication in conjunction with session key establishment. However, it is very difficult to memorize such keys and therefore these protocols usually have little implication of providing user authentication. Furthermore, those schemes require the keys and some other participant-specific information to be stored in some tamper-proof security module at each entity. For applications where a security module is not available or user authentication is prevailing, authenticated key exchange protocols which are secure against key-guessing attacks are needed. Protocols designed to provide mutual authentication and key exchange, while also secure against offline key-guessing attacks or the so-called offline dictionary attacks, are called Password Authenticated Key Exchange protocols.

The objective of a password authenticated key exchange protocol can be described as follows. After two communicating parties execute the scheme and when both parties terminate and accept, each of them should have certain assurance that it knows each other's true identity (authentication) and it shares a new and

A.H. Chan and V. Gligor (Eds.): ISC 2002, LNCS 2433, pp. 150–161, 2002.

random session key only with its intended partner and the key is derived from contributions of both parties (key exchange). These goals are essentially the same as those of cryptographic key based authenticated key exchange schemes. But unlike the cryptographic key based authenticated key exchange schemes, these two communicating parties do not have any pre-shared cryptographic symmetric key, certificate or information of any trusted third party. Instead they only have a password shared between them. Usually the password is picked from a relatively small password space which can be enumerated efficiently by an adversary.

We focus on designing a password authenticated key exchange scheme which is suitable for implementation on a type of distributed network, called imbalanced (asymmetric) network. An imbalanced network consists of two sets of entities, namely a set of powerful servers and a set of low-power clients. The servers are having similar computational power and memory capacity to current desktop machines while the clients are only comparable to those microprocessor-based smart cards, wearable devices in a PAN (Personal Area Network), low-end PDAs (Personal Digital Assistants) or cellular phones. The scheme is going to be designed for communications between a client and a server. In addition, we assume that the bandwidth of the network is low. A typical cellular network in which a mobile unit communicating with a base station, and a Bluetooth-based PAN in which an earpiece communicating with a handset are two typical examples of imbalanced networks.

1.1 Related Results

Since the first set of password authenticated key exchange schemes called EKE was proposed by Bellovin and Merritt [2] in 1992, there have been many new proposals suggested in recent years [6,10,15,3,11,7]. A more comprehensive list of these schemes can be found in [8] and Jablon's research links[1]. Most of these schemes are based on Diffie-Hellman key exchange. In an imbalanced network however, the large modular exponentiation operation, which needs to be carried out by both communicating parties, may take a long time for a low-power device to compute. As an example, one modular exponentiation taken in a 512-bit cyclic subgroup with 160-bit prime order spends 27 seconds to complete when running on a 16MHz Palm V [13]. This becomes very noticeable when the client is a smart card, a low-end PDA or a tiny wearable Bluetooth device embedded with a very limited microcontroller.

In [2], the authors investigated the feasibility of using RSA to instantiate the EKE protocol. If the RSA public exponent is short, the encryption operation can be done efficiently and the corresponding protocol may be very suitable for the imbalanced network. However, they pointed out that an e-residue attack may be feasible if the receiving party has no way to verify whether the public exponent is fraudulent or not, that is to check if the public exponent is relatively prime to $\phi(n)$ without knowing the factorization of n where n is the RSA modulus. To thwart this attack, the authors considered an interactive protocol to allow a

---
[1] http://www.integritysciences.com/links.html

receiver to detect a fraudulent value of the public exponent. However, we find that the interactive protocol is insecure. In Sect. 2, we describe an attack against the interactive protocol. We also propose a modified version such that it prevents the attack and at the same time achieves better efficiency when compared with the original one.

In 1997, Lucks proposed a scheme called OKE (Open Key Exchange) [10] which is based on RSA. It was later found to be insecure against a variant of e-residue attacks due to MacKenzie, et al. [11]. In [11], the authors modified OKE such that a *large* prime is chosen to be the RSA public exponent. This ensures that the public exponent is relatively prime to $\phi(n)$. On the other hand, this defeats the purpose of using RSA for low-power clients in an imbalanced network because the computational complexity of the protocol is no less than most of the protocols based on Diffie-Hellman key exchange.

Another issue of these schemes is that all of them are actually providing key *transport* instead of key exchange, namely the secrecy of the final session key depends on the secrecy of a session key contribution generated by one party only instead of both parties. Hence if that party's session key contribution is compromised, the session key is compromised. In the key exchange case however, the final session key is derived from the session key contributions of both parties. Compromising only one party's session key contribution does not compromise the final session key. Therefore in our work, we prefer to design a password authenticated key *exchange* scheme.

1.2   Overview of Our Results

We propose a password authenticated key exchange protocol based on RSA scheme with short public exponents. We show how e-residue attacks can be prevented by using a modified interactive protocol. We also evaluate its performance when implemented on a low-power client such as a 16MHz Palm V and discuss its efficiency on data transmission.

The subsequent sections are organized as follows. In the next section, we describe an e-residue attack against an instantiation of EKE protocol called RSA-EKE. We modify the corresponding interactive protocol and show that the modified version can both prevent the e-residue attack and improve the network efficiency. In Sect. 3, we propose our RSA-based password authenticated key exchange scheme and specify the security requirements of each component in the scheme. We then evaluate the performance of the scheme in Sect. 4 and discuss the feasibility of implementing the scheme on a low-end PalmPilot such as a 16MHz Palm V. Finally in Sect. 5, we conclude the paper with some further remarks.

2   The E-residue Attack and the Interactive Protocol

In this section we describe an instantiation of EKE protocol based on RSA, abbreviated as RSA-EKE, and explain its vulnerability against an e-residue attack.

For simplicity of description, we adopt the following notations throughout the paper.

Let

- A be a server and B be a low-power client.
- ID_A and ID_B denote the identities of A and B respectively.
- $r \in_R \{0,1\}^l$ denote a random binary string r of length l, and $\{0,1\}^l$ denote the set of all l-bit binary strings.
- pw denote a password shared between A and B. It is picked from a password space PW according to certain probability distribution.
- E_K, D_K be a symmetric encryption algorithm and respectively the decryption algorithm defined by a symmetric key $K \in \{0,1\}^l$.
- H, T, G_1, G_2, G_3 and h be distinct cryptographic hash functions.
- (n, e) be a RSA public key pair such that n be the public modulus and e be the public exponent.

The RSA-EKE protocol without the interactive protocol is illustrated in Fig. 1. In the protocol, A and B are sharing a password pw. R is a random

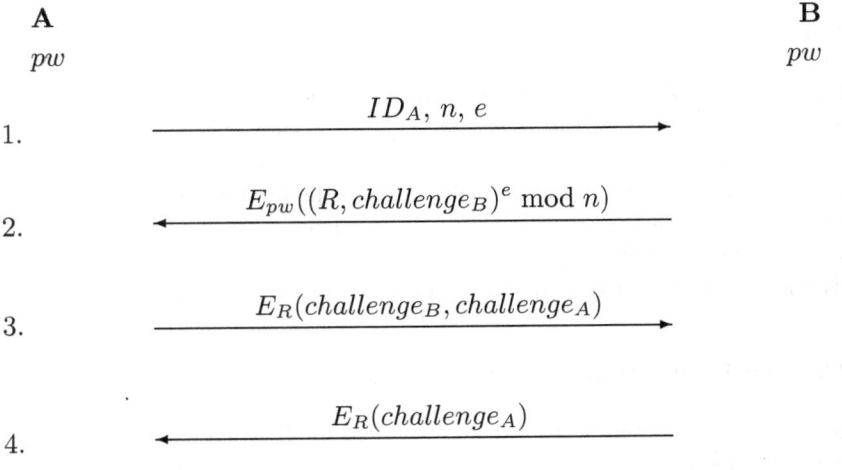

Fig. 1. RSA-EKE without Interactive Protocol

session key, and $challenge_A$ and $challenge_B$ are two random numbers used to authenticate B and A respectively.

In [2], several issues on using RSA have been pointed out. One of the related issues raised by the authors is the e-residue attack.

2.1   *E*-residue Attack

To ensure that the RSA scheme works correctly, the public exponent e has to be relatively prime to $\phi(n)$. An active attacker can launch an e-residue attack by impersonates the server A and sends (n', e') to the client B where $(e', \phi(n')) \neq 1$. The encryption function $x \to x^{e'} \bmod n'$ is no longer a permutation on $\mathbf{Z}_{n'}$. The encryption function maps elements to the set of e-residues, which is only a proper subset of $\mathbf{Z}_{n'}$. Since the adversary knows the factorization of n', it is easy for the adversary to check whether an element $a \in \mathbf{Z}_{n'}$ is an e-residue. Hence after receiving $E_{pw}(y)$ in step 2, where $y = (R, \textit{challenge}_B)^e \bmod n$, the adversary can use a trial password pw' to obtain $y' = D_{pw'}(E_{pw}(y))$ and checks whether y' is an e-residue or not. If it is not, then the trial password pw' is not the correct password and therefore can be removed from the password space PW.

Obviously this attack would not work if B can determine whether e is relatively prime to $\phi(n)$. So the following problem is crucial to resist the e-residue attack.

Problem: Given two composite n and e such that $3 \leq e < n$. Determine if e is relatively prime to $\phi(n)$.

In [12], the authors pointed out that it is not known whether there exists a polynomial-time algorithm to solve this problem in general. In [11], the authors proposed two methods to enforce the relative primality of $\phi(n)$ and e. The first method is to set e to be a prime greater than n so to guarantee that $(e, \phi(n)) = 1$. The second method is to set e to be a prime such that it is greater than $\sqrt{n}$ and $(n \bmod e)$ does not divide n. It can be shown that this also guarantees that e is relatively prime to $\phi(n)$ [9]. The drawback for these two methods is that the value of e is relatively large; thereby defeats the advantage of using a small e to improve the performance. To attain high efficiency of computation for the low power clients, small public exponents are needed. In order to thwart e-residue attacks, interactive protocols based on challenge and response may be used.

2.2   An Interactive Protocol

We now revisit a preliminary idea mentioned in [2] in detecting fraudulent values of e. The idea is based on the fact that for odd integer n and e ($e \geq 3$) such that $(e, \phi(n)) \neq 1$, any e-residue modulo n should have at least 3 e-th roots. As described in [2], a client B can verify e interactively, by asking A to decrypt a number of encrypted messages under (n, e). Specifically B picks N integers $m_i \in_R \mathbf{Z}_n$, where N is a security parameter (say 10) and sends $\{c_i \equiv m_i^e \pmod{n}\}_{1 \leq i \leq N}$ to A. A computes the e-th root of each c_i as m_i' and sends $\{m_i'\}_{1 \leq i \leq N}$ back.

For $1 \leq i \leq N$, if $(e, \phi(n)) = 1$, each c_i should have a unique e-th root and $m_i' = m_i$. On the other hand, if $(e, \phi(n)) \neq 1$, each c_i should have at least 3 e-th roots and they are equally likely. The probability that A guesses all the N e-th roots correctly is therefore at most 3^{-N}.

Although the authors of [2] could not find any immediate weakness in the RSA-EKE, they were correct in being concerned about the security of the protocol being compromised by an intruder using a server A as a decryption oracle. In the following, we show how an attacker E can impersonate B and use this decryption oracle in guessing the password shared between A and B.

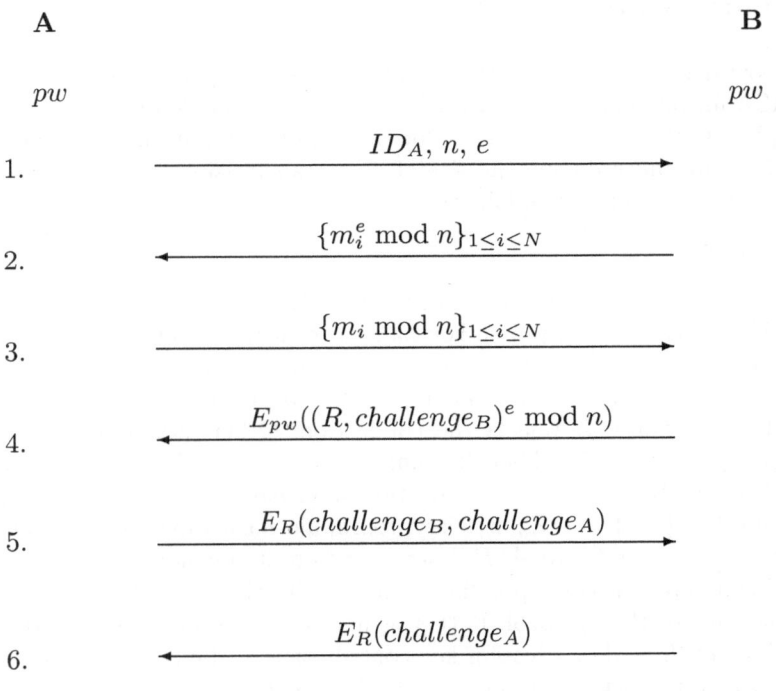

A

pw

1. $\xrightarrow{\quad ID_A,\, n,\, e \quad}$

2. $\xleftarrow{\quad \{m_i^e \bmod n\}_{1 \le i \le N} \quad}$

3. $\xrightarrow{\quad \{m_i \bmod n\}_{1 \le i \le N} \quad}$

4. $\xleftarrow{\quad E_{pw}((R, challenge_B)^e \bmod n) \quad}$

5. $\xrightarrow{\quad E_R(challenge_B, challenge_A) \quad}$

6. $\xleftarrow{\quad E_R(challenge_A) \quad}$

B

pw

Fig. 2. RSA-EKE with Interactive Protocol

The RSA-EKE with the interactive protocol is illustrated in Fig. 2. Suppose that during one successful run of the protocol between A and B, an adversary E gets the messages of the fourth and fifth flows, that is $msg_4 = E_{pw}((R, challenge_B)^e \bmod n)$ and $msg_5 = E_R(challenge_B, challenge_A)$ respectively. Assume that the same public key (n, e) is used for multiple sessions. Then E can impersonate B and communicate with A by randomly chooses N trial passwords $\{pw_i'\}_{1 \le i \le N}$ from the password space PW. It then impersonates B and communicates with A. In the second flow, it sends $\{D_{pw_i'}(msg_4)\}_{1 \le i \le N}$ to A while expecting $\{(D_{pw_i'}(msg_4))^d \bmod n\}_{1 \le i \le N}$ in reply. We can see that for any i $(1 \le i \le N)$, if $pw_i' = pw$, then the corresponding reply must contain the correct value of R and $challenge_B$. E can check this via msg_5. Hence if the checking fails, pw must be a wrong guess and E then removes it from PW. Thus E can check N passwords in one impersonation.

This attack can be prevented if the server A cannot be used as a decryption oracle. This can be accomplished by modifying it slightly via adding a cryptographic hash function. In the next section, we propose the modification.

3   Our Protocol

We now describe a new password authenticated key exchange protocol based on RSA for imbalanced networks. Our objectives include making computational complexity at the client side as low as possible, requiring minimum memory requirement and reducing the size of data transmission. The protocol is shown in Fig. 3 and described as follows.

In the protocol,

- A and B are sharing a password $pw \in PW$.
- A generates a RSA public key pair (n, e) using a public key generator and selects $r_A \in_R \{0, 1\}^l$. She sends (n, e) and r_A to B.
- B checks if (n, e) is a valid public key by using an Interactive Protocol. If it is invalid, B rejects the connection. Otherwise, it first picks $r_B \in_R \{0, 1\}^l$, $s_B \in_R \mathbf{Z}_n$. Then it computes $\pi = T(pw, \mathrm{ID}_A, \mathrm{ID}_B, r_A, r_B)$ where ID_A and ID_B are the identification information of A and B, respectively and $T : \{0, 1\}^* \to \mathbf{Z}_n$ is a cryptographic hash function. It sends r_B and $z = s_B^e + \pi \bmod n$ to A. B destroys π from its memory.
- A computes the corresponding π and obtains the value of s_B from the second message of the protocol. It then generates a temporary symmetric encryption key K and B's session key contribution c_B by computing $G_1(s_B)$, and $G_2(s_B)$, respectively where $G_1 : \{0, 1\}^* \to \{0, 1\}^l$ and $G_2 : \{0, 1\}^* \to \{0, 1\}^l$ are two distinct cryptographic hash functions. It then picks its own session key contribution $c_A \in_R \{0, 1\}^*$ and sends $E_k(c_A, \mathrm{ID}_B)$ to B. It later computes the session key σ as $G_3(c_A, c_B, \mathrm{ID}_A, \mathrm{ID}_B)$ and destroys s_B, c_A, c_B and K from its memory.
- B computes K and c_B from s_B accordingly. It decrypts the incoming message and checks if it contains its own identity ID_B along with some l-bit binary string. If it is false, B terminates the protocol run with failure. Otherwise, it denotes the l-bit binary string as c_A' and uses it as A's session key contribution and computes the session key σ' accordingly. It then destroys s_B, c_A', c_B from its memory. $h(\sigma')$ is then sent back to A and the connection is accepted.
- A checks if the incoming message $h(\sigma') = h(\sigma)$. If it is true, then A accepts the connection. Otherwise, it terminates the protocol run with failure.

To ensure our protocol is applicable to the imbalanced networks in terms of efficiency, we need to use short RSA public exponents. To resist e-residue attacks,

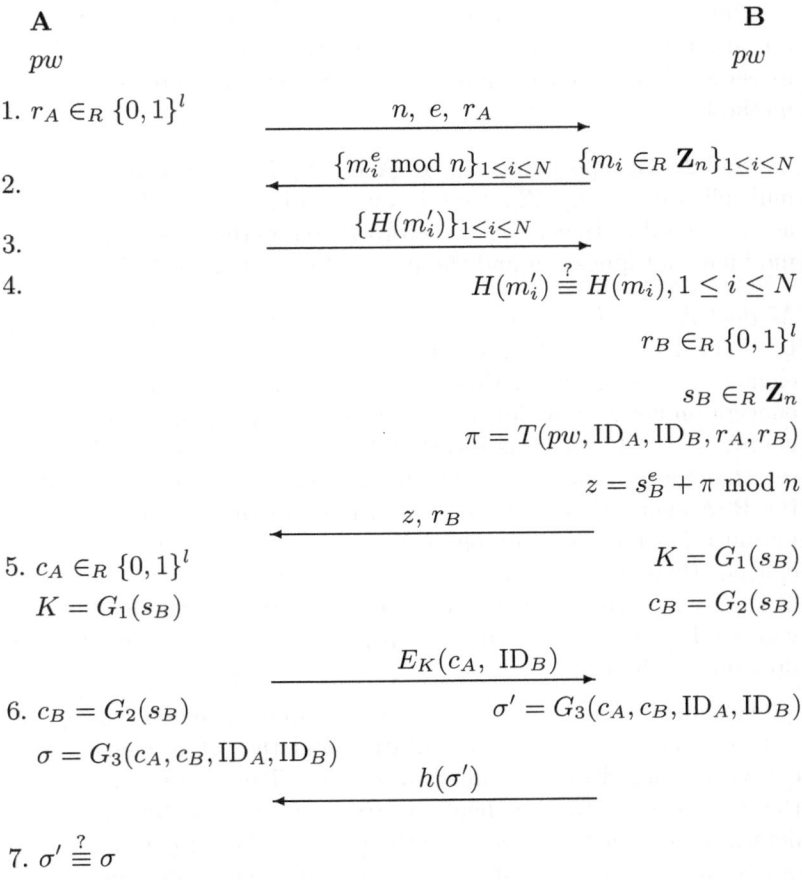

Fig. 3. Password Authenticated Key Exchange Using RSA

our scheme includes an interactive protocol in step 2 and 3 shown in Fig. 3. By having A returning hash values of the decrypted challenge numbers, that is $\{H(m_i)\}_{1 \leq i \leq N}$. The hash function H is defined as $H : \{0,1\}^* \to \{0,1\}^{Q'(l)}$ where Q' is some polynomial function. We conjecture that in this way, A can no longer be used as a decryption oracle in helping an adversary to invert RSA.

In Fig. 3, z is computed as an encrypted random element in $\mathbf{Z}_n$ followed by a modular addition of π where π is a function of the password pw with some nonces r_A and r_B and identification information. In fact, the RSA encryption algorithm can be treated to be a trapdoor one-way permutation over $\mathbf{Z}_n$ and we can also consider the modular addition operation as a permutation over the same set of elements.

Once we generalize these two operations as trapdoor permutation and permutation over the same set of elements, we may be able to apply them to other methods with the associativity issue [5] considered. Here below are the two other methods.

Method 1. By specifying the RSA encryption algorithm performed over the multiplicative group $\mathbf{Z}_n^*$, that is by choosing $s_B \in_R \mathbf{Z}_n^*$, we can compute z as $s_B^e \cdot \pi \bmod n$. Hence the 'password-keyed' permutation now becomes a simple modular multiplication and the protocol is similar to [10,11].

Method 2. Let $T : \{0,1\} \to \{0,1\}^{|n|-1}$ and the password-keyed permutation be defined as $z = y \oplus \pi$ for all $y \in \{0,1\}^{|n|-1}$. Since more than half of the elements in $\mathbf{Z}_n$ is small than $2^{|n|-1}$, the expected number of times the RSA encryption needs to perform before picking a $s_B \in_R \mathbf{Z}_n$ such that $y = s_B^e \bmod n$ is only $|n| - 1$ bits long is less than 2. On the efficiency of this method, we can see that more than half of the chance that the client only needs to carry out the RSA encryption once (instead of twice or more). Since the password-keyed permutation requires only one ($|n|$-1)-bit XOR operation, this method is more efficient than the previous two in the majority case. However for less than half of the chance, this scheme is expected to carry out the RSA encryption twice, which takes one more modular multiplication if e = 3 when compared with the previous methods.

We now review the first method we proposed, namely using modular addition as a password-keyed permutation and the set of elements that the RSA encryption algorithm is defined over is $\mathbf{Z}_n$. This method when compared with the other two allows the client to carry out only one RSA encryption and it is deterministic. Furthermore since the password-keyed permutation requires only one $|n|$-bit addition operation, this method is more efficient than the other two in the majority case.

A secure symmetric encryption scheme in our protocol can be instantiated by most of the well-known block ciphers or stream ciphers. It is also straightforward to construct one by given a pseudorandom function family. Let $f : Keys(l) \times Dom(l) \to \{0,1\}^{Q''(l)}$ be a pseudo-random function family where $Q''(l)$ is some polynomial function. The symmetric encryption scheme can be defined as $E_K(x) = (r, f(K,r) \oplus x)$ for all $x \in \{0,1\}^{Q''(l)}$ where $r \in_R Dom(l)$. Alternatively, we can use some appropriate hash function that behaves like a random oracle [1], $H_4 : \{0,1\}^{2l} \to \{0,1\}^{Q''(l)}$ and define the symmetric encryption scheme as $E_K(x) = (r, H_4(K,r) \oplus x)$. This construction allows a target application to build up the encryption scheme from a common hash function which may have already been used to construct T, G_1, G_2, G_3, H and h instead of implementing a block cipher or a stream cipher.

4   Efficiency

In an imbalanced network, the servers are generally assumed to be powerful, and all the operations of the key exchange scheme can be carried out at the server side efficiently. Hence we focus on evaluating the efficiency at the client side in terms of computational complexity as well as network and storage requirements. First we look into the efficiency issue and show that the interactive protocol is efficient enough in our target applications if some appropriate value of N is chosen.

4.1   The Interactive Protocol

One concern of this interactive protocol is that it is expensive in terms of the amount of messages sent and the number of encryptions needed to be carried out by the low-power client.

On the amount of messages needed to be sent, this interactive protocol adds two more flows and the size of the first flow of the interactive protocol is $N|n|$ bits. Suppose $N = 10$ and $|n| = 512$ bits, this flow takes about 640 msec to transmit if the network throughput is 8kbps. The second flow added by the interactive protocol is a sequence of hash values. If H maps an input to a binary string of 160-bit long, 200 bytes are needed to be sent. Therefore this interactive protocol adds about 840 msec to the total data transmission time of the scheme.

4.2   Computational Complexity

With respect to the computation complexity, B needs to compute N modular exponentiations with the exponent e. If e is small and has a small number of ones in its binary representation, the total number of modular multiplications/squares may still be relatively small when compared with schemes based on Diffie-Hellman key exchange. For example, if $e = 3$ and $|n| = 512$, one encryption essentially takes two 512-bit modular multiplications. As each 512-bit modular multiplication takes about 107 msec when implemented on a 16MHz Palm V [14], the encryptions for preparing the first flow of the interactive protocol take about 2.14 seconds.

With respect to the decryption, it is widely known that each operation can be done within 5 milliseconds on a machine with 1GHz Intel processor. Hence the interactive protocol can barely make any significant impact on the performance at the server side.

As a summary on the computational complexity at the client side, it needs to perform $2(N + 1)$ modular multiplications, one modular addition and $N + 5$ hashes. As we measured on a 16MHz Palm V, one 512-bit modular addition takes 3.28 msec to complete and less than 4.6 msec is required to digest 80 bytes of data if hash functions are based on SHA-1. Therefore, the scheme including the interactive protocol takes less than 2.5 seconds of pure computation.

4.3   Network and Storage Efficiency

There are six message flows in a single run of the protocol. As mentioned above, the interactive protocol spends 840 msec to transmit on a 8kbps network. By including the time for transmitting other flows, the scheme takes a total of about one second for transmission.

On the storage requirement, the client needs to have $N \cdot |n|$ bits of dynamic memory for storing $\{m_i^e \bmod n\}_{1 \le i \le N}$ and another $NQ'(l)$ bits of memory for storing $\{H(m_i)\}_{1 \le i \le N}$ if the second flow is sent to A in one single message flow. This implies that the low-power device should have about 840 bytes of dynamic memory for data. For those devices which do not have that much of data memory, the second flow can be subdivided into several flows so that only a portion of $\{m_i^e \bmod n\}_{1 \le i \le N}$ and $\{H(m_i)\}_{1 \le i \le N}$ are kept in the data memory at a time.

4.4   Further Optimization – Public Key Caching

In some situation, B may cache (n, e) for multiple sessions after one run of the interactive protocol. Hence it can save about 2.98 seconds for session key establishment in each of the subsequent sessions. Then each subsequent session only needs 300 msec of pure computation and its network efficiency is also improved to less than 300 msec.

In general, A may publish its RSA public key in advance or use the same public key to communicate with other participants besides B, without risking its security. In addition, this allows the clients to cache the value of (n, e) in their local memory and saves them from conducting the interactive protocol with A in any further runs of the protocol.

An even prominent gain of caching A's public key is to allow the client to further improve performance via pre-computation. As shown in the previous section, if (n, e) is cached, B can randomly pick s_B and precompute $y = x^e \bmod n$ before running the protocol. This allows B to reduce 214 msec of runtime on a PalmPilot. If r_B and the corresponding K and c_B are also pre-generated, this leaves B to carry out only three hashes, one $|n|$-bit modular addition and one symmetric key decryption during the runtime of the protocol. These operations require a total of less than 30 milliseconds of computation time when implemented on a 16MHz Palm V with some suitable symmetric key decryption algorithm such as Rijndael [4]. The obvious limitation of deploying this optimization is the memory requirement of storing A's public key and those pre-computed values. We notice that this requires $(2|n| + 4l + |e|)/8 \approx 212$ bytes of data to be stored, which may not fit in some extremely memory-limited devices such as in sensor networks. On the other hand, it is very suitable for applications running on smart card systems, wearable devices and PalmPilots.

5   Conclusion Remarks

It is clear that if the server's private key is compromised, an adversary can launch offline dictionary attack to find out the password and get all the s_B's of previous sessions. However, knowing just the password may not help reveal the session keys of previous sessions. Hence our scheme provides half forward secrecy. Since the client may be a weak device while the server can support much stronger security measures than the client, we believe that forward secrecy on the client side is a crucial feature.

Under the security requirements for each component of the scheme which are specified in the previous sections, we can show, in [13], that the scheme is secure under the random oracle model [1].

References

1. Mihir Bellare and Phillip Rogaway. Random oracles are practical: A paradigm for designing efficient protocols. In *First ACM Conference on Computer and Communications Security*, pages 62–73, Fairfax, 1993. ACM.
2. S. M. Bellovin and M. Merritt. Encrypted key exchange: Password based protocols secure against dictionary attacks. In *Proceedings 1992 IEEE Symposium on Research in Security and Privacy*, pages 72–84. IEEE Computer Society, 1992.
3. Victor Boyko, Philip MacKenzie, and Sarvar Patel. Provably secure password-authenticated key exchange using diffie-hellman. In *Proc. EUROCRYPT 2000*, pages 156–171, 2000.
4. J. Daemen and V. Rijmen. AES proposal: Rijndael. *AES Algorithm Submission*, Sep 1999. http://www.nist.gov/aes.
5. L. Gong, M. A. Lomas, R. M. Needham, and J. H. Saltzer. Protecting poorly chosen secrets from guessing attacks. *IEEE Journal on Selected Areas in Communications*, 11(5):648–656, 1993.
6. David P. Jablon. Strong password-only authenticated key exchange. *Computer Communication Review, ACM*, 26(5):5–26, 1996.
7. Jonathan Katz, Rafail Ostrovsky, and Moti Yung. Efficient password-authenticated key exchange using human-memorable passwords. In *Proc. EUROCRYPT 2001*. Springer-Verlag, 2001. Lecture Notes in Computer Science No. 2045.
8. Taekyoung Kwon. Ultimate solution to authentication via memorable password. *Contribution to the IEEE P1363 Study Group*, May 2000.
9. H. W. Lenstra, Jr. Divisors in residue classes. *Mathematics of Computation*, 42(165):331–340, 1984.
10. Stefan Lucks. Open key exchange: How to defeat dictionary attacks without encrypting public keys. In *Proc. of the Security Protocols Workshop*, pages 79–90, 1997. LNCS 1361.
11. Philip MacKenzie, Sarvar Patel, and Ram Swaminathan. Password-authenticated key exchange based on RSA. In *Proc. ASIACRYPT 2000*, pages 599–613, 2000.
12. Philip MacKenzie and Ram Swaminathan. Secure network authentication with password identification. Submitted to IEEE P1363a, 1999.
13. Duncan S. Wong. On the design and analysis of authenticated key exchange schemes for low power wireless computing platforms. Ph.D. Thesis, July 2002.
14. Duncan S. Wong, Hector Ho Fuentes, and Agnes H. Chan. The performance measurement of cryptographic primitives on palm devices. In *Proc. of the 17th Annual Computer Security Applications Conference*, Dec 2001.
15. Thomas Wu. The secure remote password protocol. In *1998 Internet Society Symposium on Network and Distributed System Security*, pages 97–111, 1998.

Quantifying Privacy Leakage through Answering Database Queries

Tsan-sheng Hsu, Churn-Jung Liau, Da-Wei Wang, and Jeremy K.-P. Chen

Institute of Information Science
Academia Sinica, Taipei, Taiwan
{tshsu,liaucj,wdw}@iis.sinica.edu.tw

Abstract. We assume a database consists of records of individuals with private or sensitive fields. Queries on the distribution of a sensitive field within a selected population in the database can be submitted to the data center. The answers to the queries leak private information of individuals though no identification information is provided. Inspired by decision theory, we present a quantitative model for the privacy protection problem in such a database query or linkage environment in this paper. In the model, the value of information is estimated from the viewpoint of the querier.

To estimate the value, we define the information state of the data user by a class of probability distributions on the set of possible confidential values. We further define the usefulness of information based on how easy the data user can locate individuals that fit the description given in the queries. These states and the usefulness of information can be modified and refined by the user's knowledge acquisition actions. The value of information is then defined as the expected gain of the privacy receiver and the privacy is protected by imposing costs on the answers of the queries for balancing the gain.

Keywords: Privacy, Data table, Decision logic, Quantitative model, Value of information.

1 Introduction

There are many technical problems to be addressed for privacy protection. The most basic one is to avoid unauthorized users access to the confidential information. Some significant works on controlling disclosure of private information from databases have been done[4,5,6,8,9,10,15,22,23]. Recently, an epistemic logic has been proposed to model the privacy protection problem in a database linking context[11]. In [2], a prototype system is designed to implement this logical model in the context of querying a medical database. The safety criteria of the data is defined rigorously in the logic and data to be disclosed must be generalized to meet this requirement. The safety criteria defined in the requirement are purely qualitative so we can only identify the situation in which the exact confidential information came to the users' knowledge. However, in many cases, even if the

A.H. Chan and V. Gligor (Eds.): ISC 2002, LNCS 2433, pp. 162–176, 2002.

private information is only known with some imprecision, there is still a risk of privacy leakage. Therefore it is very important to have the capability of risk assessment in the model of privacy protection.

Someone may benefit from the privacy leakage, but it may also be harmful for others. For example, the health information of a customer would be valuable in the decision-making of an insurance company. However, the dissemination of an individual's health information without his consent in advance is definitely an invasion of his privacy. Thus the value of confidential information would be an incentive towards invasion of privacy. The information brokers may try to collect and sell personal information for their own interest. On the other hand, it is usually difficult to estimate the damage caused by privacy leakage. However, to discourage the invasion of privacy, the damage of the victim must be appropriately compensated by the one disseminating the information. Therefore, the evaluation of gain and loss of privacy leakage is a crucial problem in privacy protection.

In this paper, we try to tackle the problem from the aspects of information value. We focus on the following database query environment. In a data center, private information about individuals are collected. There are private or sensitive fields as well as identification fields in each record. Queries on the distribution of a sensitive field within a selected population in the database can be submitted to the data center. The answers to the queries leak private information of individuals though no identification information is provided.

We study a quantitative model for the privacy protection problem in such a database query environment. It is for modeling the value of information from the viewpoint of the querier. We will model the value of information as the expected gain of knowledge of the information. In the model, we need to represent the knowledge states of an user receiving some kind of information. We further define the usefulness of information based on how easy the data user can locate individuals that fit the description given in the queries. The knowledge states and the usefulness of information can be changed or refined by receiving some answer to the user's query. Thus we also need a formalism to represent the data to be protected and a language to describe which kinds of queries are allowed. The data table and decision logic proposed in [17] will be employed as the data representation formalism and the query language respectively.

In the rest of the paper, we first review the data table formalism and the decision logic in our application context. The basic components of our models— the information states and knowledge acquisition actions—is defined in section 3. In section 4, the model for information value and its use in privacy protection are presented. Finally, the results are summarized in the concluding section.

2 Data Representation and Query Language

To state the privacy protection problem, we must first fix the data representation. The most popular data representation is by data table([17]). The data in many application domains, for example, medical records, financial transactions, employee data, etc., can be represented as data tables. A data table can be seen as a simplification of a relational database, since the latter in general consists of a number of data tables. A formal definition of data table is given in [17].

Definition 1 *A data table[1] is a pair $T = (U, A)$ such that*

- *U is a nonempty finite set of individuals, called the population or the universe,*
- *A is a nonempty finite set of primitive attributes, and*
- *every primitive attribute $a \in A$ is a total function $a : U \to V_a$, where V_a is the set of values of a, called the domain of a.*

The attributes of a data table can be divided into three sets. The first contains the *key attributes*, which can be used to identify to whom a data record belongs, therefore these attributes are always masked off in response to a query. Since the key attributes uniquely determine the individuals, we can assume that they are associated with elements in the universe U and omit them from this point. Second, we have a set of *easy-to-know attributes*, the values of which are easily discovered by the public. For example, in [21], it is pointed out that some attributes like birth-date, gender, ethnicity, etc., are included in some public databases such as census data or voter registration lists. The last kind of attributes is the *confidential type*, the values of which are mainly the goals we have to protect. Sometimes, there is an asymmetry between the values of a confidential attribute. For example, if the attribute is a HIV test result, the revelation of a '+' value may cause a serious privacy invasion, whereas it does not matter to know that an individual has a '−' value. For simplification, we assume there is exactly one confidential attribute in a data table. Thus a data table is usually written as $T = (U, A \cup \{c\})$ where A is the set of easy-to-know attributes and c is the confidential one.

Let $V_c = \{s_0, s_1, \ldots, s_{t-1}\}$ be the set of possible values for the confidential attribute c. It is assumed that the *a prior* information of the user is the probability distribution of the population on V_c. In other words, we assume that the user knows the value $\frac{|\{u \in U | c(u) = s_i\}|}{|U|}$ for all $0 \le i \le t - 1$. Then the user can improve his knowledge by investigating some sampled individuals of the population or querying the data center that stores the data table. By investigation, the user can discover the exact value of the confidential attribute of the chosen individuals. However, much effort is necessary to do the investigation. On the other hand, a query may ask for the probability distribution of sensitive fields in a specific subset of the population. Once the query is correctly answered, the user not only knows the probability distribution of the specific sub-population, but also that of its complement on V_c. Thus we need a language to specify a subset of individuals. To achieve this purpose, we suggest to use the decision logic(DL) proposed in [17]. The DL is originally designed for the representation of rules induced from a data table by data mining techniques. However, it is also

---

[1] Also called knowledge representation system, information system, or attribute-value system

perfectly suitable for the query of a data table since each formula of the logic is satisfied by some individuals in the data table.

Syntactically, an atomic formula for the data table $T = (U, A \cup \{c\})$ is of the form (a, v), where $a \in A$ is an easy-to-know attribute and $v \in V_a$ is a possible value of the attribute a. The well-formed formulas (wff) of the logic is closed under the Boolean connectives negation($\neg$), conjunction($\wedge$), disjunction($\vee$), and implication($\rightarrow$). For the semantics, an individual $u \in U$ satisfies an atomic formula (a, v), written as $u \models_T (a, v)$ iff $a(u) = v$. Intuitively, any individual satisfying (a, v) has v as the value of his attribute a. The satisfaction of other wffs can then be defined recursively as usual.

From the semantics of decision logic, we define the truth set of a wff φ with respect to the data table T, denoted by $|\varphi|_T$, as $\{u \in U \mid u \models_T \varphi\}$. Thus each wff φ specifies a subset of individuals $|\varphi|_T$ in the data table. When a query φ is submitted by an user to the data center, this means this user wants to know the distribution of the sub-population $|\varphi|_T$ on V_c. If the query is correctly answered, the user would also simultaneously know the distribution of the sub-population $U - |\varphi|_T$ by the axioms of probability. In other words, a correctly answered query would partition the population into two sub-populations and the distributions thereof on the confidential attribute values are known respectively. In this way, the user can subsequently query the data center to refine his knowledge regarding the distributions of the different sub-populations on the confidential attribute values. To model the evolution of the user's information after different queries, we need a formal representation of user's information states. The next section will be devoted to the definitions of such representation.

3   The Information States

From here on, let us fix a data table $T = (U, A \cup \{c\})$. Let $V_c = \{s_0, s_1, \ldots, s_{t-1}\}$ be the set of possible values for the confidential attribute and let $U = \{u_1, \ldots, u_n\}$ be the set of individuals. A *logical partition* of U is a subset of DL wffs $\Pi = \{\varphi_1, \varphi_2, \ldots, \varphi_m\}$ such that $|\varphi_1|_T \cup \cdots \cup |\varphi_m|_T = U$ and $|\varphi_i|_T \cap |\varphi_j|_T = \emptyset$ if $i \neq j$. Each $|\varphi_i|_T$ is called an equivalence class of Π. A piece of information (or knowledge) known to the user is given by a logical partition of U, a set of probability distributions indexed by the wffs of the partition, and the number of investigated individuals. In the following, we use $|\varphi|$ to denote the cardinality of $|\varphi|_T$.

Definition 2 *An information state (or a knowledge state) $\mathcal{I}$ for the set of possible private attribute values V_c and the set of individuals U is a triplet*

$$(\Pi, (\mu_i)_{0 \leq i \leq t-1}, (\kappa_i)_{0 \leq i \leq t-1})$$

where Π is a logical partition on U and for all $0 \leq i \leq t-1$, $\mu_i : \Pi \to [0, 1]$ and $\kappa_i : \Pi \to \mathcal{N}$ ($\mathcal{N}$ denotes the set of natural number) are functions satisfying the following constraints for any $\varphi \in \Pi$,

(i) $\sum_{i=0}^{t-1} \mu_i(\varphi) = 1$,

(ii) $|\varphi| \cdot \mu_i(\varphi)$ is a natural number, and

(iii) $\kappa_i(\varphi) \leq |\varphi| \cdot \mu_i(\varphi)$

For ease of description, we use the vector notations in denoting μ_i's and κ_i's. Thus $\boldsymbol{\mu} = (\mu_0, \ldots, \mu_{t-1})$ and $\boldsymbol{\kappa} = (\kappa_0, \ldots, \kappa_{t-1})$ denotes vector mappings which can be applied to elements of Π and the result of such application is a vector consisting of the results of applying its component functions to the element. The dimension of each vector will be self-evident from the context and not explicitly specified. By the vector notation, an information state defined above can be denoted by $(\Pi, \boldsymbol{\mu}, \boldsymbol{\kappa})$. Let $\mathcal{I}$ be such an information state, then $(\Pi, \boldsymbol{\mu})$ is called a *partial knowledge state* compatible with $\mathcal{I}$. Note that a partial knowledge state may be compatible with various information states.

Within an information state, the user partitions the population into a number of subpopulations. He knows the probability distribution of each subpopulation on the confidential attribute values. Intuitively, $\mu_i(\varphi)$ is the proportion of the individuals in sub-population $|\varphi|_T$ which have confidential attribute value s_i, whereas $\kappa_i(\varphi)$ is the number of investigated individuals in sub-population $|\varphi|_T$ which have confidential attribute value s_i. Since each DL wff φ is composed from atomic formulas with easy-to-know attributes only, it can be assumed that it takes little effort for the user to verify whether a given individual satisfies φ. Furthermore, it can also be assumed that the cardinality of the truth set of each φ is known to the public. However, note that it may sometimes be very difficult for the user to locate an individual satisfying a specific φ from the whole population U.

The information states of an user can be subsequently changed by his investigation of some individuals in a specific sup-population and by his queries posed to and the answers obtained from the data center. This is a process of knowledge refinement and can be modeled by the knowledge acquisition actions as follows.

A logical partition Π_2 is a refinement of another logical partition Π_1, denoted by $\Pi_2 \sqsubseteq \Pi_1$, if for all $\varphi_2 \in \Pi_2$, there exists $\varphi_1 \in \Pi_1$ such that $|\varphi_2|_T \subseteq |\varphi_1|_T$. It is clear that if $\Pi_2 \sqsubseteq \Pi_1$, then each $|\varphi_1|_T$ such that $\varphi_1 \in \Pi_1$ can be written as a union of the truth sets of some wffs in Π_2.

Definition 3 *Let $\mathcal{I}_1 = (\Pi_1, \boldsymbol{\mu_1}, \boldsymbol{\kappa_1})$ and $\mathcal{I}_2 = (\Pi_2, \boldsymbol{\mu_2}, \boldsymbol{\kappa_2})$ be two information states. $\mathcal{I}_2$ is a refinement of $\mathcal{I}_1$, also denoted by $\mathcal{I}_2 \sqsubseteq \mathcal{I}_1$, if both of the following conditions are satisfied:*

1. $\Pi_2 \sqsubseteq \Pi_1$.
2. *For each $\varphi \in \Pi_1$, if $|\varphi|_T = \bigcup_{1 \leq i \leq l} |\varphi_i|_T$ for some set $\{\varphi_1, \ldots, \varphi_l\} \subseteq \Pi_2$, then*

$$|\varphi| \cdot \boldsymbol{\mu_1}(\varphi) = \sum_{i=1}^{l} |\varphi_i| \cdot \boldsymbol{\mu_2}(\varphi_i),$$

and

$$\boldsymbol{\kappa_1}(\varphi) \leq \sum_{i=1}^{l} \boldsymbol{\kappa_2}(\varphi_i).$$

Note that the arithmetics (addition and multiplication) and comparison between vectors (and scalars) are defined as usual. For example, the addition of two vectors is carried out point-wise and results in a vector of the same dimension.

In our framework, there are two kinds of knowledge acquisition actions which can refine the user's information states. The first one is the query action. Each query action is represented by a wff φ in DL. The intended answer of the query is the distribution of the confidential values within the selected population $|\varphi|_T$ in the database. The other is the investigation action, which is specified by a wff φ and a positive integer number k. This means that the user have investigated k individuals from the set $|\varphi|_T$ in this action. For the uniformity of the representation, each knowledge acquisition action is written as $\alpha = (\varphi, k)$ for some DL wff φ and $k \geq 0$. When $k > 0$, it is an investigation action, whereas it is a query one if $k = 0$.

Definition 4 *1. A knowledge acquisition action $(\varphi, 0)$ is applicable under the information state $\mathcal{I}_1 = (\Pi_1, \mu_1, \kappa_1)$ and results in a state $\mathcal{I}_2 = (\Pi_2, \mu_2, \kappa_2)$ if*

   a) there exists $\varphi' \in \Pi_1$ such that $|\varphi|_T \subseteq |\varphi'|_T$,
   b) $\Pi_2 = \Pi_1 - \{\varphi'\} \cup \{\varphi, \varphi' \wedge \neg\varphi\}$,
   c) $\mathcal{I}_2$ is a refinement of $\mathcal{I}_1$,
   d) $\kappa_2(\psi) = \kappa_1(\psi)$ for any $\psi \in \Pi_1 - \{\varphi'\}$, and
   e) $\kappa_2(\varphi) + \kappa_2(\varphi' \wedge \neg\varphi) = \kappa_1(\varphi')$.

2. A knowledge acquisition action (φ, k) where $k > 0$ is applicable under the information state $\mathcal{I}_1 = (\Pi_1, \mu_1, \kappa_1)$, and $\mathcal{I}_2 = (\Pi_2, \mu_2, \kappa_2)$ is a resultant state of the application if

   a) $\varphi \in \Pi_1$ and $k \leq |\varphi| - \sum_{i=0}^{t-1} \kappa_i(\varphi)$
   b) $\Pi_1 = \Pi_2$,
   c) $\mu_1 = \mu_2$,
   d) $\kappa_2(\psi) = \kappa_1(\psi)$ for any $\psi \neq \varphi$, and
   e) $\sum_{i=0}^{t-1} \kappa_{2i}(\varphi) = \sum_{i=0}^{t-1} \kappa_{1i}(\varphi) + k$.

Since the goal of the user is to refine his knowledge by the queries, a rational user would pose his queries so that his knowledge would be improved by the answers of the queries. Thus if the user's information state is (Π_1, μ_1, κ_1), then he poses a query about a subset of an equivalence class in Π_1. This is the requirement of Condition 1a in Definition 4. Then, after the query is answered, the corresponding equivalence class is partitioned into two parts — one satisfying φ and the other not, so we have the Condition 1b in Definition 4. Condition 1c in Definition 4 further requires that the answer is correct so that the resultant information state is a refinement of the original one. Furthermore, since the query action does not cause any new individuals being investigated, the κ_2 function agrees with κ_1 in the part of the population which is not split by the query, while for the split part, the number of investigated individuals is not changed in total. This is reflected respectively in Conditions 1d and 1e of the definition.

In the case of investigation action, we assume the user will only investigate the individuals in a sub-population represented by a wff in Π_1. The assumption is inessential, since, if the investigated individuals are across some different sub-populations, the corresponding investigation action can be decomposed into a sequence of actions satisfying the applicability condition. Since it is assumed that the user knows the total number of individuals in $|\varphi|_T$ and those which have been investigated by him so far is equal to $\sum_{i=0}^{t-1} \kappa_i(\varphi)$, he would not try to investigate more individuals than all remaining ones. This is exactly required by the applicability condition of Definition 4.2a. Conditions 2b to 2d are obvious since these values are not affected by the investigation. What the investigation can affect is the total number of the investigated individuals in $|\varphi|_T$ and this is reflected in Condition 2e.

4   The Value of Information

To quantitatively determine the value of information, we must have a user model. Let us consider the case where the user is an agent trying to use the private information to aid his decision in a game. The game is played between the agent and individuals in the population U. The agent can decide the rate he want to charge an individual for playing the game (i.e., the admission fee). The rate is decided on a personalized basis so that each individual may be charged with different rates. However, once an individual agrees to play the game with the agent and pay the fee asked by the agent, he will have a chance to get back some reward which will be the loss of the agent. The reward of an individual is determined by his confidential attribute value. Let r_i denote the reward of an individual with the confidential attribute value s_i for $0 \leq i \leq t-1$, then $\rho = (r_0, r_1, \ldots, r_{t-1}) \in \Re^t$ is called the loss vector of the agent.

Let $\mathcal{I}_0 = (\{\top\}, \mu_0, \kappa_0)$ be the initial information state of the user, where $\top$ denotes any tautology in the DL and $\kappa_0(\varphi) = (0, \ldots, 0)$. Let ρ be a given loss vector. The agent first decides the *base rate* of the game on the expected loss according to his initial information state, i.e., $R_0 = \rho \cdot \mu_0(\top)$. Thus, in the initial state, the expected payoff of the agent for playing the game is zero. However, once he acquires pieces of information and reaches a new information state, he can utilize the acquired information for making some profit.

We further assume that each individual will go into the game if he is charged with the base rate. However, he can refuse to do so if the agent charges him with a rate higher than the base one. The higher the rate, the more likely the individual refuses to play the game. If the information state is $\mathcal{I} = (\Pi, \mu, \kappa)$, where $\Pi = \{\varphi_1, \ldots, \varphi_m\}$, a reasonable decision of the agent for the rate of an individual u satisfying φ is as follows:

1. if u has been investigated and it is known that the confidential attribute value of u is s_i, then the most profitable decision of the agent would be to charge the individual with $\max(R_o, r_i)$ so that the agent's payoff is $\max(R_o - r_i, 0)$;
2. if the individual has not been investigated, the agent knows the probability of the confidential attribute value of u being s_i to be

$$p_i(\varphi) = \frac{|\varphi| \cdot \mu_i(\varphi) - \kappa_i(\varphi)}{|\varphi| - \sum_{i=0}^{t-1} \kappa_i(\varphi)}. \tag{1}$$

In this case, the most reasonable decision of the agent would be to charge the individual with $\max(R_o, \sum_{i=0}^{t-1} p_i(\varphi) \cdot r_i)$ so that the agent's expected payoff would be $\max(R_o - \sum_{i=0}^{t-1} p_i(\varphi) \cdot r_i, 0)$

Thus, in average, the agent can have the following expected payoff B_φ in playing the game with an individual satisfying φ:

$$B_\varphi = \max(R_o - \sum_{i=0}^{t-1}(p_i(\varphi) \cdot r_i), 0) \cdot \frac{|\varphi| - \sum_{i=0}^{t-1} \kappa_i(\varphi)}{|\varphi|} \qquad (2)$$
$$+ \sum_{i=0}^{t-1} \max(R_o - r_i, 0) \cdot \frac{\kappa_i(\varphi)}{|\varphi|}$$

Thus, by using the knowledge about the individuals' confidential attributes, the agent can raise the rates of those who may incur a greater loss to him in order to avoid the possible loss. The value of the information is then dependent on how much he can benefit from obtaining the information. The expected gain of the agent with regard to each individual is computed by

$$B_{\mathcal{I}} = \sum_{\varphi \in \Pi} B_\varphi \cdot \frac{|\varphi|}{|U|},$$

if he decides the rates according to the two principles above.

Example 1 The scenario described above usually occurs between an insurance company and its customers. The base rate is applied to a typical customer if the company does not have any further information about his health condition. However, for the customers of high risk, the company would raise their rates. Thus the health information of the customers would be valuable to the insurance company. To avoid the leakage of privacy, the data center may correspondingly raise the cost of answering a query so that the information value for the company is counter-balanced. The company would not have the incentive to obtain the private information. ■

The notions of the value of information have been extensively studied in decision theory[7,14]. In our model above, if investigation actions are not allowed, all information states are of the form $(\Pi, \boldsymbol{\mu}, \boldsymbol{\kappa_0})$, so $\kappa_{0i}(\varphi) = 0$ and $p_i(\varphi) = \mu_i(\varphi)$ for all $0 \le i \le t - 1$ and $\varphi \in \Pi$. Consequently, $B_{\mathcal{I}}$ would be simplified into

$$\sum_{\varphi \in \Pi} \max(R_o - \boldsymbol{\mu}(\varphi) \cdot \boldsymbol{\rho}, 0) \cdot \frac{|\varphi|}{|U|}$$

which is the value of partial information defined in [14] if our user model is appropriately formulated as a decision problem of the agent. While in our case the partial information is obtained by querying the data center, another approach for obtaining partial information by sampling is suggested in [14]. Though sampling is similar to investigation, the information obtained from these two kinds of actions are quite different. For the sampling actions, even though the chosen individuals may be thoroughly investigated, only the statistical information of these investigated individuals would be kept. In fact, it is the statistical information which would be used in the prediction of the status of the whole population. However, for the investigative actions, the user would indeed keep the personal information of each investigated individual and not do the statistical inference from the investigated individuals to the whole population.

On the other hand, if no query actions are possible, the information states are always of the form $(\{\top\}, \boldsymbol{\mu_0}, \boldsymbol{\kappa})$. Once all individuals have been fully investigated (though this is hardly possible in any practical case) the information state becomes a perfect state $\mathcal{I} = (\{\top\}, \boldsymbol{\mu_0}, \boldsymbol{\kappa})$, where $\kappa_i(\top) = \mu_{0i}(\top) \cdot |U|$, so $p_i(\top) = 0$ for all $0 \le i \le t - 1$. Consequently, $B_{\mathcal{I}}$ would be simplified into

$$\sum_{i=0}^{t-1} \max(R_o - r_i, 0) \cdot \mu_{0i}(\top)$$

which is precisely the value of perfect information defined in [14]. Thus we have modeled the value of hybrid information in the above-defined framework.

5   Privacy Protection by Pricing Mechanism

5.1   Basic Scheme

According to the user model above, the user can improve his payoff from 0 to $B_{\mathcal{I}}$ when his information state is evolved from the initial state to $\mathcal{I}$. If the information is free of charge, the user would gladly receive it and consequently, the privacy of the individuals may be invaded. Thus, one approach to privacy protection is to impose costs on the answers of the queries so that the user cannot make a profit from obtaining the private information. This can be achieved by including a pricing mechanism in the data center. However, since the answer to a query may have different effects under different information states, the pricing mechanism must be adaptive according to the query history of the user. In general, it is very difficult to design an adaptive pricing mechanism since the users may have to pay different prices for the same queries under different situations. Therefore, instead of charging each query separately, we shall consider a more restricted setting. Assume that each user is allowed to ask a batch of queries only once. Afterward, he can do any investigative actions he wants. However, the data center would not answer his queries afterwards. Thus the pricing mechanism of the data center is to decide the cost of each batch of queries so that the user cannot benefit from receiving the answers of the queries.

Let $(\Pi, \boldsymbol{\mu}, \boldsymbol{\kappa})$ be the information state of the user after a sequence of queries and follow-up investigative actions, where $\Pi = \{\varphi_1, \varphi_2, \dots, \varphi_m\}$. Since the data center has no control on how the user will carry out his investigation after receiving the answers, it can only guarantee that the cost is high enough so that the user cannot make a profit from the answers of the queries, no matter what investigation be done. Thus, based only on the partial knowledge state $\mathcal{P} = (\Pi, \boldsymbol{\mu})$, the data center must estimate the maximum payoff the agent can have under different information states compatible with $\mathcal{P}$. Let $\mathbf{k} = (k_1, \ldots, k_m)$ be an m-tuple of non-negative integers and define

$$F_{\mathbf{k}} = \{\kappa \mid \sum_{i=0}^{t-1} \kappa_i(\varphi_j) = k_j, \forall 1 \leq j \leq m\}$$

as the set of κ functions which denote the possible investigation results when a specific number of individuals has been investigated. The set of information states compatible with $\mathcal{P}$ and $\mathbf{k}$ is defined as

$$\mathcal{IS}(\mathcal{P}, \mathbf{k}) = \{(\mathcal{P}, \kappa) \mid \kappa \in F_{\mathbf{k}}\}$$

and the maximal value of information of the agent under $\mathcal{P}$ and $\mathbf{k}$ is defined as

$$B(\mathcal{P}, \mathbf{k}) = \max\{B_{\mathcal{I}} \mid \mathcal{I} \in \mathcal{IS}(\mathcal{P}, \mathbf{k})\}.$$

We now further assume that a cost function $\gamma_{inv} : \Phi \times \mathcal{Z}^+ \rightarrow \Re^+$ is available to both the user and the data center, where Φ is the set of DL wffs and $\mathcal{Z}^+$ and $\Re^+$ are respectively the set of positive integer and real numbers. The intended meaning of $\gamma_{inv}(\varphi, k)$ is the cost of the investigation of k individuals satisfying φ. It can be assumed that γ_{inv} is a super-linear function in its second argument. Thus, when the user poses a batch of queries Q, the data center can know what the resultant partial knowledge state $\mathcal{P}$ would be once the answer is released. Therefore, the price of Q must be decided before releasing the information. The price $price(Q)$ of the answers to the batch of queries should be decided such that

$$|U| \cdot B(\mathcal{P}, \mathbf{k}) - \sum_{i=1}^{m} \gamma_{inv}(\varphi_i, k_i) \leq price(Q) \tag{3}$$

holds for any $\mathbf{k}$. The lowest solution of $price(Q)$ for (3) is

$$\max_{\mathbf{k}} |U| \cdot \max\{B_{\mathcal{I}} \mid \mathcal{I} \in \mathcal{IS}(\mathcal{P}, \mathbf{k})\} - \sum_{i=1}^{m} \gamma_{inv}(\varphi_i, k_i) \tag{4}$$

where the domain of $\mathbf{k}$ is finite since $0 \leq k_i \leq |\varphi_i|$.

5.2   Usefulness of Information

In our pricing mechanism, the data center assumes that the user can play the above-mentioned game with all individuals in U and charge them based on the total gain he can achieve. However, this may be an over-estimation since the user cannot play the game with all individuals when the population is large. To circumvent the problem, we may assume that the user must spend some resources for playing the game with the individuals. Let $\gamma_{ply} : \Phi \times \mathcal{Z}^+ \rightarrow \Re^+$ be another cost function such that $\gamma_{ply}(\varphi, l)$ denotes the cost of the user playing the game with l individuals satisfying φ. Given an m-tuple of non-negative integers $\mathbf{l} = (l_1, \ldots, l_m)$ and an information state $\mathcal{I}$, define

$$B_{\mathcal{I}}^{\mathbf{l}} = \sum_{i=1}^{m} B_{\varphi_i} \cdot l_i.$$

The price in (4) can be replaced by

$$\max_{\mathbf{k},\mathbf{l}}(\max\{B_{\mathcal{I}}^{\mathbf{l}} \mid \mathcal{I} \in \mathcal{IS}(\mathcal{P}, \mathbf{k})\} - \sum_{i=1}^{m} \gamma_{inv}(\varphi_i, k_i) - \sum_{i=1}^{m} \gamma_{ply}(\varphi_i, l_i)) \qquad (5)$$

where both the domains of $\mathbf{k}$ and $\mathbf{l}$ are restricted to $0 \le k_i, l_i \le |\varphi_i|$.

Intuitively, each l_i and k_j represent the *usefulness* of information. Given two equivalent classes in a logical partition, it may be easier to find potential members in one equivalence class than in the other depending on the conditions each equivalence class satisfied. It may also be true that it is easier, and thus cost-effective, to investigate members in one equivalence class than in the other. These two may be closely related, but not necessarily the same.

Example 2 Assume we again use the insurance company model mentioned in Example 1. Assume the world population is represented by all adults in the country. An equivalence class may be characterized as being the people living in the same county while another equivalence class is described as the people with weight between 60 to 65 kilograms. It is easy for the first group of people to be investigated and then to be added as customers, while it is relatively difficult for the second group of people. ∎

Thus the data center can decide the price of the answers to the batch of queries Q by a two-level maximization procedure in (4) or (5). The outer level maximization would depend on the form of the cost functions γ_{inv} and/or γ_{ply}, so it is unlikely to find an analytic solution for it. However, the inner maximization can be reduced to a set of m maximization of B_φ for each $\varphi \in \Pi$. More specifically, given φ and $0 \le k \le |\varphi|$, it is to find $\kappa(\varphi)$ which maximizes B_φ among all κ satisfying $\sum_{i=0}^{t-1} \kappa_i(\varphi) = k$ and $\kappa_i(\varphi) \le |\varphi| \cdot \mu_i(\varphi)$ for all $0 \le i \le t - 1$. This is in turn equivalent to the following constraint optimization problem in the integer domain:

$$\text{Maximize } \max(R_0 - \sum_{i=0}^{t-1} \frac{n_i - x_i}{N - k} \cdot r_i, 0) \cdot \frac{N-k}{N} + \sum_{i=0}^{t-1} \max(R_0 - r_i, 0) \cdot \frac{x_i}{N}$$
$$\text{s.t.}$$
$$x_0 + x_1 + \cdots + x_{t-1} = k \qquad (6)$$
$$0 \le x_i \le n_i \ (0 \le i \le t-1)$$

where N and n_i's correspond to $|\varphi|$ and $|\varphi| \cdot \mu_i(\varphi)$'s respectively. The solution of Equation (6) can be given by the following proposition for $k \le N$. Without loss of generality, we assume $r_0 \ge r_1 \ge \cdots \ge r_{t-1}$ for the loss vector in the proposition.

Proposition 1 *Assume* $N = \sum_{i=0}^{t-1} n_i$

1. *if $k = N$, then the solution of Equation (6) is $x_i = n_i$ for $0 \leq i \leq t-1$ and its maximum value is*

$$\sum_{i=0}^{t-1} \max(R_0 - r_i, 0) \cdot \frac{n_i}{N};$$

2. *if if $k < N$ and l is the smallest natural number such that $\sum_{i=0}^{l} n_i > k$, then the solution of Equation (6) is*

$$x_i = \begin{cases} n_i & \text{if } i < l, \\ k - \sum_{i=0}^{l-1} n_i & \text{if } i = l, \\ 0 & \text{if } i > l, \end{cases}$$

and its maximum value is

$$\max(R_0 - \sum_{i=l+1}^{t-1} \frac{n_i}{N-k} \cdot r_i + \frac{\sum_{i=0}^{l} n_i - k}{N-k} \cdot r_l, 0) \cdot \frac{N-k}{N}$$

$$+ \sum_{i=0}^{l-1} \max(R_0 - r_i, 0) \cdot \frac{n_i}{N} + \max(R_0 - r_l, 0) \cdot \frac{k - \sum_{i=0}^{l-1} n_i}{N}.$$

The individuals who will incur more loss to the agent are high risk ones. For the low risk individuals, the investigation cannot improve the payoff for the agent. However, for the high risk ones, the investigation can indeed decrease the loss for the agent by raising their admission fees appropriately. The more high risk individuals have been investigated, the more loss the agent can avoid, so the maximum payoff occurs when the investigation is carried out from the most risky individuals to the least risky ones. This intuition is verified by the preceding proposition.

6 Related Works

To quantify the value of information is by no means a novel problem. However, the quantitative models for privacy protection provides a new angle to look at the problem. As shown in section 4, our model for the value of information has generalized a standard notion in decision theory[14,7]. While the decision-theoretic analysis [14] emphasizes the value of information from the decision maker's viewpoint, our model is mainly concerned with privacy protection by the information provider. For the former, a decision maker can decide if he will purchase a piece of information according to the value of the information. For the latter, the information provider can charge the user of the information with appropriate rates.

An alternative model for the value of information in the privacy protection context is proposed in [1,2]. In their model, the value of information is estimated by the expected cost the user must pay for achieving the perfect knowledge state from the given information. The estimation is based on the rationale that the more investigation efforts a piece of information can reduce, the more valuable it is. However, without regarding the user model, the value of information defined there may not reflect the real situation.

Besides the decision theoretic analysis, the value of information can also be estimated by some information theoretic measures. The central notion of such measures is the entropy introduced by Shannon[20]. In the machine learning literatures, it is used to define the information gain of an attribute for a classification problem[16]. Though the information gain is an useful index in selecting the most informative features for the classification problem, it still suffers the same problem as the value of information defined in [1,2] since it does not take into account the fact that some confidential attribute values are more sensitive than others.

The sensitivity of different attribute values are taken into account in the average benefit and average cost models proposed in [3]. However, while only query actions are allowed there, we also consider the investigative actions in modelling the value of information.

In contrast with the quantitative approach of this paper, some qualitative criteria for privacy protection have been proposed in [11,12,18,19,21]. These criteria are designed to protect personal sensitive information in the release of a microdata set, i.e. a set of records containing information on individuals. The main objective is to avoid the re-identification of individuals or in other words, to prevent the possibility of deducing which record corresponds to a particular individual even though the explicit identifier of the individual is not contained in the released information. On the other hand, our models are concerned with the release of statistical information which is less specific than microdata in general. However, microdata release can also be handled in our framework when the queries are specific enough. Let us define a complete specification formula (CSF) as a DL wff of the form $\wedge_{a \in A}(a, v_a)$, where A is the set of all easy-to-know attributes and v_a is a value in the domain of A. The answer to the batch of queries Q consisting of all CSF's is equivalent to the microdata release of the whole data table T. Therefore, our models are applicable in a more general context.

7   Conclusion

In this paper, we present a quantitative model for privacy protection. In the model, a formal representation of the user's information states is given, and we estimate the value of information for the user by considering a specific user model. Under the user model, the privacy protection task is to ensure that the user cannot profit from obtaining the private information.

It must be emphasized that the value of information is defined with respect to the particular user model. When other user models are considered, the value of information may be different. Some examples can be seen in [13]. A problem for the pricing mechanism arises naturally since different users may put different values on the same information. This means that we may have to set different prices for different kinds of users on the same information. However, this is not so odd as it seems at first glance. In fact, differentiating prices have been employed in the software market. Differences usually occur in educational and commercial uses.

There are further complicated problems in privacy protection which can not be resolved from a purely technical aspect. For example, our schemes cannot prevent a group of users from collectively investigating private information by individually querying the data center. This must be considered from a legal aspect. Upon releasing data to a user, the user must sign a contract prohibiting him from revealing the data to others. The legal possibility for the collusion of a group of users is thus blocked. In future works, we would like to investigate how technology and law can be fully combined in the protection of privacy.

References

1. Y.-C. Chiang. Protecting privacy in public database (in Chinese). Master's thesis, Graduate Institute of Information Management, National Taiwan University, 2000.
2. Y.-C. Chiang, T.-s. Hsu, S. Kuo, and D.-W. Wang. Preserving confidentially when sharing medical data. In *Proceedings of Asia Pacific Medical Informatics Conference*, 2000.
3. Y.T. Chiang, Y.C. Chiang, T.-s. Hsu, C.-J. Liau, and D.-W. Wang. How much privacy? – a system to safe guard personal privacy while releasing database. In *Proceedings of the 3rd International Conference on Rough Sets and Current Trends in Computing*, LNCS. Springer-Verlag, 2002.
4. F. Y. Chin and G. Özsoyoğlu. Auditing and inference control in statistical databases. *IEEE Transactions Software Engineering*, 8:574–582, 1982.
5. L. H. Cox. Suppression methodology and statistical disclosure control. *Journal of the American Statistical Association*, 75:377–385, 1980.
6. D. E. R. Denning. *Cryptography and Data Security*. Addison-Wesley, 1982.
7. G.D. Eppen and F.J. Gould. *Quantitative Concepts for Management*. Prentice Hall, 1985.
8. F. Duarte de Carvalho, N. P. Dellaert, and M. de Sanches Osório. Statistical disclosure in two-dimensional tables: General tables. *Journal of the American Statistical Association*, 428:1547–1557, 1994.
9. D. Gusfield. A graph theoretic approach to statistical data security. *SIAM Journal on Computing*, 17:552–571, 1988.
10. T.-s. Hsu and M. Y. Kao. Security problems for statistical databases with general cell suppressions. In *Proceedings of the 9th International Conference on Scientific and Statistical Database Management*, pages 155–164, 1997.
11. T.-s. Hsu, C.-J. Liau, and D.-W. Wang. A logical model for privacy protection. In *Proceedings of the 4th International Conference on Information Security*, LNCS 2200, pages 110–124. Springer-Verlag, 2001.
12. A.J. Hundepool and L.C.R.J. Willenborg. "μ- and τ-ARGUS: Software for statistical disclosure control". In *Proceedings of the 3rd International Seminar on Statistical Confidentiality*, 1996.
13. J. Kleinberg, C.H. Papadimitriou, and P. Raghavan. "On the value of private information". In *Proc. 8th Conf. on Theoretical Aspects of Rationality and Knowledge*, 2001.

14. D.V. Lindley. *Making Decisions*. John Wiley & Sons, 1985.
15. T.S. Mayer. Privacy and confidentiality research and the u.s. census bureau recommendations based on a review of the literature. Technical Report RSM2002/01, U.S. Bureau of the Census, 2002.
16. T. Mitchell. *Machine Learning*. McGraw-Hill, 1997.
17. Z. Pawlak. *Rough Sets–Theoretical Aspects of Reasoning about Data*. Kluwer Academic Publishers, 1991.
18. P. Samarati. "Protecting respondents' identities in microdata release". *IEEE Transactions on Knowledge and Data Engineering*, 13(6):1010–1027, 2001.
19. P. Samarati and L. Sweeney. Protecting privacy when disclosing information: k-anonymity and its enforcement through generalization and suppression. Technical report SRI-CSL-98-04, Computer Science Laboratory, SRI International, 1998.
20. C.E. Shannon. "The mathematical theory of communication". *The Bell System Technical Journal*, 27(3&4):379–423,623–656, 1948.
21. L. Sweeney. "Guaranteeing anonymity when sharing medical data, the Datafly system". In *Proceedings of American Medical Informatics Association*, 1997.
22. W. E. Winkler. The state of record linkage and current research problems. Technical Report RR99/04, U.S. Bureau of the Census, 1999.
23. W. E. Winkler. Record linkage software and methods for merging administrative lists. Technical Report RR01/03, U.S. Bureau of the Census, 2001.

A New Offline Privacy Protecting E-cash System with Revokable Anonymity

Weidong Qiu[1], Kefei Chen[2], and Dawu Gu[2]

[1] University of Hagen, Dept. of Communication Systems
D-58084 Hagen, Germany
weidong.qiu@fernuni-hagen.de
[2] Dept of Computer Science and Engineering Shanghai Jiaotong University
200030 Shanghai, China
{kfchen,dwgu}@mail1.sjtu.edu.cn

Abstract. Some privacy-protecting electronic payment systems [2,13, 15,17] have been proposed to realize the revocable anonymity among users. In this paper, organizing all users into a group, we present a new fair off-line electronic cash system (E-Cash for short). This new E-Cash system is more efficient and more secure. The system is able of coin tracing and owner tracing. The anonymity of the system can be revocable under certain conditions by an off-line trusted third authority, the system is untraceable (under normal cases), unlinkable and double-spending resistant. Furthermore, compared with the previous E-Cash systems, our payment protocol is more efficient in computing.

Keywords. Privacy protecting, electronic payment, E-Cash, revokable anonymity, fair off-line system.

1 Introduction

Many electronic payment systems offering unconditional anonymity have been proposed in the recent years (e.g. [1,9]). However, these unconditional privacy protecting systems sometimes could be misused by criminals for blackmailing or money laundering [25]. It has been proposed that anonymity revokable systems with a trusted third party involved (e.g. the government or the authorities of law enforcement), should be designed to prevent the payment systems from being misused.

The concept of fair E-Cash system was put forth independently by E. Brickell [2] and M. Stadler [23] in 1995. It offers a compromise between the need of the privacy protection of users and effectively preventing the misuse by criminals. On one hand, the bank and the merchant can't obtain the identities of users by themselves. But on the other hand, under some special circumstances[1], with the help of the bank, the trusted third party can remove the anonymity of the transaction and recognize the user's identity.

---

[1] For example, under the cases where there are suspect criminal activities,e.g black-mailing or money laundering

A.H. Chan and V. Gligor (Eds.): ISC 2002, LNCS 2433, pp. 177–190, 2002.

Based on the system of Brands [1], E. Brickell proposed a fair E-Cash system [2], in which a trustee must be involved in the transactions. J. Camenisch extended his anonymous payment system [9] to be a fair payment system[10]. In J. Camenisch's system, users have two accounts in bank: personal account and anonymous account. It is still an on-line system which means that all three parties (the bank, the merchant and the users) will be involved during a single transaction. J. Camenisch improved the system's efficiency in [4].

In 1996, Y. Frankel, U. Tsiounis and M. Yung proposed a fair off-line E-Cash system (FOLC) [15]. G. Davida, Y. Frankel, Y. Tsiounis and M.Young improved the efficiency of FOLC system [13]. Using interactive knowledge proofs, these systems need more communication among the bank, the users and the merchants. Furthermore, both systems of J. Camenisch and G. Davida [4,15] have to search in a database at the bank to be able of owner tracing. But it is not the case in our real life: The trusted third party should be responsible for revoking the anonymity rather than the bank. Bo Yang and Yuming Wang proposed a fair electronic payment system with a hardware electronic wallet [26]. In this system, an anonymous account was set on a hardware based electronic wallet where users could store their money withdrawn from their account in a bank. The hardware based wallet is composed of a PC and a Smart card, which makes it a little inconvenient and expensive for the users. Sander, Pfitzmann and Kügler proposed a new way to offer conditional anonymity without any trustees [17,20,22].

Since the concept of group signature scheme was first introduced by Chaum and van Heyst in 1991 [11], many various group signatures have been proposed [3,6,8,12]. A group signature scheme allows the members of the group to sign messages anonymously on behalf of the group. The group has a common open public key which could be used to verify the signature without revealing any information of the signer's identity. Furthermore, the group manager has the ability to remove the anonymity of signatures.

In 1999, Jacques Traoré presented a new group signature scheme [24] and constructed a privacy-protecting fair off-line E-Cash system . In this system, the properties of group signatures were used to realize the revokable anonymity of electronic cash. But coin tracing is not available and even worse the bank could trace the coin by itself in their system[2].

In this paper, integrating with the J. Camenisch's high efficient group signature scheme [5], we propose a new high efficient fair off-line E-Cash system (especially in payment protocol). It needs less communication for using non-interactive proofs of knowledge. The anonymities of users can be revoked in our double-spending resistant system and our system has the ability to trace both the electronic coin (coin tracing) and the owner of the electronic coin (owner tracing). Furthermore, the system is easy to describe and various electronic coins don't need different signing keys of the bank.

---

[2] During their payment protocol, the bank could get all information which it need to compute the electronic coin.

This paper is organized as follows: In section 2, we define the notations we adopt in this paper and then we introduce the non-interactive proofs of knowledge which will be used in our system. In Section 3, we describe our new fair off-line E-Cash system and show how to proceed with owner tracing and coin tracing. We discuss the security of this system in section 4. Some related work will be discussed in section 5. Finally, we conclude our paper in the last section.

2   Notations and Building Blocks

In this section, we describe some notations and building blocks for proofs of knowledge which will be used throughout this paper.

- The notation $x =?y$ means whether x and y are equal or not.
- The notation $N = \{n \mid n = pq,\ p < q,\ p = 2p' + 1, q = 2q' + 1\}$ is a set where p, q, p', q' are all prime numbers and are of equal length.
- $[a, b]$ denotes the following set: $\{a, a + 1, ..., b - 1, b\}$.
- m will denote a plain message which is related to the signature of proof of knowledge and could be an empty string ζ.
- $c[i]$ denotes the i bit position of the string c.
- $x \in_R E$ means that x is chosen uniformly at random from the set E.
- $G =< g >=< g_1 >=< g_2 >$ is a multiplicative group with the order having the bit length l_g. g, g_1, g_2 are the group's generators.
- The notations ϵ, l_g, l_1, l_2, k, $\tilde{l}$, are security parameters, where k is a fixed output length of a secure one way hash function $H(\cdot) : \{0,1\}^* \rightarrow \{0,1\}^k$; l_g is the length of the group's order; $\epsilon > 1$, k, l_1, $l_2 < l_g$, $\tilde{l} = \epsilon(l_2 + k) + 1$.

Other notations will be given as needed.

Now we introduce some building blocks which will be used by our system.

According to literature [5], these building blocks which called signatures on proof of knowledge(SPK for short), are signature schemes derived from statistical zero-knowledge proofs of knowledge[3]. Under some assumptions (e.g. modified strong RSA assumption and Diffie-Hellman decision assumption[5]), Fujisaki and Camenisch proved that the blocks considered in this paper are valid honest-verifier statistical zero-knowledge proof of knowledge [16].

We introduce three building blocks in the following, borrowing some notations from [5]. The first two show the knowledge of a discrete logarithm that lies in a certain interval. The third one, group-signature block, shows how can a group member generate the group's signatures.

Definition 1. *A proof of knowledge of the discrete logarithms of y with respect to g, which also proves that $\log_g y$ is in $[2^{l_1}, 2^{l_1} + 2^{l_2}]$ is a pair $(c, s) \in \{0, 1\}^k \times$*

---

[3] The approach of security analysis on these blocks, defined as random oracle model, has been formalised in [21]. As showed by Camenisch [5], although it was proved that this method doesn't work in general protocols, the blocks considered here are stilled believed to be valid.

$[-2^{l_2+k}, 2^{\epsilon(l_2+k)}]$ *satisfying* $c = H(g||y||g^{s-c2^{l_1}}y^c||m)$. *This proof of knowledge is denoted by*

$$SPK\{(\alpha) : y = g^\alpha \wedge (2^{l_1} - 2^{\epsilon(l_2+k)+1} < \alpha < 2^{l_1} + 2^{\epsilon(l_2+k)+1})\}(m).$$

If the discrete logarithm $x \in [2^{l_1}, 2^{l_1} + 2^{l_2}]$ is known such that $y = g^x$ holds, we could compute that proof as follows:

- choose $r \in_R \{0,1\}^{\epsilon(l_2+k)}$ and compute $t := g^r$
- compute the pair $c := H(g||y||t||m)$ and $s := r - c(x - 2^{l_1})(in Z)$.

A verifier can check the equation $c =? H(g||y||g^{s-c2^{l_1}}y^c||m)$ and whether $s \in [-2^{l_2+k}, 2^{\epsilon(l_2+k)}]$ to decide whether to accept the proof or not.

We now give definition 2, which is easy to obtain from definition 1.

Definition 2. *A proof of knowledge of the discrete logarithms of y_1 with respect to g and of the discrete logarithms of y_2 with respect to h, which also proves that $\log_g y_1$ is in $[2^{l_1}, 2^{l_1} + 2^{l_2}]$ is a triple $(c, s_1, s_2) \in \{0,1\}^k \times [-2^{l_2+k}, 2^{\epsilon(l_2+k)}] \times Z$. We denote this proof of knowledge by*

$$SPK\{(\alpha, \beta) : y_1 = g^\alpha \wedge y_2 = h^\beta \wedge (2^{l_1} - 2^{\epsilon(l_2+k)+1} < \alpha < 2^{l_1} + 2^{\epsilon(l_2+k)+1})\}(m)$$

We could construct that proof and get the triple easily just as we did in Definition 1.

Definition 3. *A seven tuple $(c, s_1, s_2, s_3, a, b, d) \in \{0,1\}^k \times [-2^{l_2+k}, 2^{\epsilon(l_2+k)}] \times [-2^{l_g+l_1+k}, 2^{\epsilon(l_g+l_1+k)}] \times [-2^{l_g+k}, 2^{\epsilon(l_g+k)}] \times G^3$ satisfying $c = H(g|| h||y||z||a|| ||d||z^cb^{s_1-c2^{l_1}}/y^{s_2}||a^{s_1-c2^{l_1}}/g^{s_2}||a^cg^{s_3}||d^cg^{s_1-c2^{l_1}}h^{s_3}|| m)$ is a group signature of a message $m \in \{0,1\}^*$ with respect to the knowledge $u^e = z$ (see [5]) and could be denoted as:*

$$SPK\{(\eta, \vartheta, \xi) : z = b^\eta/y^\vartheta \wedge a^\eta/g^\vartheta = 1 \wedge a = g^\xi \wedge d = g^\eta h^\xi$$
$$\wedge (2^{l_1} - 2^{\epsilon(l_2+k)+1} < \eta < 2^{l_1} + 2^{\epsilon(l_2+k)+1})\}(m).$$

As a member of the group, one can sign a message $m \in \{0,1\}^*$ on the group's behalf as follows:

1. Choose an integer $w \in \{0,1\}^{l_g}$, and compute $a := g^w$, $b := uy^w, d := g^e h^w$,
2. Choose $r_1 \in_R \{0,1\}^{\epsilon(l_2+k)}$, $r_2 \in_R \{0,1\}^{\epsilon(l_g+l_1+k)}$, $r_3 \in_R \{0,1\}^{\epsilon(l_g+k)}$,
3. Compute $t_1 := b^{r_1}(1/y)^{r_2}$, $t_2 := a^{r_1}(1/g)^{r_2}$, $t_3 := g^{r_3}$, $t_4 := g^{r_1} h^{r_3}$,
4. Compute $c := H(g||h||y||z||a||b||d||t_1||t_2||t_3||t_4||m)$,
5. Compute $s_1 := r_1 - c(e - 2^{l_1})$, $s_2 := r_2 - cew$, $s_3 := r_3 - cw$, $s_1, s_2, s_3 \in Z$.

The seven tuple $(c, s_1, s_2, s_3, a, b, d)$ is the result of group signature $SPK\{(e, we, w)\}(m)$. It is easy to show that this result satisfies the equation in the definition 3. In addition, when verifying the group signature, the interval of s_1, s_2, s_3 should also be checked.

3   New Fair and Offline E-cash System

Usually, an E-Cash system is composed of a set of protocols in which three participants are involved : a user, a merchant and a bank. Basically, three protocols will be included in an E-Cash system: *withdrawal protocol* involving the user and the bank, *payment protocol* involving the user and the merchant and *deposit protocol* involving the merchant and the bank. In an off-line system, these three protocols proceed separately, whereas in an on-line case, the bank will participate in a single transaction in which payment and deposit protocols will take place simultaneously. In our system, where the fair property will be deployed, one more party (the trusted third party) and two more protocols (registration protocol at the trusted third party and tracing protocol for revoking the anonymity) will be added.

When we analyze the security of an E-Cash system the following aspects should be considered:

– anonymity (or revokable anonymity in fair E-Cash systems case),
– unforgeability,
– undeniability,
– unlinkability,
– double-spending resistance.

Just as mentioned in the previous section, a fair E-Cash system should keep users anonymous. On the other hand, under certain conditions, the system could remove the anonymities of users to help tracing the suspects. This allows the trusted third party, e.g. law enforcement authority, to catch users who are misusing electronic coins for criminal activities while protecting the privacy of the honest users. For this reason, our system consists of one more tracing protocol. As pointed out by previous systems, two mechanisms exist to revoke the anonymities of users:

1. **Coin tracing:** given the bank's view of the withdrawal protocol, the trusted third party can compute the electronic coin and trace it. This allows to trace the blackmailed electronic coins.
2. **Owner tracing:** to prevent money-laundering in privacy protecting E-Cash systems, with the bank's view of the payment protocol, the trusted third party can reveal the owner's identity of the suspicious electronic coins.

In this section, we propose a fair off-line E-Cash system using the buliding blocks given in the previous section. As in [24], we organize all users into a group and the trusted third party acts as a group manager who is responsible for removing the anonymities of users. Our scheme is simple and direct.

3.1   System Parameters

The Trusted Third Party (TTP):
The TTP does the following to set up the system's parameters:

1. Chooses a cyclic group $G = <g>$. Let l_g be the bit length of the group's order which is large enough. A possible group can be a cyclic subgroup of $Z_{n'}^*$, where $n' = pq$, $p, q \neq 1 (mod\ 8)$, $p \neq q\ (mod\ 8)$, $p = 2p' + 1$, $q = 2q' + 1$ and p, q are large random primes with order nearly $2^{l_g/2}$. The method that proved n' to be a product of two large primes can be found in [7],

2. Chooses two integers $z, h \in_R G$ satisfying the modified strong RSA assumption and Diffie-Hellman decision assumption[4]

3. selects randomly an integer $x \in \{0, \ldots, 2^{l_g} - 1\}$ as the secret key, and then computes the public key $y := g^x$

4. selects a secure one way hash function $H(\cdot)$

5. chooses security parameters : $\hat{l}$, l_1, l_2, ϵ. An example parameters are as follows[5]:
$$\epsilon = 9/8,\ l_g = \hat{l} = 1200,\ l_1 = 860,\ l_2 = 600,\ k = 160,$$

6. publishes z, g, h, G, l_g, y, and proves that z, h were chosen randomly.

The Bank (B):

1. chooses an RSA modulus n, a public exponent e_b and the corresponding private key d_b where e_b, d_b satisfy $e_b \cdot d_b \equiv 1\ mod\ (\varphi(n))$.

2. Publishes n, e_b.

3.2   Registration Protocol at the Trusted Third Party

First of all, users should register at TTP to obtain a membership license of the group. We describe the protocol in figure 1.

The license will be used in the withdrawal protocol, in the payment protocols and in the process of registration protocol at the bank.

We derived the registration protocol from the member registration protocol of Camenisch's group signature scheme. We needn't blind signatures in our registration protocol. Users still need to prove that $\tilde{e}$ is the product of two primes (the methods can be derived from [14]). Furthermore, $\hat{l}, l_1, l_2$ must be chosen so that $\tilde{e}$ can't be factored. The range constraint on e is to prevent the dishonest users from generating the license themselves without TTP being involved [5].

The registration protocol in TTP also ensures that the third party can not learn the secret e and can not counterfeit the honest users. In addition, without knowing the factoring of n', the dishonest users can not obtain the legal licenses by themselves.

3.3   Registration Protocol at the Bank

Now users should establish an account in the bank where they deposit and withdraw money.

To set up an account in the bank, users and the bank carry out the protocol as showed in figure 2.

---

[4] Further information on these assumptions and security analysis of the building blocks and the group signature scheme can be found in the literature[5].

[5] More choices could be available at [18,19]

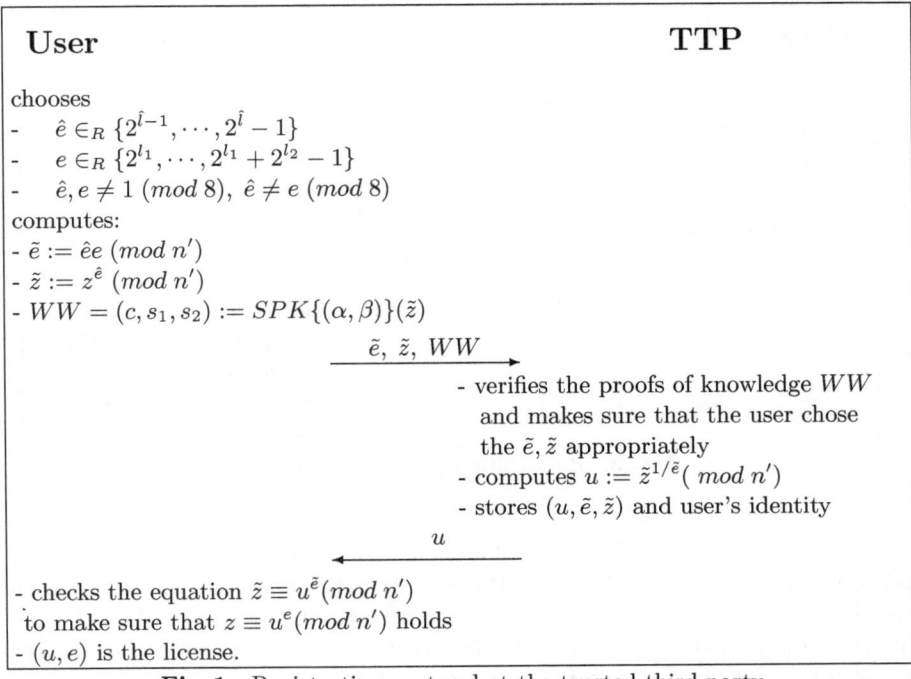

Fig. 1. Registration protocol at the trusted third party

In the registration protocol, YY is verified in order to make sure the user has been registered at the trusted third party and its identity has been authenticated by the trusted third party. The user's account ID_U is anonymous.

3.4 The Withdrawal Protocol

Users should show their account ID_U to the bank before they withdraw amount V from this account.

If there are enough funds left on that account, the bank and the user could carry out the withdrawal protocol as described in figure 3.

In our protocol, T' is designed for coin tracing so that only under the cooperation of the trusted third party and the bank, the identity of the user could be revealed. Neither TTP nor the bank can do that kind of tracing independently.

$T_1, T_2, T_3, P_1, P_2, P_3, P_4$ are used as non-interactive proofs of the knowledge. Furthermore, the amount and user's license are contained in our electronic coin $U_\$$. The bank does not need different signing keys for various value electronic coins.

3.5 The Payment Protocol

Now the user can pay merchants by the electronic coin $U_\$$. Users and merchants can perform the payment protocol as described in figure 4 to make a purchase.

User	Bank
- chooses randomly $x_U \in_R \{0, \cdots, l_g\}$ - computes $ID_U := g^{x_U}$ - computes: $ZZ = (c, s) := SPK\{(x_U) : ID_U = g^{x_U}\}(\zeta)$ $YY = (c, s_1, s_2, s_3) := SPK\{(e, we, w)\}(ID_U)$ $\xrightarrow{\hspace{1cm} ZZ,\ YY,\ ID_U \hspace{1cm}}$	- verifies YY - verifies the proofs of the knowledge, stores ID_U and amount B money in user's database

Fig. 2. Registration protocol at the bank

The payment protocol consists of two parts: firstly, the merchant verifies that the user's electronic coin $U_\$$ holds the signature from the bank. Then, the user convinces the merchant that he owns a valid license from TTP and the license's information has been embedded into the electronic coin $U_\$$ by the non-interactive proofs of knowledge block defined in section 2. Let $m = ID_U||date/time$ where date/time is the date of the payment.

The merchant confirms that the user owns a valid license and the license was embedded into the electronic coin $U_\$$ by verifing YY(checking the equation defined in definition 3 in the section 2). The merchant verifies the equation $T =?(T_1||T_2||T_3||P_1||P_2||\ P_3||P_4||V)$ to ensure the integrity of user's electronic coin $U_\$$.

Finally, the merchant sends the electronic coin $U_\$$, TT, YY, $H(T||T')$ to the bank to proceed the the deposit protocol described in the following section.

3.6   The Deposit Protocol

After the user spent his electronic coin $U_\$$, the merchant should get credited the corresponding value from the bank with the deposit protocol. As we mentioned in the last section, the merchant sends the transcript of the execution of the payment protocol to the bank. Just as the merchant did, the bank verifies the signature of the electronic coin $U_\$$ to make sure that this electronic coin was issued by itself. If the signature is valid, then the bank searches the pair $(U_\$, s_3)$ in the deposit database. This results in two possibilities:

– No items exist in the database
   The bank verifies the embedded license using the following equation:
   $$c = H(g||h||y||z||T_1||T_2||T_3||z^c T_2^{s_1 - c2^{l_1}} / y^{s_2}$$
   $$||T_1^{s_1 - c2^{l_1}} / g^{s_2}||T_1^c g^{s_3}|T_3^c g^{s_1 - c2^{l_1}} h^{s_3}||m).$$
   If the equation holds, the bank stores a 5 tuple $(T_1, T_2, c, s_3, date/time)$ in the deposit database and transfers the amount V to the merchant's account.

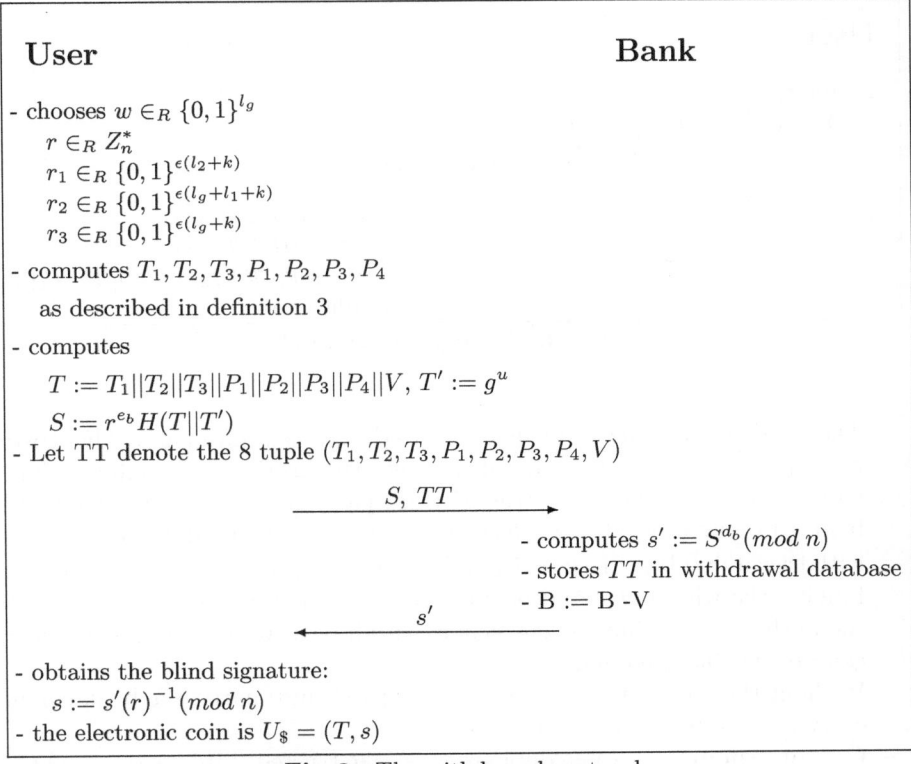

Fig. 3. The withdrawal protocol

- There is an item in the database
  It shows that there must be dishonesty between the user and the merchant. If date/time is the same, then without doubt, the merchant tries to be credited twice. Otherwise, the user is double-spending his electronic coin. There should be another (c', s_3') in the database. The bank can compute the randomly chosen integer w as follows: $w := (s_3 - s_3')/(c - c')$ and furthermore the bank computes the license's information $u := T_2/y^w$ and sends it to TTP. TTP will search in the database and get the user's identity corresponding to the computed u.

3.7 The Tracing Protocol

In anonymity revokable E-Cash systems, there are two kinds of tracing mechanisms to remove the anonymities (see [13]). In this section, we describe how these two tracing models have been realized.

- **Coin tracing.** In our scheme, given the bank's view of the withdrawal protocol, the trusted third party can compute the corresponding electronic coin and trace it. It happens as follows:

User	Merchant
- computes: $YY = (c, s_1, s_2, s_3) := SPK\{(e, we, w)\}(m)$	

$$\xrightarrow{U_\$, T', YY, TT, ID_U}$$

- checks the equations:
$$s^{eb} \equiv H(T\|T')(mod\ n)$$
$$T =?(T_1\|T_2\|T_3\|P_1\|P_2\|P_3\|P_4\|V)$$
- verifies YY

Fig. 4. The payment protocol

The bank provides the user's indentity to the trusted third party. The trusted third party searches in its database, gets the user's license information u and computes g^u. Then the trusted third party returns it to the bank. The bank can now compute the electronic coin $U_\$$ with the data stored in the withdrawal database: $U_\$:= (TT, \{H(TT\|g^u)\}^{d_b}(mod\ n))$

Linking the withdrawal and payment/deposit, this tracing protocol enables the authorities to find the suspicious withdrawal. In addition, coin tracing can prevent blackmailing.

Without the knowledge of g^u from the trusted third party, the bank can not carry out the coin tracing protocol.

– **Owner tracing.** In some dubious cases, the trusted third party can expose the identity of the owner of the specific electronic coin with the information obtained during the deposit protocol from the bank. The owner tracing protocol in our scheme can be described as follows:

The bank gives the view of T_1, T_2 during the deposit protocol to the trusted third party. The trusted third party computes the license information $u := T_2/T_1^x$, searches in the database to get the user's identity corresponding to the specific license information u and then returns the identity to the bank. Since the identity of the owner of the specific electronic coin could be exposed, the owner tracing protocol can prevent some criminal activities such as illegal purchases and money laundering described in [25].

4   Security Analysis

Some important aspects of security of a fair off-line electronic payment system have been introduced in the previous section. We will analyze the security of the proposed scheme in some detail in this section.

1. **Revokabe anonymity**

   During the withdrawal/payment protocols, the license's content, u, e, are all encrypted using ElGamal algorithm or appeared with the representation of g^e, g^u. There is no other efficient way to get the value (u, e) except to break the ElGamal encryption algorithm or to solve the Discrete Logarithm Problem.

Also, (c, s_1, s_2, s_3) didn't reveal any information about the user's license. Learning whether a specific electronic coin belongs to the user who owns the license (u, e) equals to judging whether the equation $log_g T_1 = log_y(T_2/u')$ holds or not. This is difficult according to the Diffie-Hellman decision assumption (see [16,5]).

The bank and the merchant can only get 3 equations from the payment and deposit protocols,:

$$T_1 = g^w, T_2 = uy^w, T_3 = g^e g^w,$$
$$P_1 = T_2^{r_1}(1/y)^{r_2}, P_2 = T_1^{r_1}(1/g)^{r_2}, P_3 = g^{r_3}, P_4 = g^{r_1}g^{r_3},$$
$$s_1 = r_1 - c(e - 2^{l_1}), s_2 = r_2 - cew, s_3 = r_3 - cw.$$

Obviously, it is impossible to obtain the values of 5 unknown elements $((e, r_1, r_2, r_3, w))$ [6] only with 3 equations listed above. So it is difficult to get the license's part u $(u = T_2/y^w)$ without knowing w.

Since no useful information can be available from the withdrawal, payment and deposit protocols, we conclude that our scheme can protect the user's privacy and keep the scheme anonymous. However, as we have shown in the last section, the anonymity of users can be removed with the cooperation between the bank and the trusted third party in certain special cases.

2. **Unforgeability**

The choice of the secure parameters of the system make it difficult to factor the integer $\tilde{e}$, which means that even the trusted third party can not know the user's secret e during the registration protocol in TTP. Therefore, the trusted third party is unable to disguise itself as a registered user.

The bank needs the user's secret value g^u to compute the electronic coin $U_\$$. As we have pointed out, the bank can not obtain any information about user's license (u, e) during the withdrawal and deposit protocols. So it is impossible for the bank to generate the electronic coin $U_\$$ for itself and spend it.

The merchants and the dishonest users can't do it better than the bank, since they can't get more useful information than the bank gets during a transaction.

Under the Modified Strong RSA Assumption, no one can forge a valid license (u, e) if the factors of the system parameter n are unknown. In our scheme, only the trusted third party knows the factors of n'.

3. **Undeniability**

According to the literature [5], T_1, T_2 and T_3, computed in the withdrawal protocol prove unconditionly the knowledge of the license (u, e). The user who is the owner of a license, can not deny the transaction since no one else could generate such T_1, T_2 and T_3 without knowing the license (u, e). This ensures that the system is undeniable.

4. **Unlinkability**

Various random integers, $w \in_R \{0,1\}^{l_g}$, $r \in_R Z_n^*$, $r_1 \in_R \{0,1\}^{\epsilon(l_2+k)}$, $r_2 \in_R \{0,1\}^{\epsilon(l_g+l_1+k)}$, $r_3 \in_R \{0,1\}^{\epsilon(l_g+k)}$, are selected as the same user

---

[6] e is an important part of the user's license (u, e).

withdraws two different electronic coins from the bank. The useful information we can get in the withdrawal and payment protocols of any two different electronic coins from the same user, $T_1, T_2, T_3, P_1, P_2, P_3, P_4$ and $T_1', T_2', T_3', P_1', P_2', P_3', P_4'$ are different. To know whether these two different electronic coins belong to the same user equals to decide whether the equation $log_g(T_1/T_1)' = log_y(T_2/T_2') = log_h(T_3/T_3')$ holds or not. This is also difficult under the Diffie-Hellman decision assumption.

Fortunately, although the secret g^u is needed to compute the various electronic coins for the same user, the value does not need to be transmitted to the bank. Consequently, without this value, the bank can not link the various electronic coins from the same user.

5. **Double-spending Resistant**
   See the deposit protocol in section 3.6.
6. **Traceability**
   See the tracing protocol in section 3.7.

5   Related Work

There are several other fair off-line E-Cash systems offering revokable anonymity, e.g. [15,4,13,26,24,22,20,17]. The first fair off-line electronic cash system has been presented by Frankel [15]. Some other schemes improved the efficiency [4,13]. These systems generally utilize the interactive knowledge proofs which need more computation and communication during a transaction.

New approaches have been used in Sander, Pfitzmann revokable anonymity cash systems [22,20]. They abandoned the idea of a trusted third party involved. These systems are not blind signature based and their security relies on the ability of the bank to maintain the integrity of a public database [22]. We don't think that schemes which are not based on blind signature are more secure than those blind signature based ones. But they surely offer a new direction to solve the conditional anonymity problem. Also these systems lack the ability of tracing (e.g. owner tracing and coin tracing). Kügler's system [17] solves the tracing problems but it is an on-line system.

Compared with the Traoré's system, our system is able of coin tracing and does not need different signing keys for various values of electronic coins. In addition, our system more efficient in payment protocol. In Traoré's system, three non-interactive proofs of knowledge blocks are used, while only one is needed in our payment protocol. As we all know, payment protocol is a most often using protocol in E-Cash systems. Furthermore, the proof of knowledge of roots of representations used in Traoré's system is more computation consuming.

6   Conclusion

A fair off-line electronic cash system based on non-interactive proofs of knowledge has been presented in this paper. Integrating with group signature tool, the system provides users conditional anonymity. User's anonymity can be removed by proceeding coin tracing or owner tracing under cooperating of the bank and the trusted third party.

Our fair off-line electronic cash system is secure (as analyzed in section 4), simple and natural to describe. Furthermore, the system is more efficient than the other known systems.

Acknowledgement. This work was supported by the German Academic Exchange Service (DAAD) project "International Quality Networks". We are grateful to professor Firoz Kaderali for his support and acknowledge the helpful discussions with Biljana Cubaleska.

References

1. S. Brands. Untraceable off-line cash in wallet with observers. In *Advances in Cryptology – CRYPTO '93*, volume 773 of *Lecture Notes in Computer Science*, pages 302–318. Springer Verlag, 22–26 August 1993.
2. E. Brickell, P. Gemmell, and D. Kravitz. Trustee-based tracing extensions to anonymous cash and the making of anonymous change. In *Proceedings of the 6th Annual ACM-SIAM Symposium on Discrete Algorithms*, pages 457–466, Jan 1995.
3. J. Camenisch. Efficient and generalized group signatures. In *Advances in Cryptology – EUROCRYPT '97*, volume 1233 of *Lecture Notes in Computer Science*, pages 465–479. Springer Verlag, 1997.
4. J. Camenisch, U.M. Maurer, and M. Stadler. Digital payment systems with passive anonymity-revoking trustees. In *ESORICS'96*, pages 33–43, 1996.
5. J. Camenisch and M. Michels. A group signature scheme based on an rsa-variant. *BRICS Technical Report RS-98-27(A preliminary version of this paper appeared in Advances in Cryptology-ASIACRYPT'98)*, Nov 1998.
6. J. Camenisch and M. Michels. A group signature scheme with improved efficiency. In *Advances in Cryptology – ASIACRYPT'98*, volume 1514 of *Lecture Notes in Computer Science*, pages 160–174. Springer Verlag, 1998.
7. J. Camenisch and M. Michels. Proving in zero-knowledge that a number is the product of two safe primes. In *Theory and Application of Cryptographic Techniques*, pages 107–122, 1999.
8. J. Camenisch and M.Stadler. Efficient group signatures for large groups. In *Advances in Cryptology – CRYPTO '97*, volume 1296 of *Lecture Notes in Computer Science*, pages 410–424. Springer Verlag, 1997.
9. J. Camenisch, J. Piveteau, and M. Stadler. An efficient payment system protecting privacy. In *Computer Security – ESORICS '94*, volume 875 of *Lecture Notes in Computer Science*, pages 207–215. Springer Verlag, 1994.
10. J. Camenisch, J. Piveteau, and M. Stadler. An efficient fair payment system. In *Proc.ACM Conference on Computer and Communications Security*, pages 88–94, 1996.
11. D. Chaum and E. van Heyst. Group signatures. In *Advances in Cryptology - EUROCRYPT '91*, volume 547 of *Lecture Notes in Computer Science*, pages 257–265. Springer Verlag, 1991.

12. L. Chen and T. P. Pedersen. New group signature schemes. In *Advances in Cryptology – EUROCRYPT '98 – International Conference on the Theory and Application of Cryptographic Techniques, Proceedings*, volume 950 of *Lecture Notes in Computer Science*, pages 171–181. Springer Verlag, 1994.

13. G. Davida, Y. Frankel, Y. Tsiounis, and M. Yung. Anonymity control in E-cash systems. In *Financial Cryptography: First International Conference*, volume 1318 of *Lecture Notes in Computer Science*, pages 1–16. Springer Verlag, 1997.

14. J. Van de Graaf and R. Peralta. A simple and secure way to show the validity of your public key. In *Advances in Cryptology – CRYPTO '87*, volume 293 of *Lecture Notes in Computer Science*, pages 128–134. Springer Verlag, 1988.

15. Y. Frankel, Y. Tsiounis, and M. Yung. "Indirect discourse proofs": Achieving efficient fair off-line e-cash. In *Advances in Cryptology: Proceedings of ASIACRYPT 1996*, volume 1163 of *Lecture Notes in Computer Science*, pages 286–300. Springer Verlag, 1996.

16. E. Fujisaki and T. Okamoto. Statistical zero-knowledge protocols to prove modular polynomial relations. In *Advances in Cryptology – CRYPTO '97*, volume 1294 of *Lecture Notes in Computer Science*, pages 16–30. Springer Verlag, 1997.

17. D. Kügler and H. Vogt. Fair tracing without trustees. In *Financial Cryptography – Fifth International Conference, FC'2001 Proceedings*, Lecture Notes in Computer Science. Springer Verlag, 2001.

18. J.F. Misarsky. A multiplicative attack using lll algorithm on RSA signatures with redundancy. In *Advances in Cryptology – CRYPTO '97*, volume 1294 of *Lecture Notes in Computer Science*, pages 231–234. Springer Verlag, 1997.

19. J.F. Misarsky. How to design RSA signatures schemes. In *Public Key Cryptography, First International Workshop on Practice and Theory in Public Key Cryptography, PKC '98*, volume 1431 of *Lecture Notes in Computer Science*, pages 14–28. Springer Verlag, 1998.

20. B. Pfitzmann and A. Sadeghi. Self-escrowed cash against user blackmailing. In *Financial Cryptography – Fourth International Conference, FC'2000 Proceedings*, volume 1962 of *Lecture Notes in Computer Science*, pages 42–45. Springer Verlag, 2000.

21. D. Pointcheval and J. Stern. Security proofs for signature schemes. In *Theory and Application of Cryptographic Techniques*, volume 1070 of *Lecture Notes in Computer Science*, pages 387–398. Springer Verlag, 1996.

22. T. Sander and A. Ta-Shma. Auditable, anonymous electronic cash. In *Advances in Cryptology – CRYPTO '99 – 19th Annual International Cryptology Conference, Proceedings*, volume 1666 of *Lecture Notes in Computer Science*, pages 555–572. Springer Verlag, 1999.

23. M. Stadler, J. Piveteau, and J. Camenisch. Fair blind signatures. In *Advances in Cryptology – EUROCRYPT '95*, volume 921 of *Lecture Notes in Computer Science*, pages 209–219. Springer Verlag, 1995.

24. J. Traoré. Group signature and their relevance to privacy-protecting offline electronic cash systems. In *ACISP99*, volume 1587 of *Lecture Notes in Computer Science*, pages 228–243. Springer Verlag, 1999.

25. S. von Solms and D. Naccache. On blind signatures and perfect crime. *Computer and Security*, 11(6):581–583, 1992.

26. Bo Yang and Yuming Wang. Fair payment system with electronic wallet. *Journal of Computer*, 22(8):792–796, 1999.

Receipt-Free Sealed-Bid Auction

Masayuki Abe and Koutarou Suzuki

NTT Laboratories
1-1 Hikari-no-oka, Yokosuka, Kanagawa, 239-0847 Japan
{abe,koutarou}@isl.ntt.co.jp

Abstract. This paper points out the risk of bid-rigging in electronic sealed-bid auctions and provides a receipt-free sealed-bid auction scheme to prevent it. The scheme enjoys receipt-freeness, secrecy of bidding price and public verifiability and uses a chameleon bit-commitment technique. It requires a bidding booth and a one-way untappable channel from each bidding booth to each auctioneer.

Keywords. Sealed-bid auction, bid-rigging, receipt-free, chameleon bit-commitment.

1 Introduction

Sealed-bid auctions are a basic mechanism for establishing the price of goods and are widely used in the real world. However, they are subject to bid-rigging by a coercer/buyer. To bid-rig a sealed-bid auction, a coercer/buyer orders other bidders to bid the price he specifies to cheat the auction. For instance, the coercer/buyer orders other bidders to bid very low prices, he then can win the auction at an unreasonably low price. Hence, if bid-rigging occurs, the auction fails to establish the appropriate price, so it is important to prevent bid-rigging.

To make other bidders obey his order, the coercer punishes bidders who do not cast the ordered bidding price, and the buyer rewards for bidders who cast the ordered bidding price. Fortunately, traditional paper-based sealed-bid auctions provide some escape from bid-rigging. There is no receipt that provides a way for a bidder to prove his bidding price, since his bidding price is sealed and kept secret unless he wins. So a bidder can conceal his bidding price, and can escape from the collusion of bid-rigging. This encourages escape from bid-rigging and suppresses bid-rigging.

However, since existing electronic sealed-bid auction schemes issue a receipt that provides a way for a bidder to prove his bidding price, these schemes permit bid-rigging. For instance, if each bidder publishes a commitment of his bidding price, the commitment plays the role of a receipt, i.e., the bidder can prove his bidding price to the coercer/buyer by opening his commitment. By using the receipt, the coercer/buyer can verify whether each bidder has bid as ordered, so the bidder who break a collusion of bid-rigging is always identified and punished. So there are more risks of bid-rigging in electronic sealed-bid auctions than in paper-based sealed-bid auctions.

A.H. Chan and V. Gligor (Eds.): ISC 2002, LNCS 2433, pp. 191–199, 2002.

Moreover, the coercer/buyer can bid after he verifies all bidding prices, and can always win the auction using this knowledge. So the receipt has more serious impact in sealed-bid auction than in voting where the coercer can verify each vote but cannot affect the result of the voting.

This paper proposes a receipt-free sealed-bid auction that eliminates receipts to prevent bid-rigging. The scheme enjoys receipt-freeness, secrecy of bidding price and public verifiability and uses a chameleon bit-commitment technique [BCC88]. It requires a bidding booth and a one-way untappable channel from each bidding booth to each auctioneer. This is the first proposal of receipt-free scheme in electronic sealed-bid auction, though there are some receipt-free schemes in electronic voting.

In section 2, we explain sealed-bid auction and bid-rigging using receipt. In section 3, we explain requirements and physical assumptions, introduce our receipt-free sealed-bid auction scheme and discuss its security and efficiency. In section 4, we conclude the paper.

1.1   Related Works

There is a lot of research on sealed-bid auctions. Kikuchi, Harkavy and Tygar presented an anonymous sealed-bid auction that uses encrypted vectors to represent bidding prices [KHT98]. Harkavy, Tygar and Kikuchi proposed a Vickrey auction, where the bidding price is represented by polynomials that are shared by auctioneers [HTK98]. Kudo used a time server to realize sealed-bid auctions [Kud98]. Cachin proposed a sealed-bid auction using homomorphic encryption and an oblivious third party [Cac99]. Sakurai and Miyazaki proposed a sealed-bid auction in which a bid is represented by the bidder's undeniable signature of his bidding price [SM99]. Stubblebine and Syverson proposed an open-bid auction scheme that uses a hash chain technique[SS99]. Naor, Pinkas and Sumner realized a sealed-bid auction by combining Yao's secure computation with oblivious transfer [NPS99]. Juels and Szydlo improved this scheme [JS02] Sako proposed a sealed-bid auction in which a bid is represented by an encrypted message with a public key that corresponds to his bidding price [Sak00]. Kobayashi, Morita and Suzuki proposed a sealed-bid auction that uses only hash chains [SKM00,KMSH01]. Omote and Miyaji proposed a sealed-bid auction that is efficient [OM00]. Kikuchi proposed a $M + 1$-st price auction, where the bidding price is represented by the degree of a polynomial shared by auctioneers [Kik01]. Baudron and Stern proposed a sealed-bid auction based on circuit evaluation using homomorphic encryption [BS01]. Chida, Kobayashi and Morita proposed a sealed-bid auction with low round complexity [CKM01]. Abe and Suzuki proposed a $M + 1$-st price auction using homomorphic encryption [AS02]. Lipmaa, Asokan and Niemi proposed a $M + 1$-st price auction without threshold trust [LAN02]. Brandt proposed a $M + 1$-st price auction where bidders compute the result by themselves [Bra02]. Suzuki and Yokoo proposed a combinatorial auction using secure dynamic programming [SY02,YS02]. In all of these schemes, however, each bidder issues an encrypted bidding price or commitment of bidding price, and these become the receipt of the bidding price. No receipt-free sealed-bid auction scheme has been proposed.

In the field of electronic voting, there is some research on receipt-freeness. Benaloh and Tuinstra proposed the concept of receipt-freeness and provided a receipt-free voting scheme [BT94]. Niemi and Renvall provided a receipt-free voting scheme using zero-way permutation [NR94]. Sako and Kilian proposed a receipt-free voting scheme using mix-net [SK95]. Okamoto proposed a receipt-free voting scheme using blind signature and chameleon bit-commitment [Oka96, Oka97]. Hirt and Sako proposed a receipt-free voting scheme using "mix then vote" construction [HS00].

2   Sealed-Bid Auction and Bid-Rigging

In this section, we explain sealed-bid auctions and bid-rigging via receipts.

2.1   Sealed-Bid Auction

The sealed-bid auction is a type of auction in which bids are kept secret during the bidding phase. In the bidding phase, each bidder sends his sealed bidding price. In the opening phase, the auctioneer opens the sealed bids and determines the winning bidder and winning price according to a rule : the bidder who bids the highest (or lowest) price of all bidders is the winning bidder and their bidding price is the winning price (Here we accept the case where several bidders submit identical highest bids). Since there is no difference essentially between the highest price case and the lowest price case, we discuss only the former hereafter.

Bidding : Let A be an auctioneer and $B_1, \cdots, B_b$ be m bidders. The auctioneer shows some goods for auction (e.g. a painting from a famous painter) and calls the bidders to bid their price for this item. Each bidder B_i then decides his price, and seals his price (e.g. by envelope) and puts his sealed price into the auctioneer's ballot box.

Opening : After all bidders have input their sealed prices, the auctioneer opens his ballot box. He reveals each sealed price and finds the bidder who bid the highest price. The bidder who bid the highest price wins and he can buy the item at his bid price.

2.2   Bid-Rigging Using Receipt

Sealed-bid auctions are subject to bid-rigging by a coercer. To bid-rig a sealed-bid auction, a coercer/buyer orders other bidders to bid the price he specifies to cheat the auction. To make other bidders obey his order, the coercer punishes bidders who do not cast the ordered bidding price, and the buyer rewards for bidders who cast the ordered bidding price. For instance, the coercer/buyer orders other bidders to bid very low prices, he then can win the auction at an unreasonably low price. Hence, if bid-rigging occurs, the auction fails to establish the appropriate price.

Existing electronic sealed-bid auction schemes issue a *receipt* that provides a way for a bidder to prove his bidding price. For instance, if each bidder publishes a commitment of his bidding price, the commitment plays the role of a receipt, i.e., the bidder can prove his bidding price by opening his commitment. By using the receipt, the coercer/buyer can verify whether each bidder has bid as ordered, so the bidder who break a collusion of bid-rigging is always identified and punished. Hence, there are more risks of bid-rigging in electronic sealed-bid auctions than in paper-based sealed-bid auctions where there is no receipt.

Moreover, the coercer/buyer can affect the result of the auction using receipt as follows. The coercer/buyer checks the bidding prices of other bidders using their receipts, bids slightly higher bidding price than these prices, and always wins the auction. So the receipt has more serious impact in sealed-bid auction than in voting where the coercer can verify each vote but cannot affect the result of the voting.

3   Receipt-Free Sealed-Bid Auction

In this section, we explain the requirements and physical assumptions, introduce our receipt-free sealed-bid auction, and discuss its security and efficiency.

3.1   Requirements

To prevent bid-rigging and achieve a fair auction, the sealed-bid auction must satisfy the following requirements.

Receipt-freeness : Anyone, even the bidder himself, must not be able to prove any information about the bidding price except what can be found from the result of the auction. If a bidder can prove his bidding price, a coercer/buyer can perform bid-rigging as described above.

Secrecy of bidding price : All bidding prices except winning price must be kept secret even from the auctioneer. If someone can see the bidding prices before opening, he can pass the prices to a colluding bidder in order to cheat the auction. If someone can see the bidding prices even after opening, the information can be utilized to cheat the next auction.

Public verifiability : Anyone must be able to verify the correctness of the auction. Since all bidding prices except winning price are kept secret, verifiability is necessary to convince all bidders.

3.2   Physical Assumptions

To achieve receipt-freeness, the proposed sealed-bid auction uses the following physical assumptions, like in the existing receipt-free voting scheme.

Bidding booth : In the bidding booth, bidder can perform bidding procedure freely from control or observation by of coercer/buyer. One cannot control or watch the bidder in the bidding booth. The bidding booth can be implemented as a traditional voting booth. In sealed-bid auctions of public works, the auctions are usually held in a public office. Hence, the assumption of the bidding booth is not so impractical. We assume that in our scheme each bidder performs his bidding procedure in the bidding booth.

One-way untappable channel : One-way untappable channel is a one-way communication channel from one point to another point, no eavesdropper can see the messages sent through the channel. This means that messages are hidden and not committed. If we send encrypted messages, the messages are hidden but committed. Hence, the untappable channel is a stronger assumption than the usual secure channel that can be implemented using encryption. The untappable channel can be implemented by exclusive fiber or physical envelope. We assume that in our scheme, a one-way untappable channel from each bidder to each auctioneer is available.

3.3 Proposed Receipt-Free Sealed-Bid Auction

The basic idea of the proposed receipt-free sealed-bid auction is to represent bidding price p by a sequence of chameleon bit-commitments where the message that means "I bid" is committed at the p-th position. We distribute the auctioneer among plural entities to prevent the auctioneer from cheating.

Preparation : Let $\{A_i | i = 1, 2, \cdots, a\}$ be auctioneers and $\{B_j | j = 1, 2, \cdots, b\}$ be bidders.

Auctioneer A_1 publishes a price list $P = \{l | l = 1, 2, \cdots, m\}$ of the auction, large primes $p = 2q + 1, q$ and a generator g of order q subgroup of $\mathbf{Z}_p^*$, and messages $M_0, M_1 \in \mathbf{Z}_q$ that mean "I do not bid","I bid" respectively.

Bidding : In the bidding phase, each bidder B_j bids in the *bidding booth* as follows. He chooses his secret key $x_j \in \mathbf{Z}_q$ of chameleon bit-commitment and publishes his public key $h_j = g^{x_j}$ with his signature.

Bidder B_j decides his bidding price $p_j \in P$. He chooses his secret seeds $r_{l,j} \in \mathbf{Z}_q$ ($l = 1, 2, \cdots, m$) randomly and computes a sequence of chameleon bit-commitments

$$C_{l,j} = \begin{cases} g^{M_1} h_j^{r_{l,j}} & (l = p_j) \\ g^{M_0} h_j^{r_{l,j}} & (l \neq p_j) \end{cases}$$

for $l = 1, 2, \cdots, m$. He publishes the sequence of commitments $(C_{1,j}, C_{2,j}, \cdots, C_{m,j})$ with his signature.

Bidder B_j then proves to each auctioneer A_i that bidder B_j knows the secret key $\log_g h_j = x_j$ of the chameleon bit-commitment and the discrete logs $\log_g C_{l,j}$ by the interactive zero-knowledge proof.

Finally, bidder B_j makes t-out-of-a secret shares $r_{l,j}^i$ for secret seeds $r_{l,j}$. He then sends i-th shares $r_{l,j}^i$ ($l = 1, 2, \cdots, m$) of secret seeds $r_{l,j}$ ($l = 1, 2, \cdots, m$) with his signature to i-th auctioneer A_i through the *one-way untappable channel* from bidder B_j to each auctioneer A_i.

Opening : In the opening phase, all auctioneers iterate the following steps for each price $l = m, m-1, \cdots, 1$ to determine winning (maximum) bidding price $p_{win} = max_j\{p_j\}$ and winning bidders.

Each auctioneer A_i publishes shares $r_{l,j}^i$ $(j = 1, 2, \cdots, b)$ of l-th secret seeds $r_{l,j}$ of all bidders B_j.

All auctioneers then recover secret seeds $r_{l,j}$ and check the following equalities

$$C_{l,j} = g^{M_1} h_j^{r_{l,j}} \; (j = 1, 2, \cdots, b)$$

for all bidders B_j. If there exist j's for which the above equality holds, auctioneers publish that the winning bidders are these B_j's and their winning price p_{win} is l, and stop opening. Otherwise, auctioneers A_i conclude that no bidder bids at this price l, decrease price l by 1 and iterate the process.

3.4   Security

The proposed scheme satisfies the properties listed in Section 3.1.

Secrecy of bidding price : Since bids are opened from the highest price to the price at which the wining bidders bid, no bids under the winning price are opened. Since secret seed $r_{l,j}$ is distributed to plural auctioneers by t-out-of-a secret sharing, unopened secret seeds $r_{l,j}$ are unconditionally secure if the number of collusive auctioneers is less than or equal to threshold t. Since chameleon bit-commitment $C_{l,j}$ unconditionally conceals committed message M_0, M_1 if secret seed $r_{l,j}$ is not provided, unopened bidding prices are unconditionally secure. Hence, all bidding prices except winning price are unconditionally secure even from the auctioneer.

Receipt-freeness : By the interactive zero-knowledge proof in the bidding phase, it is guaranteed that bidder B_j knows secret key $\log_g h_j = x_j$ and discrete logs $\log_g C_{l,j}$. Thus he can compute solution $r_{l,j,\epsilon}$ of equality $\log_g C_{l,j} = M_\epsilon + x_j r_{l,j,\epsilon}$, and can freely open the chameleon bit-commitment $C_{l,j}$ as message M_ϵ that he wants by showing solution $r_{l,j,\epsilon}$. Since unopened secret seeds $r_{l,j}$ are never revealed, he can open the commitment as he wants, and so cannot prove his bidding price.

Notice that we cannot use the non-interactive proof, since the non-interactive proof cannot guarantees freshness of the knowledge. If we use the non-interactive proof, a coercer can force a bidder to use the non-interactive proof made beforehand by the coercer without revealing the secret to the bidder.

Public verifiability : Since published commitments $C_{l,j}$ and opened shares $r_{l,j}^i$ of secret seeds are signed by bidder B_j, no one except bidder B_j himself can modify or forge these commitments and shares. So anyone can verify the correctness of the auction, by checking the validity of these commitments $C_{l,j}$, shares $r_{l,j}^i$ and signatures.

3.5   Efficiency

We discuss communication and computational complexity of our auction. Here, the number of auctioneer, bidders, bidding prices is a, b, m, respectively.

Table 1 shows the communication pattern, the number of communication rounds and volume per communication round in our scheme. BB is bulletin board, and data is sent to the bulletin board BB to publish it. $B_j \Rightarrow A_i$ means the one-way untappable channel from B_j to A_i. The communication cost is linear of the number of bidding prices m, so it might be heavy for a large price range, same as existing schemes. Since communications from bidder B_j to auctioneer A_i is required only in the bidding phase, our scheme achieves the "bid and go" concept.

Table 2 shows the computational complexity per one bidder and per all auctioneers in our scheme. The complexity of each bidder and all auctioneers is linear of the number of bidding prices m, so it might be heavy for a large price range, same as existing schemes.

Notice that we can reduce the costs of the interactive zero-knowledge proofs of $1+m$ statements for a auctioneers as follows. We can gather the proofs of $1+m$ statements by parallelizing them. We can gather the a auctioneers by using one public common challenge, i.e., we can use the public-coin honest verifier zero-knowledge proof where the challenge is made by collaboration of all auctioneers. (In practice, we may use simpler challenge and response system, i.e., the verifiers collaboratively make a random challenge and the prover signs on the challenge by using the Schnorr signature.) So we need $3b$ rounds communication and $1+m$ proof generations for the proof of $1 + m$ statements for a auctioneers

Table 1. The communication complexity of our scheme.

	pattern	round	volume
Bidding (Commit)	$B_j \rightarrow BB$	b	$O(m)$
Bidding (Proof)	$B_j, A_i \leftrightarrow BB$	$3b$	$O(m)$
Bidding (Secret Share)	$B_j \Rightarrow A_i$	$b \times a$	$O(m)$
Opening	$A_i \leftrightarrow BB$	$a \times m$	$O(b)$

Table 2. The computational complexity of our scheme.

	computational complexity
One Bidder	m chameleon BCs, $1 + m$ proofs and m secret sharings
Auctioneers	m interpolations and verfications of the commitments

4   Conclusion

We have pointed out the risk of bid-rigging in electronic sealed-bid auctions and provided a receipt-free sealed-bid auction scheme to prevent it. The scheme enjoys receipt-freeness, secrecy of bidding price and public verifiability and uses a chameleon bit-commitment technique. It requires a bidding booth and a one-way untappable channel from each bidding booth to each auctioneer.

References

[AS02]   M. Abe and K. Suzuki, "M+1-st Price Auction using Homomorphic Encryption", *Proceedings of Public Key Cryptography 2002*, LNCS 2274, pp. 115–124, (2002).

[Bra02]   F. Brandt, "A verifiable, bidder-resolved Auction Protocol", *Proceedings of workshop on "Deception, Fraud and Trust in Agent Societies" in Autonomous Agents and Multi-Agent Systems 2002*, workshop proceedings, (2002).

[BS01]   O. Baudron and J. Stern, "Non-interactive Private Auctions", *Proceedings of Financial Cryptography 2001*, to be published, (2001).

[Cac99]   C. Cachin, "Efficient Private Bidding and Auctions with an Oblivious Third Party", *Proceedings of 6th ACM Conference on Computer and Communications Security*, pp. 120–127, (1999).

[CKM01]   K. Chida, K. Kobayashi and H. Morita, "Efficient Sealed-bid Auctions for Massive Numbers of Bidders with Lump Comparison", *Proceedings of ISC 2001*, LNCS 2200, pp. 408–419, (2001).

[HTK98]   M. Harkavy, J. D. Tygar and H. Kikuchi, "Electronic Auctions with Private Bids", *Proceedings of Third USENIX Workshop on Electronic Commerce*, pp. 61–74, (1998).

[KHT98]   H. Kikuchi, M. Harkavy and J. D. Tygar, "Multi-round Anonymous Auction Protocols", *Proceedings of first IEEE Workshop on Dependable and Real-Time E-Commerce Systems*, pp. 62–69, (1998).

[JS02]   A. Juels and M. Szydlo, "A Two-Server, Sealed-Bid Auction Protocol", *Proceedings of Financial Cryptography 02*, to be published, (2002).

[Kik01]   H. Kikuchi, "(M+1)st-Price Auction Protocol", *Proceedings of Financial Cryptography 2001*, to be published, (2001).

[KMSH01]   K. Kobayashi, H. Morita, K. Suzuki and M. Hakuta, "Efficient Sealed-bid Auction by using One-way Functions", *IEICE Trans. Fundamentals*, Vol.E84-A NO.1, (Jan. 2001).

[Kud98]   M. Kudo, "Secure Electronic Sealed-Bid Auction Protocol with Public Key Cryptography", *IEICE Trans. Fundamentals*, Vol.E81-A NO.1, pp. 20–27, (Jan. 1998).

[LAN02]   H. Lipmaa, N. Asokan and V. Niemi, "Secure Vickrey Auctions without Threshold Trust", *Proceedings of Financial Cryptography 02*, to be published, (2002).

[NPS99]   M. Naor, B. Pinkas and R. Sumner, "Privacy Preserving Auctions and Mechanism Design", *Proceedings of ACM conference on E-commerce*, pp. 129–139, (1999).

[OM00]   K. Omote and A. Miyaji, "An Anonymous Auction Protocol with a Single Non-trusted Center Using Binary Trees", *Proceedings of ISW2000*, LNCS 1975, pp. 108–120, (2000).

[OM02]   K. Omote and A. Miyaji, "A Second-price Sealed-Bid Auction with the Discriminant of the p-th Root", *Proceedings of Financial Cryptography 02*, to be published, (2002).

[Sak00]   K. Sako, "Universally verifiable auction protocol which hides losing bids", *Proceedings of Public Key Cryptography 2000*, pp. 35–39, (2000).

[SKM00]   K. Suzuki, K. Kobayashi and H. Morita, "Efficient Sealed-Bid Auction using Hash Chain", *Proceedings of ICISC 2000*, LNCS 2015, pp. 183–191, (2000).

[SM99]   K. Sakurai and S. Miyazaki, "A bulletin-board based digital auction scheme with bidding down strategy", *Proceedings of 1999 International Workshop on Cryptographic Techniques and E-Commerce*, pp. 180–187, (1999).

[SS99]   S. G. Stubblebine and P. F. Syverson, "Fair On-line Auctions Without Special Trusted Parties", *Proceedings of Financial Cryptography 99*, LNCS 1648, (1999).

[SY02]   K. Suzuki and M. Yokoo, "Secure Combinatorial Auctions by Dynamic Programming with Polynomial Secret Sharing", *Proceedings of Financial Cryptography 02*, to be published, (2002).

[YS02]   M. Yokoo and K. Suzuki, "Secure Multi-agent Dynamic Programming based on Homomorphic Encryption and its Application to Combinatorial Auctions", *Proceedings of Autonomous Agents and Multi-Agent Systems 2002*, ACM Press, (2002).

[BCC88]   G. Brassard, D. Chaum and C. Crépeau, "Minimum Disclosure Proofs of Knowledge", *Journal of Computer and System Sciences*, Vol.37, No.2, pp. 156–189, (1988).

[BT94]   J. Benaloh and D. Tuinstra, "Receipt-Free Secret-Ballot Elections", *Proceedings of STOC 94*, pp. 544–553, (1994).

[NR94]   V. Niemi and A. Renvall, "How to Prevent Buying of Votes in Computer Elections", *Proceedings of ASIACRYPT 94*, LNCS 917, pp. 164–170, (1994).

[HS00]   M. Hirt and K. Sako, "Efficient Receipt-Free Voting Based on Homomorphic Encryption", *Proceedings of EUROCRYPT 2000*, LNCS 1807, pp. 539–556, (2000).

[Oka96]   T. Okamoto, "An Electronic Voting Scheme", *Proceedings of IFIP 96*, Advanced IT Tools, pp. 21–30, (1996).

[Oka97]   T. Okamoto, "Receipt-Free Electronic Voting Schemes for Large Scale Elections", *Proceedings of 5th Security Protocols*, LNCS 1361, pp. 25–35, (1997).

[SK95]   K. Sako and J. Kilian, "Receipt-Free Mix-type Voting Scheme", *Proceedings of EUROCRYPT 95*, LNCS 921, pp. 393–403, (1995).

Exclusion-Freeness in Multi-party Exchange Protocols

Nicolás González-Deleito and Olivier Markowitch

Université Libre de Bruxelles
Bd. du Triomphe – CP212
1050 Bruxelles
Belgium

{ngonzale,omarkow}@ulb.ac.be

Abstract. In this paper we define a property for multi-party protocols called *exclusion-freeness*. In multi-party protocols respecting the
strongest definition of this property, participants are sure that they will
not be excluded from a protocol's execution and, consequently, they do
not have to trust each other any more. We study this property on a well-
known multi-party fair exchange protocol with an online trusted third
party and we point out two attacks on this protocol breaking the fairness property and implying excluded participants. Finally, we propose
a new multi-party fair exchange protocol with an online trusted third
party respecting the strong exclusion-freeness property.

1 Introduction

The important growth of open networks such as the Internet has lead to the study
of related security problems. Achieving the exchange of electronic information is
one of these security challenges. An exchange protocol (contract signing, certified
mail, ...) allows therefore two or more parties to exchange electronic information. Such kind of protocols are said to be *fair* if the exchange is realized in such
a way that, at the end of the protocol, any honest participant has received all
the expected items corresponding to the items that he has provided. Fair exchange protocols often use a trusted third party (TTP) helping the participants
to successfully realize the exchange.

Depending on its level of involvement in a protocol, a TTP can be said *inline*,
online or *offline*. Inline and online trusted third parties are both involved in each
instance of a protocol, but the first one acts as a mandatory intermediary between
the participants. An offline TTP is used when the participants in a protocol are
supposed to be honest enough to do not need external help in order to achieve
fairness; the TTP will be involved only if some problems emerge. Consequently,
such protocols are called *optimistic*.

Fair exchange between two parties has been extensively studied and several
solutions have been proposed in the online [10,11,7] as in the offline [12,2,5,3,9]
case. The multi-party setting has also been studied and it has been noticed that
the topology of the exchange plays an important role.

A.H. Chan and V. Gligor (Eds.): ISC 2002, LNCS 2433, pp. 200–209, 2002.
© Springer-Verlag Berlin Heidelberg 2002

In [1] a generic optimistic protocol with a general topology (each entity can communicate with the set of entities of his choice) is described. However, during this protocol a participant may receive an affidavit from the TTP instead of the expected item. The protocol achieves then what it is called *weak fairness*.

In practice, many proposed multi-party fair exchange protocols [6,4,8] suppose that each party exchanges an item against another and that the exchange's topology is a ring. In other words, each participant P_i offers to participant P_{i+1} a message m_i in exchange of a message m_{i-1} offered by participant P_{i-1}. Of course, all subscripts have to be read mod n, where n is the number of participants in the exchange. (We will omit this hereafter.)

The multi-party fair exchange protocol proposed in [6] is based on an online TTP, whereas [4,8] supposed the TTP as being offline. Participants in the protocol described in [4] have to trust, in addition of the TTP, the initiator of the exchange for not becoming passive conspirators. A modified version of this protocol, in which participants do not longer need to trust that participant, was proposed in [8].

Our aim is to introduce a property devoted to multi-party protocols called *exclusion-freeness*. We illustrate it in the framework of an existing multi-party fair exchange protocol with an online TTP. We describe two attacks on this protocol in which the fairness property is broken and where participants are excluded from the exchange. A modified version of this protocol respecting the strongest flavor of exclusion-freeness is finally proposed. The study of that property on optimistic multi-party fair exchange protocols is the subject of an ongoing work. At the present time, it does not seem possible to obtain the same sort of results presented in this paper on that kind of protocols.

The remaining of this paper is organized as follows. In the next section we introduce the concept of exclusion-freeness and some other definitions and notations. In section 3 we describe the multi-party fair exchange protocol with an online TTP proposed by Franklin and Tsudik [6] and present our attacks on this protocol. Finally, we propose in section 4 a new multi-party fair exchange protocol with an online TTP, in which participants cannot be excluded from the exchange.

2   Definitions and Notations

Although not explicitly said in the literature, a protocol allowing an exchange of items is composed of a preliminary *setup phase*, followed by an *exchange phase*. During the setup phase, entities willing to participate in a given exchange's execution agree on the set of entities who will take part in this exchange, on the items to be exchanged and on how these items will be exchanged during the exchange phase. Upon completion of that setup phase, the exchange phase is performed by the means of a fair exchange protocol.

Definition 1. *We say that a participant has been* excluded *from an exchange if (1) he has taken part in the setup phase, (2) it has been agreed during that phase* *that he would participate in the exchange phase, (3) a non-empty set of other participants involved in the exchange has prevented him to successfully complete the corresponding exchange phase.*

In the following sections we will look at two multi-party fair exchange protocols with an online TTP. In order to study their exclusion issues, we introduce the following definitions.

Definition 2. *A* passive conspirator *of a coalition of participants excluding some other entities from a multi-party protocol's run is an honest participant who (1) is not excluded, (2) cannot prevent this coalition to succeed, (3) by its idleness contributes to keep the excluded participants uninformed about the protocol's execution which takes place.*

Definition 3. *A multi-party protocol is said to be* weakly exclusion-free *if, at the end of any execution of this protocol, any excluded participant is able to prove to an external adjudicator that he has been excluded.*

Definition 4. *A multi-party protocol is called* strongly exclusion-free *if, at the end of any execution of this protocol, there will be no excluded participants.*

As a consequence of these definitions, we note that in a protocol not providing strong exclusion-freeness any honest participant has to trust the remaining participants for not being excluded.

The following definitions deal with the quality of the communication channels and with the basic properties that an exchange protocol must respect.

Definition 5. *A communication channel is said to be* operational *if the messages inserted into it are delivered within a known amount of time. A* resilient *communication channel delivers data after a finite, but unknown, amount of time. Finally, a communication channel is* unreliable *if it is neither operational nor resilient.*

Definition 6. *Disregarding the quality of the communication channels, an exchange protocol is said to be* consistent *if when all the participants implied in the exchange are honest then they all obtain their expected information.*

Definition 7. *An exchange protocol is said to be* fair *if, at the end of any execution of this protocol, any honest participant has received all the expected items corresponding to the items that he has provided.*

Through this paper we will use the following notations:

- $A \rightarrow B$: denotes Alice sending a message to Bob;
- $A \Rightarrow \beta$: denotes Alice multicasting a message to the set of participants β (a one-to-many communication);
- $A \Rightarrow$: denotes Alice broadcasting a message (a one-to-any communication);
- $E_{e_A}(m)$ is the result of applying an asymmetric encryption algorithm E to the plaintext m under Alice's public key e_A.

3   A Fair Exchange Protocol with an Online TTP

We describe here the multi-party fair exchange protocol with an online trusted third party proposed by Franklin and Tsudik [6]. The protocol assumes that the exchange is cyclic, i.e. an entity P_i, $i \in [1, n]$, sends his secret information m_i to P_{i+1} in exchange of P_{i-1}'s secret information m_{i-1}; P_n sends his information to P_1.

In their protocol, the authors assume the presence of a third party which is *semi-trusted*. Such a third party is trusted to ensure the fairness during a protocol's run, but as long as all the entities involved in the protocol remain honest the semi-trusted third party will not succeed in trying to learn the information to be exchanged. The authors also consider that all the exchanged messages are private and authentic.

The scheme is based on the use of a homomorphic one-way function f and a n-variable function F_n such that

$$F_n \left(x_1, f \left(x_2 \right), \ldots, f \left(x_n \right) \right) = f \left(x_1 x_2 \cdots x_n \right).$$

The authors propose that $f(y) = y^2 \bmod N$ and $F_n(y_1, y_2, \ldots, y_n) = y_1^2 y_2 \cdots y_n \bmod N$, where N is the product of two large distinct primes.

At the end of the setup phase:

- each participant knows the identity of the remaining participants in the exchange;
- the participants in the exchange have agreed on the identity of the TTP that will be contacted during the protocol's execution and on the functions f and F that will be used;
- and the descriptions of the messages to be exchanged, $f(m_i)$, $i \in [1, n]$, are made public.

3.1   The Protocol

Each user P_i begins the protocol by choosing a random value R_i and sending it to P_{i+1}.

Upon receiving R_{i-1}, each entity P_i computes $C_i = m_i \cdot R_i^{-1}$ and

$$A_i = F_n \left(m_i, f \left(m_1 \right), \ldots, f \left(m_{i-1} \right), f \left(m_{i+1} \right), \ldots, f \left(m_n \right) \right),$$

and sends them to the TTP along with $f(R_i)$.

The TTP compares the received A_i. If they are all equal, it computes $C = C_1 \cdots C_n$. It also computes $F_{n+1} \left(C, f \left(R_1 \right), \ldots, f \left(R_n \right) \right)$, which should be equal to $f \left(m_1 \cdots m_n \right)$, and verifies whether one A_i is equal to this last computation. If all the checks pass, the TTP broadcasts $\mathcal{C} = \{ C_j \,|\, 1 \leq j \leq n \}$ to all the entities.

After having received $\mathcal{C}$ from the TTP, each P_i can verify for which C_j, $j \in [1, n]$, $f(C_j \cdot R_{i-1})$ is equal to $f(m_{i-1})$, and obtain then m_{i-1}.

Here is a summary of that protocol:

1. $\forall i \in [1, n]$:

   $P_i \rightarrow P_{i+1}$: R_i.

2. $\forall i \in [1, n]$:

   $P_i \rightarrow TTP$: $A_i, C_i, f(R_i)$.

3. $TTP \Rightarrow$: $\mathcal{C}$.

3.2 An Attack Aiming to Break the Fairness Property

Unfortunately, this protocol is not fair. When communicating with the TTP an entity, say P_i, can choose a random value $\tilde{R}$ distinct from the R_i transmitted to P_{i+1} at the previous step of the protocol and can therefore transmit to the TTP the "normal" A_i, $C_i = m_i \cdot \tilde{R}^{-1}$ and $f(\tilde{R})$.

The TTP will not be able to realize that the random $\tilde{R}$ provided by P_i is different from the random R_i received by P_{i+1}. Indeed, the TTP compares all the received A_j, which are not related to R_i nor $\tilde{R}$, and computes

$$F_{n+1}(C_1 \cdots C_n, f(R_1), \ldots, f(R_{i-1}), f(\tilde{R}), f(R_{i+1}), \ldots, f(R_n)),$$

which should be equal to any A_j.

On the other hand, P_{i+1} will obtain from the TTP the set of all C_j (where $j \in [1, n]$). P_{i+1} has to compute $\hat{m}_j = C_j \cdot R_i$, for all $j \in [1, n]$ until $f(\hat{m}_j) = f(m_i)$. Unfortunately, for P_{i+1} this last equality will never be verified. He will not retrieve his expected item and the fairness will then be broken.

Recall that P_i excludes P_{i+1} from the exchange with the passive assent of the remaining participants, who become passive conspirators of P_i.

3.3 An Attack Aiming to Exclude Participants from the Exchange

Franklin and Tsudik describe [6] two types of deviances of the third party causing the lost of fairness for the target entities. These misbehaviors lead honest participants to become passive conspirators of the third party. The authors discuss therefore about ways to counter such a behavior from the third party when all the participants in the protocol are honest.

However, these solutions imply that participants do not longer trust the TTP for being honest, which is contradictory with the definition of a semi-trusted third party. It is unusual to reduce the trust accorded to a TTP at the price of having all the participants to trust each other. This is particularly unrealistic in a multi-party framework. Considering that a TTP is a trusted entity, it seems to us that it is either considered that it behaves correctly, or it is not a trusted third party.

We present now a second exclusion attack with passive conspirators not mentioned by the authors of the original paper.

Suppose that P_i decides to exclude P_{i+1} from the exchange. If the one-way function f is, as in [6], such that $f(a) \cdot f(b) = f(ab)$, which with discrete arithmetic one-way functions is a reasonable assumption, then P_i can act as described hereunder.

P_i follows normally the protocol, except that he does not send his random value R_i to P_{i+1}. The protocol does not say that the entities have to wait to receive the random value of the previous entity before sending their own random to the next one. Then, P_{i+1} sends his random to P_{i+2}, etc. The only entity having not received his expected random value is then P_{i+1}. Therefore, in order to remain in a fair state, P_{i+1} does not continue the protocol because he will be not able to retrieve m_i without R_i.

All the entities except P_i and P_{i+1} contact the TTP as described in the second step of the protocol. P_{i+1} does not send anything and P_i contacts the TTP by sending to the latter $C_i = m_i \cdot R_i^{-1}$,

$$A_i = F_n(m_i, f(m_1), \ldots, f(m_{i-1}), f(m_{i+1}), \ldots, f(m_n)),$$

and $f(R_i) \cdot f(m_{i+1})$ instead of $f(R_i)$.

For all j in $[1, n]$, with $j \neq i + 1$, $A_j = f(m_1 \cdots m_n)$. The TTP computes then

$$F_n(C_1 \cdots C_i \cdot C_{i+2} \cdots C_n, f(R_1), \ldots, f(R_{i-1}),$$
$$f(R_i) \cdot f(m_{i+1}), f(R_{i+2}), \ldots, f(R_n)),$$

which is equal to all the A_j, and cannot therefore detect that P_{i+1} has not contacted him.

Note that P_{i+1} is excluded but remains in a fair state (he does not receive m_i and does not send m_{i+1}). However, P_{i+2} sends his message m_{i+2} without receiving P_{i+1}'s message m_{i+1}. The fairness is then broken.

This attack allows P_i to exclude P_{i+1} and P_{i+2} with the passive assent of the remaining participants. Therefore, under our assumptions, this protocol is not strongly nor weakly exclusion-free, it implies passive conspirators and does not respect the fairness property.

4   A Strongly Exclusion-Free Fair Exchange Protocol

We present now a variant of the multi-party fair exchange protocol with an online trusted third party described in the previous section, partially inspired by the two-party protocol of Franklin and Reiter [7]. The exchange topology is still a ring. The communication channels between participants are unreliable and those used between each participant and the TTP are supposed to be resilient.

Through this section we will use the following additional notations:

- f_x is a flag indicating the purpose of a message in a given protocol, where x identifies the corresponding message in that protocol;
- $S_A(m)$ denotes the digital signature of Alice over the message m;
- in the description of a protocol's message, $S_A(\star)$ denotes the digital signature of Alice over all information preceding this signature;
- $\mathcal{P}$ is the set $\{P_0, P_1, \ldots, P_{n-1}\}$ of all the participants in the exchange;

- *label* is an information identifying a protocol's run; it results from applying $\mathcal{P}$ and the descriptions of all the messages to be exchanged to a one-way hash function.

At the end of the setup phase:

- each participant knows the identity of the remaining participants in the exchange;
- the participants in the exchange have agreed on the identity of the TTP that will be contacted during the protocol's execution and on the functions f and F that will be used;
- the set $\mathcal{P}$ and the label are known by all the participants in the exchange;
- and the descriptions of the messages to be exchanged, $f(m_i)$, $i \in [0, n-1]$, are made public.

We use a label in order to prevent exclusion attacks. This label will allow the TTP to verify if all the agreed participants are taking part in the exchange phase. During the protocol, when receiving a signed message, each entity checks the validity of the signature. If the verification fails, the message is not considered.

4.1   The Protocol

As in the original protocol, each participant P_i chooses a random value R_i and sends it, in a private way, to P_{i+1}.

Upon receiving R_{i-1}, each P_i computes $C_i = m_i \cdot R_i^{-1}$ and

$$A_i = F_n(m_i, f(m_0), \ldots, f(m_{i-1}), f(m_{i+1}), \ldots, f(m_{n-1})),$$

and sends $E_{e_{TTP}}(C_i)$ and A_i to the TTP along with $f(R_i)$ and $f(R_{i-1})$, the label and the set $\mathcal{P}$ agreed during the setup phase of the protocol.

In order to avoid attacks from entities not belonging to $\mathcal{P}$, for each received message the TTP verifies if its sender is included in the set $\mathcal{P}$ found in the message. The TTP also verifies if this set and the public information corresponding to all the participants in $\mathcal{P}$ are consistent with the label that has been sent. If not, the TTP discards the message.

After a deadline chosen by the TTP, the latter verifies if the set of identities of the participants having contacted him with the same label is equal to the corresponding set $\mathcal{P}$. If so, the TTP checks if for each $i \in [0, n-1]$ the $f(R_i)$ sent by P_i is equal to the $f(R_i)$ sent by P_{i+1} and if the $f(R_{i-1})$ sent by P_i is equal to the $f(R_{i-1})$ sent by P_{i-1}.

If these two first checks succeed, the TTP verifies that all the received A_i are equal. If so, he computes $C = C_0 \cdots C_{n-1}$ and $F_{n+1}(C, f(R_0), \ldots, f(R_{n-1}))$.

If this second computation is equal to any A_i, then the TTP multicasts $\mathcal{C} = \{C_j \mid 0 \leq j \leq n-1\}$ to all the participants in the exchange. Any participant P_i can therefore verify for which C_j, with j in $[0, n-1]$, $f(C_j \cdot R_{i-1}) = f(m_{i-1})$ holds, and can retrieve m_{i-1}.

Here are the three steps of that protocol:

1. $\forall i \in [0, n-1]$:

   $P_i \rightarrow P_{i+1}$: $f_1, P_{i+1}, label, E_{e_{P_{i+1}}}(R_i), S_{P_i}(\star)$.

2. $\forall i \in [0, n-1]$:

   $P_i \rightarrow TTP$: $f_2, TTP, label, \mathcal{P}, A_i, E_{e_{TTP}}(C_i), f(R_i), f(R_{i-1}), S_{P_i}(\star)$.

3. $TTP \Rightarrow \mathcal{P}$: $f_3, \mathcal{P}, label, \mathcal{C}, S_{TTP}(\star)$.

4.2   Analysis

Property 1. The protocol is consistent.

If all the participants in the exchange are honest, then all the random values R_i, with i in $[0, n-1]$, will be properly exchanged and every participant will be able to contact the TTP during the second step of the protocol. All the verifications on the identities of the participants contacting the TTP and on the items to exchange will then succeed and the TTP will multicast the set $\mathcal{C}$ to all the participants in $\mathcal{P}$, who will be able to retrieve their corresponding expected information $m_{i-1} = C_{i-1} \cdot R_{i-1}$, with i in $[0, n-1]$.

Property 2. The proposed protocol is fair.

When the first step of the protocol has been completed, only participants having received the ciphered random value will contact the TTP. The remaining participants will stop the protocol in order to stay in a fair state.

After a chosen deadline, the TTP will verify if the set of identities of the participants having contacted him with the same label is equal to the corresponding set $\mathcal{P}$ included in their messages. (As the labels are identical, the sets $\mathcal{P}$ that they provide should also be identical.) The TTP will only continue if *all* the agreed participants realize that second step of the protocol.

The TTP will also verify if the exchanged random values are those submitted to him during the second step of the protocol and if the received C_j, with j in $[0, n-1]$, are consistent with the items to exchange agreed during the setup phase of the protocol.

If the above tests succeed, the TTP will multicast $\mathcal{C}$ to all the participants in the exchange and every entity will be able to recover his expected message. Otherwise, the TTP will not multicast $\mathcal{C}$ and the fairness property will also be respected as no participant will receive anything.

Property 3. The proposed protocol achieves strong exclusion-freeness under the assumption that the underlying signature scheme is secure against forgery attacks.

As described above, after a chosen deadline the TTP will verify if the set of identities of the participants having contacted him with the same label is equal to the corresponding set $\mathcal{P}$ agreed during the setup phase of the protocol. If some participants have not realized that second step, then the TTP will stop the protocol.

Unless some dishonest entity is able to impersonate a participant having been excluded from an exchange's execution by forging his digital signature, the TTP will stop the protocol before verifying if the items to be exchanged are those agreed during the setup phase of the protocol. Therefore, any exclusion attack will be aborted by the TTP.

5 Conclusion

We have defined the notion of being excluded from an exchange's execution and clarified the concept of a passive conspirator of a coalition excluding some other participants from an exchange. We have introduced the notions of weak and strong exclusion-freeness, and we have pointed out that the participants in a protocol respecting the strong exclusion-freeness property do not longer need to trust each other for not being excluded from an execution of this protocol.

We have illustrated those notions in the framework of multi-party fair exchange protocols with an online TTP. Therefore, we have described a well-known fair exchange protocol and we have presented two attacks on it breaking the fairness property and leading moreover to passive conspirators and excluded participants.

Finally, we have proposed a new multi-party fair exchange protocol with an online TTP, in which participants cannot be excluded from the exchange, i.e. respecting the strong exclusion-freeness property. The study of exclusion-freeness aspects in optimistic multi-party fair exchange protocols is the subject of an ongoing work. At the present time, achieving the same sort of results on that kind of protocols does not seem possible.

References

1. N. Asokan, M. Schunter, and M. Waidner. Optimistic protocols for multi-party fair exchange. Research Report RZ 2892 (# 90840), IBM Research, Dec. 1996.
2. N. Asokan, V. Shoup, and M. Waidner. Asynchronous protocols for optimistic fair exchange. In *Proceedings of the IEEE Symposium on Research in Security and Privacy*, pages 86–99. IEEE Computer Society Press, May 1998.
3. N. Asokan, V. Shoup, and M. Waidner. Optimistic fair exchange of digital signatures. *IEEE Journal on Selected Areas in Communications*, 18(4):593–610, Apr. 2000.
4. F. Bao, R. Deng, K. Q. Nguyen, and V. Vardharajan. Multi-party fair exchange with an off-line trusted neutral party. In *DEXA'99 Workshop on Electronic Commerce and Security*, Sept. 1999.
5. F. Bao, R. H. Deng, and W. Mao. Efficient and practical fair exchange protocols with off-line TTP. In *Proceedings of the 19th IEEE Computer Society Symposium on Research in Security and Privacy*, pages 77–85. IEEE, May 1998.
6. M. Franklin and G. Tsudik. Secure group barter: Multi-party fair exchange with semi-trusted neutral parties. In *Proceedings of the International Conference on Financial Cryptography*, volume 1465 of *Lecture Notes in Computer Science*, pages 90–102. Springer-Verlag, 1998.

7. M. K. Franklin and M. K. Reiter. Fair exchange with a semi-trusted third party. In *4th ACM Conference on Computer and Communications Security*, pages 1–5. ACM Press, Apr. 1997.
8. N. González-Deleito and O. Markowitch. An optimistic multi-party fair exchange protocol with reduced trust requirements. In *Proceedings of the 4th International Conference on Information Security and Cryptology*, volume 2288 of *Lecture notes in Computer Science*, pages 258–267. Springer-Verlag, Dec. 2001.
9. O. Markowitch and S. Saeednia. Optimistic fair-exchange with transparent signature recovery. In *Proceedings of the 5th International Conference on Financial Cryptography*, Lecture notes in Computer Science. Springer-Verlag, Feb. 2001.
10. N. Zhang and Q. Shi. Achieving non-repudiation of receipt. *The Computer Journal*, 39(10):844–853, 1996.
11. J. Zhou and D. Gollmann. A fair non-repudiation protocol. In *IEEE Symposium on Security and Privacy*, Research in Security and Privacy, pages 55–61. IEEE Computer Security Press, May 1996.
12. J. Zhou and D. Gollmann. An efficient non-repudiation protocol. In *Proceedings of the 10th IEEE Computer Security Foundations Workshop*, pages 126–132. IEEE Computer Society Press, 1997.

A Realistic Protocol for Multi-party Certified Electronic Mail

Josep Lluís Ferrer-Gomila, Magdalena Payeras-Capellà, and
Llorenç Huguet-Rotger

Universitat de les Illes Balears
Carretera de Valldemossa km. 7.5, Palma de Mallorca, 07071, Spain
{dijjfg, mpayeras, dmilhr0}@clust.uib.es

Abstract. In some cases, users need to notify the same information to multiple recipients, with the requirement that these recipients have to send an acknowledgement of receipt. In this paper we present an optimistic protocol for multi-party certified electronic mail. A Trusted Third Party (TTP) can take part in a protocol run, but only in case of exception. Fairness is guaranteed for all parties being involved in a transaction. At the end of a protocol run, every party possesses enough evidence to prove the final state of the exchange. Parties can contact the TTP when they want (without temporal constraints). The presented protocol is the best one in terms of efficiency: only three steps have to be followed in the exchange sub-protocol.

1 Introduction

S/MIME and PGP can help to substitute postal mail by electronic mail, but at the moment e-mail does not provide all services offered by postal companies. One of these services is certified mail. Certified electronic mail (and paper mail) is a service offered to users, when they want to obtain a receipt from the recipient. In some applications (e.g., notice of a general meeting of shareholders) the same certified message has to be sent to a set of recipients.

Certified electronic mail is a kind of fair exchange of values: the originator has an item (a message and a non-repudiation of origin token) to be exchanged for a recipient's item (the receipt). A protocol for certified electronic mail has to accomplish some requirements, as we will describe. First, the exchange has to be fair. Nobody wants to send its item if they don't have the guarantee that they will receive the expected item. A certified electronic mail protocol is fair if it provides the originator and recipients with enough evidence after the completion of the protocol, without giving to a party an advantage over the other at any stage of the protocol run [15]. Our protocol meets the fairness and the non-repudiation requirements.

We can not assume, generally, that parties have the same computational power. So, solutions based on the gradual release of secrets, as [8, 12], have to be discarded [5], in spite of the good property of not needing Trusted Third Parties (TTP). Then, we

A.H. Chan and V. Gligor (Eds.): ISC 2002, LNCS 2433, pp. 210–219, 2002.
© Springer-Verlag Berlin Heidelberg 2002

must use practical protocols that need a TTP, as [1, 2, 3, 4, 9, 10, 14, 15, 16, 17]. But TTPs can become a bottleneck. Therefore, a desirable property is to reduce TTP's involvement. Our protocol relies on the existence of a subsidiary TTP, or in terms of [2], it is an optimistic protocol: the TTP only intervenes if an exception occurs, and not in every protocol run. Parties will exchange their items, following the sequence of steps specified in the protocol. They hope to receive the expected item from the other party, and this will be the case if the protocol ends successfully. Otherwise, if one party is trying to cheat (or there are communication failures) the other party may contact the TTP to solve the unfair situation.

From a juridical point of view, a question arises: who can act as a TTP? The response is that any company (e.g., an Internet Service Provider) can, with the condition that it can be made accountable of its acts. In other words, TTP's intervention has to be verifiable: if it misbehaves, parties have to be able to prove it in courts. Our protocol meets the verifiability requirement.

An interesting property for fair exchange protocols is to be asynchronous. It means that parties can contact the TTP when they want, without losing fairness. We achieve this property in our protocol.

A sometimes ignored property is efficiency. But reality proves that, after security, it is a conditioning property to determine protocols viability [6]. In fact, in some cases (e.g., micro-payments) it is important to achieve a good balance between security and efficiency. Specifically, for certified *electronic mail*, we must think that every message exchanged by means of an off-line communication protocol (like e-mail) increases the total delay time. Our protocol is the best optimistic solution in terms of efficiency: three steps in the exchange sub-protocol.

In short, we present a multi-party protocol for certified electronic mail with the following characteristics: fair, optimistic, asynchronous, verifiable and very efficient. In section 2 we look over some previous protocols. In section 3 we outline our approach by describing the multi-party protocol for certified electronic mail, and in section 4 we discuss the dispute resolution. In section 5 we point out a security analysis, related to fairness and verifiability of the TTP. We end the paper with a brief conclusion.

2 Previous Work: ASW, ZDB, and MK

Two-party protocols for certified electronic mail were proposed in [3] and [14]. Formal requirements for fair exchange were formulated in [3], and reformulated in [14]: effectiveness, fairness, timeliness, non-repudiation and verifiability of third party. Another desirable property to be met is efficiency, and an optional one is privacy.

ASW [3] and ZDB [14] protocols are two-party, and they have, both, three sub-protocols: *exchange, abort* and *resolve*. In the normal case, only the *exchange* sub-protocol is executed, with four steps in both protocols. We agree with [14] that ASW protocol has some drawbacks (inefficient dispute resolution, performance degradation with large messages, etc.). With regard to ZDB protocol, it has some disadvantages (four steps in the *exchange* sub-protocol, inefficient *resolve* sub-protocol, etc.). But, in any case, both protocols are two-party.

In the literature we can find a few multi-party fair exchange protocols. Most of them are about contract signing [18], and only a few handle certified electronic mail or non-repudiation of receipt. A very interesting protocol is MK [11], a multi-party protocol with two sub-protocols: *main* and *recovery*. In the normal case, only the *main* sub-protocol is executed, with four steps. We want to improve this protocol in three issues: only three steps in the *exchange* sub-protocol, without temporal constraints and without needing *ftp* servers.

3   An Efficient Multi-party Protocol

The sender of the certified mail, A, and the set of recipients, B, will exchange messages and non-repudiation evidence directly, with the *exchange* sub-protocol. If they cannot get the expected items from the other party, the TTP (T) will be invoked, by initiating the *cancel* or *finish* sub-protocols.

In the following description, we have not included elements to link messages of an exchange, nor operations to achieve confidentiality, in order to simplify the explanation. Our protocol is thought having in mind RSA [13], but it is easy to extend the proposed protocol to an arbitrary asymmetric cryptographic scheme. The notation and elements used in the protocol description are as follows:

X, Y	concatenation of two messages (or tokens) X and Y
$H(X)$	a collision-resistant one-way hash function of message X
$Sign_i(X)$	digital signature of principal i on message X
$i \rightarrow j: X$	principal i sends message (or token) X to principal j
$A \Rightarrow B: X$	A sends message (or token) X to a set of entities B
M	message to be sent certified from A to the set B
K	"symmetric" key selected by A
$c = E_K(M)$	symmetric encryption of message M with key K, producing the ciphertext c
$k_T = PU_T(K)$	key K enciphered with the public key of the TTP (it means that only the TTP, who knows the correspondent private key, can decrypt it)

$h_A = Sign_A[H(c), B, k_T]$	signature of A on the concatenation of the *hash* of c, B and k_T; this token is part of the evidence of non-repudiation for every recipient B_i
$h_{Bi} = Sign_{Bi}[H(c), k_T]$	signature of B_i on the concatenation of the *hash* of c and k_T, evidence of non-repudiation for A
$k_A = Sign_A(K, B')$	key K concatenated with B', all signed by A, second part of non-repudiation evidence for B_i, if B_i is included in B'
$k_T' = Sign_T(K, B_i)$	key K and identity of B_i, signed by the TTP, alternative second part of non-repudiation evidence for B_i

The *exchange* sub-protocol is as follows:

1. $A \Rightarrow B$: c, k_T, B, h_A
2. $B_i \rightarrow A$: h_{Bi} where $B_i \in B$, and $i \in \{1, ..., |B|\}$
3. $A \Rightarrow B'$: K, B', k_A

where B_i is a particular recipient, and A is finishing the *exchange* sub-protocol with the subset of recipients B'.

If the protocol run is fully completed, the originator A will hold non-repudiation of receipt evidence from all recipients, h_{Bi}, and every recipient, B_i, will hold the message M and non-repudiation of origin evidence, h_A and k_A. Every recipient, B_i, has the key K, and then he can decrypt the ciphertext c using that key K. So, the protocol meets the effectiveness requirement.

If some of the recipients don't send the message of the step 2, those recipients won't receive the message of the last step. In fact, this last message contains the list of recipients that have completed the protocol for A (A can be cheating, but later we will see that recipients can repair unfair situations). So, cheating recipients cannot use the message 3 received by other recipients (observe that a cheating recipient can intercept the communication channel, or a recipient that has received the last message can provide him a copy).

If some party, A or/and some/all of the recipients, do not follow the *exchange* sub-protocol, they need to correct the unfair situation by initiating the *cancel* or *finish* sub-protocols, in order the situation returns to be fair. If A affirms (truly or cheating) that she has not received message 2 from some of the recipients, A may initiate the following *cancel* sub-protocol:

1'. $A \rightarrow T$: $H(c), k_T, B, h_A, B'', h_{AT}$
2'. T: FOR (all $B_i \in B''$)
                IF ($B_i \in B''$-finished) THEN *retrieves* h_{Bi}
                IF ($B_i \notin B''$-finished) THEN *appends* B_i *in* B''-cancelled
3'. $T \rightarrow A$:   *all* h_{Bi} *retrieved*, B''-cancelled,
                $Sign_T$("cancelled", B''-cancelled, h_A), h_B'

where A has not finished the *exchange* sub-protocol with the subset of recipients B''. The token h_{AT} (= $Sign_A[H(c), k_T, h_A, B'']$) is an evidence that A has demanded TTP's intervention, and the token h_B' (= $Sign_T(B''$-finished)) is a signature of the TTP on the subset B''-*finished* to prove its intervention.

The TTP will verify the correctness of the information given by A. If it is not the case, the TTP will send an error message to A. Otherwise, it will proceed in one of two possible ways, for every recipient in the subset B''. Some recipients can already have contacted the TTP (see paragraph below). The TTP has registered which of them have contacted with him (B''-*finished*). The TTP had given the key K (decrypting k_T with its private key) to the members of subset B''-*finished*, and now it has to give their non-repudiation tokens to A. So, it retrieves these stored non-repudiation tokens, h_{Bi}, and will send them to A, and a token to prove its intervention, h_B'. For recipients that have not contacted with the TTP previously, the TTP will send a message to A to *cancel* the transaction, and it will store the recipients that have not finished (*B"-cancelled*) in order to satisfy future petitions from them. Whatever case, now, we are in a fair situation.

If some recipient, B_i, affirms (truly or cheating) that he has not received message 3, B_i may initiate the following *finish* sub-protocol:

	2'. $B_i \rightarrow T$:	$H(c), k_T, B, h_A, h_{Bi}, h_{BiT}$
IF ($B_i \in$ B"-cancelled)	3'. $T \rightarrow B_i$:	$Sign_T(\text{"cancelled"}, h_{Bi})$
ELSE	3'. $T \rightarrow B_i$:	K, k_T'
	T:	*appends* B_i *in* B"-finished, *and stores* h_{Bi}

where the token h_{BiT} (= $Sign_{Bi}[H(c), k_T, h_A, h_{Bi}]$) is an evidence that B_i has demanded TTP's intervention.

The TTP, also, will verify the correctness of the information given by B_i. If it is not the case, the TTP will send an error message to B_i. Otherwise, it will proceed in one of two possible ways. If B_i is included in the subset *B"-cancelled*, it means that A had previously contacted the TTP (see paragraph above). The TTP had given a message to A in order to *cancel* the transaction, and now it has to send a similar message to B_i. If B_i is not included in the subset *B"-cancelled*, it means that A has not cancelled the transaction for him. So, the TTP will send the key K (obtained by the decryption of k_T with its private key) and a non-repudiation token. So, B_i will be able to decrypt the ciphertext c, and will have non-repudiation tokens. In this case the TTP will store the non-repudiation token, h_{Bi}, and will append B_i to the *B"-finished* list, in order to satisfy future petitions from A. Again, whatever case, now, we are in a fair situation.

As a partial conclusion, the protocol meets the fairness requirement. On the other hand, observe that we have not established any temporal constraint: the protocol satisfies the timeliness requirement. Therefore, it is not necessary to specify a deadline to finish the protocol. When A has sent the message 1, she has to wait the message 2 from every B_i, but whenever she wants she can contact the TTP to *cancel* the execution (in case she doesn't receive messages 2, or even if she has received it but she wants to cheat). The same can be said about recipients (B_i), if they don't receive message 3. So we can affirm that our protocol is asynchronous. Being independent of any time parameter is a great advantage in relation to other solutions that we find in the literature.

4 Dispute Resolution

After a protocol run is completed (with or without TTP's intervention), disputes can arise between participants. We can face with two possible types of disputes: repudiation of origin and repudiation of receipt. An arbiter has to evaluate the evidence held and brought by parties, to resolve these two types of disputes. As a result of this evaluation, the arbiter will determine who is right.

In the case of repudiation of origin, a recipient B_i is claiming that he received the message M from A, while A denies having sent M to B_i. B_i has to provide the following information to an arbiter: M, c, k_T, B, h_A and k_A-B' or k_T'. The arbiter will check, successively:

- if h_A is A's signature on $(H(c), B, k_T)$; if this check is positive, and B_i is included in B, the arbiter will assume that A had sent c to B_i
- if k_A is A's signature on (K, B'), or if k_T' is the TTP's signature on (K, B_i); if this check is positive, and B_i is included in B', the arbiter will assume that either A or the TTP had sent the key K to B_i
- if the decryption of c, $D_K(c)$, is equal to M

If all checks are positive, the arbiter will side with B_i. If one or more of the previous checks fail, the arbiter will reject B_i's demand. If the evidence held by B_i proves that he is right, and A holds a message like $Sign_T$("cancelled", B''-cancelled, h_A) and B_i is included in B''-cancelled, it means that the TTP had acted improperly (see section 5).

In the case of repudiation of receipt (repudiation of B_i), A is claiming that a recipient B_i received M, while B_i denies having received M. A has to provide the following information to an arbiter: M, c, k_T, h_{Bi} and K. The arbiter will check:

- if h_{Bi} is B_i's signature on $(H(c), k_T)$; if this check is positive the arbiter will assume that B_i had received c and k_T, and that he was committed to obtain the key K (and therefore the message M)
- if k_T is the encryption of K under the public key of the TTP; if this check is positive, the arbiter will assume that B_i was able to obtain the key K from the TTP (if he had not received from A)

If the previous checks fail, the arbiter will reject A's demand. If checks are positive, the arbiter will not side with A immediately. First the arbiter must "interrogate" B_i. If B_i contributes a message like $Sign_T$("cancelled", h_{Bi}), it means that B_i had contacted with the TTP, and the TTP observed that A had already executed the cancel sub-protocol for him. For this reason the TTP sent the cancel message to B_i. Now it is demonstrated that A has tried to cheat. Therefore, the arbiter will reject A's demand, and the arbiter will side with B_i. If B_i cannot contribute the cancel message, then the arbiter will check if the decryption of c, $D_K(c)$, is equal to M. If this final check is positive, the arbiter will side with A. Otherwise, if the previous check fails, the arbiter will reject A's demand. If the evidence held by A proves she is right, and B_i holds a message like $Sign_T$("cancelled", h_{Bi}), it means that the TTP had acted improperly (see section 5).

As a conclusion, the protocol satisfies the non-repudiation requirement.

5 Fairness and Verifiability

We have seen that the presented protocol meets the following requirements: effectiveness, fairness, non-repudiation and timeliness. Here we will analyze, in more depth, the accomplishment of the fairness requirement, and the verifiability of the TTP.

Claim 1. The protocol satisfies the fairness requirement.

Proof. We consider all possible unfair situations:

☐ A didn't receive any message from some B_i after sending message 1 in the *exchange* sub-protocol

A can initiate the *cancel* sub-protocol. If B_i has not *finished* the protocol, the TTP will not *finish* the protocol at a later time for him. Thus, B_i can not obtain the second part of the non-repudiation token. If B_i has already *finished* the protocol, A will obtain h_{Bi} and h_B' from the TTP, that can be used to prove that B_i received M.

☐ B_i didn't receive K, B' and k_A, after sending message 2 in the *exchange* sub-protocol

B_i may initiate the *finish* sub-protocol to obtain K and k_T' from the TTP. If A has not *cancelled* the protocol, the TTP will send K and k_T' to B, and it will not *cancel* the protocol at a later time. Thus, A can not obtain a *cancel* message from the TTP, and B_i has h_A and k_T' to prove he received M from A. If A has already *cancelled* the protocol, B_i will obtain a *cancel* message from the TTP, that can be used to prove that B_i did not receive M.

Remark 1. A possible criticism [7] is the following. Assume A is dishonest, sends the first message to B_i, *cancels* the exchange with the TTP, receives second message from B_i, and stops. If B_i contacts with the TTP it will get a *cancel* message, that seems inconsistent with the fact that A already "has" evidence from B_i. But, look at section 4, and you will see that B_i can prove that A is a cheating party, and so, B_i is not compelled to consequences of that certified mail. So, and very important, the three-steps asynchronous protocol is fair, even if A tries to cheat.

Remark 2. A second criticism is the following. Assume B_i needs to present a proof to another party C that A sent the message. Is it true that "C needs not only to verify the signature of A, but C has also to contact the TTP that A did not *cancel* the exchange"? It is not true: if B_i has the first message and the third message (this last message from A or from the TTP) the certified message has been sent (A can not pretend that the exchange is *cancelled*).

Remark 3. A third criticism is as follows. Assume A needs to present a proof to another party C that B_i received the certified mail. C needs not only to verify the receipt of B_i, but C has also to contact the TTP (or B_i) to verify that A did not *cancel* the exchange. It is true. A can have the second message from B_i, but she can also have a *cancel* message obtained from the TTP without sending the third message to B_i, and so the message has not been received. As a conclusion C needs to verify with the TTP or B_i if the message has been received or not, but the protocol remains fair.

Thus, the protocol satisfies the fairness requirement for A and recipients (B_i), without advantages for somebody at any point of a protocol run. Any party can conduct the protocol to a symmetric situation invoking the TTP. So, we can affirm that strict fairness has been achieved.

Claim 2. The TTP is verifiable.

Proof. The possible misbehaviors of the TTP are:

☐ A receives h_{Bi} and h_B', while B_i receives the *cancel* token

If A uses h_{Bi} and h_B' to prove that B_i received M, B_i can use the *cancel* token to prove the TTP's misbehavior. If A received h_{Bi} and then she cancelled the exchange (and so she did not receive h_B'), she can not use h_{Bi} to prove that B_i received M. Remember that the TTP has the h_{AT} token, that makes clear A's misbehavior.

☐ B_i receives k_T' while A receives the *cancel* token

If B_i uses h_A and k_T' to prove that A sent M to B_i, A can use the *cancel* token to prove the TTP's misbehavior. It should be noted that if B_i uses h_A and k_A to prove that A sent M to B_i, A can not use the *cancel* token to prove the TTP's misbehavior, since the TTP did not issue conflicting evidence (it is obvious that A is misbehaving).

6 Conclusion

We have presented a multi-party protocol for certified electronic mail with the following characteristics: fair, optimistic, asynchronous, verifiable and very efficient. Fairness is guaranteed provided the existence (and possible involvement) of a trusted third party, that plays a subsidiary role (only intervenes in case of exception), and in a verifiable way. Our protocol is the best optimistic solution to date in terms of efficiency: three steps in the *exchange* sub-protocol. Finally, the described protocol does not require any deadline to guarantee fairness: each party can contact the TTP when it wants.

References

1. Giuseppe Ateniese, Breno de Medeiros and Michael T. Goodrich: "TRICERT: Distributed Certified E-mail Schemes"; Proceedings of ISOC 2001 Network and Distributed System Security Symposium (NDSS'01), pages 47–56, San Diego, California, February 2001.
2. N. Asokan, Matthias Schunter and Michael Waidner: "Optimistic protocols for fair exchange"; Proceedings of 4th ACM Conference on Computer and Communications Security, pages 7–17, Zurich, Switzerland, April 1997.
3. N. Asokan, Victor Shoup and Michael Waidner: "Asynchronous Protocols for Optimistic Fair Exchange"; Proceedings of the IEEE Symposium on Research in Security and Privacy, pages 86–99, Oakland, California, May 1998.
4. Feng Bao, Robert H. Deng and W. Mao: "Efficient and practical fair exchange protocols with off-line TTP"; Proceedings of the IEEE Symposium on Research in Security and Privacy, pages 77–85, Oakland, California, May 1998.
5. Michael Ben-Or, Oded Goldreich, Silvio Micali and Ronald L. Rivest: "A Fair Protocol for Signing Contracts"; IEEE Transactions on Information Theory, Vol. 36, n. 1, pages 40–46, January 1990.
6. Matthew Berry, Andrew Hutchison and Elton Saul: "Predicting the performance of transactional electronic commerce protocols"; Seventh Annual Working Conference on Information Security Management & Small Systems Security, Kluwer Academic Publishers, pages 161–175, Amsterdam, The Netherlands, September-October 1999.
7. Colin Boyd and Peter Kearney: "Exploring Fair Exchange Protocols Using Specification Animation"; Proceedings of Third International Information Security Workshop, ISW 2000, LNCS 1975, Springer Verlag, pages 209-223, Wollongong, Australia, December 2000.
8. Ivan Bjerre Damgard: "Practical and provably secure release of a secret and exchange of signatures"; Advances in Cryptology – Proceedings of Eurocrypt'93, LNCS 765, Springer Verlag, pages 200–217, Lofthus, Norway, May 1993.
9. Robert H. Deng, Li Gong, Aurel A. Lazar and Weiguo Wang: "Practical Protocols for Certified Electronic Mail"; Journal of Network and Systems Management, Vol. 4, n. 3, pages 279–297, September 1996.
10. Matthew K. Franklin and Michael K. Reiter: "Fair exchange with a semi-trusted third party"; Proceedings of 4th ACM Conference on Computer and Communications Security, pages 1–6, Zurich, Switzerland, April 1997.
11. Olivier Markowitch and Steve Kremer: "A Multi-party Optimistic Non-repudiation Protocol"; Proceedings of Third International Conference on Information Security and Cryptology, ICISC 2000, LNCS 2015, Springer Verlag, pages 109–122, Seoul, Korea, December 2000.
12. Tatsuaki Okamoto and Kazuo Ohta: "How to simultaneously exchange secrets by general assumptions"; Proceedings of IEEE Symposium on Research in Security and Privacy, pages 14–28, Fairfax, Virginia, November 1994.
13. Ronald L. Rivest, Adi Shamir and Leonard M. Adleman: "A Method for Obtaining Digital Signatures and Public Key Cryptosystems"; Communications of the ACM, 21(2), pages 120–126, 1978.
14. Jianying Zhou, Robert Deng and Feng Bao: "Some Remarks on a Fair Exchange Protocol"; Proceedings of Third International Workshop on Practice and Theory in Public Key Cryptosystems, PKC 2000, LNCS 1751, Springer Verlag, pages 46–57, Melbourne, Victoria, Australia, January 2000.

15. Jianying Zhou and Dieter Gollmann: "A Fair Non-repudiation Protocol"; Proceedings of the IEEE Symposium on Research in Security and Privacy, pages 55–61, Oakland, California, May 1996.
16. Jianying Zhou and Dieter Gollmann: "An Efficient Non-repudiation Protocol"; Proceedings of 10th IEEE Computer Security Foundations Workshop, pages 126–132, Rockport, Massachusetts, June 1997.
17. Josep L. Ferrer, Magdalena Payeras and Llorenç Huguet: "An Efficient Protocol for Certified Electronic Mail"; Proceedings of Third International Information Security Workshop, ISW 2000, LNCS 1975, Springer Verlag, pages 237–248, Wollongong, Australia, December 2000.
18. Josep L. Ferrer, Magdalena Payeras and Llorenç Huguet: "Efficient Optimistic N-Party Contract Signing Protocol"; Proceedings of Fourth International Information Security Conference, ISC 2001, LNCS 2200, Springer Verlag, pages 394–407, Málaga, Spain, October 2001.

A Nyberg-Rueppel Signature for Multiple Messages and Its Batch Verification

Shunsuke Araki

Dept. of Computer Science and Electronics, Kyushu Institute of Technology,
680-4 Kawazu, Iizuka, Fukuoka 820-8502, Japan.
araki@cse.kyutech.ac.jp

Abstract. We propose a Nyberg-Rueppel message recovery signature scheme for multiple messages which produces one signature for multiple messages and has its batch verification of the signature for multiple messages. The length of the signature is shorter than the sum of length of corresponding signatures produced by the ordinary digital signature scheme, separately. In the signature generation and the verification of our scheme, the number of exponentiations is constant independent of the number of messages.

1 Introduction

In signature generation or verifications of such ordinary digital signature schemes as the ElGamal signature[2] and the Nyberg-Rueppel message recovery signature[6], the computational cost increases in proportion to the number of messages. For multiple messages, a signer or a verifier would require a method whose computational cost is smaller than one of a typical method that a signer uses repeatedly an ordinary scheme.

Fiat proposed the batch RSA[3] in order for a signer to generate multiple signatures efficiently. Additionally, in the digital signature based on the discrete logarithm problem, DSA type batch verification protocols[4,5] were proposed in order to verify efficiently multiple signatures. But signatures' generation needs interactive communication between a signer and a verifier. Bellare, Garay and Rabin proposed the fast batch verification[1] for modular exponentiation and digital signatures in order for a verifier to verify efficiently multiple signatures. In their schemes, a signer produces signatures by using such ordinary schemes as the ElGamal scheme and the Nyberg-Rueppel schemes. Then a verifier can check the validity of messages in their batch verification improved the verifying computation cost for multiple signatures. Since their scheme is only the verification, the signing computational cost increases in proportion to the number of messages.

Suppose a software distribution system via a computer network. A software provider must sign a software program sent to a user via a computer network, such as Internet, in order to guarantee its validity. For use of the software, a user must verify the signature in order to check that it is free from computer

A.H. Chan and V. Gligor (Eds.): ISC 2002, LNCS 2433, pp. 220–228, 2002.

viruses. Generally, a software program consists of many files. For example, an operating system consists of a kernel, libraries, many sub-programs, manual files, and so on. Though the kernel is necessary for all users without exception, sub-programs are not always needed by all users. If the provider signs all files of the software by using a typical method that a signer uses repeatedly such ordinary signature scheme as the ElGamal signature, the signing generation makes a signer spend the computational costs in proportion to increases in the number of files, though the verification cost does not increase by using the Bellare-Garay-Rabin batch verification[1]. If the provider signs a hash value of all files in the ordinary signature scheme, the computational costs is constant independent of the number of files. However, a verifier must obtain all files from necessary files to unnecessary files, even if he/she wants to do a file.

Suppose the following situation: A signer requires that the signing cost is smaller than one of a typical method, since he/she must sign multiple messages which are such messages as files in a software program. A verifier desires that he/she obtain only any messages as his/her wish, since he/she does not necessary need all messages. We want to propose a method whose computational cost is smaller than the typical method that an ordinary scheme is used repeatedly, whose signature is more flexible than one that a hash value of all messages is signed,

In this paper, we propose a Nyberg-Rueppel message recovery signature for multiple messages and its batch verification as the solution of the above situation in order to improve the signing and verifying computational cost. First, we review the Nyberg-Rueppel message recovery signature scheme[6] based on the discrete logarithm problem, which we call the NR-signature. Next, we show a Nyberg-Rueppel message recovery signature for multiple messages, its batch verification and a comparison between our scheme and other similar schemes.

2   Related Works

In this section, we review the Nyberg-Rueppel message recovery signature[6] as the basic scheme of our proposal and show the Bellare-Garay-Rabin batch verification algorithm[1] applying to the verification of the NR-signature.

2.1   Nyberg-Rueppel Message Recovery Signature

Nyberg and Rueppel proposed the message recovery signature schemes[6] based on the discrete logarithm problem.

The trusted authority decides the following system parameters and publishes them:

- p : a large prime
- q : a large prime satisfying $q|p-1$
- g : an element in $\mathbf{Z}_p^*$ whose order is q

All users must decide the following parameters:

- x : a secret key in $\mathbf{Z}_q^*$
- y : a public key satisfying $y \equiv g^x \pmod{p}$

A signer Alice signs a message $m(\in \mathbf{Z}_p^*)$, and produces the signature (r, s) as follows:

1. Choose a random number k in $\mathbf{Z}_q^*$
2. Compute a message commitment r satisfying $r \equiv mg^{-k} \pmod{p}$
3. Compute a signature equation s satisfying $s \equiv k - rx \pmod{q}$
4. Output (r, s) as the signature of the message m

She sends a receiver the signature (r, s) of the message m. The verification of the signature (r, s) for the message m can be performed by checking the following relation:

$$m \equiv rg^s y^r \pmod{p}.$$

2.2   Bellare-Garay-Rabin Batch Verification

Bellare, Garay and Rabin proposed the fast batch verification algorithms in [1]. In this paper, we will compare our method and a method with the small exponents test as their batch verification algorithm. In [1], they showed the batch verification algorithm for the DSS. We show their small exponents test applying to the NR-signature as their batch verification algorithm. For messages and their signatures (m_1, r_1, s_1), ..., (m_n, r_n, s_n), a verifier checks whether they are valid as follows:

1. Pick $l_1, ..., l_n \in \{0, 1\}^l$ at random, where the security parameter is $l \geq |q|$
2. Compute $A = \sum_{i=1}^{n} s_i l_i \pmod{q}$, $B = \sum_{i=1}^{n} r_i' l_i \pmod{q}$,
   $R = \prod_{i=1}^{n} r_i^{l_i} \pmod{p}$ and $M = \prod_{i=1}^{n} m_i^{l_i} \pmod{p}$,
   where $r_i' = r_i \pmod{q}$ for $(1 \leq i \leq n)$
3. If $M = Rg^A y^B \pmod{p}$ then accept, else reject.

3   A Nyberg-Rueppel Signature for Multiple Messages and Its Batch Verification

In this section, we propose a Nyberg-Rueppel message recovery signature for multiple messages and its batch verification in order to improve signing and verifying computational costs.

3.1   Scheme

A signer signs n messages $(m_1, ..., m_n)$, where m_i $(1 \leq i \leq n)$ is in $\mathbf{Z}_p$ and generates a signature as follows:

1. Choose a random number k in $\mathbf{Z}_q^*$
2. Compute $r \equiv g^{-k} \pmod{p}$

3. Compute message commitments r_{m_i} satisfying $r_{m_i} \equiv m_i r \pmod{p}$, where $1 \leq i \leq n$

4. Compute a signature equation s satisfying $s \equiv k - h(r_{m_1}, ..., r_{m_n})x \pmod{q}$, where $h(\cdots)$ is a collision-resistant hash function and outputs the digest whose length is about $|q|$

5. Output $(r_{m_1}, ..., r_{m_n}, s)$ as the signature of messages $m_1, ..., m_n$

She sends a receiver the signature $(r_{m_1}, ..., r_{m_n}, s)$ of messages $m_1, ..., m_n$. The following relation shows the validity of m_i:

$$m_i \equiv r_{m_i} g^s y^{h(r_{m_1}, ..., r_{m_n})} \pmod{p}.$$

The validity of j messages is checked as follows:

1. Compute $\kappa \equiv g^s y^{h(r_{m_1}, ..., r_{m_n})} \pmod{p}$
2. Check $m_i \equiv r_{m_i} \kappa \pmod{p}$, where $0 < i \leq j$

Note that each of the following signature equations[6] can be used in our scheme by substituting $h(r_{m_1}, ..., r_{m_n})$ for r:

$$sk \equiv \pm 1 \pm rx \pmod{q}, \quad rk \equiv \pm 1 \pm sx \pmod{q},$$
$$k \equiv \pm s \pm rx \pmod{q}, \quad sk \equiv \pm r \pm x \pmod{q},$$
$$rk \equiv \pm s \pm dx \pmod{q}, \quad k \equiv \pm r \pm sx \pmod{q}.$$

3.2 Security

We clarify a relation between the security of the original NR-signature and a scheme whose signature equation has a hash value of a message commitment, and then show that the security of our scheme equal to one of the scheme.

Let the scheme I as the original NR-signature be the following equations;

$$r \equiv mg^{-k} \pmod{p}, \quad s_1 \equiv k - r_1' x \pmod{q}, \text{ where } r_1' \equiv r \pmod{q},$$

the scheme II the following equations:

$$r \equiv mg^{-k} \pmod{p}, \quad s_2 \equiv k - r_2' x \pmod{q}, \text{ where } r_2' = h(r).$$

Theorem I: *The scheme II has at least the same security as the scheme I.*

Proof: It is easy to find $\bar{r}_1$ satisfying $\bar{r}_1 \neq r \pmod{p}$ and $\bar{r}_1 \equiv r' \pmod{q}$, where there are $p - 1/q$ candidates of $\bar{r}_1$. However, it is hard to find $\bar{r}_2$ satisfying $\bar{r}_2 \neq r \pmod{p}$ and $h(\bar{r}_2) = r_2'$, since $h(\cdot)$ is the collision-resistant hash function. Therefore, in forgery of signatures for a redundancy of r, the scheme II has at least the same security as the scheme I. □

According to theorem I, our scheme for $n = 1$ has at least the same security as the NR-signature. We show that there is no algorithm to generate invalid signatures for arbitrary messages.

Theorem II: *In our scheme, there is no algorithm to generate invalid signatures for arbitrary messages.*

Proof: Let $\mathcal{A}$ be an algorithm to generate an invalid signature for arbitrary messages in our scheme. We define $\mathcal{A}$ as follows:

$$(\bar{r}_{\bar{m}_{3,1}}, ..., \bar{r}_{\bar{m}_{3,n}}, \bar{s}) = \mathcal{A}(m_{3,1}, ..., m_{3,n}, r_{m_{3,1}}, ..., r_{m_{3,n}}, s_3, \bar{m}_{3,1}, \bar{m}_{3,n}, g, y),$$

where $m_{3,1}, ..., m_{3,n}$ are messages, $(r_{m_{3,1}}, ..., r_{m_{3,n}}, s)$ a valid signature, $\bar{m}_{3,1}, ..., \bar{m}_{3,n}$ bogus messages, $(\bar{r}_{\bar{m}_{3,1}}, ..., \bar{r}_{\bar{m}_{3,n}}, \bar{s})$ a invalid signature, g a system parameter, y a public key, $n \geq 2$. Additionally, the number of bogus messages must be the same one as valid messages.

Let $\mathcal{B}$ be an algorithm to generate an invalid signature for an arbitrary messages in the scheme II. We define $\mathcal{B}$ as follows:

$$(\bar{r}_{\bar{m}_2}, \bar{s}_2) = \mathcal{B}(m_2, r_2, s_2, \bar{m}_2),$$

where m_2 is a messages, (r_2, s_2) its signature, $\bar{m}_2$ a bogus message, $(\bar{r}_2, \bar{s}_2)$ its invalid signature.

Suppose that the hash function in our scheme satisfies the following condition: if $a_i = 0$ then $h(a_1, ..., a_i, ..., a_n) = h(a_1, a_2, ..., a_{i-1}, a_{i+1}, ..., a_n)$.

$\mathcal{B}$ is represented by using $\mathcal{A}$ as follows:

$$(\bar{r}_2, \bar{s}_2) = \mathcal{B}(m_2, r_2, s_2, \bar{m}_2) = \mathcal{A}(m_2, 0, ..., 0, r_2, 0, ..., 0, s_2).$$

If there were an algorithm $\mathcal{A}$, the scheme II would allow that attackers generate invalid signatures for arbitrary messages. However, there is no algorithm $\mathcal{A}$ in our scheme, since there is no algorithm $\mathcal{B}$ in the scheme II with the same security as the original NR-signature scheme.   □

Suppose $n > 1$ and $1 \leq i \leq n$. We assume that a signer produces a signature $(r_{m_1}, ..., r_{m_n}, s)$ for messages $m_1, ..., m_n$. We consider the security that our scheme has multiple message commitments r_{m_i} where $1 \leq i \leq n$. In the following part, two situations are considered.

1. Success Probability Finding Signer's Secret Key

Attackers may try to get signer's secret key using some signature equations s. They always have more unknown parameters than signature equations, which hide k and x, while she generates signatures without re-using the same k.

$$s' \equiv k' - h(r_{m'_1}, ..., r_{m'_n})x \pmod{q}$$
$$s'' \equiv k'' - h(r_{m''_1}, ..., r_{m''_n})x \pmod{q}$$
$$\vdots$$

If we pay attention to i-th message m_i, our scheme arrives at the original NR-signature since the inputs $r_{m_1}, ..., r_{m_n}$ of the hash function except r_{m_i} are regarded as the part of the hash function in the verification of the signature (m_i, r_{m_i}, s). In other words, $r_{m_1}, ..., r_{m_n}$ except r_{m_i} are inner values of the hash function in the signature equation s of our scheme.

A success probability finding a signer's secret key is $1/q$ and then it is infeasible that attackers find one from any signature equations. Therefore, the security of our scheme is the same as the original NR-signature.

2. Forgery of Signer's Messages

Attackers may try to forge signer's signature for arbitrary messages by using a valid signature.

When $n = 1$, our scheme outputs (r_{m_1}, s_1), the security is equal to one of the original NR-signature.

Suppose $n > 1$ and an invalid message is $\bar{m}_i (\neq m_i)$. They easily compute an invalid message commitment r as follows:

$$\bar{r}_{\bar{m}_i} \equiv \bar{m}_i (g^{-s} y^{-h(r_{m_1}, \ldots, r_{m_n})})$$
$$\equiv \bar{m}_i g^{-k} \pmod{p}.$$

Since $\bar{r}_{\bar{m}_i} \neq r_{m_i}$, they must compute $\bar{r}_{\bar{m}_j} (j \neq i)$ satisfying the following equation in order to use the same signature equation s:

$$h(r_{m_1}, \ldots, r_{m_i}, \ldots, r_{m_n}) = h(r_{m_1}, \ldots, \bar{r}_{\bar{m}_i}, \ldots, \bar{r}_{\bar{m}_j}, \ldots, r_{m_n}), \tag{1}$$

Even if they can compute $\bar{r}_{\bar{m}_j}$, they does not succeed in forging the j-th message since $\bar{m}_j (\equiv \bar{r}_{\bar{m}_j} g^s y^{h(r_{m_1}, \ldots, r_{m_n})} \pmod{p})$ is not meaningful message. However, it is hard to find $\bar{r}_{\bar{m}_j}$ satisfying equation (1) in the collision-resistant hash function.

3.3 Efficiency

We compare our method using the scheme presented in section 3.1 with the following two similar methods using the NR-signature in the situation that a signer wants to sign n messages $M_1, \ldots, M_n$:

The method I. A signer produces a signature of a hash value calculated from all messages by using the NR-signature scheme. Then the signature is (r_m, s) for the hash $m(= h(M_1, \ldots, M_n))$.

The method II. A signer produces NR-signatures of all messages, respectively. Then the signatures are $(r_{m_1}, s_1), \ldots, (r_{m_n}, s_n)$ for the hashes $(m_1, \ldots, m_n)(= H(M_1), \ldots, H(M_n))$. A verifier checks their signatures by using the Bellare-Garay-Rabin batch verification which is shown in Section 2.2.

In this section, we consider that the hash value $m = H(M)$ in $\mathbf{Z}_p$ is signed, where $H(\cdot)$ is a collision-resistant hash function and the length of an original message M is far longer than one of the hash value m.

Table 1 shows the comparison between our method and the method I and II. We compare them about random numbers, the signing and verifying cost, the signature's length and necessary data in verifications of i messages. So the computational cost is represented as the number of multiplications over $\mathbf{Z}_p$ or $\mathbf{Z}_q$.

Table 1. Comparison between our method and method I and II

	Method I	Method II	Our method
random numbers	1	n	1
signing cost	$2 + \mathrm{EC}_{Z_p}(|q|)^{*1}$	$2n + n\mathrm{EC}_{Z_p}(|q|)$	$1 + n + \mathrm{EC}_{Z_p}(|q|)$
length	$|p| + |q|$	$n|p| + n|q|$	$n|p| + |q|$
verifying cost^{*2}	$2 + 2\mathrm{EC}_{Z_p}(|q|)$	$3i + 1.5li + 2\mathrm{EC}_{Z_p}(|q|)$	$1 + i + 2\mathrm{EC}_{Z_p}(|q|)$
necessary data^{*2}	$\mathbf{M}^{*3}, r, s;$	$M_j, r_{m_j}, s_j;_{j=1,...,i}$	$M_j, \mathbf{r_m}^{*4}, s;_{j=1,...,i}$

(^{*1}: $\mathrm{EC}_{Z_p}(|q|)$ is the number of multiplications required to compute an exponentiation)

(^{*2}: They are described in the i messages verifications)

(^{*3}: $\mathbf{M}$ is equal to $M_1, ..., M_n$)

(^{*4}: $\mathbf{r_m}$ is equal to $r_{m_1}, ..., r_{m_n}$)

In the signature generation, the method I needs a random number and $2 + \mathrm{EC}_{Z_p}(|q|)$ multiplications and produces a signature whose length is $|p| + |q|$, where $\mathrm{EC}_{Z_p}(|q|)$ is the number of multiplications required to compute a modular exponentiation over $\mathbf{Z}_p$ and $|q|$ is the length of the exponent. The method II needs n random numbers and $2n + n\mathrm{EC}_{Z_p}(|q|)$ multiplications and produces signatures whose length is $n|p| + n|q|$, since she must not use the random number which is already used for other messages. On the other hand, our method needs a random number and $1 + n + \mathrm{EC}_{Z_p}(|q|)$ multiplications and the signature's length of our scheme is $n|p| + |q|$. In the signature generation, the method I is the most efficient of them. However, our method's cost is far smaller than the method II's one.

In the verifications of i messages, where $0 < i \leq n$, the method I needs $2 + 2\mathrm{EC}_{Z_p}(|q|)$ multiplications since a verifier checks only one signature but needs all original message $M_1, ..., M_n$ in order to calculate a hash m. The method II needs i messages $M_1, ..., M_i$ and i pairs (r_j, s_j) and $3 + 1.5li + 2\mathrm{EC}_{Z_p}(|q|)$ multiplications, where l is the security parameter and satisfies $l \leq |q|$, since the verification uses the small exponents test[1]. The cost of the method II is more than one of others if $i \geq |q|$ since $\mathrm{EC}_{Z_p}(|q|) \simeq 1.5|q|$ multiplications under the normal square-and-multiply method. Our signature needs i messages $M_1, ..., M_i$ and $r_{m_1}, ..., r_{m_n}$ and s and $1 + i + 2\mathrm{EC}_{Z_p}(|q|)$ multiplications. The verifying cost of our method is more efficient than the cost of the method II.

Each of them has some advantages over others.

In the software distributing situation shown in the introduction, the software provider calculates the hash values of the program files and signs them. The method I is not suitable for this situation. Under the method I, a verifier would waste time in order to get all program files which are necessary and unnecessary, since he must calculate a hash of all program files. The method II isn't suitable for this situation, too. In the method II, the computational cost of the signatures' generation increases in proportion to the number of programs, though the verification is about same cost as the others. Our scheme is suitable for this situation.

A signer can produce a signature for multiple programs in the constant computational cost, though she can't divide the signature into some signatures. A verifier can check multiple programs in the constant computational cost without getting unnecessary program files.

Table 2. Concrete example in a software distribution

	Method I	Method II	Our method
random numbers	1	5000	1
signing cost[*1]	770	3,850,000	5,769
length	192B	960KB	640KB
verifying cost[*1]	1,538	100,536	2,537
necessary data[*2]	2.5GB + 192B	500MB + 192KB	500MB + 640KB

([*1]: The cost shows the number of multiplications)
([*2]: In i messages' verifications)

We give a concrete example as follows: $|p|$ is 1024bits, $|q|$ is 512bits, i-th message length $|M_i|$ is 500KBytes, the number of messages n is 5000, the security parameter l of the small exponent test is 64. Suppose a verifier needs to verify 1000 messages ($i = 1000$). We expect that the above parameters is suitable since each of applications in the FreeBSD operating system, which are called "packages", have about 500KBytes on average, their number is about 6000. Table 2 shows the concrete example with above values.

Our method has the necessary data size which is smaller than one of the method I, though the size of our method is larger than one of the method II. Our method is more efficient than the method II except the necessary data size. Therefore, our method is suitable for such an application as a software distribution via a computer network.

4   Conclusion

We proposed a Nyberg-Rueppel message recovery signature for multiple messages and its batch verification. Our scheme has such advantages as the number of exponentiation in the signature generation and the verification are constant independent of the number of messages. Our scheme solved the following situation: a signer must sign multiple messages which are far large than their signatures, and then a receiver want to verify only some messages at a time. Additionally, we showed the concrete example in the software distribution.

References

1. Bellare, M., Garay, J. A., Rabin, T.: Fast Batch Verification for Modular Exponentiation and Digital Signatures. Advances in Cryptology-EUROCRYPTO'98, Lecture Notes in Computer Science Vol. 1403, Springer-Verlag, (1998) 236–250

2. ElGamal, T.: A Public Key Cryptosystem and A Signature Scheme Based on Discrete Logarithms. IEEE Trans. on Information Theory, Vol. IT-31 (1985) 469–472
3. Fiat, A.: Batch RSA. Advances in Cryptology-CRYPTO'89, Lecture Notes in Computer Science, Vol. 435, Springer-Verlag, (1989) 175–185
4. Harn, L.: DSA Type Secure Interactive Batch Verification Protocols. Electronics Letters, Vol. 31, No. 4, (1995) 257–258
5. Naccache, D., M'räihi, D., Vaudenay, S., Ráphaeli, D.: Can D.S.A. be Improved? – Complexity Trade-Offs with the Digital Signature Standard-. Advances in Cryptology-EUROCRYPT'94, Lecture Notes in Computer Science, Vol. 950, Springer-Verlag, (1995) 77–85
6. Nyberg, K., Rueppel, R.A.: Message Recovery for Signature Schemes Based on the Discrete Logarithm Problem. Advances in Cryptology-EUROCRYPT'94, Lecture Notes in Computer Science, Vol. 950, Springer-Verlag, (1995) 175–190

Comments to the UNCITRAL Model Law on Electronic Signatures

Apol·lònia Martínez-Nadal and Josep Lluís Ferrer-Gomila

Universitat de les Illes Balears
Carretera de Valldemossa km. 7.5, Palma de Mallorca, 07071, Spain
{dpramn0, dijjfg}@clust.uib.es

Abstract. Electronic signatures, together with certificates, are offered as a substitutive solution of hand-written signatures for a wide scale electronic commerce. The use of these electronic authentication techniques has suggested the need for a specific legal framework to reduce uncertainties, specially regarding to the legal effect that may result from the use of such techniques. The risk of diverging legislative approaches taken in various countries calls for uniform legislative provisions to establish the basic rules of what is inherently an international phenomenon, where not only technical but legal interoperability is essential. So, these new legal issues should be addressed in an internationally acceptable legal framework. This is the objective of the UNCITRAL Model Law on electronic signatures (2001). The aim of this paper is comment and criticise the content of this Model Law, studying their different precepts. The paper concludes with some observations that show that the Model Law, although positive, presents important oversights.

1 Introduction

Nowadays the use of new technologies to facilitate commercial transactions electronically is becoming more frequent. Then hand-written signatures are not possible and neither are any of the functions they perform. From the technological point of view, digital signatures are offered as substitutes for hand-written signatures together with certificates and certification authorities (also known as certifying entities, certifiers, or certification service providers).

The increased use of these electronic authentication techniques has suggested the need for a specific legal framework to reduce uncertainties, specially regarding to the legal effect that may result from the use of such modern techniques. From a legal point of view, these elements (which may be referred to, generally, as "electronic signatures") have been the object of various initiatives, differing in origin, nature and application. Amongst these, it must be mentioned the Utah Digital Signature Law (1996), the first law to attempt regulation of electronic signatures, certificates and certification authorities. Since then, a great number of states or entities have also enacted or are preparing legislation to rule electronic signatures (USA, Germany, Italy, Spain, Argentina, European Union, etc.).

A.H. Chan and V. Gligor (Eds.): ISC 2002, LNCS 2433, pp. 229–243, 2002.
© Springer-Verlag Berlin Heidelberg 2002

Anyway, we consider that local or national legislation is not enough. The risk that diverging legislative approaches being taken in various countries with respect to electronic signatures calls for uniform legislative provisions to establish the basic rules of what is inherently an international phenomenon, where legal (as well as technical) interoperability is essential. Different and diverging legislation can produce difficulties in reaching a common understanding of the new legal issues that arose from the increased use of digital signatures. So, these new legal issues should be addressed in an internationally acceptable legal framework.

Attending to the need of uniform legislation, and after some years of works, the United Nations Commission on International Trade (UNCITRAL) adopted the Model Law on Electronic Signatures on 5 July 2001. This new Model Law rules the legal effectiveness that may be expected from a given electronic signature, adopting an approach under which the legal effectiveness of a given electronic signature technique may be pre-determined (or assessed prior to being actually used). Moreover, by establishing with appropriate flexibility a set of basic rules of conduct for the various parties that may become involved in the use of electronic signatures the Model Law may assist in shaping more harmonious commercial practices in cyberspace. By incorporating the procedures prescribed in the Model Law in its national legislation, the different enacting States would establish harmonised legislative framework to address more effectively the issues of electronic signatures.

As the UNCITRAL Model Law on Electronic Commerce (1996), the new Model Law on electronic signatures is in the form of a legislative text that is recommended to States for incorporation into their national law. Unlike an international convention, model legislation does not require the State enacting it to notify the United Nations or other States that may have also enacted it. However, States are strongly encouraged to inform the UNCITRAL Secretariat of any enactment of the new Model Law (or any other model law resulting from the work of UNCITRAL). In incorporating the text of the model legislation into its legal system, a State may modify or leave out some of its provisions. In the case of a convention, the possibility of changes being made to the uniform text by the States parties is much more restricted. Model legislation is then more flexible but this flexibility, however, also means that the degree of, and certainty about, harmonisation achieved through model legislation is likely to be lower than in the case of a convention.

Regarding the question of application of Model Law to use of electronic signatures in international and domestic transactions, it is recommended that application of the Model Law be made as wide as possible. Particular caution should be used in excluding the application of the Model Law by way of a limitation of its scope to international uses of electronic signatures, since such a limitation may be seen as not fully achieving the objectives of the Model Law. The legal certainty to be provided by the Model Law is necessary for both domestic and international trade, and a duality of regimes governing the use of electronic signatures might create a serious obstacle to the use of such techniques.

In preparing and adopting the Model Law on Electronic Signatures the United Nations Commission on International Trade Law was mindful that the Model Law would be a more effective tool for States modernising their legislation if background and explanatory information were provided to Governments and legislators to assist them in using the Model Law. It's the Guide to enactment of the UNCITRAL Model Law on electronic signatures. For example, it was decided in respect of a number of issues not to settle them in the Model Law but to address them in the Guide so as to provide guidance to States enacting the Model Law.

The Model Law on electronic signatures is now object of analysis, albeit in brief, in order to understand the fundamental aspects of the subject and the basic legal principles as regards electronic signatures established in the Model Law that probably will inspire the legislation of a great number of countries. First we will analyse its sphere of application; next, basic subjective and objective notions; we'll continue with the essential question of legal effects of electronic signature and we'll end this analysis with the study of the conduct that must perform the different parties. Finally, this work will finish with some conclusions, suggestions and reflections.

2   Sphere of Application

The Model Law contains an explicit indication that its focus was on the types of situations encountered in the commercial area. According to Article 1 "This Law applies where electronic signatures are used in the context of commercial activities". So, the "Sphere of application" of Model Law would be only commercial uses, and non-commercial (e.g., administrative) uses would be excluded. Anyway, the Guide to enactment of the UNCITRAL Model Law explains that the term "commercial" should be given non a strict but a wide interpretation so as to cover matters arising from all relationships of a commercial nature, whether contractual or not, and provides indications as to what is meant thereby.

Furthermore, UNCITRAL admits that nothing in the Model Law should prevent an enacting State from extending the scope of the Model Law to cover uses of electronic signatures outside the commercial sphere. For example, while the focus of the Model Law is not on the relationships between users of electronic signatures and public authorities, the Model Law is not intended to be inapplicable to such relationships.

3   Definitions. Basic Notions: Subjective and Objective Elements

Article 2 establishes for the purposes of the Model Law the basic notions, which can be classified in two categories: objective notions: electronic signature, certificate and data message; and subjective notions: signatory, certification service provider and relying party.

3.1   Objective Notions

(a) *"Electronic signature"* means data in electronic form in, affixed to or logically associated with, a data message, which may be used to identify the signatory in relation to the data message and to indicate the signatory's approval of the information contained in the data message (art. 2, paragraph a).

This notion of "electronic signature" is intended to cover all traditional uses of a hand-written signature for legal effect: the identification of the signatory and the intent to sign. It's a wide and technologically-neutral definition, similar to the notion of electronic signature established in other legislation (e.g., European Directive on electronic signatures, 1999). The reason of this neutrality, according to Guide, is that the scope of the Model Law is to provide for the coverage of all factual situations where electronic signatures are used, irrespective of the specific electronic signature or authentication technique being applied. However, the Guide admits that in the preparation of the Model Law, special attention has been given to "digital signatures", i.e., those electronic signatures obtained through the application of dual-key cryptography, which were regarded by the UNCITRAL Working Group on Electronic Commerce as a particularly widespread technology. Observe that due to this neutrality it seems that the juridical concept of electronic signature is not equivalent to the technical concept of digital signature: a digital signature is an electronic signature but not always an electronic signature will be a digital signature. Because according to the Model Law another authentication techniques (currently available on the market or still under development) relying on techniques other than public-key cryptography can offer the technical means by which some or all of the functions identified as characteristic of hand-written signatures can be performed in an electronic environment. Such techniques may be referred to broadly as "electronic signatures".

So, UNCITRAL has intended to develop uniform legislation that can facilitate the use of both digital signatures and other forms of electronic signatures. Anyway, we consider this neutral definition too wide, in the sense that it could include techniques that are not really electronic signatures because they don't satisfy the function of authentication (probably techniques such as authentication through a biometrics device based on hand-written signatures, the use of personal identification numbers, digitised versions of hand-written signatures, and other methods). This problem is solved in other legislation establishing a second concept of electronic signature which must fulfil some additional requirements that gives more security to the concept (e.g., the advanced electronic signature of European Directive). In UNCITRAL Model Law on electronic signatures there's no a clear definition of this second concept of qualified or enhanced electronic signatures. Anyway, we consider that, as we shall see, the content and the requirements of art. 6 establishes implicitly this second concept of electronic signatures.

Furthermore, given the rapidity of technological development, this neutrality surely allows the doors to be left open for future technologies; however, on the other hand, carried to this extreme, it leaves without resolution many of the questions posed now by the digital signature, which is probably the only secure form of electronic signature available today. We do understand that it doubtless would have been better to adopt a technically open position, in order to not discourage the means for other secure technologies in the future to come forward, but, at the same time, focusing on the regulation of the digital signature, given the predominance of the function performed by the public key cryptography in the recent practices of electronic commerce.

(b) *"Certificate"* means a data message or other record confirming the link between a signatory and signature creation data (art. 2, paragraph b).

The purpose of the certificate is to recognise, or confirm a link between signature creation data and the signatory. This notion uses a concept ("signature creation data") that is not defined in the Model Law. Another legislation uses and defines this concept (e.g., the European Directive on electronic signatures: those unique data, such as codes or *private cryptographic keys*, which are used by the signatory to create an electronic signature). Only Guide of Model Law explains that the terms "signature creation data" is intended to designate those secret keys, codes, or other elements that, in the process of creating an electronic signature, are used to provide a secure link between the resulting electronic signature and the person of the signatory. For example, in the context of digital signatures relying on asymmetric cryptography, the cryptographic key pair; in the context of electronic signatures based on biometrics devices, the biometrics indicator, such as a fingerprint or retina-scan data.

Observe that while in general legislation on electronic signatures defines the certificate as a link of a person to a signature verification data (e.g., European Directive), in the Model Law the certificate establishes a link between a person (the signatory) and the opposed element: the signature creation data. In fact, the certificates of digital signature contain as basic requirement the identity of the subscriber and the public or verification key, the certificate establishes a direct link between this two elements (and only and indirect link between the subscriber and the private or signature key, which does not appear in the certificate).

Differing from other legislation the Model Law doesn't approach in this definition the essential question of confirmation or verification of the identity of the signatory (e.g., European Directive defines the certificate in general, as "an electronic attestation which links signature-verification data to a person and confirms the identity of that person"). This verification is essential for the security of the electronic signature. And it is also essential that the certification service provider assumes liability for this role and function. In practice, distinct ways of verification of identity are used (physical presence, presentation of accreditation documentation, submission of information on-line). Among them, the only one that offers security is physical identification (even so, this is not completely safe, as an impostor could assume an identity and not be detected, not even by a diligent service provider) Although from the commercial point of view it is understandable that the certification service providers offer products with differing costs and levels of security, from the legal point of view this commercial diversification doesn't allow the basic function of the certificates. Furthermore, if an excessive flexibility in commercial practices is permitted in order to facilitate the growth of certification providers the certification system will become degraded and will never achieve its final aim, which although bordering on other subjective commercial interests, is, we mustn't forget, the security of electronic commerce.

(c) *"Data message"* means information generated, sent, received or stored by electronic, optical or similar means including, but not limited to, electronic data interchange (EDI), electronic mail, telegram, telex or telecopy (art. 2, paragraph c).

The definition of "data message" is taken from article 2 of the UNCITRAL Model Law on Electronic Commerce as a broad notion encompassing all messages generated in the context of electronic commerce, including web-based commerce. The notion of "data message" is not limited to communication but is also intended to encompass computer-generated records that are not intended for communication. Thus, the notion of "message" includes the notion of "record". The reference to "similar means" is intended to reflect the fact that the Model Law was not intended only for application in the context of existing communication techniques but also to accommodate foreseeable technical developments.

3.2 Subjective Notions

Together to the previous objective notions, the Model Law defines three other subjective notions referred to the parties that normally act with respect to electronic signatures: signatories, certification services providers and relying parties. The Guide remarks that this parties corresponds to one possible PKI (Public Key Infrastructure) model, but other models are already commonly used in the marketplace (e.g., where no independent certification authority is involved). The Guide explains that focusing on the functions performed in a PKI environment and not on any specific model also makes it easier to develop a fully media-neutral rule to the extent that similar functions are served in non-PKI electronic signature technology.

(a) *"Signatory"* means a person that holds signature creation data and acts either on its own behalf or on behalf of the person it represents (art. 2, paragraph d)

The signatory is defined simply as "a person". The Guide explains that any reference in the new Model Law to a "person" should be understood as covering all types of persons or entities, whether physical, corporate or other legal persons.

This explanation seems to solve the debated question of the nature of the person who can sign electronically. In a paper-based environment legal entities cannot strictly be signatories of documents drawn up on their behalf, because only natural persons can produce authentic hand-written signatures. Electronic signatures, however, can be conceived so as to be attributable to companies, or other legal entities (including governmental and other public authorities), and there may be situations where the identity of the person who actually generates the signature, where human action is required, is not relevant for the purposes for which the signature was created. Nevertheless, according to the Guide, under the Model Law, the notion of "signatory" cannot be severed from the person or entity that actually generated the electronic signature, since a number of specific obligations of the signatory under the Model Law are logically linked to actual control over the signature creation data. However, in order to cover situations where the signatory would be acting in representation of another person, the phrase "or on behalf of the person it represents" has been retained in the definition of "signatory". The extent to which a person would be bound by an electronic signature generated "on its behalf" is a matter to be settled in accordance with the law governing, as appropriate, the legal relationship between the signatory and the person on whose behalf the electronic signature is generated, on the one hand, and the relying party, on the other hand. That matter, as well as other matters pertaining to the underlying transaction, including issues of agency and other questions as to who bears the ultimate liability for failure by the signatory to comply with its obligations under article 8 (whether the signatory or the person represented by the signatory) are outside, according to the Guide, the scope of the Model Law.

(b) *"Certification service provider"* means a person that issues certificates and may provide other services related to electronic signatures (art. 2, paragraph e).

As a minimum, the certification service provider as defined for the purposes of the Model Law would have to provide certification services, possibly together with other services. No distinction has been drawn in the Model Law between situations where a certification service provider engages in the provision of certification services as its main activity or as an ancillary business, on a habitual or an occasional basis, directly or through a subcontractor. The definition covers all entities that provide certification services within the scope of the Model Law, i.e., "in the context of commercial activities". However, in view of that limitation in the scope of application of the Model Law, entities that issue certificates for internal purposes and not for commercial purposes would not fall under the category "certification service providers" as defined in article 2.

(c) *"Relying party"* means a person that may act on the basis of a certificate or an electronic signature (art. 2, paragraph f).

The Model Law concludes the definition of subjective elements with the notion of 'Relying party", often forgotten in other legislation. According to the Guide, the definition of "relying party" is intended to ensure symmetry in the definition of the various parties involved in the operation of electronic signature schemes under the Model Law. Observe that he is not only the person who relies on a certificate but also the person who relies simply on an electronic signature. Thus, the electronic signatures schemes ruled in the Model Law are not always based in a certificate.

4   Legal Effects of Electronic Signatures

4.1   Rule of Equivalent Function for Reliable Signatures
Art. 6, Paragraph 1 and 2)

Article 6 is one of the core provisions of the Model Law, because approaches the question of legal effects of electronic signatures. In particular, art. 6, paragraph 1 and 2, of Model Law establishes that:

"1. Where the law requires a signature of a person, that requirement is met in relation to a data message if an electronic signature is used that is as reliable as was appropriate for the purpose for which the data message was generated or communicated, in the light of all the circumstances, including any relevant agreement.

2. Paragraph 1 applies whether the requirement referred to therein is in the form of an obligation or whether the law simply provides consequences for the absence of a signature"

The purpose of that provision is to ensure that, where any legal consequence would have flowed from the use of a hand-written signature, the same consequence should flow from the use of a reliable electronic signature. In the preparation of the Model

Law, the view was expressed that (either through a reference to the notion of "enhanced electronic signature" or through a direct mention of criteria for establishing the technical reliability of a given signature technique) a dual purpose of article 6 should be to establish: (1) that legal effects would result from the application of those electronic signature techniques that were recognised as reliable; and (2), conversely, that no such legal effects would flow from the use of techniques of a lesser reliability. It's thus the rule of equivalent function between hand-written signatures and reliable electronic signatures.

4.2   Requirements for a Reliable Signature (Art. 6, Paragraph 3)

However, the problem is the determination of what constitutes a reliable method of signature in the light of the circumstances. This determination can be made *ex post* by a court, possibly long after the electronic signature has been used. In contrast, the Model Law creates a benefit in favour of certain techniques, which are recognised as particularly reliable. That is the purpose of paragraph (3) of art. 6 ("An electronic signature is considered to be reliable for the purpose of satisfying the requirement referred to in paragraph 1 if: …", which is expected to create certainty, at or before the time any such technique of electronic signature is used (*ex ante*), that using a recognised technique will result in legal effects equivalent to those of a hand-written signature. Thus, paragraph (3) is an essential provision if the Model Law is to meet its goal of providing certainty as to the legal effect to be expected from the use of particularly reliable types of electronic signatures. Subparagraphs (a) to (d) of paragraph (3) are intended to express objective criteria of technical reliability of electronic signatures:

a) "The signature creation data are, within the context in which they are used, linked to the signatory and to no other person" (paragraph 3, subparagraph a). Subparagraph (a) focuses on the objective characteristics of the signature creation data, which must be "linked to the signatory and to no other person". According to the Guide, from a technical point of view, the signature creation data could be uniquely "linked" to the signatory, without being "unique" in itself. The linkage between the data used for creation of the signature and the signatory is the essential element. While certain electronic signature creation data may be shared by a variety of users, for example where several employees would share the use of a corporate signature-creation data, that data must be capable of identifying one user unambiguously in the context of each electronic signature.

b) "The signature creation data were, at the time of signing, under the control of the signatory and of no other person" (paragraph 3, subparagraph a). Subparagraph (b) deals with the circumstances in which the signature creation data is used. At the time it is used, the signature creation data must be under the sole control of the signatory. In relation to the notion of sole control by the signatory, a question is whether the signatory would retain its ability to authorise another person to use the signature data on its behalf. Such a situation might arise where the signature data is used in the corporate context where the corporate entity would be the signatory but would require a number of persons to be able to sign on its behalf. When the signatory loose the sole control of signature data (e.g., in case of robbery), and these data can be used a third non authorised party, it's necessary to revoke the link of those data to the signatory (in case of digital signatures, the certificate must be revoked) and eventually important questions of liability should be solved. The first question (revocation) is approached later by Model Law in art. 8; however, there are no rules in order to allocations risks and liabilities in this situations.

c) and d) "Any alteration to the electronic signature, made after the time of signing, is detectable" (paragraph 3, subparagraph c); and "Where a purpose of the legal requirement for a signature is to provide assurance as to the integrity of the information to which it relates, any alteration made to that information after the time of signing is detectable" (paragraph 3, subparagraph d). Subparagraphs (c) and (d) deal with the issues of integrity of the electronic signature and integrity of the information being signed electronically. It would have been possible to combine the two provisions to emphasise that, where a signature is attached to a document, the integrity of the document and the integrity of the signature are so closely related that it is difficult to conceive of one without the other. Where a signature is used to sign a document, the idea of the integrity of the document is inherent in the use of the signature. However, it was decided that the Model Law should follow the distinction drawn in the UNCITRAL Model Law on Electronic Commerce between articles 7 and 8. Although some technologies provide both authentication (article 7 of the UNCITRAL Model Law on Electronic Commerce) and integrity (article 8 of the UNCITRAL Model Law on Electronic Commerce), those concepts can be seen as distinct legal concepts and treated as such. Since a hand-written signature provides neither a guarantee of the integrity of the document to which it is attached nor a guarantee that any change made to the document would be detectable, the functional equivalence approach requires that those concepts should not be dealt with in a single provision.

4.3   Predetermination of Status of Electronic Signature: Satisfaction of Requirements of Art. 6 (Art. 7)

Article 7 ("Satisfaction of article 6") establishes in paragraph 1 that: "[Any person, organ or authority, whether public or private, specified by the enacting State as competent] may determine which electronic signatures satisfy the provisions of article 6 of this Law".

Article 7 describes the role played by the enacting State in establishing or recognising any entity that might validate the use of electronic signatures or otherwise certify their quality. The purpose of article 7 is to make it clear that an enacting State may designate an organ or authority that will have the power to make determinations as to what specific technologies may benefit from the presumptions or substantive rule established under article 6. Like article 6, article 7 is based on the positive idea that what is required to facilitate the development of electronic commerce is certainty and predictability at the time when commercial parties make use of electronic signature techniques, not at the time when there is a dispute before a court.

5 Basic Rules of Conduct for the Parties Involved

Article 8 (and articles 9 and 11) had been initially planned to contain rules regarding the obligations and liabilities of the various parties involved (the signatory, the relying party and any certification services provider). However, it was difficult to achieve consensus as to the contents of such rules. So, those issues are left to applicable law outside the Model Law. So, the Model Law does not deal in any detail with the issues of liability that may affect the various parties involved in the operation of electronic signature systems. On the contrary, other legislations, such as the European Directive, rule liability of certification service providers but do not regulate in a particular and systematic way the rights and obligations of the parties participating in the certification system. Any way, as we shall see, although there's not specific regulation of liability in UNCITRAL Model law, some of the rules on the conduct of parties contribute to clarify the question of liability.

5.1 Conduct of the Signatory

Article 8 rules the conduct of the signatory establishing in paragraph 1 that "Where signature creation data can be used to create a signature that has legal effect, each signatory shall…:"

"(a) Exercise reasonable care to avoid unauthorised use of its signature relation data". The obligation in paragraph (1) (a), in particular, to exercise reasonable care to prevent unauthorised use of a signature data, constitutes a basic obligation that is, for example, generally contained in certificate practice statements and legislation on electronic signatures. This obligation can be one the criteria to solve the question of allocation of risks in case of compromise of the signature creation data, a question not approached by the Model Law.

"(b) Without undue delay, utilize means made available by the certification service provider pursuant to article 9 of this Law, or otherwise use reasonable efforts, to notify any person that may reasonably be expected by the signatory to rely on or to provide services in support of the electronic signature if: (i) The signatory knows that the signature creation data have been compromised; or (ii) The circumstances known to the signatory give rise to a substantial risk that the signature creation data may have been compromised".

Paragraph (1) (b) establishes the obligation of notification to relying parties in case of compromise of the signature creation data. But there is not a clear regulation of liability of the different parties in this case. This paragraph refers to the notion of "person who may reasonably be expected by the signatory to rely on or to provide services in support of the electronic signature". Depending on the technology being used, such a "relying party" may be not only a person who might seek to rely on the signature, but also a person such as a certification service provider, a certificate revocation service provider and any other interested party.

"(c) Where a certificate is used to support the electronic signature, exercise reasonable care to ensure the accuracy and completeness of all material representations made by the signatory that are relevant to the certificate throughout its life cycle or that are to be included in the certificate." Paragraph (1) (c) applies where a certificate is used to support the signature data. The "life-cycle of the certificate" is intended to be interpreted broadly as covering the period starting with the application for the certificate or the creation of the certificate and ending with the expiry or revocation of the certificate.

After establishing the obligations of the signatory in paragraph 1, paragraph 2 approaches the question of the consequences in case of non-fulfilment of those requirements:

"2. A signatory shall bear the legal consequences of its failure to satisfy the requirements of paragraph 1."

Observe that paragraph (2) does not specify either the consequences or the limits of liability, both of which are left to national law of every state. However, even though it leaves the consequences of liability up to national law, paragraph (2) serves to give a clear signal to enacting States that liability should attach to a failure to satisfy the obligations set forth in paragraph (1). Paragraph (2) is based on the conclusion reached by the Working Group at its thirty-fifth session that it might be difficult to achieve consensus as to what consequences might flow from the liability of the signature data holder. Depending on the context in which the electronic signature is used, such consequences might range, under existing law, from the signature data holder being bound by the contents of the message to liability for damages.

5.2   Conduct of the Certification Service Provider

Independent of whether a licensing system were or were not established with or without its own set of exigencies, every provider of certification services would have to comply, in order to be considered a trusted third party, with a certain series of fundamental requisites in order to generate trust and security in its organisation and activities both before and after the issuing of a certificate. These requisites as they appear in Art. 9 ("Conduct of the certification service provider") paragraph 1 of the Model Law ("1. Where a certification service provider provides services to support an electronic signature that may be used for legal effect as a signature, that certification service provider shall: ...") are basically classified as follows:

"(a) Act in accordance with representations made by it with respect to its policies and practices". Subparagraph (a) expresses the basic rule that a certification service provider should adhere to the representations and commitments made by that supplier, for example in a certification practices statement or in any other type of policy statement.

"(b) Exercise reasonable care to ensure the accuracy and completeness of all material representations made by it that are relevant to the certificate throughout its life cycle or that are included in the certificate". Subparagraph (b) replicates in the context of the activities of the certification service provider the standard of conduct set forth in article 8(1)(c) with respect to the signatory.

"(c) Provide reasonably accessible means that enable a relying party to ascertain from the certificate: (i) The identity of the certification service provider; (ii) That the signatory that is identified in the certificate had control of the signature creation data at the time when the certificate was issued; (iii) That signature creation data were valid at or before the time when the certificate was issued." Subparagraph (c) defines the essential contents and the core effect of any certificate under the Model Law.

"(d) Provide reasonably accessible means that enable a relying party to ascertain, where relevant, from the certificate or otherwise:…"

"(i) The method used to identify the signatory". We consider this provision positive because in order to inspire confidence a certificate would have to establish or incorporate, amongst other things, the degree of investigation developed by the authority to confirm the identity of the signatory. It also may be useful to homologate the certificates; that is to say, establish classes or categories of certificates generally accepted by the certifying entities and widely known throughout the community of users, in which would be fixed definite types of certificate issued by each authority, permitting the relying party an approximate idea of the value of each certificate.

"(ii) Any limitation on the purpose or value for which the signature creation data or the certificate may be used". The liability of certification authority without a specific legislation, under the general regulations for liability, is potentially high and unforeseeable, given the indefinite number of operations covered by a same certificate. Because of this, and in order to stimulate the development of certification authorities which could be halted in cases of unforeseeable or unlimited risk, different legislation and legislative initiatives do expressly admit or favourably contemplate the existence of possible limitations to the liability of the providers of certification services (it must be pointed out that the existence of limitations to liability of the signatories can be equally as necessary). In the same fashion the Model Law, establishes distinct limits to liability which benefit the providers of certification services.

"(iii) That the signature creation data are valid and have not been compromised"

"(iv) Any limitation on the scope or extent of liability stipulated by the certification service provider"

"(v) Whether means exist for the signatory to give notice pursuant to article 8, paragraph 1 (b), of this Law" (whether means exist for the signatory to give notice that a signature device has been compromised)

"(vi) Whether a timely revocation service is offered".

"(e) Where services under subparagraph (d) (v) are offered, provide a means for a signatory to give notice pursuant to article 8, paragraph 1 (b), of this Law and, where services under subparagraph (d) (vi) are offered, ensure the availability of a timely revocation service". Subparagraph (e) is not intended to apply to certificates such as transactional certificates, which are one-time certificates, or low-cost certificates for low-risk applications, both of which might not be subject to revocation.

"(f) Utilize trustworthy systems, procedures and human resources in performing its services". For the assessment of the trustworthiness of the systems, procedures and human resources utilized by the certification service provider, the Model Law provides an open-ended list of indicative factors in art. 10. That list is intended to provide a flexible notion of trustworthiness, which could vary in content depending upon what is expected of the certificate in the context in which it is created.

After establishing obligations for certifications provider in paragraph 1, paragraph 2 or art. 9 approach but do no solve the question of the legal consequences of the non-fulfilment: "A certification service provider shall bear the legal consequences of its failure to satisfy the requirements of paragraph 1. Paragraph (2) mirrors the basic rule of liability set forth in article 8(2) with respect to the signatory. The effect of that provision is to leave it up to national law to determine the consequences of liability."

5.3   Conduct of the Relying Party (Art. 11)

Article 11 ("Conduct of the relying party") establishes that:
"A relying party shall bear the legal consequences of its failure:
(a) To take reasonable steps to verify the reliability of an electronic signature; or
(b) Where an electronic signature is supported by a certificate, to take reasonable steps:
(i) To verify the validity, suspension or revocation of the certificate; and
(ii) To observe any limitation with respect to the certificate."
Article 11 reflects the idea that a party who intends to rely on an electronic signature should bear in mind the question whether and to what extent such reliance is reasonable in the light of the circumstances. While article 11 might place a burden on relying parties, particularly where such parties are consumers, it may be recalled that the Model Law is not intended to overrule any rule governing the protection of consumers. However, the Model Law might play a useful role in educating all the parties involved, including relying parties, as to the standard of reasonable conduct to be met with respect to electronic signatures. In addition, establishing a standard of conduct under which the relying party should verify the reliability of the signature through readily accessible means may be seen as essential to the development of any public-key infrastructure system.

As to the possible impact of establishing as a general obligation that the relying party should verify the validity of the electronic signature or certificate, a question arises where the relying party fails to comply with the requirements of article 11. Should it fail to comply with those requirements, the relying party should not be precluded from availing itself of the signature or certificate if reasonable verification would not have revealed that the signature or certificate was invalid. Such a situation may need to be dealt with by the law applicable outside the Model Law.

6   Conclusions

In conclusion, the following observations may be made about the UNCITRAL Model Law of electronic signatures, that in general is positive but presents yet important oversights:

1. In the first place, the Model Law is positive because offers to those countries where legislative authorities are in the process of preparing legislation on electronic signature the guidance of an international instrument. The risk that diverging

legislative approaches be taken in various countries with respect to electronic signatures calls for uniform legislative provisions to establish the basic rules of what is inherently an international phenomenon, where legal (as well as technical) interoperability is essential.

2. In the second place, it was considered that, although digital signatures play a predominant role in the emerging electronic-commerce practice, the uniform rules should be adopt the media-neutral approach. Given the rapidity of technological development, this neutrality surely allows the doors to be left open for future technologies; however, on the other hand, carried to this extreme, it leaves without resolution many of the questions posed now by the digital signature, which is the only secure form of electronic signature available today. We do understand that it doubtless would have been better to adopt a technically open position, in order to not discourage the means for other secure technologies in the future to come forward, but, at the same time, focusing on the regulation of the digital signature, given the predominance of the function performed by the public key cryptography in the recent practices of electronic commerce.

3. There doesn't exist a complete vision of the certificate and its life cycle, with those distinct stages through which the certificate may pass (issue, distribution, use, revocation and/or suspension and expiry). And with regard to a question as important as the revocation of a certificate, the Model Law does not consider propoerly the distribution and assignation of liability among the different parties (certifying entity, subscriber and third user) during the period of the revocation (from, for example, the date of compromise of the private key to the effective publication of the revocation of that key); in that sense, the content of Model Law is partial and incomplete. In consequence, there are yet unresolved questions, not approached (or only partially) by the legislator. For example, what would happen if, as the consequence of the loss of a private key, that key were used for an illegitimate purpose by another party? What would happen if the applicant of the certificate had requested a revocation but the certifying entity hadn't in fact cancelled the certificate out of negligence, or if it were still checking the request? What would happen if the decision to revoke a certificate had been taken but wasn't yet known to the third relying party by reason of the time taken for publication of the information by the system (for example, periodically updated revocation lists)? And what would happen if the provider of the certification service revoked a certificate accidentally? All these questions should be solved by the national law of the enacting states and, if not, certification practice statements will be the essential rule..

4. There does not exist a complete vision of the persons implicated in the certification system (basically, the certification service provider, the subscriber and the user of the certificate). It's true that the personal elements are defined in the Model Law (even there is definition of the third party who puts their trust in the certificate. However, there do not exist detailed regulations about, e.g., the first of these personal elements, the providers. There are no provisions on matters so important as whether the certification authorities certifying the validity of cryptographic key pairs should be public entities or whether private entities might act as certification authorities; or whether the process of allowing a given entity to act as a certification authority should

take the form of an express authorization, or "licensing", by the State, or whether other methods should be used to control the quality of certification authorities if they were allowed to operate in the absence of a specific authorization. The Model Law does not deal with those issues which should be approached in respective national laws..

5. The Model Law does not approach the delicate theme of liability. This is an essential but a non-resolved question in these initial stages of commercial and legal development of certification entities. And this uncertainties could seriously affect its progress. Hence the need to establish and delineate very clearly the rules and conditions of liability derived from the issuing and use of certificates, taking into account the interests of all parties contracted in the electronic transaction (not only the certifier but also, e.g., a consumer subscriber or user of a certificate).

References

1. ABA (American Bar Association), *Digital signature guidelines, Legal infrastructure for Certification Authorities and secure electronic commerce*, August 1, 1996, USA.
2. COMMISSION OF THE EUROPEAN COMMUNITIES, *Directive of the European Parliament, and the Council for a common framework on electronic signature (13 december 1999)*.
3. MARTINEZ NADAL, A., *Comercio electrónico, firma digital y autoridades de certificación*, Madrid, 2001.
4. UNCITRAL (Commission of the United Nations for the International commercial Law), *Model Law on Electronic commerce*, 1997.
5. UNCITRAL (Commission of the United Nations for the International commercial Law), *Model Law on electronic signatures*, 2001.
6. UNCITRAL (Commission of the United Nations for the International commercial Law), *Guide to Enactment of the Uncitral Model Law on electronic signatures, 2001*.

An Anonymous Loan System Based on Group Signature Scheme

Rie Shigetomi[1], Akira Otsuka[2], Takahide Ogawa[3], and Hideki Imai[2]

[1] Graduate School of Mathematics and Computer Science,
Tsuda College,
2-1-1, Tsuda-machi, Kodaira-shi, Tokyo 187-8577 JAPAN
sigetomi@ma.tsuda.ac.jp
[2] Institute of Industrial Science, University of Tokyo,
4-6-1, Komaba, Meguro-ku, Tokyo 153-8505 JAPAN
otsuka@imailab.iis.u-tokyo.ac.jp
imai@iis.u-tokyo.ac.jp
[3] Tsuda College
ogawa@tsuda.ac.jp

Abstract. Recently, paper based transactions are being replaced by digitized transactions in a rapid pace. These kinds of digitized data are useful compared to paper based data in the sense of the flexibility of the data. Loan services, (for example, Library, Rental video, debt etc.,) are among the services that makes use of sophisticated digitized transactions. Loan services handle a lot of personal information, which enables the analysis of personal hobby and tastes, or even life style. Hence, administrators who control the loan information are able to obtain personal information of customers, which leads to a large privacy problem. We have examined a way to avoid this privacy problem. One solution is to use "An Anonymous Loan" that the user can be anonymous while borrowing and returning, but the anonymity is unveiled only after the due date without return. We will suggest An Anonymous Loan System using tamper resistance device and Group Signature Scheme.

Keywords. Group Signature, Privacy Protection, Optimistic Protocol, Timed-release Encryption, Anonymity Revocation

1   Introduction

Companies collect and accumulate the record of a service they have provided; that is, when, to whom, and how the service was provided. These records are the accumulation of consumers' tastes, and could be used to analyze their hobby or life style. This means, these records could be used to keep the consumers under observation.

This could lead to a large privacy problem, and there should be careful consideration on these situations. This is so with paper based transaction, and is

A.H. Chan and V. Gligor (Eds.): ISC 2002, LNCS 2433, pp. 244–256, 2002.
© Springer-Verlag Berlin Heidelberg 2002

a serious privacy problem with digitized transactions, where the data handling could be done more flexibly [7][9].

In "Loan Service", – Library, Rental video, Rental car, debt, etc.–, is one of the most vulnerable service to this privacy problem, as records of each transaction is kept by the company or organization that provides the service. Loan service is also one of the most sophisticated service offered digitally. Suppose examples of records of loan service: which book a person borrow from library, which movie DVD a person rent from rental video shop, how much money a person borrowed from a bank, etc.. We can easily see that organization controlling these records could use it to analyze personal hobbies, tastes, or even living standards of the consumer. Therefore, there should be careful consideration on privacy problem.

To avoid this problem, each user (that is, the customer) must be able to control the accumulation of records of loan service. In other words, she (or he) must be able to force the loan organization not to keep that records of her service. This could be done only if she is provided loan service anonymously. Otherwise, the loan organization can control her record if she gives her name to the organization. However, there lies a fundamental difficulty in realizing anonymity in loan service.

That is because there are cases where a user might not do a returning service until the due date: the returning service is to return books, or to pay back money or etc.. If the organization provides loan service under allowing the user to remain anonymous, nobody, including the loan organization, can identify his name. This allows the user to act irresponsible, and make it impossible for the organization to take control their items and provide services.

Therefore, there is a requirement for "An Anonymous Loan" that loans anonymously, but identifies the user's name on unreturning cases. These requirements could be written in the following way:

1. at the beginning of protocol, each user should be anonymous,
2. if a special event happens (user does the returning service), she is guaranteed anonymity forever, and
3. after a certain date (due date) has passed and there is no event, her secret (her name) is unveiled.

This problem is not able to be solved using general Anonymity Revocation Scheme. Anonymity Revocation Scheme promises to keep the anonymity for the user, unless when an event happens – when an adversary acts maliciously [1][5][8].

In our problem, however, anonymity should not be unveiled when an event happens, but anonymity should be unveiled when no event happens until the due date. This event is the returning service by user. The requirements for our system is as follows: the anonymity of user is unveiled when, and only when the due date has passed, and the user has not done the returning service.

This could be neither done with Timed-Release Encryption [10][12]. In Timed-Release Encryption, a message is unveiled at a certain point in the future, and this message cannot be canceled. That means that with Timed-Release Encryption, anonymity of the user on returning cases cannot be guaranteed.

Therefore we suggest "An Anonymous Loan System" which uses a tamper resistant device. The tamper resistant device keeps the a key to users' identification. and deletes the key when user does the returning service. The tamper resistant device notifies whatever it keeps on a specified time (that is, the due date). If the user has done the returning service by the specified time, her anonymity is kept. If he has not, the loan organization is able to track down her identification using the key.

We have realized such system by adopting "Group Signature Scheme" to anonymity revocation [3][6]. On the unreturning case, only the data related to the current case must be unveiled. Also, unlinkability – the property where each transaction is independent to each other – is satisfied.

In this paper, we will suggest new problem, "An Anonymous Loan", and construct "An Anonymous Loan System" using Group Signature Scheme and tamper resistant device.

This paper is organized as follows: we will show related work in section 2, the preliminaries in section 3, the definition of "An Anonymous Loan System" in section 4, a construction in section 5, proof of the construction satisfied "An Anonymous Loan System" in section 6 and conclusion respectively.

2 Related Work

This work has some ideas in common with Anonymity Revocation and Timed-Release Encryption.

Optimistic Approach is one way of realizing Anonymity Revocation. Optimistic approach was originally introduced by Asokan et al. [1][2] and was extended by Camenisch et al. [4][5]. This protocol is used in the unreturning case, where the due date has passed and the user's name must be unveiled.

There are work on encryption scheme concerning on "Time", and Timed-release encryption is one of them.

Timed-Release Encryption Problem was first discussed by May [11]and was extended by Rivest et al.[12] and Crescenzo et al. [10]. Rivest suggested that the idea has three schemes: Time-Lock Puzzle, Online Time-Server and Off-line Time-Server.

The first one, Time-Lock Puzzle, uses computational complexity; that is the difficulty to solve the encryption. The idea is that the time to recover a secret is given by the minimum computational effort needed by any machine, serial or parallel, to perform some computation which enables one to recover the secret. However this idea depends on CPU-machine of receiver. As the CPU-machine of the receiver increases, the sender must choose a longer key, thus taking a longer time to encrypt the secret. The receiver must also consume an amount of CPU-machine to decrypt any message.

The second one, Online Time-server, uses a trusted third party (TTP) to release message at the appointed time. The idea is to use TTP to store the message M until its desired release time t. However in this model, TTP has to store M, which is inefficient. The same thing could be accomplished with less cost by the next model: TTP encrypts the document and hands the encrypted document to the receiver, but publishes the secret key only at time t. The cost is reduced since, as all TTP has to keep is only the secret key. In addition, distributed TTP using secret sharing is also suggested in order to reduce the trust on a single TTP, but to keep the story simple we will only use TTP. The distributed TTP scheme is easily applied upon our simple construction. Crescenzo et al. [10] has suggested a more efficient model.

The third one, off-line Time-Server, also uses a trusted third party(TTP) but the time-server is on a tamper-device, so it is difficult to control the exact time.

3   Preliminaries

Next, we will define two encryptions, Group Signature Scheme and Timed-Release Encryption.

3.1   Group Signature Scheme

Group Signature scheme was introduced by Chaum et al. in 1991 [8] and has been extended by multiple approaches [3][4] [5][6]. The group signature scheme allows a group member to sign messages anonymously on behalf of the group. However, in exceptional cases such as legal disputes, any group signature can be "Opened" by a designated entity.

The participants are group members, a membership manager, and a revocation manager [6]. The membership manager is responsible for the system setup and adding group members while the revocation manager has the ability to revoke the anonymity of signatures.

The Model. A group signature scheme consists of the following procedures:

- GS_setup: An interactive setup protocol between the membership manager, the group members, and the revocation manager. The public output is the group's public key Y. The private outputs are the individual secret keys x_G for each group member, the secret key x_M for the membership manager, and the secret key x_R for the revocation manager.
- GS_sign: A signature generation algorithm that on an input of a message m, an individual group member's secret key x_G, and the group's public key Y, outputs a signature σ.
- GS_verify: A verification algorithm that on input a message m, a signature σ , and the group's public key Y, returns 1 if and only if σ was generated by any group member using sign on input $sign$ on input x_G, m, and Y.
- $GS\_tracing$: A tracing algorithm that on input of a signature σ, a message m, , the revocation manager's secret key x_R, and the group's public key Y returns the identity ID of the group member who issued the signature σ together with an argument arg of this fact.

- *GS_vertracing*: A tracing-verification algorithm that on input of a signature σ, a message m, the group's public key Y, the identity ID of a group member, and an argument arg outputs 1 if and only if arg was generated by *tracing* with respect to m, σ, Y, x_R.

The following informally stated security requirements must be held:

- GS Anonymity of signatures: It is not feasible to find out the group member who signed a message without knowing the revocation manager's secret key.
- GS Unlinkability of signatures: It is infeasible to decide whether two signatures have been issued by the same group member or not.
- GS Traceability of signatures: The revocation manager can reveal the identity of the signer later.

In our protocol, the Time Keeping Device act as the revocation manager, while the organization act as the group manager.

3.2   Timed-Release Encryption

We have already introduced Timed-Release Encryption in section 2. We will show the second solution of Rivest et al. [12] which was extended Crescenzo [10].

The setting is as follows. There are three participants: the sender, the receiver and the server. First, the sender transmits to the receiver an encrypted messages and a release-time. Then, the receiver is allowed into a conversation with a server. The server and the receiver engage in a conditional oblivious transfer such that if the release-time is not less than the current time defined by the server, the receiver gets the message. Otherwise, the receiver gets nothing. Furthermore, the server does not lean any information about the release-time or the identity of the sender. In particular, the server does not lean whether the release-time is less than, equal to, or greater than the current time.

The sender can get *pkey* from the server for encryption his or her messages. At the release-time, the receiver can get *skey* from the server if he or she wants to. Hence, the server gives the pair, *pkey* and *skey*, which first is the public key and the other is the secret key that opens at release-time.

The Model. Timed-Release Encryption consists of the following algorithms:

- TS_p: A encryption algorithm that takes the time server's public key *pkey* and the sender's message m as the input. The output is the encrypted message.
- TS_s: A decryption algorithm that takes the time server's secret key *skey* as the input. The outputs is the decrypted message, that means, the sender's message m.

The following informally stated security requirements must be held:

- TS security: It is not feasible to find out the sender's message m before release time without the time server.

4 An Anonymous Loan System

In this section, we will define "An Anonymous Loan System".

4.1 Notation

An Anonymous Loan System is for specific kinds of services.

Services with time limit. *A loan system* is for services with time limit, defined as follows: We have two types of players, a user P and an organization V, and there is a pair of services, a main service and a returning service. The organization V offers the main service to the user P at first, with a promise that the user P would do the returning service to the organization V on a specific time K in the future.

A *financial loan service* is a typical service of this kind. An authorized user is permitted to transact an item with the organization (*Loan Party*) under the time limit K, where K is, in other words, called the due date.

Description of States. Service with time limit takes several states as in figure [1]. Let S be a set of states of P. S has five states:

- s_0 : Non-Member
  P is not a member of V.
- s_1 : Member
  P has applied for the membership of V for *service with time limit K* from V.
- s_2 : Switch on
  V provided P *main service*.
- s_3 : Switch off
  P did *returning service* to V before K.
- s_4 : Explosion
  User P did not do *returning service* to V before K.

The Model. We consider interactions among sets of users and transactions.

1. *User*
   We have a set of n users $U = \{u_1, u_2, \ldots u_n\}$ all assumed to be polynomial-time turing machines. Each user has an ID denoted by $UserID$. UserID may be published by multiple organizations, (i.e. users may choose where they have their ID published) thus UserID is unique for each pair of user and organization.

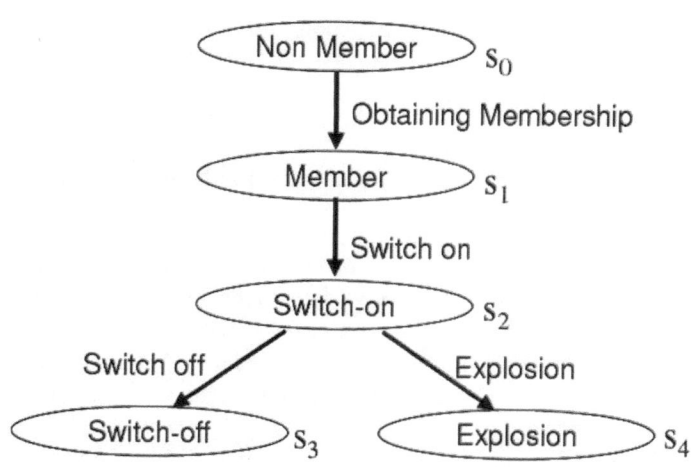

Fig. 1. Description of States

2. *Transaction*

We have a set of transactions $T = \{t_1, t_2, \ldots\}$. When some item is transacted between an organization and a user, there is a transaction. Each transaction has an unique ID denoted by *TransactionID*. Each transaction is supposed to carry all the information necessary to run the loan business such as *UserID*, loaned item information, the due date and etc. Transactions are managed by each organization and published by them.

Each transaction is in one of the states defined above. Let T be a set of transactions and S be a set of states. We consider a mapping $f_S : T \mapsto S$ which relates each transaction to a state.

With this mapping f_S, we can divide a set of transactions T into four subsets T_1, T_2, T_3 and T_4 such that

$T_1 = \{t |\ t \in T, f_S(t) = s_1\}$,
$T_2 = \{t |\ t \in T, f_S(t) = s_2\}$,
$T_3 = \{t |\ t \in T, f_S(t) = s_3\}$ and
$T_4 = \{t |\ t \in T, f_S(t) = s_4\}$.

4.2   Definition

We will define two requirements for An Anonymous Loan System.

Definition 1. *Honest-user Anonymity*

1. *Untraceability : Given $t \in T_2 \cup T_3$, and $U = \{u_1, u_2, \ldots u_n\}$, it is computationally infeasible for an probabilistic polynomial-time adversary to find $u_k \in U$ ($k \in \{1, \ldots, n\}$)who engaged in t.*

2. *Unlinkability:* Given $t_i, t_j \in T_2 \cup T_3$ $(i, j \in \{1, \ldots, n\})$, and $U = \{u_1, u_2, \ldots u_n\}$, *it is computationally infeasible for an probabilistic polynomial-time adversary to decide whether there exists same user u_k who engaged in t_i, t_j.*

A system is said to satisfy the **honest-user anonymity** if it satisfies untraceability and unlinkability simultaneously.

Definition 2. *Over-duedate Traceability*

Given $t \in T_4$ and $U = \{u_1, u_2, \ldots u_n\}$, if the user u_k who engaged in t is efficiently unveiled, then it is said that a system satisfies **over-duedate traceability**.

Problem Setting. If a loan system satisfies honest-user anonymity and over-duedate traceability, then the system is called "An Anonymous Loan System".

5 Construction

In this section, we will define the construction for "An Anonymous Loan System" using Group Signature Scheme.

5.1 Definition of Players

Our scheme is four-party protocol, User P, Organization V, Time Server TS and Time Keeping Device IC. We give a definition for each of the three players and relations using figure [2].

User P. User P is a person receiving *service with time limit*. P should receive the permission to be provided *service with time limit* from the Organization.

Organization V. The Organization V provides *service with time limit* to the permitted members. V holds a Time Keeping Device published by the Trusted Time Server. V also serves as the group manager of the Group Signature Scheme.

Time Server TS. On a time K, Time Server TS announces a secret key *skey*. The public key *pkey*(corresponding to *skey*) is announced before K. *skey* and *pkey* is on Timed-Release Encryption.

Time Keeping Device IC. The Time Keeping Device IC is a tamper resistant device like IC card. IC acts as an revocation manager of the group signature scheme, thus it has a revocation key, x_R.

When the information and *pkey* are inputted, IC saves those informations. IC is allowed to do the following three operations:

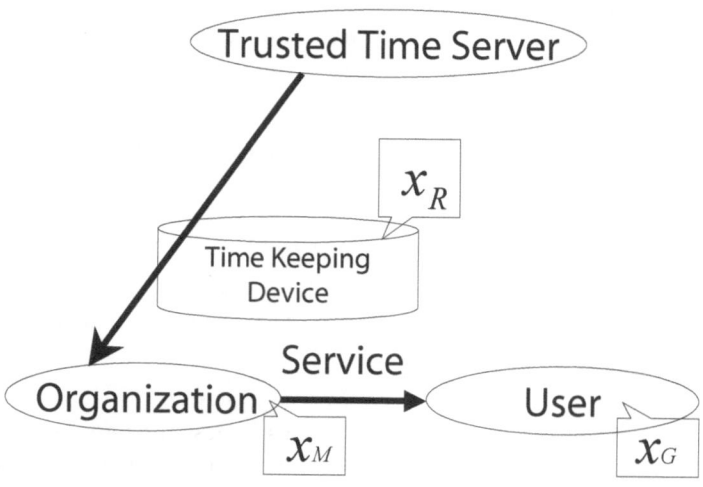

Fig. 2. Construction

1. When information and *pkey* are inputted, IC is allowed to save the information encrypted using TS_p.
2. It is allowed to delete the information saved at (a).
3. It is allowed to output the information stored in (a) when a valid skey is inputted.

Assumption 1. We assume that the Time Server TS, including the Time Keeping Device IC, is honest.

5.2   Proposed Protocol

Since we have already proved description of states in section 4.1, we will propose protocol using Group Signature Scheme. This section will propose protocol described in section 4.1.

Obtaining Membership. P must first apply for *the service with time limit* from V.

First, P asks for a membership to V. V then decides whether to grant membership to P. If V decides to reject, P cannot obtain membership. On the other hand, if V decides to grant membership to P, V issues UserID $u \in U$.

Then, GS_setup is conducted by players P, V and IC. Consequently, P gets x_G, V gets x_M, and IC gets x_R respectively.

When all of this succeeds, P obtains membership of V.

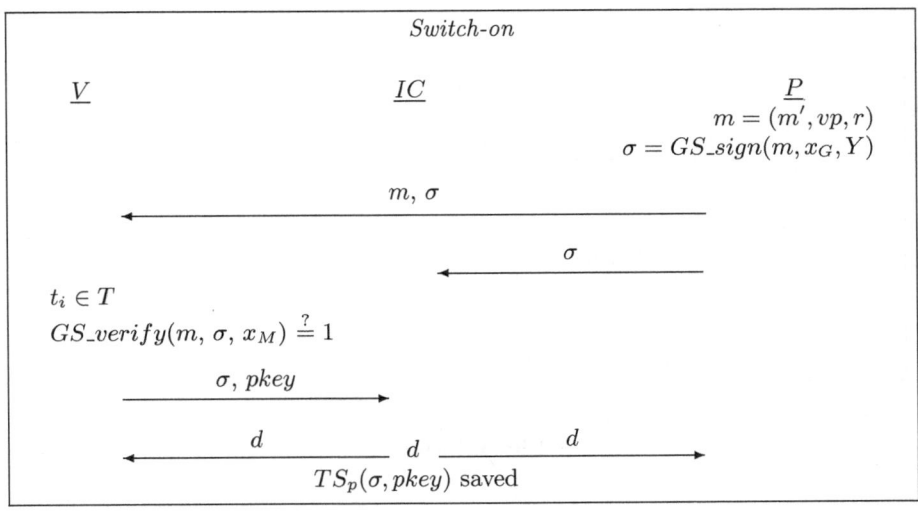

Fig. 3. Switch-on

Switch-on. Next, we will discuss about P using *main service* provided by V with figure[3]. This is done in the next three procedure: P ask for the service; V checks for P's right; V provides the service if authorized.

First, P creates message m, which includes the data m' of which *main service* P wants to receive, V's public key vp and a random number r, so $m = (m', vp, r)$.

P signs m using the group signature scheme:

$$\sigma = GS\_sign(m, x_G, Y).$$

After that, P sends (m, σ) to V and IC.

V checks the validity of σ by

$$GS\_verify(m, \sigma, x_M) \overset{?}{=} 1.$$

If the above equation holds, V decides a due date K and generates a TransactionID $t_i \in T$, which is a unique number for each transaction, and sends (m, σ) and $pkey$ to IC.

If IC receives the same signature σ from P and V, IC saves $TS_p(\sigma, pkey)$ and outputs d to V and P.

Switch-off. Thirdly, this is the case where P does *returning service* before K, for *main service* provided by V. [4].

Thus, V must delete the data in IC. This is done by sending σ and $Sign_V(\sigma)$ which is signed by V to IC. Then, IC checks the input data is correct, and searches the saved data related to σ and deletes $TS_p(\sigma, pkey)$. Hence, the information about the user who received the service is deleted. IC creates a message z, representing the deletion has finished successfully, and sign z. Then IC sends z and the signed z, $Sign_{IC}(z)$ to P and V.

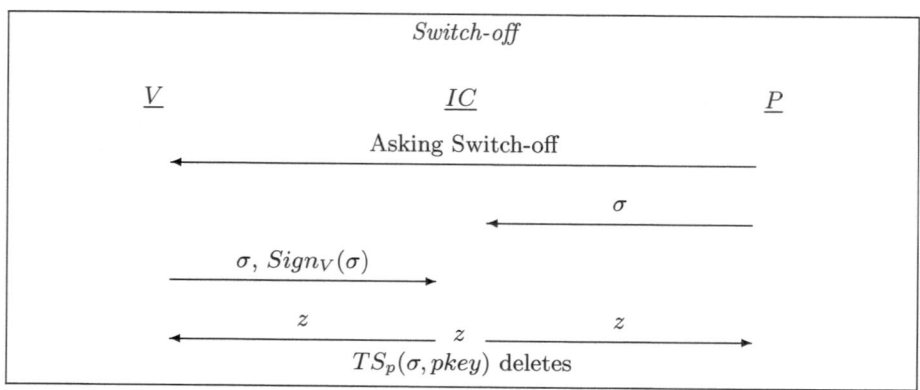

Fig. 4. Switch-off

Explosion. In the case where P does not proceed *returning service* in the due date, IC unveils the UserID as in figure[5]. V sends *pkey, skey m* and σ to IC. This could be done only after K, as *skey* is known to V only after TS opens *skey*.

After IC checks the inputs, that is *pkey* and *skey*, IC searches the saved data related to *pkey* and *skey*, and computes σ.

$$TS_s(TS_p(\sigma), skey) = \sigma$$

Then, IC computes User ID.

$$GS\_trace(m, \sigma,\ x_R) = (u\ , arg).$$

IC sends the User ID u to V, hence, V knows the User ID and calculates

$$GS\_vertracing(\sigma, m, Y, u, arg) \overset{?}{=} 1$$

for checking.

6   Theorem and Proof

In this section, we will suppose construction in section 5 satisfies problem setting in section 4.5.

6.1   Theorem 1

We defined the following problem setting in 4.5:

- Honest-user Anonymity
- Over-duedate Traceability.

Construction in 5 confirms these problem setting.

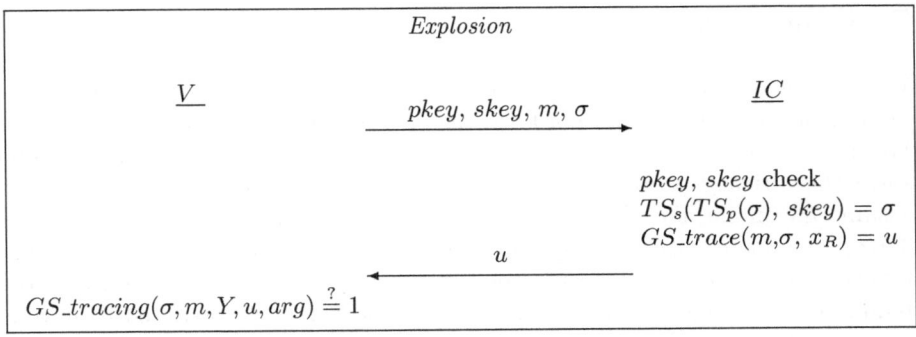

Fig. 5. Explosion

6.2   Proof

Honest-user Anonymity. In this case, we have to discuss about the situations in the proposed protocol: **Switch-on** and **Switch-off**.

Switch-on

1. Untraceability:
   IC only contains the User ID encrypted by the Timed-Release Encryption. Therefore, Malicious V cannot trace the identity of the honest user because of TRE Security and tamper resistance device. In addition, V cannot trace the User ID from σ because of GS Anonymity of the Group Signature Scheme.
2. Unlinkability:
   This case concludes GS Unlinkability of the Group Signature Scheme.

Switch-off

1. Untraceability:
   From Assumption 1, all the transcripts in IC correctly returned by an honest user are deleted. Therefore, malicious V cannot trace the identity of the honest user once items are returned. Also, malicious P cannot input $Sign_V(\sigma)$ because IC checks the relation between $Sign_V(\sigma)$ and σ which includes V's public key .
2. Unlinkability:
   This case concludes GS Unlinkability of the Group Signature Scheme.

Over-duedate Traceability. In this case, we have to discuss about the situation, **Explosion**.
V can get the User ID from a Time Keeping Device. This case concludes GS Traceability of the Group Signature Scheme. In the situation where malicious user sends fake ID and group signature to IC, he (or she) is not able to create a fake Group Signature or fake σ. This case concludes GS Traceable of the Group Signature Scheme.

7 Conclusion

We have made an analysis on the digitized form of loan services, and stated a privacy problem that would not have been a large problem paper based systems. We have proposed a system named "An Anonymous Loan System" that could solve this privacy problem. Trivial solution to anonymous loan system is to assume an online TA. We think it is important to divide up the function of TA apart and to reduce the required trust on each part. Our scheme requires two trusted parties: Time Server and Time Keeping Device. However, the trust required to each party is greatly reduced: Time Server is restricted to have an access only to broadcast channel and have no communication links with the other players. On the other hand, Time Keeping Device can communicate with the other players, but is restricted to manage the status of each transaction.

References

1. N. Asokan, V. Shoup, and M. Waidner: Optimistic fair exchange of digital signatures. IEEE Journal on Selected Areas in Communications, vol. 18, pp. 591–610, Apr. 2000.
2. N. Asokan, M. Schunter, and M. Waidner: Optimistic protocol for fair exchange. Proc. of ACM-CCS '97, pp. 8–17, 1997.
3. G. Ateniese, J. Camenisch, M. Joye, and G. Tsudik: A Practical and Provably Secure Coalition-Resistant Group Signature Scheme, CRYPTO 2000, LNCS 1880. pp. 255–270, 2000.
4. J. Camenisch and I. Damgard: Verifiable Encryption and applications to group signatures and signature sharing. Tech. Rep. RS-98-32, Brics, Department of Computer Science, University of Aarhus, Dec. 1998.
5. J. Camenisch and A. Lysyanskaya: Efficient Non-transferable Anonymous Multi-show Credential System with Optional Anonymity Revocation. Advances in Cryptology - EUROCRYPT2001, vol.1976 of LNCS, pages 331–345, Springer, 2000.
6. J. Camenisch and M. Michels: A Group Signature Scheme Based on an RSA-Varian. Tech. Rep. RS-98-27, Brics, Department of Computer Science, University of Aarhus, 1998.
7. D. Chaum, R.L. Rivest and A.T. Sherman (Eds.): Blind Signatures for Untraceable Payments, Advances in Cryptology Proceedings of Crypto 82, pp. 199–203, Springar, Plemum, 1983.
8. D. Chaum: Group Signatures, Advances in Cryptology - EUROCRYPT '91, pp. 257–265, Springar, LNCS 547,1991.
9. D. Chaum: Security without Identification: Card Computers to make Big Brother Obsolete, Communications of the ACM, v. 28, n. 10, pp. 1030–1044, Oct 1985.
10. G. D. Crescenzo, R. Ostrovsky and S. Rajagopalan: Conditional Oblivious Transfer and Timed-Release Encryption. Advances in Cryptology-EUROCRYPT '99, pp. 74–89, Springer, LNCS vol. 1592. 1999.
11. T. C. May: Timed-release crypto, Febuary 1993. http://www.hks.net/cpunks/cpunks-0/1460.html.
12. R. L. Rivest, A. Shamir, and D. A. Wagner: Time-Lock Puzzles and Timed-Release Crypto, http://theory.lcs.mit.edu/ rivest

Traceability Schemes for Signed Documents[*]

Shoko Yonezawa[1], Goichiro Hanaoka[1], Junji Shikata[2], and Hideki Imai[1]

[1] Institute of Industrial Science, University of Tokyo,
4-6-1 Komaba, Meguro-ku, Tokyo 153-8505, Japan
{shoko,hanaoka}@imailab.iis.u-tokyo.ac.jp, imai@iis.u-tokyo.ac.jp
[2] Graduate School of Environment and Information Sciences,
Yokohama National University,
79-7, Tokiwadai, Hodogaya-ku, Yokohama, 240-8501, Japan
shikata@mlab.jks.ynu.ac.jp

Abstract. Illegal distribution of signed documents can be considered as one of serious problems of digital signatures. In this paper, to solve the problem, we propose three protocols concerning signature schemes. These schemes achieve not only traceability of an illegal user but also universal verifiability. The first scheme is a basic scheme which can trace an illegal receiver, and the generation and tracing of a signed document are simple and efficient. However, in this scheme, it is assumed that a signer is honest. The second scheme gives another tracing method which does not always assume that a signer is honest. Furthermore, in the method, an illegal user can be traced by an authority itself, hence, it is efficient in terms of communication costs. However, in this scheme it is assumed that there exists only a legal verification algorithm. Thus, in general, this scheme cannot trace a modified signed document which is accepted by a modified verification algorithm. The third one is a scheme which requires no trusted signer and allows a modified verification algorithm. It can trace an illegal receiver or even a signer in such a situation. All of our schemes are constructed by simple combinations of standard signature schemes, consequently, one can flexibly choose suitable building blocks for satisfying requirements for a system.

1 Introduction

The digital signature is one of the important techniques in modern cryptography. Compared to handwritten signatures in the real world, the digital signature is based on some secret information known only to a signer. Everyone can check the validity of a signature with public information corresponding to the secret information. Since forgery of a signature without using the signer's secret information is computationally infeasible, anyone can confirm the fact that the signer has surely generated such a signature.

A message with a digital signature, which we call a *signed document*, strongly guarantees the relationship between its signer and the message. More specifically,

---

[*] The second author is supported by a research fellowship from Japan Society for the Promotion of Science (JSPS).

A.H. Chan and V. Gligor (Eds.): ISC 2002, LNCS 2433, pp. 257–271, 2002.

for a signed document, it can be efficiently verified that the signer agrees with the contents of the document. Although signed documents can play very important roles in many applications such as e-commerce, a serious problem could also arise in the usage of signed documents. Namely, since signed documents can be easily copied, a dishonest receiver of a signed document can illegally distribute the signed document to a number of other users, which may cause serious damage to a signer. For example, suppose that Alice borrows $100,000 from Bob and Alice generates a signed document for the debt with her signature. In this case, Bob can illegally distribute the signed document. Consequently, since everyone can check the validity of the signature, Alice's economic condition will be known to many other people. There is essentially no way to prevent copying a signed document, hence, it seems difficult to prevent illegal distribution of it. Thus, it is desired that a signed document has either (or both) of the following properties: (1) a signed document cannot be verified solely and additional secret information is required for its verification, (2) in order to illegally distribute a signed document, a receiver of it needs to take a certain risk for the illegal distribution.

1.1 Related Works

There are two known approaches with the aim of resolving the problem: the first approach is to prohibit arbitrary entities from verifying a signature by limiting verifiable entities, and the second is to restrain distribution of a signed document by imposing some penalty on an illegal distributor of a signed document.

The methods in the first approach include undeniable signatures [9,11] and designated confirmer signatures [10]. Undeniable signatures, introduced by Chaum and van Antwerpen [11], can be verified only with the signer's cooperation. A user cannot check the validity of an undeniable signature without a signer. That is, a signer can control signature verification in this scheme, which protects from the damage caused by illegal distribution. This scheme, however, has drawbacks that the signer could be forced to cooperate in the verification process of a signature or else, verification could be impossible in case when the signer is absent. Designated confirmer signatures [10] overcome this problem by delegating the ability to verify signatures to some designated entity, called *confirmer*. When a user verifies a signature, he asks a confirmer for the validity of the signature. Thus, any user except a confirmer must interact with a confirmer to verify signatures in this scheme. However, this property may be undesirable in the case where many users want to verify signatures, since communication cost for a confirmer becomes greater.

On the other hand, the idea of the second approach is to add the property of *traceability*, which enable us to trace the original receiver if he illegally distributes a signed document, to signature schemes. More specifically, in these schemes, an authorized entity can trace the originator of a signed document generated by these scheme whereas anyone can verify the validity of a signed document similar to standard digital signatures. Such schemes achieve restraint on distribution of signed documents, as well as universal verifiability for signature schemes. These kinds of researches involve [6,16,17]. In [6], a fingerprinting technique is used to trace an original receiver. However, this scheme is quite inefficient because of the fingerprinting technique. A more efficient scheme was proposed in [16,17], which uses proof of knowledge of discrete logarithm [13,15], identification of a double spender in an off-line electronic cash [7] and a signcryption scheme [18]. The scheme consists of two parties, a signer and a receiver, and a signer can trace the illegal receiver by himself. A signature can be issued by a 3-move interaction, while verification and tracing of signatures require no interaction. Moreover, this scheme has *asymmetricity*, the property that a signer cannot intentionally forge a signed document so that a receiver would be traced back. To provide this property, a receiver generates some information and keeps it secret from a signer. However, in the scheme, it is necessary to record a transaction log of each signing protocol to trace an original receiver. This leads to a signer's burden when he issues many signatures. And, since a receiver must show his identity to a signer, it is not suitable for some applications which require the property of protecting users' anonymity.

1.2   Our Contribution

The purpose of this paper is to propose new schemes for restraint on distribution of signed documents which meet both *universal verifiability* and *traceability*. Moreover, we also take into account the property of *anonymity*. Our schemes can be briefly described as follows: there are three parties, a signer, a receiver and a registration center. A receiver who has correctly registered at the center can anonymously request a signed document to a signer. Any verifier can check the validity of the signature by using the public information without any interaction, while cannot reveal receiver's identity. The registration center can trace back to the original receiver by using only center's secret information, and therefore a signer does not need to record transaction logs as in [16,17].

To achieve the above purpose, we first define two models, a *traceability signature scheme for honest verifiers* (HTSS) and a *traceability signature scheme for dishonest verifiers* (DTSS). Then, we actually propose three new schemes along with the models. The first scheme, Scheme 1, allows a 2-move signature issuing. In this scheme, the registration center can trace the original receiver by *2-party trial*. However, in this scheme it is required to assume that a signer is honest. To be able to assume that a signer is not always honest, a signing protocol should be *asymmetric*, that is, a signed document is generated based on the receiver's secret which a signer does not know. Considering this issue, we next propose two asymmetric constructions, Scheme 2 and Scheme 3. In Scheme 2, a receiver chooses a secret information so that a signer cannot know. Then he outputs a signed document by combining the secret with data from a signer. This makes a signing protocol asymmetric, that is, since only a receiver can output such a valid signed document, a signer cannot forge a signed document. In addition, we consider a worse case where there exists a modified verification algorithm which accepts a modified invalid signed document. Although Scheme 2 assumes that the worse case does not occur, in Scheme 3, the registration center can trace an originator of an illegally distributed signed document with 3-party trial even in the worst case. All our schemes are successfully constructed by combining the cryptographic techniques of digital signature schemes, group signature schemes [4,12] and that of partially blind signature schemes [1,2,3].

1.3 Applications

The remarkable point of our schemes is to satisfy both universal verifiability and traceability. This makes verification and tracing of our schemes quite efficient. Our schemes are suitable for applications where a number of verifiers exist, and many signatures are issued. In addition, our schemes have anonymity of receivers, and thus are suitable for applications that desire receivers' anonymity.

Such applications may include a database system, a software protection system, and a contents distribution system. Here, we consider an example of such an application. Suppose, in a database system, that a user wants to obtain information from the database server, where the stored data is accessible to registered members. By applying our schemes, a user registered in the system can anonymously retrieve data with a server's signature. Namely, the user's privacy on the information which he accessed can be protected from any adversary even including the server. Furthermore, a signature guarantees the integrity of the information. Also, anyone can verify the validity of this information. Finally, the system can still trace the original receiver of the information even if the user distributes the information beyond the server's intention.

2 Preliminaries

In this section, we give a brief review about group signature schemes and partially blind signature schemes. These cryptographic techniques are used as building blocks to propose our schemes in Section 4.

2.1 Group Signatures

A group signature scheme [12,8,4] is a signature scheme which has the following property: a group member can sign messages anonymously on behalf of the group; and the identity of the original signer can be revealed by certain entity in case of dispute. More formally, a group signature scheme is defined as follows:

Definition 1. *(Group signature scheme) [4] A group signature scheme consists of the following procedures:*

GKG: *A key generation algorithm for the group manager GM , GKG, is a probabilistic algorithm that outputs her secret key x_M and public key y_M.*

GReg: *GReg is an interactive protocol between the group manager and a group member U. Their common inputs are the group member's identity ID_U and y_M. If both parties accept, the group member's output is her secret key x_U and their common output is U's membership key y_U.*

GSig: GSig *is a probabilistic algorithm that on input of* x_U, y_M, *and a message m outputs a group signature s on m.*

GVer: GVer *is an algorithm that on input of the group public key* y_M, *an alleged signature s, and a message m outputs 1 if and only if the signature is valid.*

GTrace: GTrace *is an algorithm which on input of the group manager's secret key* x_M, *the group public key* y_M, *a message m, and a signature s on m outputs the identity* ID_U *of the originator of the signature and a proof V that* ID_U *is indeed the originator.*

The following security requirements must hold:

Correctness of signature generation: *All signatures on any messages generated by any honest group member using* GSig *will be accepted by verification algorithm.*

Anonymity and unlinkability of signatures: *Given two signature-message pair, it is only feasible for the group manager to determine which group member(s) generated any of the signatures or whether the signatures have been generated by the same group member.*

Unforgeability of signatures: *It is feasible to sign messages only to group members (i.e., users that have run the registration protocol with the group manager) or to the group manager herself.*

Unforgeability of tracing: *The group manager cannot falsely accuse a group member of having originated a given signature.*

No framing: *Even if the group manager and some of the group members collude, they cannot sign on behalf of non-involved group members.*

Unavoidable traceability: *The group manager cannot accuse a signer falsely of having originated a given signature.*

2.2 Partially Blind Signatures

A partially blind signature scheme [1,2,3] is a signature scheme that allows a user to obtain a digital signature on message (clr, bld) from a signer, such that the signer does not get any information on bld nor on the resulting signature. The message consists of a clear part clr which is sent to a signer as its original form, and a blinded part bld which is kept secret to a signer. More formally, a partially blind signature scheme is defined as follows:

Definition 2. *(Partially blind signature scheme) [3] A partially blind signature scheme consists of the following procedures:*

PKG: *A key generation algorithm that outputs a public key* y_S *and corresponding secret key* x_S.

PSig: *An interactive 2-party protocol between a signer S and a user U. Their common inputs are a clear part of a message, clr, and the signer's public key* y_S. *The signer's public input is its secret key* x_S *and that for the user is a blinded part of message, bld. The user's output is a signature s on message* (clr, bld).

PVer: *An algorithm on input of* y_S, *clr, bld and s outputs 1 if and only if the signature is valid.*

3   Model

3.1   Models for Traceability Signature Schemes

In this section, we define the model and security requirements of our schemes. More specifically, we formally present definitions of two models of traceability signature schemes: a *traceability signature scheme for honest verifier* (HTSS); and a *traceability signature scheme for dishonest verifier* (DTSS). A traceability signature scheme for honest verifier assumes a normal setting, that is, only a correct verification algorithm which accepts a signed document generated by a correct signing protocol is permitted. On the other hand, a traceability signature scheme for dishonest verifier allows a modified verification algorithm as well as a correct one.

Definition 3. *(Traceability signature scheme for honest verifier) A* traceability signature scheme for honest verifier (HTSS) *involves a signer, a receiver and a registration center. A traceability signature scheme consists of the six procedures* (TKG-RC, TKG-S, TReg, TSig, TVer, TTrace):

TKG-RC: *A key generation algorithm for the registration center,* TKG-RC, *is a probabilistic algorithm that outputs a pair of matching secret key and public key,* (x_C, y_C), *for the registration center.*

TKG-S: *A key generation algorithm for a signer,* TKG-S, *is a probabilistic algorithm that outputs a pair of matching secret key and public key,* (x_S, y_S), *for the signer.*

TReg: TReg *is an interactive two-party protocol between the registration center and a receiver. Their common inputs are the receiver's identity* ID_R *and the registration center's public key* y_C. *The registration center's secret input is the secret key* x_C. *As a result, the receiver obtains some secret* x_R *and related information* y_R *and the registration center obtains and stores* y_R *and* ID_R.

TSig: TSig *is an interactive two-party protocol between a signer and a receiver* (TSig-S, TSig-R). *Their common input consists of a message* m *and the registration center's public key* y_C. *The signer's secret input is her secret key* x_S. *The receiver's secret input are his secret key* x_R *and additional secret information* z_R. *As a result, the receiver obtains a signed document. Here, a signed document is a data structure consisting of a message part* msg *and a signature part* sig. *The message part contains the message* m *and some additional information and the signature part is a signature of* msg. *A signed document* $\langle msg, sig \rangle$ *is called* valid *if* sig *could have been generated from* msg *by the use of* TSig.

TVer: TVer *is an algorithm that on input of the signer's public key* y_S *and a signed document outputs* 1 *or* 0. TVer *outputs* 1 *if and only if the signed document is valid.*

TTrace: TTrace *is an algorithm for the registration center which outputs a fraudulent user following to a tracing rule. Tracing rule is a method to trace the originator, which originally outputs the signed document* $\langle msg, sig \rangle$ *among*

*the signer or the receiver, from the signed document according to the scheme.
The inputs are a signed document SD, the registration center's public key
y_C and secret key x_C and its list of y_R's and ID_R's.*

We require that the following conditions hold.

Correctness: All protocols should terminate successfully whenever its players are
honest (no matter how other players behaved in other protocols).

Universal verifiability: Any signed documents generated by TSig are verifiable
for any verifier.

Anonymity of receivers: A signer cannot know a receiver who requested a signed
document to him. Moreover, given a valid signed document, to determine the
original receiver is computationally hard except the registration center.

Unforgeability: It is feasible to generate a signed document only by TSig, more
specifically,

- No receiver R can output a signed document $\langle msg, sig \rangle$ which satisfies
$(\mathsf{TSig\text{-}S}(x_S), \mathsf{TSig\text{-}R}(x_{R'}, z_{R'})) (m, y_C) \rightarrow \langle msg, sig \rangle$ for another receiver
R'.
- No signer S can output a signed document $\langle msg, sig \rangle$ which satisfies
$(\mathsf{TSig\text{-}S}(x_S), \mathsf{TSig\text{-}R}(x_R, z_R)) (m, y_C) \rightarrow \langle msg, sig \rangle$ for a receiver R without running an actual protocol.
- The registration center RC cannot output a signed document $\langle msg, sig \rangle$
which satisfies $(\mathsf{TSig\text{-}S}(x_S), \mathsf{TSig\text{-}R}(x_R, z_R)) (m, y_C) \rightarrow \langle msg, sig \rangle$ for a
receiver R and a signer S.

Traceability: The tracing rule and hence TTrace can specify an originator from
a signed document. Here, the tracing rule must satisfy the following requirements : (1) a receiver cannot output a signed document which another
receiver could be falsely traced. (2) a signer cannot output a signed document which an innocent receiver could be falsely traced. (3) the registration
center cannot output a signed document which an innocent receiver could
be falsely traced by requesting a signed document for a signer instead of the
receiver.

The above model implicitly does not allow the existence of a modified verification algorithm which accepts certain signed document rejected by TVer. This
implies that the model has a strong assumption that these algorithms behave exactly. It is reasonable for various applications since, in ordinary case, the system
distributed in the market is such algorithms that work correctly. However, it is
not necessarily reasonable for all applications since it is possible that the algorithms forged as not to follow this protocol will be distributed in the market. We
should take such a situation into account. Therefore, in addition to Definition 3,
we give another definition which allows a modified verification algorithm.

Definition 4. *(Traceability signature scheme for dishonest verifier) Let* (TKG-
RC, TKG-S, TReg, TSig, TVer, TTrace) *be a traceability signature scheme for
honest verifier described in Definition 3. Consider an additional procedure* TVer' :

TVer': *Let S be the set of the signed documents generated by* TSig. *TVer' is an algorithm such that, for* TVer *and any signed document SD, there exists a computationally feasible conversion f, where f satisfies* TVer$(SD) =$ TVer$'(f(SD))$ *such that $f(SD) \notin S$.*

Then, the scheme is a traceability signature scheme for dishonest verifier (DTSS) *if it allows an adversary to attempt to create the algorithm* TVer' *defined above.*

3.2   Models for Tracing

The behavior of TTrace is defined by a tracing rule. The aim of tracing is showing to the judge the proof that someone is surely the originator of a signed document. The way of tracing can be categorized by who take part in the tracing. The tracing rule that the registration center only takes part in the protocol is called *2-party trial* [14], and that the registration center and an accused receiver take part in is called *3-party trial*. Since 2-party trial is more efficient than 3-party trial, the tracing algorithm is desired to be 2-party trial. However, some schemes, given in Definition 4 for instance, are too complicated to trace by 2-party trial. 3-party trial is yet undesirable in terms of communication costs. Therefore, let us think about the tracing rule that works by 3-party trial just in the worst case. It can trace a signed document which satisfies some condition. More precisely, a signed document accepted by TVer' can be traced with 3-party trial. We call this kind of tracing an *optimistic 3-party trial*. In this paper, we show HTSSs with 2-party trial and a DTSS with optimistic 3-party trial. The 2-party trial and optimistic 3-party trial are formally defined as follows:

Definition 5. *(2-party trial) For any signed document, the tracing rule is 2-party trial if it can trace the originator of a signed document SD only by the registration center.*

Definition 6. *(Verifiable-invalid) Let S be a set of signed documents generated by* TSig. *Note that if a signed document SD is valid if and only if $SD \in S$. For any signed document SD, if there exists (*TVer$'$, f) *such that* TVer$(SD) =$ TVer$'(f(SD))$ *where f is a computationally feasible conversion and $f(SD) \notin S$, then $f(SD)$ is called* verifiable-invalid. *In other words, an invalid signed document is* verifiable-invalid *if it is a valid signed document for* TVer'.

Definition 7. *(Optimistic 3-party trial) For any signed document, the tracing rule is* optimistic 3-party trial *if it can trace not only the originator of a valid signed document SD with 2-party trial but also the originator of a verifiable-invalid signed document with 3-party trial.*

As mentioned above, being distributed the modified software seems exceptional. The possibility of such cases will be little. This is why we use the term "optimistic" the same meaning as [5]. In the next section, we propose the three schemes following the above definitions. Two of those are HTSSs with 2-party trial. These are not enough if we need to consider a situation in which there exists TVer′ as in Definition 4. The other is a DTSS with optimistic 3-party trial, which can trace the originator even if there exists TVer′.

4   Proposed Schemes

In this section, we show three realizations of traceability signature schemes. As already mentioned, the first two schemes, Scheme 1 and Scheme 2, are HTSSs with 2-party trial, and the third scheme, Scheme 3, is a DTSS with optimistic 3-party trial. All schemes use generic group signature schemes, which regard the registration center in a traceability signature scheme as the group manager and a receiver as a group member. The registration center can trace a group signature generated by a receiver. If a signed document includes a group signature generated by a receiver, the registration center can trace the identity of the receiver. Moreover, a group signature enables a receiver to avoid being known his identity to a signer. We also use partially blind signature schemes in Scheme 3 in order to avoid revealing a receiver's secret and resulting signature to a signer.

In the sequel, let (GKG, GReg, GSig, GVer, GTrace) be a group signature scheme, (KG, Sig, Ver) a digital signature scheme and (PKG, PSig, PVer) a partially blind signature scheme. Let H be a collision-resistant hash function $H : \{0,1\}^* \to \{0,1\}^k$. The following subsections describe the schemes in detail and security analyses.

4.1   Basic Scheme

Scheme 1 is a basic scheme, which we call a symmetric HTSS. In Scheme 1, a receiver, after the registration, requests a signature from a signer. He sends to a signer a message m, its request req, which may be the title of a document, a date and so on, and a group signature gs on $m\|req$. Since a group signature has anonymity, a receiver can contact with a signer without revealing his identity. If the group signature is valid, a signer sends a signature s on $m\|req\|gs$. The receiver outputs $SD = (m, req, gs, s)$ as a signed document. If the signed document SD is regarded as illegally distributed one, the registration center can trace the original receiver by opening gs in SD.

Scheme 1 *(Symmetric HTSS)*

TKG-RC: The registration center runs GKG to get the key pair (y_C, x_C) and publishes y_C.

TKG-S: A signer S runs KG to get the key pair (y_S, x_S) and publishes y_S.

TReg: The registration center and a receiver R run GReg. The receiver gets y_R and x_R. The center gets and stores ID_R and y_R. This protocol will be done once for each receiver.

TSig: Let m be a message to be signed and req the request for m. The receiver R first generates a group signature on $H(m\|req)$ by computing $gs := \mathsf{GSig}(x_R, y_C, H(m\|req))$, and sends (m, req, gs) to the signer S. The signer checks the validity of gs by $\mathsf{GVer}(y_C, gs, H(m\|req)) \overset{?}{=} 1$. If GVer outputs 1, the signer computes the signature on m and gs by $s := \mathsf{Sig}(x_S, m\|req\|gs)$, and sends s to the receiver. The receiver outputs $SD = \langle msg, sig \rangle = \langle (m, req, gs), s \rangle$ as a signed document.

TVer: A verifier checks the validity of SD by $\mathsf{Ver}(y_S, m\|req\|gs, s) \overset{?}{=} 1$.

TTrace: The registration center traces an originator of SD by the following tracing rule.

> **Tracing rule for Scheme 1:** The registration center computes GTrace $(x_C, y_C, H(m\|req), gs)$ and obtains the fraudulent receiver's identity ID_R.

Scheme 1 is an HTSS with 2-party trial. In fact, it is easily shown that it satisfies the following properties:

Correctness : It is obvious from the construction.

Universal verifiability : For $SD = \langle (m, req, gs), s \rangle$, s is generated by Sig, where Sig is a signing algorithm of a suitable digital signature scheme. It can be verifiable for any verifier due to the property of a digital signature scheme.

Anonymity of receivers : During TSig, a receiver sends his identity as a group signature gs. Because of the property of a group signature scheme, gs has anonymity of an original signer, namely, a receiver. Similarly, SD output by a receiver does not reveal his identity from gs.

Unforgeability : For a receiver R, in order to get a signed document SD which can be traced another receiver R' via TSig, he must make a group signature gs whose originator is traced to be R'. It is impossible from the property of group signatures. Similarly, S and RC cannot make such a gs. Therefore, SD is unforgeable.

Traceability : Since a signer is supposed to be honest, a valid SD is output by a receiver. Such SD can be traced according to the tracing rule.

A group signature gs has two roles. One is to confirm that the (anonymous) receiver has correctly registered the system, and the other is to assure that the signed document which is to be generated by TSig will be traceable. Since a signature generated by a signer is that of a message including gs, a signed document can be successfully traced after distributed.

Scheme 1 does not satisfy the property of traceability in a strict sense. It is impossible to tell which is the originator of the signed document, that is, the receiver or the signer if we do not assume that a signer is honest. This is the intrinsic limitation in this construction, since a signer has the same information as a receiver from which the word "symmetric" comes.

4.2   Asymmetric Scheme (1)

The second construction, Scheme 2, is briefly described as follows (see also Fig.1.): A receiver chooses a random number r and keeps it secret from a signer. The receiver sends to a signer the hash value of r in addition to (m, req, gs). After a signer returns $(m, req, gs, H(r), s)$, where s is a signature of $m\|req\|gs\|H(r)$, the receiver publishes r and outputs $SD = (m, req, gs, H(r), r, s)$ as a signed document. Since the signer does not know r, he cannot output SD. Verification consists of two procedures, that is, checking the consistency between r and $H(r)$ in SD and verifying the validity of s. If a signed document which passes the above verification is distributed, the registration center concludes that the originator of the document is a receiver and traces him.

In our models, Scheme 2 is an HTSS with 2-party trial. In fact, the registration center can trace the originator of a valid signed document with no interaction among others.

Scheme 2 *(Asymmetric HTSS)*

TKG-RC: The registration center runs GKG to get the key pair (y_C, x_C) and publishes y_C.

TKG-S: A signer S runs KG to get the key pair (y_S, x_S) and publishes y_S.

TReg: The registration center and a receiver R run GReg. The receiver gets y_R and x_R. The center gets and stores ID_R and y_R.

TSig: Let m be a message to be signed and req the request for m. The receiver R chooses a random number r secretly, generates a group signature on $H(m\|req)\|H(r)$ by computing $gs := \mathsf{GSig}\,(x_R, y_C, H(m\|req)\|H(r))$ and sends $(m, req, H(r), gs)$ to a signer. The signer checks the validity of gs by $\mathsf{GVer}(y_C, gs, H(m\|req)\|H(r)) \overset{?}{=} 1$. If GVer outputs 1, the signer computes a signature on (m, req, gs) and $H(r)$ by $s := \mathsf{Sig}\,(x_S, m\|req\|gs\|H(r))$, and sends s to the receiver. The receiver checks the validity of s. Finally, the receiver outputs $SD = \langle msg, sig \rangle = \langle (m, req, gs, H(r)), (s, r) \rangle$ as a signed document.

TVer: When gaining $SD = \langle (m, req, gs, H(r)), (s, r') \rangle$, a verifier first checks the validity of attached random number r', that is, computes $h = H(r')$ and compares it to $H(r)$ in SD. If $h \neq H(r)$, the verifier rejects SD as an invalid signed document. If it passes this check, the verifier next checks $\mathsf{Verify}(y_S, m\|req\|gs\|H(r), s) \overset{?}{=} 1$.

TTrace: The registration center traces an originator of SD by the following tracing rule.

Tracing rule for Scheme 2: The registration center first checks the validity of SD by running TVer. If the signed document is valid, he runs $\mathsf{GTrace}(x_C, y_C, H(m\|req)\|H(r), gs)$ and obtains the fraudulent receiver's identity ID_R.

Scheme 2 is an HTSS with 2-party trial. In contrast to Scheme 1, a signer's fraudulence is considered here. A signer cannot output a signed document accepted by TVer since TVer checks the consistency between r and $H(r)$ in SD,

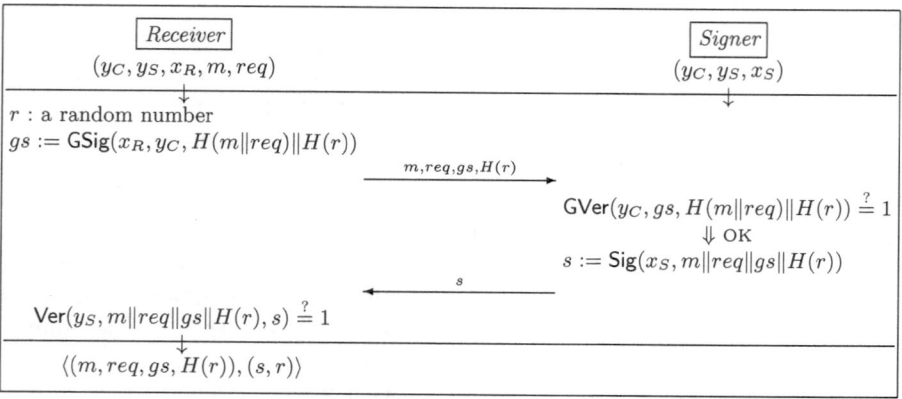

Fig. 1. Scheme 2 (TSig Protocol)

where r could be only known to a receiver. If TVer works correctly, a signer cannot attack.

4.3   Asymmetric Scheme (2)

We should note that Scheme 2 has a problem that it cannot trace the originator of a signed document if there exists a modified verification algorithm. In Scheme 2, if there exists TVer$'$ which does not check the consistency between r and $H(r)$ in SD (see Definition 4), a signer can output a signed document $SD' = \langle msg, sig \rangle = \langle (m, req, gs, H(r)), (s, r') \rangle$, which is generated by replacing r with r'. Such SD would be accepted by TVer$'$ and a receiver R would be traced. To avoid this problem, it is desired that a signer must not know the resulting signature part sig of SD.

Considering the above problem, in Scheme 3 we use partially blind signature schemes to hide a resulting signature from a signer. More precisely, a receiver and a signer run a signing protocol of a partially blind signature scheme regarding $(m, req, gs, H(r))$ as a clear part and r as a blinded part, respectively. The receiver can obtain the signature s on $(m, req, gs, H(r), r)$ (See Fig.2.). This scheme is an optimistic 3-party trial. In fact, a receiver can claim his innocent by showing his signed document which he surely received from the signer even if the signer forges the signed document for himself by using the information sent by the receiver.

Scheme 3, which is a DTSS with optimistic 3-party trial, is proposed as follows.

Scheme 3 *(Asymmetric DTSS)*

TKG-RC: The registration center runs GKG to get the key pair (y_C, x_C) and publishes y_C.

TKG-S: A signer S runs PKG to get the key pair (y_S, x_S) and publishes y_S.

TReg: The registration center and a receiver R run GReg. The receiver gets y_R and x_R. The center gets and stores ID_R and y_R.

TSig: Let m be a message to be signed and req the request for m. The receiver R chooses a random number r and generates a group signature on $H(m\|req)\|H(r)$ by computing $gs := $ GSig $(x_R, y_C, H(m\|req)\|H(r))$. The receiver runs a protocol PSig with the signer S on the receiver's input $cls = (m, req, H(r), gs)$ and $bld = r$. The signer checks GVer$(y_C, gs, H(m\|req)\|H(r)) \overset{?}{=} 1$ during the protocol, and if satisfied the signer continues the protocol. Finally, the receiver gains the signature s on (cls, bld). If the receiver can confirm the validity of s, he outputs $SD = \langle msg, sig \rangle = \langle (m, req, gs, r, H(r)), s \rangle$ as a signed document.

TVer: When gaining $SD = \langle (m, req, gs, r', H(r)), s \rangle$, a verifier first checks the validity of attached random number r', that is, computes $h = H(r')$ and compares it to $H(r)$ in SD. If $h \neq H(r)$, the verifier rejects SD as an invalid signed document. If it passes this check, the verifier next checks PVer$(y_S, (m, req, gs, H(r)), r, s) \overset{?}{=} 1$

TTrace: The registration center traces an originator of SD by the the following tracing rule.

Tracing rule for Scheme 3:
> if TVer$(SD) = 1$
>> The originator is the receiver;
>> $ID_R = $ GTrace$(x_C, y_C, H(m\|req)\|H(r), gs)$;
> **else if** SD is verifiable-invalid
>> $ID_R = $ GTrace$(x_C, y_C, H(m\|req)\|H(r), gs)$;
>> **if** the receiver can show another signed document which he surely received from the signer
>>> The originator is the signer;
>> **else** the originator is the receiver;

We explain the tracing rule in more detail. In the case that SD is valid, the tracing is the same as in Scheme 2. We consider the case that SD is verifiable-invalid. Suppose that a signer or a receiver tries to output a verifiable-invalid signed document. Consider the case where a signer is dishonest, after a signer issued a valid signed document $SD = \langle (m, req, gs, r, H(r)), s \rangle$ to a receiver, the signer would output $\langle (m, req, gs, r', H(r)), s' \rangle$ by choosing r' at uniformly random, and make a partially blind signature s' on $(m, req, H(r), gs)$ and r'. In this case, the receiver should have received the signed document SD which was correctly issued by the signer. The receiver can prove his innocence by showing SD. Whereas, when a receiver outputs a verifiable-invalid signed document, the receiver should request a signed document on $clr = (m, req, H(r), gs)$ and $bld = r''$, namely, the receiver will blind the random number r'' inconsistent of $H(r)$ and receive a signed document $\langle (m, req, gs, r'', H(r)), s \rangle$. In this case, the receiver cannot show another signed document. Therefore, the signed document can be traced with optimistic 3-party trial.

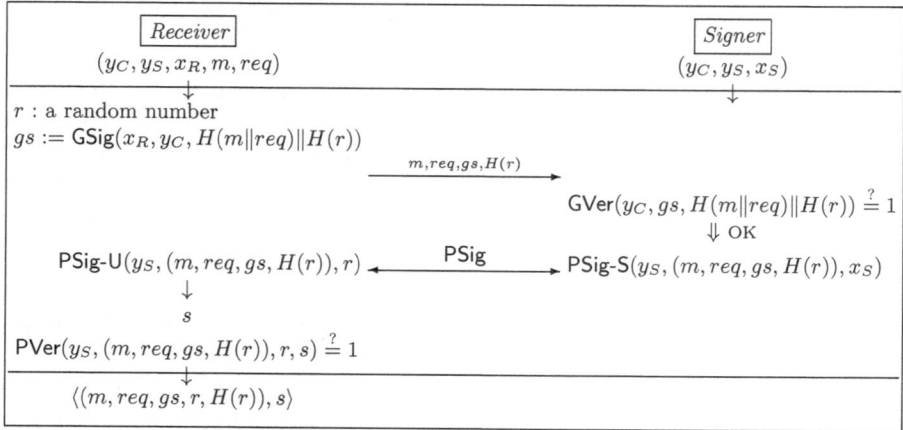

Fig. 2. Scheme 3 (TSig Protocol)

Scheme 3 can trace the originator even if we assume the existence of TVer' (see Definition 4), while Scheme 2 is not sufficient if we need to consider a situation in which there exists TVer'. However, we should note that such a situation can be ignored in certain applications.

5   Conclusion

In this paper, we proposed signature schemes which provide traceability of an illegal user. In our schemes, an original receiver of a signature would be traced when the signature that the receiver had was illegally distributed to other verifiers, therefore, illegal leakage of a digital signature could be restrained. We first constructed a basic scheme which can trace illegal users, assuming that a signer was honest. In this scheme, group signatures were utilized as important building blocks for providing both traceability and anonymity of users. Next, by extending our basic scheme, a scheme equipped with another tracing method was proposed. A remarkable point of this scheme was to enable us to assume that a signer was not always honest. Moreover, in the scheme, the registration center could trace an illegal user with no interaction among other parties. However, this scheme implicitly assumed that an adversary does not modify a signature so that one could verify the validity of the original signature by using the modified signature and a modified verification algorithm. Thus, in this scheme an illegal user who leaked the modified signature would not be traced. Therefore, by introducing partially blind signatures, we finally proposed a scheme which assumed that a signer was not always honest and could withstand attacks that an adversary utilized a modified verification algorithm. All of our schemes were constructed by simple combinations of standard digital signatures, group signatures and partially blind signatures, consequently, one can flexibly choose suitable building blocks for satisfying requirements for a system.

References

1. M. Abe and J. Camenisch, "Partially Blind Signature Schemes," In Proc. of the 1007 Symposium on Cryptography and Information Security (SCIS'97), Fukuoka, Japan, 1997.
2. M. Abe and E. Fujisaki, "How to Date Blind Signatures," In Advances in Cryptology – ASIACRYPT'96, LNCS 1163, pp. 244–251, Springer-Verlag, 1996.
3. M. Abe and T. Okamoto, "Provably Secure Partially Blind Signatures," In Advances in Cryptology – CRYPTO2000, LNCS 1880, pp. 271–286, Springer-Verlag, 2000.
4. G. Ateniese, J. Camenisch, M. Joye and G. Tsudik, "A Practical and Provable Secure Coalition-Resistant Group Signature Scheme," In Advances in Cryptology – CRYPTO2000, LNCS 1880, pp. 255–270, Springer-Verlag, 2000.
5. N. Asokan, V. Shoup and M. Waidner, "Optimistic Fair Exchange of Digital Signatures," In Advances in Cryptology – EUROCRYPT'98, LNCS 1403, pp. 591–606, Springer-Verlag, 1998.
6. K. Baba, K. Iwamura, Y. Zheng and H. Imai, "A Protocol to Detect Who Has Leaked a Signed Document," In Proc. of the 1999 Symposium on Cryptography and Information Security (SCIS'99), Kobe, Japan, pp. 257–262, 1999.
7. S. Brands, "Untraceable Off-line Cash in Wallets with Observers," In Advances in Cryptology – CRYPTO '93, LNCS 773, pp. 302–318, Springer-Verlag, 1994.
8. J. Camenisch and M. Stadler, "Efficient Group Signature Schemes for Large Groups," In Advances in Cryptology – CRYPTO'97, LNCS 1296, pp. 410–424, Springer-Verlag, 1997.
9. D. Chaum, "Zero-Knowledge Undeniable Signatures," In Advances in Cryptology – EUROCRYPT'90, LNCS 473, pp. 458–464, Springer-Verlag, 1991.
10. D. Chaum, "Designated Confirmer Signatures," In Advances in Cryptology – EUROCRYPT'94, LNCS 950, pp. 86–91, Springer-Verlag, 1994.
11. D. Chaum and H. van Antwerpen, "Undeniable Signatures," In Advances in Cryptology – CRYPTO'89, LNCS 435, pp. 212–216, Springer-Verlag, 1990.
12. D. Chaum and E. van Heyst, "Group Signatures," In Advances in Cryptology – EUROCRYPT'91, LNCS 547, pp. 257–265, Springer-Verlag, 1991.
13. A. Fiat and A. Shamir, "How to Prove Yourself: Practical Solutions to Identification and Signature Problems," In Advances in Cryptology – CRYPTO'86, LNCS 263, pp. 186–194, Springer-Verlag, 1987.
14. B. Pfitzmann and M. Waidner, "Anonymous Fingerprinting," In Advances in Cryptology – EUROCRYPT'97, LNCS 1233, pp. 88–102, Springer-Verlag, 1997.
15. C. P. Schnorr, "Efficient Identification and Signatures for Smart Cards," In Advances in Cryptology – EUROCRYPT'89, LNCS 434, pp. 688–689, Springer-Verlag, 1990.
16. Y. Watanabe, Y. Zheng and H. Imai, "Traitor Traceable Signature Scheme," In Proc. of ISIT2000, Sorrento, Italy, pp. 462, 2000.
17. Y. Watanabe, Y. Zheng and H. Imai, "Software Copyright Protection in the Presence of Corrupted Providers," In Proc. of International Symposium on Information Theory and Its Applications(ISITA2000), Honolulu, Hawaii, U.S.A., pp. 501–504, 2000.
18. Y. Zheng, "Digital Signcryption or How to Achieve Cost(Signature & Encryption) << Cost(Signature) + Cost(Encryption)," In Advances in Cryptology – CRYPTO '97, LNCS 1294, pp. 165–179, Springer-Verlag, 1997.

Proofs of Knowledge for Non-monotone Discrete-Log Formulae and Applications

Emmanuel Bresson and Jacques Stern

Ecole normale supérieure,
45 rue d'Ulm, 75230, Paris, France
{Emmanuel.Bresson, Jacques.Stern}@ens.fr.

Abstract. This paper addresses the problem of defining and providing proofs of knowledge for a general class of exponentiation-based formulae. We consider general predicates built from modular exponentiations of secret values, combined by products and connected with the logical operators "AND", "OR", "NOT". We first show how to deal with non-linear combination of secret exponents. Next,we extend the work by Brands [4] to a strictly larger class of predicates, allowing a more liberal use of the logical operator "NOT". We sketch two applications by which we enhance group signatures schemes with revocation of identity and multi-signer features. Such features can be useful to protect privacy or for collaborative use of group signatures, respectively.

1 Introduction

1.1 Proof of Knowledge

Zero-knowledge has been introduced by Goldwasser, Micali and Rackoff in [23] to quantify the amount of information leaked in an interactive protocol. The (interactive) protocols are thus proved zero-knowledge when they reveal no information apart from the validity of the statement. Almost at the same time, the concept of *proof of knowledge* [21] introduced the notion of extractor for a secret and became a building block in public-key cryptography. The property of zero-knowledge is useful as soon as one wants to perform some operations with secret values without revealing them. Classical examples are authentication, identification [5,20,21], digital signatures [21] and group signatures [10,18].

From a more general point of view, the idea of satisfying boolean statements (*predicates*) without leaking any information has been first introduced by Chaum *et al.* [13,15,22]. Numerous schemes [14] allow to combine several proofs to prove more elaborated statements about discrete logarithms; the very first only covered the case of a single equations connected by "AND" statement. In 1994, De Santis *et al.* [25] and Cramer *et al.* [19] independently discovered a general method to deal with the "OR" connective. Using their method, one can design proof systems for monotone formulae (i.e. statements without negations). An application to group signature was made in an earlier paper [18] that mentioned [19]. Both

A.H. Chan and V. Gligor (Eds.): ISC 2002, LNCS 2433, pp. 272–288, 2002.

papers were based on a protocol proposed by Schoenmakers in [26]. Later, Camenisch and Stadler [11,7] introduced a formal model for building and proving general linear relations about discrete logarithms, and combining them by the logical operators "OR" and "AND".

In 1997, Brands [4] described a general method allowing to prove *any* boolean combination of linear or affine relations on secrets exponents, including relations obtained by "NOT" operator. Note that, strictly speaking, this method does not encompass the entire class of boolean formulae obtained by connecting exponentiations of elements since one may wish to state that an exponential term differs from an element whose discrete logarithm is *unknown*. This will be precisely where the core of our paper can be found.

1.2 Contributions

Our contribution is on two points. We first explain how to prove non-linear relations on secret values and give as an example a protocol to *efficiently* prove knowledge of roots of discrete logarithms.

Next we define zero-knowledge proofs for statements involving negations (i.e. operator "NOT"), in a framework which is strictly larger than the one used in [4]. We explain why in some situations that we believe to be practical, the scheme proposed in [4] is not sufficient. As a concrete application of this particular extension, we give two examples related to group signatures. The first formalizes the work of [6,27] to perform member revocation while the second introduces multi-signer features in that context.

2   A General Class of Exponentiation-Based Formulae

We describe here a formal class of *predicates*, seen as boolean statements built from modular exponentiations of secret values, combined by products and connected with the logical operators "AND", "OR", "NOT".

2.1 Preliminaries

We follow the notation of [4,3]. We denote a polynomial-time prover by $\mathcal{P}$ and a possibly unlimited verifier by $\mathcal{V}$. The notation $x \in_R S$ means that x is chosen in the set S randomly; we assume uniform distribution, unless otherwise specified. Finally, we fix a cyclic group G of prime-order q (e.g. a subgroup of $\mathbb{Z}_p^*$, where p is a large prime and $q|p-1$). Note that q is made public. For any polynomial integer m, for any element y and generators $g_1, \ldots, g_m$ in G, we say that $(x_1, \ldots, x_m) \in \mathbb{Z}_q^m$ is a *representation* of y with respect to the g_i's if $y = \prod_{i=1}^m g_i^{x_i}$. Without loss of generality, we assume that the generators appearing in such a product are different.

The following lemma is a critical part of our construction.

Lemma 1 (see [17]). *Under the discrete logarithm assumption, it holds that no probabilistic polynomial-time algorithm, on input q and a randomly chosen, polynomial-sized tuple of generators $(g_1, \ldots, g_m)$, can output with non-negligible probability an element $h \in G$ and two different representations of h with respect to some of the g_i's.*

2.2   Knowledge of Representations

In the remaining of this paper, we consider a polynomial-sized family of generators $g_1, \ldots, g_m$ of G, whose relative discrete logarithms are unknown. An *atomic representation-based predicate* relatively to some variables $(x_1, \ldots, x_k)$ is build from a representation of a public value y w.r.t. a subset of the basis $g_1, \ldots, g_m$:

$$(T) \qquad : \qquad y = \prod_{l \in [1,k], j \in S} g_j^{x_l} \qquad \text{where } S \subseteq [1, m], \#(S) = k.$$

To avoid using two different indices for the bases and the variables, we consider an appropriate injective function π from $[1, k]$ onto $[1, m]$ such that the predicate can be re-written as follows:

$$(T) \qquad : \qquad y = \prod_{l \in [1,k]} g_{\pi(l)}^{x_l}$$

Depending on the values of $x_1, \ldots, x_k$, the above equation may be satisfied or not, and the predicate is seen as *true* or *false* for this set of values. Proving such atomic representation predicate means proving knowledge of values x_i such that the underlying equality holds. Camenish and Stadler [11] formalize this notion through *knowledge specification* and *knowledge specification set*.

We assume that $\mathcal{P}$ holds a set of values satisfying (T). Using standard zero-knowledge interactive protocol, $\mathcal{P}$ can prove knowledge of such private values $(x_1, \ldots, x_k)$. We denote such a proof:

$$ZKPK\big[\sigma_i \ : \ T(\sigma_1, \ldots, \sigma_k)\big] = ZKPK\big[\sigma_i \ : \ y = \prod_{l \in [1,k]} g_{\pi(l)}^{\sigma_l}\big]$$

which means "some secrets σ_i are known that make T *true*".

Proofs for Monotone Formulae. The prover is able to prove knowledge of the conjunction of two predicates by running a "multiple proof" in which it commits to several values using the same random number, receives a unique challenge, and gives a set of values as an answer. A predicate containing only "AND" connectives is referred to as a *conjunctive representation predicate* or CR-predicate on a set of variables $(\sigma_1, \ldots, \sigma_v)$:

$$T(\sigma_1, \ldots, \sigma_v) \qquad : \qquad \bigwedge_{i=1}^{k} \left(y_i = \prod_{l \in S_i} g_{\pi_i(l)}^{\sigma_l} \right)$$

where for each $i \in [1, k]$, S_i is a subset of $[1, v]$ of cardinality at most m and π_i is an injective function from S_i onto $[1, m]$.

Also the technique by Cramer *et al.* [19] can be used to prove knowledge for a disjunction of atomic predicates. This technique is now classical and consists in running a simulator on the predicates for which the secrets are unknown, and in completing the proof on *known* secrets by an adequate "share" of the given challenge. Such extensions appear in the literature and details are omitted here. The reader can refer to [10]. Thus, we can generically obtain proofs for any *disjunctive-conjunctive representation predicate* (DCR-predicate) on variables $(\sigma_1, \ldots, \sigma_{v_i})_{1 \le i \le n}$ written as:

$$(T) \qquad : \qquad \bigvee_{i=1}^{n} \bigwedge_{j=1}^{k_i} \left(y_{ij} = \prod_{l \in S_{ij}} g_{\pi_{ij}(l)}^{\sigma_l} \right)$$

where for each $i \in [1, n]$ and each $j \in [1, k_i]$, S_{ij} is a subset of $[1, v_i]$ of cardinality at most m and π_{ij} is an injective function from S_{ij} onto $[1, m]$.

Remark 1. DCR-predicates capture as a particular case proofs of knowledge of discrete logarithms or representations, as well as equality of discrete logs ("AND") or knowledge of one discrete log out of n (disjunctive predicate).

They also can be used to demonstrate *roots of representation* with the technique explained in [10]. However, in section 4, we show that a much more efficient technique can be used to demonstrate such statements (*logarithmic* size instead of *linear* size).

2.3   Case Where $\#(G)$ Is Unknown

When $\#(G)$ is not public, the answers cannot be reduced modulo q anymore, and zero-knowledge is only statistical. We take the example of $G = Q_N$, where Q_N is the set of quadratic residues modulo N. If N is the product of two safe primes $p = 2p' + 1$ and $q = 2q' + 1$, then Q_N is a cyclic group, and a random element is a generator with overwhelming probability, as shown in the following lemma:

Lemma 2. *Let* p, q, p', q' *be four prime numbers such that* $p = 2p' + 1$ *and* $q = 2q' + 1$ *and let* $N = pq$. *In that case, if an element* $w \in Q_N^* \backslash \{1\}$ *has order* $\mathrm{ord}(w) < p'q'$, *then either* $\gcd(w - 1, N)$ *or* $\gcd(w + 1, N)$ *is a non-trivial factor of* N.

3   Case of Monotone Formulae

3.1   Proving Linear Relations

We first recall known results on demonstrating linear relations between secret values using representation-based predicates. Following Brands formalization [4], we consider a prover $\mathcal{P}$ having knowledge of some secret values $x_1, \ldots, x_k$. The following result shows how a linear relation between the x_i's can be efficiently proven without revealing any additional information.

We assume $\mathcal{P}$ has published $h = g_1^{x_1} g_2^{x_2}$ as its public key. Let a, b be some public values in $\mathbb{Z}_q$ and assume that $\mathcal{P}$ wants to prove knowledge of two secrets σ_1, σ_2 such that the following predicate (T) : $h = g_1^{\sigma_1} g_2^{\sigma_2} \wedge (b = a\sigma_1 + \sigma_2)$ is true.

It can be shown [4] that under lemma 1, is is equivalent for $\mathcal{P}$ to prove knowledge of σ_1 and σ_2 satisfying (T) or to prove knowledge of the discrete logarithm of hg_2^{-b} to the base $g_1 g_2^{-a}$. To see that, let s be this discrete logarithm. From the definition of s, we easily get $h = g_1^s g_2^{b-as}$. According to lemma 1, $\mathcal{P}$ can know at most one representation of h to the bases g_1 and g_2. Thus we have $x_1 = s$ and $x_2 = b - as$. Hence, predicate (T) is true.

Also it must be noted that $g_1 g_2^{-a}$ is generator of G with overwhelming probability; we assume that it is always the case (for instance if a is chosen by the verifier).

These proofs can then be combined using standard techniques described in the previous section. We refer the reader to [4,11] for more details.

3.2 Extension to Quadratic Relations

We now deal with the method for proving non-linear relations. More precisely, in this section, we describe how to prove that a secret value is the product of two other secret values (or the square of another secret). Although such a technique is implicitly used in many papers, we put forward here the very conditions needed for a safe use.

Let T be a conjunctive representation predicate as defined in section 2: T : $\bigwedge_{i=1}^n y_i = \prod_l g_{\pi_i(l)}^{x_l}$ and consider the following, new predicate:

$$T' \quad : \quad (T) \wedge \left(x_i x_j = x_k \bmod q\right)$$

This is not a representation predicate anymore. However, we claim that $\mathcal{P}$ can still prove the validity of (T') when knowing the secrets x_l by using the following technique:

Protocol 1.

---

1. $\mathcal{V}$ sends to $\mathcal{P}$ a random generator h of G.
2. $\mathcal{P}$ chooses an integer $r \in_R \mathbb{Z}_q^*$ and sends to $\mathcal{V}$: $y' = g^{x_i} h^r$.
3. $\mathcal{P}$ performs the following proof of knowledge:

$$ZKPK\left[\sigma_1, \ldots, \sigma_k, \rho, \tau \; : \; (T) \wedge \left(y' = g^{\sigma_i} h^\rho\right) \wedge \left(y'^{\sigma_j} = g^{\sigma_k} h^\tau\right)\right] \quad (1)$$

We underline that it is of prime importance that $\mathcal{P}$ has no control over g and h, and that g, h are generators of G with overwhelming probability.

This protocol allows to add any non-linear relation to an arbitrary conjunctive predicate, as stated in the following theorem:

Theorem 1. *Let* (T) *be a conjunctive predicate on the variables* $(\sigma_1, \ldots, \sigma_k)$. *Then under lemma 1,* **Protocol 1** *is a zero-knowledge proof of knowledge for the predicate* $(T') := (T) \wedge (x_i x_j = x_k \bmod q)$.

Proof. We prove the following three properties.

Completeness. The verification is straightforward.

Soundness. The soundness property is computational. Let $\mathcal{E}$ be a knowledge extractor for the proof (1). We show that $\mathcal{E}$ is also a knowledge extractor for predicate (T'), provided lemma 1 holds.

Let $(z_1, \ldots, z_k, r, t)$ the secrets extracted by $\mathcal{E}$. If we raise the equation $y' = g^{z_i} h^r$ to the power of z_j, we get:

$$y'^{z_j} = g^{z_i z_j} h^{r z_j} = g^{z_k} h^t$$

Now, if g and h are randomly chosen by the verifier, lemma 1 applies and we have with overwhelming probability $z_i z_j = z_k \bmod q$. That is, returning $(z_1, \ldots, z_k)$ makes an extractor for predicate (T').

Zero-Knowledge. It is easy to see that if r is uniformly distributed over $\mathbb{Z}_q$, sending y' to the verifier does not reveal any helpful information. Also, the proof performed in the third step of the protocol does not reveal anything either. $\square$

Corollary 1. *When running* **Protocol 1** *with* $i = j$, *one can prove that a secret exponent is the square of another secret exponent.*

This simple remark allow us to build new, efficient scheme for proving knowledge of more complex statements, including polynomial relations, as explained in the next section.

4   Application to Efficient Protocols

While proving knowledge of discrete logarithms or representation is feasible in efficient ways by classical means, proving the knowledge of a root of a discrete logarithm is much more difficult. Two ideas have been proposed so far, which remain quite inefficient or constrained to particular values.

4.1   A Generic Bit-by-Bit Solution [28]

M. Stadler proposed in [28] a bit-by-bit protocol which allows to prove knowledge of the e-th root of the discrete logarithm of an element y, relatively to a base element g. That is, given $y, g \in G$ and $e > 2$, one proves knowledge of x such that $y = g^{x^e}$.

This can be done as follows. Let ℓ denote a security parameter.

Protocol 2.

---

1. $\mathcal{P}$ chooses $r_1, \ldots, r_\ell \in_R \mathbb{Z}_n^*$ and sends $t_i = g^{r_i^e}$ to $\mathcal{V}$, for $i = 1, \ldots, \ell..$

2. $\mathcal{V}$ sends a random ℓ-bit challenge c to $\mathcal{P}$.

3. $\mathcal{P}$ answers with $(s_1, \ldots, s_\ell)$ where $s_i = r_i$ if $c[i] = 0$ and $s_i = r_i/x$ otherwise.

4. $\mathcal{V}$ accepts if for all $i = 1, \ldots, \ell$: $t_i = \begin{cases} g^{s_i^e} & \text{if } c[i] = 0, \\ y^{s_i^e} & \text{otherwise.} \end{cases}$

4.2   An Alternative Solution for Small e Only [10]

In [10], another solution acceptable for small values of e appears. The resulting proof being linear in e, the usefulness is very limited in practice. One cannot use it for $e > 160$, for instance.

Let consider another generator h of group G such that the discrete logarithm of h to the base g is unknown. The basic idea is to prove a conjunctive predicate made of some statements like $y_i = g^{\sigma_i} \wedge (\sigma_i = x \times \sigma_{i-1})$, and $y_0 = g$ such that one recursively gets $\sigma_i = x^i$. However, such a solution reveals partial information about x, namely all the intermediate values g^{x^i}. The solution consists in "blinding" these intermediate values using another generator h whose discrete logarithm to the base g is unknown (this can be done by having $\mathcal{V}$ choosing h).

More precisely, $\mathcal{P}$ performs the following two steps. In the first step, $\mathcal{P}$ computes $e - 1$ random values y_1 through y_{e-1} as $y_i = h^{r_i} g^{x^i}$ where r_i is a random secret exponent. $\mathcal{P}$ sends these values to $\mathcal{V}$. In the second step, $\mathcal{P}$ proves the following representation predicate:

$$ZKPK\Big[\sigma_1, \ldots, \sigma_e, \rho : y_1 = h^{\sigma_1} g^\rho \quad \wedge \quad y_2 = h^{\sigma_2} y_1^\rho \quad \wedge \quad \ldots$$
$$\wedge \quad y_{e-1} = h^{\sigma_{e-1}} y_{e-2}^\rho \quad \wedge \quad y = h^{\sigma_e} y_{e-1}^\rho \Big]$$

According to this proof, and independently of lemma 1, y is actually of the form $h^\tau g^{\rho^e}$, where ρ and $\tau = \sigma_e + \cdots + \sigma_2 \rho^{e-2} + \sigma_1 \rho^{e-1}$ are proven to be known by $\mathcal{P}$. Also, according to lemma 1, $\mathcal{P}$ can know at most one representation of y to the bases g and h. It follows that: $\tau \equiv \rho^e \bmod q$, which means that ρ satisfies $y = g^{\rho^e}$. It is easy to see that no information is leaked by the values y_i's if the exponent r_i's are randomly and independently chosen.

4.3   Our Solution in $\mathcal{O}(\log e)$ Size

We now describe a method that can be used for larger values of e. Let ℓ be a security parameter. Our protocol can be used for any $e < 2^{\ell/2}$ and leads to proof of size $\mathcal{O}(\log e)$. Such improvment has been also suggested in [7, p. 64]. In this section, we give the first formal protocol together with a proof of security. Typically, for $\ell = 160$ our protocol outperforms both Camenish-Stadler protocol [10] and Stadler protocol [28].

The main idea is as follows. First when proving both $A = g^\sigma$ and $A^\rho = g^\tau$, for some values A and g, one proves that $\tau = \sigma \rho$. That is, we prove that a secret exponent is the product of two other secret exponents. Second, we note that if

$e = 2^k + 2^i + 2^j + \cdots$, one can write $x^e = x^{2^k} x^{2^i} x^{2^j} \cdots$. It follows that a statement like $y = g^{x^e}$ can be written as

$$y = g^{x^{2^k} x^{2^i} x^{2^j} \cdots}$$

Hence using the binary representation of e (which is $\mathcal{O}(\log e)$ long), we obtain a new form of the statement g^{x^e} wherein x^e is the product of some exponents. Let us now go into details.

Let k be $\lfloor \log_2 e \rfloor$ so that $e = \sum_{i=0}^{k} e[i] 2^{k-i}$, where $e[i]$ is the i-th most significant bit of e. We denote by e_j the integer made of the $j+1$ most significant bits of e, that is $\sum_{i=0}^{j} e[i] 2^{j-i}$. Note that we have $e_k = e$ and $e_0 = e[0] = 1$. Finally, $<e>$ denote the Hamming weight of e, that is $\sum_{i=0}^{k} e[i]$.

Now we perform a sequence of operations reflecting a square-and-multiply exponentiation.

Protocol 3.

---

1. $\mathcal{V}$ chooses at random a generator h of G and sends it to $\mathcal{P}$.
2. $\mathcal{P}$ chooses at random $k+1$ secret exponents r_0 through r_k, as well as $<e> -1$ random exponents s_i for all $i \in [1, k]$ such that $e[i] = 1$. Then the following values are made public:

$$v_i = g^{x^{e_i}} h^{r_i} \quad \text{for all } i \in [0.k]$$
$$w_i = g^{x^{2e_{i-1}}} h^{s_i} \quad \text{for all } i \in [1, k] \text{ such that } e[i] = 1$$

3. $\mathcal{P}$ performs the following proof of knowledge:

$$ZKPK\Big[\sigma_0, \ldots, \sigma_k, \rho_0, \ldots, \rho_k \ : \ v_0 = g^{\sigma_0} h^{\rho_0} \ \wedge$$
$$\Big(\bigwedge_{i=1}^{k} \big(v_i = g^{\sigma_i} h^{\rho_i} \wedge (\sigma_i = \sigma_0^{e[i]} \sigma_{i-1}^2)\big)\Big) \wedge y = g^{\sigma_k}\Big] \qquad (2)$$

Note that according to Theorem 1, a statement of the form $\sigma_i = \sigma_0^{e[i]} \sigma_{i-1}^2$ can be demonstrated by proving an additional representation of the form $v_i = v_{i-1}^{\sigma_{i-1}} h^{t_i}$ in case $e[i] = 0$ and two additional representations of the form $v_i = w_{i-1}^{\sigma_0} h^{t_i} \wedge w_{i-1} = v_{i-1}^{\sigma_{i-1}} h^{t'_i}$ in case $e[i] = 1$.

Theorem 2. *Let g be a generator of G and e be a $(k+1)$-bit integer of Hamming weight $<e>$. Then under lemma 1, **Protocol 3** is a zero-knowledge proof of knowledge of the e-th root of the discrete logarithm of y to the base g.*

Proof. We have to show the following three properties.

Completeness. Consider $\mathcal{P}$ who knows all values $x, \{r_i\}, \{s_j\}$. An easy verification ensures that for all $i \in [0, k]$, $\sigma_i = x^{e_i}$ and $\rho_i = r_i$ form a correct set of secrets for the protocol, since we have $\sigma_i = x^{e_i} = x^{e[i]+2e_{i-1}} = x^{e[i]}(x^{e_{i-1}})^2 = \sigma_0^{e[i]} \sigma_{i-1}^2$.

Soundness. The soundness property is computational. If h is randomly chosen by the verifier, lemma 1 applies and we can consider a knowledge extractor $\mathcal{E}$ for the proof (2). Let $(z_0, \ldots, z_k, r_0, \ldots, r_k)$ the secrets extracted by $\mathcal{E}$. One can easily check that for any $i \in [1, k]$ one has: $z_i = z_0^{e_i}$ and in particular $z_k = z_0^e$. Therefore, $y = g^{z_0^e}$, that is, z_0 is the e-th root of the discrete logarithm of y to the base g.

Zero-Knowledge. It is easy to see that if the $\{r_i\}$ and $\{s_j\}$ are uniformly distributed over $\mathbb{Z}_q$, no information is leaked when revealing $v_0, \ldots, v_k$ and the w_i's. Also the proof performed in the third step of the protocol is zero-knowledge and thus does not reveal anything either.   □

5   How to Deny a Predicate

5.1   Motivation

We now turn to the second contribution of our work. In this section, we explain how a prover can convince a verifier that he knows some secret values $(x_1, \ldots, x_k)$ which verify some equalities but do not verify other ones. Generalization to negate several predicates is easy. The technique can be useful in several situations:

1. A user wants to prove that he did not use a particular secret or random value in some signature or encryption he produced.
2. The prover has committed to some values x_i and wants to prove $\prod_i g_i^{x_i} \neq Y$ for a public value Y (whose representation is not known).

The protocols proposed by Brands [4] can solve the first example, but not the second one. Briefly speaking, these protocols allow a prover $\mathcal{P}$ holding a secret x *namely a discrete logarithm* to convince any verifier $\mathcal{V}$ that x differs from another *known* discrete logarithm. The main (and indeed, critical) point of these protocols, is that the prover must know these two secrets in order to perform the interaction.

What if the prover wants to demonstrate a statement like: "I know the discrete log of y to the base g, and it differs from the (unknown) discrete log of z to the base h" ? Consider the situation where Alice's public key is $Y_A = g^{x_A}$ and Bob's public key is $Y_B = h^{x_B}$. Alice knows x_A but not x_B; at the same time, she can easily verify that $x_A \neq x_B$ by computing h^{x_A}, which then must differ from Y_B. This is not achievable by Brands' protocols in which one needs to know both x_A and x_B at the same time.

That's why we claim that, even for linear relations, Brands' method only applies to a restricted class of non-monotone predicates. Indeed, Brands consider only predicates where relations hold in $\mathbb{Z}_q$. Our consider the case of relations between data obtained by exponentiating these secrets, namely, relations holding in G. This clearly leads to a larger class of formulae.

The following theorem illustrate the previously known result:

Proposition 1 (Brands, [4]). *We denote by (x_1, x_2) the set of secrets known to $\mathcal{P}$ and by $h \in G$ the (public) product $g_1^{x_1} g_2^{x_2}$. Let $T(\sigma_1, \sigma_2)$ be the predicate: $h = g_1^{\sigma_1} g_2^{\sigma_2}$ and a, b be some public values in $\mathbb{Z}_q$.*

Then, under lemma 1, $\mathcal{P}$ can prove the predicate $T'(\sigma_1, \sigma_2) = T(\sigma_1, \sigma_2) \wedge (\sigma_1 \neq a + b\sigma_2)$ if and only if it is able to prove knowledge of a representation of g_1 with respect to $g_1^a h^{-1}$ and $g_1^b g_2$.

The sketch of the proof consists in considering a knowledge extractor for the representation of g_1 and to use lemma 1 to identify these representations with the trivial representation of g_1.

5.2   Equivalent Formulation of a Negation

We are based on the fact that denying an atomic predicate is equivalent to proving a conjunction of representation predicates, relative to some well-chosen public parameters. This is also the underlying idea in [4]. But our protocol uses additional values, which allow "blinding" techniques. Some examples of this technique can be found in [12,6].

A Basic Situation. We consider Alice holding public key $Y_A = g^{x_A}$. Bob's public key is Y_B, but the corresponding secret key $X_B = \log_h Y_B$ is, of course, not known. If Alice wants to prove that she is actually Alice and not Bob, she runs the following protocol.

Protocol 4.

---

1. $\mathcal{P}$ chooses an exponent $r \in_R \mathbb{Z}_q^*$ and gives to the verifier $w = (h^{x_A}/Y_B)^r$.
2. The verifier $\mathcal{V}$ checks that $w \neq 1$.
3. $\mathcal{P}$ proves the following predicate:

$$ZKPK\,[\sigma, \rho, \tau \quad : \quad (Y_A = g^\sigma) \wedge (w = h^\tau / Y_B^\rho) \wedge (\tau = \sigma\rho)] \quad (3)$$

Theorem 3. *The above protocol is a zero-knowledge proof of knowledge for the predicate $T(\sigma) : Y_A = g^\sigma \wedge (\sigma \neq \log_h Y_B)$, provided that lemma 1 holds.*

Proof. **Completeness.** Verification is straightforward.

Soundness. The soundness property is computational. Since h and Y_B are not chosen by $\mathcal{P}$, lemma 1 applies and we can consider a knowledge extractor $\mathcal{E}$ for the proof (3). Let (s, r, t) the secrets extracted by $\mathcal{E}$. According to (3), we have $t = sr$ which leads to $w = h^t Y_B^{-r} = (h^s/Y_B)^r$. Consequently, the fact that $w \neq 1$ implies $h^s \neq Y_B$, that is $s \neq \log_h Y_B$. Hence, returning s makes an extractor for predicate $Y_A = g^\sigma \wedge (\sigma \neq \log_h Y_B)$.

Zero-Knowledge. Since h^{x_A}/Y_B is a generator with overwhelming probability (in fact, this is always the case if q is a prime), w is completely random over $G \backslash \{1\}$ if r is uniformly distributed over $\mathbb{Z}_q^*$. It follows that neither w nor the zero-knowledge proof performed in the third step does reveal helpful information. $\square$

General Linear Relations. We now consider $\mathcal{P}$ holding $(x_1, \ldots, x_k)$ and whose public key is $h = \prod_1^k g_i^{x_i}$, where π is an adequate permutation. Let $(\alpha_0, \ldots, \alpha_k)$ some fixed coefficients, Y be a public element in G (whose no representation is known) and (T) be the following predicate:

$$\neg(\log_g Y = \alpha_0 + \alpha_1 x_1 + \cdots + \alpha_k x_k \bmod q)$$

Note the validity of such predicate can clearly be checked by $\mathcal{P}$ by raising g to the power of the above linear combination. Now assume $\mathcal{P}$ wants to convince $\mathcal{V}$ of the validity of the statement without revealing the x_i's. To that goal, $\mathcal{P}$ runs the following protocol:

Protocol 5.

---

1. $\mathcal{P}$ chooses $r \in_R \mathbb{Z}_q^*$ and sends $w = (g^{\alpha_0 + \alpha_1 x_1 + \cdots + \alpha_k x_k}/Y)^r$ to $\mathcal{V}$.
2. The verifier $\mathcal{V}$ checks that $w \neq 1$.
3. $\mathcal{P}$ proves knowledge for the following predicate on variables $\rho, \sigma, \tau, \omega_1, \ldots, \omega_k$:

$$ZKPK\left[\rho, \sigma, \tau, \omega_i \; : \; \left(hg^{\alpha_0} = g^\sigma \prod_{i=1}^k \left(g^{-\alpha_i} g_i\right)^{\omega_i}\right) \wedge \left(w = g^\tau/Y^\rho\right) \wedge \left(\tau = \rho\sigma\right)\right]$$

Corollary 2. *The above* **Protocol 5** *is a proof of knowledge for the predicate* $T(\omega_i) \; : \; h = \prod(g_i^{\omega_i}) \wedge (\alpha_0 + \alpha_1\omega_1 + \cdots + \alpha_k\omega_k \neq \log_g Y \bmod q)$, *provided that lemma 1 holds.*

Proof. **Completeness.** Verification is straightforward.

Soundness. The soundness property is computational. Since g and Y are not chosen by $\mathcal{P}$, lemma 1 applies and we can consider a knowledge extractor $\mathcal{E}$ for the above proof in step 3. Let $(s, r, t, u_1, \ldots, u_k)$ the secrets extracted by $\mathcal{E}$. Since $\mathcal{P}$ cannot know two different representations of h with respect to $g_1, \ldots, g_k$, we have with overwhelming probability $s = \alpha_0 + \sum_1^k \alpha_i u_i$. Also the second statement and the third one lead to $w = g^{rs}/Y^r = (g^s/Y)^r$. From $w \neq 1$, it follows that $s = \alpha_0 + \sum_1^k \alpha_i u_i \neq \log_g Y$. Hence, returning $u_1, \ldots, u_k$ makes an extractor for predicate $h = \prod(g_i^{\omega_i}) \wedge (\alpha_0 + \alpha_1\omega_1 + \cdots + \alpha_k\omega_k \neq \log_g Y)$.

Zero-Knowledge. Since $g^{\alpha_0 + \cdots + \alpha_k x_k}/Y$ is a generator of the cyclic group G with overwhelming probability, w is completely random over $G\backslash\{1\}$ if r is uniformly distributed over $\mathbb{Z}_q^*$. It follows that neither w nor the zero-knowledge proof performed in the third step does reveal helpful information. □

6   Applications

In this section, we show some applications of our technique to classical group signature schemes. We emphasize that our solutions are generic, and we define a class of group signature schemes for which we can get some additional properties. Such schemes are derived from some general schemes for large groups originally proposed in 1997 by Camenish and Stadler [10].

6.1   Group Signatures

The concept of group signature, although extremely useful, appeared relatively recently in cryptography [16,18]. It allows a member of a group to sign documents anonymously on behalf of the group, in an unlinkable but publicly verifiable way. As a feature, a group signature scheme considers a *group leader*, also called *group manager*. The group manager deals with membership, and is allowed to "open" a group signature in order to reveal the identity of the actual signer. This can be necessary in case of legal dispute. However, he is not a trusted party and the security of a group signature scheme must consider attacks involving him. To provide separability, we can consider two different entities, a *membership manager* and a *revocation manager*. The latter should be needed only to open signatures. Separability is considered in [9,24]. However, in this paper, and to avoid confusion in the context of member exclusion, we call him the *judge* rather than the revocation manager.

A group signature scheme consists of the following five procedures:

- KEY GENERATION ($\mathcal{KG}$) : provides every player with its initial data.
- JOIN ($\mathcal{J}$) : adds a member to a group.
- SIGN ($\mathcal{S}$) allows a member to sign messages.
- VERIFY ($\mathcal{V}$) : checks validity of a group signature.
- OPEN (Ω) : allows an authority to reveal the identity of a signer.

Requirements. We briefly recall the desirable security requirements for a group signature scheme. Additionally to the usual properties of correctness (i.e., a correctly generated signature is always accepted by the verification algorithm), a group signature scheme must ensure that signatures are anonymous and unlinkable: it must be computationally infeasible to find the identity of the signer within the group. Moreover, deciding whether two signatures have been issued by the same member has to be hard. Also the scheme must ensure that opening is always possible, without cheating (i.e. the judge, when revealing the signer's identity, cannot falsely accuse an honest member). The last property is coalition resistance, which have been proven for the first time in the recent scheme [1]. Coalition resistance means that a subset of dishonest members cannot generate a valid group signature which, in case of opening, would reveal an honest (non-colluding) member as the signer.

6.2   A Class of Group Signature Schemes

The class of group signatures that we define contains the most recent and efficient schemes [1,8,10]. It is characterized by the following criteria:

- Computations are made in a group $G = \langle g \rangle$ in which the discrete logarithm problem is hard.
- The *judge* holds an ElGamal public key $y = g^w$ which is an element of G. The secret key is w.

- When registering, each member chooses a secret *membership key* x and receives a *membership certificate* for which demonstration of the corresponding secret key can be done using disjunctive-conjunctive representation predicate as defined in section 2.
- A group signature on a message m consists of a verifiable ElGamal encryption, under the judge's public key, of the public membership key, as well as an *anonymous* ZK proof of knowledge for the membership certificate and the corresponding secret key. It means that the proof can be verified using only the group public key, and not a particular member's key. We generically denote by $\mathcal{T}$ the underlying predicate contained in the zero-knowledge proof, and by (A, B) the ElGamal encryption containing the signer's identity.

Definition 1 (Camenish-Stadler -derived group signatures). *We call a CS-Group Signature Scheme any group signature scheme that uses algorithms matching the above features.*

6.3   Member Revocation

In this section, we illustrate the use of our technique to achieve member revocation in a group signature scheme. Revocation of members consists in preventing some officially excluded members to sign document on behalf of the group (for instance, after some abusive use). The general and most delicate problem encountered is how to preserve anonymity of *past signatures* for a revoked member? For instance, if one reveals its secret key, its previously issued signatures might be linked, which is undesirable.

We provided the first solution to the member revocation problem in [6]. We explain below how it is related to our general technique. Later, Song [27] proposed a slightly different solution; the resulting scheme is more efficient (in constant size rather than in linear size), however, it *implicitly* assumes that the registration of a new member is done using an authentic, private channel between the membership manager and the joining member[1]; nevertheless such an assumption follows [1]. Note that this is not necessarily the case in [6], where the revocation mechanism is done via Zero-Knowledge proofs, and was originally designed for [10]. In this section, we propose a more abstract and general framework which allows such member revocation for all efficient recent schemes [1,8, 10].

6.4   Our Method

We can use the technique of section 5 to build a revocation feature for any CS-group signature scheme. The protocol described in section 5 can be used to demonstrate that a given fair ElGamal encryption $(A, B) = (g^r, Y_A y^r)$ does

---

[1] If it is not the case, any signature can be opened in a linear time (in the number of members).

not contain a fixed plaintext Y_B. To do so, it is sufficient to prove the following predicate:

$$ZKPK\Big[\rho \; : \; \rho = \log_y(B/Y) \neq \log_g A\Big]$$

This yields to a simple mechanism of revocation. Firstly, the authority publishes via a CRL (Certificate Revocation List) the identities of revoked members. Now, the signer becomes able to show anonymously that he is not on the blacklist using non-montone DCR-proofs, since a CS-group signature is partially made of an ElGamal encryption of the signer's identity.

Theorem 4. *Let S be a CS-group signature scheme and let us denote (A, B) the ElGamal encryption of the signer's identity, and $\mathcal{T}(\sigma_i)$ the predicate contained in the zero-knowledge proof of knowledge. Then member revocation is achieved by proving the following predicate instead of $\mathcal{T}$:*

$$ZKPK\Big[\rho, \sigma_i \; : \; (\mathcal{T}(\sigma_i)) \wedge A = g^\rho \wedge \rho \neq \log_y(B/Y)\Big] \tag{4}$$

where Y is the identity of a revoked member.

The generic transformation thus works as follows. Instead of proving $\mathcal{T}$ when signing a document, a member is required to prove (4), that is to show that he holds a membership certificate, but that he is not a revoked member. If several members are revoked, one has to prove a linear number of negations. We refer the reader to [6] for further details.

6.5   Multi-signer Group Signatures

We are now interested in providing multi-signer features to any CS-group signature scheme. A multi-signer mechanism for a group signature scheme consists in generating extended group signatures that can convince a verifier that a minimal number of members have actually cooperated to produce the signature, while hiding their identity at the same time. In other words, the signers (e.g., the majority among a board of directors), can prove they have cooperatively generated such a signature, while remaining anonymous. The main point lies in the fact that a group signatures being anonymous, the signers have to prove that the same group member did not sign many times.

A multi-signer (threshold) feature is of interest when a document needs to be signed by several persons who cooperate to authenticate the document while hiding their identities. For instance, several parties have to agree on a contract and prove that at least half of the group signed it, without revealing exactly who. In this section, we show how to extend our result in section 5 to correctly provide an efficient solution to such a scenario. We consider the case where two signers want to cooperate, and refer this scenario as a *double-signer mechanism*.

We first note that the problem is different from the one of member revocation. In the former, the signer has to prove that the identity contained in the signature (within the ElGamal encryption) differs from a *public* value, namely the identity of the revoked member. The subtlety in proving that two members $\mathcal{P}_1$ and $\mathcal{P}_2$ have actually signed is that one must prove that the identity in the first encryption differs from the *hidden* identity contained in the second encryption. More formally, if member $\mathcal{P}_1$ and member $\mathcal{P}_2$ have encrypted their respective identities Y_1 and Y_2 under ElGamal, using the judge's public key (g, y) they have to prove in Zero-Knowledge that $Y_1 \neq Y_2$. A first solution has been proposed in [7, p.118]. However, this solution was designed to suit the scheme by Camenisch and Stadler [10] only. Our solution is more generic, and can be applied to more efficient and secure scheme, such like [1].

We present the following protocol:

Protocol 6.

---

1. $\mathcal{P}_1$ and $\mathcal{P}_2$ choose an exponent $u \in_R \mathbb{Z}_q^*$ and compute $T = (Y_1/Y_2)^u$. They send it to $\mathcal{V}$.
2. $\mathcal{V}$ checks that $T \neq 1$.
3. $\mathcal{P}_1$ and $\mathcal{P}_2$ prove knowledge for the following predicate:

$$\left[\sigma_1, \sigma_2, \rho, \tau \; : \; A_1 = g^{\sigma_1} \wedge A_2 = g^{\sigma_2} \wedge T = (B_1/B_2)^{\rho} y^{\tau} \wedge \left(\frac{A_1}{A_2} \right)^{\rho} = g^{-\tau} \right]$$

Theorem 5. *Under lemma 1, the above protocol is a proof of knowledge of (μ, ν) for the predicate: $T(\sigma_1, \sigma_2) \; : \; (A_1 = g^{\sigma_1}) \wedge (B_1 = Y_1 y^{\sigma_1}) \wedge (A_2 = g^{\sigma_2}) \wedge (B_2 = Y_2 y^{\sigma_2}) \wedge (Y_1 \neq Y_2)$*

Proof. Let $(A_1, B_1) = (g^r, y^r Y_1)$ and $(A_2, B_2) = (g^s, y^s Y_2)$ be the encryptions of Y_1 and Y_2, respectively.

Completeness. Verification is easy.

Soundness. Let $\mathcal{E}$ be an extractor for the proof of knowledge performed in the third step of the protocol and (s_1, s_2, r, t) be the values output by $\mathcal{E}$. From the first, second and fourth statement, we get: $(s_1 - s_2)r = -t$. It follows that:

$$T = \left(\frac{B_1/y^{s_1}}{B_2/y^{s_2}} \right)^r$$

Consequently the fact that T differs from 1 ensures that the plaintext corresponding to (A_1, B_1) differs from the plaintext corresponding to (A_2, B_2). Hence, returning (s_1, s_2) makes a knowledge extractor for the predicate: $T(\sigma_1, \sigma_2) \; : \; (A_1 = g^{\sigma_1}) \wedge (B_1 = Y_1 y^{\sigma_1}) \wedge (A_2 = g^{\sigma_2}) \wedge (B_2 = Y_2 y^{\sigma_2}) \wedge (Y_1 \neq Y_2)$.

Zero-Knowledge. We note that if r and s are randomly chosen, B_1/B_2 is a generator with overwhelming probability, thus T is randomly distributed over $G \backslash \{1\}$. Also the proof performed in step 3 does not leak any information neither. $\qquad \square$

Corollary 3. *Let S be a CS-group signature scheme in which a signature is made of an ElGamal encryption (A, B) of the signer's identity, together with a proof of knowledge for a predicate $T(\rho_i)$. Then a double-signer mechanism is achieved by providing in the signature*

- $(A_1, B_1) = (g^{s_1}, h^{s_1} Y_1)$ and $(A_2, B_2) = (g^{s_2}, h^{s_2} Y_2)$ for $s_1, s_2 \in_R \mathbb{Z}_q^*$.
- the following proof of knowledge:

$$ZKPK\Big[\rho_i^1, \rho_i^2, \sigma_1, \sigma_2) \; : \; \mathcal{T}(\rho_i^1) \; \wedge \; \mathcal{T}(\rho_i^2) \; \wedge \; (A_1 = g^{\sigma_1}) \; \wedge \; (B_1 = Y_1 y^{\sigma_1})$$
$$\wedge \; (A_2 = g^{\sigma_2}) \; \wedge \; (B_2 = Y_2 y^{\sigma_2}) \; \wedge \; (Y_1 \neq Y_2)\Big]$$

where Y_1, Y_2 are the identities of two different signers.

Proof. It is easy to see that the first two ElGamal encryptions allows the judge to recover the signers' identities. Also the zero-knowledge proof can be generated only by two different members (soundness). Finally, the signature is anonymous (apart the fact that two people have signed) and unlinkable , due to the security of ElGamal and the zero-knowledgeness. □

7   Conclusion

In this paper, we extended in several ways the class of boolean predicates that can be efficiently proved by means of zero-knowledge proofs. We showed how to compose such predicates to demonstrate polynomial relations among variables, as well as negations of predicates. Also we gave generic applications of such mechanisms to group signature schemes.

References

1. G. Ateniese, J. Camenisch, M. Joye, and G. Tsudik. A practical and provably secure coalition-resistant group signature scheme. In M. Bellare, editor, *Proc. of Crypto '00*, volume 1880 of *LNCS*, pages 255–270. Springer-Verlag, August 2000.
2. M. Bellare and P. Rogaway. Random oracles are practical: a paradigm for designing efficient protocols. In *Proc. of ACM CCS '93*, pages 62–73. ACM Press, November 1993.
3. S. A. Brands. Untraceable off-line cash in wallets with observers. In D. R. Stinson, editor, *Proc. of Crypto '93*, volume 773 of *LNCS*, pages 302–318. Springer-Verlag, August 1994.
4. S. A. Brands. Rapid demonstration of linear relations connected by boolean operators. In W. Fumy, editor, *Proc. of Eurocrypt '97*, volume 1233 of *LNCS*, pages 318–333. Springer-Verlag, May 1997.
5. G. Brassard and C. Crépeau. Non transitive transfer of confidence: a perfect zero-knowledge interactive protocol for SAT and beyond. In *Proc. of FOCS '86*, pages 188–195. IEEE Press, October 1986.
6. E. Bresson and J. Stern. Efficient revocation in group signatures. In K. Kim, editor, *Proc. of PKC '01*, volume 1992 of *LNCS*, pages 190–206. Springer-Verlag, February 2001.
7. J. Camenisch. *Group Signature Schemes and Payment Systems Based on the Discrete Logarithm Problem*. PhD thesis, ETH Zürich, 1998.
8. J. Camenisch and M. Michels. A group signature scheme with improved efficiency. In K. Ohta and D. Pei, editors, *Proc. of Asiacrypt '98*, volume 1514 of *LNCS*, pages 160–174. Springer-Verlag, October 1999.

9. J. Camenisch and M. Michels. Separability and efficiency for generic group signature schemes. In M. Wiener, editor, *Proc. of Crypto '99*, volume 1666 of *LNCS*, pages 106–121. Springer-Verlag, August 1999.
10. J. Camenisch and M. Stadler. Efficient group signatures schemes for large groups. In B. Kaliski, editor, *Proc. of Crypto '97*, volume 1294 of *LNCS*, pages 410–424. Springer-Verlag, August 1997.
11. J. Camenisch and M. Stadler. Proofs systems for general statements about discrete logarithms. Technical Report TR 260, ETH Zürich, Zürich, CH, March 1997.
12. R. Canetti and S. Goldwasser. An efficient threshold PKC secure against adaptive CCA. In J. Stern, editor, *Proc. of Eurocrypt '99*, volume 1592 of *LNCS*, pages 90–106. Springer-Verlag, May 1999.
13. D. Chaum. Demonstrating that a public predicate can be satisfied without revealing any information about how. In A. M. Odlyzko, editor, *Proc. of Crypto '86*, volume 263 of *LNCS*, pages 195–199. Springer-Verlag, August 1986.
14. D. Chaum, J. H. Evertse, and J. van de Graaf. An improved protocol for demonstrating possession of discrete logarithms and some generalizations. In D. Chaum and W. L. Price, editors, *Proc. of Eurocrypt '87*, volume 304 of *LNCS*, pages 127–141. Springer-Verlag, May 1987.
15. D. Chaum, J. H. Evertse, J. van de Graaf, and R. Peralta. Demonstrating possession of a discrete logarithm without revealing it. In A. M. Odlyzko, editor, *Proc. of Crypto '86*, volume 263 of *LNCS*, pages 200–212. Springer-Verlag, August 1986.
16. D. Chaum and E. van Heyst. Group signatures. In D. W. Davies, editor, *Proc. of Eurocrypt '91*, volume 547 of *LNCS*, pages 257–265. Springer-Verlag, May 1992.
17. D. Chaum, E. van Heyst, and B. Pfitzmann. Cryptographically strong undeniable signatures, unconditionally secure for the signer. In J. Feigenbaum, editor, *Proc. of Crypto '91*, volume 576 of *LNCS*, pages 470–484. Springer-Verlag, August 1992.
18. L. Chen and T. P. Pedersen. New group signature schemes. In A. De Santis, editor, *Proc. of Eurocrypt '94*, volume 950 of *LNCS*, pages 171–181. Springer-Verlag, May 1995.
19. R. Cramer, I. B. Damgård, and B. Schoenmakers. Proofs of partial knowledge and simplified design of witness hiding protocols. In Y. G. Desmedt, editor, *Proc. of Crypto '94*, volume 839 of *LNCS*, pages 174–187. Springer-Verlag, August 1994.
20. U. Feige, A. Fiat, and A. Shamir. Zero-knowledge proofs of identity. *J. of Cryptology*, 1(2):77–94, Summer 1988.
21. A. Fiat and A. Shamir. How to prove yourself : Practical solutions to identification and signature problems. In A. M. Odlyzko, editor, *Proc. of Crypto '86*, volume 263 of *LNCS*, pages 186–194. Springer-Verlag, August 1986.
22. Z. Galil, S. Haber, and M. Yung. A private interactive test of a boolean predicate and minimum-knowledge public key cryptosystem. In *Proc. of FOCS '85*, pages 360–371. IEEE Press, October 1985.
23. S. Goldwasser, S. Micali, and C. W. Rackoff. Knowledge complexity of interactive proofs. In *Proc. of STOC '85*, pages 291–304. ACM Press, May 1985.
24. J. Kilian and E. Petrank. Identity escrow. In H. Krawczyk, editor, *Proc. of Crypto '98*, volume 1462 of *LNCS*, pages 169–185. Springer-Verlag, August 1998.
25. A. De Santis, G. Di Crescenzo, G. Persiano, and M. Yung. On monotone formula closure of SZK. In *Proc. of FOCS '94*, pages 454–465. IEEE Press, November 1994.
26. B. Schoenmakers. Efficient proofs of or. Manuscript, 1993.
27. D. X. Song. Practical forward secure group signature schemes. In P. Samarati, editor, *ACM CCS '01*, pages 225–234. ACM Press, November 2001.
28. M. Stadler. Publicly verifiable secret sharing. In U. M. Maurer, editor, *Proc. of Eurocrypt '96*, volume 1070 of *LNCS*, pages 190–199. Springer-Verlag, May 1996.

Inversion/Division Systolic Architecture for Public-Key Cryptosystems in $GF(2^m)$

Nam-Yeun Kim[1], Dae-Ghon Kho[2], and Kee-Young Yoo[1]

[1] Department of Computer Engineering,
Kyungpook National University, Deagu, KOREA 702-701
knyeun@hanmail.net, yook@knu.ac.kr
[2] Department of Computer Education,
Daegu National University of Education, Daegu, KOREA, 705-715
jdkho@taegu-e.ac.kr

Abstract. Finite field arithmetic operations have been widely used in the areas of network security and data communication applications, and high-speed and low-complexity design for finite field arithmetic is very necessary for these applications. The current paper presents a new AB^2 algorithm along with its systolic implementations in $GF(2^m)$. The proposed algorithm is based on the MSB-first scheme using the standard basis representation. In addition, parallel-in parallel-out systolic architectures are also introduced using this algorithm as a foundation. The proposed architectures have a low hardware complexity and small latency compared to conventional architectures. In particular, the hardware complexity of AB^2 and inversion/division array are about 25% lower than Wang's over $GF(2^m)$, while the latency of AB^2 and inversion/division array are about 40% and 49.6% lower, respectively. Furthermore, since the proposed architectures incorporate simplicity, regularity, modularity, and pipelinability, they are well suited to VLSI implementation and can also be utilized as the basic architecture for a crypto-processor.

1 Introduction

Finite fields $GF(2^m)$ are widely used in communication areas, such as error-correcting codes [1], cryptography [2, 3, 4], digital signal processing [5], and so on. As such, a high speed and low-complexity design for finite field arithmetic is crucial for better security, wider bandwidths, and higher portability in personal communications [6].

Finite field architectures are classified into three types according to the basis representation of the field elements; standard, normal, and dual basis. The standard basis and normal basis representations are used for cryptographic applications, however, the dual basis representation is unsuitable for the large finite fields involved in cryptography [7]. The normal basis representation is very efficient for performing squaring, exponentiation or finding the inverse element, while normal-basis multipliers need a basis conversion. The standard basis offers

A.H. Chan and V. Gligor (Eds.): ISC 2002, LNCS 2433, pp. 289–299, 2002.

the most regular and extensible features for hardware implementation and is easiest to use among the other representations [7]. Therefore, the current paper uses the standard basis representation.

Addition, multiplication, exponentiation, and inversion are the most important computations in finite field arithmetic [1]. Among these finite field operations, the power-sum $(AB^2 + C)$ has already been established as an efficient basic operation for public key cryptosystems [3, 4, 5] over $GF(2^m)$. For example, when implementing a non-supersingular Elliptic Curve Cryptosystem(ECC) over $GF(2^m)$, the sum of two points on the elliptic curve requires a number of multiplications, inversions, and additions. The inverse operation can be computed by applying Fermat's theorem: $x^{2^m} = x$ for all $x \in GF(2^m)$, which takes m multiplications to complete the inverse operation (x^{-1}). In this case, AB^2 operations can also be used as an efficient method. However, since these operations are rather time-consuming, they require the design of high-speed and low-complexity circuits.

For a high-speed multiplier over $GF(2^m)$, Jain [8] proposed the LSB and MSB-first algorithms for multiplication, squaring, and exponentiation using semi-systolic arrays. However, the broadcasting problem becomes more difficult when the bit length m becomes larger. For a simple cell complexity, Lee [9] developed the $AB^2 + C$ bit-parallel systolic architecture in $GF(2^m)$ based on irreducible all one polynomials(AOP) of degree m, plus various other bit-parallel low-complexity multipliers have been proposed for cryptographic applications, for example, those in [10]. Recently, Wei [11] and Wang et al.[12] both proposed multipliers for $AB^2 + C$ computing over $GF(2^m)$, however, none are very suitable for cryptographic applications, due to the complexity and latency involved.

Conventional approaches for computing inversion and division in $GF(2^m)$ include the table lookup method and Euclid's algorithm. Yet neither method is easily realized in a VLSI circuit when large fields are used [12]. To overcome this problem, a number of systolic architectures for computing inverses and divisions in $GF(2^m)$ have been reported in previous literature. Wang et al. [12] proposed a parallel-in parallel-out systolic array with a maximum throughout for computing inversion/division in $GF(2^m)$. Wei [13] developed three high-speed computation algorithms to perform exponentiations, multiplicative inversions, and divisions over $GF(2^m)$. However, their arrays still have some shortcomings for cryptographic applications due to their high circuit complexity and long latency. As such, further research on efficient inversion/division architectures is needed.

Accordingly, the current paper presents a new AB^2 algorithm along with the related systolic architectures. The proposed algorithm supports the MSB-first scheme with pipelinability. Moreover, the proposed AB^2 and inversion/division architectures can reduce the cell complexity and latency. In addition, the architectures are well suited to VLSI implementation and can be easily applied to crypto-processors.

The rest of the paper is organized as follows. Section 2 gives a description of the proposed AB^2 algorithm in $GF(2^m)$. Then parallel-in parallel-out AB^2 and inversion/division systolic architectures are presented in section 3. Their relative performances are analyzed in section 4 and some final conclusions are given in section 5.

2 Algorithm

The current paper considers the arithmetic operations in one of the extension fields of GF(2). The extension degree is denoted by m, so that the field can be represented as GF(2^m). A finite field GF(2^m) has 2^m elements and it is assumed that all the $(2^m - 1)$ non-zero elements of GF(2^m) are represented using the standard basis; $\{1, x^1, x^2, \cdots, x^{m-1}\}$. Let $A(x)$ and $B(x)$ be two elements in GF(2^m), where $A(x) = a_{m-1}x^{m-1} + a_{m-2}x^{m-2} + \cdots + a_1x + a_0$ and $B(x) = b_{m-1}x^{m-1} + b_{m-2}x^{m-2} + \cdots + b_1x + b_0$, where a_i and $b_i \in GF(2)(0 \leq i \leq m-1)$. A finite field of GF($2^m$) is isomorphic to GF(2)$[x]/F(x)$, where $F(x)$ is an irreducible polynomial of degree m over GF(2) that generates the field and is expressed as $F(x) = x^m + f_{m-1}x^{m-1} + f_{m-2}x^{m-2} + \cdots + f_1x + f_0$. If α is the root of $F(x)$, then $F(\alpha) = 0$, and $F(\alpha) \equiv \alpha^m = f_{m-1}\alpha^{m-1} + f_{m-2}\alpha^{m-2} + \cdots + f_1\alpha + f_0$, $F'(\alpha) \equiv \alpha^{m+1} = f'_{m-1}\alpha^{m-1} + f'_{m-2}\alpha^{m-2} + \cdots + f'_1\alpha + f'_0$ where f_i and $f'_i \in GF(2)(0 \leq i \leq m-1)$. To compute the AB^2 operation, the proposed algorithm commences with the following equation:

$$
\begin{aligned}
P &= AB^2 \bmod F(x) \\
&= A(b_{m-1}\alpha^{2m-2} + b_{m-2}\alpha^{2m-4} + \cdots + b_1\alpha^2 + b_0) \bmod F(x) \\
&= (\cdots(\cdots((Ab_{m-1})\alpha^2 \bmod F(x) + Ab_{m-2})\alpha^2 \bmod F(x) + \cdots + Ab_{m-i})\alpha^2 \\
&\quad \bmod F(x) + \cdots + Ab_1)\alpha^2 \bmod F(x) + Ab_0
\end{aligned}
\tag{1}
$$

where the computation sequence of eq.(1) is written as follows:

> Input   : $A(\alpha), B(\alpha)$ and $F(\alpha)$
> Output   : $P(\alpha) = A(\alpha)B(\alpha)^2 \bmod F(\alpha)$
> STEP 1 : $P_1 = Ab_{m-1} \bmod F(\alpha)$
> STEP 2 : For $i = 2$ to m
> STEP 3 : $P_i = (P_{i-1}\alpha^2 + Ab_{m-i}) \bmod F(\alpha)$

where the result P is equal to P_m. As shown in the upper computation sequence, the first term is very simple without any modulo reduction.
Beginning with the first term of eq.(1), Ab_{m-1}, the subsequent terms in the above equation are accumulated until reaching the end. The procedure of the new algorithm is as follows:
First,

$$
\begin{aligned}
P_1 &= Ab_{m-1} \\
&= \sum_{k=0}^{m-1} a_k b_{m-1}\alpha^k
\end{aligned}
$$

$$= \sum_{k=0}^{m-1} p_k^1 \alpha^k$$

$$(2)$$

where, eq. (3) can be obtained;

$$p_k^1 = a_k b_{m-1} \tag{3}$$

In the general case,

$$P_i = (P_{i-1}\alpha^2 + Ab_{m-i}) \bmod F(x)$$

$$= (\sum_{k=0}^{m-1} p_k^{i-1}\alpha^k\alpha^2 + \sum_{k=0}^{m-1} a_k b_{m-i}\alpha^k) \bmod F(x)$$

$$= (\sum_{k=0}^{m-1} p_k^{i-1}\alpha^{k+2} + \sum_{k=0}^{m-1} a_k b_{m-i}\alpha^k) \bmod F(x)$$

$$= (p_{m-1}^{i-1}\alpha^{m+1} + p_{m-2}^{i-1}\alpha^m + \cdots + p_0^{i-1}\alpha^2 + a_{m-1}b_{m-i}\alpha^{m-1} + a_{m-2}b_{m-i}\alpha^{m-2}$$
$$+ \cdots + a_1 b_{m-i}\alpha + a_0 b_{m-i}) \bmod F(x)$$

$$= \sum_{k=0}^{m-1} p_k^i \alpha^k$$

$$(4)$$

From the above procedures, eq. (5) can be derived.

$$p_k^i = p_{m-1}^{i-1} f_k' + p_{m-2}^{i-1} f_k + a_k b_{m-i} + p_{k-2}^{i-1}; \tag{5}$$

Thus the product P for AB^2 in $GF(2^m)$ can be computed efficiently using the above new algorithm.

3   Systolic Architectures in $GF(2^m)$

This section proposed a systolic AB^2 multiplier and a inversion/division systolic architecture.

3.1 AB^2 Multiplier

Based on the AB^2 algorithm, a corresponding parallel-in parallel-out AB^2 systolic architecture can be obtained by following the process in [14, 15]. Fig.1 shows the proposed systolic AB^2 circuit over $GF(2^4)$. The inputs A, F, and F' enter the array in parallel from the top row, while B is from the leftmost column. The output P is transmitted from the bottom row of the array in parallel. In Fig.1, there is a traverse line in the (i, k) cell. This is required to pass the signal from the $(i-1, k-1)$ cell to the $(i, k+1)$ cell. When the cell is located in the first row;

$k = m - 1$, p_k^i must be connected to the p_{m-1}^i signal line, while p_k^{i-1} must be connected to the p_{m-2}^i signal line. Fig. 2 shows PE1, which represents the logic circuits of the top cells of the array, while Fig. 3 shows PE2, which represents the logic basic circuits. Fig. 3 shows the basic cell for the general case where the circuit function is primarily governed by eq. (5), where the k-th bit (p_k^i) of P_i is the partial product. If the cell is located in the lowest two columns, p_{k-2}^{i-1} is zero. Note that the cells in the first row only need to calculate p_k^1, as shown in Fig. 2. As such, the top cell circuit is very simple and reduces the total cell complexity compared to previous architectures. Since the vertical path of each cell only requires two delay elements, except for the cells in the first row, the latency is $3m - 1$.

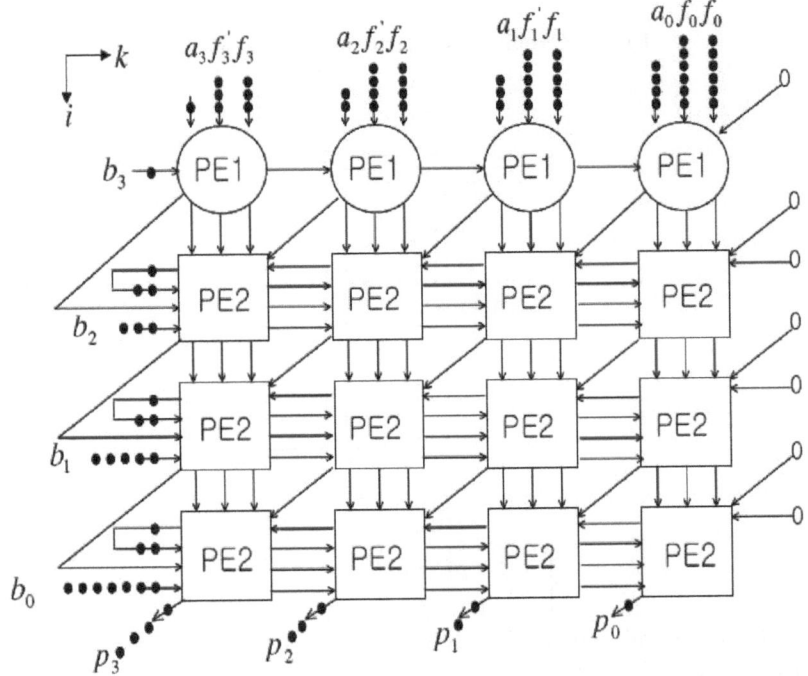

Fig. 1. Architecture for AB^2 in $GF(2^4)$

Another version of AB^2 multiplier can be derived by merging two adjacent cells of the Fig. 1 in the horizontal direction. The operation for AB^2 multiplication is changed as follows after the merging process as shown in Fig. 4. The top cell of the circuit in Fig. 4 computes the following two operations shown in Fig. 5:

$$p_k^0 = 0, 0 \le k \le m - 1;$$

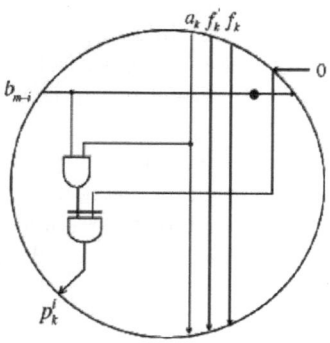

Fig. 2. Circuit for PE1(Processing Element 1)

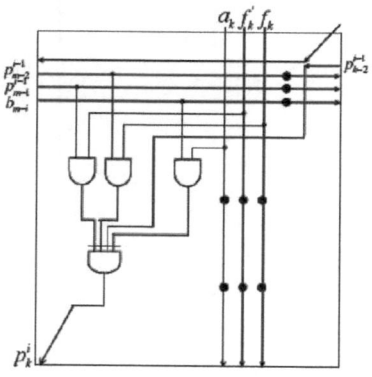

Fig. 3. Circuit for PE2

$$\begin{cases} p_k^1 = p_k^0 \oplus a_k b_{m-i}; \\ p_{k-1}^1 = p_{k-1}^0 \oplus a_{k-1} b_{m-i}; \end{cases}$$

the k-th general cell of Fig. 4 in iteration i computes the following four operations shown in Fig. 6;

$$p_{-1}^{i-1} = 0, 1 \le i \le m;$$

$$\begin{cases} p_k^i = p_{m-1}^{i-1} f_k' \oplus p_{m-2}^{i-1} f_k \oplus a_k b_{m-i} \oplus p_{k-2}^{i-1}; \\ p_{k-1}^i = p_{m-1}^{i-1} f_{k-1}' \oplus p_{m-2}^{i-1} f_{k-1} \oplus a_{k-1} b_{m-i} \oplus p_{k-3}^{i-1}; \end{cases}$$

Consequently, the top cell circuits are very simple and can reduce the total cell complexity compared to other related architectures. The output P is transmitted out of the bottom row of the array in parallel.

3.2   Inversion/Division Architecture

Finite field division in $GF(2^m)$ can be performed using multiplication and inversion, that is, $A/B = A^{-1}$, where the A and B are the elements of $GF(2^m)$.Here,

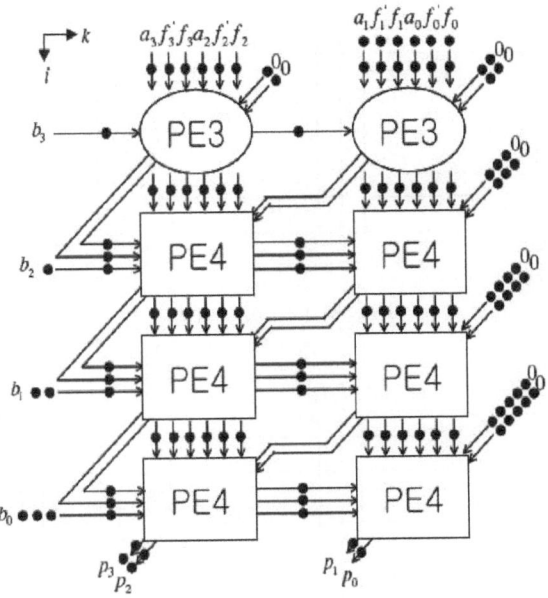

Fig. 4. Modified architecture for AB^2 in GF(2^4)

the multiplicative inverse of the field elements B can be obtained by recursive squaring and multiplication, since the field element B can be expressed as $B^{-1} = B^{2^m-2} = (B(B(B \cdots B(B(B)^2)^2 \cdots)^2)^2)^2$.

$$D = A \cdot B^{-1} = A(B(B(B \cdots B(B(B)^2)^2 \cdots)^2)^2)^2 \qquad (6)$$

Here, AB^2 operations can also be used as an efficient method. The equation can be computed as [13]:

STEP 1 : $R = B$;

STEP 2 : For $i = m - 2$ downto 1

STEP 3 : $R = B \cdot R^2$;

STEP 4 : $R = A \cdot R^2$;

The result is $R = A \cdot B^{-1}$ and when $A = 1$, the algorithm realizes the inversion operation B^{-1}. In this case, AB^2 operations can be used to compute the operations in steps 3 and 4. Fig. 7 shows a systolic architecture of inversion/division for GF(2^4), which consists of $m - 1$ AB^2 circuits. The architecture inputs two elements A and B, and two modulo polynomials, F and F', then obtains the output element $P = AB^{-1}$ or $P = B^{-1}$ (when $A = 1$). Elements B, F, and F' enter the first AB^2 circuit, while element A enters the last one after certain delays.

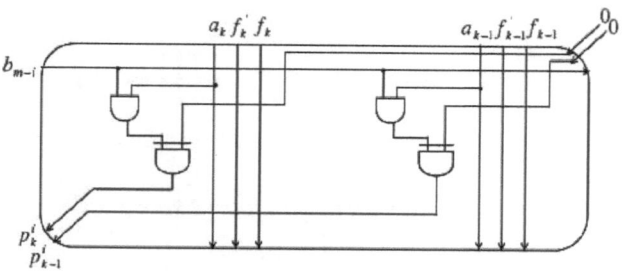

Fig. 5. Circuit for PE3

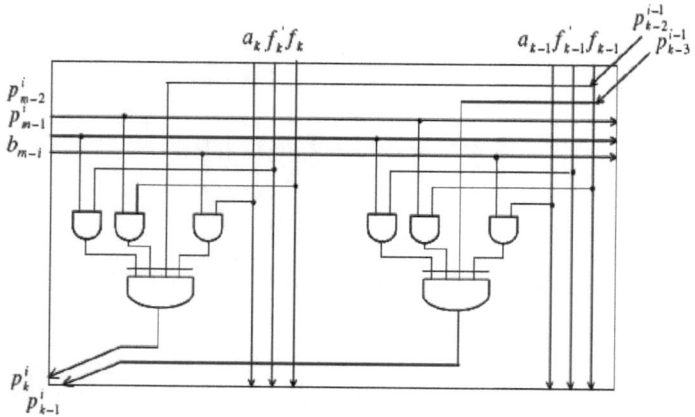

Fig. 6. Circuit for PE4

4   Analysis

The new arrays were simulated and verified using an ALTERA MAX+PLUS simulator and FLEX10K device. Tables 1 and 2 present comparisions between the proposed architectures and the related circuits described in [12]. The following assumptions were made in the comparison: 1) T_{AND2} and T_{XORi} denote the propagation delay through a 2-input AND gate and i-input XOR gate, respectively, and 2) the 3-input XOR gate and 4-input XOR gate were constructed using two and three 2-input XOR gates, respectively [16].

In table 1, it was assumed that the two arrays had the same propagation delay of $T_{AND2} + T_{XOR4}$ through one cell, as a result the proposed AB^2 architecture reduced the cell complexity by $m(\text{AND} + \text{XOR}) + (4m^2 + 3.5m)$Latches. The latency of the architecture in [12] was $2m + m/2$, whereas that of the proposed architecture was $m + \lceil m/2 \rceil$. That is, the hardware complexity and latency were approximately 25% and 40% lower than that for [12] in $GF(2^m)$, respectively. Table 2 compares two inversion/division arrays with the same propagation delay of $T_{AND2} + T_{XOR4}$ through one cell. It is clear that the proposed array was more efficient in terms of latency and cell complexity than [12]. The proposed

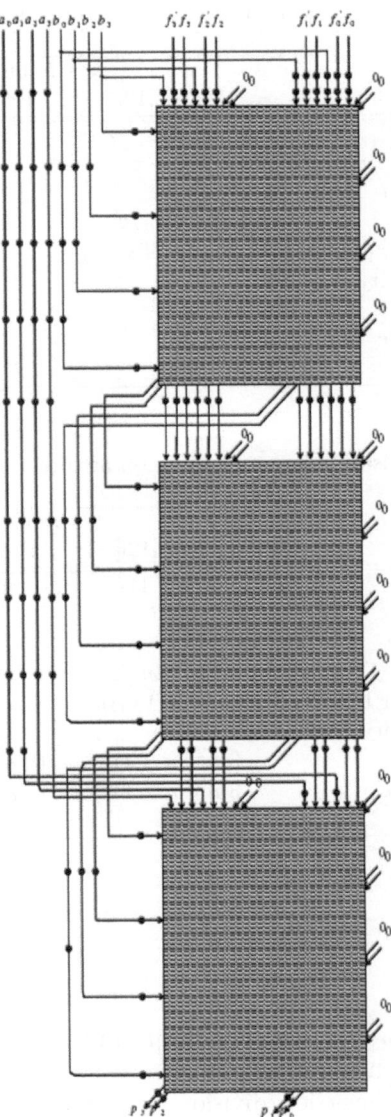

Fig. 7. Systolic architecture of inversion/division using Fig.4 in $GF(2^4)$

architecture reduced the cell complexity by $m(m-1)(\text{AND} + \text{XOR}) + (4m^2 + 3.5m)(m-1)$Latches. The latency of the architecture in [12] was $2m^2 - 3m/2$, whereas that of the proposed architecture was $m^2 - m/2$. That is, the latency of the proposed inversion/division arrays was 49.6% lower than that for [12] in $GF(2^m)$.

Table 1. Comparison of AB^2 architectures in GF(2^m)

Item	Circuit	
	Wang [12]	Proposed [Fig. 4]
No.of cells	$m^2/2$	$m \times \lceil m/2 \rceil$
Function	$AB^2 + C$	AB^2
Throughput	1	1
Latency	$2m + m/2$	$m + \lceil m/2 \rceil$
Computation time per basic cell	$T_{AND2} + T_{XOR4}$	$T_{AND2} + T_{XOR4}$
Cell Complexity		
1. AND gate	$3m^2$	$3m^2 - m$
2. XOR gate	$3m^2$	$3m^2 - m$
3. Latches	$8.5m^2$	$4.5m^2 - 3.5m$

Table 2. Comparison of inversion/division architectures in GF(2^m)

Item	Circuit	
	Wang [12]	Proposed [Fig. 7]
No.of cells	$m^2(m-1)/2$	$m^2(m-1)/2$
Function	A/B	A/B
Throughput	1	1
Latency	$2m^2 - 3m/2$	$m^2 - m/2$
Computation time per basic cell	$T_{AND2} + T_{XOR4}$	$T_{AND2} + T_{XOR4}$
Cell Complexity		
1. AND gate	$3m^2(m-1)$	$(3m^2 - m)(m-1)$
2. XOR gate	$3m^2(m-1)$	$(3m^2 - m)(m-1)$
3. Latches	$8.5m^2(m-1)$	$(4.5m^2 - 3.5m)(m-1)$

5 Conclusion

The current paper explored a new algorithm and a systolic architectures to improve the multiplication performance when calculating AB^2 multiplication systolic architectures and inversion/division by using AB^2 as the general circuit in GF(2^m). The proposed algorithm is based on the MSB-first scheme using the standard basis representation in GF(2^m). A comparison with related systolic architectures revealed that the proposed systolic architectures exhibited a lower complexity and latency than conventional architectures. With AB^2 multiplication, the area, size, and power consumption are all significantly reduced as a large number of latches can be removed after merging. Moreover, the proposed architectures include simplicity, regularity, modularity, and pipelinability.

Acknowledgement. This work was supported by grant No. 2000-2-51200-001-2 from the Korea Science & Engineering Foundation

References

[1]   W.W. Peterson, E.J. Weldon: Error-correcting codes. MIT Press, MA (1972)

[2]   D.E.R. Denning: Cryptography and data security. Addison-Wesley, MA (1983)

[3]   IEEE P1363/D9(Draft Version 9): Standard Specifications for Public Key Cryptography, IEEE standards Draft, USA (1999)

[4]   T. ElGamal: A public key cryptosystem and a signature scheme based on discrete logarithms, IEEE Trans. on Info. Theory, vol. 31(4) (1985) 469–472

[5]   I.S. Reed and T.K. Truong: The use of finite fields to compute convolutions.IEEE Trans. Inform. Theory,21 (1975) 208–213

[6]   W.C. Tsai, S.-J. Wang: Two systolic architectures for multiplication in GF(2^m). IEE Proc. Cmput. Digit. Tech, Vol. 147 (2000) 375–382

[7]   S. G. Moon, J.M. Park, Y. S. Lee: Fast VLSI arithmetic algorithms for high-security elliptic curve cryptographic applications. IEEE Transactions on Consumer Electronics, Vol. 47, No. 3 (2001) 700–708

[8]   S.K. Jain, L. Song, K.K. Parhi: Efficient semisystolic architectures for finite field arithmetic, IEEE Trans. VLSI Syst. (1995) 101–113

[9]   C.Y. Lee, E.H. Lu, L.F. Sun: Low-complexity Bit-parallel Systolic Architecture for Computing $AB^2 + C$ in a Class of Finite Field GF(2^m), IEEE Trans. On Circuits and Systems, Vol. 48 (2001) 519–523

[10] C.H. Liu, N.F. Huang, C.Y. Lee: Computation of AB^2 Multiplier in GF(2^m) Using an Efficient Low-Complexity Cellular Architecture, IEICE Trans. Fundamentals, Vol. E83-A, (2000) 2657–2663

[11] S.W. Wei: A Systolic Power-Sum Circuit for GF(2^m). IEEE Trans. Computers. **43** (1994) 226–229

[12] C.L. Wang and J.H. Guo: New systolic arrays for $C + AB^2$, inversion, and division in GF(2^m). IEEE Trans. Computers **49** (2000) 1120–1125

[13] 13. S. W. Wei : VLSI Architectures for Computing Exponentiations, Multiplicative Inverses, and Divisions in GF(2m). Proc. 1995 IEEE Int'l Symp. Circuits and Systems (1995) 203–206

[14] S. Y. Kung: VLSI Array Processors. Prentice-Hall. **43** (1987)

[15] K. Y. Yoo: A Systolic Array Design Methodology for Sequential Loop Algorithms. Ph.D. thesis, Rensselaer Polytechnic Institute, New York (1992)

[16] Daniel D. Gajski: Principles of Digital Design. Prentice-Hall international, INC. (1997)

Efficient Bit Serial Multiplication Using Optimal Normal Bases of Type II in $GF(2^m)$

Soonhak Kwon[1] and Heuisu Ryu[2]

[1] Institute of Basic Science, Sungkyunkwan University,
Suwon 440-746, Korea
shkwon@math.skku.ac.kr
[2] Electronics and Telecommunications Research Institute,
Taejon 305-350, Korea
hsryu@etri.re.kr

Abstract. Using the self duality of an optimal normal basis of type II in a finite field $GF(2^m)$, we present a design of a bit serial multiplier of Berlekamp type. It is shown that our multiplier does not need a basis conversion process and a squaring operation is a simple permutation in our basis. Therefore our multiplier provides a fast and an efficient hardware architecture for a bit serial multiplication of two elements in $GF(2^m)$, which is suitable for a cryptographic purpose.

Keywords: Finite field, bit serial multiplication, dual basis, optimal normal basis of type II

1 Introduction

Arithmetic of finite fields, especially finite field multiplication, found various applications in coding theory, cryptography and digital signal processing. Therefore an efficient design of a finite field multiplier is needed. A good multiplication algorithm depends on the choice of basis for a given finite field. One of the most widely used finite field multipliers is the Berlekamp's bit serial multiplier [1],[2],[3]. Because of its low hardware complexity, it has been used in Reed-Solomon encoders which have been utilized in various practical applications such as a deep space probe and a compact disc technology. Let us briefly explain Berlekamp's multiplier over a finite field. We are mainly interested in the finite field $GF(2^m)$ with characteristic two because it is suitable for a hardware implementation, but the basic theory can be easily extended to an arbitrary finite field. A finite field $GF(2^m)$ with 2^m elements is regarded as a m-dimensional vector space over $GF(2)$. Therefore it has a basis over $GF(2)$. One may choose a standard polynomial basis but there exist other types of basis which are useful for their specific purposes.

Definition 1. *Two bases $\{\alpha_1, \alpha_2, \cdots, \alpha_m\}$ and $\{\beta_1, \beta_2, \cdots, \beta_m\}$ of $GF(2^m)$ are said to be dual if the trace map, $Tr : GF(2^m) \to GF(2)$, with $Tr(\alpha) = \alpha + \alpha^2 + \cdots + \alpha^{2^{m-1}}$, satisfies $Tr(\alpha_i \beta_j) = \delta_{ij}$ for all $1 \le i, j \le m$, where $\delta_{ij} = 1$ if $i = j$, zero if $i \ne j$. A basis $\{\alpha_1, \alpha_2, \cdots, \alpha_m\}$ is said to be self dual if $Tr(\alpha_i \alpha_j) = \delta_{ij}$.*

A.H. Chan and V. Gligor (Eds.): ISC 2002, LNCS 2433, pp. 300–308, 2002.

Let α be an element in $GF(2^m)$ be such that $\{1, \alpha, \alpha^2, \cdots, \alpha^{m-1}\}$ is a basis of $GF(2^m)$ over $GF(2)$. Let $\{\beta_0, \beta_1, \cdots, \beta_{m-1}\}$ be the dual basis of $\{1, \alpha, \alpha^2, \cdots, \alpha^{m-1}\}$. For any $x \in GF(2^m)$, by considering both polynomial basis and its dual basis expression of x, we may express x as

$$x = \sum_{i=0}^{m-1} x_i \alpha^i = \sum_{i=0}^{m-1} [x]_i \beta_i.$$

Let $y = \sum_{i=0}^{m-1} y_i \alpha^i$ be another element in $GF(2^m)$. Then we have the dual basis expression

$$xy = \sum_{k=0}^{m-1} [xy]_k \beta_k,$$

where

$$[xy]_k = Tr(\alpha^k xy) = Tr(\alpha^k x \sum_{i=0}^{m-1} y_i \alpha^i)$$
$$= \sum_{i=0}^{m-1} y_i Tr(\alpha^{i+k} x) = \sum_{i=0}^{m-1} y_i [\alpha^k x]_i.$$

Note that $[\alpha^k x]_i$ is the ith coefficient of the dual basis expression of $\alpha^k x$. On the other hand, we have

$$[\alpha^k x]_i = Tr(\alpha^i \alpha^k x) = [\alpha^{k-1} x]_{i+1}, \quad i = 0, 1, 2, \cdots, m - 2.$$

Also letting $f_0 + f_1 X + f_2 X^2 + \cdots + f_{m-1} X^{m-1} + X^m \in GF(2)[X]$ be the irreducible polynomial of α over $GF(2)$,

$$[\alpha^k x]_{m-1} = Tr(\alpha^{m-1} \alpha^k x) = Tr(\sum_{i=0}^{m-1} f_i \alpha^i \alpha^{k-1} x)$$
$$= \sum_{i=0}^{m-1} f_i Tr(\alpha^i \alpha^{k-1} x) = \sum_{i=0}^{m-1} f_i [\alpha^{k-1} x]_i.$$

Therefore for each k and i, $[\alpha^k x]_i$ can be computed by the feedback shifting process of previous expression $[\alpha^{k-1} x]_j, j = 0, 1, \cdots, m - 1$. The multiplication $[xy]_k = \sum_{i=0}^{m-1} y_i [\alpha^k x]_i$ is realized by the following hardware arrangement using a feedback shift register [1].

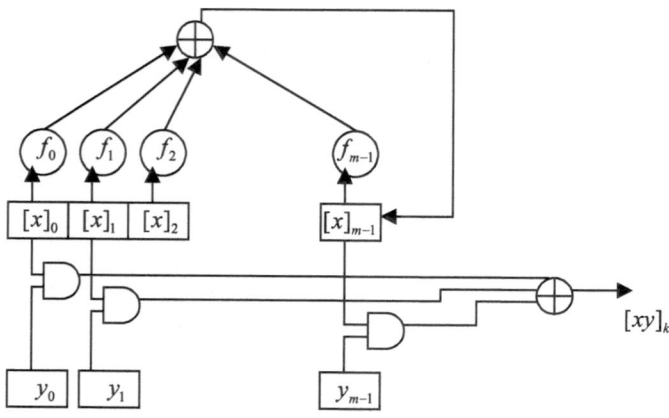

Fig. 1. Bit serial arrangement of Berlekamp's dual basis multiplier

After k-clock cycles, we get $[xy]_k$, the kth coefficient of the dual basis expression of xy. As is obvious from above algorithm, Berlekamp's bit serial multiplier uses a dual basis. In other words, to multiply two elements in a finite field, one input y is expressed in terms of a standard polynomial basis, the other input x is expressed in terms of its dual basis and the resulting output xy is expresed in terms of the dual basis. Therefore we need a basis conversion process in Berlekamp's algorithm, which necessarily increases the hardware complexity in its implementation. This problem is solved in the cases when the corresponding finite field is generated by a root of an irreducible trinomial [2] or a pentanomial of a special kind [3]. A bit serial multiplier applicable for all types of irreducible polynomials is presented in [8]. But it has an increased hardware complexity and the operations are relatively slow compared with Berlekamp's multiplier if the basis conversion is unnecessary. One more drawback of Berlekamp's multiplier is that exponentiation, inverse finding procedures are very time consuming when compared with bit parallel multipliers (especially with Massey-Omura type multipliers using normal bases [5],[6],[7]). Not to mention its high speed because of parallel processing, bit parallel normal basis multipliers are quite effective in such operations as exponentiation and inversion since squaring operation is just a cyclic shift in normal basis expression. So various types of normal basis multipliers are being studied. Among them, so called optimal normal basis multipliers [6],[7] require least number of gates than other types of parallel multipliers. There are two types of optimal normal bases [4], namely, type I and type II. Our aim in this paper is to present a design of a bit serial multiplier using a type II optimal normal basis which satisfies the following three properties. First, it is generally faster than Berlekamp's bit serial multiplier, since our multiplier has a shorter longest delay path than Berlekamp's multiplier. Second, squaring operation is just a permutation in our basis. Therefore, exponentiation and inverse finding operations are much faster than Berlekamp's multiplier. Third, it needs no basis conversion process which is usually required in dual basis multipliers.

2   Normal Basis and Optimal Normal Basis of Type II

Let α be an element of $GF(2^m)$ of degree m and let $f(X) = f_0 + f_1 X + \cdots + f_{m-1}X^{m-1} + X^m$ be the irreducible polynomial of α over $GF(2)$. Then we have

$$0 = f(\alpha) = f_0 + f_1\alpha + f_2\alpha^2 + \cdots + f_{m-1}\alpha^{m-1} + \alpha^m.$$

From this, it is clear that

$$0 = f(\alpha)^{2^i} = f(\alpha^{2^i}), \quad i = 0, 1, 2, \cdots, m-1,$$

since $f_0, f_1, \cdots, f_{m-1}$ are in $GF(2)$ and the characteristic of $GF(2^m)$ is two. In other words, all the zeros of $f(X)$ are $\alpha, \alpha^2, \alpha^{2^2}, \cdots, \alpha^{2^{m-1}}$. If all the conjugates, $\alpha, \alpha^2, \alpha^{2^2}, \cdots, \alpha^{2^{m-1}}$, of α are linearly independent over $GF(2)$, then they form a basis for $GF(2^m)$ over $GF(2)$.

Definition 2. *A basis of $GF(2^m)$ over $GF(2)$ of the form $\{\alpha, \alpha^2, \cdots, \alpha^{2^{m-1}}\}$ is called a normal basis.*

It is a standard fact [4] that there is always a normal basis in $GF(2^m)$ for any $m \geq 1$. If an element A in $GF(2^m)$ is expressed with respect to a normal basis $\{\alpha, \alpha^2, \cdots, \alpha^{2^{m-1}}\}$, i.e. if $A = a_0\alpha + a_1\alpha^2 + \cdots + a_{m-1}\alpha^{2^{m-1}}$, then one easily notices

$$A^2 = a_{m-1}\alpha + a_0\alpha^2 + a_1\alpha^{2^2} + \cdots + a_{m-2}\alpha^{2^{m-1}}.$$

That is, A^2 is a right cyclic shift of A with respect the basis $\{\alpha, \alpha^2, \cdots, \alpha^{2^{m-1}}\}$. On the other hand, a normal basis expression of a product AB of two different elements A and B in $GF(2^m)$ is not so simple. This is because the expression $\alpha^{2^i}\alpha^{2^j} = \sum_{k=0}^{m-1} a_k^{ij}\alpha^{2^k}$ may be quite complicated if one does not choose a normal basis properly. Therefore, to find an efficient bit serial multiplication using a normal basis, one has to choose a normal basis so that the coefficients a_k^{ij} in the expression $\alpha^{2^i}\alpha^{2^j}$ are zero for many indices i, j and k. There are not so many normal bases satisfying this condition, but we have one example of such normal basis and it is stated in the following theorem. A detailed proof can be found in [4].

Theorem 1. *Let $GF(2^m)$ be a finite field of 2^m elements where $2m+1 = p$ is a prime. Suppose that either $(\star)$ 2 is a primitive root $(\bmod\ p)$ or $(\star\star)$ -1 is a quadratic nonresidue $(\bmod\ p)$ and 2 generates all the quadratic residues $(\bmod\ p)$. Then letting $\alpha = \beta + \beta^{-1}$ where β is a primitive pth root of unity in $GF(2^{2m})$, we have $\alpha \in GF(2^m)$ and $\{\alpha, \alpha^2, \cdots, \alpha^{2^{m-1}}\}$ is a basis over $GF(2)$.*

Definition 3. *A normal basis in theorm 1 is called an optimal normal basis of type II.*

Using the assumptions in the previous theorem, one finds easily

$$\alpha^{2^s} = (\beta + \beta^{-1})^{2^s} = \beta^{2^s} + \beta^{-2^s} = \beta^t + \beta^{-t},$$

where $0 < t < p = 2m + 1$ with $2^s \equiv t \pmod{p}$. Moreover, replacing t by $p - t$ if $m + 1 \le t \le 2m$, we find that $\{\alpha, \alpha^2, \cdots, \alpha^{2^{m-1}}\}$ and $\{\beta + \beta^{-1}, \beta^2 + \beta^{-2}, \cdots, \beta^m + \beta^{-m}\}$ are same sets. That is, $\alpha^{2^s}, 0 \le s \le m - 1$ is just a permutation of $\beta^s + \beta^{-s}, 1 \le s \le m$. Above observation leads to the following definition.

Definition 4. *Let β be a primitive pth ($p = 2m + 1$) root of unity in $GF(2^{2m})$. For each integer s, define α_s as*

$$\alpha_s = \beta^s + \beta^{-s}.$$

Then for each integer s and t, we easily find

$$\alpha_s \alpha_t = (\beta^s + \beta^{-s})(\beta^t + \beta^{-t}) = \alpha_{s-t} + \alpha_{s+t}.$$

In other words, a multiplication of two basis elements has a simple expression as a sum of two basis elements.

Lemma 1. *An optimal normal basis $\{\alpha^{2^s} | 0 \le s \le m - 1\}$ of type II in $GF(2^m)$, if it exists, is self dual.*

Proof. After a permutation of basis elements, it can be written as $\{\alpha_s | 1 \le s \le m\}$. Note that

$$Tr(\alpha_i \alpha_j) = Tr((\beta^i + \beta^{-i})(\beta^j + \beta^{-j})) = Tr(\alpha_{i-j} + \alpha_{i+j}).$$

If $i = j$, then we have $Tr(\alpha_{2i}) = Tr(\alpha^{2^s})$ for some $0 \le s \le m - 1$. Thus the trace value is $\alpha + \alpha^2 + \cdots + \alpha^{2^{m-1}} = 1$ because of the linear independence. If $i \ne j$, then there are s and t with $0 \le s, t \le m - 1$ such that $\alpha_{i-j} = \alpha^{2^s}$ and $\alpha_{i+j} = \alpha^{2^t}$. Therefore

$$Tr(\alpha_{i-j} + \alpha_{i+j}) = Tr(\alpha_{i-j}) + Tr(\alpha_{i+j}) = Tr(\alpha^{2^s}) + Tr(\alpha^{2^t}) = 1 + 1 = 0.$$

$\square$

From now on, we assume $\{\alpha^{2^s} | 0 \le s \le m - 1\}$ is an optimal normal basis of type II in $GF(2^m)$ and $\{\alpha_s | 1 \le s \le m\}$ is a basis obtained after a permutation of the basis elements of the normal basis. For a given $A = \sum_{i=1}^{m} a_i \alpha_i$ with $a_i \in GF(2)$, by using lemma 1, we have

$$a_s = \sum_{i=1}^{m} a_i Tr(\alpha_s \alpha_i) = Tr(\alpha_s \sum_{i=1}^{m} a_i \alpha_i) = Tr(\alpha_s A),$$

for all $1 \le s \le m$. We also extend above relation by defining a_s as $a_s = Tr(\alpha_s A)$ for all integers s, where $\alpha_s = \beta^s + \beta^{-s}$ from definition 4. Then for any integer s, we get the following properties.

Lemma 2. *We have $\alpha_s = 0 = a_s$ if $2m + 1$ divides s, and*

$$\alpha_{2m+1+s} = \alpha_s = \alpha_{2m+1-s} = \alpha_{-s}, \quad a_{2m+1+s} = a_s = a_{2m+1-s} = a_{-s},$$

for all s.

Proof. We have $\alpha_s = \beta^s + \beta^{-s} = 0$ if and only if $\beta^s = \beta^{-s}$, that is, $\beta^{2s} = 1$. And this happens whenever $2m + 1 = p$ divides s since β is a primitive pth root of unity. Now $\alpha_{2m+1+s} = \beta^{2m+1+s} + \beta^{-(2m+1+s)} = \beta^s + \beta^{-s} = \alpha_s$ is obvious because $\beta^{2m+1} = 1$. Also $\alpha_{2m+1-s} = \beta^{2m+1-s} + \beta^{-(2m+1-s)} = \beta^{-s} + \beta^s = \alpha_s$. The result for a_s instantly follows from the result for α_s. □

3   Multiplication Algorithm

Using lemma 1 and 2, we are ready to give the following assertion, which explains a bit serial multiplication in $GF(2^m)$ using an optimal normal basis of type II.

Theorem 2. *Let $A = \sum_{i=1}^{m} a_i\alpha_i$ and $B = \sum_{i=1}^{m} b_i\alpha_i$ be elements in $GF(2^m)$. Then we have $AB = \sum_{k=1}^{m}(ab)_k\alpha_k$, where the kth coefficient $(ab)_k$ satisfies*

$$(ab)_k = \sum_{i=1}^{2m+1} b_i a_{i-k}.$$

Proof. By lemma 1, $\{\alpha_k | 1 \le k \le m\}$ is self dual. Thus

$$(ab)_k = Tr(\alpha_k AB) = Tr(\alpha_k A \sum_{i=1}^{m} b_i\alpha_i)$$

$$= \sum_{i=1}^{m} b_i Tr(\alpha_k \alpha_i A) = \sum_{i=1}^{m} b_i Tr(\alpha_{i-k} A + \alpha_{i+k} A)$$

$$= \sum_{i=1}^{m} b_i (Tr(\alpha_{i-k} A) + Tr(\alpha_{i+k} A)) = \sum_{i=1}^{m} b_i(a_{i-k} + a_{i+k})$$

$$= \sum_{i=1}^{m} b_i a_{i-k} + \sum_{i=1}^{m} b_i a_{i+k}.$$

On the other hand, the second summation of above expression can be written as

$$\sum_{i=1}^{m} b_i a_{i+k} = \sum_{i=1}^{m} b_{m+1-i} a_{m+1-i+k}$$

$$= \sum_{i=1}^{m} b_{m+i} a_{m+i-k}$$

$$= \sum_{i=m+1}^{2m} b_i a_{i-k},$$

where the first equality follows by rearranging the summands and the second equality follows from lemma 2. Therefore we get

$$(ab)_k = \sum_{i=1}^{m} b_i a_{i-k} + \sum_{i=1}^{m} b_i a_{i+k} = \sum_{i=1}^{2m} b_i a_{i-k}.$$

Since $b_{2m+1} = 0$ by lemma 2, $(ab)_k = \sum_{i=1}^{2m+1} b_i a_{i-k}$ is obvious from above result.   □

In fact, lemma 2 says that we also have

$$(ab)_k = \sum_{i=1}^{2m+1} b_i a_{i-k} = \sum_{i=1}^{2m+1} b_i a_{i+k}.$$

4   Bit Serial Arrangement Using an Optimal Normal Basis of Type II

Using theorem 2, we may express $(ab)_k$ as a matrix multiplication form of a row vector and a column vector,

$$(ab)_k = (a_{1-k}, a_{2-k}, \cdots, a_{2m-k}, a_{2m+1-k})(b_1, b_2, \cdots, b_{2m}, b_{2m+1})^T,$$

where $(b_1, b_2, \cdots, b_{2m}, b_{2m+1})^T$ is a transposition of the row vector $(b_1, b_2, \cdots, b_{2m}, b_{2m+1})$. Then we have

$$(ab)_{k+1} = (a_{-k}, a_{1-k}, \cdots, a_{2m-1-k}, a_{2m-k})(b_1, b_2, \cdots, b_{2m}, b_{2m+1})^T.$$

Since $a_{-k} = a_{2m+1-k}$ by lemma 2, we find that $(a_{-k}, a_{1-k}, \cdots, a_{2m-1-k}, a_{2m-k})$ is a right cyclic shift of $(a_{1-k}, a_{2-k}, \cdots, a_{2m-k}, a_{2m+1-k})$ by one position. From this observation, we may realize the multiplication algorithm in the shift register arrangement shown in Fig. 2. The shift register is initially loaded with $(a_0, a_1, \cdots, a_{2m})$ which is in fact $(0, a_1, \cdots, a_m, a_m, \cdots, a_1)$. After k clock cycles, we get $(ab)_k$, the kth coefficient of AB with respect to the basis $\{\alpha_1, \cdots, \alpha_m\}$.

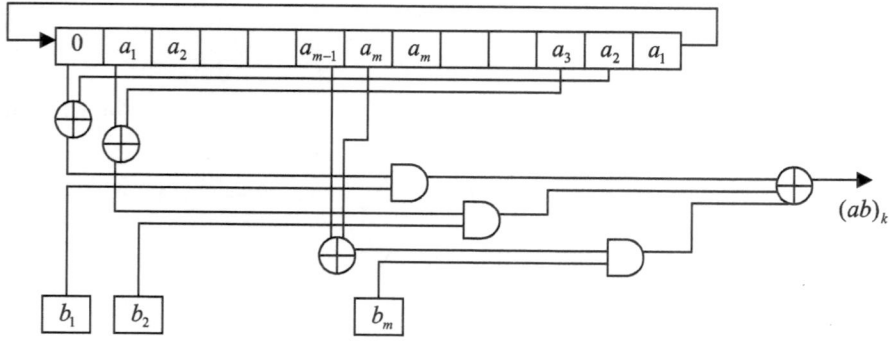

Fig. 2. Bit serial multiplier using an optimal normal basis of type II

Compared with Berlekamp's dual basis multiplier in Fig. 1, our design of bit serial multiplier requires $m + 1$ more flip-flops (in the expression of the input A). However, since our multiplier does not need XOR operations among the elements $a_i s$ to determine a shifting element unlike the case of Berlekamp's multiplier where $\sum_{i=0}^{m-1} f_i[x]_i$ has to be computed before a shifting operation, our multiplier has a shorter longest delay path than Berlekamp's multiplier. Consequently, our bit serial arrangement can be clocked faster than the dual basis arrangement by Berlekamp. Also, since our multiplier is using a normal basis, such arithmetical operations as squaring, exponentiation and inversion can be very efficiently computed. Moreover we do not need a basis conversion process which is required in dual basis multipliers. Note that a bit parallel multiplier using an optimal normal basis of type II is discussed in [6], where it is suggested to find a bit serial version of the bit parallel construction in [6]. So our multiplier gives a modest answer for the suggestion. To the author's knowledge, this is the first design of a bit serial multiplier using an optimal normal basis of type II. It should be mentioned that a bit serial multiplier using an extended AOP basis (which is not a normal basis but may be viewed as a variant of type I optimal normal basis) is discussed in [10],[11].

5   Conclusions

In this paper, we have proposed a bit serial multiplier in $GF(2^m)$ using a type II optimal normal basis. We showed that our multiplier has good properties of both dual basis and normal basis multipliers. Though it has a slightly increased hardware complexity when compared with a dual basis multipier of Berlekamp, our multiplier is faster since it has a shorter longest delay path. Also, since our basis is self dual, we do not have to worry about the basis conversion process which is required in Berlekamp's dual basis multiplier. Moreover, our multiplier has a simple squaring operation because we use a normal basis like other Massey-Omura type multipliers. Another advantage of our multiplier is that the hardware structure of our bit serial arrangement is regular. In other words, it does not depend on a particular choice of m for $GF(2^m)$ as long as there exists an optimal normal basis of type II. On the other hand, the structure of Berlekamp's bit serial multiplier depends on the irreducible polynomial $f(X) = f_0 + f_1 X + f_2 X^2 + \cdots + f_{m-1} X^{m-1} + X^m$, where only the coefficient f_i with $f_i = 1$ contributes to the summation $\sum_{i=0}^{m-1} f_i[x]_i$. Therefore, the hardware structure of Berlekamp's multiplier is different for varing choices of m for $GF(2^m)$.

Acknowledgements. The first author was supported in part by KRF 2000–015–DP0005.

References

1. E.R. Berlekamp, "Bit-serial Reed-Solomon encoders," *IEEE Trans. Inform. Theory*, **28**, pp. 869–874, 1982.
2. M. Wang and I.F. Blake, "Bit serial multiplication in finite fields," *SIAM J. Disc. Math.*, **3**, pp. 140–148, 1990.
3. M. Morii, M. Kasahara and D.L. Whiting, "Efficient bit-serial multiplication and the discrete-time Wiener-Hopf equation over finite fields," *IEEE Trans. Inform. Theory*, **35**, pp. 1177–1183, 1989.
4. A.J. Menezes, *Applications of finite fields*, Kluwer Academic Publisher, 1993.
5. Ç.K. Koç and B. Sunar, "Low complexity bit-parallell canonical and normal basis multipliers for a class of finite fields," *IEEE Trans. Computers*,**47**, pp. 353–356, 1998.
6. B. Sunar and Ç.K. Koç, "An efficient optimal normal basis type II multiplier," *IEEE Trans. Computers*,**50**, pp. 83–87, 2001.
7. M.A. Hassan, M.Z. Wang and V.K. Bhargava, "A modified Massey-Omura parallel multiplier for a class of finite fields," *IEEE Trans. Computers*,**42**, pp. 1278–1280, 1993.
8. M.A. Hasan and V.K. Bhargava, "Division and bit-serial multiplication over $GF(q^m)$," *IEE Proc. E*, **139**, pp. 230–236, 1992.
9. I.S. Hsu, T.K. Truong, L.J. Deutch and I.S. Reed, "A comparison of VLSI architecture of finite field multipliers using dual, normal or standard bases," *IEEE Trans. Computers*,**37**, pp. 735–739, 1988.
10. C.H. Lee and J.I. Lim, "A new aspect of dual basis for efficient field arithmetic," *Public Key Cryptography*, Lecture Notes in Computer Science **1560**, pp. 12–28, 1999.
11. G. Drolet, "A new representation of elements of finite fields $GF(2^m)$ yielding small complexity arithmetic circuits," *IEEE Trans. Computers*,**47**, pp. 938–946, 1998.

Conditional Cryptographic Delegation for P2P Data Sharing

Yuji Watanabe and Masayuki Numao

IBM Research, Tokyo Research Laboratory
1623-14 Shimotsuruma, Yamato-shi,
Kanagawa, 242-8502, Japan
{muew,numao}@jp.ibm.com

Abstract. A cryptographic approach that enables a peer to transfer the right to access the encrypted data provided predetermined conditions are satisfied is presented in this paper. Our approach involves a third trusted service, called "delegation check (DC) servers" to check single or multiple conditions according to the rules. A peer (delegator) delegates the right to decrypt the ciphertext to other peers (proxies) under certain conditions. The proxy can decrypt the ciphertext only after it passes the verification check of the DC server. Our system has the following properties: (1) A sender does not need to know whether or not the delegation occurs. (2) DC servers are involved only when the proxy decrypts the ciphertext. (3) Neither the DC server nor a proxy can know the private decryption key of the delegator unless both of them collude with each other.

Two types of techniques, a basic scheme and an extended scheme, are presented. The basic scheme is relatively efficient, while the security is maintained under the assumption that the DC server does not deviate from the protocol. In order to tolerate the deviation of the DC server, the extended scheme allows the delegator to direct the proxy to use a group of servers when decrypting the ciphertext. A notable feature in our scheme is that the delegator can independently choose which of the two without any interaction with the DC servers or the proxy. Moreover, the choice of the scheme does not require any modification of the operations that the server performs.

1 Introduction

1.1 Background

Peer-to-peer (P2P) technology has recently received a lot of attention due to its effective use of network bandwidth and computing resources (like [1]). P2P computing can be regarded as the sharing of computer resources by connecting peers directly. Recent advances in PC computing power as well as various kinds of network connections allow stand-alone clients to act as servers (called "servant"). For instance, a data sharing system using P2P technology (a P2P data sharing, for short) provides massive information storage virtually by enabling a peer

A.H. Chan and V. Gligor (Eds.): ISC 2002, LNCS 2433, pp. 309–321, 2002.

to search all over the network for the intended information and download it from other peers. This contributes to effective use of surplus storage resources, and furthermore, to sharing the information and knowledge among peers. In the P2P data sharing scenario, the shared data is stored not only in the private storage but also in a free disk space of other peers. When the data is confidential, cryptographic techniques are employed in order to prevent unauthorized peers from accessing the protected data while to allow authorized peers to do so. For example, suppose a user wants to keep a large private data but does not have enough free-space. In this case, the user encrypts the data and stores it in the free disk-space of other's PC. When the data is required, the user retrieves the encrypted data and decrypts it with his private decryption key. In some cases, the data is required by another user. If the user who has the decryption key is on-line, the data is accessible by requesting the decryption. However, unlike the conventional structure of a database statically managed by a central server, a P2P network consists of various types of peers, including pervasive devices, so it is required to cope with frequent peer disconnections from and rejoins to the network. In this case, smooth processing may be hindered by disconnected peers since accessing the encrypted data requires a peer who has the corresponding decryption key to decrypt the ciphertext. For example, the user requesting the data has to wait for the rejoin of the user who has the decryption key. In this case, if the right to decrypt the ciphertext is transferable into other connected peers while in a disconnected state, one can construct a robust and secure P2P data sharing with wide accessibility. For example, it is desirable to allow the user who is going to shut off the power on the PC to transfer the right to decrypt his private data into another on-line peer until the user rejoins to the network. What is important here is that the term of the delegation should be limited during the user's absence. Namely, once the user rejoins to the network, the delegated peer should not be able to access the data.

This paper describes a cryptographic approach which enables a peer to transfer (delegate) the right to access the data encrypted by its private key when predetermined conditions (the term of validity, accessing entity, etc.) are satisfied. Our approach involves a third trusted service, called "delegation check (DC) servers" to check single or multiple conditions according to the rules. One peer (the delegator) delegates the right to decrypt the ciphertext to other peers (proxies) under certain conditions. The proxy can decrypt the ciphertext only after it passes the verification check of the DC server. This system has the following properties: (1)A peer who generates a ciphertext does not need to know whether or not the delegation occurs. (2)DC servers are involved only when the proxy decrypts the ciphertext, so generating the ciphertext does not require any interaction with the DC servers unless an exception occur (e.g. cancellation of delegation, change of the term of validity, etc.). Since all the DC servers have to do is to publish a server's public key, the resources required for DC servers are relatively small. (3)Neither the DC server nor a proxy can know the private decryption key of the delegator unless both of them collude with each other.

Two types of techniques, a basic scheme and an extended scheme, are presented in this paper. The basic scheme is relatively efficient, while the security is maintained under the assumption that the DC server does not deviate from the protocol. In order to tolerate the deviation of the DC server, the extended scheme allows the delegator to direct the proxy to use a group of servers when decrypting the ciphertext. This is done by applying a distributed decryption technique which is usually used for avoiding a single point of trust. A notable feature in our scheme is that the delegator can independently choose which of the two without any interaction with the DC servers or the proxy. Moreover, the choice of the scheme does not require any modification of the operation that the server performs.

1.2 Related Work

In communication using public key cryptography, the sender of the message computes the ciphertext by encrypting the message with a recipient's public encryption key. Then, the sender transmits it to the recipient over an insecure channel. The person with the private decryption key (we call this person the "delegator", hereafter) can obtain the message by decrypting the ciphertext. Here we consider a case where the decryption of the ciphertext is required for processing sequential operations, but cannot be performed due to the absence of the delegator.

For example, suppose a user A wants to keep a large private data but does not have enough free-space. In this case, A encrypts the data and stores it in the free disk-space of other's PC. When the data is required, A retrieves the encrypted data and decrypts it with his private decryption key. But in some cases, the data is required by another user B. If A is on-line, the data is accessible by B requesting the decryption to A, while if A is off-line, B has to wait for the rejoin of A.

Such a case may happen frequently, especially when the delegator consists of a pervasive device, which might often be disconnected from the network. In order to avoid interruptions of processing, it is desired to allow the delegator to delegate the right to decrypt the ciphertext to a proxy before being disconnected. When decryption is required but the delegator is disconnected, interruption of sequential processing is avoided by requesting the proxy specified by the delegator beforehand to execute the decryption.

There are several research projects which focus on the delegation of the right to decrypt the ciphertext, called "proxy cryptosystems" [2][3][4]. A proxy cryptosystem is a transformation converting the ciphertext to another ciphertext corresponding to a different proxy's key. A trivial way to do so is to compute the message by decrypting the ciphertext and then re-encrypting it with a new key, which implies access to the original ciphertext in this transformation. The main goal of proxy cryptosystems is to convert ciphertext between keys without access to the original message. [2] describes efficient transformations that allow the delegator to forward specific ciphertexts to the proxy. The transforming function in [2] must be kept secret and applied online by the delegator message-by-message.

[3] shows an (atomic) transforming function which allows an untrusted party to convert the ciphertext without access to either the private decryption key or a new proxy key. Their transforming function is symmetric in the sense that the delegator must trust the proxy who can learn the private key of the delegator through the transformation. [4] presents an asymmetric transforming function by which the delegator can transfer the right to decrypt to the proxy without revealing any information about the private key. The transformation is performed under quorum control: if the quorum is honest, no information about the private key can be leaked.

We consider a different model regarding communication from the previous systems[2][3][4]. In our protocol, the delegator gives the proxy a new key, which allows the proxy to decrypt the ciphertext under the control of the DC servers. No communication between the delegator and the DC servers is required. The DC servers are involved only when the proxy decrypts the ciphertext. This property is quite different from [4]. Moreover, the proxy decryption is performed without revealing the private key of the delegator.

Time-controlled access to the data is a fundamental requirement when considering delegation. A cryptographic technique for protecting time-sensitive information is known as "time-release cryptosystem"[5][6][7], which allows the sender to encrypt the message so that it cannot be accessed before the release-time.

We consider a different model from the previous schemes. In the example mentioned above, it is desirable to allow A who is going to shut off the power on the PC to transfer the right to decrypt A's private data into another on-line peer until A rejoins to the network, while once A re-participants, the delegated peer should not be able to access the data. Furthermore, the following properties should be satisfied in practice. (1) Conditions on the decryption are generated by the delegator, while in the time-release crypto, the sender designates the condition. A major goal of our scheme is to construct the conditional delegation scheme without any modification of the sender's process. (2) Delegating the right of decryption within a certain period of time is a fundamental and quite desirable property of practical delegation. Our protocol easily copes with such timing constraints as conditions.

1.3   Preliminaries

Definitions. The system we envision contains the following four parties.

- sender (S) : a party that sends a message after encrypting it with the (original) recipient's public key, denoted by e_R.
- delegator (R) : a party that has a pair of the private decryption key d_R and the corresponding public key e_R, and delegates the right of decryption to the proxy.
- proxy (P) : a party that decrypts the ciphertext on behalf of R.
- delegation check (DC) server(s) (T) : a party that confirms whether the proxy fulfills the conditions which were designated by R beforehand. T holds a private key d_T corresponding to a public key e_T.

Our protocol uses the following two protocols as main building blocks.

- $\Psi(d_R, \phi)$: the delegation key generation protocol which takes R's private key d_R and the designated condition ϕ as inputs and outputs the delegation key σ.
- $\Gamma(\sigma, \phi, c)$: the two-party protocol between T and P, after which P obtains the plaintext corresponding to c if T verifies ϕ, otherwise, P cannot get any information on the plaintext.

The description of the condition ϕ must be an interpretable form so that T can verify it independently. Suppose R describes ϕ as "The right to decrypt is delegated to P from time t_1 to t_2," for example. In this case, during the execution of Γ, T must be able to examine whether the current time is between the time t_1 and t_2 and T actually communicates P. After this verification, P can decrypt c and obtain the message.

Model. We assume the following model of "conditional cryptographic delegation."

1. S computes a ciphertext c by encrypting a message m with a key e_R and sends c to R.
2. When R transfers the ability of decryption P under a condition ϕ, R computes the delegation key $\sigma = \Psi(d_R, \phi)$ and sends the pair (ϕ, σ) to P.
3. If ϕ is valid, P can decrypt c by interactive protocol Γ which takes ϕ, σ and c as inputs.

Parameters. The following parameters are used in the protocol. Let G_q be a group of prime order q, such that computing the discrete logarithm of G_q is infeasible. For simplicity, we take as G_q the subgroup of Z_p of order q such that g is a generator of G_q and p is a prime with respect to $q|p-1$. Alternatively, the group of points of an elliptic curve over a finite field is available. After this, we assume all arithmetic to be modulo p where applicable, unless otherwise stated. Let $H(\cdot)$ denote an ideal collision-resistant cryptographic hash function. We assume this function maps from the integer space to Z_q. Let E be a public key encryption from a message space $\mathcal{M}$ to a ciphertext space $\mathcal{C}$. We can adopt any public key encryption scheme as E, e.g., [8][9][10][11]. Let us refer to $E(e, m)$ as the encryption of a message m with the public encryption key e, and $D(d, c)$ as the decryption of a ciphertext c with the private decryption key d.

Apart from E, our protocol assumes an ElGamal cryptosystem [9] as the sender's encryption function. To encrypt a value m using the public key $y = g^x$, where x is corresponding private key, a value $r \in_u Z_q$ is chosen uniformly at random and the pair $(c_1, c_2) = (g^r, my^r)$ is calculated. The resulting ciphertext to m consists of the pair (c_1, c_2). In order to decrypt this and obtain m, the recipient with x calculates $m = c_2/c_1{}^x$.

2 Protocol

Suppose P, who is the proxy of R under a condition ϕ, tries to decrypt the ciphertext which S sends to R. To encrypt the message m, S chooses $r \in Z_q$

and computes $c_1 = g^r$, $c_2 = m(e_R)^r$. Then, S sends the ciphertext (c_1, c_2) to R and P over a public insecure channel. The basic scheme and the extended version are presented below. The difference between them is the dependence on the reliability on T.

2.1 Basic Scheme

We present the basic scheme in which the DC server T is assumed to be honest, i.e., T does not deviate from the protocol. Such deviation includes collusion with other parties and the leakage of T's secret information.

1. protocol Ψ

   Ψ is the delegation key generation protocol by which the delegator R with the decryption key $d_R (\in Z_q)$ transfers the conditional right of decryption to P. At first, R chooses $v \in \mathcal{M}$ uniformly at random, and then computes the delegation key $\sigma = < u_T, u_P > = < E(e_T, v), d_R - H(\phi, v) >$. Both σ and ϕ are sent to P over a secure channel.

2. protocol Γ

   Γ is the proxy decryption protocol, a two-party protocol between the DC server T and the proxy P, in which P decrypts the ciphertext (c_1, c_2) with the delegation key σ under the condition ϕ. The communication between T and P is made over a secure channel such as SSL.

   a) P sends u_T, ϕ and c_1 to T. Note that u_P and c_2 are not sent to T.

   b) T evaluates ϕ. If valid, T computes $c_T = c_1^{H(\phi, D(d_T, u_T))}$ and sends it back to P, otherwise, T returns an error message.

   c) After receiving c_T, P can compute m as $m = c_2 c_1^{-u_P} c_T^{-1}$.

If the delegation key σ is properly formed, the decryption of u_T with T's decryption key d_T is v, namely $D(d_T, u_T) = v$. Hence, one can see that after receiving c_T, P obtains m by

$$c_2 c_1^{-u_P} c_T^{-1} = c_2 c_1^{-u_P} c_1^{-H(\phi, v)} = c_2 c_1^{d_R} = m \quad .$$

P can learn m if and only if ϕ is valid and P knows σ which is given by R from the following observation.

- If ϕ is invalid, T does not send c_T to P. P who has u_P can compute c_T from m as $c_T = c_2 c_1^{-u_P} m$ and vice versa. So, given u_T, u_P, c_1 and c_2, the computational difficulty for P to compute m is equivalent to that of computing c_T, which requires T's private key d_T because if E is secure which means that the attacker cannot get the value of $D(d_T, u_T)$, $H(\phi, D(d_T, u_T))$ cannot be computed due to the one-way property of H.

- The value u_T in σ is tightly coupled to ϕ since computing u_T corresponding to $\phi'(\neq \phi)$ without d_R is as hard as inverting the one-way function H. Therefore, P can use only the given condition.

It is required that the execution of the proxy decryption protocol does not reveal any information on d_R to either P or T, since the knowledge of d_R means the ability to decrypt any ciphertext sent to R.

- P cannot compute d_R from σ due to the security of E and the hardness of inverting H.
- T does not learn any information about d_R since u_T does not contain any information about d_R. This is the major difference from the scheme in which R send just d_R and ϕ directly to T. In our scheme, T offers the support for decryption but T cannot decrypt the ciphertext alone. Even T obtaining u_T requires u_P (P's part of the delegation key) in order to decrypt the ciphertext.

2.2   Extended Scheme

The security of the basic scheme depends on the reliability of the DC server T, that evaluates the condition ϕ. Moreover, P can compute the private key of R by obtaining v which only T knows internally. To reduce such dependence on T, we show an extended scheme, in which, a group of servers jointly play the role of the DC server, so after a quorum of them checks the validity of ϕ, P can decrypt the ciphertext. We use the idea similar to the group key distribution technique in [12] in order to implement the quorum access control. The difference from the ordinary threshold cryptosystem is that even more than the quorum of the servers (even if all servers) cannot get any information about the private decryption key d_R without cooperating with the proxy.

1. protocol Ψ
   Ψ is the delegation key generation protocol Ψ by which the delegator R with the decryption key $d_R(\in Z_q)$ transfers the right of decryption to P under a condition which is verified by a quorum of servers. Let ϕ be the condition that R wants to designate.
   R selects a group of n servers $T_1, \ldots, T_n$. Let i be the ID of T_i, Λ be the set of the ID of n servers, and (e_i, d_i) be a pair of a public and private key, respectively. For each T_i, R chooses v_i in Z_q and computes $u_{T_i} = E(e_i, v_i)$. Then, R forms a polynomial of degree n such that $f(0) = d_R$ and $f(i) = H(\phi, v_i)$ for $i \in \Lambda$, which can be obtained by

$$f(x) = \lambda_0(x) \times d_R + \sum_{i \in \Lambda} \lambda_i(x) \times H(\phi, v_i) \bmod q$$

where $\lambda_i(x)$ is a function to compute the Lagrange coefficient given by

$$\lambda_i(x) = \prod_{i \in \Lambda, j \neq i} (x - j)/(i - j) \bmod q \quad .$$

Let t be the quorum number of servers required to perform the proxy decryption Γ. R chooses a set of $n - t + 1$ integers $\Omega = \{i_0, \ldots, i_{n-t}\}$ from $Z_q \setminus (\Lambda \cup \{0\})$ and computes $\tau_j = f(j)$ for $j \in \Omega$ in order to compute $u_P = \{(j, \tau_j) \mid j \in \Omega\}$. The delegation key σ consists of u_P and $u_{T_1}, \ldots, u_{T_n}$. The value σ and ϕ are sent to P over a secure channel.

2. protocol Γ

The proxy decryption protocol Γ for the extended scheme is a protocol between the proxy P and t out of n servers $T_1, \ldots, T_n$. After communicating with t servers which verify the condition ϕ, P can decrypt the ciphertext (c_1, c_2) with the delegation key σ. The communication between P and the servers is made over a secure channel such as SSL. Suppose P communicates with $T_1, \ldots, T_t$ and the set of their IDs is $\mathcal{T} = \{1, \ldots, t\}$ without loss of generality. For each of them, P iterates the following process.

a) P sends u_{T_i}, ϕ and c_1 to T_i.

b) T_i evaluates ϕ. If valid, T_i computes $c_{T_i} = c_1{}^{H(\phi, D(d_i, u_{T_i}))}$ and sends it back to P, otherwise, T_i returns an error message.

After receiving $c_{T_1}, \ldots, c_{T_t}$ from t servers, P can compute m as

$$m = c_2 c_1{}^{-\Sigma_{i \in \Omega} \theta_i \tau_i} \left(\prod_{i \in \mathcal{T}} c_{T_i}{}^{-\theta_i} \right)$$

where

$$\theta_i = \prod_{j \in \Omega \cup \mathcal{T}, j \neq i} j \times (j - i)^{-1} \bmod q \quad .$$

We assume at most $t - 1$ servers might collude with the proxy P. To model this case, suppose the attacker A can arbitrarily control $t - 1$ dishonest servers $T_1, \ldots, T_{t-1}$ and the proxy P without loss of generality, that is, A knows their private key $d_1, \ldots, d_{t-1}$ and all inputs to $T_1, \ldots, T_{t-1}$ and P. Even in this case, A cannot learn m as long as ϕ is verified to be invalid due to the following observation. Suppose T_t is the honest server. If ϕ is invalid, A cannot obtain c_{T_t} from T_t. A who knows $u_{T_1}, \ldots, u_{T_{t-1}}$ and u_P can compute c_{T_t} from m as $c_{T_t} = \{m^{-1} c_2 c_1{}^{-\Sigma_{i \in \Omega} \theta_i \tau_i} (\prod_{i \in \mathcal{T} \setminus \{t\}} c_{T_i}{}^{-\theta_i})\}^{-\theta_t}$ and vice versa. So, given $u_{T_1}, \ldots, u_{T_{t-1}}$, u_P, c_1 and c_2, the computational difficulty for A to compute m is equivalent to that of computing c_{T_t}, which requires T_t's private key d_{T_t} because if E is secure which means that the attacker cannot get the value of $D(d_{T_t}, u_{T_t})$, $H(\phi, D(d_{T_t}, u_{T_t}))$ cannot be computed due to the one-way property of H. Moreover, A cannot compute R's private key d_R for the following reason: In the extended scheme, d_R is represented with $d_1, \ldots, d_t$ by

$$d_R = \theta_t \times H(\phi, D(d_t, u_{T_t})) + \sum_{i \in \mathcal{T} \setminus \{t\}} \theta_i \times H(\phi, D(d_i, u_{T_i})) + \sum_{i \in \Omega} \theta_i \tau_i$$

and therefore, computing d_R requires the value of $H(\phi, D(d_t, u_{T_t}))$, which cannot be obtained without d_t due to the security of E and the one-way property of H.

One desirable property is that R's private key d_R is not revealed even when all of the servers collude unless P is dishonest. As one can see from the construction of Ψ in the extended scheme, $u_{T_1}, \ldots, u_{T_n}$ are randomly produced and thus do not contain any information on d_R. This fact implies that P cannot deny the leakage due to the non-repudiation property, i.e., P cannot deny the deviation from the protocol to R when a problem has occurred, such as the exposure of the private key. This increases the liability to manage the proxy key carefully.

The two schemes presented here can be implemented in a seamless manner. The difference between the basic scheme and the extended one is in the roles of the delegator R and the proxy P. Specifically, the operation using T in the basic scheme is equivalent to one done by the servers in the extended scheme. Moreover, R can choose n and t independently for each execution of Ψ without any communication with the servers. This is quite practical, especially when a service provider over the network plays the role of the DC sever.

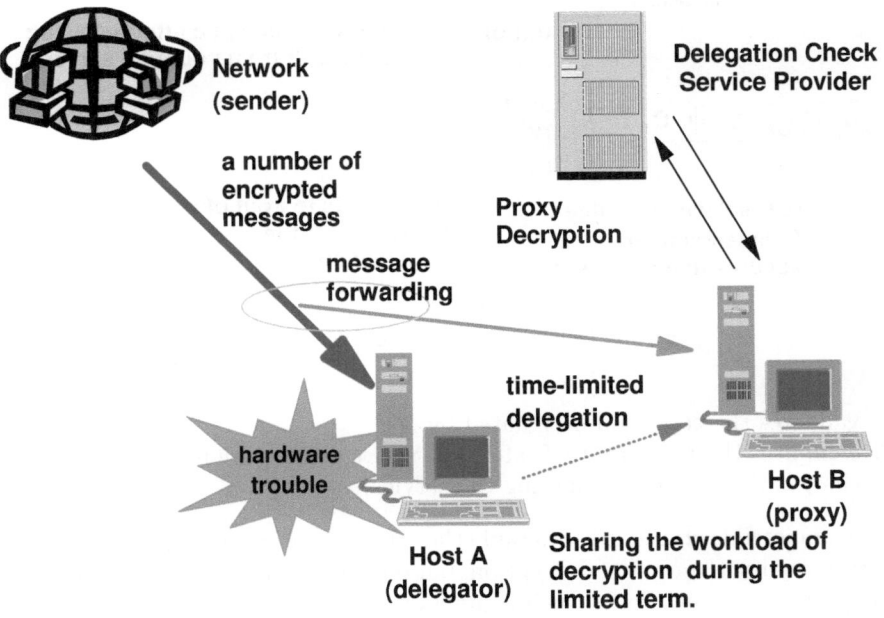

Fig. 1. Delegation Check Service Provider

3   Application

3.1   Delegation Check Service Provider

Suppose a party A wants to delegate to another other party B the right to access the data encrypted with A's public key. For example, when A is unable to perform decryption due to such reasons as a traffic increase or a temporary failure (Fig.1), it is desirable to allow another reliable party to execute the decryption on behalf of A. Also, the delegated right should revert to A after A's recovery or re-connection. In order to support conditional decryption by B, A can make use of a service provider that offers the function of a DC server. This service provider provides the clients with the following services.

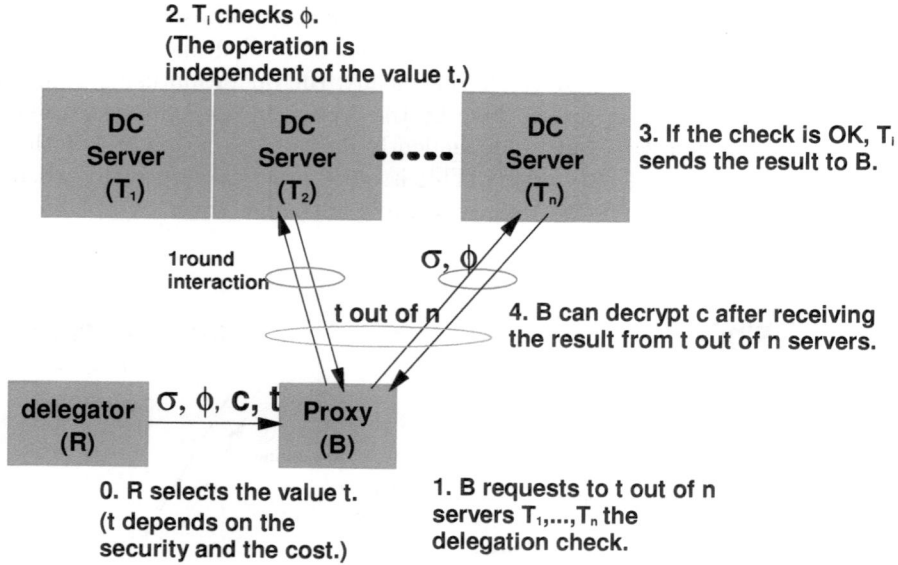

Fig. 2. Delegation with Multiple DC Server

1. validates the condition designated by A
2. computes the response to B after the above confirmation.
3. charges A some fee for offering the service.

In a commercial service, it is desirable that the delegator has to pay a charge not for transferring the right of decryption, but only for the proxy decryption (Fig.2). Our protocol is suitable for such commercial services in the sense that the DC server participates only during the execution of the proxy decryption protocol Γ. Moreover, our protocol allows the delegator to choose any number of n and t for each delegation. This property is also suitable for real world applications. The larger the t the delegator chooses to guard against the server's misbehavior, the higher the charge the delegator has to pay for the service.

As shown in Fig.3, The sender may possibly be the same party as the delegator.

For example, suppose a party Alice encrypts confidential information and puts the ciphertext into a public P2P data sharing system (Fig.4). Before disconnection, Alice wants to transfer the right to access the information to Bob until re-participation. In this case, Alice plays the sender who encrypts the message, as well as the role of the delegator who has the private key at the same time.

3.2   PIN Control for Mobile Devices

For example, suppose a party A encrypts confidential information and puts the ciphertext in a public P2P data sharing system. Before disconnection, A wants

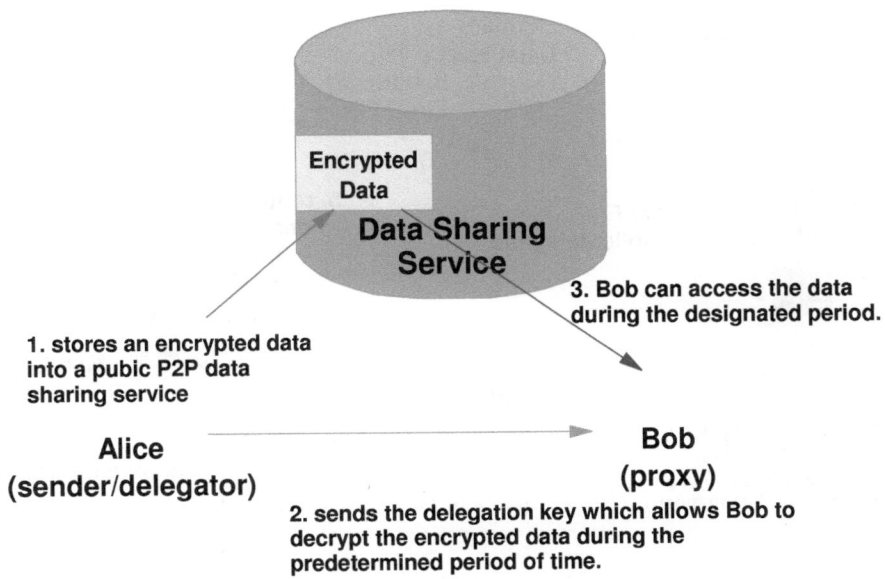

Fig. 3. Access Control for Self-Encrypted Data

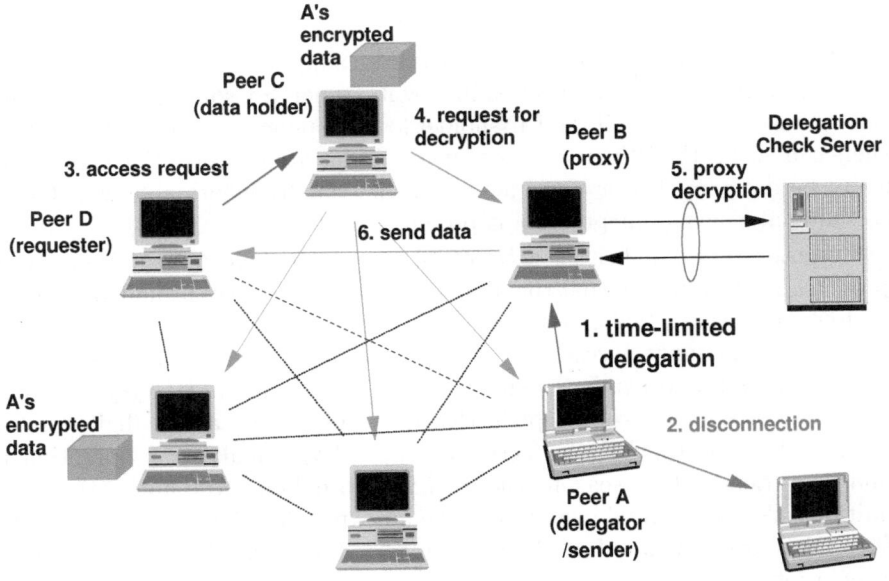

Fig. 4. Delegation for P2P Data Sharing

to transfer the right to access the information to B until re-participation. In this case, A plays not only the role of the sender who encrypts the message, but also one of the delegator.

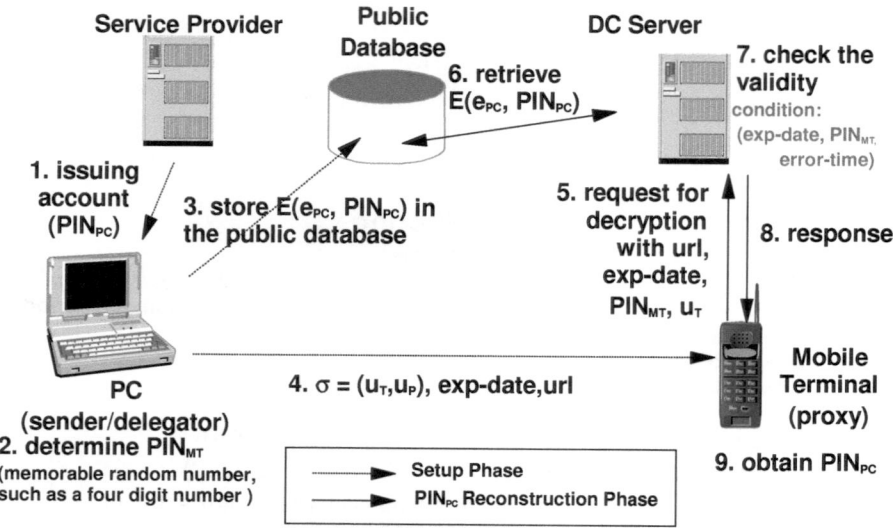

Fig. 5. PIN Control for Mobile Devices

In a pervasive computing world, pervasive devices, such as cellular phones, are often used for accessing the network. A mobile user might want to keep their PIN that is required to access to the service in the memory of such device in order to save the cumbersome input or to prevent it from slipping in his/her mind. On the other hand, the PIN should be accessible by its owner. So, some countermeasures are required so that even if the PIN-holder lost the phone containing the PIN, no others can access the PIN unless certain conditions are satisfied. Such conditions should be designated in a user-friendly but personally identifiable way. One of the candidates using our protocol is presented in Fig. 5.

Suppose a user who has the account for PC, denoted as PIN_{PC}, wants to set up the mobile terminal so that the user can access the service through it. Another requirement is that PIN_{PC} is accessible only by the user and the others, even the DC server, cannot access PIN_{PC}. To authorize the user who operates the mobile terminal, another PIN denoted as PIN_{MT} is used. PIN_{MT} is enough short random number to be kept in the user's mind, e.g., a four digit number. Using PIN_{MT} as the PIN for accessing the PIN_{PC} makes the operation by hand user-friendly but weakens the security. To enhance the authenticity, the additional device-oriented constraints like an expiration date, the limit number of mistakes are designated as the condition for the proxy decryption. To store the encryption of PIN_{PC} in the public database, each of the user's devices that might access to the service do not have to keep the encryption. For example, the condition can be designated as "the PIN_{PC} can be shown on the display if matching the input PIN to PIN_{MT} is confirmed until the mistakes is not over three times." This situation is considered to one where the mobile user plays the roles of the sender (PC), the delegator (PC), and the proxy (mobile terminal) at the same time.

4 Conclusion

In this paper, we presented a cryptographic method to enable a peer to transfer the right to access encrypted data provided predetermined conditions are satisfied. Our approach involves a DC server to check a predetermined condition according to the rule. A delegator transfers the right to decrypt the ciphertext to a proxy under certain conditions. The proxy can decrypt the ciphertext only after it passes the verification check of the DC server. Two types of techniques, a basic scheme and an extended scheme, were presented. The basic scheme is relatively efficient, safeguarding the security under the assumption that the DC server does not deviate from the protocol. In order to reduce the dependency regarding the reliability of the DC server, the extended scheme allows the delegator to direct the proxy to use a group of servers. Our protocol has the desirable properties that the delegator can independently choose which of the two schemes to use without any interaction with the DC servers or the proxy, and the choice of the scheme does not require any modification of the operations that the server performs.

References

1. B. Horne, B. Pinkas, and T. Sander. Escrow services and incentives in peer-to-peer networks. In *Proc. of ACM EC'01*, 2001.
2. M. Mambo and E. Okamoto. Proxy cryptosystems: Delegation of the power to decrypt ciphertexts. In *IEICE Trans. Fund. Electronics Communications and Comp. Sci. E80-A/1*, pages 54–63, 1997.
3. M. Blaze, G. Bleumer, and M. Strauss. Divertible protocols and atomic proxy cryptography. In *Proc. of EUROCRYPT'98*, pages 127–144, 1998.
4. M. Jakobsson. On quorum controlled asymmetric proxy re-encryption. In *Proc. of PKC'99*, pages 112–121, 1999.
5. R. L. Rivest, A. Shamir, and D. A. Wagner. Time-lock puzzles and timed-release crypto. In *MIT/LCS/TR-684*, 1996.
6. M. Kudo. Secure electronic sealed-bid auction protocol with public key cryptography. In *IEICE Trans. Fundamentals, E81-A, 1,*, pages 20–26, 1998.
7. G. D. Crescenzo, R. Ostrovsky, and S. Rajagopalan. Conditional oblivious transfer and timed-release encryption. In *Proc. of EUROCRYPT'99*, pages 74–89, 1999.
8. R. Rivest, A. Shamir, and L. Adleman. A method for obtaining digital signatures and public key cryptosystems. *Communication of the ACM*, 21(2):120–126, 1978.
9. T. El Gamal. A public key cryptosystem and a signature scheme based on discrete logarithms. In *Proc. of CRYPTO'84*, pages 10–18, 1984.
10. M. Bellare and P. Rogaway. Optimal asymmetric encryption. In *Proc. of EUROCRYPT'94*, pages 92–111, 1994.
11. R. Cramer and V. Shoup. A practical public key cryptosystem provably secure against adaptive chosen ciphertext attack. In *Proc. of CRYPTO'98*, pages 13–25, 1994.
12. J. Anzai, N. Matsuzaki, and T. Matsumoto. A quick group key distribution scheme with "entity revocation". In *Proc. of ASIACRYPT'99*, pages 333–347, 1999.

Certification of Public Keys within an Identity Based System

L. Chen[1], K. Harrison[1], A. Moss[2], D. Soldera[1], and N.P. Smart[2]

[1] Hewlett-Packard Laboratories,
Filton Road,
Stoke Gifford,
Bristol, BS34 8QZ,
United Kingdom.
{liqun_chen, keith_harrison, david_soldera}@hpl.hp.com
[2] Computer Science Department,
Woodland Road,
University of Bristol,
Bristol, BS8 1UB,
United Kingdom.
{moss, nigel}@cs.bris.ac.uk

Abstract. We investigate a number of issues related to the use of multiple trust authorities in the type of identifier based cryptography enabled by the Weil and Tate pairings. An example of such a system is the Boneh and Franklin encryption scheme. We examine how to create an efficient hierarchy of multiple trust authorities and then go on to examine some application areas of pairing based cryptography.

1 Introduction

In 1984 Shamir [10] introduced the concept of identity based cryptography and proposed a signature scheme based on the RSA assumption. Over the years a number of researchers tried to propose secure and efficient identity based encryption algorithms, but with little success. This state of affairs changed in 2001 when two identity based encryption algorithms were proposed, one by Cocks [4] based on the quadratic residuosity assumption and another by Boneh and Franklin [1] based on the Weil pairing, although using a variant based on the Tate pairing is more efficient. A number of identity based signature algorithms based on the Tate pairing also exist, e.g. [3], [7] and [9].

The creation of these identity based schemes made it possible to approach the problem of creating a public-key infrastructure from a new angle. To this end Horwitz and Lynn [8] describe a way of coping with a hierarchy of trust authorities using only identity-based encryption. However, this advantage of only being based on identifiers comes with a disadvantage that the proposed system only works with two levels of keys and that a certain amount of collusion leads to the whole system being broken. This paper addresses the same issues as [8] and provides a more scalable solution.

A.H. Chan and V. Gligor (Eds.): ISC 2002, LNCS 2433, pp. 322–333, 2002.

The paper is structured as follows, in the next section we set up notation and recap on a number of pairing based schemes. In section 3 we describe how a hybrid of traditional PKI and IBE may be created that could overcome some of the current scalability issues with traditional PKIs. We show how the short signature of Boneh, Lynn and Shacham [2] lends itself naturally to use in the certificates of a hybrid traditional-PKI/IBE system. In section 4 we describe a scalable hierarchy of trust authorities using a combination of IBE and short signatures. In section 5 we look at some applications that would require a scalable and efficient hierarchy of trust authorities. Section 6 draws some conclusions from this paper.

2   Notation and Pairing Based Schemes

2.1   The Tate Pairing

Let G_1 and G_2 denote two groups of prime order q in which the discrete logarithm problem is believed to be hard and for which there exists a computable bilinear map

$$t : G_1 \times G_1 \longrightarrow G_2.$$

We shall write G_1 with an additive notation and G_2 with a multiplicative notation, since in real life G_1 will be the group of points on an elliptic curve and G_2 will denote a subgroup of the multiplicative group of a finite field.

Since the mapping is bilinear, we can move exponents/multipliers around at will. For example if $a, b, c \in \mathbb{F}_q$ and $P, Q \in G_1$ then we have

$$t(aP, bQ)^c = t(aP, cQ)^b = t(bP, cQ)^a = t(bP, aQ)^c = t(cP, aQ)^b = t(cP, bQ)^a$$
$$= t(abP, Q)^c = t(abP, cQ) = t(P, abQ)^c = t(cP, abQ)$$
$$= \ldots$$
$$= t(abcP, Q) = t(P, abcQ) = t(P, Q)^{abc}$$

These tricks will be used repeatedly throughout this document.

We define the following cryptographic hash functions

$$H_1 : \{0, 1\}^* \longrightarrow G_1,$$
$$H_2 : \{0, 1\}^* \longrightarrow \mathbb{F}_q,$$
$$H_3 : G_2 \longrightarrow \{0, 1\}^*.$$

2.2   Types of Public/Private Key Pairs

We require the following two types of keys:

- A standard public/private key pair is a pair (R, s) where $R \in G_1$ and $s \in \mathbb{F}_q$ with
$$R = sP$$
for some given fixed point $P \in G_1$.

- An identifier based key pair is a pair $(Q_{\texttt{ID}}, S_{\texttt{ID}})$ where $Q_{\texttt{ID}}, S_{\texttt{ID}} \in G_1$ and there is some trust authority (TA) with a standard public/private key pair given by $(R_{\texttt{TA}}, s)$, such that the key pair of the trust authority and the key pair of the identifier are linked via

$$S_{\texttt{ID}} = sQ_{\texttt{ID}} \text{ and } Q_{\texttt{ID}} = H_1(\texttt{ID}),$$

where ID is the identifier string.

2.3 Cryptographic Primitives

We recap on the following three cryptographic primitives.

Short Signatures. This scheme, due to Boneh, Lynn and Shacham [2], allows the holder of the private part s of a standard public/private key pair to sign a bit string. Let m denote the message to be signed

- **Signing :**
  Compute $V = sH_1(m)$.
- **Verification :**
  Check whether the following equation holds

$$t(P, V) = t(R, H_1(m))$$

Since this is the first time we have used the pairing it is worth demonstrating why the equation should hold for a valid signature.

$$
\begin{aligned}
t(P, V) &= t(P, sH_1(m)) &&\text{Since } V = sH_1(m), \\
&= t(P, H_1(m))^s &&\text{By linearity in the second coordinate,} \\
&= t(sP, H_1(m)) &&\text{By linearity in the first coordinate,} \\
&= t(R, H_1(m)) &&\text{Since } R = sP.
\end{aligned}
$$

Identifier Based Encryption. This scheme, due to Boneh and Franklin [1], allows the holder of the private part $S_{\texttt{ID}}$ of an identifier based key pair to decrypt a message sent to her under the public part $Q_{\texttt{ID}}$. We present only the simple scheme which is only ID-OWE, for an ID-CCA scheme one applies the Fujisaki-Okamoto transformation [6]. Let m denote the message to be encrypted then:

- **Encryption :**
  Compute $U = rP$ where r is a random element of $\mathbb{F}_q$. Then compute

$$V = m \oplus H_3(t(R_{\texttt{TA}}, rQ_{\texttt{ID}}))$$

Output the ciphertext (U, V).

- **Decryption :**
Decryption is performed by computing

$$
\begin{aligned}
V \oplus H_3(t(U, S_{\text{ID}})) &= V \oplus H_3(t(rP, sQ_{\text{ID}})) \\
&= V \oplus H_3(t(P, Q_{\text{ID}})^{rs}) \\
&= V \oplus H_3(t(sP, rQ_{\text{ID}})) \\
&= V \oplus H_3(t(R_{\text{TA}}, rQ_{\text{ID}})) \\
&= m.
\end{aligned}
$$

Identifier Based Signatures. There are a number of such schemes based on the Tate pairing, we present the one due to Hess [7], which is not only efficient but has a security proof relative to the computational Diffie-Hellman problem in G_1. Let m denote the message to be signed then:

- **Signing :**
Compute $r = t(P, P)^k$ where k is a random element of $\mathbb{F}_q$. Apply the hash function H_2 to $m\|r$ to obtain $h = H_2(m\|r)$. Compute

$$
U = hS_{\text{ID}} + kP.
$$

Output (U, h) as the signature on the message m.
- **Verification :**
Compute

$$
r = t(U, P) \cdot t(Q_{\text{ID}}, -R_{\text{TA}})^h.
$$

Accept the signature if and only if $h = H_2(m\|r)$.

3   A Hybrid PKI/IBE

3.1   Combining a Traditional PKI with IBE

In [8] a way of coping with a hierarchy of trust authorities is presented. The approach is for trust authorities to produce keys for trust authorities further down the hierarchy. There is only one standard public/private key pair in the whole system, which belongs to the root trust authority. All other keys are identifier based key pairs and as such the hierarchy produced can be considered as a pure identifier based infrastructure.

However, this advantage of only being based on identifiers comes with a disadvantage that the proposed system only works with two levels of keys and that a certain amount of collusion leads to the whole system being broken. Thus this type of hierarchical approach as a means to replacing traditional, X509 like, PKI systems seems to suffer from worse scalability issues than X509.

As a solution we propose a hybrid system which merges traditional PKI solutions with identifier based solutions. We assume a multitude of standard public/private key pairs held by trust authorities, with user keys being identity based. A number of points need to be made

- This model of multiple trust authorities is more likely to resemble the "real world" where no global hierarchy is in place.
- We do not assume that trust authorities are embodied in reputable organisations, for example some applications may want trust authorities to be embedded into ones PDA. However, we do not exclude global trust authorities such as Verisign or Microsoft in our model.

Hence, multiple trust authorities can exist but we assume encryption and signatures are made using identifier based keys. With multiple trust authorities one of course needs some way of authenticating, or cross certifying, the authorities as in a traditional form of PKI solution.

So has this hybrid PKI/IBE based solution bought us anything? It appears to have created a level of complication, but our belief is that this makes the system more scalable. A common problem with traditional PKI is that whilst it is very good at authenticating domain names, as in the use of SSL, it is rather poor in authenticating large numbers of individual users. On the other hand, identifier based systems are very good at identifying individual users, but poor when it comes to multiple trust domains (as the paper [8] demonstrates).

We use two analogies for the state of affairs we envisage:

- The first is from the world of telecommunications. In this world there are two systems (often run by two separate companies). There is the *local loop* which is the copper wires (or fibre optic cables) from your home to the exchange and then there is the global long distance telephone system. One should think of the local loop being identifier based and the long distance network being PKI based.
- The email system has a similar discontinuity between what are essentially local and global names. Take the email address

$$\texttt{Alice@people.iacr.org}$$

The `people.iacr.org` part is a global name which can be authenticated efficiently using standard certificate chains. The problems arise when one tries to push down the PKI solution to the next level. The `Alice` part is therefore more easily dealt with using identifier based systems.

3.2   Certificates Using Short Signatures

We examine this hierarchy of TA's in more detail using the above email address as an example. We let the three TA's each with their own standard public/private key pairs.

Entity	Private Key	Public Key
org	s_1	$R_{\texttt{org}} = s_1 P$
iacr	s_2	$R_{\texttt{iacr}} = s_2 P$
people	s_3	$R_{\texttt{people}} = s_3 P$

The entity `Alice` is issued an identifier based key pair from the trust authority `people`, namely

$$S_{\text{Alice}} = s_3 R_{\text{Alice}} \text{ and } Q_{\text{Alice}} = H_1(\text{Alice}).$$

Now suppose someone, Bob, wishes to send the entity denoted by

`Alice@people.iacr.org`

an email or someone wishes to verify that entity's signature. Bob first needs to obtain a trusted copy of the public key of the `people` trust authority.

Supposing Bob already trusts the public key of the trust authority `org`. They could simply verify a certificate chain down to the public key of `people` using standard certificate formats, but since each trust authority has the correct type of standard public/private key pair we can use the short signature scheme of Boneh, Lynn and Shacham.

The certificate of the trust authority `iacr`, as produced by the trust authority `org` would then look like

$$(\text{Subject}, \text{Issuer}, \text{Key}, \text{Signature}) = (\text{iacr}, \text{org}, R_{\text{iacr}}, V)$$

where

$$V = s_1 H_1(R_{\text{iacr}} \| \text{iacr}).$$

Note that we can use the same code to perform certificate checking and verification as one would use to produce identifier based encryption and signatures. This will be an advantage on small devices which may only allow small code footprints.

4   Hierarchies of Linked Trust Authorities

In the previous section we assumed that the various trust authorities were not linked via their identities but simply had traditional public/private key pairs. In this section we examine what happens when the trust authorities are linked in an identifier based hierarchy.

Entity	Standard Private Key	Standard Public Key	ID Based Private Key	ID Based Public Key
org	s_1	$R_{\text{org}} = s_1 P$	-	-
iacr	s_2	$R_{\text{iacr}} = s_2 P$	$S_{\text{iacr}} = s_1 Q_{\text{iacr}}$	$Q_{\text{iacr}} = H_1(\text{iacr})$
people	s_3	$R_{\text{people}} = s_3 P$	$S_{\text{people}} = s_2 Q_{\text{people}}$	$Q_{\text{people}} = H_1(\text{people})$
Alice	-	-	$S_{\text{Alice}} = s_3 Q_{\text{Alice}}$	$Q_{\text{Alice}} = H_1(\text{Alice})$

We now have the chance to authenticate public keys in another way. If a user trusts the standard public key of any TA in the hierarchy (either `org`, `iacr` or `people`), this TA will become the root of trust to the user; and then this TA's corresponding standard private key will become the master key to the user. In this section, we consider an example where a user trusts the standard public key of iacr, i.e. $s_2 P$. Based on this trust he wishes to authenticate the identifier based public key of Alice, which has been issued by the trust authority people. We shall see that both iacr and people are able to offer this authentication service.

4.1   Transferring Trust at the Upper Level

One obvious way of doing this is for iacr to sign people's standard public key, using the short signature scheme, as above. Since iacr's standard public key is trusted, the verifier will then trust people's standard public key and so will trust Alice's identifier based public key.

We can represent this transfer of trust from iacr to people via

$$\text{iacr} \longrightarrow \text{people},$$

since the certification is performed by iacr.

4.2   Transferring Trust at the Lower Level

There is another obvious solution, which is for people to sign its own standard public key using an identifier based signature scheme, with the identifier based private key supplied to people by iacr. Since iacr's standard public key is trusted, the verifier trusts people's identifier based public key and will then trust the signature on people's standard public key. Just as before the verifier will then trust Alice's identifier based public key.

We represent this transfer of trust from iacr to people via

$$\text{iacr} \longleftarrow \text{people},$$

since now the certification is performed by the trust authority people.

4.3   Balanced Trust Transferal

However, there is another more natural way which can be deployed by either iacr or people and which to the user is transparent as to who actually produced the authentication of people's public key. A situation which we can represent diagrammatically via

$$\text{iacr} \longleftrightarrow \text{people}.$$

The system we provide below provides implicit authentication of the key R_{people}, in that explicit authentication is only obtained once the key R_{people} has been seen 'in action', in other words it is used to verify a signature.

The verifier is assumed to know and trust the standard public key R_{iacr}. They wish to obtain implicit trust that people's standard public key R_{people} is linked to the entity which iacr is claiming to be people. Once this linkage is established the verifier can then use Alice's public key.

One of the following stages is then executed:

- If the authenticating party is people, then people generates a random value of $r \in \mathbb{F}_q$ and publishes

$$C_1 = rS_{\texttt{people}} = rs_2Q_{\texttt{people}},$$
$$C_2 = rQ_{\texttt{people}},$$
$$C_3 = rR_{\texttt{people}}.$$

- If the authenticating party is iacr, then iacr generates a random value of $r \in \mathbb{F}_q$ and publishes

$$C_1 = rs_2Q_{\texttt{people}},$$
$$C_2 = rQ_{\texttt{people}},$$
$$C_3 = rR_{\texttt{people}}.$$

The verifier can then check that the linkage is as claimed by checking the following two equations hold

$$t(C_2, R_{\texttt{people}}) = t(rQ_{\texttt{people}}, R_{\texttt{people}})$$
$$= t(Q_{\texttt{people}}, rR_{\texttt{people}})$$
$$= t(Q_{\texttt{people}}, C_3),$$
$$t(P, C_1) = t(P, rs_2Q_{\texttt{people}})$$
$$= t(s_2P, rQ_{\texttt{people}})$$
$$= t(R_{\texttt{iacr}}, C_2).$$

These two equations demonstrate that the discrete logarithms are related as they should be.

5 Applications of Pairing Based Systems

We now examine some novel applications of the pairing based cryptosystems given at the beginning of this paper. All of the following applications assume that the trust authorities are in fact trusted by all users, and hence all require some form of certification like those proposed in the prior sections.

5.1 Delegation of Rights

Up to now when we have used identifiers they have really been identities. Traditional PKI sometimes makes a distinction between an identity certificate (represented by a 4-Tuple in SPKI for example [5]) and an authorisation certificate (represented by a 5-Tuple in SPKI). Since strings correspond to keys in an identifier based system, we can replace identity strings in our discussion above with authorisation strings.

For example given a SPKI s-expression which describes some access rights, we can write down immediately the corresponding identifier public key corresponding to this s-expression. There is no need to bind the s-expression to the key, since the s-expression *is* the key.

We now describe how delegation of authorisations can be handled. Suppose we have some trust authority (say Alice) who has control of some resource. Suppose Alice has a standard public/private key pair given by

$$R_{\texttt{Alice}} = sP.$$

Assume that Bob has a public key given by $M_{\texttt{Bob}}$, this could either be a standard public key or an identifier based one.

Alice wishes to pass authorisation to use this resource to Bob. In SPKI this is represented by the 5-tuple

(Issuer, Subject, Delegate, Authorization, Validity),

where the standard SPKI format is to have Issuer and Subject being hashes of public keys, Delegate being a Yes/No flag, Authorization being the description of what is being authorised and Validity being the validity period.

Alice forms the s-expression given by

$$\sigma = M_{\texttt{Bob}}\|\texttt{Delegate}\|\texttt{Authorization}\|\texttt{Validity}$$

and then forms the public/private key pair given by

$$S_\sigma = sQ_\sigma \text{ where } Q_\sigma = H_1(\sigma).$$

Alice then gives the private key S_σ to Bob.

For Bob to now use this resource he needs to demonstrate

- He knows the private key corresponding to $M_{\texttt{Bob}}$, i.e. he is Bob.
- He knows the private key corresponding to Q_σ, i.e. Alice has given him the authorisation.

To demonstrate the two facts he can either produce a signature or engage in a challenge-response protocol using the two corresponding private keys.

Now consider the case where the Delegate field is set to Yes. In this case Bob is allowed to delegate some, or all, of his authorisation from Alice to a third party, say Charlie. In this case Bob himself needs to act as a trust authority and so must have a standard public/private key pair

$$R_{\texttt{Bob}} = tP.$$

Bob can then create a delegation

$$\tau = M_{\texttt{Charlie}}\|\texttt{Delegate'}\|\texttt{Authorization'}\|\texttt{Validity'}$$

in the same way as Alice did. To use the resource Charlie needs to present both σ and τ, and needs to prove

- He knows the private key corresponding to M_{Charlie}, i.e. he is Charlie.
- He knows the private key corresponding to Q_τ, i.e. Bob has given him the authorisation.

But how is Alice's original authorisation σ going to be authenticated? First Alice should use Bob's key R_{Bob} within the s-expression for σ, where we interpret this as saying only the key R_{Bob} is allowed to delegate. Finally Bob needs to pass onto Charlie some information which proves that Alice gave him authorisation by revealing the value of S_σ to him. This last task is accomplished in one of two ways:

- As in the last section by Bob publishing

$$C_1 = rS_\sigma, C_2 = rQ_\sigma, C_3 = rR_{\text{Bob}}.$$

The advantage of this method is that Alice could also produce this information for Charlie, however the disadvantage is the relatively large bandwidth considerations.
- Bob could sign, using the private key S_σ and the earlier identifier based signature scheme, the message given by Q_τ.

Composition of the delegated authorisations can be accomplished using the standard SPKI 5-Tuple reduction rules. Notice that, one can even remove the delegation field from the s-expressions, since to delegate we require a standard public/private key. We can bind the authorisation to a standard public key when delegations are allowed and an identifier based public key when delegations are not allowed.

5.2 Creating Groups

We give an example where the use of trust authorities, even at the user level, gives a number of added advantages when combined with the identity based encryption and signature schemes. Note, this application requires the trust authorities standard public key to itself be trusted. Hence, the following application assumes the existence of some form of certification for the trust authorities public keys as we have discussed in the rest of this paper.

Imagine a city in which there is a city wide local public wireless network. For example Bristol University, Hewlett-Packard and a number of other organisations plan to roll out such an infrastructure across Bristol in the near future. Suppose you arrive in this city for a conference and you are good friends with Alice, who lives in this city. You would ideally like Alice to pick you up from the airport, but if she is not available then one of Alice's friends you would trust to do this. Therefore you broadcast a message over the network when you land saying, "I've arrived at the airport! I am completely lost! Could one of Alice's friends pick me up?".

Clearly if this was broadcast in the clear then you would leave yourself open for any unscrupulous person to come and try and mug you. Whilst this may not be a major problem in a relatively peaceful city, but it may be a problem in some cities. The question arises, how can you encrypt to Alice's friends when you may not know who they are?

To overcome this problem consider the situation in which people are their own trust authorities and issue keys to certain subsets of their acquaintances. In our example Alice is a trust authority and has a public/private key given by

$$R_{\texttt{Alice}} = sP.$$

She then, when she meets her friends, gives them a public/private key not according to the actual name but simply under the identifier `Friend`. Such a device to create, distribute and accept keys can be embedded into either a PDA or into some wearable computer that people in the city use to interact with the wireless network.

In this way our hapless traveller, just arrived for the conference, can encrypt a message to all of Alice's friends by using the pair of keys

$$R_{\texttt{Alice}} \text{ and } Q_{\texttt{Friends}}.$$

This encrypted message can then be broadcast to the whole city, knowing that only Alice's friends can decrypt it.

5.3 Addition of Multiple Short Signatures

Although not an application of identifier based cryptography as such, the following illustrates another advantage of the short signature scheme based on pairings. Suppose we have three users Alice, Bob and Charlie with standard public/private key pairs given by

$$R_A = aP, \ R_B = bP, \ R_C = cP.$$

Now suppose they wish to all commit to some document by signing it. For example the document could be a treaty and the three parties could be heads of state, or the document could be a will and the three parties could be the person and two witnesses.

Suppose the document is represented by the string s. They can then generate individual signatures by computing

$$V_A = aH_1(s),$$
$$V_B = bH_1(s),$$
$$V_C = cH_1(s).$$

However, one only needs to store a single signature given by

$$V = V_A + V_B + V_C.$$

Since this can be verified by using the "virtual" public key obtained by computing

$$R = R_A + R_B + R_C.$$

6 Conclusion

We have shown how one can create simple certificate chains for identifier based cryptosystems using either the short signature system of Boneh, Lynn and Shacham or using the identifier based signature scheme of Hess and others. We have argued that this is more efficient than using a traditional X.509 based solution due not only to bandwidth but also because the code required to produce the certificate chains can reuse a lot of the routines needed for the end applications of identity based signatures and encryption. Thus code foot print will be smaller.

We have also given a method of certification in a hierarchy of trust authorities which can be performed either by entities certifying down the chain of trust or by entities certifying up the chain of trust. The advantage of this scheme is that it is transparent to the verifying party as to who actually performed the certification.

Finally we have examined a number of application domains of pairing based cryptography, all of which produce advantages over standard public key cryptographic systems.

References

1. D. Boneh and M. Franklin. Identity based encryption from the Weil pairing. *Advanced in Cryptology – CRYPTO 2001*, Springer-Verlag LNCS 2139, 213–229, 2001.
2. D. Boneh, B. Lynn and H. Shacham. Short signatures from the Weil pairing. *Advances in Cryptology – ASIACRYPT 2001*, Springer-Verlag LNCS 2248, 514–532, 2001.
3. J. C. Cha and J. H. Cheon. An identity-based signature from gap Diffie-Hellman groups. Preprint 2002.
4. C. Cocks. An identity based encryption scheme based on quadratic residues. *Cryptography and Coding*, Springer-Verlag LNCS 2260, 360–363, 2001.
5. C. Ellison and B. Frantz. SPKI certificate theory. Internet RFC 2693, 1999.
6. E. Fujisaki and T. Okamoto. Secure integration of asymmetric and symmetric encryption schemes. *Advances in Cryptology – CRYPTO '99*, Springer-Verlag LNCS 1666, 537–554, 1999.
7. F. Hess. Efficient identity based signature schemes based on pairings. To appear *Selected Areas in Cryptography – 2002*.
8. J. Horwitz and B. Lynn. Hierarchical identity-based encryption. *Advances in Cryptology – EUROCRYPT 2002*, Springer-Verlag LNCS 2332, 466–481, 2002.
9. K. Paterson. ID-based signatures from pairings on elliptic curves. Preprint 2002.
10. A. Shamir. Identity based cryptosystems and signature schemes. *Advanced in Cryptology – CRYPTO '84*, Springer-Verlag LNCS 196, 47–53, 1985.

A New Public Key Cryptosystem for Constrained Hardware

Jiande Zheng

No. 307 Zheng Chang Zhuang, Feng Tai District, Beijing 100039, China
zhengjd@public3.bta.net.cn

Abstract. This paper reports a research on the development of an efficient public key cryptosystem that uses simple matrix operations to encrypt and decrypt messages. The new cryptosystem has the following advantages: a) It is "self-sufficient" and needs not to be integrated with any symmetric cryptosystem. This new asymmetric cryptosystem is supposed to work directly on large quantity of user data and provide an average encryption/decryption speed much higher than mixed cryptosystems currently in use; b) It is good for implementation with constrained hardware. Both encryption and decryption are performed with simple algorithms and require less computing power than existing public key cryptosystems.

1   Introduction

Numerous public-key cryptosystems have been proposed since the invention of public-key cryptography in 1976 by Whitfield Diffie and Martin Hellman [1]. All of these systems rely on the difficulty of some mathematical problems for their security. These systems, classified according to the mathematical problems on which they are based, are integer factorization systems (of which RSA[2] and Rabin[3] are the best known examples), the discrete logarithm systems (such as the Diffe-Hellman key exchange scheme[1], the Elgamal cryptosystem[4]), and the Elliptic Curve Cryptosystem[5]. Each particular system has certain security and performance attributes, which translate into advantages and disadvantages relative to a solution that meets a user's needs.

The algebraic problem of reducing a high degree matrix to its canonical form by similarity transformations is also very difficult. Its complexity is equivalent to the solution of a polynomial equation with the same degree, which is well known to be incapable of deterministic algebraic solution in terms of limited number of additions, subtractions, multiplications and divisions, when its degree is higher than 4[7]. This feature is used in the paper to build a new type of cryptosystem that is good for implementation with constrained hardware platforms. We expect the new public key cryptosystem to be the most efficient one ever proposed.

A.H. Chan and V. Gligor (Eds.): ISC 2002, LNCS 2433, pp. 334–341, 2002.
© Springer-Verlag Berlin Heidelberg 2002

2   The Basic Method

An $r \times r$ matrix $\mathbf{A}$ and an r-dimension vectors $\mathbf{b}_1$, all defined on $GF(p)$, p is a prime number, are chosen subject to the following:
1) $r>4$
2) $\mathbf{A}$ is computed with the following equation:

$$\mathbf{A} = \mathbf{H} \text{ diag } (\lambda_1, \lambda_2, \lambda_3 \ldots \lambda_r) \, \mathbf{H}^{-1} \text{ (mod p)}, \tag{1}$$

where λ_i, i=1,2,...r, are selected as distinct eigenvalues of $\mathbf{A}$,

$$\mathbf{H} = [\mathbf{h}_1 \ \mathbf{h}_2 \ \ldots \mathbf{h}_r] \tag{2}$$

is a modulo p invertible matrix, $\mathbf{h}_i$, i=1,2,...r will be eigenvectors of $\mathbf{A}$.
3) $\mathbf{b}_1$ is located in a subspaces spanned by some eigenvectors of $\mathbf{A}$:

$$\mathbf{b}_1 = (\alpha_1\mathbf{h}_1 + \alpha_2\mathbf{h}_2 + \ldots \alpha_m\mathbf{h}_m)(\text{mod p}), \quad 1<m<r. \tag{3}$$

$(\mathbf{A}, \mathbf{b}_1)$ is used as the public key, while λ_i, i=1,2,...r are used as the private key.
The encryption process begins with the calculation of another r-degree matrix $\mathbf{Y}$ and another r-dimensional vector $\mathbf{d}$:

$$\mathbf{Y} = (k_1\mathbf{A}^{r-1} + k_2\mathbf{A}^{r-2} + \ldots + k_r\mathbf{I})(\text{mod p}), \tag{4}$$

where $k_i \in GF(p)$, i=1,2,...r are random numbers,

$$\mathbf{d} = (\mathbf{Y}^2\mathbf{b}_1 + \mathbf{Y}\mathbf{b}_2)(\text{mod p}), \tag{5}$$

$\mathbf{b}_2$ is selected as a system parameter. The data to be encrypted should be grouped into r-dimensional vectors, denoted as z_1, z_2, ... z_s, all elements of these vectors are integers within $GF(p)$. The encryption is completed by the calculation of

$$\mathbf{C} = \mathbf{Y}[z_1 \ z_2 \ \ldots \ z_s](\text{mod p}), \tag{6}$$

and the ciphertext is given as $(\mathbf{C}, \mathbf{d})$.
To rebuild $\mathbf{Y}$ for the decryption of the message one notices that $\mathbf{Y}$ has the same eigenvector set as $\mathbf{A}$ and satisfies

$$\mathbf{Y} = \mathbf{H} \text{ diag}(\mu_1, \mu_2, \mu_3 \ldots \mu_r) \, \mathbf{H}^{-1} \text{ (mod p)}, \tag{7}$$

where $\mu_1, \mu_2, \mu_3 \ldots \mu_r$ are eigenvalues of $\mathbf{Y}$, $\mu_i \in GF(p)$, i=1,2,...r. Multiplying both sides of (5) with $\mathbf{H}^{-1}$ and one obtains

$$\mathbf{H}^{-1}\mathbf{d} = (\mathbf{H}^{-1}\mathbf{Y}^2\mathbf{H}\mathbf{H}^{-1}\mathbf{b}_1 + \mathbf{H}^{-1}\mathbf{Y}\mathbf{H}\mathbf{H}^{-1}\mathbf{b}_2)(\text{mod p})$$

$$= [\text{diag}(\mu_1^2, \mu_2^2, \ldots \mu_r^2) \, \mathbf{H}^{-1}\mathbf{b}_1 + \text{diag}(\mu_1, \mu_2, \ldots \mu_r)\mathbf{H}^{-1}\mathbf{b}_2](\text{mod p}). \tag{8}$$

Since $\mathbf{b}_1$ is located in the subspaces spanned by the first m eigenvectors of $\mathbf{A}$,

$$[0 \ I_{r-m}]\mathbf{H}^{-1}\mathbf{b}_1 \, (\text{mod p}) = 0. \tag{9}$$

Let

$$[\alpha_1 \ \alpha_2 \ ...\alpha_r]^T = \mathbf{H}^{-1}\mathbf{b}_1(\mathrm{mod} \ p), \tag{10}$$

$$[\beta_1 \ \beta_2... \ \beta_r]^T = \mathbf{H}^{-1}\mathbf{b}_2(\mathrm{mod} \ p), \tag{11}$$

$$[\delta_1 \ \delta_2 \ ... \ \delta_r]^T = \mathbf{H}^{-1}\mathbf{d}(\mathrm{mod} \ p). \tag{12}$$

We get from (8), (9) , (10), (11) and (12)

$$\delta_i = (\alpha_i\mu_i^2 + \beta_i\mu_i)(\mathrm{mod} \ p), \quad i=1, 2,...m, \tag{13}$$

$$\delta_i = \beta_i\mu_i \ (\mathrm{mod} \ p), \ i=m+1, \ m+2,...r. \tag{14}$$

With $\mathbf{Y}$ identified by (7), (13) and (14), the message can be recovered by the reverse operation of (6):

$$\mathbf{z}_j = \mathbf{Y}^{-1}\mathbf{c}_j(\mathrm{mod} \ p) = \mathbf{H}\mathrm{diag}(\mu_1^{-1},...\mu_m^{-1}, \mu_{m+1}^{-1}...\mu_r^{-1})\mathbf{H}^{-1}\mathbf{c}_j(\mathrm{mod} \ p), \tag{15}$$

where $j=1,2,...s$, $\mathbf{c}_j$ is the jth column of $\mathbf{C}$.   A small m will help to reduce computational efforts required by (13). However m should not be smaller than 2, otherwise an eigenvector of $\mathbf{A}$ will be exposed. Since there are two solutions to (13) for each i, $1\leqslant i\leqslant m$, at least an element of $\mathbf{z}_1$ should be set to a specific value for the identification of correct μ_i.

3   Security Analyses

The random matrix $\mathbf{Y}$ plays a key roll in the proposed cryptosystem. For the security of the encrypted messages it is desirable that the eigenvalues of $\mathbf{Y}$ distribute over the whole GF(p). This requirement is met by $\mathbf{Y}$ obtained from (4). To verify the fact we get from (1), (4) and (7)

$$\mu_i = (k_1\lambda_i^{r-1} + k_2\lambda_i^{r-2} +...+ k_r)(\mathrm{mod} \ p), \ i=1,2,...r \tag{16}$$

Equation (16) can be rewritten as

$$\boldsymbol{\mu}^T = [\mu_1 \ \mu_2 \ ...\mu_r] = [k_1 \ k_2 \ ...k_r] \ \mathbf{V} \ (\mathrm{mod} \ p) \tag{17}$$

where $\mathbf{V}$ denotes a Vandermonde matrix given below:

$$\mathbf{V} = \begin{bmatrix} \lambda_1^{r-1} & \lambda_2^{r-1} & ... & \lambda_r^{r-1} \\ \lambda_1^{r-2} & \lambda_2^{r-2} & ... & \lambda_r^{r-2} \\ ... & ... & ... & ... \\ 1 & 1 & ... & 1 \end{bmatrix} \tag{18}$$

We have

$$\det(\mathbf{V}) \pmod p$$

$$= [(\lambda_2-\lambda_1)\ldots(\lambda_r-\lambda_1)]\ [(\lambda_3-\lambda_2)\ldots(\lambda_r-\lambda_2)]\ldots[(\lambda_r-\lambda_{r-1})] \pmod p \neq 0 \qquad (19)$$

The rows in $\mathbf{V}$ form a full basis for the r-dimensional space defined on GF(p) and μ can be any vector in this space. This completes our verification.

There are two immediate attacks against the proposed cryptosystem. The first attack is to reduce matrix $\mathbf{A}$ to its canonical form. This is equivalent to find the solution for the following equation:

$$\det(\lambda I - \mathbf{A}) \pmod p = 0. \qquad (20)$$

Equation (20) is an r-degree (r>4) polynomial equation, as mentioned earlier, it is incapable of deterministic algebraic solution in terms of limited number of additions, subtractions, multiplications and divisions. Another attack is to find out k_1, $k_2,\ldots k_r$ in (4), with the information provided by (5). The following equation can be obtained by combining (4) and (5) together:

$$[(k_1\mathbf{A}^{r-1}+k_2\mathbf{A}^{r-2}\ldots+k_r\mathbf{I})^2\mathbf{b}_1 + (k_1\mathbf{A}^{r-1}+k_2\mathbf{A}^{r-2}\ldots+k_r\mathbf{I})\,\mathbf{b}_2 - \mathbf{d}] \pmod p = 0 \qquad (21)$$

This vector equation is equivalent to r joint quadratic equations with r variables, which can be reduced to a univariate polynomial equation, but usually with a degree higher than 2r. The complexity of solving (21) is basically the same as that of solving (20).

It takes time to find out if there is any attack that is more effective. Meanwhile further researches could strengthen the security of the proposed cryptosystem. First, the choices of λ_i, i=1,2,…r, are worth of study and it is probable that the complexity of equation (20) could be significantly increased if λ_1, $\lambda_2,\ldots \lambda_r$ are not limited to integers within GF(p). Second, a non-prime number n can be used to replace the prime number p as the modulus for encryption and decryption algorithms. A cryptosystem based on the problem of reducing a matrix to its canonical form defined on Z_n, a ring of integers, will be substantially more secure than a cryptosystem based on the same problem defined on GF(p), a Galois field, if the factors of n are kept secret. However, replacing GF(p) by Z_n will at the same time complicate the computations. There should be a tradeoff between the security and the efficiency.

4   Reduction of Key Size

One notices from the second section that the size of the private key $(\lambda_1, \lambda_2, \ldots\lambda_r)$ is rq, where q is the size of the eigenvalues. To reduce the size of public key we select

$$\mathbf{H} = [\mathbf{h}(\lambda_1)\ \ \mathbf{h}(\lambda_2)\ \ldots\mathbf{h}(\lambda_r)], \qquad (22)$$

where

$$\mathbf{h}(\lambda) = [\lambda^{r-1}\ \lambda^{r-2}\ \ldots\lambda^2\ \lambda\ 1]^T \pmod p \qquad (23)$$

and $\mathbf{A}$ will become the companion matrix of its eigenfunction

$$\det(\lambda I - A)(\bmod p) = (\lambda - \lambda_1)(\lambda - \lambda_2)\ldots(\lambda - \lambda_r)(\bmod p)$$

$$= (\lambda^r + f_1\lambda^{r-1} + f_2\lambda^{r-2} \ldots + f_r)(\bmod p), \tag{24}$$

which can be expressed as

$$A = \begin{bmatrix} -f_1 & -f_2 & \ldots & -f_{r-1} & -f_r \\ 1 & & \ldots & \ldots & 0 \\ & 1 & \ldots & \ldots & 0 \\ & & & & 0 \\ & & \ldots & \ldots & 0 \\ & & & 1 & 0 \end{bmatrix} \tag{25}$$

It requires only r parameters, i.e., f_1, f_2 ...f_r, to determine the above matrix. There are also r numbers in b_1, and the actual size of the public key will be 2rq. If the modulus is chosen as a non-prime number n, we suggest that n be selected a little smaller than rq, otherwise replacing p by n in equation (20) will be of no significance.

5   Implementation with Constrained Hardware

Constrained computing power is not a problem for the proposed cryptosystem since it does not require complicated operations such as exponentiations with big exponents. However measures should be taken for the cryptosystem to work on hardware environments with limited memory. To reduce the memory required for keeping the matrix Y during encryption process, (4) and (6) is combined to give

$$c_j = Y z_j \ (\bmod p)$$

$$= (k_1 A^{r-1} + k_2 A^{r-2} + \ldots + k_r I)z_j \ (\bmod p) \tag{26}$$

$$= (A(\ldots(A(k_1 A z_j + k_2 z_j) + k_3 z_j)\ldots + k_{r-1}z_j) + k_r z_j)(\bmod p), j=1,2,\ldots s$$

(26) can be completed for z_j, j=1,2,...s separately using the following recursive algorithm:

$$\left. \begin{array}{l} \xi_1 = k_1 z_j \ (\bmod p) \\[4pt] \xi_{t+1} = (A\xi_t + k_{t+1}z_j \ )(\bmod p), t = 1,2,\ldots r-1 \\[4pt] c_j = \xi_r \end{array} \right\} \tag{27}$$

with A given by (25), the above recursive algorithm has a simple scalar form as given below:

$$\xi_{i1} = k_1 z_{ij} \ (\text{mod } p), \quad i = 1,2,\ldots r$$
$$\xi_{1,t+1} = (-f_1\xi_{1t} - f_2\xi_{2t}\ldots-f_r\xi_{rt} + k_{t+1}z_{1j})(\text{mod } p), \quad t = 1,2,\ldots r\text{-}1$$
$$\xi_{i,t+1} = (\xi_{i-1,t} + k_{t+1}z_{ij})(\text{mod } p), \quad i=2, 3,\ldots r, \quad t = 1,2,\ldots r\text{-}1$$
$$c_{ij} = \xi_{ij}, \quad i = 1,2,\ldots r \tag{28}$$

where c_{ij}, ξ_{ij} and z_{ij} are ith element of $\mathbf{c}_j$, ξ_j and $\mathbf{z}_j$ respectively.
The solution of (14) can be given as

$$\mu_i = \delta_i\beta_i^{-1}(\text{mod } p), \quad i=m+1, m+2,\ldots r, \tag{29}$$

where $\beta_i^{-1}(\text{mod } p)$ can be computed beforehand. To reduce computational efforts, equation (13) is modified to

$$(\delta_i\mu_i^{-2} - \beta_i\mu_i^{-1} - \alpha_i)(\text{mod } p) = 0, \quad i=1, 2,\ldots m \tag{30}$$

and solved directly for μ_i^{-1} instead of μ_i.
Next we develop a recursive algorithm to simplify the calculation of $\mathbf{H}^{-1}\mathbf{c}_j(\text{mod } p)$ in (15) so as to make it good for implementation with constrained memory. Let

$$\mathbf{G}_k = \begin{bmatrix} \lambda_2^{k-1} & \cdots & \lambda_k^{k-1} & \\ \lambda_2^{k-2} & \cdots & \lambda_k^{k-2} & \\ \cdots & \cdots & \cdots & \\ 1 & \cdots & 1 & \\ & & & \mathbf{I}_{r-k} \end{bmatrix} \tag{31}$$

$$k=2,3,\ldots r$$

$$\mathbf{T}_k = \begin{bmatrix} 1 & -\lambda_k & & & \\ & 1 & \cdots & & \\ & & \cdots & 1 & -\lambda_k \\ & & & 1 & \\ & & & & \mathbf{I}_{r-k} \end{bmatrix} \quad r \times r \tag{32}$$

$$\mathbf{R}_k = \begin{bmatrix} (\lambda_1 - \lambda_k)^{-1} & & & & & \\ & (\lambda_1 - \lambda_k)^{-1} & & & & \\ & & \cdots & & & \\ & & & (\lambda_1 - \lambda_k)^{-1} & & \\ -1 & -1 & \cdots & -1 & 1 & \\ & & & & & \mathbf{I}_{r-k} \end{bmatrix}_{r \times r} \tag{33}$$

$$k = 2, 3, \ldots r$$

where $\mathbf{I}_k$, $1 \leq k \leq r$, denotes the $k \times k$ unit matrix. We have

$$\mathbf{G}_r = \mathbf{H},$$
$$\mathbf{G}_1 = \mathbf{T}_1 = \mathbf{R}_1 = \mathbf{I}_r,$$

and

$$\mathbf{T}_k \mathbf{G}_k \mathbf{R}_k = \mathbf{G}_{k-1}. \tag{34}$$

From (34) we get

$$\mathbf{G}_k^{-1} = \mathbf{R}_k \mathbf{G}_{k-1}^{-1} \mathbf{T}_k \tag{35}$$

One obtains from the above equations

$$\mathbf{H}^{-1} = \mathbf{G}_r^{-1} = \mathbf{R}_r \mathbf{G}_{r-1}^{-1} \mathbf{T}_r = \mathbf{R}_r \mathbf{R}_{r-1} \mathbf{G}_{r-2}^{-1} \mathbf{T}_{r-1} \mathbf{T}_r = \mathbf{R}_r \mathbf{R}_{r-1} \ldots \mathbf{R}_2 \mathbf{T}_2 \ldots \mathbf{T}_{r-1} \mathbf{T}_r \tag{36}$$

Let c_{ij} and z_{ij} denote ith elements of $\mathbf{c}_j$, and $\mathbf{z}_j$ respectively, the recursive algorithm is given below:

$$\begin{aligned}
& \xi_{i1} = z_{ij}, \ i = 1, 2, \ldots r \\
& \xi_{i,t+1} = (\xi_{it} - \lambda_{r-t+1} \xi_{i+1,t})(\bmod\ p), \ i = 1, 2, \ldots r-t, \\
& \xi_{i,t+1} = \xi_{it}, \ i = r-t+1, \ldots r, \\
& \hspace{5cm} t = 1, 2, \ldots r-1 \\
& \eta_{i1} = \xi_{ir}, \ i = 1, 2, \ldots r \\
& \eta_{it} = \eta_{i,t-1}(\lambda_1 - \lambda_t)^{-1}, \ i = 1, 2, \ldots t-1, \\
& \eta_{tt} = \eta_{t,t-1} - \eta_{1,t-1} - \eta_{2,t-1} \ldots - \eta_{t-1,t-1}, \\
& \eta_{it} = \eta_{i,t-1}, \ i = t+1, t+2, \ldots r, \\
& \hspace{5cm} t = 2, 3, \ldots r
\end{aligned} \tag{37}$$

and the result is expressed as

$$\mathbf{H}^{-1} \mathbf{c}_j (\bmod\ p) = [\eta_1 \ \eta_2 \ldots \eta_r]^T \tag{38}$$

To speed up the decryption process $(\lambda_i-\lambda_j)^{-1}$, $1 \leqslant i \leqslant j$, should also be computed before hand and stored in EEPROM or flash for use. It will not be a serious challenge to the capacity of EEPROM, which is normally 16K-bytes even for a cute Smart Card.

6   Further Discussions

The cipher text produced by the new cryptosystem can be divided into two parts. The first part is **C**, which is the encrypted form of the message. The second part is **d**, which is virtually the encrypted form of a session key. It is used for the recovery of **Y**, a dependency of $(k_1, k_2,\dots k_r)$, which plays the same role as that played by session keys in mixed cryptosystems. One may also consider the proposed cryptosystem as an integration of asymmetric and symmetric algorithms. The asymmetric algorithms are used to compute **d** and rebuild **Y**, while the symmetric algorithms are used to calculate **C** and recover z_1, z_2, … z_s. An improvement can be made by selecting $\alpha_i=\beta_i$, i=1, 2,…m, and using $\mathbf{Y}^2 + \mathbf{Y}$ instead of **Y** for symmetric encryption described by (6). This improvement will eliminate the necessity to solve quadratic equations given by (13). Let L stands for bit-length of the modulus, total time required by the asymmetric part of the new cryptosystem will be $O(L^2)$ for fixed r. This reveals the superiority of the new cryptosystem since total time required by major existing cryptosystems, such as RSA, Elgamal and Rabin cryptosystems, to encrypt and decrypt a message is $O(L^3)$[6].

The symmetric algorithm given by (6) is not the only choice. In fact one may group the message into an $r \times r$ matrix **M**, and encrypt it simply by computing $\mathbf{C}=\mathbf{M}+\mathbf{Y}+\mathbf{Y}^2$ modulo p or n. One may also use the elements of $\mathbf{Y}+\mathbf{Y}^2$, or some combinations of the elements as secret keys, and encrypt the message with some existing symmetric algorithms, thus giving a new implementation of the mixed cryptosystem.

References

1.   Diffie, W. and Hellman, M.E.: New directions in cryptography, IEEE Transactions in Information Theory, vol. IT-22, (1976)
2.   Rivest R. L. et al: A Method for Obtaining Digital Signatures and Public-Key Cryptosystems, Communications of the ACM, vol . 21(1978)
3.   Rabin, M. O.: Digital Signatures and Public Key Functions as Intractable as Factorization, MIT Laboratory for Computer Science, Technical Report, MIT/LCS/TR-212(1979)
4.   Elgamal, T.: A Public Key Cryptosystem and a Signature Scheme Based on the Discrete Logarithm, IEEE Trans. On Information Theory, vol. 31(1985)
5.   Koblitz, N.: Elliptic curve cryptosystems, Mathematics of Computation, Vol 48(1987)
6.   Schneier, B.: Applied Cryptography, John Wiley & Sons, NY(1996)
7.   Wells, D. , The Penguin Dictionary of Curious and Interesting Numbers, Penguin Books, New York(1986)

A Distributed and Computationally Secure Key Distribution Scheme[*]

Vanesa Daza, Javier Herranz, Carles Padró, and Germán Sáez

Dept. Matemàtica Aplicada IV, Universitat Politècnica de Catalunya
C. Jordi Girona, 1-3, Mòdul C3, Campus Nord, 08034-Barcelona, Spain
{vdaza,jherranz,matcpl,german}@mat.upc.es

Abstract. In [16], Naor, Pinkas and Reingold introduced schemes in which some groups of servers distribute keys among a set of users in a distributed way. They gave some specific proposals both in the unconditional and in the computational security framework. Their computationally secure scheme is based on the Decisional Diffie-Hellman Assumption. This model assumes secure and authenticated communication between users and servers. Furthermore it requires users to do some expensive computations in order to obtain a key.

In this paper we modify the model introduced in [16]. Our model makes the user's computations easier, because most computations of the protocol are carried out by servers, keeping to a more realistic situation. Furthermore, this new model requires only authenticated channels between users and servers.

We propose a basic scheme, that makes use of ElGamal cryptosystem, and that fits in with this model in the case of a passive adversary. Then we add zero-knowledge proofs and verifiable secret sharing to prevent from the action of an active adversary. We consider general structures (not only the threshold ones) for those subsets of servers that can provide a key to a user and for those tolerated subsets of servers that can be corrupted by the adversary. We find necessary combinatorial conditions on these structures in order to provide security to our scheme.

1 Introduction

When a group of users wish to communicate securely over insecure channels, either symmetric or public key cryptosystems are used. Public key schemes present some drawbacks both from the communication and the computational point of view. On the other hand, when symmetric algorithms are considered in order to solve this problem, the question is then how to set up an efficient protocol to give each group of users a common key.

The solution of setting a server responsible of the distribution and management of the secret keys was introduced in [17] by Needham and Schroeder. This idea of a Key Distribution Center was formalized in [3]. This model presents

---

[*] This work was partially supported by Spanish *Ministerio de Ciencia y Tecnología* under project TIC 2000-1044.

A.H. Chan and V. Gligor (Eds.): ISC 2002, LNCS 2433, pp. 342–356, 2002.

some drawbacks. A single server that is in charge of the distribution of keys to a group of users presents some weak points. It is a possible bottleneck of the system and it must be trusted. Among the proposed solutions in order to remove this drawback, the use of Distributed Key Distribution Centers is one of the most accepted.

The model in which the task of a single server is distributed among a set of servers, the Distributed Key Distribution Center model, was introduced in [16]. Schemes fitting this model are called Distributed Key Distribution Schemes. Some specific realizations were proposed both in the information theoretic model, where no limits in the computational power of an adversary are assumed, and in the computationally secure framework, where the computational capability of an adversary is bounded.

With regard to the information theoretic point of view some studies have been done since then: in [5] an exhaustive study on the amount of information needed to set up and manage such a system was presented. They considered *threshold* access structures, that is, those sets of servers that are authorized to provide keys have at least t servers (t is the threshold). Afterwards, in [6] it was extended to a model considering *general* access structures. Moreover, a relation between distributed key distribution schemes and secret sharing schemes was shown.

However, in this paper we focus on computationally secure distributed key distribution schemes. Previously, in [16] such a scheme was proposed, based on the Decisional Diffie-Hellman Assumption [11], as an application of their scheme for evaluating a pseudo-random function in a distributed way. This scheme assumes secure communication between users and servers. Moreover, it requires users to do some expensive computations in order to get a key.

We propose a new model for describing distributed key distribution schemes, in which authenticated channels between servers and users are necessary, instead of secure and authenticated channels (as they are in the proposal of [16]). We provide an explicit construction realizing this new model. The use of the homomorphic properties of the ElGamal cryptosystem [12] allows the servers to carry out most computations of the protocol. Note that this fact fits with a more real world oriented situation, in which servers are supposed to have more powerful computational resources. The basic scheme is secure against a *passive adversary* which can corrupt some set of servers and obtain all their secret information, but can not force them to change their correct role in the protocol. Those subsets of servers that can be corrupted by the adversary are given by an *adversary structure* $\mathcal{A}$, which must be monotone decreasing: if a set of servers $B_1 \in \mathcal{A}$ can be corrupted, and $B_2 \subset B_1$, then the set of servers $B_2 \in \mathcal{A}$ can be corrupted, too.

But we want our scheme to be secure even under the most powerful attacks. In this case, in which we accept the presence of an *active adversary* which is able to alter the behavior of the corrupted players during the protocol, we must add some mechanisms in order to maintain the security and the correctness of the scheme. These tools are basically the use of verifiable secret sharing and non-interactive zero-knowledge proofs of knowledge.

In all cases, we consider general adversary and access structures in the set of servers, not only the threshold ones. That is, those subsets of dishonest servers tolerated by the system as well as those subsets of servers that can provide a valid key to a user are not necessarily those with a maximum (or minimum) number of players. This general framework modelizes situations in which servers do not have all the same power or the same susceptibility to be corrupted. We state the combinatorial conditions that these structures must satisfy if we want our schemes to run securely.

Organization of the paper. In Section 2 we review some cryptographic tools that we will need throughout the rest of the paper, such as ElGamal encryption or basics on zero-knowledge proofs, and we also present the model of distributed key distribution schemes described in [16]. In Section 3 we explain secret sharing schemes for general access structures, and how they can be used by a set of participants to jointly generate a random secret shared value. In Section 4 we propose a new model in order to minimize users' computations and we propose a distributed key distribution scheme for this model, computationally secure against both passive and active adversaries. We give an explicit construction for the passive case, based on the homomorphic properties of ElGamal encryption scheme. Then, we introduce all the techniques that we use in order to provide robustness for the active case to our proposal. All our results consider general structures, not only threshold ones. Finally, in Section 5 we conclude the work summarizing our contribution and future research.

2   Preliminaries

In this section we describe some cryptographic tools that we will need later on. We will also explain the model of computationally secure Distributed Key Distribution Schemes introduced in [16].

2.1   ElGamal Encryption

In [12], ElGamal proposed a public-key probabilistic encryption scheme. We explain here an specific version of this scheme, but it can be generalized to work in any finite cyclic group (see [15], Section 8.4.2, for example).

The public parameters of the scheme are two large primes p and q, such that $q|p-1$, and a generator g of the multiplicative subgroup of $\mathbb{Z}_p^*$ with order q. Every user U generates both his public and private keys by choosing a random element $x \in \mathbb{Z}_q^*$ and computing $y = g^x \bmod p$. The public key of user U is (p,q,g,y) and his private key is x.

If a user wants to encrypt a message $m \in \mathbb{Z}_p$ for user U, he chooses a random element $\beta \in \mathbb{Z}_q^*$, and computes $r = g^\beta \bmod p$ and $s = my^\beta \bmod p$. The ciphertext of message m that is sent to user U is $c = (r,s)$.

When U wants to recover the original message m from the ciphertext $c = (r, s)$, he computes

$$m = sr^{-x} \bmod p$$

The semantic security of ElGamal cryptosystem is equivalent to the Decisional Diffie-Hellman Assumption [11]. One of the most useful features of this encryption scheme is its *homomorphic property*: if $c_i = (r_i, s_i)$ is a ciphertext corresponding to the plaintext m_i, for $i = 1, 2$ then $c = (r_1 r_2, s_1 s_2)$ is a ciphertext corresponding to plaintext $m = m_1 m_2$. This property is the one we need for the encryption scheme that we will use in our proposal of a new distributed and computationally secure key distribution scheme.

2.2 Zero-Knowledge Proofs of Knowledge

A zero-knowledge proof of knowledge allows a prover to demonstrate knowledge of a secret while revealing no information about it to the verifier of the proof, other than the mentioned knowledge and what the verifier was able to deduce prior to the protocol run. Zero-knowledge protocols are examples of interactive proof systems, in which a prover and a verifier exchange multiple messages, typically dependent on random numbers which they may keep secret. In these systems, there are security requirements for both the prover and the verifier: for the prover, security means that the protocol should be zero-knowledge, that is, the verifier gains no information on the secret; for the verifier, it means that the protocol should be a proof of knowledge: complete and sound. Intuitively, these two conditions mean that, with overwhelming probability, a honest verifier accepts a proof if and only if the prover is also honest. See [15], Section 10.4.1, for a comprehensive definition of these concepts.

Interactive proof systems can be transformed into non-interactive protocols, following the techniques and ideas of [14] and [19]. The security of such a non-interactive system is argued by showing that the plain interactive protocol is secure and then replacing the verifier with a collision resistant and random hash function; this approach has been formalized as the random oracle model [2].

In the context of this paper, we are specially interested in zero-knowledge proofs of the validity of statements about discrete logarithms. This topic has been deeply studied in works such as [8,9]. We will use notation introduced by Camenisch and Stadler [9]: for instance, the statement

$$PK \{ (\alpha, \beta) : A = g_1^\alpha g_2^\beta \wedge B = g_3^\alpha \}$$

denotes a zero-knowledge proof of knowledge of values α and β such that $A = g_1^\alpha g_2^\beta$ and $B = g_3^\alpha$. By convention, Greek letters $(\alpha, \beta, \ldots)$ denote quantities whose knowledge is being proved, while all other parameters are known to the verifier (in this case, the values A, B, g_1, g_2, g_3).

2.3 Previous Computational Distributed Key Distribution Schemes

In [16] it was introduced the notion of Distributed Key Distribution Schemes in order to avoid the main drawbacks that the existence of a single Key Distribution

Scheme had. They considered a set of servers $\mathcal{S} = \{S_1, \ldots, S_n\}$ and a group of users $\mathcal{U} = \{U_1, \ldots, U_m\}$ (they also referred to them as clients). Each user U has private communication with at least t servers. Let $\mathcal{C} \subset 2^{\mathcal{U}}$ a family of sets of users, the *conferences*, who want to communicate securely among them.

Initialization: Each server S_i receives a share α_i of some random secret α, shared among the servers by means of Shamir secret sharing scheme. The generation of these values can be performed by either a central authority or jointly by a group of servers.

Regular Operation: if a user U in a conference $C \in \mathcal{C}$ needs the key of this conference, he proceeds as follows:

- He contacts t servers $S_1, \ldots, S_t$ and asks them for the key of the conference C. Each conference C is related to a public value h_C.
- Each server S_i, for $i = 1, \ldots, t$, verifies that the user is allowed to ask for that key and, if so, computes the value $h_C^{\alpha_i}$ and sends it to him through their private channel.
- After receiving the information from the servers, the user is able to compute the conference key κ_C as follows: $\kappa_C = h_C^\alpha = \prod_{i=1}^{t}(h_C^{\alpha_i})^{\lambda_i}$, where λ_i are the Lagrange interpolation coefficients.

3   Joint Generation of a Random Shared Secret Value

In this section we explain some basics on secret sharing schemes, and how these schemes can be used by a set of players to jointly generate shares of a random secret value. These protocols are secure against passive adversaries. If the adversary is active, verifiable secret sharing schemes must be used. We consider a framework which is more general than the threshold one.

3.1   Secret Sharing Schemes

In a *secret sharing scheme*, a dealer distributes shares of a secret value among a set of players $\mathcal{P} = \{P_1, \ldots, P_n\}$ in such a way that only authorized subsets of players (those in the called *access structure*) can recover the secret value from their shares, whereas non-authorized subsets do not obtain any information about the secret. The access structure is usually noted Γ. It must be monotone increasing, i.e. any subset containing an authorized subset will also be authorized.

Secret sharing schemes were introduced independently by Shamir [21] and Blakley [4] in 1979. Shamir proposed a *threshold* scheme, i.e. subsets that can recover the secret are those with at least t members (t is the threshold). Other works have proposed schemes realizing more general structures, such as *vector space secret sharing schemes* [7]. An access structure Γ is realizable by such a scheme defined in a finite field $\mathbb{Z}_q$, for some prime q, if there exists a positive integer r and a function $\psi : \mathcal{P} \cup \{D\} \longrightarrow (\mathbb{Z}_q)^r$ such that $W \in \Gamma$ if and only if $\psi(D) \in \langle \psi(P_i) \rangle_{P_i \in W}$. Here D denotes a special entity (real or not), outside the set $\mathcal{P}$. If a dealer wants to distribute a secret value $x \in \mathbb{Z}_q$, he takes a random element $\mathbf{v} \in (\mathbb{Z}_q)^r$, such that $\mathbf{v} \cdot \psi(D) = x$. The share of a participant $P_i \in \mathcal{P}$ is $x_i = \mathbf{v} \cdot \psi(P_i) \in \mathbb{Z}_q$. Let W be an authorized subset, $W \in \Gamma$; then, $\psi(D) = \sum_{P_i \in W} \lambda_i^W \psi(P_i)$, for some $\lambda_i^W \in \mathbb{Z}_q$. In order to recover the secret, the players of W compute

$$\sum_{P_i \in W} \lambda_i^W x_i \ = \ \sum_{P_i \in W} \lambda_i^W \mathbf{v} \cdot \psi(P_i) \ = \ \mathbf{v} \cdot \sum_{P_i \in W} \lambda_i^W \psi(P_i) \ = \ \mathbf{v} \cdot \psi(D) \ = \ x \mod q \, .$$

Simmons, Jackson and Martin [22] introduced *linear secret sharing schemes*, that can be seen as vector space secret sharing schemes in which each player can be associated with more than one vector. They proved that any access structure can be realized by a linear secret sharing scheme (in general, the construction they proposed results in an inefficient secret sharing scheme). From now on in our work, we will consider any possible access structure Γ, so we will know that there exists a linear secret sharing scheme realizing this structure. For simplicity, however, we will suppose that this scheme is a vector space one defined by a function ψ over $\mathbb{Z}_q$. See [24] for a comprehensive introduction to secret sharing schemes.

3.2   The Passive Adversary Case

In many protocols, it is interesting to avoid the presence of a dealer who knows all the secret information of the system. The role of the dealer can be distributed among the players, as long as the secret is chosen at random. This distributed protocol must be protected against the presence of some coalition of players corrupted by an adversary. The monotone decreasing family of these tolerated coalitions of corrupted servers is defined as the adversary structure $\mathcal{A}$. If the adversary is passive, the only required condition is $\Gamma \cap \mathcal{A} = \emptyset$, and the distributed generation of a random secret value can be performed by any authorized subset $A \in \Gamma$, as follows:

- Each player $P_i \in A$ chooses at random a value $k_i \in \mathbb{Z}_q$, and distributes it among all players in $\mathcal{P}$, using the corresponding vector space secret sharing scheme. That is, P_i chooses a random vector $\mathbf{v_i} \in (\mathbb{Z}_q)^r$ such that $\mathbf{v_i} \cdot \psi(D) = k_i$. Then P_i sends to each player P_j in $\mathcal{P}$ his share $k_{ij} = \mathbf{v_i} \cdot \psi(P_j)$. The generated random secret will be $x = \sum_{i \in A} k_i$.
- Each player $P_j \in \mathcal{P}$ computes his share of the secret x as $x_j = \sum_{i \in A} k_{ij}$.

In effect, suppose that an authorized subset of players $W \in \Gamma$ wants to recover the secret x. We know that there exist values $\{\lambda_j^W\}_{j \in W}$ such that $\psi(D) = \sum_{j \in W} \lambda_j^W \psi(P_j)$. Then players in W can obtain the secret x from their shares:

$$\sum_{j \in W} \lambda_j^W x_j = \sum_{j \in W} \lambda_j^W \sum_{i \in A} k_{ij} = \sum_{j \in W} \sum_{i \in A} \lambda_j^W \mathbf{v_i} \cdot \psi(P_j) = \sum_{i \in A} \mathbf{v_i} \sum_{j \in W} \lambda_j^W \psi(P_j) =$$

$$= \sum_{i \in A} \mathbf{v_i} \psi(D) = \sum_{i \in A} k_i = x$$

We denote an execution of this distributed protocol, in the passive adversary scenario, with the following expression:

$$(x_1, \ldots, x_n) \quad \overset{(\mathcal{P}, \Gamma, \mathcal{A})}{\longleftrightarrow} \quad x$$

3.3   The Active Adversary Case: Verifiable Secret Sharing

If the adversary is active, some players of $\mathcal{P}$ can cheat during the protocols. *Verifiable secret sharing schemes* were introduced in order to tolerate this kind of situations. The two most used verifiable secret sharing schemes are the proposals of Pedersen [18] and Feldman [13], which are both based on Shamir's secret sharing scheme. Whereas the security of secret sharing schemes is unconditional, that is, subsets that are not in the access structure do not obtain any information about the secret, independently of their computational capability, the security of some verifiable secret sharing schemes is based on some computational assumption; for instance, Feldman's scheme is secure assuming that the discrete logarithm problem in some finite field is hard.

Now we explain the joint generation of a random secret value, shared among players in $\mathcal{P}$ according to the access structure Γ, and secure against the action of an active adversary who can corrupt a subset of players in the adversary structure $\mathcal{A}$. It must be performed by a subset R of players satisfying that for all $B \in \mathcal{A}$, we have $R - B \in \Gamma$. We denote by $\Omega = \Omega(\Gamma, \mathcal{A})$ the monotone increasing family formed by those subsets R. This family is not empty if and only if $\mathcal{A}^c \subset \Gamma$, where $\mathcal{A}^c = \{\mathcal{P} - B \mid B \in \mathcal{A}\}$. In effect, $\mathcal{P} \in \Omega$ if and only if for all $B \in \mathcal{A}$ we have that $\mathcal{P} - B \in \Gamma$, and this is equivalent to $\mathcal{A}^c \subset \Gamma$.

In the threshold case, where $\Gamma = \{W \subset \mathcal{P} : |W| \geq t\}$ and the adversary structure is usually taken as $\mathcal{A} = \{B \subset \mathcal{P} : |B| < t\}$, we have that $\Omega = \{R \subset \mathcal{P} : |R| \geq 2t - 1\}$. This family is not empty if and only if $n \geq 2t - 1$.

The protocol for generating a random secret value in a distributed way can be performed by a subset $R \in \Omega$ as follows:

- Each player $P_i \in R$ chooses at random a value $k_i \in \mathbb{Z}_q$, and distributes it among all players in $\mathcal{P}$, using the following (verifiable) vector space secret sharing scheme (it is a generalization of the threshold scheme of Feldman [13]). Let q and p be large primes such that $q|p-1$. Let g be a generator of a multiplicative subgroup of $\mathbb{Z}_p^*$ with order q. P_i chooses a random vector $\mathbf{v_i} = (v_i^{(1)}, \ldots, v_i^{(r)}) \in (\mathbb{Z}_q)^r$ such that $\mathbf{v_i} \cdot \psi(D) = k_i$. Then P_i sends to each player P_j in $\mathcal{P}$ his share $k_{ij} = \mathbf{v_i} \cdot \psi(P_j)$. He also makes public the commitments $V_{i\ell} = g^{v_i^{(\ell)}}$, for $1 \leq \ell \leq r$.
- Each player $P_j \in \mathcal{P}$ verifies the correctness of his share k_{ij} by checking that

$$g^{k_{ij}} = \prod_{\ell=1}^{r} (V_{i\ell})^{\psi(P_j)^{(\ell)}}$$

If this check fails, P_j makes public a complaint against P_i.

- If player $P_i \in R$ receives complaints from players that form a subset that is not in $\mathcal{A}$, he is rejected. Otherwise, P_i makes public the shares k_{ij} corresponding to the players that have complained against him. If any one of these published shares do not satisfy the previous verification equation, P_i is also rejected.
- We denote by $Qual \subset R$ the (public) set of players that pass this verification phase. Due to the definition of the structure Ω, we have that $Qual$ belongs to Γ.
- The generated random secret will be $x = \sum_{i \in Qual} k_i$. Note that, since $Qual \in \Gamma$, we have that $Qual \notin \mathcal{A}$, and so any subset in $\mathcal{A}$ cannot obtain the secret x from their initial secret values k_i. Each player $P_j \in \mathcal{P}$ computes his share of the secret x as $x_j = \sum_{i \in Qual} k_{ij}$.

An authorized subset of players could obtain the value of x from their shares exactly in the same way explained for the passive case.

Note that the values $D_j = g^{x_j}$ can be publicly computed by all players as follows:

$$D_j = g^{\sum_{i \in Qual} k_{ij}} = \prod_{i \in Qual} g^{k_{ij}} = \prod_{i \in Qual} \prod_{\ell=1}^{r} (V_{i\ell})^{\psi(P_j)^{(\ell)}}$$

We denote the output of this protocol with the expression:

$$(x_1, \ldots, x_n) \overset{(\mathcal{P}, \Gamma, \mathcal{A})}{\longleftrightarrow} (x, \{D_j\}_{1 \le j \le n})$$

4   Our Computationally Secure Distributed Key Distribution Scheme

In [16] a construction based on the decisional Diffie-Hellman assumption was presented. However, this proposal requires a user to compute $O(t)$ exponentiations in order to compute a key (where t is the minimum number of servers the user must contact with), in addition to the verification of the information that he receives from each (possibly dishonest) server. Meanwhile, a server computes only a single exponentiation in order to help the user. This may not correspond to real situations, where it is possible to take profit of the computational power of the servers. Thus, we are interested in a scheme minimizing the computational effort of the user. Next we will set up the new model of computationally secure distributed key distribution scheme that we will use from now on. Afterwards, we will present an explicit construction based on ElGamal encryption. We will take into account both passive and active adversaries. When we describe the protocol, first, we will consider a passive adversary, and later on, we will note which changes should be made in the protocol to provide security against an active adversary.

4.1   Setting up the Model

Let $\mathcal{U} = \{U_1, \ldots, U_m\}$ be a set of m users and $\mathcal{S} = \{S_1, \ldots, S_n\}$ a set of n servers. Let $\Gamma \subset 2^{\mathcal{S}}$ be a general monotone increasing access structure, formed by those subsets of servers that are allowed to recover a secret from their shares; and let $\mathcal{A} \subset 2^{\mathcal{S}}$ be a general monotone decreasing adversary structure, formed by those subsets of dishonest servers that the system is able to tolerate. These two structures must satisfy $\mathcal{A} \cap \Gamma = \emptyset$. For simplicity, we assume that the access structure Γ can be realized by a vector space secret sharing scheme. That is, there exist a positive integer r and a function $\psi : \mathcal{S} \cup \{D\} \longrightarrow (\mathbb{Z}_q)^r$ such that $A \in \Gamma$ if and only if $\psi(D) \in \langle \psi(S_i) \rangle_{S_i \in A}$.

Let $\mathcal{C} \subset 2^{\mathcal{U}}$ be a family of sets of users (conferences). Every user in a conference needs to know the conference key in order to communicate securely with other members of the conference. To obtain the conference key, the user must contact with every server in some subset $A \subset \mathcal{S}$. Let $\mathcal{R} \subset 2^{\mathcal{S}}$ be the family of such sets of servers, which can provide conference keys. This family $\mathcal{R}$ must be monotone increasing, and will be different depending on the kind of adversary (passive or active) that we consider. We say that a set A of servers in $\mathcal{R}$ is *robust*. We divide a distributed key distribution scheme into three different phases:

Initialization Phase. We assume that the initialization phase is performed by a robust subset of servers, that jointly performs the generation of shares $\{\alpha_i\}_{i \in \mathcal{S}}$ of a random value α, realizing the access structure Γ, by using the protocols explained in Section 3. Each server has a share α_i of α and any set that is not in Γ can obtain no information of this random secret value α.

Key Request and Computational Phase. A user U_j in a conference $C \in \mathcal{C}$ contacts with a robust subset $A \in \mathcal{R}$ of servers asking for the key of the conference C, which we will call κ_C. Every server $S_i \in A$ checks for membership of U_j in C. If he belongs to, server S_i computes a share of the conference key using α_i and a value related with the conference C. Afterwards, server S_i encrypts his share of the key by means of a suitable homomorphic encryption scheme with the public key of user U_j. The contacted group of servers A, by using homomorphic properties of the used cryptosystem, is able to compute an encryption of the conference key κ_C from the encryptions of the shares of the key.

Key Delivery Phase. Either a single server in A or the whole set A (depending on the behavior of the adversary, passive or active, respectively) sends the computed result to user U_j through an authenticated channel. Using his private key, the user will be able to decrypt this message obtaining in this way the conference key.

4.2   Our Proposal for the Passive Adversary Case

Now we propose a method to construct a Distributed Key Distribution Scheme computationally secure against a passive adversary who corrupts servers on a subset in $\mathcal{A}$, following the model introduced in Section 4.1. We use ElGamal cryptosystem [12], and take profit from its homomorphic properties.

We have an access structure Γ, such that the condition $\Gamma \cap \mathcal{A} = \emptyset$ holds. In this passive case, we have that the family of robust subsets is $\mathcal{R} = \Gamma$. Let p and q be two large primes such that $q | p - 1$. Let H be a hash function (collision and pre-image resistant) that inputs a conference in $\mathcal{C}$ and outputs an element in $\mathbb{Z}_p^*$. We assume that each user U_j has a public ElGamal key (p, q, g, y_j) corresponding to a private key $x_j \in \mathbb{Z}_q^*$; that is, $y_j = g^{x_j} \bmod p$, where g is an element with order q in $\mathbb{Z}_p^*$. Here we present our scheme:

Initialization Phase

A subset in $\mathcal{R} = \Gamma$ jointly performs the passive version of the protocol in Section 3.2 for the generation of a random shared secret, which results in

$$(\alpha_1, \ldots, \alpha_n) \overset{(\mathcal{S}, \Gamma, \mathcal{A})}{\longleftrightarrow} \alpha$$

where $\alpha, \alpha_i \in \mathbb{Z}_q$ are random.

Key Request and Computational Phase

A user U_j in a conference $C \in \mathcal{C}$ asks for the conference key κ_C to a robust subset of servers $A \in \mathcal{R}$. These servers check the membership of the user in the conference and perform the following distributed encryption protocol. Note that $A \in \mathcal{R} = \Gamma$ is an authorized set of servers and we are assuming that the access structure Γ is realized by a vector space secret sharing scheme defined by the function ψ. Thus, there exist values $\{\lambda_i^A\}_{S_i \in A}$ in $\mathbb{Z}_q$ such that $\psi(D) = \sum_{S_i \in A} \lambda_i^A \psi(S_i)$ and so $\alpha = \sum_{S_i \in A} \lambda_i^A \alpha_i \bmod q$ (in the threshold case, these values $\{\lambda_i^A\}_{S_i \in A}$ would be the Lagrange interpolation coefficients). Servers in A proceed as follows:

- Each server $S_i \in A$ applies the hash function H to the conference C, obtaining $h_C = H(C) \in \mathbb{Z}_p^*$. The conference key will be $\kappa_C = h_C^\alpha$. Then each $S_i \in A$ encrypts the value $h_C^{\alpha_i} \bmod p$ using the ElGamal public key of user U_j, which is (p, q, g, y_j). That is:

  - Server S_i chooses a random element $\beta_i \in \mathbb{Z}_q^*$.
  - He computes $r_i = g^{\beta_i} \bmod p$ and $s_i = h_C^{\alpha_i} y_j^{\beta_i} \bmod p$.
  - Server S_i broadcasts the ciphertext $c_i = (r_i, s_i)$.

- Now each server $S_i \in A$ can compute the encryption (r, s) of the conference key $\kappa_C = (h_C)^\alpha$ as follows:

$$r = \prod_{S_i \in A} r_i^{\lambda_i^A} = (g)^{\sum_{S_i \in A} \lambda_i^A \beta_i} \bmod p$$

$$s = \prod_{S_i \in A} s_i^{\lambda_i^A} = (h_C)^{\sum_{S_i \in A} \lambda_i^A \alpha_i} (y_j)^{\sum_{S_i \in A} \lambda_i^A \beta_i} = h_C^\alpha (y_j)^{\sum_{S_i \in A} \lambda_i^A \beta_i} \bmod p$$

Since the elements $\{\beta_i\}_{S_i \in A}$ are random, we have that the element $\sum_{S_i \in A} \lambda_i^A \beta_i$ is also random, and so (r, s) is a valid ElGamal encryption of the message h_C^α. We also note that the resulting ciphertext (r, s) does not depend on the authorized subset $A \in \Gamma$ that has been considered.

Key Delivery Phase

The ciphertext $c = (r, s)$ is sent by some server $S_i \in A$ to user U_j, who decrypts it (he is the only one who can do this) and obtains automatically the conference key $\kappa_C = h_C^\alpha$.

4.3   Achieving Robustness against an Active Adversary

Next we will consider an adversary who corrupts servers on a subset in $\mathcal{A}$, in an active way; that is, those corrupted servers may not follow the protocol properly. The condition $\Gamma \cap \mathcal{A} = \emptyset$ is still necessary, of course. In this active scenario, the family $\mathcal{R}$ of robust subsets of servers will be $\mathcal{R} = \Omega(\Gamma, \mathcal{A})$ defined as in Section 3. Note that the condition $\mathcal{A}^c \subset \Gamma$ is necessary and sufficient in order to make sure that the family $\mathcal{R}$ is not empty (again, the justification is explained in Section 3).

The following changes must be introduced in each one of the phases:

Initialization Phase

We require a robust subset of servers to perform this phase. They jointly generate a random shared secret, using verifiable secret sharing (see Section 3.3) to detect corrupted servers:

$$(\alpha_1, \ldots, \alpha_n) \quad \overset{(\mathcal{S}, \Gamma, \mathcal{A})}{\longleftrightarrow} \quad (\alpha, \{D_i\}_{1 \leq i \leq n})$$

where g is an element with order q in $\mathbb{Z}_p^*$ and $D_i = g^{\alpha_i}$ are the public commitments associated with the shares α_i's of the secret value α.

Note that although the adversary corrupts a tolerated set of servers, these corrupted servers will be detected; the remaining servers of the robust subset will belong to the access structure Γ, because of the definition of the family $\mathcal{R}$, and they will able to finish the protocol correctly.

Key Request and Computational Phase

Now a user must ask for a conference key κ_C to a robust subset A of servers. After this, every server S_i in A broadcasts a ciphertext $c_i = (r_i, s_i)$ of its share $h_C^{\alpha_i}$ of the conference key as in the passive case.

We must deal with the case of corrupted servers who want to boycott the system, by broadcasting a ciphertext $\tilde{c}_i = (\tilde{r}_i, \tilde{s}_i)$ which does not correspond to the plaintext $h_C^{\alpha_i}$.

We will detect these corrupted servers if we impose them to do a determined proof of knowledge. After the joint generation of the secret shared value α, all servers know public commitments $D_i = g^{\alpha_i}$ to the value α_i, for $1 \leq i \leq n$. Each server, after broadcasting $c_i = (r_i, s_i)$, must prove that he knows values α_i and β_i such that $D_i = g^{\alpha_i}$, $r_i = (g)^{\beta_i}$ and $s_i = (h_C)^{\alpha_i}(y_j)^{\beta_i}$. The rest of servers will play the role of a verifier in this non-interactive proof of knowledge. So, following the notation of Section 2.2, each server must perform :

$$PK \{ (\alpha_i, \beta_i) : \ D_i = g^{\alpha_i} \ \wedge \ r_i = g^{\beta_i} \ \wedge \ s_i = (h_C)^{\alpha_i}(y_j)^{\beta_i} \}$$

where $D_i, r_i, s_i, g, h_C, y_j$ are elements known to the verifiers. We present now a protocol to achieve this non-interactive proof of knowledge; it is similar to the one that appears in [1], and uses standard techniques introduced by Camenisch [8], Stadler [23] and Camenisch and Stadler [9]. In the random oracle model, the security of this protocol can be proved using the same strategies as them.

The proof $PK\{(\alpha, \beta) : A = g_1^\alpha \wedge B = g_2^\beta \wedge C = g_3^\alpha g_4^\beta\}$ is as follows: let $\ell \leq k$ be two security parameters and $\hat{H} : \{0,1\}^* \to \{0,1\}^k$ be a hash function. The prover does the following:

1. Generate 2ℓ numbers $u_1, \ldots, u_\ell$ and $v_1, \ldots, v_\ell$ at random in $\mathbb{Z}_q^*$
2. Compute, for $1 \leq i \leq \ell$, the values $t_i = g_1^{u_i}$, $t_i' = g_2^{v_i}$ and $t_i'' = g_3^{u_i} g_4^{v_i}$
3. Compute $c = \hat{H}(A, B, C, g_1, g_2, g_3, g_4, t_1, \ldots, t_\ell, t_1', \ldots, t_\ell', t_1'', \ldots, t_\ell'')$
4. Compute, for $1 \leq i \leq \ell$

$$\text{if } c[i] = 0 \text{ then } w_i = u_i \text{ and } w_i' = v_i$$
$$\text{if } c[i] = 1 \text{ then } w_i = u_i - \alpha \text{ and } w_i' = v_i - \beta$$

5. The proof of knowledge is the tuple $(c, w_1, \ldots, w_\ell, w_1', \ldots, w_\ell')$

The verifier of the proof must do the following:

1. Compute, for $1 \leq i \leq \ell$

$$\text{if } c[i] = 0 \text{ then } \tilde{t}_i = g_1^{w_i} , \tilde{t}_i' = g_2^{w_i'} \text{ and } \tilde{t}_i'' = g_3^{w_i} g_4^{w_i'}$$
$$\text{if } c[i] = 1 \text{ then } \tilde{t}_i = A g_1^{w_i} , \tilde{t}_i' = B g_2^{w_i'} \text{ and } \tilde{t}_i'' = C g_3^{w_i} g_4^{w_i'}$$

2. Compute $c' = \hat{H}(A, B, C, g_1, g_2, g_3, g_4, \tilde{t}_1, \ldots, \tilde{t}_\ell, \tilde{t}_1', \ldots, \tilde{t}_\ell', \tilde{t}_1'', \ldots, \tilde{t}_\ell'')$
3. If $c' = c$, then accept the proof; otherwise, reject the proof.

Each server S_i verifies the proofs published by the rest of servers, until he obtains accepted partial ciphertexts from a subset of servers in Γ. Notice that this subset in Γ always exists, because of the definition of the family $\mathcal{R}$. Then S_i can use the correct values $c_j = (r_j, s_j)$ corresponding to servers S_j in this subset in Γ to compute, exactly in the same way as we have shown in Section 4.2, an encryption (r, s) of the conference key $\kappa_C = h_C^\alpha$, using the homomorphic properties of ElGamal cryptosystem.

Key Delivery Phase

Each server in A sends the encryption of the conference key to user U_j. After receiving these messages, user U_j selects from the whole list of received values, the one which has been sent by all the servers of a subset that is not in $\mathcal{A}$. This implies that there exists at least one honest server in this subset (otherwise, the subset would be in $\mathcal{A}$), and so the corresponding ciphertext must be the correct one. For example, in the threshold case the user must select the value that he receives from at least t different servers. U_j decrypts the valid ciphertext by means of his private key, obtaining in this way the required conference key.

4.4 Some Remarks

Note that, although ElGamal cryptosystem is probabilistic, all the honest servers obtain the same ciphertext (r, s) of the requested conference key, because of the deterministic way in which they must calculate this ciphertext from the probabilistic ciphertexts (r_i, s_i).

In the case of a passive adversary, all servers follow the protocol correctly. So, a user could ask a single server for the key instead of an entire robust subset. This server will then contact with a robust subset, and the protocol will follow as we explain in Section 4.2. In the active case, this is not possible because the users do not know which servers are honest, thus they could ask wrongly a corrupted server, who could boycott the protocol.

The fact that we denote as robust the subsets of servers that can provide a valid conference key to a user is not accidental. We define these robust subsets in such a way that their members can execute the protocol correctly even if they contain some subset of players corrupted by the adversary. Roughly speaking, that is the definition of a robust distributed protocol, and for this reason we use the terminology of robust subsets.

And last but not least, note that in some way, the model we propose can be rewritten as a Multi-party protocol. Indeed, the protocol in which servers compute shares of the encryption of a conference key from their shares of the random secret value α fits in a Multi-party framework. This could be used in order to prove security properties of the protocol by means of using techniques of Canetti [10] to prove security in Multi-party protocols.

5 Conclusion

In this paper we introduce a new model for distributing keys in a distributed way in the computationally secure framework, and we design a protocol realizing it. This model minimizes the computations that every user has to carry out in order to obtain a key, and transmits them to the servers, which are supposed to have more powerful computational resources. In order to fit this protocol into a real oriented scenario we introduce techniques to provide robustness against both passive and active adversaries who can corrupt some groups of servers. We consider general structures, not only threshold ones, for both subsets of servers that can provide a valid key to a user and subsets of servers that can be corrupted by the adversary. We find the combinatorial conditions that these structures must satisfy if we want our scheme to run securely.

In our model, we require secure and authenticated channels among the servers only in the initialization phase. In the rest of phases, servers only need an authenticated broadcast channel among them. In the communication between a user and a server, authenticated channels are needed, but not secure ones, because the information that servers send to users is encrypted. This last point is an improvement with respect to the model in [16], because in that proposal secure and authenticated channels between servers and users were required. Even the requirement of secure channels among the servers can be eliminated (in our proposal as well as in [16]), if the secret sharing schemes that servers use in the initialization phase are *publicly verifiable* (see [23,20] for the details). The use of these schemes, however, reduces the efficiency of the distributed generation of a random secret shared value in Section 3.

In the passive case, a user only needs to decrypt a value (basically, one exponentiation) in order to obtain the requested key. Recall that in the proposal of [16] each user had to compute $O(t)$ exponentiations to get the key. In the active case, he must in addition compare a list of values and detect the correct ciphertext. However this is still quite more efficient than the same operation in the scheme of [16], where the user must verify all the information that he receives from each server (for example, verifying proofs of knowledge, which can be expensive), in order to distinguish the honest servers from the corrupted ones.

Some interesting questions arise from this work: first of all, it must be defined in a formal way all security requirements that must satisfy a distributed key distribution scheme and prove the security of our scheme based on this security model. Maybe the strategy is to see these schemes as Multi-Party protocols, and apply the security results of Canetti [10] in this scenario. It would be also interesting to check if other cryptosystems could fit in with our model, and if so, to study the efficiency of the consequent schemes. Likewise, some other security requirements such as proactivity or resharing would be desirable.

References

1. G. Ateniese, D. Song and G. Tsudik. Quasi-efficient revocation in group signatures. *Proc. of Sixth International Financial Cryptography Conference* (2002).
2. M. Bellare and P. Rogaway. Random oracles are practical: a paradigm for designing efficient protocols. *First ACM Conference on Computer and Communications Security* pp. 62–73 (1993).
3. M. Bellare and P. Rogaway. Provably secure session key distribution: the three party case. *Proc. 27th Annual Symposium on the Theory of Computing, ACM,* 1995.
4. G.R. Blakley. Safeguarding cryptographic keys. *Proceedings of the National Computer Conference, American Federation of Information.* Processing Societies Proceedings **48** pp. 313-317 (1979).
5. C. Blundo and P. D'Arco. Unconditionally secure distributed key distribution schemes. Preprint available at http://www.dia.unisa.it/paodar.dir
6. C. Blundo, P. D'Arco, V. Daza and C. Padró. Bounds and constructions for unconditionally secure distributed key distribution schemes with general access structures. *Proc. of the Information Security Conference (ISC 2001).* LNCS 2200, Springer-Verlag, pp. 1–17 (2001).
7. E.F. Brickell. Some ideal secret sharing schemes. *J. Combin. Math. and Combin. Comput.* **9** pp. 105-113 (1989).
8. J. Camenisch. Group signature schemes and payment systems based on the discrete logarithm problem. PhD thesis, ETH Zurich. *Diss. ETH No. 12520* (1998).
9. J. Camenisch and M. Stadler. Efficient group signature schemes for large groups. *Advances in Cryptology: CRYPTO'97,* LNCS 1294, Springer-Verlag, pp. 410-424 (1997).

10. R.Canetti. Security and composition of multi-party cryptographic protocols. *Journal of Cryptology* **13** (1) pp. 143–202, (2000).
11. W. Diffie and M.E. Hellman. New directions in cryptography. *IEEE Trans. Information Theory*, IT-**22** (6) pp. 644–654 (1976).
12. T. ElGamal. A public key cryptosystem and a signature scheme based on discrete logarithms. *IEEE Trans. Information Theory* **31** pp. 469–472 (1985).
13. P. Feldman. A practical scheme for non-interactive verifiable secret sharing. *Proceedings of the 28th IEEE Symposium on the Foundations of Computer Science.* IEEE Press, pp. 427–437 (1987).
14. A. Fiat and A. Shamir. How to prove yourself: practical solution to identification and signature problems. *Advances in Cryptology: CRYPTO'86*, LNCS 263, Springer, pp. 186–194 (1987).
15. A.J. Menezes, P.C. van Oorschot and S.A. Vanstone. *Handbook of Applied Cryptography.* CRC Press Inc., Boca Raton (1997).
16. M. Naor, B. Pinkas and O. Reingold. Distributed pseudo-random functions and KDCs. *Advances in Cryptology: Eurocrypt'99*, LNCS 1592, Springer-Verlag, pp. 327–346 (1999).
17. R. M. Needham and M. D. Schroeder. Using encryption for authentication in large networks of computers. *Communications of the ACM*, vol. **21** pp. 993–999 (1978).
18. T.P. Pedersen. Non-interactive and information-theoretic secure verifiable secret sharing. *Advances in Cryptology: CRYPTO'91*, LNCS 576, Springer-Verlag, pp. 129–140 (1991).
19. C. Schnorr. Efficient identification and signatures for smart cards. *Advances in Cryptology: CRYPTO'89*, LNCS 435, Springer-Verlag, pp. 239–252 (1989).
20. B. Schoenmakers. A simple publicly verifiable secret sharing scheme and its applications to electronic voting. *Advances in Cryptology: CRYPTO'99*, LNCS 1666, Springer-Verlag, pp. 148–164 (1999).
21. A. Shamir. How to share a secret. *Communications of the ACM* No. **22** pp. 612–613 (1979).
22. G. J. Simmons, W. Jackson and K. Martin. The geometry of secret sharing schemes. *Bulletin of the ICA* **1** pp. 71–88 (1991).
23. M. Stadler. Publicly verifiable secret sharing. *Advances in Cryptology: Eurocrypt'96*, LNCS 1070, Springer-Verlag, pp. 190–199 (1996).
24. D.R. Stinson. *Cryptography: Theory and Practice.* CRC Press Inc., Boca Raton (1995).

On Optimal Hash Tree Traversal for Interval Time-Stamping

Helger Lipmaa

Laboratory for Theoretical Computer Science
Department of Computer Science and Engineering
Helsinki University of Technology
P.O.Box 5400, FI-02015 HUT, Espoo, Finland
{helger}@tcs.hut.fi

Abstract. Skewed trees constitute a two-parameter family of recursively constructed trees. Recently, Willemson proved that suitably picked skewed trees are space-optimal for interval time-stamping. At the same time, Willemson proposed a practical but suboptimal algorithm for nonrecursive traversal of skewed trees. We describe an alternative, extremely efficient traversal algorithm for skewed trees. The new algorithm is surprisingly simple and arguably close to optimal in every imaginable sense. We provide a detailed analysis of the average-case storage (and communication) complexity of our algorithm, by using the Laplace's method for estimating the asymptotic behavior of integrals. Since the skewed trees can be seen as a natural generalization of Fibonacci trees, our results might also be interesting in other fields of computer science.

Keywords: Analysis of algorithms, implementation complexity, interval time-stamping, Laplace's method for integrals, tree traversal.

1 Introduction

Hash trees were originally introduced by Merkle in [Mer80]. Since then, hash trees together with their generalization to arbitrary graphs have been used in many different application areas of cryptography. The hash tree paradigm is very flexible since one has a large freedom of choosing the trees that are the "best" for a particular area.

Cryptographic time-stamping is a prime example area where a large amount of work has been done to devise graph families that are "optimal" in some well-defined sense [BLLV98,BL98,BLS00]. In particular, Buldas, Lipmaa and Schoenmakers proved in [BLS00] that the family of complete binary trees is optimal in the "usual" time-stamping scenario.

The kind of time-stamping where one must show that a certain document was stamped during some interval of time is called *interval time-stamping*. It has been argued informally for a long time that interval time-stamping is an important flavor of time-stamping, necessary to establish whether a certain document was signed during the period of validity of the signing key. (See, for example, [BLLV98].)

Recently, Buldas and Willemson [Wil02b] have described a two-parameter family of trees $\mathfrak{S}(d, w)$ that we call the *skewed (hash) trees*. This family is constructed recursively,

A.H. Chan and V. Gligor (Eds.): ISC 2002, LNCS 2433, pp. 357–371, 2002.

so that $\mathfrak{S}(d, w)$ is constructed from the trees $\mathfrak{S}(d-1, w-1)$ and $\mathfrak{S}(d-1, w)$. Willemson [Wil02b] gave an elegant combinatorial proof that a suitable chosen subfamily of $\mathfrak{S}(d, w)$ results in about 1.4 times shorter interval time-stamps than the family of complete binary trees $\mathfrak{T}(d)$ that is optimal in the non-interval scenario [BLS00]. Willemson also proved that this subfamily is optimal in this sense.

But (there is always a but), to be practically applicable, a family of hash trees must have an efficient graph traversal algorithm. The family of complete binary trees has an almost trivial traversal algorithm. Existence of such an algorithm, however, is caused by the extremely simple constitution of complete binary trees. A priori it is not clear at all that, given some tree family, there is a similar efficient algorithm that takes the tree parameters as inputs and thereafter performs the functionality of hash traversal.

While the skewed trees promise short time stamps, their recursive construction does not seem to make them well-suited for nonrecursive graph traversal that is actually used in applications. Willemson proposed in [Wil02b] a very interesting alternative combinatorial interpretation of skewed hash trees and described a traversal algorithm, based on this. However, the resulting algorithm is quite complicated. Moreover, its complexity forced Willemson actually to suggest that one would use a certain suboptimal subfamily $\{\mathfrak{S}(d, w)\}$ of skewed trees. Even in the latter case, during Willemson's algorithm one must store $\ell = \min(d+1, w+1)$ counters and ℓ hash values that amounts in the overall storage requirement of $(1 + o(1))\ell \cdot (\log_2 d + k)$ bits, where k is the output length of the employed hash function.

We propose a more efficient algorithm (Algorithm 1 on page 363) for traversing the whole family $\mathfrak{S}(d, w)$. We feel that such a generality is very important since this makes it very easy to switch to an arbitrary skewed tree very quickly, if needed. In particular, Algorithm 1 works for the subfamily of optimal skewed trees. During Algorithm 1 it is only necessary to store up to d hash values at every time moment and it is only necessary to do up to d hash computations every time when a new document is stamped. Both values are clearly the best that can be achieved when one is concerned about the worst-case.

Our algorithm is surprisingly simple. Its construction depends on somewhat subtle properties of well-known functions like addition, doubling and Hamming weight (population count). However, possession of an elegant algorithm is not a specific property of the skewed hash trees: As we will show later, one can derive as elegant, though a differently-looking, implementation for mirrored skewed trees. Both algorithms, when reduced to work on family $\{\mathfrak{T}(d)\}_d$ give rise to the well-known algorithm for traversing the complete binary trees. Based on this (may be slightly surprising) fact we conjecture that our approach works for many different families of recursively constructed tree families.

Our pseudocode implementation of the algorithm is very clean (the pseudocode for the *update* operation consists of five lines), and therefore potentially interesting by itself. Existence of a clean pseudocode implementation is a very desirable property of algorithms since it potentially reduces the work needed to debug real-life implementations. We hope that due to the cleanliness, our algorithm is almost immune to implementation errors. More precisely, between the invocations, our example implementation maintains a small stack, accessed only by the **push** and **pop** operations, and an additional d-bit counter. The stack consists solely of the hash values, necessary for incremental computing of the hash root; the counter encodes information about the current location in tree.

We provide a complexity analysis of our algorithm and argue that our storage complexity is almost optimal. In fact, the computational work done while traversing an arbitrary skewed hash tree is only slightly more complex than the computational work that must be done in the special case of complete binary trees. Thus we show that this very important flavor of time-stamping, the interval time-stamping, is almost as practical as the usual time-stamping were one must only prove that a document was stamped before a certain event. We think that the double-simplicity of skewed trees (the simplicity of its recursive construction and the simplicity of the nonrecursive traversal algorithm) is yet another witness of the immeasurable beauty and effectiveness of mathematics.

The most elaborated part of the analysis deals with the average-case storage complexity. (Which, by virtue of the algorithm, is practically equal to the average-case communication complexity.) By using the Laplace's method [dB82] for estimating the asymptotic behavior of integrals, we develop a surprisingly precise asymptotic approximation to the average-case storage complexity of our algorithm. For example, we find that the average-case storage is maximized when $w \approx \sqrt{d}$, then being $\approx (d - \sqrt{d})k + d$, where k is the output value of the employed hash function.

We hope that Lagrange's method could also be useful for analysing other cryptographic algorithms. We also hope that the skewed trees, being a simple generalization of Fibonacci trees, are of independent interest in the theory of data structures and other areas of computer science.

Road-map. In Section 2 we will introduce the kind reader to preliminaries. In particular, in Section 2.3 we will give a short description of the graph family $\mathfrak{S}(d, w)$ together with an explanation of its use in time-stamping. In Section 3 we describe our algorithm and give a proof of its correctness. In Section 4 we analyze the efficiency of our algorithm.

2   Preliminaries

2.1   Tree Traversal

By (hash) tree traversal, we mean the next problem: Given a tree with leaves $x_1, \dots, x_n$ that has a prespecified shape, one must incrementally compute the hash of the root of the tree, as the leaf values $x_0, x_1, \dots, x_{n-1}$ arrive, in this order, from an external source. A canonical example application area is time-stamping [HS91,BLLV98,Lip99], where the time-stamping authority outputs the root hash (the "round stamp") of a predefined authentication graph $\mathfrak{G}$ after the documents $x_0, \dots, x_{n-1}$ have arrived sequentially from several clients. The documents x_i are positioned at the leaves of $\mathfrak{G}$ from left to right. Moreover, after the ith document has been inserted to the tree, the time-stamping authority TSA must immediately return to the client a so called *freshness token* (often called the *head* of a stamp) that consists of the minimal amount of information that proves that the ith stamp is dependent of all previous ones. Immediate return is necessary to prevent the authority from cheating.

If the latter requirement of immediate return could be omitted, one could always use a trivial traversal algorithm where the authority constructs the graph G post factum, after arrival of the last document, and only then returns the freshness tokens to every client. However, as already mentioned, this would not be an acceptable solution due to the security reasons.

There is also an efficiency reason. Since documents can arrive to the time-stamping authority from very different sources, it is well possible that at some point they arrive in large bursts. To guarantee that the TSA continues to work under such extreme situations, one must take care that the *maximal* workload of the server would be minimized. Here, the workload includes, in particular, the cost of updating the contents of memory, so as to make it possible to output the root hash without any extra delay after the last document arrives.

Other practical requirements for hash tree traversal include minimal amount of the memory usage at every time moment. Since the potential number of documents stamped during one round is huge (say, in order of 2^{48}), it is clearly impractical to store n elements, or to do n hashing, at any given time. Instead, one would like to upper bound both the number of hashings done when a document arrives and the maximum amount of memory that is used to store the hash values at any given time moment, by sequentially computing the hash values G after arrival of every document.

Last but not least, it is desirable for an algorithm to have minimal implementation complexity: That is, it must be short in description (to fit in low-memory devices) and easily implementable (to minimize implementation errors).

2.2 Interval Time-Stamping

The main goal of interval time-stamping is to enable one to prove that a document was stamped in a finite interval: That is, later than some other document but before than yet another document. One of the original motivations for interval time-stamping was probably first written down in [BLS00], where the next argument was given.

Namely, in many slightly different schemes it is assumed that the time-stamping authority (TSA) links submitted time-stamps by using some linkage-based authentication graph [HS91,BdM91,BHS92,BLLV98,Lip99,BLS00]. However, this approach is often criticized for the following reason. Let $H_1, \ldots, H_n$ be the stamping requests during a round. Before "officially" closing the round, the TSA may issue additional time stamps for H_n, H_{n-1}, $\ldots$, H_1 in reverse order. After that the TSA is able, for any pair of stamps of H_i and H_j, to present proofs for the statements "H_i was stamped before H_j" and "H_j was stamped before H_i". Therefore, a critical reader might think that using linking schemes and signed receipts does not give any advantage compared to simple hash-and-sign scheme.

Interval time-stamping allows one to alleviate the situation as follows. First, a client requests a stamp L_n of a nonce from the TSA. Subsequently, she stamps her signature σ on the actual document X and L_n. The TSA may then issue additional stamps for X and σ. However, no one is able to back-date new documents relative to σ without cooperating with the signer. This example shows that interval time-stamping is fundamentally useful in certificate management since without it, one cannot really avoid the reordering attacks. We refer to [Wil02b] for more examples.

The given example can be seen as an intuition, that an interval time-stamp consists of two separate parts, or more precisely, that an interval time-stamp is the union of two

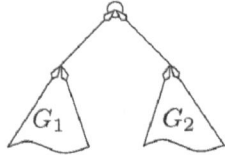

Fig. 1. The composed tree $\mathfrak{G}_1 \otimes \mathfrak{G}_2$

stamps: of the stamp of the nonce (*the freshness token*), and of the stamp on (X, σ) (*the existence token*). As shown in [Wil02b], to optimize the size of an interval time stamp, one must choose a tree G where the maximal sum of the lengths of freshness token and existence tokens is minimal. In graph-theoretic terms, the ith freshness token is defined as a (nonunique) set S of nodes with minimal cardinality, such that every leaf $j < i$ of G has some set in S as its parent. The ith existence token is defined as a set S of nodes with minimal cardinality such that the root hash can be "computed" from $S \cup \{i\}$ but not from S alone. In the next subsection we describe the concrete tree family that has been proven to provide minimal time stamp lengths.

2.3   Definition of the Skewed Trees

We will assume throughout this paper that d and w are nonnegative integers, used to parametrize different graph families. Define the family $\mathfrak{G}(d, w)$ (that we call *skewed trees*) of directed rooted trees recursively as follows [Wil02b]:

1. Set $\mathfrak{G}(0, x) = \mathfrak{G}(x, 0) = I$ for an arbitrary integer $x \geq 0$, where I is the singleton graph.
2. If $d, w \geq 1$ then set $\mathfrak{G}(d, w) = \mathfrak{G}(d - 1, w - 1) \otimes \mathfrak{G}(d - 1, w)$. Here, the result of the tree composition operation $\mathfrak{G}_1 \otimes \mathfrak{G}_2$ is defined as binary directed tree with a root that has two subtrees: $\mathfrak{G}_1$ being the left subtree, and $\mathfrak{G}_2$ being the right subtree. (See Fig. 1.)

This composition operator is a standard tool of constructing the tree families. For example, the family $\{\mathfrak{T}(d)\}$ of (directed) complete binary trees is constructed by $\mathfrak{T}(d + 1) = \mathfrak{T}(d) \otimes \mathfrak{T}(d)$ and $\mathfrak{T}(0) = I$. (As a simple consequence, $\mathfrak{T}(d)$ has 2^d leaves, and $\mathfrak{T}(d) = \mathfrak{G}(d, d)$.) The family $\{\mathfrak{F}(d)\}$ of Fibonacci trees is constructed by letting $\mathfrak{F}(d) = \mathfrak{F}(d - 1) \otimes \mathfrak{F}(d - 2)$ and $\mathfrak{F}(0) = \mathfrak{F}(1) = I$. For Fibonacci trees, $d \approx c_f \log(n)$, where n is the number of leaves in $\mathfrak{F}(d)$ and $c_f = 1/\log_2((1 + \sqrt{5})/2) \approx 1.44$.

If the complete binary tree is used for interval time-stamping then the worst-case length of the interval time-stamp is $c \log_2 n$, where $c = 2$ [Wil02b]. This corresponds to the case of family $\{\mathfrak{G}(d, w)\}_d$ with $\alpha := w/d = 1$. Setting $d = 2w + 1$ (that is, $\alpha = 2 + o(1)$) improves the value of the constant to $c = 3/2 + o(1)$. However, the asymptotically optimal (and already familiar!) constant $c = c_f \approx 1.44$ is obtained by setting $\alpha := w/d \approx (3 - \sqrt{5})/2$ [Wil02b].

Therefore, if short time-stamps are desired in interval time-stamping, one has to traverse trees from the family $\mathfrak{G}(d, w)$ with particular values of d and w for which $\mathfrak{G}(d, w)$ is quite different from the complete binary trees $\mathfrak{T}(d) = \mathfrak{G}(d, d)$. One would

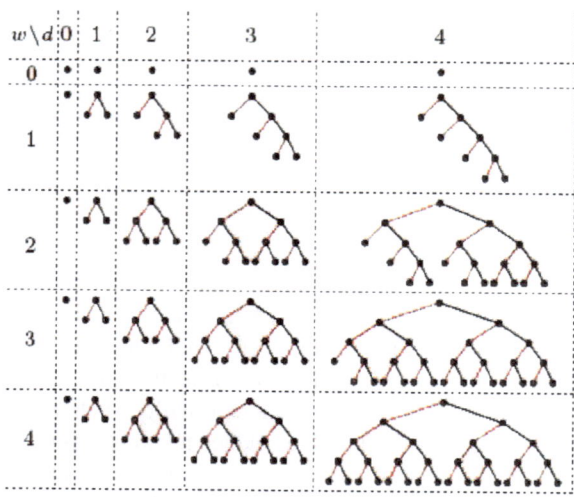

Fig. 2. The trees $\mathfrak{S}(d, w)$ for small d, w

like to have a general algorithm for traversing trees from this family that would satisfy the desiderata of Section 2.1. This is the task solved in the next section.

Finally, $\mathfrak{S}(d, w) = \mathfrak{S}(d, d)$ whenever $d > w$. Some skewed graphs are depicted by Fig. 2. It is interesting to observe some similarities and differences between the Fibonacci and the skewed trees. First, the recurrent rule for constructing the families is deceivingly similar: $\mathfrak{F}(d)$ is constructed by composing two previous Fibonacci trees while $\mathfrak{S}(d, w)$ is constructed by composing two last skewed trees from "column" $d - 1$. The Fibonacci trees are obtained as a solution to a minimum problem (they are minimum-node AVL trees for given height [Knu98]), while the optimal skewed trees are a solution to a maximum problem (they are maximum-node trees for given sum of width and height) [Bul02]. The reason why the constant c_f pops out in both cases is, while clear mathematically, still an intellectual mystery.

3   Algorithm for Traversing the Tree Family

A highly optimized algorithm for traversing the family $(\mathfrak{S}(d, w))$ of skewed trees is depicted by Algorithm 1. It consists of two procedures. The first, *initialization*, inputs the parameters d and w. It is only invoked once, during the set-up. The second, *update*, gets as input the ith data item x_i (that is, the label of the ith leaf). We will first describe the used notation and after that explain the main ideas behind this algorithm. This includes a detailed correctness proof.

3.1   Notation

We work in the RAM model where the word length is not smaller than $N = \max(w, d)$. In practice it could mean using, say, 64-bit integers. Our algorithms the Boolean bitwise

Algorithm 1 An algorithm for traversing $\mathfrak{S}(d, w)$. After *update*, contents of the stack is returned as the freshness token

```
 1  funct initialization(d, w)  ≡
 2      state := 0;
 3      if w > d then w = d fi;
 4      Store w, d;
 5      Create an empty stack of maximum possible size w.
 7  funct update(value)  ≡
 8      if state ≥ 2^d then return(Error!);  fi
 9      push(value);
10      for i := 1 to ntz(state + 1) do
11          push(H(pop(), pop()));  end
12      state := state + (1 ≪ (w̄_h(state) ∸ w)).
```

AND "$x \wedge y$" and the left shift $x \lll y = x \cdot 2^y$. Common arithmetics is implicitly done modulo 2^N but it can be sometimes done modulo d or modulo w. We denote the proper subtraction, that is well-known from the theory of primitive recursive functions, by $a \dot- b$, that is, $a \dot- b = a - b$ when $a \geq b$, and $a \dot- b = 0$ when $b > a$. Let w_h be the Hamming weight function; that is, $w_h(x)$ is equal to the number of one-bits in the binary presentation of x. (For example, $w_h(17) = 2$ and $w_h(0011) = 2$.) Let $\overline{w}_h(e) := |e| - w_h(e)$ be the number of zeros in the binary encoding of e; for example, $\overline{w}_h(01101) = 2$. Let $\mathsf{ntz}(x)$ be the number of trailing zeros of x; that is, $\mathsf{ntz}(x) = k$ iff $2^k \mid x$ but $2^{k+1} \nmid x$. For example, $\mathsf{ntz}(48) = 4$ and $\mathsf{ntz}(0000) = 4$. Both functions w_h (and thus, the function $\overline{w}_h$) and ntz can be computed in time $\log_2 w$.

Several newer processors, including the Pentium MMX, have a special instruction for proper subtraction. An efficient $O(\log_2 N)$-time algorithm for w_h has been described, say, in [LM01]. The function ntz can then be computed in time $O(\log_2 N)$ as $\mathsf{ntz}(x) := w_h(x - (x \wedge (x-1))) - 1)$. Many common processors have special instructions for both w_h (see [LM01] for a recent overview) and ntz (the instruction bsf on the Pentium, for example). This basically means that all nontrivial instructions of Algorithm 1 (namely, w_h, ntz and $\dot-$) can be seen as primitive in modern microprocessors.

We let $\alpha \mathbin{+\!\!+} \beta$ to denote the concatenation of binary strings α and β. We use a collision-resistant hash function H [Dam87]. We assume implicitly that the left argument of H is evaluated (that is, popped from the stack) earlier than the right argument of H.

3.2 Variables

Algorithm 1 uses a stack that has maximum size w, and is initially empty. The top element of the stack can be removed by using function **pop**(), and an element x can be inserted to the stack by using function **push**(x). There are no other means to access the contents of stack. Observe that like always, a stack implementation can be replaced with a possibly more efficient but less modular array implementation.

Intuitively, after an *update*, the stack contains the hash values of left children of root path that starts from the leaf that corresponds to the lastly arrived document. This set of hash values coincides with the ith freshness token [Wil02b] and therefore the whole contents of the stack must be returned to the ith client after the *update* function.

Except from the stack and parameters w and d, Algorithm 1 maintains only one internal value, *state*. Intuitively, *state* represents binary "Huffman" encoding of the location of the next leaf, labeled by say x_n, in the binary tree $\mathfrak{S}(d, w)$. Namely, by following the path from this leaf to the root, in every step one starts either from the left or from the right child and follows an arc to its parent node. Let X^i denote a run of i X-s, where i can be 0. If we encode left by $L = 0$ and right by $R = 1$, the path that starts from the root and ends with an arbitrary vertex v can be encoded as $\mathrm{enc}(v) := L^{a_d} \mathbin{+\!\!+} R^{b_d} \mathbin{+\!\!+} L^{a_{d-1}} \mathbin{+\!\!+} R^{b_{d-1}} \mathbin{+\!\!+} \cdots \mathbin{+\!\!+} L^{a_1} \mathbin{+\!\!+} R^{b_1}$ for some integers $(a_d, b_d, \ldots, a_1, b_1)$. This holds since no leaf has depth greater than d. For the jth leftmost leaf v we denote $\mathrm{enc}(v)$ often by $\mathrm{enc}(j)$. For example, in Fig. 2, the three leaves of $\mathfrak{S}(2, 1)$ are encoded as $\mathrm{enc}(0) = L = 0$, $\mathrm{enc}(1) = RL = 10$ and $\mathrm{enc}(2) = RR = 11$, respectively. (Recall that the leftmost leaf is 0.) Note that for no two leafs $i \neq j$, $\mathrm{enc}(i)$ will be a prefix of $\mathrm{enc}(j)$. Finally, $\overline{w}_h(state) = d - w_h(state)$ since we interpret *state* always as a bitstring of length d.

3.3   Correctness Proof

Theorem 1. *Algorithm 1 is a correct $\mathfrak{S}(d, w)$-traversal algorithm.*

Proof: A simple case arises when $d = w$, since $\mathfrak{S}(d, d)$ is equal to the complete binary tree $\mathfrak{T}(d)$. Its all leaves are at the same depth d, and have different d-bit encodings $\mathrm{enc}(0) := 0 \ldots 000$, $\mathrm{enc}(1) := 0 \ldots 001$, $\ldots$, $\mathrm{enc}(2^d - 1) := 1 \ldots 111$. Clearly, all encodings are different and therefore *state* $= \mathrm{enc}(j)$ is just equal to the binary d-bit representation of j.

We have a slightly more difficult case when $w \neq d$. As in the $\mathfrak{T}(d)$-case, $\mathrm{enc}(0)$ is always an all-zero string, $\mathrm{enc}(n - 1)$ is always an all-one string and that for all j, $\mathrm{enc}(j) > \mathrm{enc}(j - 1)$ always as a binary string. On the other hand, some of the nodes of $\mathfrak{S}(d, w)$ have depth smaller than w. Therefore, one must first determine during every invocation of *update* the next two things: First, what is the depth of the next node j, and second, how to compute $\mathrm{enc}(j)$ from $\mathrm{enc}(j - 1)$.

Now, let $\mathrm{depth}_{d,w}(j)$ denote the depth of the jth leaf of $\mathfrak{S}(d, w)$. Equivalently, $\mathrm{depth}_{d,w}(j)$ is the length of binary string $\mathrm{enc}(j)$, for fixed d and w. Denote $\mathrm{enc}(j) = h \mathbin{+\!\!+} t$, where $h \in \{0, 1\}$. To compute $\mathrm{depth}_{d,w}(j)$, first note that since $\mathfrak{S}(d, w) = \mathfrak{S}(d - 1, w - 1) \otimes \mathfrak{S}(d - 1, w)$ then

$$\mathrm{depth}_{d,w}(j) = \begin{cases} 1 + \mathrm{depth}_{d-1,w-1}(j') \ , & h = 0 \ , \\ 1 + \mathrm{depth}_{d-1,w}(j') \ , & h = 1 \end{cases} \ ,$$

since $h = 0$ exactly when j is in the left subtree, $\mathfrak{S}(d - 1, w - 1)$, of $\mathfrak{S}(d, w)$. (In both cases j' is a leaf of corresponding subtree with encoding $\mathrm{enc}(j') = t$.) Therefore, an arbitrary vertex $v \in \mathfrak{S}(d, w)$ is a root of the subtree $\mathfrak{S}(d - |\mathrm{enc}(j)|, w - \overline{w}_h(\mathrm{enc}(j)))$. Therefore, we have shown that

Lemma 1. *Let $\mathfrak{S}(d, w)$ be a fixed skewed tree. A binary string e is*

1. *Encoding of a leaf of* $\mathfrak{S}(d, w)$ *iff one of the two values* $d - |e|$ *and* $w - \overline{w}_h(e)$ *is* 0 *and both are nonnegative.*
2. *Encoding of an internal node of* $\mathfrak{S}(d, w)$ *iff both those values are positive;*
3. *An invalid encoding (not an encoding of any vertex of* $\mathfrak{S}(d, w)$*) iff either of those two values is negative;*

Now, let us look in more detail at the sequential generation process of encodings $\mathsf{enc}(0), \mathsf{enc}(1), \ldots, \mathsf{enc}(n - 1)$ in the case of a fixed skewed tree $\mathfrak{S}(d, w)$. For the simplicity of description we also define an alternative padded encoding function $\mathsf{penc}(j) := \mathsf{enc}(j) \mathbin{+\!\!+} 0^{d - \mathsf{depth}_{d,w}(j)}$. That is, $\mathsf{penc}(j)$ is equal to $\mathsf{enc}(j)$, padded on right with zeros to the length d.

Algorithm 1 stores the encoding of next leaf $\mathsf{penc}(j)$ as *state*. The encoding of the leftmost leaf 0, $\mathsf{enc}(0)$, consists of all zeros, and therefore $\mathsf{penc}(0) = 0^d$. Thus, the initialization *state* $:= 0$ is correct. Assume that we have computed the value $\mathsf{enc}(j - 1)$ for some j. The next node, j, has encoding $\mathsf{penc}(j) > \mathsf{penc}(j - 1)$.

To compute the encoding $\mathsf{penc}(j)$, given *state* $= \mathsf{penc}(j - 1)$, note that if $j - 1$ is a leaf with encoding $\mathsf{enc}(j - 1) = e$ then

1. If $\overline{w}_h(e) < w$ then by Lemma 1, $\mathsf{depth}_{d,w}(e) = d$. But then $e = state$ and hence also $\overline{w}_h(state) < w$. In this case the next leaf j has encoding $\mathsf{penc}(j) = state + 1$. (If the least significant bit of *state* is 0 then $w_h(state + 1) = w_h(state) + 1$, and then $state + 1$ encodes the jth leaf with $\mathsf{depth}_{d,w}(j) = d$. Otherwise, $\mathsf{enc}(j)$ will be the longest prefix of $state + 1$ that contains no more than w zeros; then $\mathsf{penc}(j) = state + 1$.)
2. Otherwise, by Lemma 1, $\overline{w}_h(e) = w$. (Then clearly $\overline{w}_h(state) \geq \overline{w}_h(e) = w$.) That is, e is equal to the longest prefix of *state* that contains exactly w zeros, and $\mathsf{depth}_{d,w}(j - 1) = d - (\overline{w}_h(state) - w) = w + w_h(state)$. In this case, no leaf can have encoding of form $e \mathbin{+\!\!+} 0^k$ for $k \geq 1$. However, $e + 1$ is a valid encoding for a vertex in $\mathfrak{S}(d, w)$. Therefore, $\mathsf{penc}(j) = state + 2^{\overline{w}_h(state) - w}$.

Now, we have shown that Algorithm 1 updates the *state* correctly: It starts with the encoding *state* $= \mathsf{penc}(0) = 0^d$ of the first node. At every step it updates *state* from $\mathsf{penc}(j - 1)$ to $\mathsf{penc}(j)$: Depending on whether $w_h(state) = w$, it follows one of the two described updating rules that can be jointly described as $\mathsf{penc}(j) = \mathsf{penc}(j) + (1 < \ll (\overline{w}_h(\mathsf{penc}(j - 1)) \mathbin{\dot{-}} w))$.

Apart from updating the state, Algorithm 1 must also update the stack, that is, it must remove from the the node labels (either original data items, corresponding to leafs, or internal hash representations) that are not anymore needed and replace them with the new ones. The intuition behind this simple procedure (starting from line 10 in Algorithm 1) is very simple.

To compute the hash chain from leaf j with encoding $\mathsf{enc}(j)$ to the root, one must have available all the hash values, corresponding to the left and right children of this path together with the endpoint of the path. Denote the set of left children of the root path that starts from leaf j by $X(j)$. (E.g., to compute the value of the root, it suffices to have available the hash values that correspond to the set $X(n - 1) \cup \{n - 1\}$, where $n - 1$ is the rightmost leaf like always.)

Now, one can compute the set $X(j)$ from $X(j - 1)$ as follows. The set $X(j - 1) \setminus X(j)$ consists of hash values of nodes with encoding $p \mathbin{+\!\!+} 0 \mathbin{+\!\!+} 1^i \mathbin{+\!\!+} 0$, where $\mathsf{enc}(j - 1) =$

Algorithm 2 An algorithm for traversing $\overline{\mathfrak{S}}(d, w)$

```
1   funct init(d, w) ≡
2       state := 0;
3       if w > d then w = d fi;
4       Store w, d;
5       Create an empty stack of maximum possible size w.
7   funct update(value) ≡
8       if state ≥ 2^d then return(Error!); fi
9       if w_h(state) < w
10          then n := ntz(state + 1); increment := 1;
11          else n := ntz((state ≫ ntz(state)) + 1); increment := 1 ⋘ (w̄_h(state) − w); fi
12      push(value);
13      for i := 1 to n do
14          push(H(pop(), pop())); end
15      state := state + increment.
```

$p + 0 + 1^k$ and $i \in [0, k − 1]$. The only element in $X(j)$ that is not in $X(j − 1)$ is the node with encoding $p + 0$. The latter node is the root of the subtree that has nodes from $(X(j − 1) \setminus X(j)) \cup \{j − 1\}$. Therefore, before the **for** -loop in Algorithm 1, the stack clearly consists of the set of hash values of nodes $X(j)$, and the **for** -loop updates the stack to the state where it contains the hash values, corresponding to the nodes from set $X(j + 1)$.   ∎

Finally, Algorithm 2 and Algorithm 3 work on families $\overline{\mathfrak{S}}(d, w)$ and $\mathfrak{T}(d)$ respectively, where $\overline{\mathfrak{S}}(d, w)$ is a mirror family of $\mathfrak{S}(d, w)$ (that is, one applies the recursive rule $\overline{\mathfrak{S}}(d, w) = \overline{\mathfrak{S}}(d, w − 1) \otimes \overline{\mathfrak{S}}(d − 1, w − 1)$ instead of the rule $\mathfrak{S}(d, w) = \mathfrak{S}(d − 1, w − 1) \otimes \mathfrak{S}(d, w − 1)$). In principal, Algorithm 2 algorithm is the same as Algorithm 1, except that the meanings of bits 0 and 1 in the encodings are switched. What is interesting is that Algorithm 2 is at least conceptually slightly more difficult than Algorithm 1. Algorithm 3 is mostly described for comparison purposes.

4 Complexity Analysis

We next analyse the complexity of *update* in Algorithm 1. The error verification and **for** - loop notwithstanding, during one run of *update*, the computer must execute two ordinary additions, one proper subtraction, one data-dependent shift left, two assignments, and once the functions $\overline{w}_h$ and ntz. There are special instructions for all these functions in many new processors and therefore the total time for this part is negligible. Instead, the *update* time depends primarily on the **for** -loop, that consists of $2 \cdot$ ntz$(state + 1)$ **pop**() operations (easy) and ntz$(state + 1)$ hash-function invocations (hard). Therefore, in the worst case, this algorithm can do up to d hash-function invocations. Moreover, the worst-case memory use is $d(k + 1)$, where k is the output size of the employed hash function (usually in the range of $160 \ldots 512$ bits): Really, one stores at any time moment a freshness token (that takes up to $d \cdot k$ bits and a d-bit *state*.

Algorithm 3 An algorithm for traversing $\mathfrak{T}(d)$, given for comparison purposes

```
1  funct init(d) ≡
2      state := 0;
3      Store d;
4      Create an empty stack of maximum possible size d.
6  funct update(value) ≡
7      if state ≥ 2^d then return(Error!); fi
8      push(value);
9      for i := 1 to ntz(state + 1) do
10         push(H(pop(), pop())); end
11     state := state + 1.
```

Hence, one could argue that the time complexity of our algorithm is close to optimal. Really, the number of hashings must be the same for all algorithms that accomplish the same task. Moreover, $d \cdot k$ bits are necessary to store the greatest freshness token. Apart from that, our algorithms uses a small number of additional instructions that can all be executed very quickly on current processors.

Next, we will estimate the average storage complexity of Algorithm 1. For this, we first define the partial binomial sum $L(d, w) := \sum_{k=0}^{w} \binom{d}{k}$.

Lemma 2. *(1)* $\mathfrak{S}(d, w)$ *has* $L(d, w)$ *leaves. (2) Let* $\ell(d, w, t)$ *be the number of leaves of* $\mathfrak{S}(d, w)$ *that are at depth* t. *Then*

$$
\ell(d, w, t) = \begin{cases}
0 , & t < w , \\
\binom{t-1}{w-1} , & t \in [w, d-1] , \\
2 \cdot \sum_{k=0}^{w-1} \binom{d-1}{k} = 2L(d-1, w-1) , & t = d , \\
0 , & t > d .
\end{cases}
$$

Proof: (1) Proof by induction [Wil02b].

(2) Proof by induction on (d, w). If $d = w = 1$ then $\ell(1, 1, t) = 1$. Otherwise, $\ell(d, w, t) = \ell(d-1, w-1, t-1) + \ell(d-1, w, t-1)$. When $t < w$ then $\ell(d, w, t) = 0$. When $t = w$ then $\ell(d, w, t) = \binom{t-2}{w-2} + 0 = 1 = \binom{t-1}{w-1}$. When $t \in [w+1, d-1]$ then $\ell(d, w, t) = \binom{t-2}{w-2} + \binom{t-2}{w-1} = \binom{t-1}{w-1}$. When $t = d$ then $\ell(d, w, t) = 2 \cdot \left(\sum_{k=0}^{w-2} \binom{d-2}{k} + \sum_{k=0}^{w-1} \binom{d-2}{k} \right) = 2 \cdot \left(\sum_{k=0}^{w-1} \binom{d-2}{k-1} + \sum_{k=0}^{w-1} \binom{d-2}{k} \right) = 2 \cdot \sum_{k=0}^{w-1} \binom{d-1}{k}$. When $t > d$ then $t = 0$. ∎

Lemma 3. *The number of hashings done on the* j*th step of Algorithm 1 is* $\mathrm{ntz}(state+1)$. *The size of the stack before the* j*th step is* $w_h(\mathrm{enc}(j))$.

Proof: The proof of the first claim is straightforward. That the second claim holds is also clear: $X(j)$ has $w_h(\mathrm{enc}(j))$ different elements, with $\mathrm{enc}(x)$ being equal to the maximum prefix of $\mathrm{enc}(j)$ that has exactly i, $0 \le i < w_h(\mathrm{enc}(j))$, ones that are appended by a 0. ∎

Theorem 2. *(1) In average, the stack contains*

$$\mathrm{ft}(d, w) = \frac{d}{2} + \frac{w - 1}{2^{d+1}(w+1) \int_0^{0.5} y^{d-w-1}(1-y)^w \, dy} \tag{1}$$

hash elements. (2) Asymptotically,

$$\mathrm{ft}(d, w) \sim \begin{cases} \frac{d}{2} + \frac{(w-1)(d-2w)}{2(w+1)} , & w \leq d/2 , \\ \frac{d}{2} + \frac{d^d(w-1)}{2^{d+1}(w+1)\sqrt{2\pi/d}\cdot(d-w)^{d-w-1/2}w^{w+1/2}} , & w \geq d/2 . \end{cases}$$

The proof of this theorem will use the next two lemmas.

Lemma 4. $L(d, w) = 2^d(d - w)\binom{d}{w} \int_0^{0.5} y^{d-w-1}(1-y)^w \, dy.$

Proof: Multiple integration by parts gives $\int y^a(1-y)^b \, dy = \frac{y^{a+1}(1-y)^b}{a+1} + \frac{b}{a+1} \int y^{a+1}(1-y)^{b-1} \, dy.$ Thus $B_1(d, w, p) := \sum_{k=0}^w \binom{d}{k}p^{d-k}(1-p)^k = (d-w)\binom{d}{w}\int_0^p y^{d-w-1}(1-y)^w \, dy.$ Therefore, since $L(d, w) = \sum_{k=0}^w \binom{d}{k}$, $L(d, w) = 2^d B_1(d, w, 1/2) = 2^d(d-w)\binom{d}{w}\int_0^{0.5} y^{d-w-1}(1-y)^w \, dy.$ ∎

Lemma 5. $L(d - 1, w - 1) = \frac{L(d,w)}{2} - \frac{1}{2} \cdot \binom{d-1}{w}.$

Proof: Define $J(a, b) := \binom{d}{w}\int_0^{0.5} y^a(1-y)^b \, dy.$ Thus, $L(d, w) = 2^d(d-w)\binom{d}{w}J(d-w-1, w).$ Now, $\int y^a(1-y)^b \, dy = \int y^a(1-y)^{b-1} \, dy - \int y^{a+1}(1-y)^{b-1} \, dy,$ and therefore $J(a, b) = J(a, b-1) - J(a+1, b-1).$ Most importantly, $J(d-w-1, w) = J((d-1)-(w-1)-1, w-1) - J(d-(w-1)-1, w-1),$ which gives us $L(d-1, w-1) = \frac{L(d,w)w}{2d} + \frac{L(d,w-1)(d-w)}{2d}.$ Given that $L(d, w-1) = L(d, w) - \binom{d}{w},$ we get that $L(d-1, w-1) = \frac{L(d,w)w}{2d} + \frac{(L(d,w)-\binom{d}{w})(d-w)}{2d} = \frac{L(d,w)}{2} - \frac{1}{2} \cdot \binom{d-1}{w}.$ ∎

Proof: [of Thm. 2.] (1) According to Lemma 3, in average the stack contains $s(d, w)/L(d, w)$ hash elements, where $s(d, w) = \sum_{j=0}^{n-1} w_h(\mathrm{enc}(j)).$ By Lemma 2, $s(d, w) = \sum_{t=w}^{d-1} \binom{t-1}{w-1}\cdot(t-w) + \sum_{k=0}^{w-1} \binom{d-1}{k}\cdot(2\cdot(d-k-1)+1) = \sum_{t=0}^{d-w-1} \binom{t+w-1}{w-1}\cdot t + (2d-1)\cdot \sum_{k=0}^{w-1} \binom{d-1}{k} - 2\cdot \sum_{k=0}^{w-1} \binom{d-1}{k}\cdot k = w\cdot\binom{d-1}{w-1} + (2d-1)\cdot L(d-1, w-1) - 2\cdot Q(d-1, w-1),$ where $Q(d, w) := \sum_{k=0}^w \binom{d}{k}\cdot k.$

Define $B_2(d, w, p) := \sum_{k=0}^w \binom{d}{k}kp^{d-k}(1-p)^k.$ Thus, $B_2(d, w, p) = d(1-p)\sum_{k=0}^{w-1} \binom{d-1}{k}p^{d-1-k}(1-p)^k = d(1-p)B_1(d-1, w-1, p).$ In particular, $Q(d, w) = 2^d B_2(d, w, 1/2) = \frac{d2^d}{2}B_1(d-1, w-1, 1/2) = dL(d-1, w-1).$ Hence, $\mathrm{ft}(d, w) = \frac{w\cdot\binom{d-1}{w+1}+(2d-1)L(d-1,w-1)-2(d-1)(L(d-2,w-2))}{L(d,w)}.$

Now, according to Lemma 5, $\mathrm{ft}(d, w) = \frac{w\cdot\binom{d-1}{w+1}+dL(d-1,w-1)+(d-1)\binom{d-2}{w-1}}{L(d,w)} = \frac{2w\cdot\binom{d-1}{w+1}+dL(d,w)-d\binom{d-1}{w}+2(d-1)\binom{d-2}{w-1}}{2L(d,w)} = \frac{d}{2} + \binom{d}{w}\frac{(w-1)(d-w)}{(w+1)2L(d,w)}.$ According to Lemma 4, $\mathrm{ft}(d, w) = \frac{d}{2} + \frac{w-1}{2^{d+1}(w+1)\int_0^{0.5} y^{d-w-1}(1-y)^w \, dy}.$

(2) We will use the standard Laplace's method [dB82] for estimating the asymptotic behavior of integrals of type $I(d) = \int_a^b e^{d\cdot h(y)}g(y) \, dy.$ Since this method is standard

in analysis but might probably be not well-known to a potential reader, we will give a somewhat longish proof without any precise explanations. A curious reader is referred to [dB82]. (For completeness, we will give a shorter alternative proof directly after this one.)

Assume that $w = \alpha d$. Rewrite the integral from (1) as a Laplace integral, $I(d) = \int_0^{0.5} y^{d-\alpha d-1}(1-y)^{\alpha d}dy = \int_0^{0.5} e^{d((1-\alpha)\ln y + \alpha \ln(1-y))}\frac{1}{y}dy = \int_0^{0.5} e^{d \cdot h(y)}g(y)dy$, where $h(y) = (1-\alpha)\ln y + \alpha \ln(1-y)$ and $g(y) = \frac{1}{y}$. Now, $h(y)$ has a unique maximum $y_0 = \min(1-\alpha, 0.5)$ in the interval $[0, 0.5]$. Due to this reason, we divide the analysis into two parts: in the first part we analyse the case $\alpha \le 0.5$ and in the second part the case $\alpha \ge 0.5$.

First case, $\alpha \le 0.5$. For applying the Laplace's method for integrals, we first rescale the integration variable by setting $s := (y - y_0)d = (y - 0.5)d$. Then $I(d) \sim \int_{0.5-\varepsilon}^{0.5} e^{dh(y)}g(y)\ dy = \frac{1}{d}\int_{-\varepsilon d}^{0} e^{dh(1/2+s/d)}g(1/2 + s/d)\ ds$, where $1/x \ll \varepsilon \ll 1/\sqrt{x}$. But $h(1/2 + s/d) = -\ln 2 - \frac{2(2\alpha-1)}{d}\cdot s - \frac{2}{d^2}\cdot s^2 + O(s^3)$ and $g(1/2 + s/d) = 2 - 4/s \cdot d + 8/s^2d^2 + O(s^3)$. Thus we can simplify $I(d)$, approximating $g(1/2 + s/d) \sim 2$. Then, $I(d) \sim \frac{2}{d}\int_{-\varepsilon d}^{0} e^{dh(1/2+s/d)}\ ds$. Furthermore, take $e^{d \cdot h(1/2+s/d)} = e^{-d\ln 2 - 2(2\alpha-1)s}\cdot e^{-2/(s^2d)+O(s^3)} \sim e^{-d\ln 2 - 2(2\alpha-1)s}\cdot (1 - \frac{2}{s^2d} + O(s^3)) \sim 2^{-d}\cdot e^{-2(2\alpha-1)s}$. Thus, $I(d) \sim \frac{2^{1-d}}{d}\int_{-\varepsilon d}^{0} e^{-2(2\alpha-1)s}\ ds \sim \frac{2^{1-d}}{d}\int_{-\infty}^{0} e^{-2(2\alpha-1)s}\ ds = \frac{2^{1-d}}{d}\cdot \left(-\frac{1}{2(2\alpha-1)}\right) = -\frac{1}{d2^d(2\alpha-1)}$. Thus, in this case, $ft(d, w) \sim \frac{d}{2} - \frac{(w-1)d2^d(2\alpha-1)}{2^{d+1}(w+1)} = \frac{d}{2} + \frac{(w-1)(d-2w)}{2(w+1)}$.

Second case, $\alpha \ge 0.5$. In this case, the function $h(y)$ has a maximum at the point $\beta := 1 - \alpha \le 0.5$. Split the integral into a local and nonlocal part: $I(d) = \int_0^{\beta-\varepsilon} e^{d\cdot h(y)}g(y)\ dy + \int_{\beta-\varepsilon}^{\beta+\varepsilon} e^{d\cdot h(y)}g(y)\ dy + \int_{\beta+\varepsilon}^{0.5} e^{d\cdot h(y)}g(y)\ dy$, where $1/x^{1/2} \ll \varepsilon \ll 1/x^{1/3}$ and the nonlocal part is exponentially small. Therefore, $I(d) \sim \int_{\beta-\varepsilon}^{\beta+\varepsilon} e^{d\cdot h(y)}g(y)\ dy$. We can expand $g(y)$ and $h(y)$ around $y = \beta$, which gives us $I(d) \sim \int_{\beta-\varepsilon}^{\beta+\varepsilon} e^{d\cdot(\alpha\ln\alpha + \beta\ln\beta - \frac{(y-\beta)^2}{2\alpha\beta} + O((y-\beta)^3))}(\frac{1}{\beta} + O(y-\beta))\ dy$. Change the variables, $s = \sqrt{d}(y-\beta)$. Thus, $I(d) \sim \frac{1}{\sqrt{d}}\int_{-\sqrt{d}\cdot\varepsilon}^{\sqrt{d}\cdot\varepsilon} e^{d\cdot(\alpha\ln\alpha + \beta\ln\beta - \frac{s^2}{2\alpha\beta d} + O(s^3))}(\frac{1}{\beta} + O(s))\ ds$. Next, discard all but the leading-order term of g, and approximate $e^{O(s^3)} \sim 1 + O(s^3)$. Thus, $I(d) \sim \frac{1}{\sqrt{d}\cdot\beta}\int_{-\sqrt{d}\cdot\varepsilon}^{\sqrt{d}\cdot\varepsilon} e^{d\cdot(\alpha\ln\alpha + \beta\ln\beta - \frac{s^2}{2\alpha\beta d})}\ ds = \frac{e^{d\cdot\alpha\ln\alpha + d\cdot\beta\ln\beta}}{\sqrt{d}\cdot\beta}\int_{-\sqrt{d}\cdot\varepsilon}^{\sqrt{d}\cdot\varepsilon} e^{-\frac{s^2}{2\alpha\beta}}\ ds = \frac{\alpha^{d\cdot\alpha}\beta^{d\cdot\beta}}{\sqrt{d}\cdot\beta}\int_{-\sqrt{d}\cdot\varepsilon}^{\sqrt{d}\cdot\varepsilon} e^{-\frac{s^2}{2\alpha\beta}}\ ds$. Expanding the integral gives $I(d) \sim \frac{\alpha^{d\cdot\alpha}\beta^{d\cdot\beta}}{\sqrt{d}\cdot\beta}\int_{-\infty}^{\infty} e^{-\frac{s^2}{2\alpha\beta}}\ ds = \frac{\alpha^{d\cdot\alpha}\beta^{d\cdot\beta}}{\sqrt{d}\cdot\beta}\cdot\sqrt{2\pi\beta\alpha} = \sqrt{2\pi/d}\alpha^{d\cdot\alpha+1/2}\beta^{d\cdot\beta-1/2}$. Therefore, in this case, $ft(d, w) \sim \frac{d}{2} + \frac{d^{d+1/2}(w-1)}{2^{d+3/2}\sqrt{\pi}(w+1)\cdot(d-w)^{d-w-1/2}\cdot w^{w+1/2}} \sim \frac{d}{2}$. ∎

Proof: [Shorter proof of Thm. 2, (2).] As before, rewrite the integral as $\int_a^b e^{d\cdot h(y)}g(y)\ dy$ with $a = 0$ and $b = 0.5$, and analyse separately the same two cases, $\alpha \ge 0.5$ and $\alpha \le 0.5$. In the first case, one uses the well-known analytic result [dB82] that $I(d) \sim \frac{g(b)e^{dh(b)}}{d\cdot h'(b)} =$

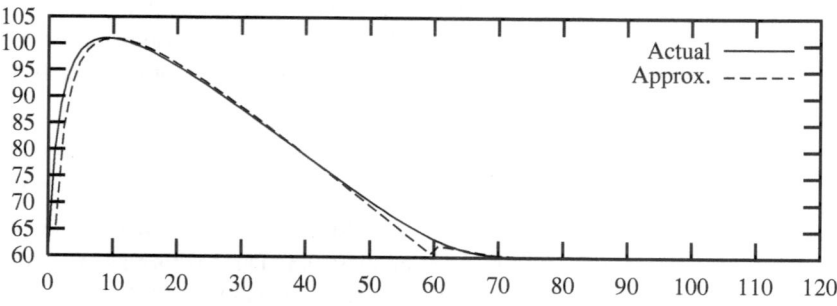

Fig. 3. Function ft(120, ·): its actual value together with approximation

$-\frac{1}{d2^d(2\alpha-1)}$, and thus $\mathrm{ft}(d,w) \sim \frac{d}{2} + \frac{(w-1)(d-2w)}{2(w+1)}$. In the second case, one has that

$I(d) \sim \frac{\sqrt{2\pi} \cdot e^{d \cdot h(\beta)} g(\beta)}{\sqrt{-d \cdot h''(\beta)}} = \sqrt{2\pi/d} \cdot \alpha^{d \cdot \alpha + 1/2} \beta^{d \cdot \beta - 1/2}$.   ■

As noted by Willemson [Wil02a], the result $\mathrm{ft}(d,w) = \frac{d}{2} + \binom{d}{w} \frac{(w-1)(d-w)}{(w+1)2L(d,w)}$ can be derived in an easier way by using the alternative representation of the skewed trees from [Wil02b, Chapter 5].

The "actual" function ft(120, ·) together with approximation from the previous theorem are depicted by Fig. 3. As it can be seen, Thm. 2 results in very precise approximation even for small d-s.

Corollary 1. *(1) For fixed d,* $\mathrm{ft}(d,w)$ *obtains the maximum value when* $w \approx \sqrt{d+2}-1$. *Then* $\mathrm{ft}(d,w) \sim d - \sqrt{d+2} + 3$. *Thus, in the maximum average storage complexity of Algorithm 1 is* $\approx (d - \sqrt{d})k + d$. *(2) Assume* $\alpha = w/d = \frac{3-\sqrt{5}}{2}$. *Then* $\mathrm{ft}(d,w) \approx \frac{d(3-\sqrt{5})(d+2+\sqrt{5})}{2d+3+\sqrt{5}} \approx \frac{3-\sqrt{5}}{2}d$ *and the total storage complexity of Algorithm 1 is* $\approx \frac{3-\sqrt{5}}{2}d \cdot k + d$.

(The double occurance of constant $\frac{3-\sqrt{5}}{2}$ in (2) is rather curious.) Finally, one can safely assume that when the protocols are designed reasonably then the communication between clients and the TSA will be dominated by the size of freshness tokens. Therefore, the average-case communication complexity of interval time-stamping is $\mathrm{ft}(d,w) \cdot (1+o(1))$ that can be computed by using Thm. 2.

Acknowledgments. This work was partially supported by the Finnish Defence Forces Research Institute of Technology. Algorithm 1 was originally presented in the rump session of Estonian Winter School of Computer Science, March 4, 2002. We would like to thank Ahto Buldas, Markus Jakobsson, Jan Willemson and anonymous referees for useful comments.

References

[BdM91]   Josh Benaloh and Michael de Mare. Efficient Broadcast Time-stamping. Technical Report 1, Clarkson University Department of Mathematics and Computer Science, August 1991.

[BHS92]   Dave Bayer, Stuart A. Haber, and Wakefield Scott Stornetta. Improving the Efficiency And Reliability of Digital Time-stamping. In *Sequences'91: Methods in Communication, Security, and Computer Science*, pages 329–334. Springer-Verlag, 1992.

[BL98]   Ahto Buldas and Peeter Laud. New Linking Schemes for Digital Time-stamping. In *The 1st International Conference on Information Security and Cryptology*, pages 3–14, Seoul, Korea, 18–19 December 1998. Korea Institute of Information Security and Cryptology.

[BLLV98] Ahto Buldas, Peeter Laud, Helger Lipmaa, and Jan Villemson. Time-stamping with Binary Linking Schemes. In Hugo Krawczyk, editor, *Advances in Cryptology — CRYPTO '98*, volume 1462 of *Lecture Notes in Computer Science*, pages 486–501, Santa Barbara, USA, 23–27 August 1998. International Association for Cryptologic Research, Springer-Verlag.

[BLS00]   Ahto Buldas, Helger Lipmaa, and Berry Schoenmakers. Optimally Efficient Accountable Time-stamping. In Hideki Imai and Yuliang Zheng, editors, *Public Key Cryptography '2000*, volume 1751 of *Lecture Notes in Computer Science*, pages 293–305, Melbourne, Victoria, Australia, 18–20 January 2000. Springer-Verlag.

[Bul02]   Ahto Buldas. Personal communication. June 2002.

[Dam87]   Ivan Bjerre Damgård. Collision free hash functions and public key signature schemes. In David Chaum and Wyn L. Price, editors, *Advances in Cryptology — EUROCRYPT '87*, volume 304 of *Lecture Notes in Computer Science*, pages 203–216, Amsterdam, The Netherlands, 13–15 April 1987. Springer-Verlag, 1988.

[dB82]   Nicholas Govert de Bruijn. *Asymptotic Methods in Analysis*. Dover, January 1982.

[HS91]   Stuart A. Haber and Wakefield Scott Stornetta. How to Time-stamp a Digital Document. *Journal of Cryptology*, 3(2):99–111, 1991.

[Knu98]   Donald E. Knuth. *The Art of Computer Programming. Volume 3: Sorting and Searching*. Addison-Wesley, 2 edition, 1998.

[Lip99]   Helger Lipmaa. *Secure and Efficient Time-stamping Systems*. PhD thesis, University of Tartu, June 1999.

[LM01]   Helger Lipmaa and Shiho Moriai. Efficient Algorithms for Computing Differential Properties of Addition. In Mitsuru Matsui, editor, *Fast Software Encryption '2001*, volume 2355 of *Lecture Notes in Computer Science*, pages 336–350, Yokohama, Japan, 2–4 April 2001. Springer-Verlag, 2002.

[Mer80]   Ralph Charles Merkle. Protocols for Public Key Cryptosystems. In *Proceedings of the 1980 Symposium on Security and Privacy*, Oakland, California, USA, 14–16 April 1980. IEEE Computer Society Press.

[Wil02a] Jan Willemson. Personal communication. July 2002.

[Wil02b] Jan Willemson. *Size-Efficient Interval Time Stamps*. PhD thesis, University of Tartu, June 2002. Available from http://home.cyber.ee/jan/publ.html, May 2002.

An Efficient Dynamic and Distributed Cryptographic Accumulator⋆

Michael T. Goodrich[1], Roberto Tamassia[2], and Jasminka Hasić[2]

[1] Dept. Information & Computer Science, University of California, Irvine
goodrich@acm.org
[2] Dept. Computer Science, Brown University, Providence, Rhode Island
{rt,jh}@cs.brown.edu

Abstract. We show how to use the RSA one-way accumulator to realize an efficient and dynamic authenticated dictionary, where untrusted directories provide cryptographically verifiable answers to membership queries on a set maintained by a trusted source. Our accumulator-based scheme for authenticated dictionaries supports efficient incremental updates of the underlying set by insertions and deletions of elements. Also, the user can optimally verify in constant time the authenticity of the answer provided by a directory with a simple and practical algorithm. This work has applications to certificate revocation in public key infrastructure and end-to-end integrity of data collections published by third parties on the Internet.

1 Introduction

Modern distributed transactions often operate in an asymmetric computational environment. Typically, client applications are deployed on small devices, such as laptop computers and palm devices, whereas the server side of these applications are often deployed on large-scale multiprocessors. Moreover, several client applications communicate with these powerful server farms over wireless connections or slow modem-speed connections. Thus, distributed applications are facilitated by solutions that involve small amounts of computing and communication on the client side, without overly burdening the more-powerful server side of these same applications. The challenge we address in this paper is how to incorporate added levels of information assurance and security into such applications without significantly increasing the amount of computation and communication that is needed at the client (while at the same time keeping the computations on the servers reasonable).

An information security problem arising in the replication of data to mirror sites is the authentication of the information provided by the sites. Indeed, there are applications where the user may require that data coming from a mirror site be cryptographically validated as being as genuine as they would be had

---

⋆ Work supported in part by the Dynamic Coalitions Program of the Defense Advanced Research Projects Agency under grant F30602–00–2–0509.

A.H. Chan and V. Gligor (Eds.): ISC 2002, LNCS 2433, pp. 372–388, 2002.

the response come directly from the source. For example, a financial speculator that receives NASDAQ stock quotes from the *Yahoo! Finance* Web site would be well advised to get a proof of the authenticity of the data before making a large trade.

For all data replication applications, and particularly for e-commerce applications in wireless computing, we desire solutions that involve short responses from a mirror site that can be quickly verified with low computational overhead.

Problem Definition. More formally, the problem we address involves three groups of related parties: trusted information sources, untrusted directories, and users. An information *source* defines a finite set S of elements that evolves over time through insertions and deletions of items. *Directories* maintain copies of the set S. Each directory storing S receives time-stamped updates from the source for S together with *update authentication information*, such as signed statements about the update and the current elements of the set. A *user* performs membership queries on the set S of the type "is element e in set S?" but instead of contacting the source for S directly, it queries a directory for S instead. The contacted directory provides the user with a yes/no answer to the query together with *query authentication information*, which yields a proof of the answer assembled by combining statements signed by the source. The user then verifies the proof by relying solely on its trust in the source and the availability of public information about the source that allows to check the source's signature. The data structures used by the source directory to maintain set S, together with the protocol for queries and updates is called an *authenticated dictionary* [25].

The design of an authenticated dictionary should address several goals. These goals include low computational cost, so that the computations performed internally by each entity (source, directory, and user) should be simple and fast, and low communication overhead, so that bandwidth utilization is minimized. Since these goals are particularly important for the user, we say that an authenticated dictionary is *size-oblivious* if the query authentication information size and the verification time do not depend in any way on the number of items in the dictionary. Size-oblivious solutions to the authenticated dictionary problem are ideally suited for wireless e-commerce applications, where user devices have low computational power and low bandwidth. In addition, size-oblivious solutions add an extra level of security, since the size of the dictionary is never revealed to users.

Applications of authenticated dictionaries include third-party data publication on the Internet, certificate revocation, and the authentication of Web services.

Previous and Related Work. Authenticated dictionaries are related to research in distributed computing (e.g., data replication in a network [5,20]), data structure design (e.g., program checking [7,28] and memory checking [6,13]), and cryptography (e.g., incremental cryptography [3]).

Previous additional work on authenticated dictionaries has been conducted primarily in the context of certificate revocation. The traditional method for certificate revocation (e.g., see [18]) is for the CA (source) to sign a statement consisting of a timestamp plus a hash of the set of all revoked certificates, called *certificate revocation list* (CRL), and periodically send the signed CRL to the directories. This approach is secure, but it is inefficient, for it requires the transmission of the entire set of revoked certificates for both source-to-directory and directory-to-user communication. Thus, this solution is clearly not size-oblivious, and even more recent modifications of this solution, which are based on delta-CRLs [12], are not size-oblivious.

The *hash tree* scheme introduced by Merkle [23,24] can be used to implement a static authenticated dictionary, which supports the initial construction of the data structure followed by query operations, but not update operations. Other certificate revocation schemes, based on variations of cryptographic hashing, have been recently proposed in [8,14], but like the static hash tree, these schemes have logarithmic verification time.

Dynamic data structures based on hierarchical hashing that efficiently support also the insertion and deletion of elements are presented in [16,25]. These data structures have logarithmic query, update and verification time.

The software architecture and implementation of an authenticated dictionary based on the above approach of [16] is described in [17]. An efficient data structure for *persistent authenticated dictionaries*, where user can issue historical queries of the type, "was element e in set S at time t?" is introduced in [1].

A general approach to the design of authenticated data structures, which is based on a hashing scheme that digests a search structure into a single hash value, and its applications to multidimensional range searching are presented in [21]. Using a similar approach, efficient data structures for various fundamental graph problems, such as path and k-connectivity queries for $k \leq 3$, and geometric problems, such as intersection and containment queries, are given in [11]. Both these approaches have logarithmic query and verification time and thus are not size-oblivious.

Our Results. In this paper we present a number of size-oblivious solutions to the authenticated dictionary problem. The general approach we follow here is to abandon the approach of the previous methods cited above that are based on applying one-way hash functions to nodes in a data structure. Instead, we make use of one-way accumulators, as advocated by Benaloh and de Mare [4]. Such an approach is immediately size-oblivious, but there is an additional challenge that has to be overcome to make this approach practical. The computations needed at the source and/or directories in a straightforward implementation of the Benaloh-de Mare scheme are inefficient. Our main contribution, therefore, is a mechanism to make the computations at the source and mirrors efficient.

We present a size-oblivious scheme for authenticated dictionaries, based on one-way accumulators, that it is dynamic and distributed, thus supporting efficient updates and balancing the work between the source and the directories. A first variation of our scheme achieves a complete tradeoff between the cost of updates at the source and of queries at the directories, with updates taking $O(p + \log(n/p))$ time and queries taking $O(n/p)$ time, where n is the size of the dictionary and p is any fixed integer parameter such that $1 \leq p \leq n$. For example, we can achieve $O(\sqrt{n})$ time for both updates and queries. A second variation of our scheme, suitable for large data sets, achieves $O(n^\epsilon)$-time performance for updates and queries, while keeping $O(1)$ verification time, where $\epsilon > 0$ is any fixed constant.

Throughout the rest of this paper, we denote with n the current number of elements of the set S stored in the authenticated dictionary. Also, we describe the verification of positive answers to membership queries (i.e., validating $e \in S$). The verification of negative answers (i.e., validating $e \notin S$) can be handled with the technique of storing in the dictionary not the items themselves, but instead pairs of consecutive elements [19].

2 Preliminaries

In this section, we discuss some cryptographic concepts used in our approach.

One-Way Accumulators. An important tool for our scheme is that of one-way *accumulator* functions [2,4,9,15,26]. Such a function allows a source to digitally sign a collection of objects as opposed to a single object.

The use of one-way accumulators originates with Benaloh and de Mare [4]. They show how to utilize an exponential one-way accumulator, which is also known as an RSA accumulator, to summarize a collection of data so that user verification responses have constant-size. Refinements of the RSA accumulator used in our construction are given by Baric and Pfitzmann [2], Gennaro, Halevi and Rabin [15], and Sander, Ta-Shma and Yung [26].

Recently, Camenisch and Lysyanskaya [9] have independently investigated dynamic accumulators. They give a zero-knowledge protocol and a proof that a committed value is in the accumulator with respect to the Pedersen commitment scheme. They also present applications to revocation for group signature, identity escrow schemes and anonymous credentials systems.

As we show in the rest of this section, the RSA accumulator can be used to implement a static authenticated dictionary, where the set of elements is fixed. However, in a dynamic setting where items are inserted and deleted, the standard way of utilizing the RSA accumulator is inefficient. Several other researchers have also noted the inefficiency of this implementation in a dynamic setting (e.g., see [27]). Indeed, our solution can be viewed as refuting this previous intuition to show that a more sophisticated utilization of the exponential accumulator can be made to be efficient even in a dynamic setting.

The most common form of one-way accumulator is defined by starting with a "seed" value y_0, which signifies the empty set, and then defining the accumulation value incrementally from y_0 for a set of values $X = \{x_1, \cdots, x_n\}$, so that $y_i = f(y_{i-1}, x_i)$, where f is a one-way function whose final value does not depend on the order of the x_i's (e.g., see [4]). In addition, one desires that y_i not be much larger to represent than y_{i-1}, so that the final accumulation value, y_n, is not too large. Because of the properties of function f, a source can digitally sign the value of y_n so as to enable a third party to produce a short proof for any element x_i belonging to X—namely, swap x_i with x_n and recompute y_{n-1}

from scratch—the pair (x_i, y_{n-1}) is a cryptographically-secure assertion for the membership of x_i in set X.

A well-known example of a one-way accumulator function is the *exponential accumulator*, $f(y, x) = y^x \mod N$ for suitably-chosen values of the seed y_0 and modulus N [4]. In particular, choosing $N = pq$ with p and q being two strong primes [22] makes the exponential accumulator function as difficult to invert as RSA cryptography [4].

The difficulty in using the exponential accumulator function in the context of authenticated dictionaries is that it is not associative; hence, any updates to set X require significant recomputations.

Implications of Euler's Theorem. There is an important technicality involved with use of the exponential accumulator function, namely in the choice of the seed $a = y_0$. In particular, we should choose a relatively prime with p and q. This choice is dictated by Euler's Theorem, which states that $a^{\phi(N)} \mod N = 1$ if $a > 1$ and $N > 1$ are relatively prime. In our use of the exponential accumulator function, the following well-known corollary to Euler's Theorem will prove useful.

Corollary 1. *If $a > 1$ and $N > 1$ are relatively prime, then $a^x \mod N = a^{x \mod \phi(N)} \mod N$, for all $x \geq 0$.*

One implication of this corollary to the authenticated dictionary problem is that the source should never reveal the values of the prime numbers p and q. Such a revelation would allow a directory to compute $\phi(N)$, which in turn could result in a false validation at a compromised directory. So, our approach takes care to keep the values of p and q only at the source.

Two-Universal Hash Functions. As in previous approaches [15,26], we use the RSA accumulator in conjunction with two-universal hash functions. Such functions were first introduced by Carter and Wegman [10].

A family $H = \{h : A \to B\}$ of functions is *two-universal* if, for all $a_1, a_2 \in A$, $a_1 \neq a_2$ and for a randomly chosen function h from H,

$$\Pr_{h \in H}\{h(a_1) = h(a_2)\} \leq \frac{1}{|B|}.$$

In our scheme, the set A consists of $3k$-bit vectors and the set B consists of k-bit vectors, and we are interested in finding random elements in the preimage of a two-universal function mapping A to B. We can use the two-universal function $h(x) = Ux$, where U is a $k \times 3k$ binary matrix. To get a representations of all the solutions for $h^{-1}(e)$, we need to solve a linear system. Once this is done, picking a random solution can be done by multiplying a bit matrix by a random bit vector, and takes $O(k^2)$ bit operations.

Choosing a Suitable Prime. We are interested in obtaining a prime solution of the linear system that represents a two-universal hash function. The following lemma, of Gennaro *et al.* [15], is useful in this context:

Lemma 1 ([15]). *Let H be a two-universal family from $\{0,1\}^{3k}$ to $\{0,1\}^{k}$. Then, for all but a 2^{-k} fraction of the functions $h \in H$, for every $e \in \{0,1\}^{k}$ a fraction of at least $\frac{1}{ck}$ of the elements in $f^{-1}(e)$ are primes, for some small constant c.*

For reasons that will become clear in the security proof given in Section 6, our scheme requires that a prime inverse be greater then $\sqrt{2^{3k}}$. Also, since the domain of H is $\{0,1\}^{3k}$, this prime is less than 2^{3k}. Thus, in order to find a suitable prime with high probability $1 - 2^{-\Omega(k)}$, we need to sample $O(k^2)$ times.

The Strong RSA Assumption. The proof of security of our scheme uses the *strong RSA assumption*, as defined by Baric and Pfitzmann [2]. Given N and $x \in Z_N^*$, the strong RSA problem consists of finding integers f, with $2 \leq f < N$, and a, such that we have $a^f = x$. The difference between this problem and the standard RSA problem is that the adversary is given the freedom to choose not only the base a but also the exponent f.

> *Strong RSA Assumption:* There exists a probabilistic algorithm B that on input 1^r outputs an RSA modulus N such that, for all probabilistic polynomial-time algorithms D, all $c > 0$, and all sufficiently large r, the probability that algorithm D on a random input $x \in Z_N$ outputs a and $f \geq 2$ such that $a^f = x \bmod N$ is no more than r^{-c}.

In other words, given N and a randomly chosen element x, it is infeasible to find a and f such that $a^f = x \bmod N$.

A Straightforward Accumulator-Based Scheme. Let $S = \{e_1, e_2, \ldots, e_n\}$ be the set of elements stored at the source. Each element e is represented by k bits. The source chooses strong primes [22] p and q that are suitably large, e.g., $p, q > 2^{\frac{3}{2}k}$. It then chooses a suitably-large base a that is relatively prime to $N = pq$. Note that N is at least 2^{3k}. It also chooses a random hash function h from a two-universal family. The source broadcasts once a, N and h to the directories and users, but keeps p and q secret. At periodic time intervals, for each element e_i of S, the source computes the *representative* of e_i, denoted x_i, where $h(x_i) = e_i$ and x_i is a prime chosen as described above. The source then combines the representatives of the elements by computing the RSA accumulation

$$A \leftarrow a^{x_1 x_2 \cdots x_n} \bmod N$$

and broadcasts to the directories a signed message (A, t), where t is the current timestamp.

Query. To prove that a query element e_i is in S, a directory computes the value

$$A_i \leftarrow a^{x_1 x_2 \cdots x_{i-1} x_{i+1} \cdots x_n} \bmod N. \tag{1}$$

That is, A_i is the accumulation of all the representatives of the elements of S besides x_i and is said to be the *witness* of e_i. After computing A_i, the directory returns to the user the representative x_i, the witness A_i and the pair (A, t), signed by the source. Note that this query authentication information has constant size; hence, this scheme is size-oblivious. However, computing witness A_i is no trivial task for the directory, for it must perform $n-1$ exponentiations to answer a query. Making the simplifying assumption that the number of bits needed to represent N is independent of n, the computation performed to answer a single query takes $O(n)$ time.

Verification. The user checks that timestamp t is current and that (A, t) is indeed signed by the source. It then checks that x_i is a valid representative of e_i, i.e., $h(x_i) = e_i$. Finally, it computes $A' \leftarrow A_i^{x_i} \bmod N$ and compares it to A. If $A' = A$, then the user is reassured of the validity of the answer because of the strong RSA assumption. The verification time is $O(1)$.

Updates. For updates, the above simple approach has an asymmetric performance (for unrestricted values of accumulated elements), with insertions being much easier than deletions. To insert a new element e_{n+1} into the set S, the source simply recomputes the accumulation A as follows

$$A \leftarrow A^{x_{n+1}} \bmod N$$

where x_{n+1} is the representative of e_{n+1}. The computation of x_{n+1} can be done in time that is independent of n (see Section 2), i.e., $O(1)$ time. An updated signed pair (A, t) is then sent to the directories in the next time interval. Thus, an insertion takes $O(1)$ time. The deletion of an element $e_i \in S$, on the other hand, will in general require the source to recompute the new value A by performing $n-1$ exponentiations. That is, a deletion takes $O(n)$ time.

Of course, if a representative x_i is relatively prime with $p-1$ and $q-1$, the source can delete e_i in constant time by computing $x \leftarrow x_i^{-1} \bmod \phi(N)$ (via the extended Euclidean algorithm) and then updating $A \leftarrow A^x \bmod N$. This deletion computation would take $O(1)$ time, but we cannot guarantee that x_i has an inverse in $Z_{\phi(N)}$ if it is an accumulation of a group of elements; hence, we do not advocate using this approach for deletions. Indeed, we will not assume the existence of multiplicative inverses in $Z_{\phi(N)}$ for any of our solutions. Thus, we are stuck with linear deletion time at the source and linear query time at a directory when making this straightforward application of exponential accumulators to the authenticated dictionary problem.

We describe in the next section an alternative approach that can answer queries much faster.

3   Precomputed Accumulations

We present a first improvement that allows for fast query processing. We require the directory to store a precomputed witness A_i for each element e_i of S, as defined in Eq. 1. Thus, to answer a query, a directory looks up the A_i value, rather than computing it from scratch, and then completes the transaction as described in the previous section. Thanks to the precomputation of the witnesses at the source, a directory can process any query in $O(1)$ time while the verification computation for a user remains unchanged.

Unfortunately, a standard way of implementing this approach is inefficient for processing updates. In particular, a directory now takes $O(n)$ time to process a single insertion, since it needs to update all the witnesses, and $O(n \log n)$ time to process a single deletion, for after a deletion the directory must recompute all the witnesses, which can be done using the algorithm given in [26]. Thus, at first glance, this precomputed accumulations approach appears to be quite inefficient when updates to the set S are required.

We can process updates faster than $O(n \log n)$ time, however, by enlisting the help of the source. Our method in fact can be implemented in $O(n)$ time by a simple two-phase approach. The details for the two phases follows.

First Phase. Let S be the set of n items stored at the source after performing all the insertions and deletions required in the previous time interval. We build a complete binary tree T "on top" of the representative values of the elements of S, so that each leaf of T is associated with the representative x_i of an element e_i of S. In the first phase, we perform a post-order traversal of T, so that each node v in T is visited only after its children are visited. The main computation performed during the visit of a node v is to compute a value $x(v)$. If v is a leaf of T, storing some representative x_i, then we compute

$$x(v) \leftarrow x_i \bmod \phi(N).$$

If v is an internal node of T with children u and w (we can assume T is proper, so that each internal node has two children), then we compute

$$x(v) \leftarrow x(u)x(w) \bmod \phi(N).$$

When we have computed $x(r)$, where r denotes the root of T, then we are done with this first phase. Since a post-order traversal takes $O(n)$ time, and each visit computation in our traversals takes $O(1)$ time, this entire first phase runs in $O(n)$ time. We again make the simplifying assumption that the number of bits needed to represent N is independent of n.

Second Phase. In the second phase, we perform a pre-order traversal of T, where the visit of a node v involves the computation of a value $A(v)$. The value $A(v)$ for a node v is defined to be the accumulation of all values stored at nodes that are *not* descendents of v (including v itself if v is a leaf). Thus, if v is a leaf associated with the representative value x_i of some element of S, then $A(v) = A_i$. For the root, r, of T, we define $A(r) = a$. For any non-root node v, let z denote v's parent and let w denote v's sibling (and note that since T is proper, every node but the root has a sibling). Given $A(z)$ and $x(w)$, we can compute the value $A(v)$ for v as follows:

$$A(v) \leftarrow A(z)^{x(w)} \bmod N.$$

By Corollary 1, we can inductively prove that each $A(v)$ equals the accumulation of all the values stored at non-descendents of v. Since a pre-order traversal of

T takes $O(n)$ time, and each visit action can be performed in $O(1)$ time, we can compute all the A_i witnesses in $O(n)$ time. Note that implementing this algorithm requires knowledge of the value $\phi(N)$, which presumably only the source knows. Thus, this computation can only be performed at the source, who must transmit the updated A_i values to the directory.

A variation of the approach presented in this section consists of precomputing at the source the exponents of the witnesses instead of the witnesses themselves. In this way, the arithmetic computations performed at the source consist of a series of modular multiplications (of bit complexity $O(k^2)$) and do not include modular exponentiations (of bit complexity $O(k^3)$). The directory, however, has to perform one modular exponentiation to compute the actual witness from its exponent when answering a query.

The precomputed accumulations approach supports constant-time queries and linear-time updates. In the next section, we show how to combine this approach with the straightforward approach of Section 2 to design a scheme that is efficient for both updates and queries.

4   Parameterized Accumulations

Consider again the problem of designing an accumulator-based authenticated dictionary for a set $S = \{e_1, e_2, \dots, e_n\}$. In this section, we show how to balance the processing between the source and the directory, depending on their relative computational power. The main idea is to choose an integer parameter $1 \leq p \leq n$ and partition the set S into p groups of roughly n/p elements each, performing the straightforward approach inside each group and the precomputed accumulations approach among the groups. The details are as follows.

Subdividing the Dictionary. Divide the set S into p groups, $Y_1, Y_2, \dots, Y_p$, of roughly n/p elements each, balancing the size of the groups as much as possible. For group Y_j, let y_j denote the product of the representatives of the elements in Y_j modulo $\phi(N)$. Define B_j as

$$B_j = a^{y_1 y_2 \cdots y_{j-1} y_{j+1} \cdots y_p} \bmod N.$$

That is, B_j is the accumulation of representatives of all the elements that are not in the set Y_j. After any insertion or deletion in a set Y_j, the source can compute a new value y_j in $O(n/p)$ time. Moreover, since the source knows the value of $\phi(N)$, it can update all the B_j values (or their exponents) after such an update in $O(p)$ time. Thus, the source can process an update operation in $O(p + n/p)$ time, assuming that the update does not require redistributing elements among the groups.

Maintaining the size of each set Y_j is not a major overhead. We need only keep the invariant that each Y_j has at least $\lceil n/p \rceil / 2$ elements at most $2\lceil n/p \rceil$ elements. If a Y_j set becomes too small, then we either merge it with one of its adjacent sets Y_{j-1} or Y_{j+1}, or (if merging Y_j with such a sets would cause an overflow) we "borrow" some of the elements from an adjacent set to bring the size of Y_j to at least $3\lceil n/p\rceil/4$. Likewise, if a Y_j set grows too large, then we simply split it in two. These simple adjustments take $O(n/p)$ time, and will maintain the invariant that each Y_j is of size $\Theta(n/p)$. Of course, this assumes that the value of n does not change significantly as we insert and remove elements. But even this condition is easily handled. Specifically, we can maintain the sizes of the Y_j's in a priority queue that keeps track of the smallest and largest Y_j sets. Whenever we increase n by an insertion, we can check the priority queue to see if the smallest set now must do some merging or borrowing to keep from growing too small. Likewise, whenever we decrease n by a deletion, we can check the priority queue to see if the largest set now must split. An inductive argument shows that this approach keeps the size of the groups to be $\Theta(n/p)$.

Turning to the task at a directory, then, we recall that a directory receives all p of the B_j values after an update occurs. Thus, a directory can perform its part of an update computation in $O(p)$ time. It validates that some e_i is in e by first determining the group Y_j containing e_i, which can be done by table look-up. Then, it computes A_i as

$$A_i \leftarrow B_j^{\Pi_{e_m \in Y_j - \{e_i\}} x_m} \bmod N,$$

where x_m is the representative of e_m. Thus, a directory answers a query in $O(n/p)$ time.

Improving the Update Time for the Source. In this section, we show how the source can further improve the performance of an update operation in the parameterized scheme. In the algorithm described above, the source recomputes y_j from scratch after any update occurs, which takes $O(n/p)$ time. We will now describe how this computation can be done in $O(\log(n/p))$ time.

The method is for the source to store the elements of each Y_j in a balanced binary search tree. For each internal node w in T_j, the source maintains the value $y(w)$, which is the product of the representatives of all the items stored at descendents of w, modulo $\phi(N)$. Thus, $y(r(T_j)) = y_j$, where $r(T_j)$ denotes the root of T_j. Any insertion or deletion will affect only $O(\log(n/p))$ nodes w in T_j, for which we can recompute their $x(w)$ values in $O(\log(n/p))$ total time. Therefore, after any update, the source can recompute a y_j value in $O(\log(n/p))$ time, assuming that the size of the Y_j's does not violate the size invariant. Still, if the size of Y_j after an update violates the size invariant, we can easily adjust it by performing appropriate splits and joins on the trees representing Y_j, Y_{j-1}, and/or Y_{j+1}. Moreover, we can rebuild the entire set of trees after every $O(n/p)$ updates, to keep the sizes of the Y_j sets to be $O(n/p)$, with the cost for this periodic adjustment (which will probably not even be necessary in practice for most applications) being amortized over the previous updates.

Theorem 1. *The parameterized accumulations scheme for implementing an authenticated dictionary over a set of size n uses data structures with $O(n)$ space at the source and directories and has the following performance, for a given parameter p such that $1 \leq p \leq n$:*

- the insertion and deletion times for the source are each $O(p + \log(n/p))$;

- *the update authentication information has size $O(p)$;*
- *the query time for a directory is $O(n/p)$;*
- *the query authentication information has size $O(1)$; and*
- *the verification time for the user is $O(1)$.*

Thus, for $p = \sqrt{n}$, one can balance insertion time, deletion time, update authentication information size, and query time to achieve an $O(\sqrt{n})$ bound, while keeping the query authentication information size and the verification time constant.

The parameterized accumulations scheme described in this section significantly improves the overhead at the source and directories for using an exponential accumulator to solve the authenticated dictionary problem. Moreover, this improvement was achieved without any modification to the client from the original straightforward application of the exponential accumulator described in Section 2.

In the next section, we show that if we are allowed to slightly modify the computation at the client, we can further improve performance at the source and directory while still implementing a size-oblivious scheme

5   Hierarchical Accumulations

In this section, we describe a hierarchical accumulation scheme for implementing an authenticated dictionary on a set S with n elements. In this scheme, the verification algorithm consists of performing a series of c exponentiations, where c is a fixed constant for the scheme. Note that the approach of Section 4 assumed that $c = 1$.

Given a fixed constant c, we define $p = n^{1/(c+1)}$ and construct the following hierarchical partition of S:

- We begin by partitioning set S into p subsets of $n_1 = n^{c/(c+1)}$ elements each, called level-1 subsets.
- For $i = 1, \ldots, c - 1$, we partition each level-i subset into p subsets of $n^{(c-i)/(c+1)}$ elements each, called level-$(i + 1)$ subsets.

Also, we conventionally say that S is the level-0 subset.

Next, we associate a value $\alpha(Y)$ to each subset Y of the above partition, as follows:

- The value of a level-c subset is the accumulation of the representatives of its elements.
- For $i = 0, \ldots, c - 1$, the value of a level-i subset is the accumulation of the representatives of the values of its level-$(i + 1)$ subsets.

Finally, we store with each level-i subset Y a data structure based on the precomputed accumulations scheme of Section 3 that stores and validates membership in the set $S(Y)$ of the values of the level-$(i + 1)$ subsets of Y.

Let e be an element of S. To prove the containment of e in S, the directory determines, for $i = 1, \ldots, c$, the level-i subset Y_i containing e and returns the sequence of values $\alpha(Y_c), \alpha(Y_{c-1}), \ldots, \alpha(Y_0)$ plus witnesses for the following $c+1$ memberships:

- $e \in Y_c$
- $\alpha(Y_i) \in S(Y_{i-1})$ for $i = c, \ldots, 1$

The user can verify each of the above memberships by means of an exponentiation. Thus, the verification time and query authentication information are proportional to c, i.e., they are $O(1)$.

Theorem 2. *The hierarchical accumulations scheme for implementing an authenticated dictionary over a set of size n uses uses data structures with $O(n)$ space at the source and directories and has the following performance, for a given constant ϵ such that $0 < \epsilon < 1$:*

- *the insertion and deletion times for the source are each $O(n^\epsilon)$);*
- *the update authentication information has size $O(n^\epsilon)$;*
- *the query time for a directory is $O(n^\epsilon)$;*
- *the query authentication information has size $O(1)$; and*
- *the verification time for the user is $O(1)$.*

We can extend the hierarchical accumulations scheme by using a more general hierarchical partitioning of the set S while keeping constant the size of the query authentication information and the verification time. The two extreme partitioning strategies are: (i) single-level partition in $O(1)$ groups of size $O(n)$, and (ii) $O(\log n)$-level partition where the size of each partition is $O(1)$ (this corresponds to a hierarchy that can be mapped into a bounded-degree tree). The insertion and deletion times and the update authentication information size are then proportional to $O(\sum_{i=1}^{c-1} g_i)$, where g_i is the size of the partition at the i-th level, and can range from $O(1)$ to $O(n)$. At the same time, the query time is proportional to $O(c + g_{c-1})$, and can range from $O(n)$ to $O(1)$.

6   Security

We now show that an adversarial directory cannot forge a proof of membership for an element that is not in S. Our proof follows a closely related constructions given in [9,15,26]. An important property of the scheme comes from representing the elements e of set S with prime numbers. If the accumulator scheme was used without this stage, the scheme would be insecure. An adversarial directory could forge the proof of membership for all the divisors of elements whose proofs it has seen.

Theorem 3. *In the dynamic accumulator schemes for authenticated dictionaries defined in the previous sections, under the strong RSA assumption, a directory whose resources are polynomially bounded can produce a proof of membership only for the elements that are in the dictionary.*

Proof. Our proof is based on related proofs given in [9,15,26]. Assume an adversarial directory D has seen proofs of membership for all the elements $e_1, e_2, \ldots e_n$ of the dictionary S. The trusted source has computed representatives $x_1, x_2, \ldots, x_n$ as suitable primes defined in Section 2. The witnesses $A_1, A_2 \ldots, A_n$ have been computed as well, either solely by the trusted source, or by balancing the work between the trusted source and the directories. The trusted source has distributed a signed pair (A, t). By the definition of the scheme in Section 2, for all $1 \le i \le n$, we have

- x_i is the prime representative of $e_i \in S$, i.e., $h(x_i) = e_i$;
- $\sqrt{2^{3k}} < x_i < 2^{3k}$;
- $A_i^{x_i} \bmod N = A$.

We need to show that directory D cannot prove the membership of a an element e_{n+1} that is not in the set S already. The proof is by contradiction. Suppose that D has has found a triplet $(e_{n+1}, x_{n+1}, A_{n+1})$ proving the membership of e_{n+1}. Then, the following must hold and can checked by the user (it is not necessary for x_{n+1} to be a prime):

- $h(x_{n+1}) = e_{n+1}$;
- $\sqrt{2^{3k}} < x_{n+1} < 2^{3k}$;
- $A_{n+1}^{x_{n+1}} \bmod N = A$.

Let $d = \gcd(x_{n+1}, x_1 x_2 \ldots x_n)$. Thus, we have $\gcd(\frac{x_{n+1}}{d}, \frac{x_1 x_2 \ldots x_n}{d}) = 1$. Define $f = \frac{x_{n+1}}{d}$. There are integers u, v such that $v \frac{x_1 x_2 \ldots x_n}{d} + uf = 1$ holds over integers. Directory D can find u and v in polynomial time using the extended Euclidean algorithm. Set $s = A_{n+1}^v a^u$. We have

$$s^f = A_{n+1}^{vf} a^{uf} = A_{n+1}^{v \frac{x_{n+1}}{d}} a^{uf} = A^{\frac{v}{d}} a^{uf} = a^{v \frac{x_1 x_2 \ldots x_n}{d} + uf} = a.$$

Thus, directory D can find in polynomial time a value s that is an f-th root of a. By the strong RSA assumption (Section 2), it must be that $f = 1$. Hence, we have $x_{n+1} = d$ and it follows that x_{n+1} divides $x_1 x_2 \ldots x_n$. But by our assumptions we have $x_{n+1} < 2^{3k}$ and $x_i > \sqrt{2^{3k}}$ for each i, which implies that $x_{n+1} = x_i$, for some $1 \le i \le n$. Thus, element e_{n+1} is already in set S, which is a contradiction.

We conclude that the adversarial directory D can find membership proofs only for those elements already in S.   □

7   Experimental Results

In this section, we present a preliminary experimental study on the performance of the dynamic accumulator schemes for authenticated dictionaries described in this paper. The main results of this study are summarized in the the charts of Figures 1–2, where the x axis represents the size of the dictionary (number of elements) and the y axis represents the average time of the given operation in

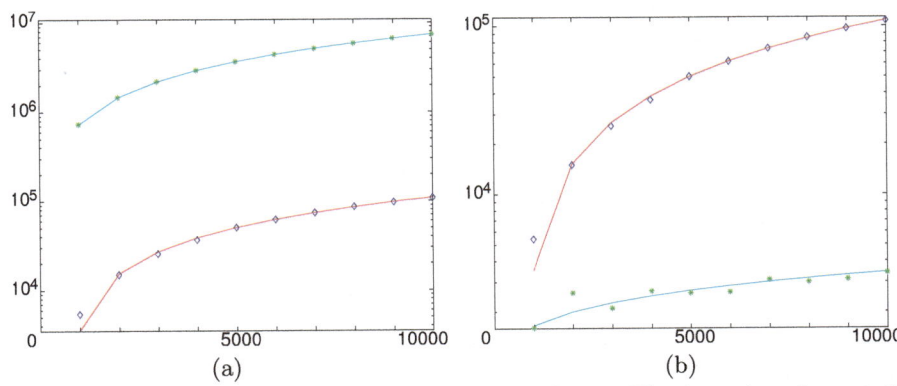

Fig. 1. Performance tradeoffs for dynamic accumulators. The insertion time at the source excludes the computation of the prime representative. Note that we use a logarithmic scale for the y-axis. **(a)** Query time at the directory (stars) when the directory computes the witness from scratch for each query (using modular exponentiations) vs. insertion time at the source (diamonds) when the source precomputes all the exponents of the witnesses (using modular multiplications). **(b)** Insertion time at the source (diamonds) without partitioning, when all the n witnesses's exponents are precomputed, vs. with partitioning (stars), when a 2-level $(n^{1/2}, n^{1/4})$ partitioning scheme is used and $O(n^{1/2})$ witnesses's exponents are precomputed.

microseconds. We denote with $(f_1(n), f_2(n), ..., f_c(n))$ a generalized hierarchical partition scheme of the dictionary with $O(f_i(n))$ elements in the i-th level group (Section 5).

The dynamic accumulator scheme has been implemented in Java and the experiments have been conducted on an AMD Athlon XP 1700+ 1.47GHz, 512MB running Linux. The items stored in the dictionary and the query values are randomly generated 165-bit integers and the parameter N of the RSA accumulator is a 200-bit integer. The variance between different runs of the query and deletion operations was found to consistently small so only a few runs were done for each dictionary size considered.

The main performance bottleneck of the scheme was found to be the computation of prime representatives for the elements. In our experiments, finding a prime representative of a 165-bit integer using the standard approach of Section 2 takes about 45 milliseconds and dominates the rest of the insertion time. The computation of prime representatives is a constant overhead that does not depend on the number of elements and has been omitted in the rest of the analysis.

Figure 1 illustrates two performance tradeoffs. Part (a) compares the performance of the two extreme naive approaches where either the source or the directory does essentially all the work. Since the source can use modular multiplication and the directory has to use modular exponentiation, it is more effective to shift as much as possible the insertion work to the source. Part (b) shows the benefits of partitioning, which allows to reduce the computation time at the source.

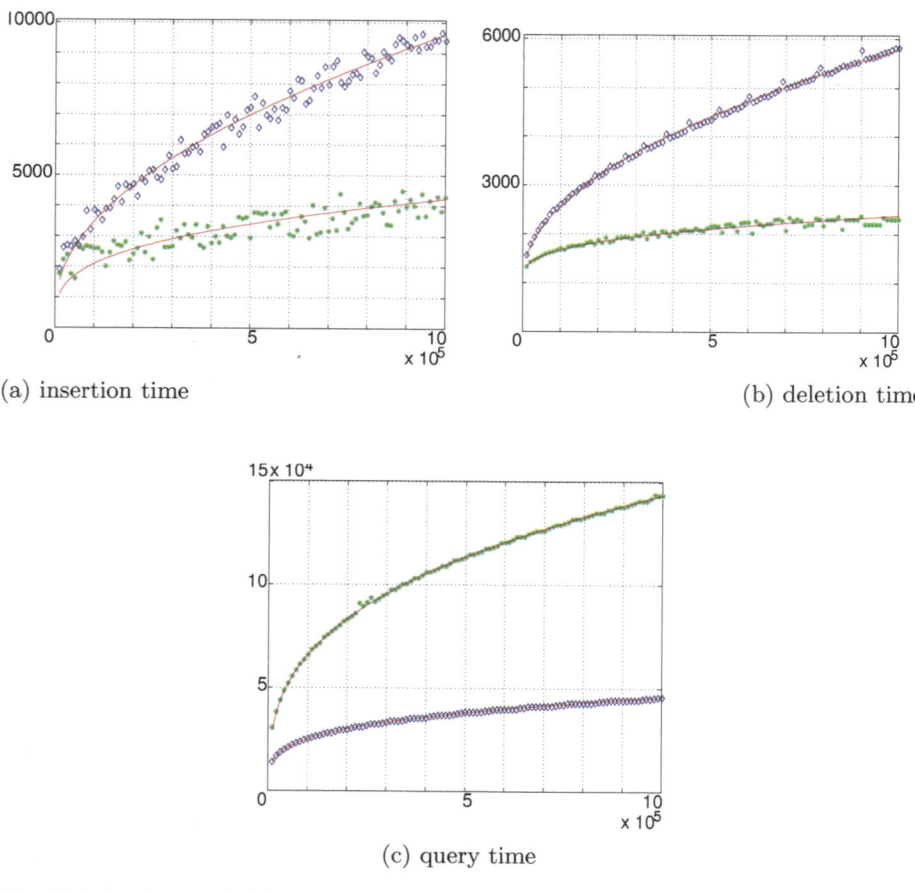

(a) insertion time   (b) deletion time

(c) query time

Fig. 2. Insertion and deletion times at the source and query time at the directory for two variants of the hierarchical accumulations approach (Section 5) on dictionaries with up to one million elements. The time for computing the prime representative of an element has been omitted from the insertion time. The stars represent a 2-level ($n^{1/2}$, $n^{1/4}$) partitioning scheme and the diamonds represent a 2-level ($n^{2/3}$, $n^{1/3}$) partitioning scheme.

Experimental results on the hierarchical accumulations method (Section 5) are presented in Figure 2. These results show that one can tune the partitioning scheme according to the processing power available at the source and the directory.

Acknowledgments. We would like to thank Andrew Schwerin, Giuseppe Ateniese, and Douglas Maughan for several helpful discussions and e-mail exchanges relating to the topics of this paper.

References

1. A. Anagnostopoulos, M. T. Goodrich, and R. Tamassia. Persistent authenticated dictionaries and their applications. In *Proc. Information Security Conference (ISC 2001)*, volume 2200 of *LNCS*, pages 379–393. Springer-Verlag, 2001.
2. N. Baric and B. Pfitzmann. Collision-free accumulators and fail-stop signature schemes without trees. In *Advances in Cryptology: Proc. EUROCRYPT*, volume 1233 of *LNCS*, pages 480–494. Springer-Verlag, 1997.
3. M. Bellare, O. Goldreich, and S. Goldwasser. Incremental cryptography: The case of hashing and signing. In *Advances in Cryptology—CRYPTO '94*, volume 839 of *LNCS*, pages 216–233. Springer-Verlag, 1994.
4. J. Benaloh and M. de Mare. One-way accumulators: A decentralized alternative to digital signatures. In *Advances in Cryptology—EUROCRYPT 93*, volume 765 of *LNCS*, pages 274–285. Springer-Verlag, 1993.
5. J. J. Bloch, D. S. Daniels, and A. Z. Spector. A weighted voting algorithm for replicated directories. *Journal of the ACM*, 34(4):859–909, 1987.
6. M. Blum, W. Evans, P. Gemmell, S. Kannan, and M. Naor. Checking the correctness of memories. *Algorithmica*, 12(2/3):225–244, 1994.
7. M. Blum and S. Kannan. Designing programs that check their work. *J. ACM*, 42(1):269–291, Jan. 1995.
8. A. Buldas, P. Laud, and H. Lipmaa. Accountable certificate management using undeniable attestations. In *ACM Conference on Computer and Communications Security*, pages 9–18. ACM Press, 2000.
9. J. Camenisch and A. Lysyanskaya. Dynamic accumulators and application to efficient revocation of anonymous credentials. In *Proc. CRYPTO 2002*. To appear.
10. I. L. Carter and M. N. Wegman. Universal classes of hash functions. In *Proc. ACM Symp. on Theory of Computing*, pages 106–112, 1977.
11. R. Cohen, M. T. Goodrich, R. Tamassia, and N. Triandopoulos. Authenticated data structures for graph and geometric searching. Technical report, Center for Geometric Computing, Brown University, 2001. http://www.cs.brown.edu/cgc/stms/papers/authDatStr.pdf.
12. D. A. Cooper. A more efficient use of delta-CRLs. In *Proceedings of the 2000 IEEE Symposium on Security and Privacy*, pages 190–202, 2000.
13. Fischlin. Incremental cryptography and memory checkers. In *Proc. EUROCRYPT*, volume 1233 of *LNCS*, pages 393–408. Springer-Verlag, 1997.
14. I. Gassko, P. S. Gemmell, and P. MacKenzie. Efficient and fresh certification. In *Int. Workshop on Practice and Theory in Public Key Cryptography (PKC '2000)*, volume 1751 of *LNCS*, pages 342–353. Springer-Verlag, 2000.
15. R. Gennaro, S. Halevi, and T. Rabin. Secure hash-and-sign signatures without the random oracle. In *Proc. EUROCRYPT*, volume 1592 of *LNCS*, pages 123–139. Springer-Verlag, 1999.
16. M. T. Goodrich and R. Tamassia. Efficient authenticated dictionaries with skip lists and commutative hashing. Technical report, Johns Hopkins Information Security Institute, 2000. http://www.cs.brown.edu/cgc/stms/papers/hashskip.pdf.
17. M. T. Goodrich, R. Tamassia, and A. Schwerin. Implementation of an authenticated dictionary with skip lists and commutative hashing. In *Proc. 2001 DARPA Information Survivability Conference and Exposition*, volume 2, pages 68–82, 2001.
18. C. Kaufman, R. Perlman, and M. Speciner. *Network Security: Private Communication in a Public World*. Prentice-Hall, Englewood Cliffs, NJ, 1995.

19. P. C. Kocher. On certificate revocation and validation. In *Proc. Int. Conf. on Financial Cryptography*, volume 1465 of *LNCS*. Springer-Verlag, 1998.
20. B. Kroll and P. Widmayer. Distributing a search tree among a growing number of processors. *ACM SIGMOD Record*, 23(2):265–276, 1994.
21. C. Martel, G. Nuckolls, P. Devanbu, M. Gertz, A. Kwong, and S. Stubblebine. A general model for authentic data publication, 2001. http://www.cs.ucdavis.edu/˜devanbu/files/model-paper.pdf.
22. A. J. Menezes, P. C. van Oorschot, and S. A. Vanstone. *Handbook of Applied Cryptography*. CRC Press, 1997.
23. R. C. Merkle. Protocols for public key cryptosystems. In *Proc. Symp. on Security and Privacy*, pages 122–134. IEEE Computer Society Press, 1980.
24. R. C. Merkle. A certified digital signature. In G. Brassard, editor, *Proc. CRYPTO '89*, volume 435 of *LNCS*, pages 218–238. Springer-Verlag, 1990.
25. M. Naor and K. Nissim. Certificate revocation and certificate update. In *Proc. 7th USENIX Security Symposium*, pages 217–228, Berkeley, 1998.
26. T. Sander, A. Ta-Shma, and M. Yung. Blind, auditable membership proofs. In *Proc. Financial Cryptography (FC 2000)*, volume 1962 of *LNCS*. Springer-Verlag, 2001.
27. B. Schneier. *Applied Cryptography: protocols, algorithms, and source code in C*. John Wiley and Sons, Inc., New York, 1994.
28. G. F. Sullivan, D. S. Wilson, and G. M. Masson. Certification of computational results. *IEEE Trans. Comput.*, 44(7):833–847, 1995.

A Second-Order DPA Attack Breaks a Window-Method Based Countermeasure against Side Channel Attacks

Katsuyuki Okeya[1] and Kouichi Sakurai[2]

[1] Hitachi, Ltd., Systems Development Laboratory,
292, Yoshida-cho, Totsuka-ku, Yokohama, 244-0817, Japan
ka-okeya@sdl.hitachi.co.jp
[2] Kyushu University,
Graduate School of Information Science and Electrical Engineering,
6-10-1, Hakozaki, Higashi-ku, Fukuoka, 812-8581, Japan
sakurai@csce.kyushu-u.ac.jp

Abstract. Möller proposed a countermeasure using window method against side channel attacks. However, its immunity to side channel attacks is still controversial. In this paper, we show Möller's countermeasure is vulnerable to a second-order differential power analysis attack. A side channel attack is an attack that takes advantage of information leaked during execution of a cryptographic procedure. An nth-order differential power analysis attack is the side channel attack which uses n different leaked data that correspond to n different intermediate values during the execution. Our proposed attack against Möller's countermeasure finds out the use of same elliptic points, and restricts candidates of the secret scalar value. In these circumstances, the attack completely detects the scalar value using Baby-Step-Giant-Step method as a direct-computational attack. For a 160-bit scalar value, the proposed attack restricts the number of candidates of the scalar to a 45-bit integer, and the direct-computational attack can actually detect the scalar value. Besides, we improve Möller's countermeasure to prevent the proposed attack. We compare the original method and improved countermeasure in terms of the computational intractability and the computational cost of the scalar multiplication.

Keywords: Elliptic Curve Cryptosystems, Side Channel Attacks, Differential Power Analysis, Higher-Order DPA Attack, Second-Order DPA Attack, Möller's Countermeasure

1 Introduction

A window-method based countermeasure proposed by Möller has been considered to be effective in preventing *side channel attacks*. However, its immunity to side channel attacks is still controversial. In this paper, we will show that *Möller's countermeasure* is vulnerable to *Differential Power Analysis (DPA) attack*, which is a kind of side channel attack.

A.H. Chan and V. Gligor (Eds.): ISC 2002, LNCS 2433, pp. 389–401, 2002.

1.1 Side Channel Attacks

Kocher *et al.* were first to propose the side channel attack [Koc96,KJJ99] in which an attacker infers secret information using leaked data from a cryptographic device while it executes cryptographic procedures. Messerges provided a definition of an nth-order DPA attack [Mes00], which uses n different leaked data that correspond to n different intermediate values during the execution. Besides, Messerges showed that some countermeasure against a first-order DPA attack is vulnerable to a second-order DPA attack [Mes00]. Coron extended the side channel attack to include elliptic curve cryptosystems [Cor99].

Proposed countermeasures against such an attack are varied up to the present. Coron proposed three countermeasures [Cor99]: randomization of the private exponent, blinding the point P and randomized projective coordinates. Countermeasures on a Koblitz curve by Hasan [Has00], those on a Montgomery-form elliptic curve by Okeya-Sakurai [OS00], those on a Jacobiform elliptic curve by Liardet-Smart [LS01], those on a Hessian-form elliptic curve by Joye-Quisquater [JQ01], those using random isomorphic elliptic curves by Joye-Tymen [JT01], those using randomized addition-subtraction chains[1] by Oswald-Aigner [OA01], and those on a Weierstrass-form elliptic curve by Brier-Joye [BJ02], Fischer *et al.* [FGKS02] and Izu-Takagi [IT02] have also been proposed.

1.2 Möller's Countermeasure

Möller [Möl01] proposed a window-method based elliptic scalar multiplication method which thwarts side channel attacks. This countermeasure was devised from window method, and always computes non-dummy addition independently on the bit of the secret scalar. This countermeasure is believed to prevent side channel attacks, however, its immunity is still controversial.

1.3 Our Contributions

We will show that Möller's countermeasure is vulnerable to a second-order DPA attack. The proposed attack consists of the following three phases.

I   An attacker detects two values which are variances of the difference between power consumption that corresponds to the computations at two moments in the scalar multiplication.
II   The attacker finds out the variance of the difference between power consumption that corresponds to the computations at two specific moments by using measurements of power consumption during the execution of scalar multiplication, and restricts candidates of the secret scalar.
III The attacker completely detects the scalar d using direct-computational attack.

---

[1] A recent paper [OS02] has shown that a basic version of the countermeasures is vulnerable to an SPA attack.

In Phase I, the attacker detects the variances for the difference between power consumptions when some points are loaded into registers. In Phase II, using the variances, the attacker finds out the time when same points are used for elliptic operations, and restricts candidates of the scalar value. In Phase III, the attacker completely detects the scalar value using Baby-Step-Giant-Step method. Whereas a straightforward application of Baby-Step-Giant-Step method fails because the operations of Giant-Step depends on those of Baby-Step, our proposed Baby-Step-Giant-Step method is devised in terms of independence between the operations of Giant-Step and those of Baby-Step.

We will estimate a number of the candidates of the scalar value which is restricted by Phases I and II. For example, in the case that the scalar is a 160-bit integer and the window width is 4, the number of candidates of the scalar value is a 45-bit integer. The direct-computational attack can actually detect the scalar value. Thus, Möller's countermeasure is vulnerable to the proposed attack.

Besides, we will propose a countermeasure to prevent the proposed attack. The countermeasure uses a large window width, which thwarts Phase III, because of the increase of the candidates of the scalar. However, the countermeasure is very slow, a fast countermeasure against the proposed attack remains as a matter to be discussed further.

The remainder of this article is organized as follows: Section 2 is a survey of side channel attacks. Section 3 describes Möller's countermeasure. Section 4 proposes a DPA attack against Möller's countermeasure. Section 5 proposes a countermeasure against the proposed DPA attack.

2   Side Channel Attacks

In cryptographic devices such as smart cards, data other than input data and output data may 'leak out' during cryptographic procedures. The computation timing of cryptographic procedures is one such kind of data. So is power consumption because the smart card uses an external power source. Kocher *et al.* developed the side channel attack in which an attacker infers stored secret information in a cryptographic device by using such leaked data [Koc,Koc96,KJJ98, KJJ99]. This type of attack, which includes timing attack [Koc,Koc96], Simple Power Analysis (SPA) attack [Koc,Koc96], and Differential Power Analysis (DPA) attack [KJJ98,KJJ99], render smart cards particularly vulnerable.

Kocher *et al.* envisioned mainly DES [DES] and RSA [RSA78] as targets for side channel attacks. Coron extended DPA attack to elliptic curve cryptosystems [Cor99].

Coron's SPA preventative scalar multiplication method using dummy operations [Cor99], the countermeasures on a Montgomery-form elliptic curve [OS00, OMS01] and those on a Weierstrass-form elliptic curve [BJ02,FGKS02,IT02] have fixed procedures independently of the secret information. This property prevents SPA attack. Randomized projective coordinates [Cor99,OS00,OMS01] and random isomorphic elliptic curves [JT01,IT02] promote an SPA attack countermeasure to a DPA attack countermeasure.

Kocher *et al.* have proposed a higher-order DPA attack [KJJ98] in which an attacker uses several power consumption data that correspond to intermediate values. More accurately, Messerges has provided a definition of an nth-order DPA attack as follows:

Definition 1 ([Mes00]). *An nth-order DPA attack makes use of n different samples in the power consumption signal that correspond to n different intermediate values calculated during the execution of an algorithm.*

In addition, Messerges showed that countermeasures using random mask for keys on private key cryptosystems against a first-order DPA attack are vulnerable to a second-order DPA attack [Mes00].

3 Möller's Countermeasure

Möller proposed a side channel attack preventative elliptic scalar multiplication method using window method [Möl01].

Let d be an integer, and $w \geq 2$ be a window width. We represent d as $d = \sum_{i=0}^{k'} b_i' \cdot 2^{wi}$, where $b_i' \in \{0, 1, \cdots, 2^w - 1\}$. We demand that k' be chosen minimal, *i.e.* $b_{k'}' \neq 0$. Next, we determine $b_i \in J := \{-2^w, 1, 2, \cdots, 2^w - 1\}$ and k such that $d = \sum_{i=0}^{k} b_i \cdot 2^{wi}$, as follows: Let $c_0 = 0$, and for $i = 0, \cdots, k' + 1$, let $t_i = b_i' + c_i$ and

$$(c_{i+1}, b_i) = \begin{cases} (1, -2^w) & \text{if } t_i = 0 \\ (0, t_i) & \text{if } 0 < t_i < 2^w \\ (2, -2^w) & \text{if } t_i = 2^w \\ (1, 1) & \text{if } t_i = 2^w + 1. \end{cases}$$

We set $k = k' + 1$ if $b_{k'+1} \neq -2^w$; otherwise $k = k'$.

With regard to the precomputation table of the scalar multiplication method, we denote the memory P_j which stores the point jP on an elliptic curve. In addition, we denote $P_j + P_{j'}$ (resp. $2P_j$) as the result of addition (resp. doubling) of the stored points.

Algorithm (Precomputation Stage)
    INPUT A scalar value d, a point $P = (x, y)$, and a window width w.
    OUTPUT The precomputation table $\{P_j\}_{j \in J}$.
    1. Generate a random number λ.
    2. $P_1 \leftarrow (\lambda x, \lambda y, \lambda)^2$
    3. For $j = 2$ to $2^w - 2$ step 2 do
        3.1 $P_j \leftarrow 2P_{j/2}$
        3.2 $P_{j+1} \leftarrow P_j + P_1$
    4. $P_{-2^w} \leftarrow -2P_{2^w-1}$

---

[2] This is in the case of projective coordinates. In the case of Chudnovsky Jacobian coordinates, $P_1 \leftarrow (\lambda^2 x, \lambda^3 y, \lambda, \lambda^2, \lambda^3)$.

Algorithm (Evaluation Stage)
  INPUT A scalar value $d = \sum_{i=0}^{k} b_i 2^{wi}$, a point P, a window width w, and
    the precomputation table $\{P_j\}_{j \in J}$.
  OUTPUT The scalar multiplied point dP.
  1. $Q \leftarrow \mathcal{O}$, where $\mathcal{O}$ is the point at infinity.
  2. For $i = k$ down to 0 do
      2.1 $Q \leftarrow 2^w Q$
      2.2 $Q \leftarrow Q + P_{b_i}$
  3. Output Q as a scalar multiplied point dP.

This countermeasure is immune to the SPA attack, because it computes the
scalar multiplied point dP with fixed procedure independently on the scalar d.
Besides, the countermeasure is believed to be immune to the DPA attack also,
because precomputed points are randomized by using randomized (projective)
coordinates in the precomputation stage, then the randomized points are used
in the evaluation stage.

4   DPA Attack versus Möller's Countermeasure

4.1   Power Leakage Model

Messerges proposed the following power leakage model [Mes00] whose leaked
information depends on the Hamming weight of the data being processed, and
confirmed that the model is valid under smart cards. Let the power consumption
$C(t)$ at the time t be expressed as $C(t) = \epsilon \cdot H(t) + L + N$, where $H(t)$, ϵ, L, and
N respectively represent the Hamming weight of the intermediate data result at
the time t, the incremental amount of power for each extra '1' in the Hamming
weight, the additive constant portion of the total power, and the noise. $\mathcal{E}[N]$
and $\mathcal{V}[N]$ respectively denote mean and variance of the noise N. The noise N is
assumed to have zero mean: $\mathcal{E}[N] = 0$.

  With respect to mean and variance of the Hamming weight of randomly
chosen bits, the following lemma holds:

Lemma 1. *The Hamming weight of randomly chosen data of bit length l has
mean $\mathcal{E}_l = \frac{l}{2}$ and variance $\mathcal{V}_l = \frac{l}{4}$.*

Proof. $\mathcal{E}_l = \frac{l}{2}$ is clear. We will show $\mathcal{V}_l = \frac{l}{4}$.
  The definition of variance provides

$$\mathcal{V}_l = \frac{1}{2^l} \sum_{k=0}^{l} \binom{l}{k} \left(\frac{l}{2} - k \right)^2 .$$

On the other hand, the definition of binomial coefficients provides

$$(1 + x)^l = \sum_{k=0}^{l} \binom{l}{k} x^k .$$

$\frac{d}{dx}\big|_{x=1}$ and $\frac{d^2}{dx^2}\big|_{x=1}$ yield

$$l \cdot 2^{l-1} = \sum_{k=1}^{l} k \binom{l}{k} \quad \text{and} \quad l(l-1) \cdot 2^{l-2} = \sum_{k=2}^{l} k(k-1) \binom{l}{k}.$$

Substituting these equations into the equation of $\mathcal{V}_l$ gives $\mathcal{V}_l = \frac{1}{4}$. □

The proposition below is useful to construct a DPA attack against Möller's countermeasure. Let $C^A[Q, P](t)$, $t \in [0, T^A]$ be the power consumption for addition of points Q and P, and $C^D[Q](t)$, $t \in [0, T^D]$ be that for doubling of a point Q, where T^A is the timing of addition, and T^D is that of doubling.

Proposition 1. *Assume that the second parameter, the point P (or P'), of addition at the time $\tilde{t}$ is loaded into registers. Then, with respect to variances of power consumption, the following relations hold:*

$$v_1 := \mathcal{V}\big[C^A[Q, P](\tilde{t}) - C^A[Q', P](\tilde{t})\big] = \epsilon \cdot \frac{r - |P|}{2} + 2\mathcal{V}[N],$$

$$v_2 := \mathcal{V}\big[C^A[Q, P](\tilde{t}) - C^A[Q', P'](\tilde{t})\big] = \epsilon \cdot \frac{r}{2} + 2\mathcal{V}[N].$$

In particular, $v_1 < v_2$ holds. Here, $Q, Q', P, P' \in E$ are randomly chosen, r denotes the bit length of the registers, and $|\cdot|$ denotes the bit length of data.

Proof. Messerges' power leakage model [Mes00] provides

$$v_1 = \mathcal{V}\big[(\epsilon \cdot H[Q, P](\tilde{t}) + L + N(\tilde{t})) - (\epsilon \cdot H[Q', P](\tilde{t}) + L + N(\tilde{t}))\big],$$

where $H[Q, P](t)$, $H[Q', P](t)$ respectively represent the Hamming weight of registers at the time t for addition of points Q, P, that for addition of points Q', P. The constant portions are canceled, and the noises are independent. Besides, since the point P is loaded into the registers at the time $\tilde{t}$, the Hamming weight of the point P of the addition $Q + P$ and that of the addition $Q' + P$ are identical and canceled. Thus, each Hamming weight may be regarded as Hamming weight of data with $r - |P|$ bit length. Assume that the Hamming weights are independent, the variance of the difference of the Hamming weights is $\frac{r-|P|}{2}$ by using Lemma 1. In consideration of the variances for the noises, we obtain

$$v_1 = \epsilon \cdot \frac{r - |P|}{2} + 2\mathcal{V}[N].$$

In the same way, in consideration of incoincidence of the Hamming weights of the points P, P', we obtain

$$v_2 = \epsilon \cdot \frac{r}{2} + 2\mathcal{V}[N].$$

□

Remark 1. v_1, v_2 depend on hardware characteristics and implementations; methods to load data from memories into registers: When data are loaded into registers, the entire data is loaded, or the potions of data are loaded one after another. In any case, $v_1 < v_2$ holds, because identical portions are loaded whenever the point P is loaded.

4.2   Proposed Attack

A proposed DPA attack to Möller's countermeasure consists of the following three phases.

I   Detect v_1 and v_2 of Proposition 1.
II   Calculate $\mathcal{C}'_s$ for $s = 0, 1, \cdots, k$, where $\mathcal{C}'_s := \{s' | \, b_s = b_{s'}\}$.
III   Find out the correspondences between $\mathcal{C}_j$ and $\mathcal{C}'_s$ using direct-computational attack, and detect the scalar d, where $\mathcal{C}_j := \{s | \, b_s = j\}$.

4.3   Phase I

We describe the method to detect v_1 and v_2 in two ways: the case that an attacker can simulate an addition device, and otherwise. First, assume that the attacker can simulate an addition device. In this case, the measurement of power consumption on the simulator detects v_1 and v_2.

Next, assume that the attacker cannot simulate an addition device. In this case, the use of scalar multiplication provides the result. Let t_s be the time when the second parameter P_{b_s} of addition at Step 2.2 of $i = s$ is loaded into registers:

$$t_s = (k - s)(T^A + wT^D) + wT^D + \tilde{t}.$$

Let the correlation function $g(t_s, t_{s'})$ on m_0 times measurements for $s \neq s'$ be

$$g(t_s, t_{s'}) := \frac{1}{m_0} \sum_{m=1}^{m_0} \left[C_m(t_s) - C_m(t_{s'}) \right]^2,$$

where $C_m(t)$ is power consumption associated with the m-th execution of Möller's countermeasure. Proposition 1 provides

$$g(t_s, t_{s'}) = \frac{1}{m_0} \sum_{m=1}^{m_0} \left[C^A[Q, P_j](\tilde{t}) - C^A[Q', P_j](\tilde{t}) \right]^2 \to v_1 \quad (\text{as } m_0 \to \infty)$$

if $b_s = b_{s'}$ $(b_s P = b_{s'} P = P_j)$, and

$$g(t_s, t_{s'}) = \frac{1}{m_0} \sum_{m=1}^{m_0} \left[C^A[Q, P_j](\tilde{t}) - C^A[Q', P_{j'}](\tilde{t}) \right]^2 \to v_2 \quad (\text{as } m_0 \to \infty)$$

if $b_s \neq b_{s'}$ $(b_s P = P_j, b_{s'} = P_{j'})$. Hence, the following proposition holds:

Proposition 2. $b_s = b_{s'}$ if $g(t_s, t_{s'}) \to v_1$; $b_s \neq b_{s'}$ if $g(t_s, t_{s'}) \to v_2$.

The attacker calculates $g(t_s, t_{s'})$ for any s and s'. If the number of the values is exactly two, $v_1 = v'_1$ and $v_2 = v'_2$ hold. In the case that the number of the values is only one, the attacker checks whether substituting $b_s = j$ $(s = 0, 1, \cdots, k)$ for some $j \in J$ yields $Q = dP$ or not. If $Q = dP$ for some j, $v_1 = v'$ holds, and furthermore $d = \sum_{i=0}^{k} j 2^{wi}$ holds. If $Q \neq dP$ for any j, $v_2 = v'$ holds. In this case, $b_s \neq b_{s'}$ holds for any $s \neq s'$. However, a usual choice of the window width, which is $k > 2^w$, for speeding up the scalar multiplication eliminates the case of $v_2 = v'$

Remark 2. The proposed attack is a second-order DPA attack, because the attack uses two different power consumption that correspond to the time t_s and $t_{s'}$.

Remark 3. Möller's countermeasure is believed to prevent the first-order DPA attacks, however, a sophisticated first-order DPA attack might break the countermeasure. The immunity to the first-order DPA attacks is still controversial.

4.4   Phase II

For a fixed s, the attacker calculates $g(t_s, t_{s'})$ for any s', and finds out $\mathcal{C}'_s$ using Proposition 2; he detects all the s' with $b_s = b_{s'}$. In the same way, he finds out $\mathcal{C}'_s$ for any s.

Remark 4. In the case that Phase I detects v_2 only, $\mathcal{C}'_s$ is the one-point set $\{s\}$ for any s.

Effect of Phases I and II. Phases I and II restrict candidates of the scalar d. We estimate a number of the candidates.

Since a correspondence between $\mathcal{C}'_s$ and $\mathcal{C}_j$ gives a candidate of the scalar d, the number of candidates of the scalar d is that of correspondences between $\mathcal{C}'_s$ and $\mathcal{C}_j$.

Proposition 3. *Let* $\mathcal{S} := \{s \mid s \le s' \text{ for any } s' \text{ with } b_s = b_{s'}\}$ *and* $q := \#\mathcal{S}$. *Then, the number of candidates of the scalar d is*

$$\prod_{m=0}^{q-1} (2^w - m).$$

Proof. The number of the candidates of the scalar d is that of the permutations of q out of 2^w. $\qquad\square$

Proposition 4. *Assume that b_i is randomly chosen. Then, the expectation of q is*

$$2^w \left(1 - \left(\frac{2^w - 1}{2^w}\right)^{k+1}\right),$$

where k denotes (the number of windows -1).

Proof. We will show that the expectation of the number of $j (\in J)$ that is not chosen is

$$2^w \cdot \left(\frac{2^w - 1}{2^w}\right)^{k+1},$$

by the induction with respect to the number of windows. In the case of the number of windows to be 1, exactly one $j (\in J)$ is chosen; hence, the expectation is $2^w - 1$.

Table 1. Numbers of candidates for scalar values

Window width w	2	3	4	5	6
$\lvert d \rvert =$ 160	5 bits	16 bits	45 bits	93 bits	132 bits
192	5 bits	16 bits	45 bits	100 bits	148 bits
256	5 bits	16 bits	45 bits	109 bits	179 bits
384	5 bits	16 bits	45 bits	117 bits	222 bits
512	5 bits	16 bits	45 bits	118 bits	252 bits

Each entry indicates the bit length of the number of candidates of a scalar d which is restricted by Phases I and II.

Next, assume that for k, the expectation of the number of j that is not chosen is

$$2^w \cdot \left(\frac{2^w - 1}{2^w} \right)^k \ (=: x).$$

Then, the probability that a newly chosen b_i is equal to some known j is $(2^w - x)/(2^w)$. Thus, for $k + 1$, the expectation of the number of j that is not chosen is

$$x \cdot \frac{x}{2^w} + (x - 1)\frac{2^w - x}{2^w} = \frac{2^w - 1}{2^w} \cdot x$$

$$= 2^w \cdot \left(\frac{2^w - 1}{2^w} \right)^{k+1}.$$

$\square$

Table 1 shows numerical examples of a number of candidates. For example, if Möller's countermeasure computes a scalar multiplied point for a 160-bit scalar d using the window width $w = 4$, then Phases I and II restrict the number of candidates to be a 45-bit integer.

4.5   Phase III

Due to Phases I and II, candidates of the scalar d are restricted. Phase III uses Baby-Step-Giant-Step method [Sha71], and completely detects the scalar d.

First of all, divide $\mathcal{S}$ into two classes $\mathcal{S}_1, \mathcal{S}_2$ with the following conditions:

1. $\mathcal{S}_1 \cap \mathcal{S}_2 = \phi$ and $\mathcal{S}_1 \cup \mathcal{S}_2 = \mathcal{S}$.
2. $\#\mathcal{S}_1 = \lfloor \#\mathcal{S}/2 \rfloor$.

A candidate $\tilde{d}$ of the scalar d is written as $\tilde{d} = \sum_{s_1 \in \mathcal{S}_1} \sum_{s' \in \mathcal{C}'_{s_1}} j_{s_1} 2^{ws'} P + \sum_{s_2 \in \mathcal{S}_2} \sum_{s' \in \mathcal{C}'_{s_2}} j_{s_2} 2^{ws'} P$. For any $s_1 \in \mathcal{S}_1$ and for any $s_2 \in \mathcal{S}_2$, j_{s_1} is not equal to j_{s_2}. Hence, it is possible to combine $\{j_{s_2}\}_{s_2 \in \mathcal{S}_2}$ with $\{j_{s_1}\}_{s_1 \in \mathcal{S}_1}$, however, it is impossible to combine $\{j_{s_2}\}_{s_2 \in \mathcal{S}_2}$ with $\{j'_{s_1}\}_{s_1 \in \mathcal{S}_1}$ that there exists $s_1 \in \mathcal{S}_1$ such that $j'_{s_1} \in \{j_{s_2} \mid s_2 \in \mathcal{S}_2\}$. Therefore, the operations of Giant-Step cannot be calculated independently on those of Baby-Step, assuming one calculates operations for $\mathcal{S}_1$ as Baby-Step and those for $\mathcal{S}_2$ as Giant-Step. As a result, Baby-Step-Giant-Step method [Sha71] cannot be used naively.

Giant-Step of our proposed Baby-Step-Giant-Step method calculates the operations for $\{j_{s_2}\}_{s_2 \in \mathcal{S}_2}$ for all the candidates $\tilde{d}$, which provides independence on the operations for Baby-Step.

Attack Algorithm (Baby-Step-Giant-Step)
INPUT Elliptic points P, $Q = dP$, a window width w, and information which is obtained by Phases I and II $(\mathcal{S}, \mathcal{C}'_s, \mathcal{S}_1, \mathcal{S}_2)$.
OUTPUT The scalar value d.

1. (Baby-Step) For any $(\cdots, j_s, \cdots) \in \bigoplus_{s \in \mathcal{S}_1} J$ with $j_s \in J - \{j_{\tilde{s}} | \tilde{s} \in \mathcal{S}_1, \tilde{s} < s\}$, compute $Q - \sum_{s \in \mathcal{S}_1} \sum_{s' \in \mathcal{C}'_s} j_s 2^{ws'} P$.

2. (Giant-Step) For any $(\cdots, j_s, \cdots) \in \bigoplus_{s \in \mathcal{S}_2} J$ with $j_s \in J - \{j_{\tilde{s}} | \tilde{s} \in \mathcal{S}_2, \tilde{s} < s\}$, compute $\sum_{s \in \mathcal{S}_2} \sum_{s' \in \mathcal{C}'_s} j_s 2^{ws'} P$.

3. Calculate $\left\{ Q - \sum_{s \in \mathcal{S}_1} \sum_{s' \in \mathcal{C}'_s} j_s 2^{ws'} P \right\} \cap \left\{ \sum_{s \in \mathcal{S}_2} \sum_{s' \in \mathcal{C}'_s} j_s 2^{ws'} P \right\}$.
   Concretely speaking, sort the values which are computed in Baby-Step, in terms of the size of the x-coordinate. In the same way, sort the values which are computed in Giant-Step. Then, seek the coincident values. The intersection is a one-point set.

4. $Q - \sum_{s \in \mathcal{S}_1} \sum_{s' \in \mathcal{C}'_s} j_s^{(1)} 2^{ws'} P = \sum_{s \in \mathcal{S}_2} \sum_{s' \in \mathcal{C}'_s} j_s^{(2)} 2^{ws'} P$ is in the intersection, then $d = \left(\sum_{s \in \mathcal{S}_1} \sum_{s' \in \mathcal{C}'_s} j_s^{(1)} 2^{ws'} \right) + \left(\sum_{s \in \mathcal{S}_2} \sum_{s' \in \mathcal{C}'_s} j_s^{(2)} 2^{ws'} \right)$.

Remark 5. The proposed Baby-Step-Giant-Step method is a deterministic algorithm with running time $O(\sqrt{n})$ and with space requirement $O(\sqrt{n})$, where

$$n = \left[\prod_{m=0}^{\lfloor (q+1)/2 \rfloor} (2^w - m) \right]^2$$

. Whether a kangaroo method [Pol78,Tes00], a space efficient probabilistic method to solve a discrete logarithm problem, is adaptable to the situation or not is an open question.

Remark 6. In the case that d is a 160-bit integer and the window width is 4, the above n is a 58-bit integer, which is within the scope of solvable elliptic curve discrete logarithm problems [ECCC].

5   Countermeasures

We propose a countermeasure to prevent the above-mentioned DPA attack as follows:

Large Window Width: The countermeasure uses a large window width. Table 1 shows that a somewhat large window width thwarts Phase III, because of the increase of the candidates of the scalar.

Table 2. Computational intractability and computational cost for Möller's countermeasure

Method	Window width	Bit length	# of candidates for scalar values	Computational cost for scalar multiplication
Original	4	160	45 bits	$1884.2M$
Large window width	7	160	152 bits	$2975.6M$
Large window width	7	170	158 bits	$3106.4M_{170}$

"Original" means the original version of Möller's countermeasure. "M" denotes multiplication on a finite field of 160 bits. "M_{170}" denotes multiplication on a finite field of 170 bits.

In the case that the window width of the large window width countermeasure is 7 and the scalar d is a 170-bit integer, the number of the candidates of the scalar is about 158-bit integer, which nearly provides 160-bit security for the countermeasure.

However, the large window width increases the computational cost[3]. The countermeasure stores the precomputation points with $\mathcal{J}^c$, and selects the coordinate systems as follows: $\mathcal{J} + \mathcal{J}^c \to \mathcal{J}^m$ for addition, $\mathcal{J}^m \to \mathcal{J}$ for doubling before addition, and $\mathcal{J}^m \to \mathcal{J}^m$ for doubling before doubling, where $\mathcal{J}, \mathcal{J}^c, \mathcal{J}^m$ respectively denote Jacobian coordinates, Chudnovsky Jacobian coordinates, and modified Jacobian coordinates. The use of the coordinate systems provides quick computation of the scalar multiplied point for the evaluation stage[4]. The computational cost of the evaluation stage is $(4w + 11)kM + (4w + 5)kS$, where M and S respectively denote multiplication and doubling on a finite field. The storage of the precomputation points with $\mathcal{J}^c$ in the precomputation stage requires $(16 \cdot 2^{w-1} - 11)M + (9 \cdot 2^{w-1} - 3)S$.

Assume that $S = 0.8M$ [LH00]. The computational cost of the countermeasure with 160 bits needs $1884.2M$ if $w = 4$; $2975.6M$ if $w = 7$. Thus, the use of the large window width countermeasure causes the $1091.4M$ increase. Besides, whereas a scalar value with 170 bits nearly achieves 160-bit security, it causes the extra increase of computational cost such as the computational cost for operations on a larger finite field and extra elliptic operations. The computational cost is 3106.4 multiplications on a 170-bit finite field. Therefore, it is unfortunately that the countermeasure is very slow. A fast countermeasure against the proposed DPA attack remains as a matter to be discussed further.

---

[3] The estimates of the computational cost in the paper are the case of elliptic curves defined over prime fields. The others are also estimable in the same way.

[4] Möller [Möl01] gave the computational cost of Möller's countermeasure. However, the computational cost is incorrect because the choice of coordinate systems was not considered. Concretely speaking, according to [Möl01], the computational cost of addition is $15M$. $\mathcal{J}^c + \mathcal{J}^c \to \mathcal{J}^m$ is the only choice of the coordinate systems for addition with $15M$. The coordinate systems of addition require the coordinate systems of doubling before the addition be $\mathcal{J}^m \to \mathcal{J}^c$. However, the computational cost of the doubling is $9M$, and differs from that in [Möl01], which is $8M$.

Remark 7. The proposed countermeasure might be vulnerable to an nth-order DPA attack ($n \geq 3$). Whether the proposed countermeasure is immune to a higher-order DPA attack or not is an open question.

Table 2 summarizes the computational intractabilities and computational costs of the methods discussed in this paper.

Acknowledgements. The authors would like to thank the anonymous referees for their useful comments.

References

[BJ02]   Brier, É., Joye, M., *Weierstrass Elliptic Curves and Side-Channel Attacks*, Public Key Cryptography (PKC 2002), LNCS2274, (2002), 335–345.

[CMO98]   Cohen, H., Miyaji, A., Ono, T., *Efficient Elliptic Curve Exponentiation Using Mixed Coordinates*, Advances in Cryptology – ASIACRYPT '98, LNCS1514, (1998), 51–65.

[Cor99]   Coron, J.S., *Resistance against Differential Power Analysis for Elliptic Curve Cryptosystems*, Cryptographic Hardware and Embedded Systems (CHES'99), LNCS1717, (1999), 292–302.

[DES]   National Bureau of Standards, *Data Encryption Standard*, Federal Information Processing Standards Publication 46 (FIPS PUB 46), (1977).

[ECCC]   ECC Challenge. Available at
            http://www.certicom.com/resources/ecc_chall/challenge.html

[FGKS02]   Fischer, W., Giraud, C., Knudsen, E.W., Seifert, J.P., *Parallel scalar multiplication on general elliptic curves over $\mathbf{F}_p$ hedged against Non-Differential Side-Channel Attacks*, International Association for Cryptologic Research (IACR), Cryptology ePrint Archive 2002/007, (2002). Available at http://eprint.iacr.org/

[Has00]   Hasan, M.A., *Power Analysis Attacks and Algorithmic Approaches to Their Countermeasures for Koblitz Curve Cryptosystems*, Cryptographic Hardware and Embedded Systems (CHES 2000), LNCS1965, (2000), 93–108.

[IT02]   Izu, T., Takagi, T., *A Fast Parallel Elliptic Curve Multiplication Resistant against Side Channel Attacks*, Public Key Cryptography (PKC 2002), LNCS2274, (2002), 280-296.

[JQ01]   Joye, M., Quisquater, J.J., *Hessian elliptic curves and side-channel attacks*, Cryptographic Hardware and Embedded Systems (CHES 2001), LNCS2162, (2001), 402–410.

[JT01]   Joye, M., Tymen, C., *Protections against Differential Analysis for Elliptic Curve Cryptography – An Algebraic Approach –*, Cryptographic Hardware and Embedded Systems (CHES 2001), LNCS2162, (2001), 377–390.

[Kob87]   Koblitz, N., *Elliptic curve cryptosystems*, Math. Comp. 48, (1987), 203–209.

[Koc]   Kocher, C., *Cryptanalysis of Diffie-Hellman, RSA, DSS, and Other Systems Using Timing Attacks*. Available at http://www.cryptography.com/

[Koc96]   Kocher, C., *Timing Attacks on Implementations of Diffie-Hellman, RSA,DSS, and Other Systems*, Advances in Cryptology – CRYPTO '96, LNCS1109, (1996), 104–113.

[KJJ98]   Kocher, C., Jaffe, J., Jun, B., *Introduction to Differential Power Analysis and Related Attacks*. Available at http://www.cryptography.com/dpa/technical/ index.html

[KJJ99]   Kocher, C., Jaffe, J., Jun, B., *Differential Power Analysis*, Advances in Cryptology – CRYPTO '99, LNCS1666, (1999), 388–397.

[LH00]   Lim, C.H., Hwang, H.S., *Fast implementation of Elliptic Curve Arithmetic in $GF(p^m)$*, Public Key Cryptography (PKC 2000), LNCS1751, (2000), 405–421.

[LS01]   Liardet, P.Y., Smart, N.P., *Preventing SPA/DPA in ECC systems using the Jacobi form*, Cryptographic Hardware and Embedded System (CHES 2001), LNCS2162, (2001), 391–401.

[Mes00]   Messerges, T.S., *Using Second-Order Power Analysis to Attack DPA Resistant Software*, Cryptographic Hardware and Embedded System (CHES 2000), LNCS1965, (2000), 238–251.

[Mil86]   Miller, V.S., *Use of elliptic curves in cryptography*, Advances in Cryptology - CRYPTO '85, LNCS218,(1986), 417–426.

[Möl01]   Möller, B., *Securing Elliptic Curve Point Multiplication against Side-Channel Attacks*, Information Security (ISC2001), LNCS2200, (2001), 324–334.

[OA01]   Oswald, E., Aigner, M., *Randomized Addition-Subtraction Chains as a Countermeasure against Power Attacks*, Cryptographic Hardware and Embedded Systems (CHES'01), LNCS2162, (2001), 39–50.

[OMS01]   Okeya, K., Miyazaki, K., Sakurai, K., *A Fast Scalar Multiplication Method with Randomized Projective Coordinates on a Montgomery-form Elliptic Curve Secure against Side Channel Attacks*, The 4th International Conference on Information Security and Cryptology (ICISC 2001), LNCS2288, (2002), 428–439.

[OS00]   Okeya, K., Sakurai, K., *Power Analysis Breaks Elliptic Curve Cryptosystems even Secure against the Timing Attack*, Progress in Cryptology - INDOCRYPT 2000, LNCS1977, (2000), 178–190.

[OS02]   Okeya, K., Sakurai, K., *On Insecurity of the Side Channel Attack Countermeasure using Addition-Subtraction Chains under Distinguishability between Addition and Doubling*, The 7th Australasian Conference in Information Security and Privacy, (ACISP 2002), LNCS2384, (2002), 420–435.

[Pol78]   Pollard, J.M., *Monte Carlo methods for index computation (mod p)*, Math. Comp. 32, (1978), 918–924.

[RSA78]   Rivest, R.L., Shamir, A., Adleman, L., *A Method for Obtaining Digital Signatures and Public-Key Cryptosystems*, Communications of the ACM, Vol.21, No.2, (1978), 120–126.

[Sha71]   Shanks, D., *Class number, a theory of factorization and genera*, In Proc. Symp. Pure Math. 20, (1971), 415–440.

[Tes00]   Teske, E., *Square-root Algorithms for the Discrete Logarithm Problem (A Survey)*, Public-Key Cryptography and Computational Number Theory, Walter de Gruyter, (2001), 283–301.

Parallelizable Elliptic Curve Point Multiplication Method with Resistance against Side-Channel Attacks

Bodo Möller

Technische Universität Darmstadt, Fachbereich Informatik
moeller@cdc.informatik.tu-darmstadt.de

Abstract. We present a new 2^w-ary elliptic curve point multiplication method with resistance against side-channel attacks. This method provides two advantages compared with previous similar side-channel attack countermeasures: It avoids a fixed table, thus reducing potential information leakage available to adversaries; and it is easily parallelizable on two-processor systems, where it provides much improved performance.

1 Introduction

Implementations of elliptic curve cryptosystems may be vulnerable to *side-channel attacks* ([12], [13]) where adversaries can use power consumption measurements or similar observations to derive information on secret scalars e in point multiplications eP. One distinguishes between *differential side-channel attacks,* which require correlated measurements from multiple point multiplications, and *simple side-channel attacks,* which directly interpret data obtained during a single point multiplication.

Randomization can be used as a countermeasure against differential side-channel attacks. In particular, for elliptic curve cryptography, *projective randomization* is a simple and effective tool [5]: If (X, Y, Z) represents the point whose affine coordinates are $(X/Z^2, Y/Z^3)$, another representation of the same point that cannot be predicted by the adversary is obtained by substituting $(r^2 X, r^3 Y, rZ)$ with a randomly chosen secret non-zero field element r. (When starting from an affine representation (X, Y), this simplifies to $(r^2 X, r^3 Y, r)$.)

Simple side-channel attacks can be easy to perform because usually the attacker can tell apart point doublings from general point additions. Thus point multiplication should be implemented using a fixed sequence of point operations that does not depend on the particular scalar. Note that it is reasonable to assume that point addition and point subtraction are uniform to the attacker as point inversion is nearly immediate (dummy inversions can be inserted to obtain the same sequence of operations for point additions as for point subtractions).

Various point multiplication methods have been proposed that use an alternating sequence of doublings and additions: The simplest approach is to use a binary point multiplication method with dummy additions inserted to avoid

A.H. Chan and V. Gligor (Eds.): ISC 2002, LNCS 2433, pp. 402–413, 2002.

dependencies on scalar bits [5]; however as noted in [15] it may be easy for adversaries to determine which additions are dummy operations, so it is not clear that this method provides sufficient security. For odd scalars, a variant of binary point multiplication can be used where the scalar is represented in balanced binary representation (digits -1 and $+1$) [22]. Also Montgomery's binary point multiplication method [17], which maintains an invariant $Q_1 - Q_0 = P$ while computing eP using two variables Q_0, Q_1, can be adapted for implementing point multiplication with a fixed sequence of point operations ([23], [18], [1], [9], [6]). With this approach, specific techniques can be used to speed up point arithmetic: The doubling and addition steps can be combined; y-coordinates of points may be omitted during the computation ([17], [1], [9], [6]); and on suitable hardware, parallel execution can be conveniently used for improved efficiency ([9], [6]).

All of the above point multiplication methods are binary. Given sufficient memory, efficiency can be improved by using 2^w-ary point multiplication methods. Here, the scalar e is represented in base 2^w using digits b_i from some digit set B:

$$e = \sum_{0 \leq i \leq \ell} b_i 2^{wi}$$

A simple way to obtain a uniform sequence of doublings and additions (namely, one addition after w doublings in the main loop of the point multiplication algorithm) is to use 2^w-ary point multiplication as usual (first compute and store bP for each $b \in B$, then compute eP using this precomputed table), but to insert a dummy addition whenever a zero digit is encountered. However, as noted above for the binary case, the dummy addition approach may not be secure. This problem can be avoided (given $w \geq 2$) by using a representation of e without digit value 0, such as

$$B = \{-2^w, 1, 2, \ldots, 2^w - 1\}$$

as proposed in [15], or

$$B = \{-2^w, \pm 1, \pm 2, \ldots, \pm(2^w - 2), 2^w - 1\}$$

for improved efficiency as proposed in [16]. A remaining problem in the method of [15] and [16] is that the use of a fixed table may allow for statistical attacks: If the same point from the table is used in a point addition whenever the same digit value occurs, this may help adversaries to find out which of the digits b_i have the same value (cf. the attacks on modular exponentiation using fixed tables in [24] and [21]). This problem can be countered by performing, whenever the table is accessed, a projective randomization of the table value that has been used. This will avoid a fixed table, but at the price of reduced efficiency.

In this paper, we present a new variant of 2^w-ary point multiplication with resistance against side-channel attacks that avoids a fixed table without requiring frequently repeated projective randomization. An additional advantage of the new method is that it is easily parallelizable on two-processor systems. The essential change in strategy compared with earlier methods for side-channel attack resistant point multiplication is that we use a right-to-left method (the scalar is processed starting at the least significant digit, cf. [25]) whereas the conventional methods work in a left-to-right fashion. Section 2 describes the new point multiplication method. Section 3 examines its efficiency in comparison with the left-to-right method of [15] and [16]. In section 4, we describe some possible variants. Section 5 summarizes our conclusions.

2   Description of the Point Multiplication Method

Our method for computing eP is parameterized by an integer $w \geq 2$ and a digit set B consisting of 2^w integers of small absolute value such that every positive scalar e can be represented in the form

$$e = \sum_{0 \leq i \leq \ell} b_i 2^{wi}$$

using digits $b_i \in B$; for example

$$B = \{0, 1, \ldots, 2^w - 1\}$$

or

$$B = \{-2^{w-1}, \ldots, 2^{w-1} - 1\}.$$

A representation of e using the latter digit set can be easily determined on the fly when scanning the binary digits of e in right-to-left direction. If e is at most n bits long (i.e. $0 < e < 2^n$), $\ell = \lfloor n/w \rfloor$ is sufficient.

Let B' denote the set $\{|b| \mid b \in B\}$ of absolute values of digits, which has at least $2^{w-1} + 1$ and at most 2^w elements. The point multiplication method uses $\#(B') + 1$ variables for storing points on the elliptic curve in projective representation: Namely, one variable A_b for each $b \in B'$, and one additional variable Q.

The method works in three stages, which we call *initialization stage*, *right-to-left stage*, and *result stage*. We will first give a high-level view of these stages before discussing the details. Let A_b^{init} denote the value of A_b at the end of the initialization stage, and let A_b^{sum} denote the value of A_b at the end of the right-to-left stage.

The *initialization stage* sets up the variables A_b ($b \in B'$) in a randomized way such that $A_b^{\text{init}} \neq \mathcal{O}$ for each b, but

$$\sum_{b \in B'} b A_b^{\text{init}} = \mathcal{O}.$$

($\mathcal{O}$ denotes the point at infinity, the neutral element of the elliptic curve group.) Then the *right-to-left stage* performs computations depending on P and the digits b_i, yielding new values A_b^{sum} of the variables A_b satisfying

$$A_b^{\text{sum}} = A_b^{\text{init}} + \sum_{\substack{0 \leq i \leq \ell \\ b_i = b}} 2^{wi} P - \sum_{\substack{0 \leq i \leq \ell \\ b_i = -b}} 2^{wi} P$$

for each $b \in B'$. Finally, the *result stage* computes

$$\sum_{b \in B' \backslash \{0\}} b A_b^{\mathsf{sum}},$$

which yields the final result eP because

$$\sum_{b \in B' \backslash \{0\}} b A_b^{\mathsf{sum}} = \underbrace{\sum_{b \in B' \backslash \{0\}} b A_b^{\mathsf{init}}}_{\mathcal{O}} + \sum_{b \in B' \backslash \{0\}} b \left(\sum_{\substack{0 \le i \le \ell \\ b_i = b}} 2^{wi} P - \sum_{\substack{0 \le i \le \ell \\ b_i = -b}} 2^{wi} P \right)$$

$$= \sum_{0 \le i \le \ell} b_i 2^{wi} P = eP.$$

Our point multiplication method is a signed-digit variant of Yao's right-to-left method [25] (see also Knuth [10, exercise 4.6.3-9] and [11, exercise 4.6.3-9] and Brickell et al. [3]) with two essential modifications for achieving resistance against side-channel attacks: The randomized initialization stage is new; and in the right-to-left stage, we treat digit 0 like any other digit.

2.1   Initialization Stage

The initialization stage can be implemented as follows:

1. For each $b \in B' \backslash \{1\}$, generate a random point on the elliptic curve and store it in variable A_b.
2. Compute the point $-\sum_{b \in B' \backslash \{0,1\}} b A_b$ and store it in variable A_1.
3. For each $b \in B'$, perform a projective randomization of variable A_b.

The resulting values of the variables A_b are denoted by A_b^{init}.

If the elliptic curve is fixed, precomputation can be used to speed up the initialization stage: Run steps 1 and 2 just once, e.g. during personalization of a smart card, and store the resulting intermediate values A_b for future use. We denote these values by A_b^{fix}. Then only step 3 (projective randomization of the values A_b^{fix} to obtain new representations A_b^{init}) has to be performed anew each time the initialization stage is called for. The points A_b^{fix} must not be revealed; they should be protected like secret keys.

Generating a random point on an elliptic curve is straightforward. For each element X of the underlying field, there are zero, one or two values Y such that (X, Y) is the affine representation of a point on the elliptic curve. Given a random candidate value X, it is possible to compute an appropriate Y if one exists; the probability for this is approximately $1/2$ by Hasse's theorem. If there is no appropriate Y, one can simply start again with a new X.

Computing an appropriate Y given X involves solving a quadratic equation, which usually (depending on the underlying field) is computationally expensive. This makes it worthwhile to use precomputation as explained above. It is also possible to reuse the values that have remained in the variables A_b, $b \ne 1$, after a previous computation, and start at step 2 of the initialization stage.

To determine $-\sum_{b \in B' \backslash \{0,1\}} b A_b$ in step 2, it is not necessary to compute all the individual products $b A_b$. Algorithm 1 can be used instead to set up A_1 appropriately if $B' = \{0, 1, \ldots, \beta\}$, $\beta \ge 2$. (Note that both loops will be skipped in

---

Algorithm 1 Compute $A_1 \leftarrow -\sum_{b \in \{2,\ldots,\beta\}} bA_b$ in the initialization stage

---

  for $i = \beta - 1$ down to 2 **do**
    $A_i \leftarrow A_i + A_{i+1}$
  $A_1 \leftarrow 2A_2$
  for $i = 2$ to $\beta - 1$ **do**
    $A_i \leftarrow A_i - A_{i+1}$
    $A_1 \leftarrow A_1 + A_{i+1}$
  $A_1 \leftarrow -A_1$

---

the case $\beta = 2$.) This algorithm takes one point doubling and $3\beta - 6$ point additions. When it has finished, the variables A_b for $1 < b < \beta$ will contain modified values, but these are representations of the points originally stored in the respective variables. If sufficient memory is available, a faster algorithm can be used to compute A_1 without intermediate modification of the variables A_b for $b > 1$ (use additional variables Q_b instead; in this case, see section 2.3 for a possible additional improvement if point doublings are faster than point additions).

The projective randomization of the variables A_b ($b \in B'$) in step 3 has the purpose to prevent adversaries from correlating observations from the computation of A_1 in the initialization stage with observations from the following right-to-left stage. If algorithm 1 has been used to compute A_1 and the points are not reused for multiple invocations of the initialization stage, then no explicit projective randomization of the variables A_b for $1 < b < \beta$ is necessary; and if $\beta > 2$, no explicit projective randomization of A_1 is necessary: The variables have automatically been converted into new representations by the point additions used to determine their final values.

2.2 Right-to-Left Stage

Algorithm 2 implements the right-to-left stage using a uniform pattern of point doublings and point additions. Initially, for each b, variable A_b contains the value A_b^{init}; the final value is denoted by A_b^{sum}. Due to special cases that must be

---

Algorithm 2 Right-to-left stage

  $Q \leftarrow P$
  for $i = 0$ to ℓ **do**
    if $b_i \geq 0$ **then**
      $A_{b_i} \leftarrow A_{b_i} + Q$
    else
      $A_{|b_i|} \leftarrow A_{|b_i|} - Q$
    $Q \leftarrow 2^w Q$

---

handled in the point addition algorithm (see [7]), uniformity of this algorithm is violated if $A_{|b_i|}$ is a projective representation of $\pm Q$; the randomization in the initialization stage ensures that the probability of this is negligible. (This is why in section 2.1 we required that precomputed values A_b^{fix} be kept secret.)

If B contains no negative digits, the corresponding branch in the algorithm can be omitted.

The obvious way to implement $Q \leftarrow 2^w Q$ in this algorithm is w-fold iteration of the statement $Q \leftarrow 2Q$, but depending on the elliptic curve, more efficient specific algorithms for w-fold point doubling may be available (see [8]).

In the final iteration of the loop, the assignment to Q may be skipped (the value Q is not used after the right-to-left stage has finished). With this modification, the algorithm uses ℓw point doublings and $\ell + 1$ point additions.

Observe that on two-processor systems the point addition and the w-fold point doubling in the body of the loop may be performed in parallel: Neither operations depends on the other's result.

2.3   Result Stage

Similarly to the computation of A_1 in the initialization stage, the result stage computation

$$\sum_{b \in B' \setminus \{0\}} b A_b^{\text{sum}}$$

can be performed without computing all the individual products $b A_b^{\text{sum}}$. In the result stage, it is not necessary to preserve the original values of the variables A_b, so algorithm 3 (from [10, answer to exercise 4.6.3-9]) can be used if $B' = \{0, 1, \ldots, \beta\}$ when initially each variable A_b contains the value A_b^{sum}. This algorithm uses $2\beta - 2$ point additions.

Algorithm 3 Compute $\sum_{b \in \{1, \ldots, \beta\}} b A_b^{\text{sum}}$ when initially $A_b = A_b^{\text{sum}}$

---
for $i = \beta - 1$ down to 1 **do**
    $A_i \leftarrow A_i + A_{i+1}$
for $i = 2$ to β **do**
    $A_1 \leftarrow A_1 + A_i$
return A_1

Elliptic curve point arithmetic usually has the property that point doublings are faster than point additions. Then the variant given in algorithm 4 is advantageous. This algorithm uses $\lfloor \beta/2 \rfloor$ point doublings and $2\beta - 2 - \lfloor \beta/2 \rfloor$ point additions.

3   Efficiency

We first examine the efficiency of our algorithm for performing a point multiplication eP in a small configuration with $w = 2$ and $B = \{-2, -1, 0, 1\}$ (i.e. with four variables A_0, A_1, A_2, Q).

Algorithm 4 Compute $\sum_{b\in\{1,\ldots,\beta\}} bA_b^{\mathsf{sum}}$ when initially $A_b = A_b^{\mathsf{sum}}$ (variant)

---

for $i = \beta$ down to 1 **do**
  if $2i \leq \beta$ **then**
    $A_i \leftarrow A_i + A_{2i}$
  if i is even **then**
    if $i < \beta$ **then**
      $A_i \leftarrow A_i + A_{i+1}$
    $A_i \leftarrow 2A_i$
  else
    if $i > 1$ **then**
      $A_1 \leftarrow A_1 + A_i$
return A_1

For elliptic curve cryptography over prime fields using Jacobian projective coordinates, a point addition can be done in 16 field multiplications, and curves are usually chosen such that a point doubling can be done in 8 field multiplications [7]. The cost for a projective randomization is 5 field multiplications. Generating a random point on the curve would be rather expensive, so we assume that points $A_0^{\mathsf{fix}}, A_1^{\mathsf{fix}}, A_2^{\mathsf{fix}}$ such that $A_1^{\mathsf{fix}} = -2A_2^{\mathsf{fix}}$ have been precomputed.

In this scenario, the initialization stage has to perform three projective randomizations; the right-to-left stage uses 2ℓ point doublings and $\ell + 1$ point additions; and the result stage can be implemented in one point doubling and one point additions. The total cost is $(\ell + 2) \cdot 16 + (2\ell + 1) \cdot 8 + 3 \cdot 5 = 32\ell + 55$ field multiplications; assuming 160-bit scalars ($\ell = 80$), we have 2615 field multiplications.

With two processors, in the loop of the right-to-left stage, the two point doublings ($2 \cdot 8 = 16$ field multiplications) can be performed in parallel with the one point addition (also 16 field multiplications), and so we can remove 16ℓ field multiplications from the tally. (We ignore the small additional savings that can be achieved through parallelization in the other stages.) Only $16\ell + 55$ field multiplications remain; for 160-bit scalars, this is 1335 field multiplications.

The 2^w-ary left-to-right method from [15] with the improvement from [16] in a similar configuration (digit set $\{-4, -1, 1, 2\}$, three points $P, 2P, 4P$ to precompute) uses one projective randomization followed be two point doublings for precomputation and then one projective randomization, 2ℓ point doublings, and ℓ point additions for determining the result. If we additionally perform a projective randomization after each except the very last point addition to avoid a fixed table, the total cost becomes $\ell \cdot 16 + (2\ell + 2) \cdot 8 + (\ell + 1) \cdot 5 = 37\ell + 21$ field multiplications. Assuming 160-bit scalars ($\ell = 80$), we have 2981 field multiplications. This is about 14 % more than with the new method on a single processor.

Now we consider similar scenarios with arbitrary window sizes $w \geq 2$ and arbitrary scalar bit lengths n. The new method ($\ell = \lfloor n/w \rfloor$, $\beta = 2^{w-1}$) performs $2^{w-1} + 1$ projective randomizations in the initialization stage; $\lfloor n/w \rfloor \cdot w$ point doublings and $\lfloor n/w \rfloor + 1$ point additions in the right-to-left stage; and 2^{w-2}

point doublings and $3 \cdot 2^{w-2} - 2$ point additions in the result stage. The total cost is

$$\left\lfloor \frac{n}{w} \right\rfloor \cdot (w \cdot 8 + 16) + 2^{w-2} \cdot 66 - 11$$

field multiplications.

Note that in the case with parallelization, $w = 2$ provides better performance than larger values of w (the right-to-left stage provides essentially the same amount of work to both processors if $w = 2$). Compared with the one-processor variant, we always save $\lfloor n/w \rfloor \cdot 16$ field multiplications, and

$$\left\lfloor \frac{n}{w} \right\rfloor \cdot w \cdot 8 + 2^{w-2} \cdot 66 - 11$$

field multiplications remain.

For arbitrary window size $w \geq 2$ and scalar bit length n, the left-to-right method from [15] as improved in [16] with additional projective randomizations to avoid a fixed table uses one projective randomization, $2^{w-2} + 1$ point doublings, and $2^{w-2} - 1$ point additions for precomputation and $\lfloor n/w \rfloor$ projective randomizations, $\lfloor n/w \rfloor \cdot w$ point doublings, and $\lfloor n/w \rfloor$ point additions for computing the result. The total cost of this is

$$\left\lfloor \frac{n}{w} \right\rfloor \cdot (w \cdot 8 + 21) + 2^{w-2} \cdot 24 - 3$$

field multiplications.

Table 1 compares the efficiency of the methods for various window sizes in the case of 160-bit scalars. Table 2 provides a similar comparison for 256-bit scalars. (Note that these efficiency comparisons do not take into account the additional cost of generating random field elements for repeated projective randomization in the left-to-right method from [15] and [16].) Table entries are printed in bold if the respective window size w provides better efficiency than smaller values of w, i.e. if w is optimal given certain bounds on memory usage.

The new method needs read-write memory for the same number of points as the left-to-right method from [16] with the same window size. (The new method needs additional read-only memory for the precomputed points A_b^{fix}.) The tables show that, when using a single processor, the left-to-right method with additional projective randomizations can be faster than the new method, but will need more read-write memory to achieve this: In the example scenarios, the left-to-right method needs $w = 5$ (17 table values) to outperform the new method with $w = 4$. (Whether the left-to-right method is actually faster in such cases depends on the speed of random number generation for projective randomization.)

4 Variants

We show some possibilities to vary the point multiplication method described in section 2.

Table 1. Number of field multiplications for a 160-bit point multiplication

w	2	3	4	5	6
New method	**2615**	**2241**	**2173**	2309	2709
New method, two processors	**1335**	1393	1533	1797	2293
L-to-R method [16], proj. rand. to avoid fixed table	2981	2430	**2213**	**2141**	2175

Table 2. Number of field multiplications for a 256-bit point multiplication

w	2	3	4	5	6	7
New method	**4151**	**3521**	**3325**	3373	3733	4693
New method, two processors	**2103**	2161	2301	2557	3061	4117
L-to-R method [16], proj. rand. to avoid fixed table	4757	3870	3485	**3300**	**3279**	3537

4.1   Projective Randomization of P

While it does not appear to be strictly necessary, we recommend to perform a projective randomization of P before beginning the right-to-left stage (algorithm 2). At small computational cost, this will further reduce the side-channel information available to potential attackers.

4.2   Scalar Randomization

Okeya and Sakurai [20] describe a second-order power analysis attack on the fixed-table point multiplication method of [15]. The attack requires power consumption traces from many point multiplications using the same scalar e (and thus the same addition chain). The basis of the attack is to detect table-value reuse by observing side-channel data that leaks information on the Hamming weight of representations of points (cf. [14]): To find out whether the i-th and j-th point addition use the same table value, compute for each power consumption trace the difference between (normalized) power consumption measurements at the two points of time when the respective table entries are read from memory; over sufficiently many point multiplications, the sample variance of these power consumption differences should converge to one of two values depending on whether the i-th and j-th point addition use the same table value or different table values.

No experimental results are given in [20]. If this attack is practical, similar attacks may be possible against most point multiplication methods using a constant sequence of operations as it may be possible to trace values based on their Hamming weight (i.e. determine whether the output of the i-th operation is used as input to the j-th operation). A countermeasure is to randomize the addition chain. This can be done by randomizing the scalar e: Compute eP with two point multiplications and one point subtraction as

$$(e + mN + \widetilde{m})P - \widetilde{m}P$$

where N is the order of the elliptic curve group and $m, \widetilde{m}$ are one-time random numbers (e.g. 32 bits long).

(Adding a multiple of the group order was originally proposed in [12], but it leaves some bias in the least significant digits [19]. Scalar splitting in the form $eP = (e+m)P - mP$ as proposed in [4] avoids this bias, but is only sufficient if m is of the same length as e, which would double the cost of a point multiplication. By combining these two ideas, we avoid the bias while keeping the overhead low.)

4.3   Avoiding Digit 0

In the point multiplication method described in section 2, if $0 \in B$, the variable A_0 is essentially a dummy variable: Its value does not affect the final result. Assume that an attacker is performing a fault attack [2] by purposefully inducing computation faults. If these faults occur only during computations with A_0, the result of the point multiplication will still be correct. Thus, verifying the result cannot reveal that a fault attack has taken place. Therefore it may be useful to avoid the dummy variable.

The point multiplication method of section 2 can be used with a digit set B that does not include the value 0, e.g.

$$B = \left\{ -2^w, \pm 1, \pm 2, \ldots, \pm(2^w - 2), 2^w - 1 \right\}$$

as in [16]. Compared with digit set $\{-2^{w-1}, \ldots, 2^{w-1} - 1\}$, this requires modifications to the algorithms used in step 2 of the initialization stage (section 2.1) and in the result stage (section 2.3). If we assume that the initialization stage uses precomputed points A_b^{fix}, only the changes to the result stage will increase the computational cost of a point multiplication. The result stage for said digit set has to compute the sum

$$\sum_{b \in \{1, \ldots, 2^{w-1}, 2^w\}} b A_b^{\text{sum}};$$

the additional cost is one point doubling and one point addition (set $A_{2^w-1} \leftarrow A_{2^w-1} + 2A_{2^w}$ before running algorithm 3 or 4).

4.4   Variant for $w = 1$

The point multiplication method as described in section 2 works only for $w \geq 2$ because of the requirement that $A_b^{\text{init}} \neq \mathcal{O}$ for each $b \in B'$, but $\sum_{b \in B'} b A_b^{\text{init}} = \mathcal{O}$. The method can be adapted to the case $w = 1$ by relinquishing the latter part of the requirement; instead, save the value A_1^{init} and change the result stage to compute $A_1^{\text{sum}} - A_1^{\text{init}}$.[1] If A_1^{init} is just a projective randomization of a precomputed random point A_1^{fix}, there is no need to save A_1^{init}, as the result stage can simply compute $A_1^{\text{sum}} - A_1^{\text{fix}}$.

4.5   Application to Modular Exponentiation

A variant of the method of section 2 can be used for modular exponentiation. For this purpose, digit set B will only contain non-negative digits.

---

[1] This variant was suggested by Tsuyoshi Takagi.

5   Conclusion

We have described a 2^w-ary right-to-left method for elliptic curve point multiplication that employs a randomized initialization stage to achieve resistance against side-channel attacks. In contrast to similar left-to-right methods, there is no inherent fixed table; thus the new method is more secure than fixed-table left-to-right methods, and in many cases faster than left-to-right methods that use repeated projective randomization to avoid a fixed table. Also the right-to-left method is easily parallelizable and provides much improved performance on two-processor systems.

References

1. BIER, É., AND JOYE, M. Weierstraß elliptic curves and side-channel attacks. In *Public Key Cryptography – PKC 2002* (2002), D. Naccache and P. Paillier, Eds., vol. 2274 of *Lecture Notes in Computer Science*, pp. 335–345.
2. BONEH, D., DEMILLO, R. A., AND LIPTON, R. J. On the importance of eliminating errors in cryptographic computations. *Journal of Cryptology 14* (2001), 101–119.
3. BRICKELL, E. F., GORDON, D. M., MCCURLEY, K. S., AND WILSON, D. B. Fast exponentiation with precomputation. In *Advances in Cryptology – EUROCRYPT '92* (1993), R. A. Rueppel, Ed., vol. 658 of *Lecture Notes in Computer Science*, pp. 200–207.
4. CLAVIER, C., AND JOYE, M. Universal exponentiation algorithm – a first step towards provable SPA-resistance. In *Cryptographic Hardware and Embedded Systems – CHES 2001* (2001), Ç. K. Koç, D. Naccache, and C. Paar, Eds., vol. 2162 of *Lecture Notes in Computer Science*, pp. 300–308.
5. CORON, J.-S. Resistance against differential power analysis for elliptic curve cryptosystems. In *Cryptographic Hardware and Embedded Systems – CHES '99* (1999), Ç. K. Koç and C. Paar, Eds., vol. 1717 of *Lecture Notes in Computer Science*, pp. 292–302.
6. FISCHER, W., GIRAUD, C., KNUDSEN, E. W., AND JEAN-PIERRE, S. Parallel scalar multiplication on general elliptic curves over $\mathbb{F}_p$ hedged against non-differential side-channel attacks. Cryptology ePrint Archive Report 2002/007, 2002. Available from http://eprint.iacr.org/.
7. INSTITUTE OF ELECTRICAL AND ELECTRONICS ENGINEERS (IEEE). IEEE standard specifications for public-key cryptography. IEEE Std 1363-2000, 2000.
8. ITOH, K., TAKENAKA, M., TORII, N., TEMMA, S., AND KURIHARA, Y. Fast implementation of public-key cryptography on a DSP TMS320C6201. In *Cryptographic Hardware and Embedded Systems – CHES '99* (1999), Ç. K. Koç and C. Paar, Eds., vol. 1717 of *Lecture Notes in Computer Science*, pp. 61–72.
9. IZU, T., AND TAKAGI, T. A fast parallel elliptic curve multiplication resistant against side channel attacks. In *Public Key Cryptography – PKC 2002* (2002), D. Naccache and P. Paillier, Eds., vol. 2274 of *Lecture Notes in Computer Science*, pp. 280–296.
10. KNUTH, D. E. *The Art of Computer Programming – Vol. 2: Seminumerical Algorithms (2nd ed.)*. Addison-Wesley, 1981.
11. KNUTH, D. E. *The Art of Computer Programming – Vol. 2: Seminumerical Algorithms (3rd ed.)*. Addison-Wesley, 1998.

12. KOCHER, P. C. Timing attacks on implementations of Diffie-Hellman, RSA, DSS, and other systems. In *Advances in Cryptology – CRYPTO '96* (1996), N. Koblitz, Ed., vol. 1109 of *Lecture Notes in Computer Science*, pp. 104–113.

13. KOCHER, P. C., JAFFE, J., AND JUN, B. Differential power analysis. In *Advances in Cryptology – CRYPTO '99* (1999), M. Wiener, Ed., vol. 1666 of *Lecture Notes in Computer Science*, pp. 388–397.

14. MESSERGES, T. S. Using second-order power analysis to attack DPA resistant software. In *Cryptographic Hardware and Embedded Systems – CHES 2000* (2000), Ç. K. Koç and C. Paar, Eds., vol. 1965 of *Lecture Notes in Computer Science*, pp. 238–251.

15. MÖLLER, B. Securing elliptic curve point multiplication against side-channel attacks. In *Information Security – ISC 2001* (2001), G. I. Davida and Y. Frankel, Eds., vol. 2200 of *Lecture Notes in Computer Science*, pp. 324–334.

16. MÖLLER, B. Securing elliptic curve point multiplication against side-channel attacks, addendum: Efficiency improvement. http://www.informatik.tu-darmstadt.de/TI/ Mitarbeiter/moeller/ecc-sca-isc01.pdf, 2001.

17. MONTGOMERY, P. L. Speeding the Pollard and elliptic curve methods of factorization. *Mathematics of Computation 48* (1987), 243–264.

18. OKEYA, K. Method of calculating multiplication by scalars on an elliptic curve and apparatus using same. European Patent EP1160661, 2001.

19. OKEYA, K., AND SAKURAI, K. Power analysis breaks elliptic curve cryptosystems even secure against the timing attack. In *Progress in Cryptology – INDOCRYPT 2000* (2000), B. K. Roy and E. Okamoto, Eds., vol. 1977 of *Lecture Notes in Computer Science*, pp. 178–190.

20. OKEYA, K., AND SAKURAI, K. A second-order DPA attack breaks a window-method based countermeasure against side channel attacks. In *Information Security – ISC 2002* (these proceedings), A. H. Chan and V. Gligor, Eds.

21. SCHINDLER, W. A combined timing and power attack. In *Public Key Cryptography – PKC 2002* (2002), D. Naccache and P. Paillier, Eds., vol. 2274 of *Lecture Notes in Computer Science*, pp. 263–279.

22. VADEKAR, A., AND LAMBERT, R. J. Timing attack resistant cryptographic system. Patent Cooperation Treaty (PCT) Publication WO 00/05837, 2000.

23. VANSTONE, S. A., AND GALLANT, R. P. Power signature attack resistant cryptography. Patent Cooperation Treaty (PCT) Publication WO 00/25204, 2000.

24. WALTER, C. D., AND THOMPSON, S. Distinguishing exponent digits by observing modular subtractions. In *Progress in Cryptology – CT-RSA 2001* (2001), D. Naccache, Ed., vol. 2020 of *Lecture Notes in Computer Science*, pp. 192–207.

25. YAO, A. C.-C. On the evaluation of powers. *SIAM Journal on Computing 5* (1976), 100–103.

Automated Analysis of Some Security Mechanisms of SCEP⋆

Fabio Martinelli, Marinella Petrocchi, and Anna Vaccarelli

Istituto per l'Informatica e la Telematica
Consiglio Nazionale delle Ricerche
Via G.Moruzzi 1 - Pisa, Italy.
{Fabio.Martinelli, Marinella.Petrocchi, Anna.Vaccarelli}@iit.cnr.it

Abstract. The paper analyzes SCEP, the Simple Certificate Enrollment Procedure, a two-way communication protocol to manage the secure emission of digital certificates to network devices. The protocol provides a consistent method
of requesting and receiving certificates from different Certification Authorities by
offering an open and scalable solution for deploying certificates which can be ben-
eficial to all network devices and IPSEC software solutions. We formally analyze
SCEP through a software tool for the automatic analysis of cryptographic protocols able to discover, at a conceptual level, attacks against security procedures.
Our method of survey contributes towards a better understanding of the structure
and aims of a protocol both for developers, analyzers and final users.

1   Introduction

The aim of this paper is to highlight how formal methods can be useful to better define
the security mechanisms and aims of security protocols and to offer a formal description
of SCEP[1], the Simple Certificate Enrollment Protocol. To the best of our knowledge,
this is the first attempt to give a formal description of this protocol, and we based our
study on the Internet Draft [7][2].

The SCEP protocol gives specifications for digital certificate enrollment, access and
revocation, for certificates and CRL queries. SCEP was developed for the distribution
of digital certificates to network devices such as routers and gateways. It seems to
offer a valid support for the development of Virtual Private Networks - VPNs - which
are communication networks realized on a public infrastructure such as the Internet.
Using a VPN involves encrypting data before sending it through the public network and
decrypting it at the receiving end, in order to achieve one or more of the following goals:

⋆ Work partially supported by Microsoft Research Europe (Cambridge); by MIUR project "ME-
FISTO: Metodi Formali per la Sicurezza ed il Tempo"; by MIUR project "Tecniche e Strumenti
Software per l'Analisi della Sicurezza delle Comunicazioni in Applicazioni Telematiche di In-
teresse Economico e Sociale"; by CNR project "Strumenti, Ambienti ed Applicazioni Innovative
per la Società dell'Informazione"; by CSP project "SeTAPS: Strumenti e Tecniche per l'Analisi
di Protocolli di Sicurezza".

[1] SCEP is the evolution of specifications developed by Verisign Inc. and Cisco Systems and it is
commercially available in both client and CA implementations.

[2] Released on May 15, 2002, it will expire on November 15, 2002. As declared by the same
authors, it has to be considered as a "work in progress".

A.H. Chan and V. Gligor (Eds.): ISC 2002, LNCS 2433, pp. 414–427, 2002.
© Springer-Verlag Berlin Heidelberg 2002

- connect users securely to their own corporate access (remote access);
- link branch offices to an enterprise network (intranet);
- extend existing infrastructure to include partners and customers (extranet).

Ideally, a VPN should behave similarly to a private network. Looking at the goals of a VPN, authentication ensures the identity of all communicating parties, may they be individual or computer resources. To correctly identify a communicating party, VPNs typically use preshared keys, but could use digital certificates, [5]. Digital certificates were born in the field of public key cryptosystems, [14]: roughly, public key cryptosystems consist of an encryption function E, a decryption function D and a pair of keys. Each pair consists of a public key k and a private key k^{-1} and each user of a public key cryptosystem holds his own pair. What is encoded with one key, can only be decoded with the other. The adjective "public" means that everyone (non only the owner of the key pair) is allowed to know the public key and so to use it. The adjective "private" means that only the user that holds that pair knows the private key which remains a closely guarded secret. These cryptographic systems may be used to guarantee both confidentiality and authentication of origin:

- Confidentiality: the sender of a message m can encrypt it with the receiver's public key k; the receiver will decrypt it with his private key k^{-1}.
- Authentication of origin: the sender encrypts message m with his private key k^{-1}; the receiver decrypts the encrypted message with the sender's public key. Authentication of origin should be guaranteed by the fact that only the sender knows the private key and thus only he could generate the encryption. These concepts are the basis for digital signature schemes, e.g. [13].

Basically, a digital certificate is an electronic document that links an identity (i.e. a person or a machine) and a public key. It is issued by a Certification Authority (CA) that can vouch for an individual identity. The way CA vouches for such links is to digitally sign the issued certificate with CA's private key. Typically, a digital certificate contains a public key, information specific to the user (a name, a company, an IP address, etc.), information specific to the Certification Authority issuer, a validity period (starting date - finishing date) and additional management information.

The paper is organized as follows. In Section 2, we present the usual scenario of security protocols and give an idea of our analysis method. In Section 3, we describe the structures of messages exchanged between parties during the phase of SCEP enrollment. Section 4 highlights the motivations for the need of some forms of correctness checks in SCEP specifications; without them, the protocol would be vulnerable to attack by adversaries. Finally, Section 5 gives some conclusions. Below, we summarize the main contributions of this paper.

1.1 Contributions

The main contributions of this paper are the following:

- (Part of) the SCEP Protocol has been formally analyzed and the results are reported in this paper. With regard to the security properties listed in the draft we did not find attacks, at least in a limited analysis scenario consisting of a finite number of participants. While this does not suffice to ensure the absolute security of the protocol in all circumstances, it does enhance the reliability of SCEP. However, we noticed a vulnerability concerning the emission of two digital certificates with the same subject name - public key binding.

- The application of automated verification tools is useful to better understand how certain mechanisms and checks ensure certain security features of communication protocols. This might be useful in revealing causes of omitted or erroneously implemented security checks. It might be also useful to render more comprehensive for those less expert some statements written in technical documents, where often it is asserted that a security check is necessary but rarely is the reason given. In order to understand the reason, we simply omit the security check in the description of the protocol, run the verification tool and wait for the result of the analysis. This methodology is particularly useful to study security protocols in a formal way by suitably changing the protocol description in order to simulate possible faults and check the relative effect (as in the common "Failure Model and Effect Assessment (FMEA)" adopted in software engineering). Our next step will be to systematically create such case studies in the security protocol analysis framework as done in [2] for safety in critical systems.

2   Analysis Approach

In standard communication protocols all interactions are achieved by means of communications, i.e. parties communicate with each other by exchanging a sequence of messages on channels of the net. Talking about security communication protocols, cryptographic functions are introduced in the structures of messages in order to guarantee the satisfaction of certain security properties. Common security properties are *secrecy* (i.e. confidentiality of exchanged messages: nobody except the legitimate participants should know the content of an exchanged secret message), *message authenticity* (i.e. no alteration of the content of a message) and *entity authentication* (i.e. capability of identifying other parties during a communication). Given the sensitive nature of the information possibly exchanged in the run of a protocol (e.g. credit card numbers, passwords, current account numbers) it appears reasonable to consider the presence in the net of third malicious parties: such intruders try to interfere with the normal execution of the protocol in order to achieve advantages for themselves. Due to the unpredictable behavior of such intruders, the design of distributed security protocols is very challenging. Several protocols that have appeared in scientific literature have been found to be flawed (e.g., see [8,15]) and this also happens by assuming the underlying cryptographic primitives reliable. Indeed, we may have some subtle attacks depending on how messages are exchanged over the network. Several methodologies for the analysis of security protocols have been developed in recent years, e.g. [1,3,9,11].

For our analysis we consider honest participants S of a protocol plus an intruder X, as a *compound system* $S|X$, i.e. a system whose components run in parallel and that can interact. Basically, our aim consists in verifying that a certain security property is satisfied by the compound system. We investigate whether, for every possible active intruder X, $S|X$ satisfies that property.

An operational language is adopted for the description of the protocols. It is a CCS process algebra style language, [12], with slight variations for the treatment of cryptographic functions, [10]. We do not need *a priori* any intruder specification and moreover we make no assumption on its behavior, X can be any term of the algebra. As the other protocol participants, X has a set of message manipulating rules that are used to model cryptographic functions such as encryption and decryption. The intruder has the capability to send and receive messages over net channels to and from other components of the system and also intercept and fake messages. He derives new messages from his initial knowledge: the set of messages we assume the intruder is in possession of at the beginning of the computation and other intercepted information obtained during the run of the protocol. Data encryption is assumed to be "opaque", i.e. a message encrypted with the public key of i cannot be decrypted by anyone but the person who knows the correspondent private key (unless the decryption key is compromised). An adversary can intercept and store an encrypted message and replay it later, but the structure of the message is not accessible to him, i.e. he cannot split the encrypted message unless he knows the decryption key. The intruder's knowledge grows as the computation evolves: we consider whether this knowledge satisfies, at a certain point of the computation, a predicate based on a specific security property. In the case of a positive answer, our analysis reports an attack against the security property. In other words, an attack is possible when X is able to force the execution of protocol to be performed in a different way, by cheating the honest parties. The development of the theory has lead to the implementation of a tool for the analysis of distributed systems with finite behavior, the Partial Model Checking Security Analyzer (PAMoCHSA), [4,6].

Following, we give the standard notation with which security protocols are usually specified in literature - for information about the operational language used to describe the protocol specifications we refer to [10] - in this paper we prefer to follow a more intuitive notation.

We then consider, with a simple example, the uncertainty about protocol specifications correctness. We will show how the security properties of a protocol may be broken without implementing cryptanalysis.

2.1 Notation

We consider a set of agents able to send and receive messages. We represent the sending and reception of a message in this way: $i \quad A \mapsto B : msg$, where msg is the exchanged message, i is the i-th communication channel, on which the exchange takes place. A and B are the sender and the receiver of msg.

As already outlined, since the net is public, we have to consider the presence of a malicious agent X, that can intercept and fake messages:

$$(1) \quad X(A) \mapsto B : msg$$
$$(2) \quad A \mapsto X(B) : msg$$

Notation (1) describes intruder X that sends a message msg to party B pretending to be party A (forgery); (2) denotes: msg, originally intended for B, is actually intercepted by X (interception).

We will use the following notation throughout the paper:

$$name_i, pin_i, etc := Name\ of\ party\ i,\ password\ of\ party\ i,\ etc.$$
$$pk_i, pk_i^{-1} \qquad := respectively,\ public\ and\ private\ key\ of\ party\ i$$
$$\{...\}_{pk_i^{-1}} \qquad := message\ signed\ by\ party\ i$$
$$\{...\}_{pk_i} \qquad := message\ encrypted\ by\ public\ key\ of\ party\ i$$
$$\{...\}_{KEY} \qquad := message\ encrypted\ by\ symmetric\ key\ KEY$$
$$Hash\{...\} \qquad := MD5\ fingerprint$$

Hash functions are a family of functions with the following main properties: i) they take as input a message of arbitrary length and produce as output a fixed length "fingerprint" of the input; ii) they are not-reversible (with high probability); iii) it is computationally infeasible to produce two messages having the same fingerprint or to produce any message having a given prespecified target fingerprint. The *Hash* function used in the SCEP implementation is MD5. We refer to the output of the MD5 *Hash* function as *MD5 fingerprint*.

2.2 A Simple Example

Consider the following example, where a user A wants to send to his $Bank$ an order to move money on the account of another user X. A may send the message "*move $1000 to X's account*" signed with its private key pk_A^{-1}:

$$A \mapsto Bank : \{\text{move \$1000 to X's account}\}_{pk_A^{-1}}$$

In communication networks, it is not possible to determine the origin of messages. This must be deduced by the content of the message itself. Since this message is signed with the private key of A, the $Bank$ should be sure that the message has been originated by A and the order is legitimate. Thus, the $Bank$ makes the money transfer. Suppose that X eaves-drops on this message. He can send it again to the $Bank$, i.e.:

$$X(A) \mapsto Bank : \{\text{move \$1000 to X's account}\}_{pk_A^{-1}}$$

The $Bank$ is unable to be sure of the sender of the message, and the signature of this message is still valid. Eventually, X gets $2000. Thus, even without breaking cryptography, the protocol is attacked.

3 The SCEP Enrollment Phase

We formally describe the Simple Certificate Enrollment Procedure (SCEP), a two-way communication protocol whose goal is the secure issuance of certificates to network devices, such as routers and gateways, using existing technology. Up to today, the last document describing SCEP is an Internet Draft available on Internet at [7]. The protocol is one of the first to be adopted by numerous vendors because it offers a common method of enrolling (i.e. requesting and receiving digital certificates) from different Certification Authorities.

SCEP supports the following operations:

– CA public key distributions;

- Certificate Enrollment;
- Certificate Revocation;
- Certificate and CRL query.

In the following, we mainly focus our attention on the enrollment phase. An enrollment procedure consists of two main phases:

- the SCEP client, identified by a subject name consisting of the Fully Qualified Domain Name (i.e. alice.somewhere.com), asks for a digital certificate. It composes its certificate request and sends it to a Certification Authority Server (CA), an entity which issues certificates and whose name will be declared in the certificate issuer name field.
- The Certification Authority tests the correctness of the received request[3]; in case of positive outcome, CA issues the certificate, digitally signs it and sends it to the applicant.

The secrecy and integrity of the private key of the Certification Authority must be preserved. (This is why the CA Server should be an off-line machine. In this case, communications between CA and the applicant pass through an on-line Registration Authority Server RA. In this paper, CA Server and RA Server are specified as one entity).

We will refer to SCEP client as user U. U generates its pair of asymmetric keys with a specific key usage (i.e. only for encryption, only for digital signature, or both). The public key to be certified and the key usage are conveyed to CA through the certificate enrollment request.

3.1 User Certificate Request

After the generation of the keys and having obtained the CA's certificate, necessary to retrieve CA's Public Key in order to enroll, the user generates its request using PKCS#10 and sends it to the CA exploiting PKCS#7. PKCS#10 and PKCS#7 were issued by RSA Labs and made public and modifiable as with PKCS#i (Public-Key Cryptography Standards). They are "de facto" standards: PKCS#10 describing the syntax for certification requests and PKCS#7 defining formats to represent data with the addition of cryptographic information, i.e. encrypted data or digital signatures. PKCS#7 provides different kinds of formats, like Signed Data (data plus digital signatures), Enveloped Data (encrypted data plus encrypted key by means of RSA), Degenerated Mode (for the distribution of certificates). Briefly, a PKCS#10 request can be formalized as follows:

$$PKCS\#10 := \{name_U, pk_U, pin_U, \{name_U, pk_U, pin_U\}_{pk_U^{-1}}\}$$

where $name_U$ is the Subject Name of the user U (Fully Qualified Domain Name plus IP Address), pk_U is the public key to be certified and pin_U is a secret that associates the subject name to that certificate request[4].

---

[3] In subsection 3.2 it is explained how CA tests the correctness of the request.

[4] This pin is used for certificate revocation (currently implemented as a manual process: User phones a CA Operator asking for revocation of its certificate, the operator replies asking for the challenge password, and if it coincides with the one contained in PKCS#10 request, the certificate will be revoked). The pin can also be used to authenticate the identity of User U, as explained in subsection 3.2.

PKCS#10 is completed by adding the digital signature of the 3-tuple Subject Name, Public Key and Pin, using the User Private Key. This signature acts as a Proof of Possession (POP), i.e. once CA has verified the signature, it has proof that whoever originated the signature holds the corresponding private key. The key usage is specified in the PKCS#10; in our formalization the key usage is not explicitly declared, the usage is intended for both encryption and signature.

Upon composing PKCS#10, U builds the Enveloped Data[5], exploiting PKCS#7 technologies:

$$EnvelopedData := \{PKCS\#10\}_{KEY}, \{KEY\}_{pk_{CA}}$$

where KEY is a randomly generated symmetric key. The construction of Enveloped Data provides the encryption of KEY with the public key of the CA, pk_{CA}, so that only CA can retrieve KEY and successively obtain the PKCS#10 as a clear-text.

To complete the enrollment request, U creates Signed Data, basically consisting of:

$$SignedData := \{EnvelopedData, \{ID, Nonce\}_{pk_U^{-1}}\}$$

- The aim of the Transaction Identifier ID is to uniquely identify the transaction. ID is the MD5 fingerprint of the public key to be certified.
- $Nonce$ is a random number generated by U, and its aim is to prove the freshness of the response from the CA to the user request.

$ID, Nonce$ are sent as "authenticated attributes" of PKCS#7, signed with private key of U. Answers[6] of CA to U's enrollment request can be of three kinds:

1. SUCCESS response: CA successfully emits the requested certificate;
2. PENDING response: CA is configured to act in manual mode. Before the emission, it has to carry out some checks to verify enrollment request correctness;
3. FAILURE response: checks have produced a negative result and CA does not emit the certificate.

When User receives a response from CA containing a *pending* "status", it can enter into polling mode, i.e. it can periodically send to CA *Get Cert Initial* messages, pressing for the certificate emission. The structure of a *Get Cert Initial* message is substantially the following:

$$GetCertInitial := \{\{name_U, ID\}_{KEY}, \{KEY\}_{pk_{CA}}, \{Nonce\}_{pk_U^{-1}}\}$$

3.2 Modeling the Enrollment Procedure

For the sake of clarity, it is worth spending a few words on User Authentication. In protocols that use public key cryptography, the association between the public keys and the identities with which they are associated must be authenticated in a secure manner. SCEP provides two authentication methods: a manual one and one based on a pre-shared secret. In manual mode, once a certificate request has been sent to CA, U has to wait until its identity can be verified using any reliable out of band method. In [7] it is suggested

---

[5] For the sake of readability the structures of Enveloped Data, Signed Data and Get Cert Initial message here are simplified (without however affecting the results of our analysis).

[6] These answers contain the same ID and $Nonce$ present in User Certificate Request.

that CA generates the MD5 fingerprint of the PKCS#10 retrieved from the User request and compares it with the one computed by the User itself. During this period, the state of the whole transaction is set to "PENDING".

Otherwise, CA can choose to act in automatic mode: before any request takes place, CA should distribute a pre-shared secret to the User - the secret is assumed to be unique for each User (the way in which the distribution takes place is subject to the CA policy). When creating an enrollment request, the User will insert the secret in the PKCS#10 (later on we refer to this secret as pin_U). Upon receiving the request, CA should check the correspondence between pin_U and the subject name included in the PKCS#10.

Enrollment procedure with out-of-band User Authentication. Formally, the enrollment procedure with manual authentication of the User can be described as follows:

Table 1. SCEP Enrollment Phase with out-of-band User Authentication.

$$1 \; U \mapsto CA : \{name_U, pk_U, pin_U, \{....\}_{pk_U^{-1}}\}_{KEY}, \{KEY\}_{pk_{CA}}, \{ID_U, Nonce_U\}_{pk_U^{-1}}$$
$$2 \; CA \mapsto U : \{ID_U, Nonce_U, \text{"pending"}\}_{pk_{CA}^{-1}}$$
$$3 \; U \mapsto CA : \{name_U, ID_U\}_{KEY}, \{KEY\}_{pk_{CA}}, \{Nonce1_U\}_{pk_U^{-1}}$$
$$4 \; CA \mapsto U : Hash\{name_U, pk_U, pin_U, \{....\}_{pk_U^{-1}}\}$$
$$5 \; U \mapsto CA : Comparison : ok/ko$$
$$6 \; CA \mapsto U : \{\{name_U, pk_U\}_{pk_{CA}^{-1}}\}_{KEY1}, \{KEY1\}_{pk_U}, \{Nonce1_U\}_{pk_{CA}^{-1}}$$

1. U connects to CA and sends enveloped PKCS#10 and authenticated attributes. ID_U is the MD5 fingerprint of pk_U. $Nonce_U$ is inserted in the authenticated attributes to prevent replay attacks from the user point of view. In this procedure, every answer from CA to U has to contain the same nonce of the previous message from U to CA.
2. CA is configured to manually authenticate the end entity, so it sends a PKCS#7 message back to U containing only authenticated attributes: "status" of transaction set to *pending*, same transaction identifier and same nonce as in the user request.
3. Upon receiving a pending status, U enters into polling mode by periodically sending *Get Cert Initial* messages to CA, until he either receives the certificate or rejection or he simply times out. (Here, we suppose user successfully obtains its certificate after the sending of the first *Get Cert Initial.*)
4. Communications over channels 4 and 5 should be intended out of band, i.e. not on the network. (The analysis tool allows these two channels to be hidden from the intruder, in order to simulate a secure communication between CA and users). This reliable out of band communication could be by phone or by surface mail. In any case, CA must securely contact U and communicate the MD5 fingerprint of the PKCS#10 received in Message 1 (Message 4). Thereafter, the user can compare the fingerprint with the one computed from its original PKCS#10 (Message 5).

5. User gives a positive or negative answer to the CA, depending on the result of the comparison.
6. Upon receiving a positive answer from the User regarding the comparison of the MD5 fingerprints, CA emits the certificate. The issued certificate is formalized here with the name of the User and its public key signed by CA's private key, $\{name_U, pk_U\}_{pk_{ca}^{-1}}$. The choice in SCEP for the distribution of certificates is PKCS#7 Degenerated Mode, enveloped and followed by the same user nonce contained in the previous *Get Cert Initial*.

Enrollment Procedure with Automatic User Authentication. When a pre-shared secret scheme is used, the enrollment procedure is simply, (Tab. 2). User Authentication is subject to the correspondence between pin_U and $name_U$.

Table 2. SCEP Enrollment Phase with Automatic User Authentication.

$$1\ U \mapsto CA : \{name_U, pk_U, pin_U, \{...\}_{pk_U^{-1}}\}_{KEY}, \{KEY\}_{pk_{CA}}, \{ID_U, Nonce_U\}_{pk_U^{-1}}$$
$$2\ CA \mapsto U : \{\{name_U, pk_U\}_{pk_{CA}^{-1}}\}_{KEY1}, \{KEY1\}_{pk_U}, \{Nonce_U\}_{pk_{CA}^{-1}}$$

4   Analysis

A formal analysis of security protocols turns out to be a useful mechanism to better understand motivations and choices for intrinsic structures of messages specified in Internet standards and drafts.

The security goals of SCEP are that no adversary can:

1. subvert the public key/identity binding from that intended;
2. discover the identity information in the enrollment requests and issued certificates;
3. cause the revocation of certificates with any non-negligible probability.

The first and second goals are met through the use of PKCS#7 and PKCS#10 encryption and digital signatures using authenticated public keys. The third goal is met through the use of a Challenge Password for revocation.

The revocation phase is not a concern to the scope of this paper but rather we consider the phase of enrollment. We formally analyze both the SCEP enrollment procedure with manual authentication of the User and the automatic procedure.

In our experiments, we consider a finite number of processes each having finite behavior. Note that, with regard to this scenario, SCEP guarantees the correct emission of certificates (i.e. Properties 1 and 2 hold).

However, we will focus our attention on particular checks suggested in [7], in order to understand some security mechanisms and the possible consequences of their absence.

In subsection 4.1 we consider the security mechanisms suggested in the Internet Draft to achieve Property 1, namely what mechanisms are involved and whether without them it would be possible to emit a certificate with a errand correspondence between the identity and the public key to be certified.

The possibility of issuing two (or more) certificates with same subject name - public key - key usage binding whose validity periods overlap is also considered. In subsection 4.2 we consider why the event should be avoided, what [7] suggests and what could happen without these suggestions.

4.1 Relevance of User Authentication

One of the security goals of SCEP is that no intruder can force CA to emit erroneous certificates in which the public key / identity binding is subverted. Here, we perform a simple analysis about the security of SCEP with out-of-band User Authentication against an active enemy that may try to interfere. We make no assumption about the behavior of this enemy. In principle, he is able to listen to, intercept and fake communications between legitimate users and CAs. We are going to check whether CA is able to emit certificates in which the name of a legitimate user is tied to a public key provided by an enemy. This is an important question, since if CA emits such a certificate it could cause the so called "*responsibility* attack". Indeed, someone could sign something and make you responsible for that signature.

We checked whether the enrollment procedure described in Tab. 1 allows the emission of a wrong certificate like $\{name_U, pk_X\}_{pk_{ca}^{-1}}$. We checked the specifications that follow the Internet Draft (i.e. including the comparison of the PKCS#10 fingerprints). The output of the tool confirms the correct emission of the certificate.

We check another specification, modified in such a way that there is no MD5 fingerprint comparison. This specification could represent either the fact that CA does not contact the User to communicate the received fingerprint (no Message 4 in Tab. 1) or the fact that the User itself omits the comparison (no Message 5 in Tab. 1). In this case, the protocol results vulnerable to a "man in the middle" attack. The tool automatically unveils the attack.

The attack procedure consists of the following steps (see also Table 3):

1. U connects to CA as in a normal execution, but its request is intercepted by X.
2. X sends to CA a certificate request containing the name of User U.
3. CA's answer contains a pending status.
4. U enters into polling mode. Its *Get Cert Initial* message is intercepted by X.
5. X simulates the polling mode.
6. Something went wrong with the comparison of MD5 fingerprint. It is possible to issue the certificate related to X request.

Note 1. The particular structure of messages in SCEP helps U to discover that he actually receives a fake certificate. Upon receiving CA's answer containing the certificate (message 6), U will not be able to open the envelope, since the symmetric key $KEY1$ is encrypted with the wrong key, pk_X. In any case, the enemy could intercept message 6, so

Table 3. No MD5 fingerprint comparison: X is able to force the emission of a certificate where its public key is tied to the name of the User U.

$$1\ U \mapsto X(CA) : \{name_U, pk_U, pin_U, \{...\}_{pk_U^{-1}}\}_{KEY}, \{KEY\}_{pk_{CA}}, \{ID_U, Nonce_U\}_{pk_U^{-1}}$$

$$2\ X(U) \mapsto CA : \{name_U, pk_X, pin_X, \{name_U, pk_X, pin_X\}_{pk_X^{-1}}\}_{KEY_X}, \{KEY_X\}_{pk_{CA}},$$
$$\{ID_X, Nonce_U\}_{pk_X^{-1}}$$

$$3\ CA \mapsto U \quad : \{ID_X, Nonce_U, \text{``pending''}\}_{pk_{CA}^{-1}}$$

$$4\ U \mapsto X(CA) : \{name_U, ID_U\}_{KEY}, \{KEY\}_{pk_{CA}}, \{Nonce1_U\}_{pk_U^{-1}}$$

$$5\ X(U) \mapsto CA : \{name_U, ID_X\}_{KEY_X}, \{KEY_X\}_{pk_{CA}}, \{Nonce1_U\}_{pk_X^{-1}}$$

$$6\ CA \mapsto U \quad : \{\{name_U, pk_X\}_{pk_{CA}^{-1}}\}_{KEY1}, \{KEY1\}_{pk_X}, \{Nonce1_U\}_{pk_{CA}^{-1}}$$

that the user does not receive the certificate. In these circumstances, the user presumably sends to CA a sequence of *GetCertInitial* messages, pressing for the certificate. The possible interceptions of *Get Cert Initial* messages by the intruder and the consequent time out interrupt of U's connection may lead U to realize that something wrong has happened.

4.2   How to Avoid the Issuance of Two Identical Certificates

For User Authentication in automatic enrollment, (Tab.2), it is recommended the use of a pre-shared secret scheme. The pre-shared secret is represented in our formalization by pin_U. As an enrollment request is received by CA server, it appears reasonable to verify the right correspondence between the applicant identity and its related secret pin_U. Further, [7] encourages CAs to enforce *certificate-name uniqueness*: at any time, there will be only one pair of keys for a given subject name and key usage combination[7]. We prefer to name the property *weak uniqueness*: it is not possible to emit two (or more) valid certificates with same subject name, public key and key usage whose validity periods overlap. The *weak uniqueness* property is in contrast with another property: it is *never* possible to emit two (or more) certificates with same subject name, public key and key usage. We call the last property *strong uniqueness*.

   In SCEP specifications U is allowed to re-use the same request when it times out from polling for a pending request, or some errors in the network occur and the connection between U and CA goes down. In any case, the second request should not create a new transaction nor should the second request be rejected. So what should the request re-emission lead to? There are some possibilities expressed in the draft:

 – If CA has already emitted the certificate and the re-emission of the request occurs less than halfway through the validity time of an existing certificate, then CA
   should realize that something went wrong in the first sending of the certificate. It

---

[7] Uniqueness is not mandatory in the draft, but the draft itself claims that all current SCEP client implementations expect the property. Moreover, the authors of the draft made examples by assuming uniqueness holds. Thus, we perform our analysis assuming the property holds.

can possibly re-send the same certificate to the applicant, without issuing another certificate.

- If CA has already emitted the certificate, and the re-emission of the request occurs more than halfway through the validity time of an existing certificate, this can be interpreted by CA as a renewal request. In that case, CA should have previously revoked the existing certificate[8].
- If CA has not yet emitted the certificate, the reception of the same request should be taken by CA as another $GetCertInitial$ message, instead of a request for a new enrollment.

Let us consider the hypothesis that CA emitted two certificates with the same subject name U, the same public key and key usage. They will differ in the serial number, say $sn1$ and $sn2$, and the respective validity periods will overlap. Suppose also that X was able to force CA to issue the last certificate, so X is conscious of its existence, while U is not. There are multiple reasons for preventing the re-transmission of the same data from creating a second certificate. The most significant reasons, according to us, are cited below:

- considering a large scale application scenario, the computational cost in generating and signing unused certificates can be high;
- a document digitally signed by U (i.e. by the public key corresponding to U's private key) could be valid longer than expected, because the not already expired certificate would validate the signature;
- U could maliciously extend his own certificate validity even when he is purposely denied the right to a new certificate; for example in a corporate environment, an employee might have access to a certain facility but only for a limited time.

Each public key to be certified is strictly connected to the Transaction Identifier ID (we remind that ID is the MD5 hash of the public key). To guarantee the *weak uniqueness* property we assume that CA records the pair $(name_U, ID_U)$.

We checked whether the automatic enrollment procedure in Tab. 2 allows the emission of two identical certificates whose validity periods overlap. We checked a specifications that expect the *weak uniqueness* property (i.e. a specifications including the record of the pair $(name_U, ID_U)$). The output of the tool confirms that it is not possible to emit two identical certificates.

We checked another specification, modified in such a way that CA omits to record the pair $(name_U, ID_U)$. An intruder X could eavesdrop on a legitimate certificate request and simply repeat it later. In this way, X can force CA to issue two identical certificates - apart from the serial number. The replay attack reported by the tool is shown in Tab. 4. Basically, the attack procedure consists of the following steps:

1. U connects to CA as usual. Its request is eavesdropped by X.
2. X connects to CA and repeats U certificate request.
3. CA emits a first valid certificate with serial number sn_1.
4. CA emits a second valid certificate with a different serial number, because it omits checks on crucial fields in the received requests. X is able to intercept the message.

Table 4. Replay Attack: if CA does not record the Transaction Identifier, the intruder is able to force the emission of a double certificate.

$1\ U \mapsto CA$	$: \{name_U, pk_U, pin_U, \{...\}_{pk_U^{-1}}\}_{KEY}, \{KEY\}_{pk_{CA}}, \{ID_U, Nonce_U\}_{pk_U^{-1}}$
$2\ X(U) \mapsto CA$	$: \{name_U, pk_U, pin_U, \{...\}_{pk_U^{-1}}\}_{KEY}, \{KEY\}_{pk_{CA}}, \{ID_U, Nonce_U\}_{pk_U^{-1}}$
$3\ CA \mapsto U$	$: \{\{name_U, pk_U, sn_1\}_{pk_{CA}^{-1}}\}_{KEY1}, \{KEY1\}_{pk_U}, \{Nonce_U\}_{pk_{CA}^{-1}}$
$4\ CA \mapsto X(U)$	$: \{\{name_U, pk_U, sn_2\}_{pk_{CA}^{-1}}\}_{KEY2}, \{KEY2\}_{pk_U}, \{Nonce_U\}_{pk_{CA}^{-1}}$

Note 2. The user itself may unconsciously contribute towards the emission of identical certificates. Suppose the user times out or the connection with the CA Server goes down for some reason. Under these circumstances CA could emit a first certificate but U may not receive anything because of the connection crash or time out. Consequently, U is allowed to re-issue the same request and the absence of checks by CA may lead to the emission of a double certificate.

Note 3. In the discussion above, we investigated the existence of certificates whose validity periods overlap. When automatic enrollment is used, *weak uniqueness* property is not enough to protect against replay attacks on expired certificates requests. An intruder X could eavesdrop on a legitimate certificate request. The automatic procedure will lead to the emission of a legitimate certificate, say $\{name_U, pk_U\}_{pk_{ca}^{-1}}$. The intruder may send the replay of the request once the legitimate certificate has been expired. This can cause a new certificate to be issued with the same subject name - public key binding. The existence of the last certificate may cause a document previously signed by U to be valid longer than expected. To avoid this vulnerability CAs should guarantee the *strong uniqueness* property.

5   Concluding Remarks

In this paper we gave a formalization of the SCEP protocol enrollment phase and performed the analysis of part of the protocol's security properties by means of a software tool. With regard to a limited scenario (finite number of processes with a finite behavior), we did not find any attack, meaning the analyzed properties hold. When automatic enrollment is used, we found a vulnerability concerning a replay attack on expired certificates requests. To deep understand certain security mechanisms in SCEP specifications, we purposely omitted particular checks suggested in the draft in some of our experiments. As a consequence, an attack regarding the emission of certificates with the public key/identity binding subverted and an attack concerning duplicate valid certificates were automatically detected. Since the technique is general and can be applied to several cryptographic protocols, it turns out to be a valid support for the analysis of RFCs, drafts and commercial products.

---

[8] Before revoking the existing certificate, CA should presumably contact the user for confirmation, but this is not specified in [7].

Acknowledgements. We would like to thank the anonymous referees for their help in the presentation of the paper. We also thank Claud Anticoli for his valued collaboration as proof reader.

References

1. M. Abadi and A.D. Gordon. Reasoning about Cryptographic Protocols in the Spi Calculus. In *Proc. of CONCUR'97*, volume 1243 LNCS, pages 59–73. Springer, 1997.
2. T. Cichocki and J. Gorski. Formal Support for Fault Modeling and Analysis. In *Proc. of SAFECOMP'01*, volume 2187 LNCS, pages 190–199. Springer, 2001.
3. R. Focardi, R. Gorrieri, and F. Martinelli. Non Interference for the Analysis of Cryptographic Protocols. In *Proc. of ICALP'00*, volume 1853 LNCS, pages 354–372. Springer, 2000.
4. A. Giani, F. Martinelli, M. Petrocchi, and A. Vaccarelli. A Case Study with PaMoChSA: a Tool for the Automatic Analysis of Cryptographic Protocols. In *Proc. of SCI-ISAS'01*, volume 5, Orlando, July 2001.
5. R. Housley, W. Ford, W. Polk, and D. Solo. RFC 2459: Internet X.509 Public Key Infrastructure Certificate and CRL Profile, IETF, 1999. http://www.ietf.org/rfc/rfc2459.txt.
6. http://pmartinelli1.iat.cnr.it:8080/pamochsa.htm.
7. X. Liu, C. Madson, D. McGrew, and A. Nourse. Internet Draft: draft-nourse-scep-06, Cisco Systems, 2002. http://www.vpnc.org/draft-nourse-scep.
8. G. Lowe and A. W. Roscoe. Using CSP to Detect Errors in the TMN protocol. *Software Engineering*, 23(10):659–669, 1997.
9. D. Marchignoli and F. Martinelli. Automatic Verification of Cryptographic Protocols through Compositional Analysis Techniques. In *Proc. of TACAS'99*, volume 1579 LNCS, 1999.
10. F. Martinelli. Analysis of Security Protocols as Open Systems. *Theoretical Computer Science (to appear)*. A preliminary version in ICTCS, World Scientific, pages 304–315, 1998.
11. C. Meadows. Formal Verification of Cryptographic Protocols: a Survey. In *ASIACRYPT'94: Advances in Cryptology*, volume 917 LNCS, pages 135–150. Springer, 1995.
12. R. Milner. *Communication and Concurrency*. Prentice Hall, 1989.
13. R. Rivest, A. Shamir, and L. Adleman. A Method for Obtaining Digital Signatures and Public Key Cryptosystems. *Comm. of the ACM*, 21(2):120–126, 1978.
14. F.B. Schneider. *Applied Cryptography*. J. Wiley & Sons, Inc, 1996.
15. V. Shmatikov and U. Stern. Efficient Finite State Analysis for Large Security Protocols. In *Proc. of CSFW'98*, pages 105–116. IEEE Computer Society Press, 1998.

An Attack on a Protocol for Certified Delivery

José R.M. Monteiro[1,2] and Ricardo Dahab[1]

[1] Institute of Computing, University of Campinas
Caixa Postal 6176, CEP 13084-971, Campinas – SP – BRASIL
{monteiro,rdahab}@ic.unicamp.br
[2] Cepesc/DT/ABIN, SPS – Área 5, Quadra 1, Bloco V
CEP 70610-200, Brasília, DF – BRASIL

Abstract. We show that the protocol for certified mail delivery of Ferrer-Gomila and others [2] may exhibit contradictory behavior when the recipient is not well behaved. As a consequence, properties such as non-repudiation of reception and fairness may not hold. We also present a solution for this weakness which has minimal cost.

1 Introduction

Fair exchange protocols provide communicating parties with assurances regarding the outcome of the exchange: each party receives the item it expects if and only if the other party also gets his or hers. Exchanges are typical of distributed system environments, where negotiations are carried over insecure channels, between mutually trusting parties (except, perhaps, for byzantine-like agreements). We are interested, however, in those exchanges which occur over the Internet between non-trusting parties, usually unknown to each other. More specifically, we are concerned with *optimistic fair exchange protocols*, with the participation of a trusted third party (TTP). The role of a TTP in an optimistic protocol is restricted to resolving conflicts between the parties, as opposed to being involved in every communication between them, thus reducing the occurrence of bottlenecks involving the TTP. In an environment of mostly well-behaved parties, this approach results in much greater efficiency.

We refer to conflicts between the parties as *exceptions*. Such exceptions may arise either from misbehavior by one of the parties, or from interference by a third party, or from faults in the communication channel. Whatever the cause, it may be unknown to the parties, who may have the TTP as their last resort for settling a dispute. A protocol possesses the *timeliness* property if the parties are guaranteed to complete their exchange in a finite amount of time, even in the presence of exceptions. Optimistic fair exchange protocols, proposed by Asokan [1] in 1998, implement timeliness through the use of local timeouts and a TTP to resolve disputes.

In Asokan's proposal, a TTP may have two options in such a situation: either deliver the expected item to the requesting party or replace it with another,

A.H. Chan and V. Gligor (Eds.): ISC 2002, LNCS 2433, pp. 428–436, 2002.

previously agreed, item. This second strategy is used by Asokan in [1] to implement his Certified Delivery Protocol. In 2000, Ferrer-Gomila, Payeras-Capellà and Huguet i Rotger [2] presented a new version of Asokan's protocol, and analyzed it under the following criteria: (i) effectiveness–i.e. the protocol actually exchanges a message for a receipt; (ii) fairness, as defined above; (iii) timeliness; (iv) non-repudiation of the actions of each party–i.e., the sender and the recipient; and (v) verifiability of the TTP–i.e., the actions of a TTP, may be checked and audited by independent sources.

Our work here points to problems in items (ii) and (iv) above. As we shall see, it is possible for one of the parties, the recipient, to induce the TTP to issue two contradictory tokens, one signaling that the exchange has been *resolved* and another *aborted*.

This paper is organized as follows: in Section 2, we describe the notation used in the remaining sections; in Section 3 we present the main protocol of Ferrer-Gomila and others in [2] and their exception handling subprotocols; Section 4 describes our attack and its impact on the protocol's dispute settling mechanisms; a solution for the described weaknesses is presented in Section 5; the last section contains the conclusions.

2   Notation

Throughout the rest of this paper, we use the same conventions adopted in [2], which we list below for completeness. Moreover, we shall refer to the protocol in [2] as the FPH protocol.

i. A and B are the parties in the exchange and T is the TTP;

ii. X, Y – concatenation of messages X and Y;

iii. $H(X)$ – application of collision-resistant hash function to message X;

iv. $PR_I[H(X)]$ – the digital signature of party I on X (which is first hashed with H), generated with I's private key PR_I; here I may be one of A, B, T;

v. M – message from A to be certifiably delivered to B;

vi. K – a symmetric encryption key;

vii. "s" denotes the string s;

viii. $c = E_K(M)$ – encryption of M using a symmetric algorithm E with secret key K producing ciphertext c; decryption of c is performed with $D_K(c)$;

ix. $k_T = PU_T(K)$ – key K encrypted with the TTP's public-key PU_T;

x. $h_A = PR_A[H(H(c), k_T)]$ – part of the evidence of non-repudiation of origin of message M for B;

xi. $h_B = PR_B[H(H(c), k_T)]$ – part of the evidence of non-repudiation of reception of message M for A;

xii. $k_A = PR_A[\text{``key=''}, K]$ - second part of the evidence of non-repudiation of origin for B;

xiii. $k_T{'} = PR_T[\text{``key=''}, K]$ - an alternative second part of the evidence of non-repudiation of origin for B;

xiv. $h_{AT} = PR_A[H(H(c), k_T, h_A)]$ – an evidence that A has requested the TTP's intervention;

xv. $h_{BT} = PR_B[H(H(c), k_T, h_A, h_B)]$ – an evidence that B has requested the TTP's intervention;

xvi. $h_B{'} = PR_T[H(h_B)]$ – the TTP's signature on h_B which proves its intervention.

3   The FPH Protocol

The FPH protocol is an optimistic protocol for certified mail delivery. Its outcome is the exchange of a message M and a receipt for it between two parties, A and B. In case of an exception, the TTP issues a certificate with the same value of a receipt or the message, whichever is necessary. The main protocol and its exception handling protocols are described in Figures 1 and 2. Our description is not exactly the same as that in [2]; some steps have been included for clarity but they do not alter the essence of the protocol.

3.1   Dispute Handling

Upon completion of the protocol, it may be necessary to handle the following abnormal completion claims:

- **Repudiation of origin.** B claims to have received M from A but A denies having sent it.
- **Repudiation of reception.** A claims to have sent M to B but B denies having received it.

An external adjudicator J should handle these claims as follows:

- **Repudiation of origin.** J requests M, c, k_T, h_A and k_A from B and verifies the signatures in h_A, k_A, $k_T{'}$ and whether $D_K(c) = M$. If all these checks are positive, then J rules in favor of B; otherwise J dismisses B's claim. Moreover, if B's evidence is correct and if A is able to provide J with the token $PR_T[H(\text{``cancelled''}, h_A)]$, then J rules that the TTP has acted incorrectly.

Protocol 1 - *FPH Protocol for Certified Delivery.*

Step Action

1 $A \to B$: c, k_T, h_A
2 If exception,
   B stops
3 $B \to A$: h_B
4 If exception,
   A runs the Cancel protocol
5 $A \to B$: k_A
6 If exception,
   B runs the Finish protocol

Subprotocol 1 - *Cancel*

Step Action

1 $A \to T$: $H(c), k_T, h_A, h_{AT}$
2 T performs:
   if *finished* **then**
      T recovers h_B
      $m := h_B, h_B{'}$;
   else
      cancelled := V;
      $m := PR_T[H(\text{``cancelled''}, h_A)]$;
   end if
3 $T \to A$: m.

Fig. 1. The FPH Protocol and Cancel Subprotocol

- **Repudiation of reception.** J requests M, c, k_T, h_B and K from A and verifies the signatures in h_A, k_A, $k_T{'}$ and whether $D_K(c) = M$. If any of these checks is not verified, then J dismisses A's claim. However, their correct verification is not enough to decide the question in A's favor. The adjudicator should now require from B a token $PR_T[H(\text{``cancelled''}, h_B)]$; if B is able to provide it, this is evidence of cheating on A's part and thus the question is resolved in B's favor; otherwise, if B cannot provide that token and, indeed, $D_K(c) = M$, then J rules in A's favor; if $D_K(c) \neq M$, then J dismisses A's claim. Finally, if A has provided correct evidence and B is able to provide a token $PR_T[H(\text{``cancelled''}, h_B)]$, then the conclusion is that the TTP has acted improperly.

Subprotocol 2 - *Finish*

Step Action

1 $B \to T: H(c), k_T, h_A, h_B, h_{BT}$
2 T performs:
    if *cancelled* **then**
       $m := PR_T[H(\text{"cancelled"}, h_B)]$;
    else
       $finished := V$;
       $m := k_T'$;
    end if
3 $T \to B: m$.

Fig. 2. The Finish Subprotocol

4   Our Attack on the FPH Protocol

Before stating our attack, we note that:

1. Tokens $h_A = PR_A[H(H(c), k_T)]$ and $h_B = PR_B[H(H(c), k_T)]$ are very similar, differing only on the signing agent.
2. The **Finish** subprotocol, described above, returns one of the following messages: (i) $PR_T[H(\text{"cancelled"}, h_B)]$; or (ii) k_T'.
3. Party B always knows ciphertext c, since it is part of the first message sent by A.
4. Ciphertext c has nothing in itself that shows it was originated by A.

4.1   Description of the Attack

After receiving the first message from A, party B initiates an execution of the **Cancel** subprotocol with the TTP. The result of the request follows.

Attack 1 - *B requests cancellation of exchange (1)*

Step Action

1 $B \to T: H(c), k_T, h_B, h_{BT}'$
2 Since $finished \neq V$, then B gets:
3 $T \to B: PR_T[H(\text{"cancelled"}, h_B)]$
4 T sets $cancelled = V$

where $h'_{BT} = PR_B[H(H(c), k_T, h_B)]$. This provides B with cancellation token $PR_T[H(\text{"cancelled"}, h_B)]$. Proceeding with the attack, B now initiates subprotocol **Finish** with the TTP, for a different exchange, say number 2.

Attack 2 - *B requests finalization of exchange (2)*

Step	Action
1	$B \to T :\ H(c), k_T, h_A, h_B, h_{BT}$
2	Since *cancelled* $\neq V$:
3	$T \to B :\ k_T{}'$
4	T sets *finished* $= V$

This provides B with token $k_T{}'$, amounting to a well resolved exchange. Finally, B sends the second message, h_B, to A, A replies with k_A and the protocol terminates. There is another possibility for B. If B decides not to answer to A, then A calls the TTP to get a cancellation token. But B has executed the subprotocol **Finish** first, thus she gets the $h_B, h_B{}'$ from the TTP. In any case, A gets h_B.

As a result of these two interactions, B has obtained from the TTP two certificates which are contradictory. This situation was made possible because: (i) the messages sent in each case to the TTP do not identify their initiator; (ii) the messages returned by the TTP do not identify uniquely an exchange; and (iii) ciphertext c has no evidence of its originator.

In a dispute with A, B can now deny having received a message from A by exhibiting token $PR_T[H(\text{"cancelled"}, h_B)]$. The dispute will be handled by J as follows.

4.2 Dispute Resolution

Even presenting all the correct information, A will not be able to convince J of its (correct) claim that it has not received a receipt for a delivered message to B. Upon obtaining from B token $PR_T[H(\text{"cancelled"}, h_B)]$, J will rule (see Section 3.1), that A has acted maliciously. Another possibility is the ruling that the TTP has acted incorrectly, which can also be verified not to be true, since it acted according to its subprotocols. Thus B succeeds in cheating A.

5 Strengthening the Protocol

The perceived weakness in the FPH protocol can be circumvented by redefining h_B as $\overline{h_B}$, where $\overline{h_B} = PR_B[H(H(c), k_T, h_A)]$, and substituting $\overline{h_B}$ for h_B in the description of the FPH protocol. The resulting tokens h_{BT} and h'_B are also relabelled $\overline{h_{BT}}$, $\overline{h'_B}$ This results in the following subprotocols:

Subprotocol 3 - *Finish2*

Step Action

1   $B \rightarrow T :\; H(c), k_T, h_A, \overline{h_B}, \overline{h_{BT}}$
2   T performs:
  if *cancelled* **then**
    $m := PR_T[H(\text{``cancelled''}, \overline{h_B})];$
  else
    $finished := V;$
    $m := k_T';$
  end if
3   $T \rightarrow B :\;\; m.$

Subprotocol 4 - *Cancel2*

Step Action

1   $A \rightarrow T :\; H(c), k_T, h_A, h_{AT}$
2   T performs:
  if *finished* **then**
    T recovers $\overline{h_B}$
    $m := \overline{h_B}, h'_B;$
  else
    $cancelled := V;$
    $m := PR_T[H(\text{``cancelled''}, h_A)];$
  end if
3   $T \rightarrow A :\;\; m.$

---

6   Analysis of the Strengthening

Given that A uses a different key K to encrypt each message m, then k_T is expected to be different for each exchange, and, consequently, h_A is also expected to be different. If no exceptions occur, message sets from different exchanges are expected to be different. In case of exception, since $\overline{h_B}$ depends on the value of h_A, it identifies the originator of exchange 2 above. Thus, the cancellation tokens returned by the TTP in the two instantiations of the protocol are different. For exchange 1, it will remain unchanged, i.e., $PR_T[H(\text{``cancelled''}, h_B)]$, and for exchange 2 it will be $PR_T[H(\text{``cancelled''}, \overline{h_B})]$. Now, the token returned to B

by the TTP upon a cancellation request depends on h_A, which is unique for each exchange.

The proposed changes do not alter timeliness or efectiveness properties of the FPH protocol, but they do have an effect on non-repudiation and fairness. We discuss these effects on the following theorems.

Theorem 1 *The proposed changes on the FPH protocol provide fairness.*

Proof: We assume that the TTP's state variables, *cancelled* and *finished* are initially set to False. If no exceptions occur, then, since the protocol is effective, fairness is granted. Otherwise, an exception will trigger the initiation of one of the two subprotocols[1]. There are two cases to consider:

Cancel2 is called. The TTP knows that A initiated the exchange, since it has received h_A. If variable *finished* is True, then variable *cancelled* will not be altered and the TTP will issue party A a certificate of successful resolution, i.e., $\overline{h_B}, \overline{h'_B}$. If, otherwise, variable *finished* is False, then *cancelled* is set to True and A gets a certificate $PR_T[H(\text{``cancelled''}, h_A)]$, indicating that the exchange has been cancelled. In any case, both A and B receive non-contradictory certificates.

Finish2 is called. The TTP knows that it is a request from B, in response to the initiation of an exchange by A, since it has received $\overline{h'_B}$, which is a function of h_A. If variable *cancelled* is True, then variable *finished* will not be altered and the TTP will issue party B a certificate indicating that the transaction has been cancelled. If, otherwise, variable *cancelled* is False, then variable *finished* is set to True and B gets from the TTP a certificate k_T', indicating that the exchange has been resolved successfully. Again, A and B get non-contradictory certificates. The proof is complete.

Theorem 2 *The proposed changes on the FPH protocol provide non-repudiation of both origin and reception.*

Proof: Let us examine each case in turn, after completion of the protocol, whichever it is.

Non-repudiation of origin. Suppose B claims to have received M from A but denies having sent M to B.
If the protocol ends without exception, then B gets c, k_A and h_A, which proves that A initiated the transaction, since $A's$ signature on c is present. Likewise, A cannot deny having sent K since k_A contains $A's$ signature.
If an exception occurs, then B gets k_T', which contains the key K signed by the TTP.

---

[1] Exceptions which do not cause the execution of one of the subprotocols are considered as having no consequence to the parties.

Non-repudiation of reception. Suppose now that A claims to have sent M to B but B denies the reception of M.

If the protocol ends without exception, then A receives $\overline{h_B}$, which proves that message M, sent to B in an exchange initiated by A, was accepted by B.

If an exception occurs, then A receives $\overline{h'_B}$, which proves that B received key K from the TTP, relative to the exchange initiated by A, having B as recipient.

This concludes the proof. We note that resolving a dispute follows the same outline of Section 3.1.

7   Conclusions

The use of symmetric messages in a protocol always brings the possibility of attacks. Specifically, in the case of the FPH protocol, messages derived from different instantiations of the protocol can be brought together to produce contradictory outcomes. This illustrates the tricky features of cryptographic protocols and the difficulty of achieving thoroughness in their analysis.

The solution presented to correct FPH's weakness is simple and the impact on the performance is minimal.

References

1. N. Asokan, *Fairness in Electronic Commerce*, University of Waterloo, 1998.
2. Ferrer-Gomila, J. L. and Payeras-Capellà, M. and Rotger, L.H., *"An Efficient Protocol for Certified Electronic Mail"*, Third International Workshop – ISW 2000 (Berlin) Lecture Notes in Computer Science, vol. 1975, Springer-Verlag 2000, pp. 237–248.

Oblivious Counter and Majority Protocol

Hiroaki Kikuchi

Dept. of Information Media Technology, Tokai University
1117 Kitakaname, Hiratsuka, Kanagawa, 259-1292 Japan.
kikn@tokai.ac.jp

Abstract. The paper presents a new protocol for counting 1-bit secrets without revealing if the bit is 1 or 0 in publicly verifiable way. Other than the conventional multi-party protocols that involve enormous number of rounds and huge bandwidth consumption, the proposed protocol, based on the Mix and Match approach [2] in which computations are dealt with ciphertexts, requires a non-interactive constant number of round and simple but verifiable computation for both of sender and counter. The expected application of proposed protocol is an (one-bit) secret voting in which voters cast a ballot encrypted by a public key and an oblivious party (counter) makes a tally of how many votes are polled. The final tally is represented as a k-digit binary *register* consisting of k ciphertexts that only collaboration of distributed authorities can decrypt. Opening only the MSB of ciphertexts allows us to see if more than half voters cast "Yes" or not without revealing the details of total number. The cost for opening is $O(\log n)$, where n is a number of voters. With the proof of knowledge, voters can prove that the vote is either 1 or 0 without revealing their privacy. The proposed protocol is universally verifiable because any third party can verify that voters, a counter and administrators do not violate the protocol. The protocol is robust against up to a constant number of malicious administrators using standard threshold scheme.

1 Introduction

Oblivious Counter is a counter that takes n ciphertexts of one-bit secret as an input and outputs the $\log n$ ciphertexts which encodes the sum of all secrets. The counter is an oblivious party who learn no information about the secrecy from inputs. The counter has no private information and thus the processes of adding are all publicly verifiable. The corresponding private key can be shared among some trusted parties called administrators, who involve at the end of the protocol in order to jointly decrypt the tally.

The most suitable application of oblivious counter is to an electronic voting, in which we have two conflicting goals; the privacy of votes and the accountability of parties. (For requirements and styles of voting, see [1]. So far, major efforts have been made for universally and publicly verifiable Mix-net.) The oblivious counter can match the requirements, i.e., each voter can casts a ciphertext of his/her private vote to the oblivious counter without care of the private vote being compromised or discarded. The double-counting and altering are prevented by an additional verification protocol.

A.H. Chan and V. Gligor (Eds.): ISC 2002, LNCS 2433, pp. 437–445, 2002.

Many electronic voting protocols have been proposed so far. In [7], Cramer Gennaro and Schoenmakers constructed a secure protocol in which a voter casts a single ciphertext with proof of knowledge. The final tally is publicly ensured to be valid by an arbitrary entity under an assumption of homomorphic property of encryption as

$$\prod E[b_i] = E[g^{\sum b_i}] = E[g^T],$$

where $b_i \in \{G, 1/G\}$ and T is the final tally which represents the difference of yes and no votes. The well-known efficient distributed decryption based on El Gamal encryption allows the protocol to be robust against a reasonable number of malicious parties amoung key holders. From the practical viewpoint, an interesting property is that the protocol is scalable, i.e., an entity counting votes can be distributed so that casting processes can be in parallel for each of smaller group. One drawback is that determining T from the decrypted final tally g^T requires an exhaustive search from possible n choices, $1, g, g^{-1}, g^2, g^{-2}, \ldots$ and results in a time of proportional to the number of voters n, $O(n)$. Although the computation can be done prior to the voting, the size of election shall be restricted.

Katz, Myers and Ostrovsky presented what they call *cryptographic counter* which allows votes to increment and decrement a cryptographic representation of tally robustly and privately. The cryptographic counter uses an encryption scheme homomorphic over Z_2, while the previous approaches require *fully* homomorphic over Z_p. The internal state in the counter is represented with an array of k ciphertexts, which are then updated on arriving ciphertext of vote according to the linear feedback shift register (LFSR) of period of $2^k - 1$. An instance of (weaker) homomorphic encryption is presented based on the quadratic residuosity assumption with non-interactive zero-knowledge proof. The protocol is efficient for both communication and computation cost in $O(\log n)$ time. One drawback of the protocol is robustness with respect to the administrators who share the corresponding secret key. Since the quadratic residuosity encryption is used as building block, the distributed key generation and the threshold decryption scheme is not trivial[1].

Both of [7,6] are efficient and practical enough to ordinary election in which the exact tally is necessary. However, these can not cover the case when only a partial result of tally is required. For example, let us consider an example of majority election in which we are interested in one bit information whether or not the total tally is more than the half of all voters and the difference must be secret. A loser may be comfortable if the difference is private. A certain cryptographical protocol needs a comparison of a given secret with arbitrary threshold value, e.g., $n/4$, or $n/8$. Our proposed protocol allows any entity to compute the partial tally without revealing other information at all.

Our idea is based on the protocol "Mix and Match" presented by Jakobsson and Juels[2]. The Mix-and-match is a multiparty protocol in which an arbitrary function is computed without revealing private input values. Other than

---

[1] In Section 3.5 of [6], it says that the threshold decryption is feasible and will be given as full version.

the GMW multiparty schemes [8], the Mix-and-match manipulates ciphertexts directly without being secret shared. New building block is introduced; Plaintext Equality Test ($\mathcal{PET}$) which examine two ciphertext to be identical or not without revealing plaintexts.

The advantage of our proposed protocol is the cost of decoding the tally. The previous approaches [7,6] require $O(n)$ time for determining T from the decrypted registers. Instead, we present $O(\log n)$ solution in this paper. Our idea is based on n-bit (up) counter which takes one bit input and outputs the n-bit number of inputs. The $\mathcal{PET}$ can be used to design the arbitrary counter, however, it requires enormous number of interaction between counter and administrators who have the shared private key. Instead, we use internal states as carry bits in conjunction with proof of disjunctive knowledge presented in [4]. Our contribution is to present up-counter protocol without AND.

2   Preliminaries and Building Blocks

2.1   Models and Assumptions

We have three parties; *voters* who has an one bit secret, say 1 or 0, and let denote by N the number of total voters, *counter*, an oblivious party who keeps a tarry of votes without revealing the result of count until the time to open the ballot boxes comes, and *administrators* who are trusted parties sharing a private key and jointly decrypt the result of count when the time to open voting box comes. We assume that some of administrators may be faulty but not more than $2/n$ can corrupt, namely, any appropriate threshold schemes such as [3] can be used to recover the corresponding plaintext in a secure way. All players agree the security parameter and the public key securely and jointly generated by the administrators. We assume an authenticated broadcast channel by which the counter can effectively publish the proof of every vote being counted in the tally, and the common public-key infrastructure for listing all legitimate voters.

2.2   Building Blocks

Modified El Gamal Cryptosystem. Let p and q be large primes such that

$$\dot{p} = 4q + 1$$

and $\mathcal{G}$ be the set of multiplicative group of order q in Z_p^*. Let g be a primitive element of $\mathcal{G}$. Note that the definition is not the standard one $p = 2q + 1$ for which -1 (mod p) does not belong to $\mathcal{G}$.

All arithmetic operations are done in modulo p, unless otherwise stated. An El Gamal encryption of message m with public key $y = g^x$ is of form $E_a[m] = (M, G) = (my^a, g^a)$, where a is a random number chosen from Z_q. To decrypt the ciphertext (M, G), we use the corresponding private key x to compute $M/G^x = mg^{xa-ax} = m$. The El Gamal cryptosystem is indistinguishable under the Decision Diffie-Hellman (DDH) assumption over $\mathcal{G}$. Namely, given two ciphertexts $E[m]$ and $E[m']$, no one can learn if $m = m'$ or not. This property allows us to construct an oblivious computation in later section.

The El Gamal cryptosystem satisfies a *homomorphism* under a multiplication of two ciphertexts, i.e., given two ciphertexts $E_a[m_a] = (M_a, G_a)$ and $E_b[m_b] = (M_b, G_b)$, the products of the ciphertexts for each element yields a new valid ciphertext $(M_a M_b, G_a G_b) = (m_a m_b y^{a+b}, g^{a+b}) = E_{a+b}[m_a m_b]$. We write this as $E[M_a] \times E[M_b]$. Obviously, the homomorphism holds not only under a multiplication but also under a division and under a raising to exponent, that are used to blind a result of Plaintext Equality Test in [2].

One more good property of the El Gamal cryptosystem is that it can be extended to use the threshold schemes [3]. A private key is jointly generated by a collaboration of t honest parties (key holders) out of n and distributed among them using $(t-1)$-degree random polynomials $f(x)$ as $f(1), f(2), \ldots, f(n)$. To decrypt a ciphertext provided with the public key $y = g^{f(0)}$, i-th party publishes $G^{f(i)}$ for $i = 1, \ldots, t$, and then computes $G^{f(1)\gamma_1} \cdots G^{f(t)\gamma_t} = G^{f(0)}$ where γ_i is the LaGrange coefficient for i. For the sake of verifiability, we can have the key holders proving that they follows the protocol correctly in the zero-knowledge proof of $f(i)$ such that $G^{f(i)}$. See [3] for details.

Various Protocols for Proof of Knowledge. We will use a proof of knowledge of private input to the counter, which is based on the variation of disjunctive and conjunctive proofs of knowledge in [4].

Conjunctive Proof of Knowledge: Let $g_1, g_2 \in \mathcal{G}$. By $PK\{(\alpha) : y_1 = g_1^\alpha \wedge y_2 = g_2^\alpha\}$, we denote a proof of knowledge of discrete logarithms of elements y_1 and y_2 to the bases g_1 and g_2. Picking random numbers r_1 and $r_2 \in Z_q$, a prover sends $t_1 = g_1^{r_1}$ and $t_2 = g_2^{r_2}$ to a verifier, who then sends back a random challenge $c \in \{0,1\}^k$. The prover shows $s = r - cx \pmod{q}$, which should hold both $g_1^s y_1^c = t_1$ and $g_2^s y_2^c = t_2$.

Disjunctive Proof of Knowledge: We denote by $PK\{(\alpha, \beta) : y_1 = g^\alpha \vee y_2 = g^\beta\}$ to mean a proof of knowledge of one out of the two discrete logarithms of y_1 and y_2 to the base g. Namely, the prover can prove that he knows a secret value under which either $y = y_1$ or $y = y_2$ must hold without revealing which identity was used. Without loss of generality, we assume that the prover knows α for which $y = g^\alpha$ holds. The prover uniformly picks $r_1, s_2 \in Z_q$ and $c_2 \in \{0,1\}^k$ and sends $t_1 = g^{r_1}$ and $t_2 = g^{s_2} y_2^{c_2}$ to the verifier, who then gives a random challenge $c \in \{0,1\}^k$, where k is a security parameter. On receiving the challenge, the prover sends $s_1 = r_1 - c_1\alpha \pmod{q}$, s_2, c_1 and c_2, where $c = c_1 \oplus c_2$. The verifier can see if the prover is likely to have the knowledge by testing both $t_1 = g^{s_1} y_1^{c_1}$ and $t_2 = g^{s_2} y_2^{c_2}$ with provability $1 - 2^{-k}$. Note that the same test can be used when t_1 and t_2 are prepared for the other knowledge β.

3   Oblivious Counter

3.1   1-Bit Counter (Half Adder)

Let $V = \{1, -1\}$ be a set of truth values meaning boolean values *false* (0) and *true* (1). Let a and b be boolean variables in V. We denote by capital letters the ciphertexts of boolean variables, e.g., $A = E_r[a]$ and $B = E_s[b]$. A *half adder* is a state-full circuit that takes two inputs, a and b, and produces *sum s* and *carry c* as outputs computed by

$$s = a \oplus b, \quad c = a \wedge b,$$

and the internal state a will be updated when (edge-triggered) clock pulse arrives, we write this by $a(t+1) = s(t)$ where t indicates the synchronous (discrete) time.

In consequence of the multiplicative homomorphism of El Gamal cryptosystem, the function EXORing of two plaintexts, a and b, is easily implemented by simply multiplying the ciphertexts A and B. Table 1 demonstrates the result of multiplication, which shows the truth table of EXOR.

Table 1. Truth Table of EXOR

$A \times B = S$	$a \oplus b = s$
$E[1] \times E[1] = E[1]$	$0 \oplus 0 = 0$
$E[1] \times E[-1] = E[-1]$	$0 \oplus 1 = 1$
$E[-1] \times E[1] = E[-1]$	$1 \oplus 0 = 1$
$E[-1] \times E[-1] = E[1]$	$1 \oplus 1 = 0$

The carry c (AND) is, however, hard to realize since the set of logical operations EXOR and negation, which is done by EXORing 1, is not sufficient for achieving the functionally completeness. The Mix and Match approach [2] is a solution to this problem, in which a truth table of AND is blinded and row-wise mixed and then the plaintext equality test ($\mathcal{PET}$) is used to figure out the *match* of the corresponding row for given input ciphertexts with the help of distributed private key dealers. Rather than involving trusted parties and many other players (MIXs), we would like to make our protocol non-interactive, i.e., avoiding the involvement of other parties except the voter who has the private input b and the counter who has the private state a.

3.2   2-Bit Counter

In this section, we show that the oblivious 2-bit counter is feasible without using the logical AND.

A voter has an one-bit secret b and wishes to have the counter add b to the oblivious tally without revealing if b is 1 or 0. First, the voter casts a pair of ciphertexts (B, C) computed by

$$(B, C) = \begin{cases} (E[b], E[1]) & \text{if } b = 1, \\ (E[b], E[A]) & \text{if } b = -1, \end{cases}$$

where A is the ciphertext of a and $E[A]$ is the corresponding re-encryption defined as $E[A] = A \times E[1]$. The element B contains one-bit secret b to be added and the element C gives the output carry digit. Note that no one can distinguish $E[A]$ from $E[1]$ from the assumption of semantically secure El Gamal cryptosystem.

Second, in order to prevent faulty voters from casting invalid pairs of cipher-texts, in particular, $(E[-1], E[1])$ and $(E[1], E[-1])$, we require voters to provide along with the B, C the proof of disjunctive knowledge

$$PK \begin{array}{l} \{(u, v) : B = E_u[1] \wedge C = E_v[1]\} \vee \\ \{(u', v') : B = E_{u'}[-1] \wedge C = E_{v'}[A]\}. \end{array}$$

We present the proof of knowledge based on zero-knowledge protocols in [4].

Given $B = (M_B, G_B)$ and $C = (M_C, G_C)$, let us define

$$\begin{array}{ll} M_{B1} = M_B, & G_{B1} = G_B, \\ M_{C1} = M_C, & G_{C1} = G_C, \\ M_{B2} = -M_B, & G_{B2} = G_B, \\ M_{C2} = M_C/M_A, & G_{C2} = G_C/G_A, \end{array}$$

where (M_A, G_A) is the current ciphertext A. Protocol specified in Table 2 ensures that the pair of ciphertexts (B, C) is either $E[1] = (M_{B1}, G_{B1})$ and $E[1] = (M_{C1}, G_{C1})$ or $E[1] = (M_{B2}, G_{B2})$ and $E[1] = (M_{C2}, G_{C2})$. The technical details of the protocol are omitted.

On receiving (B, C) and additional proof of knowledge from a voter, the counter computes the sum of input b and the previous result encoded by (A_2, A_1) (A_2 is MSB), as for each digits

$$S_1 = A_1 \times B, \quad S_2 = A_2 \times C.$$

The internal states A_1 and A_2 subsequently are updated by

$$A_1(t + 1) = S_1(t), \quad A_2(t + 1) = S_2(t).$$

An initial state for A_i is $E[1]$ additionally proved in some manner. Since any computation involved in the counter does not reveal private information of input nor the tally, the verification of procedures can be publicly done. Any party who is interested in an accountability of the counter can easily check the consistency by comparing the previously published sum $A_2(t-1), A_1(t-1)$ and the updated sum $A_2(t), A_1(t)$.

Table 3 demonstrates the states transition when "active" voter who has $b = -1$ comes every even clock. The carry digit c_1 is implemented by a duplication of the third row headed by a_1 but the duplication happens only when $b = -1$. For example, the $c_1 = -1$ at clock $t = 4$ comes from the a_1 at the same clock but the duplication at $t = 2$ does not alter the internal state s_1 at all. Hence, it can properly deal with cases when multiple "unactive" votes cast in succession.

3.3 k-Bit Counter

In switching circuit theory, the 2-bit counter is known as a half-adder for which k-bit counter can be formed by cascading k adders. The carry bits ripple from least significant bit to most significant bit. Our construction of 2-bit counter,

Table 2. Protocol for Proof of Knowledge $PK\{(u,v) : B = E_u[1] \wedge C = E_v[1]\} \vee \{(u',v') : B = E_{u'}[-1] \wedge C = E_{v'}[A]\}$

Step	$(b = 1)$	$(b = -1)$
1	The prover (voter) picks random elements $r_{B1}, r_{C1}, z_{B2}, z_{C2} \in Z_q$ and $d_2 \in \{0,1\}^k$ if $b = 1$; otherwise $r_{B2}, r_{C2}, z_{B1}, z_{C1} \in Z_q$ and $d_1 \in \{0,1\}^k$, on which he computes the followings and sends to the verifier. $$t_{B1} = g^{r_{B1}}$$ $$w_{B1} = y^{r_{B1}}$$ $$t_{B2} = g^{z_{B2}}G_{B2}^{d_2}$$ $$w_{B2} = y^{z_{B2}}M_{B2}^{d_2}$$ $$t_{C1} = g^{r_{C1}}$$ $$w_{C1} = y^{r_{C1}}$$ $$t_{C2} = g^{z_{C2}}G_{C2}^{d_2}$$ $$w_{C2} = y^{z_{C2}}M_{C2}^{d_2}$$	$$t_{B1} = g^{z_{B1}}G_{B1}^{d_1}$$ $$w_{B1} = y^{z_{B1}}M_{B1}^{d_1}$$ $$t_{B2} = g^{r_{B2}}$$ $$w_{B2} = y^{r_{B2}}$$ $$t_{C1} = g^{z_{C1}}G_{C1}^{d_1}$$ $$w_{C1} = g^{z_{C1}}M_{C1}^{d_1}$$ $$t_{C2} = g^{r_{C2}}$$ $$w_{C2} = y^{r_{C2}}$$
2	The verifier randomly picks a challenge d from $\{0,1\}^k$ and sends to the prover.	
3	The prover computes $d_1 = d \oplus d_2$ and sends d_1, d_2 and $$z_{B1} = r_{B1} - d_1 u$$ $$z_{B2}$$ $$z_{C1} = r_{C1} - d_1 v$$ $$z_{C2}$$	The prover computes $d_2 = d \oplus d_1$ and sends d_1, d_2 and $$z_{B1}$$ $$z_{B2} = r_{B2} - d_2 u$$ $$z_{C1}$$ $$z_{C2} = r_{C2} - d_2 v$$
4	The verifier accepts if $d = d_1 \oplus d_2$ and $$g^{z_{B1}}G_{B1}^{d_1} = g^{r_{B1} - d_1 u + u d_1} = t_{B1}$$ $$y^{z_{B1}}M_{B1}^{d_1} = y^{r_{B1} - d_1 u + u d_1} = w_{B1}$$ $$g^{z_{B2}}G_{B2}^{d_2} = t_{B2}$$ $$y^{z_{B2}}M_{B2}^{d_2} = w_{B2}$$ $$g^{z_{C1}}G_{C1}^{d_1} = g^{r_{C1} - d_1 v + v d_1} = t_{C1}$$ $$y^{z_{C1}}M_{C1}^{d_1} = y^{r_{C1} - d_1 v + v d_1} = w_{C1}$$ $$g^{z_{C2}}G_{C2}^{d_2} = t_{C2}$$ $$y^{z_{C2}}M_{C2}^{d_2} = w_{C2}$$	$$g^{z_{B1}}G_{B1}^{d_1} = t_{B1}$$ $$y^{z_{B1}}M_{B1}^{d_1} = w_{B1}$$ $$g^{z_{B2}}G_{B2}^{d_2} = g^{r_{B2} - d_2 u + u d_2} = t_{B2}$$ $$y^{z_{B2}}M_{B2}^{d_2} = y^{r_{B2} - d_2 u + u d_2} = w_{B2}$$ $$g^{z_{C1}}G_{C1}^{d_1} = t_{C1}$$ $$y^{z_{C1}}M_{C1}^{d_1} = w_{C1}$$ $$g^{z_{C2}}G_{C2}^{d_2} = g^{r_{C2} - d_2 v + v d_2} = t_{C2}$$ $$y^{z_{C2}}M_{C2}^{d_2} = y^{r_{C2} - d_2 v + v d_2} = w_{C2}$$

Table 3. State Transition Table of the 2-bit Counter

t	time	1	2	3	4	5	6	7	8	9
b	input	1	-1	1	-1	1	-1	1	-1	1
a_1	$= s_1(t-1)$	1	1	-1	-1	1	1	-1	-1	1
s_1	$= a_1(t) \oplus b(t)$	1	-1	-1	1	1	-1	-1	1	1
c_1	$= a_1(t) \wedge b(t)$	1	1	1	-1	1	1	1	-1	1
a_2	$= s_2(t-1)$	1	1	1	1	-1	-1	-1	-1	1
s_2	$= a_2(t) \oplus c_1(t)$	1	1	1	-1	-1	-1	-1	1	1
(a_2, a_1)	decimal	0	0	1	1	2	2	3	3	0

however, requires a carry bit being duplicated from the previous internal state (A_1). Thus, the k-bit extension is not trivial.

The idea is having voter cast with all subsequent carry bits. For simplicity, let us consider a case $k = 3$ where we wish to have C_2. The second carry bit C_2 is provided by voter as

$$C_2 = E[c_1 \wedge a_2] = \begin{cases} E[1] & \text{if } b = 1, \\ E[A_2'] & \text{if } b = -1, \end{cases}$$

where A_2' is defined as follows:

$$A_2'(t+1) = S_2'(t)$$
$$S_2'(t) = C_2'(t) \times A_2'(t) = E[c_2' \oplus a_2']$$
$$C_2'(t) = \begin{cases} E[1] & \text{if } b = 1, \\ E[A_2] & \text{if } b = -1. \end{cases}$$
$$A_2(t+1) = S_2(t)$$
$$S_2(t) = C_1(t) \times A_2(t)$$

The ballot voter has to send consists of B, C_1, C_2' and C_2. The carry bit C_1 is identical to C in the 2-bit counter protocol. We then extend the basic 2-bit counter to n-bit in which a sequence of n ciphertexts is used as register. We illustrate how 3-bit counter works in Table 4. For simplification, we assume every vote is "active". At the bottom row, we can observe that the second carry can be obtained properly.

The n-bit counter can be naturally extended; the voter fetches the current internal states $A_1, \ldots, A_k$ which have been published and updated for every new vote is added to the counter. Then, the voter computes the ciphertexts of ballot according to his private vote (b) and additional ciphertexts for bits of register and sends it with optional proof of disjunctive knowledge of conjunction of ciphertexts for all bits.

In the previous section, we see that the register decreases the cycle by half for each. Hence, with appropriate length of register, any carry bit c_m can be computed from the one-bit-left carry c_{m-1}. For instance, to implement c_3, we need three additional ciphertexts, i.e., a_3', a_3'' and a_3''', and the total of $4 + 4 = 8$ ciphertexts are necessary to cast one bit. In general, k-bit counter requires voter to send the total of 2^{k-1} ciphertexts. The possible state is equal to the number of voters, so we have $2^{k-1} = n$.

Remark 31 *The communication cost for voter is $O(n)$.*

The overhead at the counter is considerably small because it has no private information such as private key and thereby it can reduce the cost for operation. But, the update process may alter at most 2^{k-1} internal states.

Remark 32 *The computation cost for counter is $O(n)$.*

The cost of administrators is the lightest in our protocol. The administrators involved at the begging of the protocol (for key generation) and the end for distributed description of the tally $(A_k, A_{k-1}, \ldots, A_1)$, which gives the total number of "active votes".

Remark 33 *The computation cost for administrator is $O(\log n)$.*

Table 4. State Transition Table of 3-bit Counter

t	1	2	3	4	5	6	7	8
b	-1	-1	-1	-1	-1	-1	-1	-1
a_1	1	-1	1	-1	1	-1	1	-1
s_1	-1	1	-1	1	-1	1	-1	1
c_1	1	-1	1	-1	1	-1	1	-1
a_2	1	1	-1	-1	1	1	-1	-1
s_2	1	-1	-1	1	1	-1	-1	1
c'_2	1	1	-1	-1	1	1	-1	-1
a'_2	1	1	1	-1	1	1	1	-1
s'_2	1	1	-1	1	1	1	-1	1
c_2	1	1	1	-1	1	1	1	-1

4   Conclusion

We presented an oblivious counter protocol which allows us to count up "active votes" without revealing privacy of voters. The most significant bit of ciphertext conveys an one-bit information if the tally exceeds the majority of voters. With the agreement of the administrators, the tally can be gradually revealed from the most significant bit to the least significant bit without the rest of information being revealed.

References

1. M. Abe, "Universally Verifiable Mix-Net with Verification Work Independent of the Number of Mix-Servers," IEICE Trans. Fundamentals, Vol. E83-A, No.7, July 2000.
2. M. Jakobsson and A. Juels, "Mix and Match: Secure Function Evaluation via Ciphertexts," Proc. of ASIACRYPTO 2000, LNCS 1967, pp. 162-177, 2000.
3. T. P. Pedersen, "A threshold cryptosystem without a trusted party," *EURO-CRYPTO '91*, pp. 522–526, 1991.
4. R. Cramer, I. Damgard, and B. Schoenmakers, "Proofs of partial knowledge and simplified design of witness hiding protocols," *CRYPTO '94*, pp. 174–187, 1994.
5. J. Camenisch and M. Michels, "Proving in Zero-Knowledge that a Number Is the Product of Two Safe Primes," *EUROCRYPT'99*, pp. 107–122, 1999.
6. J. Katz, S. Myers and R. Ostrovsky, "Cryptographic Counters and Applications to Electronic Voting," *EUROCRYPT 2001*, 2001.
7. R. Cramer, R. Gennaro and B. Schoenmakers, "A Secure and Optimally Efficient Multi-Authority Election Scheme," *EUROCRYPT 1997*.
8. S. Goldwasser and S. Micali and A. Wigderson, "How to Play Any Mental Game, or a Completeness Theorem for Protocols with an Honest Majority," *STOC'87*, 1987.

Efficient Mental Card Shuffling via Optimised Arbitrary-Sized Benes Permutation Network

Wai Han Soo[1], Azman Samsudin[1], and Alwyn Goh[2]

[1] School of Computer Sciences, Universiti Sains Malaysia, 11800 Penang, Malaysia
{whsoo, azman}@cs.usm.my
[2] OpenSys (M) Sdn. Bhd., KLCC Tower 2, Level 23, 50088 Kuala Lumpur, Malaysia
agoh@myopensys.com

Abstract. The presumption of player distrust and untrustworthiness in mental card gaming results in the formulation of complex and compute-intensive protocols, particularly for shuffling. We present a robust, verifiable and efficient card shuffling protocol based on an optimisation of Chang-Melham arbitrary-sized (AS) Benes permutation network (PN), which can flexibly accommodates variable pack sizes, achieving optimal shuffling performance. We also outline the use of these PNs in a distributed (among η players) construction, which combines the best attributes of Abe and Jakobsson-Juels mix-net formalisms. Card shuffling can therefore be executed on a structurally simple mix-net – with only $t + 1$ PNs required for operational robustness against collusion by t cheating players, and efficient zero knowledge proofs (ZKP) to verify correct shuffling by each player. Shuffling efficiency is also enhanced by our limited application of verifiable secret sharing (VSS) on the ElGamal keys. The resultant protocol achieves an asymptotic complexity of $O(tN \lg N)$ for N inputs; which is comparable or superior to previous schemes.

Keywords. Shuffle, mental card game, mix-net, Benes permutation network.

1 Introduction

Mental gaming protocols are specifically designed to enable verifiably fair gameplay among remote parties whose a priori distrust and untrustworthiness precludes introduction of a trusted third party. Such protocols are supportive of card confidentiality, fraud detection and conditional security against player collusions, but generally require compute-expensive shuffling. This, in essence, derives from the inherent risk of dependence on a single *random* permutation of the cards in play, having control of which gains (as in physical gaming) an unfair advantage. *Fair* shuffling must therefore incorporate inputs from every player, so as to produce a permuted deck that is both random and secret.

The simplest shuffling methods are based on sequential application of individual random permutations [1-5]. This approach tends to be extremely compute-expensive due to the necessity for complex ZKPs to verify that the deck has undergone a permutation – without divulging useful information on the specific transformation –

A.H. Chan and V. Gligor (Eds.): ISC 2002, LNCS 2433, pp. 446–458, 2002.
© Springer-Verlag Berlin Heidelberg 2002

but is otherwise not tampered with. Some of these schemes [1–3] are furthermore *fragile* in their inability to handle malicious dropouts (i.e. by players with a bad hand) in mid gameplay, or (for that matter) simple connection failure; both of which are unfortunately indistinguishable from each other. Kurosawa *et al.* [4] protocol – with robust verifiable mix-net [5] based on Benaloh r^{th} residue cryptosystem and associated VSS [6, 7] – rigorously addresses gameplay robustness, but incurs very high operational overheads due to the use of VSS on every input card as well as intermediate values.

This work follows Kurosawa *et al.* in its use of mix-net, but considers constructions more appropriate for small input size (deck of cards); in particular Jakobsson-Juels [8] and Abe [9, 10], both of which are in turn based on Waksman's construction of Benes PNs [11]. The simpler Jakobsson-Juels formulation assigns a shuffling workload of one PN per player, which can be reduced via Abe's stipulation of $t + 1$ PNs for robustness against t faulty parties. Abe's mix-net therefore has a lessened workload of significantly *less* than one PN per player. Jakobsson-Juels's mix-net, on the other hand, features simpler and less compute-expensive ZKPs at each switch. The complementary nature of mix-net-level structural simplicity and switch-level ZKP efficiency motivates our formulation of a shuffling protocol incorporating both, which is subsequently demonstrated (in section 5). The security of our mix-net based shuffling is predicated on the intractability of discrete logarithm (DL) assumption for the switch-specific ElGamal re-encryptions and ZKPs. DL-based VSS [15, 16] is applied to ensure gameplay robustness. However, its usage is limited to the session-specific decryption key to obtain higher computational performance.

Mix-net based shuffling is nevertheless still restricted by the $N = 2^r$ deck-size (input) requirement of its Waksman PN constituent, which is ideal only for very few games e.g. Skat with its 32-card pack. Arbitrary-sized decks – e.g. the standard 52-card pack or Uno 108-card pack – incur a non-functional overhead due to the need of *dummy* cards to pad the deck to the nearest binary power. This is typically burdensome; as exemplified by the 50 dummies required for Tarot 78-card pack, comprising 39% of the input list and associated overheads. The employment of Chang-Melham AS-Benes PN [20] would therefore result in significantly more efficient shuffling, which is further improved by our proposed optimised AS (OAS) Benes PN (to be elaborated in section 3). Our construction is based on an efficient application of Waksman methodology, realising greater switch-level reduction compared to Chang-Melham while retaining the rearrangeable and non-blocking characteristics of a PN.

In this paper, we therefore present an efficient collaborative card shuffling protocol based on $t + 1$ OAS PN. Each player's shuffling action is publicly verifiable via efficient correctness proofs. Robustness is supported due to sharing of the decryption key. We present our gaming model and the cryptographic building blocks in section 4 before describing the card shuffling protocol in section 5.

2 Arbitrary Size (AS) Benes

Benes PN is a directed graph of bounded degree with N inputs/outputs, denoted as $PN^{(N)}$. It is rearrangeable nonblocking, i.e. capable of realising all possible input permutations with a set of edge disjoint paths. It is constructed from 2×2 switches as depicted in Figure 1(a), with the internal state being determined by a binary control signal $b \in \{0, 1\}$. An r-dimensional Benes network accepts $N = 2^r$ inputs and has $2 \lg N - 1$ stages, with each stage having $\frac{N}{2}$ switches. Waksman [11] showed that the lower bound for the number of switches required to achieve $M!$ permutations is $\Pi_{\text{Waksman}}(N) = M \lg N - N + 1$. An example is shown in Figure 1(b) for $r = 3$.

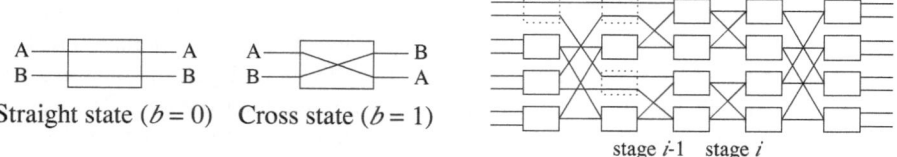

A ——————— A   A ———————— B
B ——————— B   B ———————— A

Straight state ($b = 0$)   Cross state ($b = 1$)

stage i-1   stage i

Fig. 1(a). Two states of a 2×2 switch   **Fig. 1(b).** An 8×8 Waksman PN

The restriction of 2^r input size enforced by Waksman PN is impractical for card games which use various sizes of card pack. In cases where the number of card is $2^{r-1} < N < 2^r$, we have to employ $PN^{(2^r)}$, which involves unnecessary switches and dummy inputs, thereby degrading efficiency. Chang and Melham [12] presented an extension of a typical Benes network, allowing any number of inputs, yet having equivalent permutation capability as a Benes. Such construction is realisable with the introduction of a 3×3 network, built from 1×1 and 2×2 sub-networks as shown below:

1x1 network

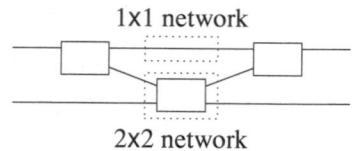

2x2 network

Fig. 2. A 3×3 Benes network

The 3×3 network can be used to form network of any size. As depicted in Figure 3, for even N, $PN^{(N)}$ can be built recursively from two even blocks of $\frac{N}{2}$-dimension AS-Benes; while odd N is based on an upper $\lfloor \frac{N}{2} \rfloor$ even block and a lower $\lceil \frac{N}{2} \rceil$ odd block permutations. Considering a 3×3 network as an atomic unit, AS-Benes has $2 \lfloor \lg N \rfloor - 1$ stages, and the number of switches is $\Pi_{\text{AS Benes}}(N) = 2 \lfloor \frac{N}{2} \rfloor + \Pi(\lceil \frac{N}{2} \rceil) + \Pi(\lfloor \frac{N}{2} \rfloor)$ where $\Pi_{\text{AS-Benes}}(1) = 0$ and $\Pi_{\text{AS-Benes}}(2) = 1$.

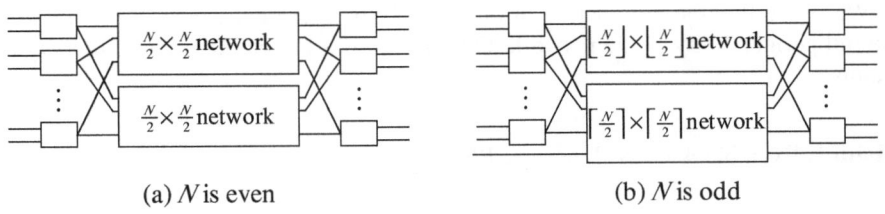

(a) N is even   (b) N is odd

Fig. 3. Construction of AS-Benes

Chang-Melham's AS-Benes is basically a regular Benes when $N = 2^r$. In such cases, Waksman's construction is more efficient as $\Pi_{\text{Waksman}}(2^r) < \Pi_{\text{AS-Benes}}(2^r)$, which motivates our formulation of an OAS-Benes via elimination of redundant switches following Waksman's technique, as outlined in the next section.

3 Optimised Arbitrary Size (OAS) Benes

As a straightforward extension of AS-Benes, our construction of OAS-Benes also consists of two block structures, even and odd blocks. Based on the topology of AS-Benes, we observe that every sub-network with even inputs can be optimised in a manner similar to Waksman. An even block with N inputs can therefore be built from two $\frac{N}{2}$-input sub-networks using $N-1$ input-output switches as shown in Figure 4(a). The odd block – following Chang-Melham's formulation – is not subjected to optimisation. We illustrate our construction with an example of 9×9 network in Figure 4(b).

upper sub-network

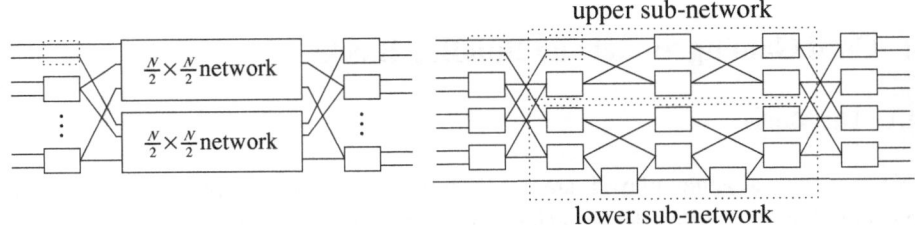

lower sub-network

Fig. 4(a). Construction of OAS-Benes   **Fig. 4(b).** A 9×9 OSA-Benes

Note that for the case of $N = 2^r$, OAS-Benes is equivalent to Waksman PN, i.e. $\Pi_{\text{OAS-Benes}}(2^r) = \Pi_{\text{Waksman}}(2^r) < \Pi_{\text{AS-Benes}}(2^r)$; and for the general case of $2^{r-1} < N < 2^r$, OAS-Benes requires less switches compared to AS-Benes. (A comparison of the PNs can be seen in Figure 9.) Thus, OAS-Benes has the most optimised construction with minimum switches to satisfy $N!$-permutation.

With $\Pi_{\text{OAS-Benes}}(1) = 0$, $\Pi_{\text{OAS-Benes}}(2) = 1$, $\Pi_{\text{OAS-Benes}}(3) = 3$,

$$\Pi_{\text{OAS-Benes}}(N) = \begin{cases} (N-1) + 2\Pi_{\text{OAS-Benes}}(\frac{N}{2}); & \text{for even } N \\ 2\lfloor \frac{N}{2} \rfloor + \Pi_{\text{OAS-Benes}}(\lceil \frac{N}{2} \rceil) + \Pi_{\text{OAS-Benes}}(\lfloor \frac{N}{2} \rfloor); & \text{for odd } N. \end{cases}$$

We prove that the elimination of one switch for every even block does not affect the full permutability of the network. OAS-Benes is a PN based on the following two claims:

Claim 1. Even block OAS-Benes is a PN.

Proof. Even block OAS-Benes is fundamentally a Benes network with the top-left switch being omitted (see Figure 4(a)). Therefore, Benes looping algorithm [20] can be applied on OAS-Benes to achieve M!-permutation. The algorithm starts from the first switch with two options, either set it to a straight or a cross state. In OAS-Benes, however, the non-existence of the first (top-left) switch is assumed to be a straight state, so that the looping algorithm is unaffected and ends successfully.

Claim 2. Odd block OAS-Benes is a PN.

Proof. In Benes network, the looping algorithm ensures that half of the inputs/outputs is routed through the upper sub-network and the other half to the lower sub-network. However, in odd block OAS-Benes, one of the sub-networks has an extra input/output connection. This irregularity requires the looping algorithm to assign paths commencing from the bigger sub-network to ensure a rearrangeable nonblocking topology. With this additional rule we can guarantee that $\left\lceil \frac{N}{2} \right\rceil$ connections will be routed to the bigger sub-network and $\left\lfloor \frac{N}{2} \right\rfloor$ connections to the smaller sub-network, satisfying our claim.

4 Card Gaming Model and Building Blocks

4.1 The Model

We consider a game played among η mutually distrustful players, without the presumption of a trusted dealer, using a deck of μ cards in a distributed environment. For communication, a bulletin board is publicly accessible in which messages can be read and appended, but deletion of data is prohibited. An adversary, who can expectedly, post as a player, is assumed to be polynomial-time bounded. The subsequent description is feasible given at least $t + 1$ ($t < \left\lfloor \frac{\eta-1}{2} \right\rfloor$) honest players during a configurable gaming session.

Our mental gaming framework depends on the underlying homomorphic public-key cryptosystem [14] for security. We denote individual card M and player P by the indices i and j respectively. $E_j(\cdot)$ and $D_j(\cdot)$ are the encryption-decryption transformations on plaintext M using P_j's public and private keys. $H(\cdot)$ is a collision resistant one-way hash function, which relies on the random oracle model for security.

The deck in play is composed of cards $(M_1,...,M_\mu)$, the back of which is a semantically secure commitment on M_i, denoted as $C_i = E(M_i)$. Our card shuffling protocol is based on the mechanism of mix-net, using OAS PN as outlined in section 3. The protocol must therefore satisfy:

- *Privacy* – The relationship between input and output sequences remains obscure to all players.
- *Robustness* – Protocol ends successfully with overwhelming probability.
- *Verifiability* – Incorrect shuffling output is detected with overwhelming probability.

4.2 Building Blocks

Our shuffling protocol is built upon the following tools:

- *Encryption algorithm* – takes as input public key y, random value α and plaintext M; it outputs ciphertext C.
- *Distributed key generation protocol* – runs by η players, taking as input a threshold t and private random strings w_j; it outputs a public key y, a list of private key shares x_j and their commitments (individual public keys) y_j.
- *Randomisation algorithm* – takes as input ciphertext C, public key y and random value β; it outputs a randomised ciphertext C' and its proof of validity.

Encryption Algorithm. Our construction is grounded on ElGamal cryptosystem [14], leveraging on the difficulty of discrete logarithm problem over a subgroup G_q of order q of Z_p^*, where p, q are large primes such that $q \mid p - 1$. Henceforth, we assume computation in G_q where applicable. Let g be a generator of G_q and $q = 2p + 1$. p, q and g are considered as system parameters. We define the private-public key pair as (x, y) such that $x \in_U Z_q$ where $\in_U$ denotes uniform random selection, and $y = g^x$. Encrypting a plaintext $M \in G_q$ yields ciphertext $C = (a, b) = (My^\alpha, g^\alpha)$ for some $\alpha \in_U Z_q$; while decryption is calculating $M = a/b^x$. The cryptosystem is semantically secure under the Decision Diffie-Hellman (DDH) assumption over G_q.

The cryptosystem is of multiplicative homomorphic nature. Let

$$(a_1, b_1) \otimes (a_2, b_2) = (a_1a_2, b_1b_2) \text{ and } (a_1, b_1) \oslash (a_2, b_2) = (a_1/a_2, b_1/b_2).$$

If $E(M_1) = (a_1, b_1)$ and $E(M_2) = (a_2, b_2)$, then

$$E(M_1M_2) = E(M_1) \otimes E(M_2) \text{ and } E(M_1/M_2) = E(M_1) \oslash E(M_2).$$

This algebraic property allows for random re-encryption of a ciphertext $C = (a, b)$ via computation of $C' = (a, b) \otimes (a', b')$ such that $(a', b') = E(1) = (y^\beta, g^\beta)$ where $\beta \in_U Z_q$. The underlying plaintexts for C and C' are equivalent, which we denote as $C \equiv C'$.

Distributed Key Generation Protocol. In our gaming environment, no trusted dealer is assumed. Thus, we apply a threshold scheme for ElGamal cryptosystem to facilitate distribution of trust among mutually suspicious players by sharing the underlying private decryption key. The ElGamal key pair (x, y) is jointly generated by all players where y is disclosed but x is shared additively via Shamir's secret sharing technique [15]. The distributed key generation protocol is due to Pedersen [16]:

- *Secret Distribution*: Each player P_j randomly selects a secret w_j and a tth degree polynomial $f_j(x) = \sum_{k=0}^{t} a_{jk} x^k$ over $\mathbf{Z}_q$, satisfying $f_j(0) = a_{j0} = w_j$. P_j then broadcasts $A_{jk} = g^{a_{jk}} \bmod p$ for $k = 0,...,t$ and secretly sends shares $s_{jt} = f_j(\ell) \bmod q$ to all other players.

- *Shares Verification*: Every player P_l ($l \in [1, \eta]$, $l \neq j$) verifies that $g^{s_{jt}} \overset{?}{=} \prod_{k=0}^{t} A_{jk}^{\ell^k} \bmod p$. If false, a complaint is broadcast against P_j.

- *Generating Key Pair*: Let Q be the set of honest players, each P_j ($j \in Q$) keeps share of private key $x_j = \sum_{l \in Q} s_{lj} \bmod q$ secretly. The distributed private key $x = \sum_{j \in Q} w_j \bmod q$ is not explicitly computed. The public key is computed as $y = \prod_{j \in Q} A_{j0}$ with public verification values being $A_k = \prod_{j \in Q} A_{jk}$ for $k = 1,...,t$. Each P_j ($j \in Q$) broadcasts individual public key $y_j = g^{x_j} \bmod p$ as a commitment of the private key share x_j.

Randomisation Algorithm. Due to the homomorphic property of ElGamal cryptosystem, a ciphertext $C = (a, b) = (My^\alpha, g^\alpha)$ for $\alpha \in_U \mathbf{Z}_q$, can be randomised by simply re-encrypting it with a random exponent $\beta \in_U \mathbf{Z}_q$:

$$C' = (a', b') = (ay^\beta, bg^\beta) = (My^v, g^v); \; v = \alpha + \beta.$$

We need ZKP for the relation $C \equiv C'$ using the prover's knowledge of the re-encryption exponent β. Another useful ZKP for our scheme is to prove that one of two ElGamal ciphertexts C_i' for $i \in \{1, 2\}$, represents a valid re-encryption of C, that is, $C \equiv C_i'$ without revealing which i. We outline both honest-verifier ZKPs from [8] as follows:

Plaintext Equivalence Proof (PEP). Ciphertexts $(a_1, b_1) = (M_1 y^{v_1}, g^{v_1})$ and $(a_2, b_2) = (M_2 y^{v_2}, g^{v_2})$ for some $v_1, v_2 \in_U \mathbf{Z}_q$ are plaintext equivalent if $M_1 = M_2$. Let $(a_1/a_2, b_1/b_2) = (y^{v_0}, g^{v_0})$ for $v_0 = v_1 - v_2$, and $(Y, G) = ((a_1/a_2)^\kappa (b_1/b_2), y^\kappa g) = ((y^\kappa g)^{v_0}, y^\kappa g)$ for $\kappa = H(y, g, a_1, a_2, b_1, b_2)$. To prove $(a_1, b_1) \equiv (a_2, b_2)$, the prover demonstrates knowledge of v_0 based on a variant of Schnorr signature algorithm [17] on (Y, G):

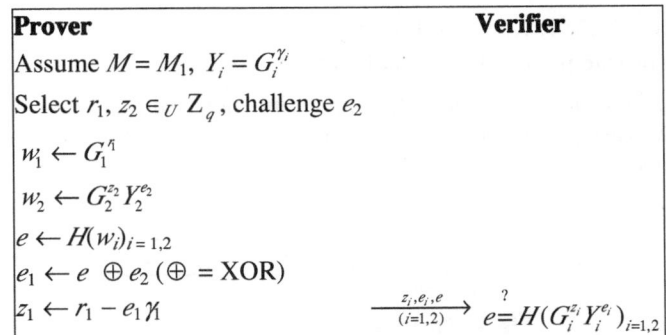

Fig. 5. *PEP* (*Y, G*)

Disjunctive PEP (D-PEP). This is an extension of *PEP*. Let $(a_1, b_1) = (M_1 y^{v_1}, g^{v_1})$ or $(a_2, b_2) = (M_2 y^{v_2}, g^{v_2})$ be re-encryptions of $(a, b) = (My^\alpha, g^\alpha)$ for some α, v_1, $v_2 \in_U Z_q$. If $M = M_i$ for $i \in \{1, 2\}$, then $(a/a_i, b/b_i) = (y^{\gamma_i}, g^{\gamma_i})$ where $\gamma_i = \alpha - v_i$ and $(Y_i, G_i) = ((a/a_i)^{\kappa_i}(b/b_i), y^{\kappa_i}g) = ((y^{\kappa_i}g)^{\gamma_i}, y^{\kappa_i}g)$ for $\kappa_i = H(y, g, a, a_i, b, b_i)$. To prove either $M = M_1$ or $M = M_2$, a prover demonstrates knowledge of γ_i. For simplicity, we assume the prover is showing $M = M_1$:

Prover	Verifier
Assume $M = M_1$, $Y_i = G_i^{\gamma_i}$	
Select $r_1, z_2 \in_U Z_q$, challenge e_2	
$w_1 \leftarrow G_1^{r_1}$	
$w_2 \leftarrow G_2^{z_2} Y_2^{e_2}$	
$e \leftarrow H(w_i)_{i=1,2}$	
$e_1 \leftarrow e \oplus e_2 \ (\oplus = \text{XOR})$	
$z_1 \leftarrow r_1 - e_1 \gamma_1$	$\xrightarrow[(i=1,2)]{z_i, e_i, e}$ $e \overset{?}{=} H(G_i^{z_i} Y_i^{e_i})_{i=1,2}$

Fig. 6. *D-PEP* (*Y_i, G_i*)

5 Card Shuffling Protocol

As previously mentioned, our mix-net based shuffling protocol incorporates:
- Optimised mix-net construction of Abe [9], which requires minimally $t + 1$ PNs for sufficient fault tolerance.
- OAS-Benes PN for accommodation of any deck sizes.
- Efficient switch-specific ZKPs of Jakobsson-Juels [8] for correct mixing.

The protocol commences with the establishment of $t + 1$ PN$^{(\mu)}$ and fair distribution of the stages among all players. Each player is thereby assigned an average of $S = (\frac{t+1}{\eta})(2\lfloor \lg N \rfloor - 1)$ adjacent stages. All players then collaboratively execute the *distributed key generation protocol* to create the group public key y and individual key pairs (x_j, y_j). Note that these keys are generated once and used throughout the gaming session as x and x_j are never exposed. Any player can prepare the deck via *encryption algorithm* using y, on each card M_i ($i \in [1, \mu]$), forming a list of publicly verifiable ElGamal ciphertexts $(C_1,...,C_\mu)$.

Shuffling the deck $(C_1,...,C_\mu)$ can be subsequently executed via sequential private permutation and re-encryption (or randomisation) at every switch of every player-hosted stage, with verification via publication of the relevant ZKP transcripts as depicted in Figure 7.

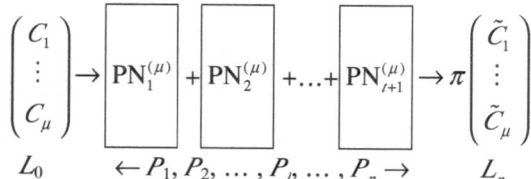

Fig. 7. Shuffling by η players using $t + 1$ $PN^{(\mu)}$

Specifically, shuffling from initial list $L_0 = \{C_{0,i}\}_{i=1,...,\mu}$ is performed sequentially by each player P_j ($j = 1,...,\eta$) as follows:

(1) Applies private permutation π_j on input list $L_{j-1} = \{C_{j-1,i}\}_{i=1,...,\mu}$ at each switch of S consecutive stages to reorder the input ciphertext pair, and runs *randomization algorithm* (using y) to obscure the action. The inputs and outputs of each switch is publicised:

$$E(M_i)=(a_i,b_i) \rightarrow \boxed{\begin{array}{c} 2 \times 2 \\ \text{switch} \end{array}} \rightarrow E(M'_i)=(a'_i,b'_i)$$
$$E(M_{i+1})=(a_{i+1},b_{i+1}) \rightarrow \qquad\qquad \rightarrow E(M'_{i+1})=(a'_{i+1},b'_{i+1})$$

Fig. 8. Input and output of a 2×2 switch

(2) Proves correctness of switch execution (i.e. the hidden action) by demonstrating either $(M_i, M_{i+1}) = (M'_i, M'_{i+1})$ OR $(M_i, M_{i+1}) = (M'_{i+1}, M'_i)$, which is equivalent to proving the following two statements with appropriate ZKPs:

Table 1. Proving correctness of mixing at each switch

Statement	Proof
$(M_i = M'_i) \vee (M_i = M'_{i+1})$	Publish transcript of *D-PEP*.
$M_i M_{i+1} = M'_i M'_{i+1}$	Compute $C = E(M_i M_{i+1})$ and $C' = E(M'_i M'_{i+1})$, publish transcript of *PEP* for $C \equiv C'$.

(3) All other players P_ℓ ($\ell \in [1,\eta], \ell \neq j$) perform verification on the proofs.

If no cheating is detected, the resulting list L_η is published on the bulletin board. This is essentially the shuffled $DECK = \{\tilde{C}_{\pi(i)} = (\tilde{a}_{\pi(i)}, \tilde{b}_{\pi(i)}) = (M_{\pi(i)} y^\gamma, g^\gamma)\}$, for some random γ and $\pi = \pi_\eta \circ ... \circ \pi_1$, derived from the initial set of cards $\{C_i = (a_i, b_i) = (M_i y^\alpha, g^\alpha)\}$ as depicted in Figure 7. Note that the privacy of π only requires a single secret permutation π_j ($j \in [1, \eta]$).

6 Analysis

The presented integration of Jakobsson-Juels [8] ZKP efficiency (reduced computation per switch), Abe [9] structural simplicity (reduced switches per player) and the presented OAS PN construction (reduced switches per PN) is certainly more versatile in terms of support for various card games. Our scheme also has compelling security and performance attributes, as subsequently outlined.

6.1 Security

Privacy. An adversary who corrupts up to t players has a negligible advantage than a random guess on the permutation π underlies L_0 and L_η because the decryption key x is shared via $(t + 1, \eta)$-VSS scheme. Furthermore, the encryption scheme is semantically secure under DDH assumption, thus no adversary can distinguish the corresponding plaintexts of the shuffled deck with non-negligible probability. Non-malleability of the encryption scheme also serves to prevent repeated ciphertext attack. The permutation remains random and private because there are $t + 1$ PNs and the honest players are in the majority, this guarantees that there is at least one PN controlled by honest players.

Robustness. With honest-verifier ZKPs (*PEP* and *D-PEP*), it is infeasible for a player or a collusion of t players to cheat without the knowledge of x. Incorrect computations by dishonest players at each switch are detected with an overwhelming probability. Therefore, if all proofs are correct, we can be assured of the equality of plaintexts between the input and output ciphertexts. Besides, gameplay robustness is also guaranteed. Disconnection – both accidental and intentional – will not halt the game because these players are in the minority, thus they can be disregarded without affecting the correctness of output due to threshold sharing of x.

Verifiability. All proof transcripts are published on the bulletin board for verification. Thus, any deviation from the protocol is always detected with overwhelming probability without the dependence on a trusted dealer.

6.2 Performance

We analyze the computational cost based on modular exponentiations in Z_p. For simplicity, we consider a single exponentiation scaled as 1 and double exponentiation costs 1.2 times single exponentiation assuming the use of simultaneous multiple exponentiation technique. The computational effort is mainly determined by the work at each switch, particularly the ZKPs, as tabulated below:

Table 2. Modular exponentiations per switch

Task	Cost
Randomisation	4
Proof	3.6
Verification	3.6

With approximately $\Pi_j = \frac{t+1}{\eta} \Pi_{\text{OAS-Benes}}(\mu)$ number of switches per player, a player thus performs $7.6\,\Pi_j$ and $3.6\,\Pi_j$ for mixing and verification respectively; the former reducible to $3.6\,\Pi_j$ via precomputation of re-encryption factors in *randomisation algorithm*. On the other hand, the latter is executed $(\eta - 1)$ times by the verifying players.

In a practical setting, assume $\eta = 5$ players with possibility of $t = 2$ cheaters, and a deck of $\mu = 52$ cards. With 3 OAS-Benes PN$^{(52)}$, each player is assigned approximately $\Pi_j = (2 + 1)(249)/5 \approx 150$ switches. The total computational cost per player (without considering precomputation) is therefore $(7.6)(150) + (5 - 1)(3.6)(150) = 3300$ on average.

Obviously, Π_j is the major factor contributing to the computation cost. Thus, employing OAS-Benes PN achieves significant efficiency gain compared to Waksman PN [11] or Chang-Melham AS-Benes [12], as evident from the graph in Figure 9. In the case of 52 cards, our construction requires only 249 switches in contrast to 321 switches needed by Waksman PN and 260 for AS-Benes, resulting in cost reduction by approximately 20% and 4% respectively.

7 Concluding Remarks

The presented shuffling protocol attains efficiency of $O(tN\lg N)$ for N inputs in terms of computation and communication, which is comparable to the schemes of Abe [9] and Jakobsson-Juels [8]. This is nevertheless substantially more efficient compared to the $O(\kappa t\eta)$ (with κ some security parameter) of the Kurosawa *et al.*'s formulation [4], which also scales linearly with the number of players η. Our formulation – in common with other PN-based schemes – would not have increased overheads for larger η, which is an important practical consideration given that many interesting card games have no restriction on the number of engaged players. The use of non-interactive ZKPs posted on the bulletin board also facilitates implementation within framework of contemporary client-server networking.

The computation overhead is nevertheless extremely high in absolute terms, particularly in comparison to *basic* protocols i.e. asymmetric encryptions and signatures. This stems from the large number of switch-specific number-theoretic computations; the total quantity of which is dependent on the size of the card-deck and also the desired robustness (for a particular gaming session) against cheaters. It should, however, be noted that our formulation is based entirely on DL cryptography, thereby motivating a theoretically straightforward restatement in terms of elliptic curve (EC) cryptography. An EC-based implementation enables order-of-magnitude efficiency gains in computation, storage and communication; all of which are important considerations if real-time gaming is to be workable within the context of typical platforms and wide-area networks (WAN).

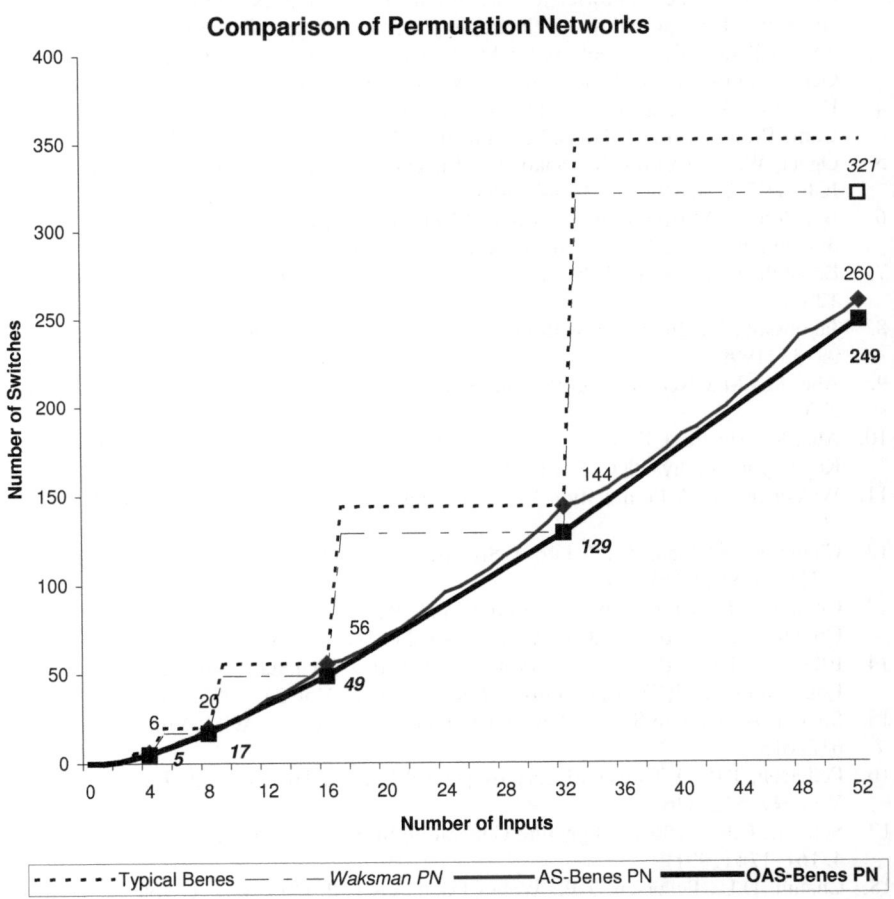

Fig. 9. Comparison of Permutation Networks

Acknowledgements. The authors wish to thank Markus Jakobsson for his helpful suggestions and Masayuki Abe for invaluable comments.

References

1. Crépeau, C.: A Secure Poker Protocol that Minimizes the Effect of Player Coalitions. Crypto 85, 73–86
2. Crépeau, C.: A zero-knowledge poker protocol that achieves confidentiality of the players' strategy or How to achieve an electronic poker face. Crypto 86, 239–247
3. Schindelhauer, C.: A Toolbox for Mental Card Games. Medizinische Universität Lübeck, Germany (1998). Available at http://www.tcs.mu-luebeck.de/Forschung/A9814.ps
4. Kurosawa, K., Katayama, Y., Ogata, W.: Reshufflable and Laziness Tolerant Mental Card Game Protocol. IEICE Trans. Fundamentals, Vol. E00-A, No. 1 (1997)
5. Ogata, W., Kurosawa, K., Sako, K., Takatani, K.: Fault Tolerant Anonymous Channel. ICICS 97. LNCS Vol. 1334, 440–444
6. Benaloh, J.: Verifiable Secret-Ballot Elections. PhD thesis. Yale University, Department of Computer Science Department, New Haven, CT (1987)
7. Benaloh, J.: Dense Probabilistic Encryption. Selected Areas in Cryptography (SAC) 94, 120–128
8. Jakobsson, M., Juels, A.: Millimix: Mixing in Small Batches. DIMACS Technical Report 99–33 (1999)
9. Abe, M.: Mix-Networks on Permutation Networks. Asiacrypt 99. LNCS Vol. 1716, 258–273
10. Abe, M., Hoshino, F.: Remarks on Mix-Network Based on Permutation Networks. Public Key Cryptography (PKC) 2001. LNCS 1992, 317–324
11. Waksman, A.: A Permutation Network. Journal of the ACM Vol. 15, No. 1 (1968) 159–163
12. Chang, C., Melham, R.: Arbitrary Size Benes Networks. Parallel Processing Letters Vol. 7, No. 3 (1997) 279–284
13. Chaum, D.L.: Untraceable Electronic Mail, Return Addresses, and Digital Pseudonyms. Communications of the ACM. Vol. 24, No. 2 (1981) 84–88
14. ElGamal, T.: A Public-Key Cryptosystem and a Signature Scheme based on Discrete Logarithms. IEEE Trans. on Information Theory. IT Vol. 31 (1985) 469–472
15. Shamir, A.: How to Share a Secret. Communications of the ACM, Vol. 22, No. 11 (1979) 612–613
16. Pedersen, T.P.: A Threshold Cryptosystem Without a Trusted Party. Eurocrypt 91. LNCS Vol. 547, 522–526
17. Schnorr, C.P.: Efficient Signature Generation by Smart Cards. Journal of Cryptology Vol. 4, 161–174 (1991)
18. Chaum, D.L., Pedersen, T.P.: Wallet Databases with Observers. Crypto 92. LNCS Vol. 740, 89–105
19. Cramer, R., Damgård, I., Schoenmakers, B.: Proofs of Partial Knowledge and Simplified Design of Witness Hiding Protocols. Crypto 94. LNCS Vol. 839, 174–187
20. Opferman, D.C., Tsao-Wu, N.T.: On A Class of Rearrangeable Switching Networks. Bell Systems Technical Journal Vol. 50, No. 5 (1971) 1579–1618

Fingerprinting Concatenated Codes with Efficient Identification

M. Fernandez and M. Soriano*

Department of Telematics Engineering. Universitat Politècnica de Catalunya.
C/ Jordi Girona 1 i 3. Campus Nord, Mod C3, UPC. 08034 Barcelona. Spain.
{marcelf,soriano}@mat.upc.es

Abstract. A fingerprinting code is a set of codewords that are embedded in each copy of a digital object, with the purpose of making each copy unique. If the fingerprinting code is c-secure, then the decoding of a pirate word created by a coalition of at most c dishonest users, will expose at least one of the guilty parties. In this paper we construct a 2-secure fingerprinting code by concatenating an inner (2,2)-separating code with an outter IPP code. The particular choice of the codes is such that allows the use of efficient decoding algorithms that correct errors beyond the error correction bound of the code, namely a simplified version of the Chase algorithms for the inner code and the Koetter-Vardy soft-decision list decoding algorithm for the outter code.

1   Introduction

In the multimedia content market, there is the need to protect both intellectual property and distribution rights against dishonest buyers. Encrypting the data only offers protection as long as the data remains encrypted, since once an authorized but fraudulent user decrypts it, nothing stops him from redistributing the data without having to worry about being caught.

The fingerprinting technique consists in making the copies of a digital object unique by inserting a different set of marks in each copy. Having unique copies of an object clearly rules out plain redistribution, but still a coalition of dishonest users can collude, compare their copies and by changing the marks where their copies differ, they are able to create a pirate copy that tries to disguise their identities. Thus, the fingerprinting problem consists in finding, for each copy of the object, the right set of marks that help to prevent collusion attacks. If the marks are the codewords of a c-secure code, then it is guaranteed that at least one of the members of the coalition can be traced back.

The construction of c-secure codes was first addressed in [2]. In that paper, Boneh and Shaw obtain a logarithmic length c-secure code by composing an inner binary code with an outter random code. Therefore, the identification

---

* This work has been supported in part by the Spanish Research Council (CICYT) Project TIC2000-1120-C03-03 (ACIMUT).

A.H. Chan and V. Gligor (Eds.): ISC 2002, LNCS 2433, pp. 459–470, 2002.

algorithm of the Boneh and Shaw code involves the decoding of a random code, that is known to be a NP-hard problem [1].

Therefore, there is a clear motivation to use the structure provided by algebraic codes in the construction of fingerprinting codes.

In [1], Barg, Blakley and Kabatiansky construct fingerprinting codes that use algebraic codes. If the codes have length n, then the decoding algorithm has complexity $\mathbf{poly}(n)$. They also show that for the case of size 2 coalitions, either one of the traitors is identified with probability 1 or both traitors are identified with probability $1-\exp(\Omega(n))$. In this paper, we show how soft-decision decoding can be introduced in the identification process, to (in some cases) improve the results in [1] and identify both traitors with probability 1.

A weaker form of traceability is provided by (t,t)-separating codes [4,9]. Loosely speaking, if a (t,t)-separating code is used in fingerprinting, then two disjoint coalitions of size t cannot come up with the same pirate, in other words, a coalition of size at most t cannot "frame" a disjoint coalition also of size at most t.

Codes with the identifiable parent property or IPP codes, introduced in [7], are 2-secure q-ary codes. The fingerprinting code we present is a binary 2-secure code with error ϵ. It is a concatenated code, where the inner code is a dual binary Hamming code that is $(2,2)$-separating and the outter code is a Reed-Solomon code having IPP.

The use of error correcting codes allows us to view the pirate fingerprint as a codeword of the fingerprinting code containing many errors. As it is shown below, the number of errors that a dishonest coalition is able to introduce into the fingerprint, will force us to be able to decode beyond the error correction bound of the code. Since we will be using concatenated codes, the basic idea is to pass the information obtained from the inner decodings, provided by a simplified version of the Chase algorithms, to a Koetter-Vardy algebraic soft-decision decoding algorithm that is used to decode the outter code. This technique provides, in many cases, better identification performance than the previously known decoding algorithms with the same complexity.

In Section 2 we introduce the basic notation used throughout the paper and the concept of IPP and separating codes. The Chase algorithms and the Koetter-Vardy algorithm are both described in Section 3. Section 4 presents the fingerprinting concatenated code. The identification process is shown in Section 5, where a simplified version of the Chase algorithms is presented, and in Section 6, where the full decoding scheme is described.

2   IPP Codes, Separating Codes, C-secure Codes, and Fingerprinting Codes

A subset C of a vector space $\mathbf{F}_q^n$ is called a *code*. The set of scalars $\mathbf{F}_q$ is called the *code alphabet*. A vector in $\mathbf{F}_q^n$ is called a *word* and the elements of C are called *codewords*, each codeword is of the form $\mathbf{x} = (x_1, \dots, x_n)$ where $x_i \in \mathbf{F}_q$, $1 \le i \le n$.

The number of nonzero coordinates in $\mathbf{x}$ is called the *weight* of $\mathbf{x}$ and is commonly denoted by $w(\mathbf{x})$. The *Hamming distance* $\mathbf{d}(\mathbf{a}, \mathbf{b})$ between two words $\mathbf{a}, \mathbf{b} \in \mathbf{F}_q^n$ is the number of positions where $\mathbf{a}$ and $\mathbf{b}$ differ. The distance between a word $\mathbf{a}$ and a subset of words $U \subset \mathbf{F}_q^n$ is defined as $\mathbf{d}(\mathbf{a}, U) := \min_{\mathbf{u} \in U} \mathbf{d}(\mathbf{a}, \mathbf{u})$. The *minimum distance* of C, denoted by d, is defined as the smallest distance between two different codewords.

A code C is a *linear code* if it forms a subspace of $\mathbf{F}_q^n$. A code with length n, dimension k and minimum distance d is denoted as a $[n, k, d]$-code.

If we take a set of n distinct elements $P = \{\nu_1, \ldots, \nu_n\} \subseteq \mathbf{F}_q$, then a *Reed-Solomon code* of length n and dimension k, consists of all codewords of the form $(f(\nu_1), \ldots, f(\nu_n))$ where f takes the value of all polynomials of degree less than k in $\mathbf{F}_q[x]$:

$$\mathrm{RS}(P, k) = \{(f(\nu_1), \ldots, f(\nu_n)) \mid f \in \mathbf{F}_q[x] \wedge \deg(f) < k\}$$

A *simplex code* or *dual binary Hamming code* S_r, is a $[2^r - 1, r, 2^{r-1}]$ code, consisting of $\mathbf{0}$ and $2^r - 1$ codewords of weight 2^{r-1}, with every pair of codewords the same distance apart.

2.1   IPP Codes

The contents in this section are based on [7].

For any two words $\mathbf{a}$, $\mathbf{b}$ in $\mathbf{F}_q^n$ we define the *set* of *descendants* $D(\mathbf{a}, \mathbf{b})$ as

$$D(\mathbf{a}, \mathbf{b}) := \{\mathbf{x} \in \mathbf{F}_q^n : x_i \in \{a_i, b_i\}, 1 \leq i \leq n\}.$$

One can see that among the set of descendants of $\mathbf{a}$ and $\mathbf{b}$, there are $\mathbf{a}$ and $\mathbf{b}$ themselves.

For a code C, the *descendant code* C^* is defined as:

$$C^* := \bigcup_{\mathbf{a} \in C, \mathbf{b} \in C} D(\mathbf{a}, \mathbf{b}).$$

For example, if $C = \{0000, 1111\}$ then $C^* = \mathbf{F}_2^4$.

If $\mathbf{z} \in C^*$ is a descendant of $\mathbf{a}$ and $\mathbf{b}$, then we call $\mathbf{a}$ and $\mathbf{b}$ *parents* of $\mathbf{z}$. If for every descendant in C^*, at least one of the parents can be identified, we say that code C has the *identifiable parent property* (IPP). Usually a word in C^* has several pairs of parents, so if the code has IPP then the intersection of those pairs will be non-empty. The IPP decoding algorithm consists in finding all pairs of parents of a given descendant $\mathbf{z} \in C^*$.

Next Theorem gives an explicit construction of IPP codes.

Theorem 1 (Holl. et al. [7]). *Let q be a prime power. If $q \geq n - 1$, then there exists a (shortened, extended or doubly extended) Reed-Solomon code over $\mathbf{F}_q$ with parameters $[n, \lceil n/4 \rceil, n - \lceil n/4 \rceil + 1]$ that has IPP.*

2.2   Fingerprinting Codes and C-secure Codes

A fingerprinting code is a set of codewords ("fingerprints"), where each codeword is to be embedded in a different copy of a digital object. The codewords must be chosen in a way that it must be possible to identify at least one guilty user in case of a collusion attack.

In a collusion attack, a coalition of users compare their copies and create a new *pirate* copy, by changing some of the marks that they can detect. Under the assumption that the coalition can only change the marks where their copies differ, the set of potential pirate copies that the coalition is able to create, is precisely the set of descendants of the codewords belonging to the members of the coalition.

A code is *totally c-secure*, if given a descendant of a coalition of size at most c, there exists a tracing algorithm that allows to find one member of the coalition with probability 1.

Since there are no totally c-secure codes for $c \geq 2$ [2] (Theorem 4.2 of that paper), then the goal is to construct codes that allow to at least identify one member of the coalition with probability greater than $1 - \epsilon$. Such codes are denoted as *c-secure codes with ϵ-error*.

2.3   (2,2)-Separating Codes

A code C is $(2, 2)$-*separating*, if for any two disjoint subsets of codewords of size two, $\{\mathbf{a}, \mathbf{b}\}$ and $\{\mathbf{c}, \mathbf{d}\}$, where $\{\mathbf{a}, \mathbf{b}\} \cap \{\mathbf{c}, \mathbf{d}\} = \emptyset$, their respective sets of descendants are also disjoint, $D(\mathbf{a}, \mathbf{b}) \cap D(\mathbf{c}, \mathbf{d}) = \emptyset$.

Next corollary from [4] gives a sufficient condition for a linear code to be (2,2)-separating.

Corollary 1 ([4]). *All linear, equidistant codes are (2,2)-separating.*

Using Corollary 1, the dual binary Hamming code is readily seen to be (2,2)-separating.

3   Algorithms That Decode Beyond the Error Correction Bound

In a codeword transmission through a communications channel, the received word is usually a corrupted version of the sent codeword due to the inherent presence of noise in the channel. If we denote by $\mathbf{c}$ the transmitted codeword and by $\mathbf{r}$ the received word, then the *error pattern* of $\mathbf{r}$ is a word $\mathbf{e}$, that satisfies $\mathbf{r} = \mathbf{c} + \mathbf{e}$. The task of the decoder is to estimate the sent codeword from the received word. If the number of errors $w(\mathbf{e})$ is greater than $\lfloor (d - 1)/2 \rfloor$, then there can be more than one codeword within distance $w(\mathbf{e})$ from the received word and the decoder may either decode incorrectly or fail to decode. This leads to the concept of *list decoding* [6,8], where the decoder outputs a list of all codewords within distance $w(\mathbf{e})$ of the received word, thus offering a potential way to recover from errors beyond the error correction bound of the code.

In *soft-decision* decoding, the decoding process takes advantage of "side information" or channel measurement information generated by the receiver, to estimate the sent codeword.

In the process of decoding fingerprinting codes, we are faced with the task of correcting a number of errors beyond the error correction bound of the code.

3.1   Chase Algorithms

In [3], three decoding algorithms that can double the error correcting capabilities of a given binary block code are presented. Using a binary decoder that corrects $\lfloor (d-1)/2 \rfloor$ errors together with channel measurement information, the Chase algorithms can correct up to $d-1$ errors. The idea is to perturb the received word with different test patterns, and then pass the perturbed word to a binary decoder to obtain a small set of possible error patterns, rather than just a single error pattern. The channel measurement information is used to choose the appropriate error pattern from the set. The difference between the three algorithms lies in the size of the set of error patterns considered.

3.2   The Koetter-Vardy Soft-Decision Decoding Algorithm

In this section, we give a brief overview of the Koetter-Vardy (KV) soft-decision decoding algorithm presented in [8], that list decodes a Reed-Solomon code beyond the error correction bound.

The KV algorithm, instead of using the received word symbols, uses probabilistic reliability information about these received symbols.

A discrete memoryless channel can be defined as two finite sets $\mathcal{X}$ and $\mathcal{Y}$ called the *input alphabet* and *output alphabet* respectively, and $|\mathcal{X}|$ functions

$$f(y|x) \in [0,1] \qquad \text{for all } x \in \mathcal{X} \tag{1}$$

where $y \in \mathcal{Y}$. We suppose that these functions are known to the decoder.

Now, if we see the input and output of a discrete memoryless channel as random variables X and Y respectively, and we suppose that X is uniformly distributed over $\mathcal{X}$, then the decoder can compute the probability that $\alpha_i \in \mathcal{X}$ was the transmitted symbol given that $\beta_j \in \mathcal{Y}$ was observed as

$$\Pr(X = \alpha_i | Y = \beta_j) = \frac{f(\beta_j|\alpha_i)}{\sum_{x \in \mathcal{X}} f(\beta_j|x)} \tag{2}$$

For the case of Reed-Solomon codes of length n and dimension k, where the input alphabet is $\mathcal{X} = \mathbf{F}_q$, we take $\alpha_1, \alpha_2, \ldots, \alpha_q$ as the ordering of the elements of $\mathbf{F}_q$. If vector $\beta = (\beta_1, \ldots, \beta_n)$ is received, then using (2) the following values can be computed

$$r_{i,j} = \Pr(X = \alpha_i | Y = \beta_j) \tag{3}$$

These values are the entries of a $q \times n$ matrix, called the *reliability matrix* and denoted by $\mathcal{R}$, that is the input to the KV algorithm.

We are interested in knowing what codewords the KV algorithm will return. With this intention, given two $q \times n$ matrices A and B over the same field, the following product is defined

$$\langle A, B \rangle := trace(AB^T) = \sum_{i=1}^{q} \sum_{j=1}^{n} a_{i,j} b_{i,j} \tag{4}$$

Also a word $\mathbf{v} = (v_1, v_2, \ldots, v_n)$ over $\mathbf{F}_q$ can be represented by the $q \times n$ matrix $[\mathbf{v}]$, with entries $[\mathbf{v}]_{i,j}$ defined as follows

$$[\mathbf{v}]_{i,j} := \begin{cases} 1 \text{ if } v_j = \alpha_i \\ 0 \text{ otherwise} \end{cases} \tag{5}$$

In [8] Koetter and Vardy state the following theorem:

Theorem 2 ([8]). *If codeword $\mathbf{u}$ is transmitted, word $\mathbf{v}$ is received and the reliability matrix $\mathcal{R}$ is constructed according to (3), then the KV soft-decision decoding algorithm outputs a list that contains the sent codeword $\mathbf{u} \in \mathrm{RS}(n, k)$ if*

$$\frac{\langle \mathcal{R}, [\mathbf{u}] \rangle}{\sqrt{\langle \mathcal{R}, \mathcal{R} \rangle}} \geq \sqrt{k-1} + o(1) \tag{6}$$

where $o(1)$ is a function that tends to zero in the asymptotic case.

4 Construction of a Concatenated Fingerprinting Code

The idea of using code concatenation in fingerprinting schemes to construct shorter codes, was presented earlier in [2].

A concatenated code is the combination of an *inner* $[n_i, k_i, d_i]$ q_i-ary code ($q_i \geq 2$) with an *outter* $[n_o, k_o, d_o]$ code over $\mathbf{F}_{q_i^{k_i}}$. The combination consists in mapping the codewords of the inner code to the elements of $\mathbf{F}_{q_i^{k_i}}$, that results in a q_i-ary code of length $n_i n_o$ and dimension $k_i k_o$. Note that the size of the concatenated code is the same as the size of the outter code.

In [5], dual binary Hamming codes are proposed as fingerprinting codes. One of the major drawbacks of that scheme is that the number of codewords grows linearly with the length of the code. To overcome this situation we use code concatenation, and combine a dual binary Hamming code with an IPP Reed-Solomon code.

So, to construct a $[n(2^r - 1), r\lceil n/4 \rceil]$ binary fingerprinting code $\mathcal{C}$, we use:

− as inner code, a $[2^r - 1, r, 2^{r-1}]$ dual binary Hamming code S_r,
− as outter code, a $[n, \lceil n/4 \rceil, n - \lceil n/4 \rceil + 1]$ IPP Reed-Solomon code over $\mathbf{F}_{2^r}$,
− together with a mapping $\phi : \mathbf{F}_{2^r} \rightarrow S_r$.

The codewords of $\mathcal{C}$ are obtained as follows, take a codeword $\mathbf{x} = (x_1, \ldots, x_n)$ from the Reed-Solomon code and compute $y_i = \phi(x_i)$, $1 \leq i \leq n$. The concatenation of the $\mathbf{y}_i$'s forms a codeword $\mathbf{y} \in \mathcal{C}$, where,

$$\mathbf{y} = (\mathbf{y}_1, \ldots, \mathbf{y}_n) \text{ such that } \mathbf{y}_i = \phi(x_i)$$

5   Simplified Chase Algorithm

In this section, we present a new decoding algorithm that decodes the descendant code of a dual binary Hamming code. Our algorithm is based on the Chase decoding algorithms presented in Section 3.

As we said before, to decode a descendant code means to find all possible pairs of parents of a given descendant. To accomplish this task for a dual binary Hamming code, we will need to "correct" up to 2^{r-2} errors, which is beyond the error correction bound of the code. To see this, suppose we have a code S_r with parameters $(2^r - 1, 2^r, 2^{r-1})$, if $\mathbf{v}$ belongs to the descendant code S_r^*, then there are three possibilities for the sets of pairs of parents:

1. A star configuration. All pairs of parents have a common element, say $\mathbf{x}$, where $\mathrm{dist}(\mathbf{x}, \mathbf{v}) \leq 2^{r-2} - 1$.
2. A "degenerated" star configuration. There is a single parent pair $\{\mathbf{x}, \mathbf{y}\}$. Now $\mathrm{dist}(\mathbf{x}, \mathbf{v}) = \mathrm{dist}(\mathbf{y}, \mathbf{v}) = 2^{r-2}$.
3. A triangle configuration. There are three possible pairs of parents: $\{\mathbf{x}, \mathbf{y}\}$, $\{\mathbf{x}, \mathbf{z}\}$ and $\{\mathbf{y}, \mathbf{z}\}$. Note that $\mathrm{dist}(\mathbf{x}, \mathbf{v}) = \mathrm{dist}(\mathbf{y}, \mathbf{v}) = \mathrm{dist}(\mathbf{z}, \mathbf{v}) = 2^{r-2}$.

Therefore, we need an algorithm that outputs all codewords of S_r within distance 2^{r-2} of $\mathbf{v}$. As it is assumed in [3], we suppose that we have a binary decoder that corrects up to $\lfloor (d-1)/2 \rfloor = 2^{r-2} - 1$ errors, so if $\mathbf{v}$ lies in a sphere of radius $2^{r-2} - 1$ surrounding any codeword, then it will be corrected by the binary decoder.

On the other hand, if there are 2^{r-2} errors in $\mathbf{v}$, then the binary decoder fails to decode. But in this case, note that the word $\mathbf{v}'$, obtained by applying a test pattern $\mathbf{p}$ of weight 1 to $\mathbf{v}$ ($\mathbf{v}' = \mathbf{v} \oplus \mathbf{p}$), can fall in a sphere of radius $2^{r-2} - 1$ around a codeword. So, using the appropriate test pattern, we are allowed to correct 2^{r-2} errors.

We define the set of *matching positions* between two words $\mathbf{a}$ and $\mathbf{b}$, $M(\mathbf{a}, \mathbf{b})$, as $M(\mathbf{a}, \mathbf{b}) := \{i : a_i = b_i\}$.

Suppose that the number of errors in a descendant word $\mathbf{v}$ is 2^{r-2}, then the algorithm will return two or three codewords, depending of how $\mathbf{v}$ was constructed. The idea of the algorithm is to efficiently find the right test pattern, using the already found candidate parents. To see how this is done, note that once a candidate parent is found, the support of the test pattern that helps to find another parent, lies in the matching positions between the candidate and the received word.

Simplified Chase Algorithm:

The algorithm uses:

- A function called *binary_decoder*$(\mathbf{v})$, that takes as its argument the descendant $\mathbf{v}$, and if it exists, outputs the unique codeword within distance $2^{r-2} - 1$ of $\mathbf{v}$.
- A function called *right_shift*$(\mathbf{p})$, that takes as its argument a test pattern $\mathbf{p}$ of weight 1, and outputs a test pattern with its support shifted one position to the right with respect to $\mathbf{p}$, i.e., *right_shift*$((0, 1, 0, 0)) = (0, 0, 1, 0)$.

- A *list* that maintains all the already used test patterns that, when applied to the received word, failed to decode into a codeword.
- Take $\mathbf{u} = (u_1, \ldots, u_r)$ and $\mathbf{v} = (v_1, \ldots, v_r)$, then $\mathbf{u} \oplus \mathbf{v}$ denotes the bitwise *exclusive or*, $\mathbf{u} \oplus \mathbf{v} = (u_1 \oplus v_1, \ldots, u_r \oplus v_r)$.

Input: S_r, Dual binary Hamming code of dimension r; descendant $\mathbf{v} \in S_r^*$.
Output: All codewords within distance 2^{r-2} of $\mathbf{v}$.

1. Set $\mathbf{u}_1 := binary\_decoder(\mathbf{v})$. If $\mathbf{u}_1 \neq \emptyset$ then output $\mathbf{u}_1$ and quit.
2. Initialization: $\mathbf{p} := (1, 0, 0, \ldots, 0)$, $list := \{\emptyset\}$.
3. Set $\mathbf{v}' := \mathbf{v} \oplus \mathbf{p}$ and run the binary decoder. Set $\mathbf{u}_1 := binary\_decoder(\mathbf{v}')$.
4. If $\mathbf{u}_1 \neq \emptyset$ then go to step 5.
   Else add $\mathbf{p}$ to $list$. Set $\mathbf{p} := right\_shift(\mathbf{p})$. Go to step 3.
5. Construct a new test pattern $\mathbf{p}$ of weight 1 that:
   - is different from all the patterns in $list$.
   - its support is one of the matching positions between $\mathbf{v}$ and $\mathbf{u}_1$.
6. Set $\mathbf{v}' := \mathbf{v} \oplus \mathbf{p}$ and run the binary decoder, $\mathbf{u}_2 := binary\_decoder(\mathbf{v}')$.
7. If $\mathbf{u}_2 \neq \emptyset$ then go to step 8.
   Else add $\mathbf{p}$ to $list$ and go to step 5.
8. Construct a new test pattern $\mathbf{p}$ of weight 1 that:
   - is different from all the patterns in $list$.
   - its support is one of the matching positions between $\mathbf{v}$, $\mathbf{u}_1$ and $\mathbf{u}_2$.
   If there are no more test patterns available, output codewords $\mathbf{u}_1$, $\mathbf{u}_2$ and quit.
9. Set $\mathbf{v}' := \mathbf{v} \oplus \mathbf{p}$ and run the binary decoder, $\mathbf{u}_3 := binary\_decoder(\mathbf{v}')$.
10. If $\mathbf{u}_3 \neq \emptyset$ then goto step 11.
    Else add $\mathbf{p}$ to $list$ and go to step 8.
11. Output codewords $\mathbf{u}_1$, $\mathbf{u}_2$ and $\mathbf{u}_3$ and quit.

6   Decoding of the Fingerprinting Concatenated Code

In this section, we present a tracing algorithm that efficiently decodes the fingerprinting codes constructed in Section 4. The decoding method we propose uses the Simplified Chase Algorithm described in Section 5, and the Koetter-Vardy Algorithm described in Section 3.

For a Reed-Solomon code with IPP, we call any codeword that is involved in the construction of a given descendant in an unambiguous way a *positive parent*. The goal of a tracing algorithm is to output a list that contains all positive parents of a given descendant. However, note that to find both parents is a strong condition, since if for example, one of the parents contributes with only $k - 1$ positions, where k is the dimension of the code, then there are multiple pairs of parents. Theorem 3 below, provides a useful condition for a codeword to be a positive parent.

Theorem 3. *Let C be a $[n, k, d]$ Reed-Solomon code with IPP, if a codeword agrees in more than $2(n-d)$ positions with a given descendant then this codeword is a positive parent of the descendant.*

Proof. If the code has minimum distance d, then two codewords can agree in at most $n - d$ positions, therefore a parent pair is only able to produce a descendant that agrees in at most $2(n - d)$ positions with any other codeword. Then any codeword that agrees with a descendant in at least $2(n - d) + 1$ positions is a parent. $\qquad\square$

6.1   Overview of the Algorithm

The decoding is done in two stages. First, we decode the inner code to obtain an n-tuple of sets of codewords. Then, with this n-tuple of sets we construct a reliability matrix that is used to decode the outter code.

Suppose we want to decode the following fingerprint:

$$\mathbf{y} = (\mathbf{y}_1, \mathbf{y}_2, \dots, \mathbf{y}_n)$$

The inner decoding consists in the decoding of each subword $\mathbf{y}_i$ using the Simplified Chase Algorithm. The output, as seen in Section 5, will be a single codeword $\{\mathbf{h}_1\}$, a pair of codewords $\{\mathbf{h}_1, \mathbf{h}_2\}$ or three codewords $\{\mathbf{h}_1, \mathbf{h}_2, \mathbf{h}_3\}$.

Then, for $i = 1, \dots, n$ we use the mapping $\phi(s_m) = \mathbf{h}_m$ to obtain the set $S_i^{(j)} = \{s_{i_1}, \dots, s_{i_j}\}$, where the superscript $j \in \{1, 2, 3\}$ indicates the cardinality of the set. Note that the elements of the $S_i^{(j)}$'s are symbols from $\mathbf{F}_{2^r}$. We denote by $\mathcal{S}^{(1)}$ the set of the $S^{(1)}$'s, by $\mathcal{S}^{(2)}$ the set of the $S^{(2)}$'s and by $\mathcal{S}^{(3)}$ the set of the $S^{(3)}$'s.

We also define the n-tuple of sets $\mathcal{S} = (S_1^{(j)}, \dots, S_n^{(j)})$, that is used to construct a reliability matrix. With this matrix we run the Koetter-Vardy algorithm obtaining a list U of potential parents. If d_o denotes the minimum distance of the outer code, then to extract the positive parents out of the list U, we use the following statements:

– If $(|\mathcal{S}^{(1)}| + |\mathcal{S}^{(2)}|) > 4(n - d_o)$, then by Theorem 3, at least one of the parents is identified with probability 1.

– If $|\mathcal{S}^{(2)}| > 2(n - d_o)$, then by Theorem 3, both parents are identified with probability 1.

– If $(|\mathcal{S}^{(1)}| + |\mathcal{S}^{(2)}|) \leq 4(n - d_o)$, then define $U_3 = \{\mathbf{u} \in U : u_p \in S_p^{(3)}, \forall S_p^{(3)} \in \mathcal{S}\}$. The only cases of positive identification are:

   • For any $S_p^{(2)} \in \mathcal{S}$, where $S_p^{(2)} = \{s_{p_1}, s_{p_2}\}$, if there are two and only two codewords $\{\mathbf{u}^1, \mathbf{u}^2\} \in U_3$, such that $u_p^1 = s_{p_1}$ and $u_p^2 = s_{p_2}$, then codewords $\mathbf{u}^1$ and $\mathbf{u}^2$ can be identified as positive parents.

   • For any $S_p^{(1)} \in \mathcal{S}$, where $S_p^{(1)} = \{s_{p_1}\}$, if there is one and only one codeword $\mathbf{u} \in U_3$, such that $u_p = s_{p_1}$, then codeword $\mathbf{u}$ can be identified as a positive parent.

6.2 Decoding Algorithm for the Fingerprinting Concatenated Code

The algorithm takes as its input a word $\mathbf{y} = (\mathbf{y}_1, \mathbf{y}_2, \dots, \mathbf{y}_n)$ of the concatenated code, and outputs the positive parents of this word in the form of codewords of the outter code.

1. For $i := 1$ to n:
   a) Decode the inner word $\mathbf{y}_i$ using the Simplified Chase Algorithm to obtain a list of at most 3 codewords $\{\mathbf{h}_1, \dots, \mathbf{h}_j\}$, $j \in \{1, 2, 3\}$.
   b) Define $S_i^{(j)} = \{s_{i_1}, \dots, s_{i_j}\}$, where $\phi(s_m) = \mathbf{h}_m$, $1 \leq m \leq j$ and $j \in \{1, 2, 3\}$ depending on the output of step 1a.

2. Initialize $\mathcal{S} = (S_1^{(j)}, \dots, S_n^{(j)})$.
   Define the subsets $\mathcal{S}^{(1)} = \{S_p^{(j)} \in \mathcal{S} : j = 1\}$, $\mathcal{S}^{(2)} = \{S_p^{(j)} \in \mathcal{S} : j = 2\}$ and $\mathcal{S}^{(3)} = \{S_p^{(j)} \in \mathcal{S} : j = 3\}$.

3. Construct the reliability matrix $\mathcal{R}$ as follows:
$$r_{i,p} := \begin{cases} \dfrac{1}{j} & \text{if } s_{p_m} = \alpha_i, \; s_{p_m} \in S_p^{(j)}, \; 1 \leq m \leq j \\ 0 & \text{otherwise} \end{cases}$$

4. Run the Koetter-Vardy algorithm using $\mathcal{R}$, obtaining a list of codewords U.

5. Use the following decision rule:

6. If $(|\mathcal{S}^{(1)}| + |\mathcal{S}^{(2)}|) > 2(n - d)$ then compute
   $U_{1,2} = \{\mathbf{u} \in U : |\{p : u_p \in S_p^{(1)} \lor u_p \in S_p^{(2)}\}| > 2(n - d)\}$.
   Note that $|U_{1,2}| \leq 2$.
   If $|U_{1,2}| = 0$ then go to Step 7, else output $|U_{1,2}|$ and quit.

7. Find a list U_3, of all codewords $\mathbf{u}^l \in U$ such that $u_p^l \in S_p^{(3)}$ for all $S_p^{(3)} \in \mathcal{S}$.
   a) For each $S_p^{(2)} \in \mathcal{S}$ do:
      If there is an $S_p^{(2)} = \{s_{p_1}, s_{p_2}\}$ for which there are exactly 2 codewords $(\mathbf{u}^1, \mathbf{u}^2) \in U_3$ such that $u_p^1 = s_{p_1}$ and $u_p^2 = s_{p_2}$, then output $\mathbf{u}^1$ and $\mathbf{u}^2$ and quit.
   b) For each $S_p^{(1)} \in \mathcal{S}$ do:
      If there is an $S_p^{(1)} = \{s_{p_1}\}$ for which there is exactly 1 codeword $\mathbf{u}^1 \in U_3$ such that $u_p^1 = s_{p_1}$, then output $\mathbf{u}^1$ and quit.
   c) Decoding Fails.

6.3 Analysis of the Algorithm

Note that if the algorithm succeeds it outputs at least one of the parents. Also note that the algorithm only outputs positive parents, so if it is used in fingerprinting schemes it never accuses innocent users.

Next, we will show that the probability that the algorithm of the previous sub-section fails can be made arbitrarily small. To see this, we first recall a Proposition from [5].

Proposition 1 ([5]). *Given* $\mathbf{x}, \mathbf{y} \in S_r$. *The probability that the coalition* $\{\mathbf{x}, \mathbf{y}\}$ *constructs a descendant word* $\mathbf{v}$, *such that there exists a* $\mathbf{z} \in S_r$ *with* $\mathbf{d}(\mathbf{v}, \mathbf{z}) = 2^{r-2}$ *is*

$$p \leq \left(\frac{1}{2}\right)^{2^{r-1}}$$

Proof. For the proof of the Proposition see [5].   □

Next theorem shows that the probability that the tracing algorithm fails, decreases exponentially with the length of the code.

Theorem 4. *Given the code from Section 4 and given a descendant word* $\mathbf{y} = (\mathbf{y}_1, \mathbf{y}_2, \ldots, \mathbf{y}_n)$ *created by a coalition of at most size two. The probability that the tracing algorithm fails is given by*

$$p \leq 2^{-[2^{r-1}[n-2(n-d)]-kr]}$$

where $d = n - \lceil n/4 \rceil + 1$ *is the minimum distance of the outter code and* k *its dimension.*

Proof. From the decoding algorithm, it can be seen that decoding can only fail if $(|S^{(3)}| \geq n - 2(n - d)$. Using Proposition 1, the probability that this happens is $(2^{-2^{r-1}})^{[n-2(n-d)]}$.

No codeword will be identified if there is a codeword in the outter code that matches all the parents positions in $S^{(1)} \cup S^{(2)}$. The outter code is a Reed-Solomon code over $\mathbf{F}_{2^r}$, so there are $2^r \binom{n}{k-1}$ of such codewords. Since we have that $2^r \binom{n}{k-1} < 2^{rk}$, the theorem follows.   □

7   Conclusions

In this paper, we have presented a fingerprinting code together with an efficient tracing algorithm. The tracing algorithm never accuses an innocent user and the probability that tracing fails can be made arbitrarily small.

The identification process consists in the decoding of a concatenated code, where both the inner and the outter code are decoded beyond the error correction bound. For the decoding of the inner code, we present a modification of the Chase algorithms, that taking advantage of the structure of the descendant code of a dual binary Hamming code, allows to efficiently search for all codewords within distance 2^{r-2}.

The outter code is decoded with the Koetter-Vardy soft-decision decoding algorithm. Using soft-decision decoding allows us to improve the tracing capabilities of the algorithms in [1], that use hard-decision decoding, where only one of the colluders can be traced with probability 1. Our approach allows, in many cases, to find both colluders with probability 1.

References

1. A. Barg, G. R. Blakley, and G. Kabatiansky. Digital fingerprinting codes: Problems statements, constructions, identification of traitors. Technical report, DIMACS 2001-52, 2001.
2. D. Boneh and J. Shaw. Collusion-secure fingerprinting for digital data. *Lecture Notes in Computer Science*, 963:452–465, 1995.
3. D. Chase. A class of algorithms for decoding block codes with channel measurement information. *IEEE Trans. Inform. Theory*, 18:170–182, 1972.
4. G. Cohen, S. Encheva, and H. G. Schaathun. On separating codes. Technical report, ENST, Paris, 2001.
5. J. Domingo-Ferrer and J. Herrera-Joancomartí. Simple collusion-secure fingerprinting schemes for images. *Proceedings of the Information Technology: Coding and Computing ITCC'00*, pages 128–132, 2000.
6. V. Guruswami and M. Sudan. Improved decoding of Reed-Solomon and algebraic-geometry codes. *IEEE Trans. Inform. Theory*, 45(6):1757–1767, 1999.
7. Henk D. L. Hollmann, Jack H. van Lint, Jean-Paul Linnartz, and Ludo M. G. M. Tolhuizen. On codes with the Identifiable Parent Property. *J. Combinatorial Theory*, 82(2):121–133, May 1998.
8. R. Koetter and A. Vardy. Algebraic soft-decision decoding of Reed-Solomon codes. *ISIT'00*, 2000.
9. Y. L. Sagalovich. Separating systems. *Probl. Inform. Trans.*, 30(2):14–35, 1994.

A Provably Secure Additive and Multiplicative Privacy Homomorphism[*]

Josep Domingo-Ferrer

Universitat Rovira i Virgili, Dept. of Computer Engineering and Maths,
Av. Països Catalans 26, E-43007 Tarragona, Catalonia. Tel. +34-977559657, Fax
+34-977559710,
jdomingo@etse.urv.es

Abstract. Privacy homomorphisms (PHs) are encryption transformations mapping a set of operations on cleartext to another set of operations on ciphertext. If addition is one of the ciphertext operations, then it has been shown that a PH is insecure against a chosen-cleartext attack. Thus, a PH allowing full arithmetic on encrypted data can be at best secure against known-cleartext attacks. We present one such PH (none was known so far) which can be proven secure against known-cleartext attacks, as long as the ciphertext space is much larger than the cleartext space. Some applications to delegation of sensitive computing and data and to e-gambling are briefly outlined.

Keywords: Privacy homomorphisms, Encrypted data processing, Cryptography, Delegation of computing and data, Multilevel security, E-gambling.

1 Introduction

The first general approach to encrypted data processing is due to the authors of [10], when they introduced the notion of privacy homomorphism (PH from now on). Basically, such homomorphisms are encryption functions $E_k : T' \longrightarrow T$ allowing a set F of operations on encrypted data without knowledge of the decryption function D_k. Knowledge of D_k allows the result of the corresponding set F' of cleartext operations to be retrieved. The availability of secure PHs is central to the development of multilevel secure computation underlying such applications as computing delegation, data delegation and e-gambling: the idea is to encrypt data at a classified level, to process them at an unclassified level and to decrypt the result at a classified level. By way of illustration, consider the following example of PH, given in [10]

---

[*] This work has been partly supported by the European Commission under project IST-2001-32012 "Co-Orthogonal Codes" and by the Spanish Ministry of Science and Technology and the European FEDER fund through project no. TIC2001-0633-C03-01 "STREAMOBILE".

A.H. Chan and V. Gligor (Eds.): ISC 2002, LNCS 2433, pp. 471–483, 2002.

Example 1. Let p and q be two large and secret primes (100 decimal digits each). Let $m = pq$ be public. Define the cleartext set as $T' = \mathbf{Z}_m$ and the set of cleartext operations as $F' = \{+_m, -_m, \times_m\}$ consisting, respectively, of addition, subtraction and multiplication modulo m. Let the ciphertext set be $T = \mathbf{Z}_p \times \mathbf{Z}_q$. Operations in the set F of ciphertext operations are the componentwise version of those in F'. Define the encryption key as $k = (p, q)$ and the encryption transformation as $E_k(a) = [a \bmod p, a \bmod q]$. Given $k = (p, q)$, the Chinese remainder theorem is used to compute $D_k([b, c])$. A technical detail is that when the unclassified level computes on encrypted data, it cannot reduce partial results to the secret moduli p and q; only reduction to the public modulus m is possible, so that in fact the unclassified level operates on $\mathbf{Z}_m \times \mathbf{Z}_m$; however, at decryption time, knowledge of the key allows the classified level to map encrypted results from $\mathbf{Z}_m \times \mathbf{Z}_m$ back to $\mathbf{Z}_p \times \mathbf{Z}_q$ prior to using the Chinese remainder theorem.

Unfortunately, it is shown in [3] that this PH can be broken —*i. e.*, p and q can be found— by a known-cleartext attack. •

Next follows a summary of the state of the art on PHs. If a PH preserves order, then it is insecure against a ciphertext-only attack. If addition is one of the ciphertext operations of a PH, then such a PH is insecure against a chosen-cleartext attack ([1]). With the exception of the RSA algorithm —which preserves only multiplication—, all examples given in [10] were broken by ciphertext-only attacks or, at most, known-cleartext attacks (see [3]); the authors of [3] invented R-additive PHs, which securely allow ciphertext addition at the cost of restricting the number of ciphertexts that can be added together. In [2], a partially homomorphic scheme for statistical computation on encrypted data was proposed that consists of a two-layer encryption: data records are first encrypted as sparse polynomials, and these are then encrypted as regular polynomials; while the first layer is homomorphic, the second is not (yet the second layer is needed because the PH in the first layer is insecure); therefore, encrypted data processing is not feasible without a trusted device able to decrypt the second layer. Lacking secure PHs that preserve more than one operation, subsequent attempts at encrypted data processing have relied on *ad-hoc* solutions ([1,15]). In [4], we presented a PH preserving addition and multiplication which was conjectured to be computationally resistant against known-cleartext attacks. In [8,12], it was wondered whether provably secure algebraic (*i.e.* additive and multiplicative) privacy homomorphisms exist; this paper is meant to answer that question.

1.1   Our Contribution

In this paper, we propose the first PH preserving both addition and multiplication that can be proven secure against known-cleartext attacks, as long as the ciphertext space is much larger than the cleartext space. In Section 2 the homomorphism is specified. In Section 3 a numerical example is given. Security is proven in Section 4. Section 5 mentions some practical applications to delegation of computing and data and to e-gambling. Section 6 is a conclusion.

2   Specification of the New PH

The PH proposed in this paper can be described as follows:

- The public parameters are a positive integer $d > 2$ and a large integer m ($\approx 10^{200}$ or maybe larger). m should have many small divisors and at the same time there should be many integers less than m that can be inverted modulo m; the first condition can be satisfied by construction of m, and the second condition can be satisfied by iterating until an m is found such that $\phi(m)$ is close to $6m/(\pi^2)$, which is the expected value of $\phi(m)$ for a random m (see Lemma 5 below).
- The secret parameters are $r \in \mathbf{Z}_m$ such that $r^{-1} \bmod m$ exists and a small divisor $m' > 1$ of m such that $s := \log_{m'} m$ is a (secret) security parameter; the influence of the sizes of m' and m on security can be seen in Table 1 below. Thus, the secret key is $k = (r, m')$.

In this case the set of cleartext is $T' = \mathbf{Z}_{m'}$. The set of ciphertext is $T = (\mathbf{Z}_m)^d$. The set F' of cleartext operations is formed basically by addition, subtraction and multiplication in T'. The set F of ciphertext operations contains the corresponding componentwise operations in T. The PH transformations can be described as

Encryption. Randomly split $a \in \mathbf{Z}_{m'}$ into secret $a_{.1}, \cdots, a_{.d}$ such that $a = \sum_{j=1}^{d} a_{.j} \bmod m'$ and $a_{.j} \in \mathbf{Z}_m$. Compute

$$E_k(a) = (a_{.1}r \bmod m, a_{.2}r^2 \bmod m, \cdots, a_{.d}r^d \bmod m) \tag{1}$$

Decryption. Compute the scalar product of the j-th coordinate by $r^{-j} \bmod m$ to retrieve $a_{.j} \bmod m$. Compute $\sum_{j=1}^{d} a_{.j} \bmod m'$ to get a.

As encrypted values are computed over $(\mathbf{Z}_m)^d$ at an unclassified level, the use of r requires that the terms of the encrypted value having different r-degree be handled separately —the r-degree of a term is the exponent of the power of r contained in the term—. This is necessary for the classified level to be able to multiply each term by r^{-1} the right number of times, before adding all terms up over $\mathbf{Z}_{m'}$.

The set F' of ciphertext operations consists of

Addition and subtraction. They are done componentwise, *i. e.* between terms with the same degree.

Multiplication. It works like in the case of polynomials: all terms are cross-multiplied in $\mathbf{Z}_m$, with a d_1-th degree term by a d_2-th degree term yielding a $d_1 + d_2$-th degree term; finally, terms having the same degree are added up.

Division. Cannot be carried out in general because the polynomials are a ring, but not a field. A good solution is to leave and handle divisions in rational format by considering the field of rational functions: the encrypted version of a/b is $E_k(a)/E_k(b)$.

In addition to the operations in F', it is also possible to multiply all components of a ciphertext vector $E_k(a)$ by a cleartext constant c. If the resulting ciphertext vector is decrypted, $ac \bmod m'$ is obtained. Whenever possible, this operation should be preferred to multiplication of two ciphertexts, as ciphertext multiplication is the only operation in F that increases the r-degree of the result.

Note 2. Unlike for the PH in Example 1, in our PH the cleartext space is unknown to the unclassified level, because the parameter m' is secret. This will be useful to prove the security of our proposal. Notice that if the unclassified level is told which is the ciphertext space, then it needs no knowledge on the cleartext space to do encrypted computations. However, one of the troubles with Example 1 was that the unclassified level cannot be revealed which is the ciphertext space (giving away the ciphertext space $\mathbf{Z}_p \times \mathbf{Z}_q$ is equivalent to revealing the secret key (p, q)); therefore, knowledge of the size $m = pq$ of the cleartext space (or another common multiple of p and q) was needed to reduce partial encrypted results.

3   Numerical Example

This example is unrealistically small but it illustrates the computation of a formula including two additions and one multiplication, namely $(x_1 + x_2 + x_3)x_4$. Although $d > 2$ is recommended for security reasons (see Remark 9 below), we will take $d = 2$ to keep computations brief and clear; thus, cleartexts will be split in two parts during encryption. The public modulus is chosen to be $m = 28$.

Classified level.

Let $r = 3$ and $m' = 7$ be the secret key. Let $(x_1, x_2, x_3, x_4) = (-0.1, 0.3, 0.1, 2)$. In order to suppress decimal positions, initial data are multiplied by 10, which yields the fractions $x_1 = \tilde{x}_1/10 = -1/10$, $x_2 = \tilde{x}_2/10 = 3/10$, $x_3 = \tilde{x}_3/10 = 1/10$ and $x_4 = \tilde{x}_4/1 = 2/1$. Numerators are randomly and secretly split mod 7 and are transformed according to the proposed PH. In this way, first and second r-degree terms are obtained

$$E_k(\tilde{x}_1) = E_k(-1) = E_k(2, 4) = (6, 8)$$
$$E_k(\tilde{x}_2) = E_k(3) = E_k(2, 1) = (6, 9)$$
$$E_k(\tilde{x}_3) = E_k(1) = E_k(4, 4) = (12, 8)$$
$$E_k(\tilde{x}_4) = E_k(2) = E_k(3, 6) = (9, 26)$$

Encrypted data are forwarded to the unclassified level, along with their denominators: (1,1) for $E_k(\tilde{x}_4)$ and (10,10) for the rest of data.

Unclassified level.

First, do the additions by directly adding the numerators in the fractions, since the denominator is 10 for all data

$$\sum_{i=1}^{3} E_k(\tilde{x}_i) = (6 + 6 + 12 \bmod 28, 8 + 9 + 8 \bmod 28) = (24, 25)$$

The denominator of the sum is obviously $(10,10)$. Then, multiply by $E_k(\tilde{x}_4)$

$$(E_k(\tilde{x}_1) + E_k(\tilde{x}_2) + E_k(\tilde{x}_3))E_k(\tilde{x}_4) = (24, 25) \times (9, 26)$$

$$= (0, 24 \times 9 \bmod 28, 24 \times 26 + 25 \times 9 \bmod 28, 25 \times 26 \bmod 28) = (0, 20, 9, 6)$$

In this way, the numerator of the result has terms up to the fourth r-degree. The denominator of the product is $10 \times 1 = 10$ for all terms. Return both numerator and denominator to the classified level.

Classified level.

Compute

$$(0 \times r^{-1} \bmod m, 20 \times r^{-2} \bmod m, 9 \times r^{-3} \bmod m, 6 \times r^{-4} \bmod m)$$

$$= (0 \times 19 \bmod 28, 20 \times 19^2 \bmod 28, 9 \times 19^3 \bmod 28, 6 \times 19^4 \bmod 28)$$

$$= (0, 24, 19, 26)$$

Now add all terms in the last step over $\mathbf{Z}_{m'}$ to obtain $6 \bmod 7 = 6$. Thus, we have $(\tilde{x}_1 + \tilde{x}_2 + \tilde{x}_3)\tilde{x}_4 = 6 \bmod m' = 6$. Finally, divide 6 by the denominator 10 returned by the unclassified level, so that the final result is $(x_1 + x_2 + x_3)x_4 = 0.6$.

4   Security of the New Privacy Homomorphism

Definition 3. *A privacy homomorphism is said to be secure against a known-cleartext attack if, for any fixed number n of known cleartext-ciphertext pairs, the probability of successful decryption of a ciphertext for which the cleartext is unknown can be made arbitrarily small by properly choosing the security parameters of the homomorphism.*

We will show in this section that the PH whose encryption function is given by Expression (1) is secure. First, it will be shown that, for a fixed number n of known cleartext-ciphertext pairs, the probability of randomly guessing the right key can be made arbitrarily small. Second, it will be shown that there is only a small probability that a ciphertext decrypts to the same cleartext using two different keys. Combining both results, security will follow. We next recall three known preliminary results:

Lemma 4. *Assume that divisibility of an integer by different primes is independent and that divisibility of randomly chosen integers by the same prime is independent. Let B be a positive integer. If positive integers $c_1, \cdots, c_n$ are randomly drawn from the interval $(0, B)$, then*

$$\lim_{B \to \infty} Pr\{\gcd(c_1, c_2, \cdots, c_n) = 1\} \approx \frac{1}{\zeta(n)} \qquad (2)$$

where $\zeta(n) = \sum_{t=1}^{\infty} t^{-n}$ is Riemann's zeta function.

Proof. Let $B \to \infty$ and see [13], section 4.4. ●

Lemma 5. *If $\phi(m)$ is Euler's totient function counting the number of integers less than m that are coprime with m, then*

$$\phi(1) + \cdots + \phi(m) = \frac{3m^2}{\pi^2} + O(m \log m) \tag{3}$$

In particular, the average order of $\phi(m)$ is $6m/\pi^2 \approx 0.608m$.

Proof. See [9], section 18.5. ●

Lemma 6. *Let $d(n)$ be the number of divisors of a positive integer n, counting 1 and n. The average order of $d(n)$ is $\log n$.*

Proof. See [9], section 18.2. ●

The first result concerning the security of the new privacy homomorphism against known-cleartext attacks regards the subset of keys consistent with the known cleartext-ciphertext pairs:

Theorem 7. *Consider a PH whose encryption function is given by Expression (1). Let n be the number of random cleartext-ciphertext pairs known by the cryptanalyst. If the r-degree of all ciphertexts is greater than 1, then the size of the subset of keys consistent with the known pairs grows exponentially with $s - n$ and has an expected value of at least $\max(6(m')^{s-n}/\pi^2, 1)$, where $s = \log_{m'} m$. Cleartext-ciphertext pairs derived from the n known pairs using the homomorphic properties do not compromise the security of the PH.*

Proof. Denote by d the maximal r-degree of ciphertexts in known message pairs. Let the n known random message pairs consist of cleartexts a_i and ciphertexts $(b_{i1}, \cdots, b_{id})$, for $i = 1, \cdots, n$. The following construction shows that if n is not too large, then there exist several keys $(\hat{r}, \hat{m}')$ consistent with the n known pairs

1. Randomly pick $\hat{r}$ such that $\hat{r}^{-1} \bmod m$ exists. Clearly, all numbers coprime to m are eligible; thus, there are $\phi(m)$ candidates.
2. For $i = 1, \cdots, n$ compute $\hat{a}_{i1}, \cdots, \hat{a}_{id}$ such that $\hat{a}_{ij} = b_{ij}\hat{r}^{-j} \bmod m$.
3. Find $\hat{m}'$ such that it divides m and verifies

$$\hat{a}_{i1} + \cdots + \hat{a}_{id} = a_i \bmod \hat{m}'$$

for $i = 1, \cdots, n$. A possibility (perhaps not unique) is to take

$$\hat{m}' = \gcd_{1 \leq i \leq n} \left(\sum_{j=1}^{d} \hat{a}_{ij} - a_i, m \right)$$

where, to keep the notation short, we have defined $\gcd_{1 \leq i \leq n}(c_i, m) := \gcd(c_1, c_2, \cdots, c_n, m)$. If $\hat{m}' \leq \max_{1 \leq i \leq n}(a_i)$ is obtained, then go to Step 1. Otherwise a key $(\hat{r}, \hat{m}')$ consistent with the known pairs has been obtained and the procedure is finished.

The probability of coming up with a good $\hat{m}'$ at Step 3 of the above construction can be lower-bounded as

$$Pr(\gcd_{1 \le i \le n} (\sum_{j=1}^{d} \hat{a}_{ij} - a_i, m) > \max_{1 \le i \le n} (a_i)) \ge Pr(\gcd_{1 \le i \le n} (\sum_{j=1}^{d} \hat{a}_{ij} - a_i, m) \ge m')$$

$$\ge Pr(\gcd_{1 \le i \le n} (\sum_{j=1}^{d} \hat{a}_{ij} - a_i, m) = m')$$

$$= Pr(A)Pr[\gcd_{1 \le i \le n} (\frac{\sum_{j=1}^{d} \hat{a}_{ij} - a_i}{m'}, m/m') = 1 | A]$$

$$\approx (\frac{1}{m'})^n \frac{1}{\zeta(n+1)} \approx \frac{1}{(m')^n} \tag{4}$$

where the last approximation is valid if n is not too small (say ≥ 10) and the ζ approximation is obtained from Lemma 4. A is the event "m' divides m and all $\sum_{j=1}^{d} \hat{a}_{ij} - a_i$, $i = 1, \cdots, n$"; clearly, by assumption m' divides m, and the probability that m' divides a random integer (such as $\sum_{j=1}^{d} \hat{a}_{ij} - a_i$) is $1/m'$; thus, $Pr(A) = (1/m')^n$. Let us check that Lemma 4 can be used:

1. In the last gcd computation, m/m' is random (because m is) and the rest of numbers can be viewed as being randomly drawn from the interval $(0, dm/m')$, since they depend on a random number $\hat{r}$.
2. dm/m' is large since m' is a small divisor of m.

Now the above construction can be run for $\phi(m)$ different values of $\hat{r}$. This means that the expected number of keys $(\hat{r}, \hat{m}')$ consistent with the known pairs is at least

$$\max(\frac{\phi(m)}{(m')^n}, 1) \approx \max(\frac{6}{\pi^2} \frac{m}{(m')^n}, 1) = \max(\frac{6}{\pi^2} (m')^{s-n}, 1)$$

where the approximation is obtained from Lemma 5. Finally, to prove the last assertion of the theorem, imagine that two known pairs are added, subtracted or multiplied by the cryptanalyst to generate a new cleartext-ciphertext pair. If this new pair is input to the gcd computation at Step 3, it is easy to see that the gcd value remains unchanged. Thus only genuine randomly split cleartext-ciphertext known pairs are to be taken into account. •

Note 8. m' must be considered as a secret parameter for the above proof of Theorem 7 to be correct. Otherwise, consistent keys would be only those having the form $(\hat{r}, m')$ and their number would be much smaller. Even if it is assumed that the enemy cryptanalyst can compute all divisors $\hat{m}'$ of m, she cannot decide which divisor is actually being used; the only clue is that $\hat{m}' > \max_{1 \le i \le n}(a_i)$, as reflected in Derivation (4).

Note 9 (On the value of d). It is recommended that $d > 2$. The shortcomings of $d = 1$ and $d = 2$ are examined below:

$d = 1$: Notice that random cleartext splitting is central to the proof of Theorem 7. Imagine that no splitting is done (*i. e.*, $d = 1$) and that one cleartext-ciphertext pair (a, b) is known. Then $b = ar \bmod m$ and r is revealed.

$d = 2$: It will be shown that, if $d = 2$, knowledge of m' allows to determine r, that is, knowledge of a part of the secret key k allows to determine the rest of k. Then for message 0, one has $E_k(0) = (ar, a'r^2)$, where $a = -a' \bmod m'$; now notice that $a'r^2/ar \bmod m'$ yields $r \bmod m'$. But how can the enemy cryptanalyst get $E_k(0)$? Assume that four cleartext-ciphertext pairs are known to her, namely $B_1 = E_k(a_1)$, $B_2 = E_k(a_2)$, $B_3 = E_k(a_3)$ and $B_4 = E_k(a_4)$. There is a high probability that two pairs of coprime numbers exist among the cleartexts; assume $\gcd(a_1, a_2) = 1$ and $\gcd(a_3, a_4) = 1$. Then u, v, u', v' exist such that $B_5 := E_k(1) = uB_1 + vB_2$ (equivalently $1 = ua_1 + va_2$) and $B_6 := E_k(1) = u'B_3 + v'B_4$ (equivalently $1 = u'a_3 + v'a_4$). Then $B_5 - B_6 = E_k(0)$. Notice that the above attack does not work without knowledge of m', so $d = 2$ is not necessarily insecure; still it is not recommended.

Note 10. Instead of using the average approximation from Lemma 5, one might think of using the Rosser-Schoenfeld lower bound on $\phi(m)/m$ ([11], p. 72) in the proof of Theorem 7. However, being based on a smooth function of m, this bound is often too conservative and can lead to a serious underestimation of the size of the subset of consistent keys. Due to this drawback and the probabilistic nature of the proof, it seems more realistic and natural to use the expected value of $\phi(m)$.

The second result concerning the security of the proposed PH regards the behaviour of keys:

Theorem 11. *The expected probability that any two keys (r_1, m_1') and (r_2, m_2') decipher a random ciphertext to the same cleartext is $O((\log m)/m)$. Therefore, this probability can be made arbitrarily small by increasing m.*

Proof. Let the two keys be (r_1, m_1') and (r_2, m_2'). Let $(b_1, b_2, \cdots, b_d)$ be a randomly chosen ciphertext. Assume that both keys decrypt to the same cleartext a. Then from the specification of the PH (Section 2):

$$a = P(r_1^{-1}) \bmod m_1' = b_1 r_1^{-1} + b_2 r_1^{-2} + \cdots + b_d r_1^{-d} \bmod m_1'$$

$$= P(r_2^{-1}) \bmod m_2' = b_1 r_2^{-1} + b_2 r_2^{-2} + \cdots + b_d r_2^{-d} \bmod m_2' \qquad (5)$$

where the inverses are modulo m. Three cases must be considered:

- If $r_1 = r_2 = r$ then $m_1' \neq m_2'$ since both keys are assumed to be different. In that case, Equation (5) holds only if both m_1' and m_2' divide $a - P(r^{-1})$. Assuming that a is such that m_1' is a divisor, from Lemma 6 the expected probability that m_2' is also a divisor is $(\log m)/m$.

- If $m'_1 = m'_2 = m$ then $r_1 \neq r_2$ since both keys are assumed different. In that case, Equation (5) holds only if m divides $P(r_1^{-1}) - P(r_2^{-1})$. From Lemma 6, this happens with an expected probability

$$\frac{\log |P(r_1^{-1}) - P(r_2^{-1})|}{|P(r_1^{-1}) - P(r_2^{-1})|} = O((\log m)/m) \tag{6}$$

- If $m'_1 \neq m'_2$ and $r_1 \neq r_2$, Equation (5) implies that there exists an integer a such that m'_1 divides $P(r_1^{-1}) - a$ and m'_2 divides $P(r_2^{-1}) - a$. Using Lemma 6, the probability of such an event can be upper bounded by

$$\max_{0 \leq a \leq \min(m'_1, m'_2) - 1} \left(\frac{\log |P(r_1^{-1}) - a|}{|P(r_1^{-1}) - a|}, \frac{\log |P(r_2^{-1}) - a|}{|P(r_2^{-1}) - a|} \right) = O((\log m)/m) \tag{7}$$

Thus in all cases the expected probability of obtaining the same cleartext from decryption of the same ciphertext using two different keys is $O((\log m)/m)$ •

Note 12. It should be noted that the security provided by the proposed scheme is based on the fact that the subset of keys consistent with the known pairs is kept large and any two different keys yield different cleartexts from the same ciphertext with a high probability. Further, in the proof of Corollary 13 it is assumed that an infinitely powerful cryptanalyst can enumerate the subset of consistent keys, but no easy way to do this is obvious. In computational terms, even if there exists only one consistent key (probability of random key guessing equal to 1 for infinite computing power), this does not mean that such a key is easy to find.

Corollary 13. *If leakage of n cleartext-ciphertext pairs is to be tolerated, then the probability of success for a known-cleartext attack with unlimited computing power can be made arbitrarily small by a proper choice of the security parameter* $s = \log_{m'} m$.

Proof. Assume that the cryptanalyst has enough computing power to enumerate the subset of keys consistent with the known pairs. From Theorems 7 and 11 it is clear that the best attacking strategy is randomly guessing the key, which has a probability of success at most equal to

$$\begin{cases} \pi^2 (m')^{n-s}/6 & \text{if } s > n \\ 1 & \text{if } s \leq n \end{cases}$$

For any $\epsilon > 0$, there exists a value of s that makes this probability smaller than ϵ. •

Table 1 illustrates the dependency between parameters with several example choices. There are at least two scenarios for parameter design:

- If n, m' and the probability of random key guessing are specified as requirements, then suitable values for s and m must be determined.

- If m' and m are fixed in advance (*i.e.* the PH is fixed), then the probability of random key guessing can be computed for each number n of known cleartext-ciphertext pairs. If more and more random pairs are leaked over time, then a proactive key renewal scheme should be enforced by the classified level in order to keep the probability of random key guessing smaller than an alarm threshold set beforehand.

Table 1. Some example parameter choices for the proposed privacy homomorphism ($l(x) = \lceil log_{10}x \rceil$ is the length of x in decimal digits).

n	s	$l(m')$	$l(m)$	Prob. rand. key guessing
5	5	20	100	1
5	6	20	120	$\approx 1.64 \times 10^{-20}$
10	11	20	220	$\approx 1.64 \times 10^{-20}$
50	50	5	250	1
50	51	5	255	$\approx 1.64 \times 10^{-5}$
50	53	5	265	$\approx 1.64 \times 10^{-15}$

5   Applications to Delegation of Computing and Data and to E-gambling

Delegation of computing and data is a major field of application for PHs. When the computations to be performed on encrypted data are of an arithmetical nature, then the PH presented in this paper is especially useful. We next sketch some practical scenarios where delegation problems appear.

A computing delegation problem happens whenever a (small) company wants to use external computing facilities to do some calculations on corporate confidential data. A very common variant of this situation is a medical research team using a (insecure) university mainframe for processing confidential healthcare records. The reason for using external facilities may be the complexity of the calculations but also the huge volume of the data set. Clearly, computation on confidential data can be delegated to an unclassified facility (denoted by data handler) if data are kept in encrypted form during computations. The data owner is only left the task of decrypting the final result of computation.

Data delegation differs from computing delegation in that the party interested in the result of computations is not the data owner, but the data handler. Data delegation problems appear in the interaction between public administrations at several levels. For example, municipalities cooperate with national statistical offices in statistical data collection. In return, municipalities would like to be able to analyze the whole collected data set (pooled from all municipalities). But only national statistical offices are usually authorized to hold nation-wide individual census data. A similar problem occurs in any federal-like structure (European Union, U.S.A., Germany, etc.). Member states cooperate with federal agencies in collecting data from individuals, companies, etc. In return, states would like to be able to analyze data at a federal level. A secure solution in both scenarios above is for the organization owning the whole data set to perform (probably for free) the analyses requested by the cooperating organizations. But then the data owning organization becomes a bottleneck and is forced to waste time and resources in uninteresting tasks. A better solution would be for the data owner to delegate data in a secure way and reduce its role in subsequent analyses to a minimum. Delegation of data can be performed by releasing them in encrypted form. The cooperating organization plays the role of the data handler in that it can compute on encrypted data and submit the results of computations to the data owner for decryption; in this way, the data owner is only left the (mechanical) job of decrypting and returning the final result. A prototype using the PH proposed here to implement such a scheme for delegation of sensitive statistical data has been sketched ([6]), completed and patented[7]; because of patent reasons, no public description of the proposed PH and its security properties had so far been offered.

In [5], availability of secure data delegation is assumed for increasing the multi-application capacity of smart cards. The basic idea is that if a very resource-demanding application is to be run on card-stored data then the card exports these data in encrypted form and the application is run on an external computing server.

Data delegation has stronger security requirements than computing delegation. In computing delegation the data handler only sees ciphertext. However, in data delegation the data owner decrypts the final result of computations and returns it as cleartext to the data handler. This means that in data delegation each time the data owner returns one decrypted result to the data handler, the data handler learns one new cleartext-ciphertext pair (or two if what is returned is an unreduced fraction). Therefore, the data owner should take care that the number n of returned decrypted results is not too large to become unsafe (given the security parameter s of the homomorphism, see Corollary 13). Once the safety limit has been reached, no more decrypted results should be returned by the data owner, unless he decides to change the key of the homomorphism and reencrypt all delegated data under the new key.

E-gambling, and more specifically electronic poker, is another recent application of the PH proposed in this paper. Cards chosen by players are homomorphically encrypted and they are manipulated in encrypted form. In e-poker, PH card encryption plays a role analogous to turning cards upside down in physical poker; computing on encrypted cards is analogous to manipulating reversed cards in the physical world. A protocol describing this application of the PH presented here is patent pending ([14]), so no further details on it can be disclosed here.

6   Conclusion

The features of the proposed homomorphism can be summarized as follows

- Addition, subtraction, multiplication and division can be carried out on encrypted data at an unclassified level.
- The proposed homomorphism is the first one to allow full arithmetic while being secure against known-cleartext attacks. Security against known-cleartext attacks can be proven provided that cleartext splitting is always used when encrypting (recommended splitting factor $d > 2$) and the ciphertext space is much larger than the cleartext space. Pairs that are derived from random pairs using the homomorphic properties do not compromise the security of the PH.
- Encryption and decryption transformations can be implemented efficiently, because they only require modular multiplications. Note that no exponentiation is needed, because the powers of r can be precomputed. Unlike exponential ciphers, the proposed PH can be fast even if the ciphertext space is very large.
- A ciphertext with r-degree d is about

$$d\frac{\log m}{\log m'} = d\log_{m'} m = ds$$

times longer than the corresponding cleartext. Although this is a storage penalty, a choice of $d = 3$ at the time of encryption should be affordable while remaining secure. For a given r-degree, the ciphertext expansion grows linearly with the security parameter s.
- Multiplication of two ciphertexts is the only operation that increases the r-degree of the resulting ciphertext. A good strategy is to use multiplication by cleartext constants instead of multiplication of two ciphertexts whenever possible.
- The equality predicate is not preserved, and thus comparisons for equality cannot be done at an unclassified level based on encrypted data. A given cleartext can have many ciphertext versions for two reasons: A) random splitting during encryption; B) the unclassified level computes over $(\mathbf{Z}_m)^d$ and only the classified level can perform a reduction to $\mathbf{Z}_{m'}$ during decryption.

Acknowledgments. Thanks go to Stefan Brands and Josep Rifà for useful talks and comments.

References

1. N. Ahituv, Y. Lapid and S. Neumann, "Processing encrypted data", *Communications of the ACM*, vol. 20, no. 9, pp. 777–780, Sept. 1987.

2. G. R. Blakley and C. Meadows, "A database encryption scheme which allows the computation of statistics using encrypted data", in *Proceedings of the IEEE Symposium on Research in Security and Privacy*. New York: IEEE CS Press, 1985, pp. 116–122.

3. E. F. Brickell and Y. Yacobi, "On privacy homomorphisms", in *Advances in Cryptology-Eurocrypt'87*, D. Chaum and W. L. Price, Eds. Berlin: Springer-Verlag, 1988, pp. 117–125.

4. J. Domingo-Ferrer, "A new privacy homomorphism and applications", *Information Processing Letters*, vol. 60, no. 5, pp. 277–282, Dec. 1996.

5. J. Domingo-Ferrer, "Multi-application smart cards and encrypted data processing", *Future Generation Computer Systems*, vol. 13, pp. 65–74, Jun. 1997.

6. J. Domingo-Ferrer and R. X. Sánchez del Castillo, "An implementable scheme for secure delegation of statistical data", in *Information Security-ICICS'97*, Lecture Notes in Computer Science 1334, Y. Han, T. Okamoto and S. Qing, Eds. Berlin: Springer-Verlag, 1997, pp. 445–451.

7. J. Domingo-Ferrer and Ricardo X. Sánchez del Castillo, "Method for secure delegation of statistical data", Spanish patent no. P9800608, granted Dec. 2000.

8. J. Feigenbaum and M. Merritt, "Open questions, talk abstracts, and summary of discussions", *DIMACS Series in Discrete Mathematics and Theoretical Computer Science*, vol. 2, pp. 1–45, 1991.

9. G. H. Hardy and E. M. Wright, *An Introduction to the Theory of Numbers*, 5th ed. Oxford: Clarendon, 1993.

10. R. L. Rivest, L. Adleman and M. L. Dertouzos, "On data banks and privacy homomorphisms", in *Foundations of Secure Computation*, R. A. DeMillo *et al.*, Eds. New-York: Academic Press, 1978, pp. 169-179.

11. J. B. Rosser and L. Schoenfeld, "Approximate formulas for some functions of prime numbers", *Illinois Journal of Mathematics*, vol. 6, no. 1, pp. 64–94, Jan. 1962.

12. T. Sander and C. F. Tschudin, "Protecting mobile agents against malicious hosts", in *Mobile Agent Security*, Lecture Notes in Computer Science 1419. Berlin: Springer-Verlag, 1998, pp. 44–60.

13. M. R. Schroeder, *Number Theory in Science and Communication*, 2nd ed. Berlin: Springer-Verlag, 1986.

14. SCYTL Online World Security. http://www.scytl.com

15. G. Trouessin, *Traitements Fiables des Données Confidentielles par Fragmentation-Rédondance-Dissémination*. Ph. D. Thesis, Univ. Paul Sabatier, Toulouse, France, 1991.

Algorithms for Efficient Simultaneous Elliptic Scalar Multiplication with Reduced Joint Hamming Weight Representation of Scalars

Yasuyuki Sakai[1] and Kouichi Sakurai[2]

[1] Mitsubishi Electric Corporation,
5-1-1 Ofuna, Kamakura, Kanagawa 247-8501, Japan
ysakai@iss.isl.melco.co.jp
[2] Kyushu University,
6-10-1 Hakozaki, Higashi-ku, Fukuoka 812-8581, Japan
sakurai@csce.kyushu-u.ac.jp

Abstract. The computational performance of cryptographic protocols using an elliptic curve strongly depends on the efficiency of the scalar multiplication. Some elliptic curve based cryptographic protocols, such as signature verification, require computation of multi scalar multiplications of $kP + lQ$, where P and Q are points on an elliptic curve. An efficient way to compute $kP + lQ$ is to compute two scalar multiplications simultaneously, rather than computing each scalar multiplication separately. We introduce new efficient algorithms for simultaneous scalar multiplication on an elliptic curve. We also give a detailed analysis of the computational efficiency of our proposed algorithms.

Keywords. Elliptic Curve Cryptosystems, Scalar Multiplication

1 Introduction

Elliptic curve cryptosystems, which were suggested by Miller [Mi85] and Koblitz [Ko87], are now widely used in various security services, such as the digital transmission content protection (DTCP), that defines a cryptographic protocol for protecting audio/video entertainment content from illegal copying, intercepting and tampering as it traverses high performance digital buses, such as the IEEE 1394 standard [DTCP].

IEEE and other standardizing bodies, such as the ANSI and the ISO, are in the process of standardizing elliptic curve cryptosystems. Therefore, it is very attractive to provide algorithms that allow efficient implementation. Elliptic curve based encryption/decryption or signature generation/verification schemes require computation of scalar multiplications. The computational performance of cryptographic protocols with elliptic curves strongly depends on the efficiency of the scalar multiplication procedure. Thus, fast scalar multiplication is essential for elliptic curve cryptosystems.

A.H. Chan and V. Gligor (Eds.): ISC 2002, LNCS 2433, pp. 484–499, 2002.

Some elliptic curve based cryptographic protocols, such as signature verification in ECDSA, require computing multi scalar multiplications of $kP + lQ$, where P and Q are points on an elliptic curve. There are several algorithms for elliptic scalar multiplication that improve computational efficiency. An efficient way to compute $kP + lQ$ is to perform two scalar multiplications simultaneously, rather than computing each scalar multiplication separately [Ak01,LL94,Mo01, So01].

In this paper, we describe an efficient method for accelerating simultaneous scalar multiplication on an elliptic curve. There is no general rule for selecting scalar multiplication algorithms. Some methods for scalar multiplication, for example the window method, use an auxiliary table of group elements, which is usually computed off-line and is stored in a non-negligible chunk of memory. Our proposed algorithms do not use such a pre-computation table.

The number of point additions involved in a simultaneous scalar multiplication depends on the *"joint hamming weight"* of the two given scalars. We need to compute point additions for each non-zero column in a joint scalar representation. One approach to reducing the number of point additions in the method known as Shamir's trick [El85,MOV97], which is a traditional simultaneous scalar multiplication algorithm, is to replace the binary representation of the integer with a representation that has fewer non-zero terms. There are such representations: the non-adjacent form (NAF) [MOV97] and the joint sparse form (JS-form) [So01]. In this paper we consider new joint scalar representations that are based on the binary, the NAF and the JS-form. Our techniques decrease the average joint hamming weight in each case. Based on our representation, we construct a new algorithm for simultaneous elliptic scalar multiplication.

By implementing the proposed algorithms with respect to binary representation and the NAF representation for randomly chosen scalars, we reduce the computational complexity in more than 73% cases in the simultaneous scalar multiplication on an elliptic curve of size 160-bit, defined over a prime field. The running time is reduced by a few percent on average in the simultaneous scalar multiplication.

The proposed algorithms improve the performance of simultaneous elliptic scalar multiplication with the binary representation, as well as with the NAF representation. Our proposed algorithms do not use an auxiliary pre-computation table. Therefore, they are effective in restricted environments where resources are limited, such as smart cards.

1.1 Notations and Assumptions

The following notations and assumptions are used throughout the paper. We denote field multiplication and squaring by $\mathcal{M}$ and $\mathcal{S}$, respectively. Point addition and doubling on an elliptic curve are denoted by $\mathcal{A}$ and $\mathcal{D}$, respectively. When we evaluate computational efficiency, we assume that one squaring has computational complexity $\mathcal{S} = 0.8\mathcal{M}$, and that the costs of field addition and multiplication by small constants can be ignored. $\lceil x \rceil$ denotes the smallest integer greater than or equal to x. $\mathbb{F}_q$ denotes a finite field with q elements. $\mathcal{O}$

denotes the point at infinity. $\tilde{1}$ denotes -1. $k \gg s$ denotes a right-shift operation by s bits, where the right-most s bits of the integer k are discarded and then s zero bits are padded on the left.

2   Elliptic Curve and Scalar Multiplication

In this section we give a brief overview of an elliptic curve and simultaneous scalar multiplication. Let p be a prime, $a, b \in \mathbb{F}_p$, $4a^3 + 27b^2 \neq 0$, and $p > 3$. An elliptic curve E defined over $\mathbb{F}_p$ is given by the equation: $E : y^2 = x^3 + ax + b$. The set of $\mathbb{F}_p$-rational points is denoted by $E(\mathbb{F}_p)$.

In cases where field inversion is significantly more expensive than multiplication, it is preferable to use weighted projective coordinates (also referred to as Jacobian coordinates), where a triplet (X, Y, Z) corresponds to the affine coordinates $(X/Z^2, Y/Z^3)$ whenever $Z \neq 0$. In terms of weighted projective coordinates, the standard algorithms, given in [IEEE], for point addition and doubling have computational complexity $12\mathcal{M} + 4\mathcal{S}$ and $4\mathcal{M} + 6\mathcal{S}$, respectively, where $\mathcal{M}$ and $\mathcal{S}$ denote field multiplication and squaring, respectively.

2.1   Simultaneous Scalar Multiplication

Encryption/decryption or signature generation/verification schemes require the computation of scalar multiplications. The computational performance of cryptographic protocols with elliptic curves strongly depends on the efficiency of the scalar multiplication procedure. Thus, fast scalar multiplication is essential for elliptic curve cryptosystems.

Some elliptic curve based cryptographic protocols, such as signature verification in ECDSA, require the multi scalar multiplication $kP + lQ$, where P and Q are points on an elliptic curve. An efficient way to compute $kP + lQ$ is to carry out two scalar multiplications simultaneously, rather than separately.

Shamir's algorithm 1, given below, is used to perform simultaneous elliptic scalar multiplications. This algorithm is well known, and is known as Shamir's trick [El85]. Here the two integers k, l are represented in binary form. Note that if scalars are represented in signed binary, then a further addition, $P - Q$, is required in the pre-computation stage.

Algorithm 1 Simultaneous Scalar Multiplication: Shamir's Trick

---

Input $P, Q \in E(\mathbb{F}_p)$, two non-negative t-bit integers $k = \sum_{i=0}^{t-1} 2^i k_i$, $l = \sum_{i=0}^{t-1} 2^i l_i$, where $k_i, l_i \in \{0, 1\}$
Output $kP + lQ \in E(\mathbb{F}_p)$

1.   **Pre-computation:** Compute $G \leftarrow P + Q$
2.   Let $A \leftarrow \mathcal{O}$
3.   For i from $t - 1$ down to 0, do the following:
  3.1. $A \leftarrow 2A$
  3.2.   if $(k_i, l_i) = (1, 0)$ then $A \leftarrow A + P$
       else if $(k_i, l_i) = (0, 1)$ then $A \leftarrow A + Q$
       else if $(k_i, l_i) = (1, 1)$ then $A \leftarrow A + G$
4.   Return A

Computational Efficiency of Shamir's Algorithm. 1 Shamir's algorithm 1 computes $kP + lQ$ by performing $t - 1$ elliptic doublings and a number of additions. The required number of elliptic additions depends on the joint hamming weight, as defined below.

Definition 1 (Joint hamming weight). *Given two positive t-bit integers k and l, consider the $2 \times t$ array whose rows are the binary or signed binary representations of the integers. The joint hamming weight (JHW) of k and l is the number of non-zero columns of the array. We denote JHW of k, l by JHW(k,l).*

Example 1. If two integers k and l have the binary representation shown below, then $JHW(k, l) = 8$.

$$k = (1\,0\,1\,0\,0\,1\,0\,1\,0\,0\,1)_2$$
$$l = (1\,0\,0\,1\,0\,0\,1\,0\,1\,0\,1)_2$$

When two randomly chosen integers k and l are represented in binary, each has a hamming weight of $t/2$ on average. Thus, JHW(k,l) equals $\frac{3}{4}t$ on average. Consequently, if we take the binary representation for two integers, Shamir's algorithm 1 has computational complexity $(\frac{3}{4}t + 1)\mathcal{A} + (t - 1)\mathcal{D}$ on average.

2.2 Representation of an Integer

As stated earlier, the required number of point additions in a simultaneous scalar multiplication depends on the joint hamming weight of the integers. An approach to reducing the number of point additions in Shamir's trick is to replace the binary representation of the integer with a representation that has fewer non-zero terms.

In this paper we will consider three representations of a non-negative integer: binary, the non-adjacent form (NAF) and the joint sparse form (JS-form) [So01].

The binary representation is unique, and has on average $t/2$ non-zero entries for a t-bit integer. Consequently, if we choose binary representation for two non-negative t-bit integers, the joint hamming weight equals $\frac{3}{4}t$ on average, as previously stated. Unlike the binary representation, the signed-digit representation of an integer is not unique. The NAF is one of the signed binary representations for a t-bit integer having at most $t + 1$ bits. No two non-zero entries are adjacent in the NAF. The NAF has the smallest possible number of non-zero entries among all signed binary representations for an integer. For example, $k = (1101110111)_2$ will be represented as $k = (100\bar{1}000\bar{1}00\bar{1})_{NAF}$, where $\bar{1}$ denotes -1. It is known that the number of non-zero entries in the NAF for a t-bit integer is $\frac{1}{3}t$. Therefore the joint hamming weight of two t-bit integers represented in the NAF will be $\frac{5}{9}t$ on average. Consequently, if we choose the NAF representation for two given scalars, Shamir's algorithm 1 has computational complexity $(\frac{5}{9}t + 2)\mathcal{A} + t\mathcal{D}$ on average. Note that in the pre-computation stage of Shamir's algorithm 1, computation of two points, $P + Q$ and $P - Q$, is required for signed binary representations.

In [So01], Solinas gave an efficient representation for two non-negative integers. The representation is called the joint sparse form (JS-form), which is a joint signed binary representation where:

- Any three consecutive columns includes a zero column.
- If two adjacent entries in a row are non zero, then they are (1 1) or (−1 −1), and the corresponding entries from the other row are (±1 0).

Example 2. The two integers $(4773)_{10}$ and $(4395)_{10}$ can be represented in JS-form as shown below.

$$\begin{pmatrix} 4773 \\ 4395 \end{pmatrix} = \begin{pmatrix} 1 & 0 & 1 & 0 & \tilde{1} & \tilde{1} & 0 & 1 & 0 & 0 & 1 & 0 & 1 \\ 1 & 0 & 0 & 0 & 1 & 0 & 0 & 1 & 1 & 0 & \tilde{1} & 0 & \tilde{1} \end{pmatrix}$$

It is easy to calculate the JS-form of two integers. The JS-form has the following properties:

- A JS-form representation exists for every positive pair of integers.
- The JS-form of two integers is unique.
- The JS-form of two integers has the least joint hamming weight among all joint signed binary representations of the two integers.
- The average joint hamming weight of two t-bit integers is $\frac{1}{2}t$.

Consequently, if we take the JS-form representation for two given integers, Shamir's algorithm 1 has computational complexity $(\frac{1}{2}t + 2)\mathcal{A} + t\mathcal{D}$ on average.

We will consider the three representations for simultaneous scalar multiplication. Our new algorithms, described in the next section, achieve a greater reduction in the average number of point additions.

3   Reducing the Joint Hamming Weight of Two Integers

In this section we describe our new algorithms, which compute two elliptic scalar multiplications simultaneously. As already stated in the previous section, the computational efficiency of Shamir's algorithm 1-based simultaneous elliptic scalar multiplication depends on the joint hamming weight of two given integers.

The algorithms that we propose are based on the following simple observation. For the two integers k, l, with the binary representations shown below, we have $JHW(k, l) = 8$. When we shift k to the right by 1 bit, we observe that $JHW(k/2, l) = 7$, so the joint hamming weight is reduced by 1.

$$\begin{array}{rl} k = & 1\ 0\ 1\ 0\ 0\ 1\ 0\ 1\ 0\ 0\ 1\ - \\ l = & 1\ 0\ 0\ 1\ 0\ 0\ 1\ 0\ 1\ 0\ 1\ - \\ k/2 = & -\ 1\ 0\ 1\ 0\ 0\ 1\ 0\ 1\ 0\ 0\ 1 \end{array}$$

3.1   Simultaneous Scalar Multiplication with Reduced Joint Hamming Weight

We apply the revised scalars, one of which is re-constructed by the right-shift, to the simultaneous scalar multiplication. The algorithm 2 below presents a method for simultaneous scalar multiplication based on the revised joint scalar representation determined by a selection algorithm.

Algorithm 2 Simultaneous Scalar Multiplication with Reduced Joint Hamming Weight

---

Input $P, Q \in E(\mathbb{F}_p)$, two non-negative t-bit integers k, l, upper bound of the shift-length s (bits)

Output $kP + lQ \in E(\mathbb{F}_p)$

1.   **Pre-computation:**

   1.1.   Select an optimal pair from the pairs (k, l), $(k \gg s', l)$, and $(k, l \gg s')$, where $0 < s' \leq s$, using **Algorithm 3** on input k, l, s.

   1.2.   If (k, l) is selected, then do the following:
$$P_s \leftarrow P,\ Q_s \leftarrow Q,\ k' \leftarrow k,\ l' \leftarrow l,\ c \leftarrow 0,\ R \leftarrow \mathcal{O}$$
    else if $(k \gg s', l)$ is selected, then do the following:
$$P_s \leftarrow 2^{s'}P,\ Q_s \leftarrow Q,\ k' \leftarrow k \gg s',\ l' \leftarrow l,\ c \leftarrow k \wedge (2^{s'} - 1),\ R \leftarrow P$$
    else if $(k, l \gg s')$ is selected, then do the following:
$$P_s \leftarrow P,\ Q_s \leftarrow 2^{s'}Q,\ k' \leftarrow k,\ l' \leftarrow l \gg s',\ c \leftarrow l \wedge (2^{s'} - 1),\ R \leftarrow Q$$

2.   **Simultaneous scalar multiplication:**

   2.1.   Compute $A \leftarrow k'P_s + l'Q_s$ using **Algorithm 1** on input P_s, Q_s, k', l'

3.   **Post-computation:**

   3.1.   Compute $A \leftarrow A + cR$

4.   Return A

In the algorithm, the pre-computation and post-computation stages should be processed. In step 1.1 of the algorithm 2, we first select a computationally "*optimal*" pair of scalars using the selection algorithm 3, which will be described in the next subsection. Once an optimal pair of scalars has been selected, we then compute the input for a traditional simultaneous scalar multiplication.

Notice that the traditional simultaneous scalar multiplication method of Shamir's algorithm 1 scans the columns of the scalar array from left (most significant) to right. Which point P, Q, or $P + Q$ should be added in the main loop is related to the value of the scalar array column. Let us consider the case that $(k \gg s', l)$ has been chosen at the selection step. The simultaneous scalar multiplication should be processed based on the right-shifted scalar k and the original l. Our algorithm also scans the columns of the scalar array from left to right. The difference is that the point added in the main loop must be $2^{s'}P$, Q, or $2^{s'}P + Q$, because the scalar k has been right-shifted by s' bits in advance. Thus, the points for input to the traditional simultaneous scalar multiplication method of Shamir's algorithm 1 should be the points $2^{s'}P$ and Q. Extra $2^{s'}$ doublings are required in the pre-computation stage.

In the post-computation stage, we must treat the discarded word of the right-shifted scalar. c is related to the discarded word produced from the right-shift. The point cP (or cQ) must be added in the last step of our algorithm.

As we have discussed above, additional computation of the pre-computation and post-computation stages is required in the algorithm 2. Although there is this increased computational cost, if the joint hamming weight is relatively reduced, the overall computational cost in the simultaneous scalar multiplication may be improved. The trade-off between the computational advantage corresponding to the reduced joint hamming weight and the cost of the extra computation can be evaluated by the equation (1) below, which will be discussed in the next subsection.

3.2   Selecting the Optimal Pair of Two Scalar Values

Let us discuss how to construct the optimal pair of scalars for a simultaneous elliptic scalar multiplication. First, if the joint hamming weight is reduced by a right-shift for one of the two scalars, how much computational efficiency can be achieved in the simultaneous scalar multiplication? In this subsection we estimate the efficiency. The problem is that even if the joint hamming weight is reduced, there is no guarantee that the computational complexity is improved in the simultaneous scalar multiplication, because:

- By shifting one of the two given scalars, the length of the row of the array whose rows are the binary (or signed binary) representations of the scalars will be increased.
- By right-shifting a scalar, some right-most bits, which may be non-zero, will be discarded.

Some additional computation related to the above considerations is required. Assume that one of the two given scalars is right-shifted by s bits. We require an extra s elliptic doublings for the input of a traditional simultaneous scalar multiplication. When the word discarded by shifting has non-zero entries, point additions corresponding to the non-zero entries are required. The number of extra point additions required can be evaluated by the reduction in the joint hamming weight. Assume that the joint hamming weight is reduced by h. Consequently, when one of the given two scalars is right-shifted by s bits, reducing the joint hamming weight by h, the computational reduction of the simultaneous scalar multiplication can be evaluated by the following.

$$Reduction = h\mathcal{A} - s\mathcal{D} \tag{1}$$

The computational improvement, "$Reduction$", also depends on the computational cost of the point additions $\mathcal{A}$ and doublings $\mathcal{D}$. It is possible to express the time that it takes to perform one point addition $\mathcal{A}$ and doubling $\mathcal{D}$ in terms of the equivalent number of field multiplications needed per point addition $\mathcal{A}$ and doubling $\mathcal{D}$. Thus, we evaluate the computational complexity of "$Reduction$" by the number of field multiplications required. In the case that weighted projective coordinates are used for point representation on an elliptic curve, $\mathcal{A} = 12\mathcal{M} + 4\mathcal{S} = 15.2\mathcal{M}$ and $\mathcal{D} = 4\mathcal{M} + 6\mathcal{S} = 8.8\mathcal{M}$. (We assume that field squaring has complexity $\mathcal{S} = 0.8\mathcal{M}$. We also assume that the costs of field addition and multiplication by small constants can be ignored.)

The selection algorithm 3 presents a method for selecting the optimal setting of the given non-negative two scalars.

Algorithm 3 Selecting an Optimal Pair

Input two non-negative t-bit integers k, l, upper bound of the shift-length s (bits)
Output (k, l) or $(k \gg s', l)$ or $(k, l \gg s')$, where $0 < s' \leq s$

1. $JHW_{00} \leftarrow JHW(k, l)$
2. $Reduction_{00} \leftarrow 0$
3. For i from 1 to s do the following:
     $JHW_{i0} \leftarrow JHW(k \gg i, l)$
     $JHW_{0i} \leftarrow JHW(k, l \gg i)$
     $Reduction_{i0} \leftarrow (JHW_{00} - JHW_{i0})\mathcal{A} - i\mathcal{D}$
     $Reduction_{0i} \leftarrow (JHW_{00} - JHW_{0i})\mathcal{A} - i\mathcal{D}$
4. Find maximal $Reduction$, then return (k, l) or $(k \gg s', l)$ or $(k, l \gg s')$ which has maximal $Reduction$

In the algorithm 3, we first compute the joint hamming weight of (k, l). Next we compute the joint hamming weight of $(k \gg s', l)$ and $(k, l \gg s')$, which is a weight between the original scalar and the shifted scalar. Then the computational efficiency "$Reduction$" is evaluated. If all $Reduction_{ij}$ for $i \neq 0, j \neq 0$ are negative, this means that the original setting (k, l) is the most effective for simultaneous scalar multiplication. In that case, the simple traditional simultaneous scalar multiplication should be processed, and our proposed algorithm 2 will be equivalent to Shamir's algorithm 1 in terms of computational cost.

Clearly, all of the steps in the algorithm 3 have a computational cost, which is linear in the bit-length. But if the upper bound of the shift-length s is relatively large, the computational cost of the selection algorithm may be non-negligible. A reasonable size should be chosen for the upper bound of the shift-length s. Setting s will be discussed in a later section.

3.3 Multi-block

We can extend the algorithm 2 to a multi-block version.

We split two given scalars k and l into several blocks. Each block has a pre-fixed bit-length. We can apply the shift algorithm 2 to each block. The multi-block version of the algorithm is described below.

Algorithm 4 Simultaneous Scalar Multiplication: Multi-Block

Input $P, Q \in E(\mathbb{F}_p)$, two non-negative t-bit integers k, l, upper bound of the shift-length s (bits), block-length b (bits)
Output $kP + lQ \in E(\mathbb{F}_p)$

1. Set $A \leftarrow \mathcal{O}$
2. For i from 1 to $\lceil t/b \rceil$ do the following:
    1.1. Pick the ith-most significant leading b bits of k and l, then set k' and l', respectively
    1.2. Compute $A \leftarrow k'P + l'Q + A$ using **Algorithm 2** on input A, P, Q, k', and l'
3. Return A

---

4   Computational Efficiency

In this section we provide evidence for the computational efficiency of our algorithms, described in the previous section.

4.1   Upper Bound of the Shift Length

We first examine the effect of the size of the upper bound of the shift-length s.

We assume an elliptic curve defined over a prime field of 160 bits, that is, scalars are of 160 bits. The block-length b in the algorithm 4 is set to 160, 80, 53, 40, or 32 bits. In the case of a 160-bit block, the multi-block method is not applied. In the case of the 80-, 53-, 40-, and 32-bit blocks, the arrays of the given scalars are split into 2, 3, 4, and 5 blocks, respectively. The upper bound of the shift-length s is set to 16 bits. That is, optimal pairs of scalars from (k, l), $(k \gg s', l)$, and $(k, l \gg s')$, where $1 \le s' \le 16$, are selected for each of the two given scalars. If (k, l) is selected as an optimal pair, this implies that the original (k, l) is more computationally efficient than any $(k \gg s', l)$ and $(k, l \gg s')$. We randomly generate 10,000 pairs of integers that have size equal to 160 bits. In each case, we apply the algorithm 3 to select an optimal pair of scalars. As stated previously, we consider three methods for the representation of scalars: binary, NAF, and JS-form.

Table 1. Number of optimal scalar pairs selected and the average reduction in computational complexity when the upper bound of the shift-length is set to 16 bits, with binary representation

Selected optimal pair	$b = 160$		$b = 80$		$b = 53$		$b = 40$		$b = 32$	
	prob.	r	prob.	r	prob.	r	prob.	r	prob.	r
(k, l)	0.27	0	0.33	0	0.37	0	0.41	0	0.44	0
$(k \gg 1, l)$ or $(k, l \gg 1)$	0.29	61	0.34	41	0.36	32	0.37	27	0.37	23
$(k \gg 2, l)$ or $(k, l \gg 2)$	0.17	64	0.17	42	0.15	34	0.14	29	0.12	26
$(k \gg 3, l)$ or $(k, l \gg 3)$	0.11	57	0.090	37	0.072	27	0.058	22	0.044	19
$(k \gg 4, l)$ or $(k, l \gg 4)$	0.066	58	0.043	37	0.028	29	0.020	24	0.013	22
$(k \gg 5, l)$ or $(k, l \gg 5)$	0.039	49	0.019	29	0.011	21	0.006	16	0.003	15
$(k \gg 6, l)$ or $(k, l \gg 6)$	0.023	52	0.008	32	0.004	22	0.002	20	0.0009	15
$(k \gg 7, l)$ or $(k, l \gg 7)$	0.012	53	0.002	36	0.0006	24	0.0003	23	0.0001	24
$(k \gg 8, l)$ or $(k, l \gg 8)$	0.006	48	0.001	35	0.0001	25	0.0001	21	0.0001	6
$(k \gg 9, l)$ or $(k, l \gg 9)$	0.003	58	0.0003	27	0	0	0	0	0	0
$(k \gg 10, l)$ or $(k, l \gg 10)$	0.0001	45	0.0001	11	0	0	0	0	0	0
$(k \gg 11, l)$ or $(k, l \gg 11)$	0.0004	82	0.0001	55	0	0	0	0	0	0
$(k \gg 12, l)$ or $(k, l \gg 12)$	0.0004	24	0	0	0	0	0	0	0	0
$(k \gg 13, l)$ or $(k, l \gg 13)$	0.0003	48	0	0	0	0	0	0	0	0
$(k \gg 14, l)$ or $(k, l \gg 14)$	0	0	0	0	0	0	0	0	0	0
$(k \gg 15, l)$ or $(k, l \gg 15)$	0	0	0	0	0	0	0	0	0	0
$(k \gg 16, l)$ or $(k, l \gg 16)$	0	0	0	0	0	0	0	0	0	0

Table 2. Number of optimal scalar pairs selected and the average reduction in computational complexity when the upper bound of the shift-length is set to 16 bits, with NAF representation

Selected optimal pair	160 prob.	r	80 prob.	r	53 prob.	r	40 prob.	r	32 prob.	r
(k, l)	0.23	0	0.30	0	0.35	0	0.39	0	0.42	0
$(k \gg 1, l)$ or $(k, l \gg 1)$	0.28	114	0.35	72	0.38	55	0.41	45	0.42	39
$(k \gg 2, l)$ or $(k, l \gg 2)$	0.15	43	0.14	30	0.13	25	0.11	21	0.094	19
$(k \gg 3, l)$ or $(k, l \gg 3)$	0.11	76	0.093	44	0.071	34	0.055	27	0.041	23
$(k \gg 4, l)$ or $(k, l \gg 4)$	0.076	62	0.052	39	0.036	30	0.022	25	0.015	21
$(k \gg 5, l)$ or $(k, l \gg 5)$	0.051	64	0.030	35	0.017	25	0.010	18	0.006	13
$(k \gg 6, l)$ or $(k, l \gg 6)$	0.036	59	0.017	36	0.008	27	0.004	21	0.002	17
$(k \gg 7, l)$ or $(k, l \gg 7)$	0.022	57	0.007	40	0.002	29	0.0006	20	0.0001	14
$(k \gg 8, l)$ or $(k, l \gg 8)$	0.014	55	0.003	25	0.0006	16	0.0001	9	0.0001	6
$(k \gg 9, l)$ or $(k, l \gg 9)$	0.007	61	0.001	26	0.0002	27	0.0001	12	0	0
$(k \gg 10, l)$ or $(k, l \gg 10)$	0.006	59	0.0005	42	0	0	0	0	0	0
$(k \gg 11, l)$ or $(k, l \gg 11)$	0.003	56	0.0002	36	0.0001	10	0	0	0	0
$(k \gg 12, l)$ or $(k, l \gg 12)$	0.001	59	0.0001	31	0	0	0	0	0	0
$(k \gg 13, l)$ or $(k, l \gg 13)$	0.002	58	0	0	0	0	0	0	0	0
$(k \gg 14, l)$ or $(k, l \gg 14)$	0.001	53	0	0	0	0	0	0	0	0
$(k \gg 15, l)$ or $(k, l \gg 15)$	0.0001	5	0	0	0	0	0	0	0	0
$(k \gg 16, l)$ or $(k, l \gg 16)$	0.0001	11	0	0	0	0	0	0	0	0

Tables 1, 2, and 3 show the experimental results for the binary representation, the NAF representation, and the JS-form representation, respectively. In these tables, "prob." denotes the probability that $(k \gg s', l)$ or $(k, l \gg s')$ is selected as an optimal pair. r denotes the average number of *"Reduction"*, which is evaluated as an equivalent number of field multiplications. When we evaluate the equivalent number of field multiplications, we assume that weighted projective coordinates are used for point representation and that well-known algorithms are used for point operation [IEEE], where point addition and doubling have computational complexity $\mathcal{A} = 12\mathcal{M} + 4\mathcal{S} = 15.2\mathcal{M}$ and $\mathcal{D} = 4\mathcal{M} + 6\mathcal{S} = 8.8\mathcal{M}$, respectively.

There is a difference between the JS-form and the others. In the case of the binary and NAF representations, we can see from tables 1 and 2 that:

- Shifting one of the two given scalars is effective in reducing the computational cost of the simultaneous scalar multiplication.
- A longer block-length is more effective than a shorter block-length. For the case of $b = 160$, the computational cost is reduced in more than 73% of cases. In the case of $b = 32$, the computational cost is reduced in more than 56% of cases.
- In more than 50% of cases, a shift-length of 1, 2, or 3 bits is optimal. In other words, cases for which the optimal shift-length is more than 3 bits are relatively rare.

Table 3. Number of optimal scalar pairs selected and the average reduction in computational complexity when the upper bound of the shift-length is set to 16 bits, with JS-form representation

Selected optimal pair	160 prob.	r	80 prob.	r	53 prob.	r	40 prob.	r	32 prob.	r
(k, l)	0.98	0	0.94	0	0.91	0	0.90	0	0.90	0
$(k \gg 1, l)$ or $(k, l \gg 1)$	0	0	0.001	12	0.006	17	0.015	15	0.026	14
$(k \gg 2, l)$ or $(k, l \gg 2)$	0.015	23	0.040	23	0.051	20	0.052	18	0.050	17
$(k \gg 3, l)$ or $(k, l \gg 3)$	0.002	16	0.014	14	0.021	12	0.024	11	0.024	9
$(k \gg 4, l)$ or $(k, l \gg 4)$	0	0	0.001	17	0.0009	15	0.0009	15	0.0009	12
$(k \gg 5, l)$ or $(k, l \gg 5)$	0.0009	8	0.003	12	0.003	8	0.002	6	0.001	7
$(k \gg 6, l)$ or $(k, l \gg 6)$	0.0001	8	0.0005	22	0.0006	13	0.0003	11	0.0001	8
$(k \gg 7, l)$ or $(k, l \gg 7)$	0.0001	14	0.0003	20	0.0001	14	0	0	0.0001	14
$(k \gg 8, l)$ or $(k, l \gg 8)$	0.0001	7	0.0001	6	0	0	0	0	0	0
$(k \gg 9, l)$ or $(k, l \gg 9)$	0	0	0	0	0	0	0	0	0	0
$(k \gg 10, l)$ or $(k, l \gg 10)$	0	0	0	0	0	0	0	0	0	0
$(k \gg 11, l)$ or $(k, l \gg 11)$	0	0	0	0	0	0	0	0	0	0
$(k \gg 12, l)$ or $(k, l \gg 12)$	0	0	0	0	0	0	0	0	0	0
$(k \gg 13, l)$ or $(k, l \gg 13)$	0	0	0	0	0	0	0	0	0	0
$(k \gg 14, l)$ or $(k, l \gg 14)$	0	0	0	0	0	0	0	0	0	0
$(k \gg 15, l)$ or $(k, l \gg 15)$	0	0	0	0	0	0	0	0	0	0
$(k \gg 16, l)$ or $(k, l \gg 16)$	0	0	0	0	0	0	0	0	0	0

- Viewed in terms of computational effort, we often achieve a 10% computational reduction, which is manifested in an equivalent reduction in the number of field multiplications required.

To achieve a computational advantage by right-shifting one of the given two scalars, the word discarded by shifting should have a relatively small hamming weight, because we cannot avoid extra point doublings, the number of which is equal to the length shifted. Thus, how much computational advantage can be achieved depends on the hamming weight of the discarded word(s).

Consequently, the optimal settings for the algorithm 2 and 3 are:

- The block-length b is set to the maximal possible length, that is, the bit-length of the field of definition.
- The upper bound of the shift-length $s = 3$ should be reasonable in terms of the computational efficiency of the simultaneous scalar multiplication.

In the case of the JS-form, the original pair (k, l) is selected as optimal in most cases. The original (k, l) values are optimal in 90% ($b = 32$) through 98% ($b = 160$) of cases. The main reason for this is that the JS-form has the most sparse form of all joint signed binary representations. That is, if one scalar is shifted, the resulting joint hamming weight often increases. The difference between the JS-form and the other representations is that, for the former, a shorter block-length b is more effective for our algorithms.

4.2 Shorter Shift Length

As we have observed in the previous subsection, we can expect that by setting $s = 3$, the upper bound of the shift-length, will seem reasonable. Tables 4, 5, and 6 give data for the 3-bit cases. In these tables, the probabilities have larger values than those in the previous examples. The reason is that, for example, although (k, l) has maximal computational reduction, if a shift-length of more than 3 bits were examined, $(k \gg s', l)$ might have a larger computational reduction. In the case of 160-bit block-length with the binary or NAF representations, which is the most efficient setting in terms of block-length, the computational cost is reduced in 70% of cases.

Table 4. Number of optimal scalar pairs selected and the average reduction in computational complexity when the upper bound of the shift-length is set to 3 bits, with binary representation

	160		80		53		40		32	
Selected optimal pair	prob.	r	prob.	r	prob.	r	prob.	r	prob.	r
(k, l)	0.31	0	0.35	0	0.39	0	0.42	0	0.45	0
$(k \gg 1, l)$ or $(k, l \gg 1)$	0.35	58	0.37	40	0.38	31	0.38	26	0.38	23
$(k \gg 2, l)$ or $(k, l \gg 2)$	0.21	61	0.18	42	0.16	33	0.14	29	0.12	26
$(k \gg 3, l)$ or $(k, l \gg 3)$	0.14	54	0.10	36	0.077	27	0.060	22	0.046	19

Table 5. Number of optimal scalar pairs selected and the average reduction in computational complexity when the upper bound of the shift-length is set to 3 bits, with NAF representation

	160		80		53		40		32	
Selected optimal pair	prob.	r	prob.	r	prob.	r	prob.	r	prob.	r
(k, l)	0.29	0	0.34	0	0.38	0	0.41	0	0.43	0
$(k \gg 1, l)$ or $(k, l \gg 1)$	0.36	101	0.39	68	0.41	53	0.42	44	0.43	38
$(k \gg 2, l)$ or $(k, l \gg 2)$	0.20	41	0.17	29	0.14	24	0.11	21	0.097	19
$(k \gg 3, l)$ or $(k, l \gg 3)$	0.14	70	0.10	43	0.075	33	0.057	26	0.042	23

Table 6. Number of optimal scalar pairs selected and the average reduction in computational complexity when the upper bound of the shift-length is set to 3 bits, with JS-form representation

	160		80		53		40		32	
Selected optimal pair	prob.	r	prob.	r	prob.	r	prob.	r	prob.	r
(k, l)	0.98	0	0.94	0	0.92	0	0.91	0	0.90	0
$(k \gg 1, l)$ or $(k, l \gg 1)$	0	0	0.001	12	0.006	16	0.012	15	0.027	14
$(k \gg 2, l)$ or $(k, l \gg 2)$	0.016	24	0.040	23	0.051	20	0.052	18	0.051	17
$(k \gg 3, l)$ or $(k, l \gg 3)$	0.002	16	0.014	14	0.022	12	0.024	11	0.024	9

Tables 7, 8, and 9 show the case that the upper bound of the shift-length is restricted to 1 bit. For the binary and NAF representations, our method is effective in more than 50% of cases.

In the case of JS-form representation, a short shift-length almost never results in computational efficiency.

Table 7. Number of optimal scalar pairs selected and the average reduction in computational complexity when the upper bound of the shift-length is set to 1 bit, with binary representation

Selected optimal pair	160		80		53		40		32	
	prob.	r	prob.	r	prob.	r	prob.	r	prob.	r
(k,l)	0.45	0	0.46	0	0.48	0	0.50	0	0.51	0
$(k \gg 1, l)$ or $(k, l \gg 1)$	0.55	51	0.54	36	0.52	28	0.50	24	0.49	21

Table 8. Number of optimal scalar pairs selected and the average reduction in computational complexity when the upper bound of the shift-length is set to 1 bit, with NAF representation

Selected optimal pair	160		80		53		40		32	
	prob.	r	prob.	r	prob.	r	prob.	r	prob.	r
(k,l)	0.48	0	0.48	0	0.49	0	0.50	0	0.51	0
$(k \gg 1, l)$ or $(k, l \gg 1)$	0.52	85	0.52	59	0.51	47	0.50	40	0.49	35

Table 9. Number of optimal scalar pairs selected and the average reduction in computational complexity when the upper bound of the shift-length is set to 1 bit, with JS-form representation,

Selected optimal pair	160		80		53		40		32	
	prob.	r	prob.	r	prob.	r	prob.	r	prob.	r
(k,l)	1.00	0	0.99	0	0.99	0	0.97	0	0.96	0
$(k \gg 1, l)$ or $(k, l \gg 1)$	0	0	0.01	13	0.01	14	0.03	13	0.04	13

4.3 Scalar Multiplication

We now apply our algorithms 2, 3, and 4 to an elliptic simultaneous scalar multiplication.

Tables 10, 11, and 12 show the computational complexity of simultaneous scalar multiplications, which are evaluated as the equivalent number of field multiplications. In each table, the upper bound of the shift-length is set to 16, 3, 1, and 0 bits. The use of 0 bits means that the traditional Shamir's algorithm

Table 10. Computational complexity of simultaneous elliptic scalar multiplication $kP + lQ$ on $E(\mathbb{F}_p)$, where $\log_2 p = 160$, weighted projective coordinates for point representation, and binary representation for scalars

shift-length (bits)	block-size (bits)	dbl/add	complexity
16	160	$160.8\mathcal{D} + 117.3\mathcal{A}$	$2050.9\mathcal{M} + 1433.8\mathcal{S} \cong 3197.9\mathcal{M}$
	80	$161.3\mathcal{D} + 117.8\mathcal{A}$	$2059.3\mathcal{M} + 1439.2\mathcal{S} \cong 3210.6\mathcal{M}$
	53	$161.6\mathcal{D} + 118.3\mathcal{A}$	$2065.7\mathcal{M} + 1442.6\mathcal{S} \cong 3219.7\mathcal{M}$
	40	$161.7\mathcal{D} + 118.6\mathcal{A}$	$2069.7\mathcal{M} + 1444.7\mathcal{S} \cong 3225.5\mathcal{M}$
	32	$161.8\mathcal{D} + 118.7\mathcal{A}$	$2071.7\mathcal{M} + 1445.5\mathcal{S} \cong 3228.1\mathcal{M}$
3	160	$160.2\mathcal{D} + 117.9\mathcal{A}$	$2055.3\mathcal{M} + 1432.6\mathcal{S} \cong 3201.3\mathcal{M}$
	80	$160.8\mathcal{D} + 118.2\mathcal{A}$	$2061.9\mathcal{M} + 1437.8\mathcal{S} \cong 3212.2\mathcal{M}$
	53	$161.2\mathcal{D} + 118.5\mathcal{A}$	$2067.3\mathcal{M} + 1441.3\mathcal{S} \cong 3220.4\mathcal{M}$
	40	$161.4\mathcal{D} + 118.8\mathcal{A}$	$2070.7\mathcal{M} + 1443.5\mathcal{S} \cong 3225.6\mathcal{M}$
	32	$161.5\mathcal{D} + 118.8\mathcal{A}$	$2072.1\mathcal{M} + 1444.6\mathcal{S} \cong 3227.7\mathcal{M}$
1	160	$159.6\mathcal{D} + 119.0\mathcal{A}$	$2066.6\mathcal{M} + 1433.4\mathcal{S} \cong 3213.3\mathcal{M}$
	80	$159.9\mathcal{D} + 119.4\mathcal{A}$	$2072.3\mathcal{M} + 1437.1\mathcal{S} \cong 3222.0\mathcal{M}$
	53	$160.2\mathcal{D} + 119.5\mathcal{A}$	$2074.7\mathcal{M} + 1439.1\mathcal{S} \cong 3226.0\mathcal{M}$
	40	$160.4\mathcal{D} + 119.5\mathcal{A}$	$2075.1\mathcal{M} + 1440.1\mathcal{S} \cong 3227.1\mathcal{M}$
	32	$160.5\mathcal{D} + 119.3\mathcal{A}$	$2074.1\mathcal{M} + 1440.4\mathcal{S} \cong 3226.4\mathcal{M}$
0	—	$159.0\mathcal{D} + 121.2\mathcal{A}$	$2090.7\mathcal{M} + 1438.9\mathcal{S} \cong 3241.8\mathcal{M}$

Table 11. Computational complexity of simultaneous elliptic scalar multiplication $kP + lQ$ on $E(\mathbb{F}_p)$, where $\log_2 p = 160$, weighted projective coordinates for point representation, and NAF representation for scalars

shift-length (bits)	block-size (bits)	dbl/add	complexity
16	160	$161.9\mathcal{D} + 85.7\mathcal{A}$	$1675.9\mathcal{M} + 1314.0\mathcal{S} \cong 2727.1\mathcal{M}$
	80	$162.3\mathcal{D} + 85.9\mathcal{A}$	$1680.5\mathcal{M} + 1317.5\mathcal{S} \cong 2734.5\mathcal{M}$
	53	$162.5\mathcal{D} + 86.2\mathcal{A}$	$1684.3\mathcal{M} + 1319.6\mathcal{S} \cong 2739.9\mathcal{M}$
	40	$162.5\mathcal{D} + 86.3\mathcal{A}$	$1685.5\mathcal{M} + 1320.1\mathcal{S} \cong 2741.6\mathcal{M}$
	32	$162.4\mathcal{D} + 86.2\mathcal{A}$	$1684.1\mathcal{M} + 1319.5\mathcal{S} \cong 2739.7\mathcal{M}$
3	160	$160.9\mathcal{D} + 86.6\mathcal{A}$	$1683.2\mathcal{M} + 1311.9\mathcal{S} \cong 2732.7\mathcal{M}$
	80	$161.5\mathcal{D} + 86.6\mathcal{A}$	$1685.2\mathcal{M} + 1315.5\mathcal{S} \cong 2737.6\mathcal{M}$
	53	$161.8\mathcal{D} + 86.6\mathcal{A}$	$1686.8\mathcal{M} + 1317.5\mathcal{S} \cong 2740.8\mathcal{M}$
	40	$162.0\mathcal{D} + 86.6\mathcal{A}$	$1686.7\mathcal{M} + 1318.4\mathcal{S} \cong 2741.4\mathcal{M}$
	32	$162.1\mathcal{D} + 86.4\mathcal{A}$	$1684.7\mathcal{M} + 1318.1\mathcal{S} \cong 2739.1\mathcal{M}$
1	160	$160.3\mathcal{D} + 87.7\mathcal{A}$	$1693.8\mathcal{M} + 1312.5\mathcal{S} \cong 2743.7\mathcal{M}$
	80	$160.6\mathcal{D} + 87.6\mathcal{A}$	$1694.0\mathcal{M} + 1314.2\mathcal{S} \cong 2745.4\mathcal{M}$
	53	$160.9\mathcal{D} + 87.4\mathcal{A}$	$1692.3\mathcal{M} + 1314.9\mathcal{S} \cong 2744.2\mathcal{M}$
	40	$161.1\mathcal{D} + 87.1\mathcal{A}$	$1689.4\mathcal{M} + 1314.8\mathcal{S} \cong 2741.2\mathcal{M}$
	32	$161.2\mathcal{D} + 86.7\mathcal{A}$	$1685.2\mathcal{M} + 1314.0\mathcal{S} \cong 2736.4\mathcal{M}$
0	—	$159.9\mathcal{D} + 90.9\mathcal{A}$	$1730.8\mathcal{M} + 1323.1\mathcal{S} \cong 2789.3\mathcal{M}$

1 is used. We examine block sizes of 160, 80, 53, 40, and 32 bits, as in the experiments in the previous sections.

Table 12. Computational complexity of simultaneous elliptic scalar multiplication $kP + lQ$ on $E(\mathbb{F}_p)$, where $\log_2 p = 160$, weighted projective coordinates for point representation, and JS-form representation for scalars

shift-length (bits)	block-size (bits)	dbl/add	complexity
16	160	$159.8\mathcal{D} + 81.5\mathcal{A}$	$1617.6\mathcal{M} + 1284.9\mathcal{S} \cong 2645.5\mathcal{M}$
	80	$160.0\mathcal{D} + 82.5\mathcal{A}$	$1618.0\mathcal{M} + 1286.2\mathcal{S} \cong 2647.0\mathcal{M}$
	53	$160.3\mathcal{D} + 81.5\mathcal{A}$	$1618.8\mathcal{M} + 1287.7\mathcal{S} \cong 2649.0\mathcal{M}$
	40	$160.5\mathcal{D} + 81.5\mathcal{A}$	$1619.6\mathcal{M} + 1298.9\mathcal{S} \cong 2650.0\mathcal{M}$
	32	$160.7\mathcal{D} + 81.5\mathcal{A}$	$1620.7\mathcal{M} + 1290.1\mathcal{S} \cong 2652.9\mathcal{M}$
3	160	$159.8\mathcal{D} + 81.5\mathcal{A}$	$1617.6\mathcal{M} + 1284.9\mathcal{S} \cong 2645.6\mathcal{M}$
	80	$160.0\mathcal{D} + 81.5\mathcal{A}$	$1618.1\mathcal{M} + 1286.0\mathcal{S} \cong 2646.9\mathcal{M}$
	53	$160.2\mathcal{D} + 81.5\mathcal{A}$	$1618.8\mathcal{M} + 1287.4\mathcal{S} \cong 2648.8\mathcal{M}$
	40	$160.5\mathcal{D} + 81.5\mathcal{A}$	$1619.6\mathcal{M} + 1288.7\mathcal{S} \cong 2650.6\mathcal{M}$
	32	$160.7\mathcal{D} + 81.5\mathcal{A}$	$1620.7\mathcal{M} + 1289.9\mathcal{S} \cong 2652.7\mathcal{M}$
1	160	$159.7\mathcal{D} + 81.6\mathcal{A}$	$1618.1\mathcal{M} + 1284.9\mathcal{S} \cong 2646.0\mathcal{M}$
	80	$159.8\mathcal{D} + 81.6\mathcal{A}$	$1618.2\mathcal{M} + 1284.9\mathcal{S} \cong 2646.1\mathcal{M}$
	53	$159.8\mathcal{D} + 81.6\mathcal{A}$	$1618.4\mathcal{M} + 1285.1\mathcal{S} \cong 2646.5\mathcal{M}$
	40	$159.8\mathcal{D} + 81.6\mathcal{A}$	$1619.1\mathcal{M} + 1285.6\mathcal{S} \cong 2647.6\mathcal{M}$
	32	$159.9\mathcal{D} + 81.7\mathcal{A}$	$1620.0\mathcal{M} + 1286.3\mathcal{S} \cong 2649.1\mathcal{M}$
0	—	$159.7\mathcal{D} + 82.0\mathcal{A}$	$1623.7\mathcal{M} + 1287.7\mathcal{S} \cong 2653.8\mathcal{M}$

We count the number of point additions and doublings required, when we take the average over a randomly generated 10,000 pairs of scalars of size equal to 160 bits. From the number of point additions and doublings required, we derive the equivalent number of field multiplications. As stated previously, we assume that weighted projective coordinates are used for point representation and that well-known algorithms are used for point operations [IEEE], where point additions and doublings have computational complexity $\mathcal{A} = 12\mathcal{M} + 4\mathcal{S} = 15.2\mathcal{M}$ and $\mathcal{D} = 4\mathcal{M} + 6\mathcal{S} = 8.8\mathcal{M}$, respectively.

We can see from the tables that the maximal computational reduction is achieved when the upper bound of the shift-length is set to 16 bits and the block-size is set to 160 bits. This observation corresponds to the tables 1, 2, and 3. Although the upper bound of the shift-length is restricted to 3 bits, the computational advantage is close to that for 16 bits.

References

[Ak01]   T. Akishita, "Fast Simultaneous Scalar Multiplication on Elliptic Curves with Montgomery Form," *Selected Areas in Cryptography, SAC2001*, LNCS, **2259** (2001), Springer-Verlag, 255–267.

[DTCP]   Digital Transmission Content Protection, http://www.dtcp.com

[El85]   T. ElGamal, "A Public Key Cryptosystem and a Signature Scheme Based on Discrete Logarithms," *IEEE Trans. on Information Theory*, **31** (1985), 469–472.

[IEEE]   IEEE P1363-2000, (2000), http://grouper.ieee.org/groups/1363/

[LL94]   C.H. Lim, P.J. Lee, "More Flexible Exponentiation with Precomputation,"
           Advances in Cryptology – CRYPTO'94, LNCS, **839** (1994), Springer-Verlag,
           95–107.
[Ko87]   N. Koblitz, "Elliptic curve cryptosystems," *Mathematics of Computation*,
           48 (1987), 203–209.
[Mi85]   V. Miller, "Uses of elliptic curves in cryptography," *Advances in Cryptology
           – CRYPTO'85*, LNCS, **218** (1986), Springer-Verlag, 417–426.
[Mo01]   B. Möller, "Algorithms for Multi Exponentiation," *Selected Areas in Crypto-
           graphy, SAC2001*, LNCS, **2259** (2001), Springer-Verlag, 165–180.
[MOV97]   A.J. Menezes, P.C. Oorschot, S.A. Vanstone, "Handbook of Applied Cryp-
           tography," *CRC Press, Inc*, (1999),
[So01]   J.A. Solinas, "Some Computational Speedups and Bandwidth Improve-
           ments for Curves over Prime Fields," available at `http://www.cacr.math.`
           `uwaterloo.ca/conferences/2001/ecc/slides.html`, (2001),

Author Index